Mc
for
Writers

Short Essays for Composition

Models for Writers

Short Essays for Composition

NINTH EDITION

Alfred Rosa
Paul Eschholz

University of Vermont

BEDFORD/ST. MARTIN'S
Boston ◆ New York

For Bedford/St. Martin's

Developmental Editor: Gregory S. Johnson
Production Editor: Ryan Sullivan
Senior Production Supervisor: Dennis J. Conroy
Marketing Manager: Karita dos Santos
Art Director: Lucy Krikorian
Copy Editor: Wendy Polhemus-Annibell
Cover Design: Donna Lee Dennison
Cover Art: Pelle Cass, Kim Cevoli, Donna Lee Dennison, and Catherine Sheridan
Composition: Macmillan India Ltd.
Printing and Binding: Haddon Craftsmen, Inc., an R.R. Donnelley & Sons Company

President: Joan E. Feinberg
Editorial Director: Denise B. Wydra
Editor in Chief: Nancy Perry
Director of Marketing: Karen Melton Soeltz
Director of Editing, Design, and Production: Marcia Cohen
Managing Editor: Erica T. Appel

Library of Congress Control Number: 2006921426

Manufactured in the United States of America.

2 1 0 9 8 7
f e d c b a

For information, write: Bedford/St. Martin's, 75 Arlington Street, Boston, MA 02116 (617-399-4000)

ISBN-10: 0-312-44637-3 ISBN-13: 978-0-312-44637-6 (paperback)
ISBN-10: 0-312-45404-X ISBN-13: 978-0-312-45404-3 (hardcover)

Acknowledgments
Acknowledgments and copyrights can be found at the back of the book on pages 602–6, which constitute an extension of the copyright page.

Preface

Models for Writers, now in its ninth edition, continues to offer students and instructors brief, accessible, high-interest essays that model rhetorical elements, principles, and patterns. As important as it is for students to read while they are learning to write college-level essays, *Models for Writers* offers more than just a collection of essays. The abundant study materials that accompany each selection help students master the writing skills they'll need for their college classes. In addition, writing activities and assignments help students stitch the various rhetorical elements together into coherent, forceful essays of their own. This approach, which has helped several million students over the past thirty years to become better writers, remains at the heart of the book.

In this ninth edition, we continue to emphasize the classic features of *Models for Writers* that have won praise from teachers and students alike. In addition, we have strengthened the book by introducing new selections and new voices and by developing key new features that provide students with the tools they need to become better readers and writers.

FAVORITE FEATURES OF *MODELS FOR WRITERS*

• **Brief, Lively Readings That Provide Outstanding Models.** Most of the 71 selections in *Models for Writers* are comparable in length (two to three pages) to the essays students will write themselves, and each clearly illustrates a basic rhetorical element, principle, or pattern. Just as important, the essays deal with subjects that we know from our own teaching experience will spark the interest of most college students. With such well-known authors as Sandra Cisneros, Isaac Asimov, Maya Angelou, Norman Mailer, Annie Dillard, Langston Hughes, and Sarah Vowell, the range of voices, cultural perspectives, styles, and degrees of complexity represented in the essays will resonate with today's students.

• **Introductory Chapters on Reading and Writing.** The chapters in Part One help students understand the writing process and use the essays they read to improve their own writing. Chapter 1, "The Writing

Process," details the steps in the writing process and illustrates them with a student essay in progress. Chapter 2, "From Reading to Writing," shows students how to use the apparatus in the text, provides them with guidelines for critical reading, and demonstrates with three student essays how they can generate their own writing from reading.

• **Expanded Rhetorical Organization.** Each of the eighteen rhetorically based chapters in *Models for Writers* is devoted to a particular element or pattern important to college writing. In Part Two, Chapters 3 through 9 focus on the concepts of thesis, unity, organization, beginnings and endings, paragraphs, transitions, and effective sentences. In Part Three, Chapter 10 illustrates the importance of controlling diction and tone, and Chapter 11, the uses of figurative language. In Part Four, Chapters 12 through 20 explore the types of writing most often required of college students: illustration, narration, description, process analysis, definition, division and classification, comparison and contrast, cause and effect, and argument.

• **Abundant Study Materials.** To help students use the readings to improve their writing, every essay is accompanied by ample study materials.

For Your Journal activities precede each reading and prompt students to explore their own ideas and experiences regarding the issues presented in the reading.

A *Thinking Critically about This Reading* question follows each essay, and it encourages students to consider the writer's assumptions, make connections not readily apparent, or explore the broader implications of the selection.

Questions for Study and Discussion focus on the selection's content and on the author's purpose and the particular strategy used to achieve that purpose, with at least one question in each series focusing on a writing concern other than the one highlighted in the chapter to remind students that good writing is never one-dimensional.

Classroom Activities provide brief exercises enabling students to work in the classroom (often in groups) on rhetorical elements, techniques, or patterns. These activities range from developing thesis statements to using strong action verbs and building argumentative evidence. Classroom activities help students apply concepts modeled in the readings to their own writing.

Suggested Writing Assignments provide at least two writing assignments for each essay, with one encouraging students to use the reading selection as a direct model and another asking them to respond to the content of the reading.

• **Concise and Helpful Chapter Introductions.** Writing instructors who use *Models for Writers* have continued to be generous in their praise for the brief, student-friendly chapter introductions, which explain the various elements and patterns. In each one, students will find numerous illuminating examples—many written by students—of the feature or principle under discussion.

• **Longer Readings in Each Part.** To provide a greater variety of essays for students and to help them progress to more demanding reading, Parts Two, Three, and Four of *Models for Writers* include at least one longer essay. Selections by Gloria Naylor, George Orwell, and James David Barber, for example, introduce students to more complex forms of the genre.

• **Flexible Arrangement.** Each chapter is self-contained so that instructors can easily follow their own teaching sequences, omitting or emphasizing certain chapters according to the needs of their students or the requirements of the course.

• **Appendix on Writing a Research Paper.** A brief, helpful appendix, including a sample documented student essay, offers guidance on conducting research using print and online sources; evaluating, quoting, and integrating sources; and using MLA citation style.

• **Glossary of Useful Terms.** Cross-referenced in many of the questions and writing assignments throughout the book, this helpful list covers rhetorical and literary terms that student writers need to know. Terms that are defined in the Glossary are shown in boldface the first time they appear in the text.

• **Instructor's Manual.** In the manual that accompanies *Models for Writers,* we offer insights into the rhetorical features of each essay as well as advice on how best to use the materials in class. Suggested answers for critical thinking questions, study questions, and classroom activities are included.

NEW TO THE NINTH EDITION OF *MODELS FOR WRITERS*

• **Engaging, Informative, and Diverse New Readings.** Twenty-four readings—one third of this edition's selections—are new, and many are on topics of current interest, such as America's consumerism, the limits of new medical technologies, the role of manners in an uncivil society, and the effects of advertising on our reading patterns. We chose these essays for their brevity, clarity, and potential for developing critical thinking and writing skills in student writers. Among the new readings included in this edition are essays by popular contemporary writers such as Greg Critser, Merrill Markoe, David McCullough, Anna Quindlen, and David Sedaris.

- **New Argument Pairs on Contemporary Issues.** Three new paired argument essays—on obesity, alternatives to incarceration, and mandatory childhood vaccinations—will spark lively debate, both in class discussions and in students' writing.

- **New "Thematic Clusters" Alternate Table of Contents.** This new alternate table of contents features focused clusters of two to seven essays that share common themes. Students and instructors attracted to the theme of one essay in *Models for Writers* can consult these clusters to find other essays in the book that address the same topic or theme.

- **New Critical Thinking Questions.** Each selection is now followed by a prompt that encourages students to think critically about their reading by exploring—in discussion or in writing—the author's meaning and assumptions as well as the broader implications of the selection.

- **New Visual Writing Prompts.** Eighteen new images are paired with professional essays, encouraging students to analyze connections between the print and visual texts.

- **New Online Reading Comprehension Quizzes.** The *Models for Writers* companion Web site now features self-scoring quizzes for every professional essay in the book.

- **New Research-Based Writing Suggestions.** Each of the paired argument essays features a research-based writing suggestion and a cross reference to the *Models for Writers* Web site, where students will find annotated links to current and reliable information online.

- **More Help with Sentence Grammar.** Chapter 1, "The Writing Process," now includes help with the editing concerns instructors across the country identified as the most problematic for their students—such as run-on sentences and misplaced modifiers. Brief explanations and hand-edited examples help students find and correct these common errors in their own writing.

- **Expanded Vocabulary Glosses.** To facilitate comprehension and to encourage close reading, every selection now features glosses that clarify difficult vocabulary words and unfamiliar cultural references.

• **Expanded Companion Web Site, bedfordstmartins.com/models.** The companion Web site for the ninth edition of *Models for Writers* features a wealth of resources for students and instructors, including Exercise Central, online reading quizzes, annotated research links, and a downloadable Instructor's Manual. The site also provides access to *Re:Writing,* Bedford/St. Martin's free online collection of plagiarism tutorials, model documents, style and grammar exercises, visual analysis activities, research guides, bibliography tools, and much more.

ACKNOWLEDGMENTS

In response to the many thoughtful and helpful reviews from instructors who use this book, we have maintained the solid foundation of the previous edition of *Models for Writers* while adding fresh new readings and additional support for writing and editing.

We are indebted to many people for their advice as we prepared this ninth edition. We are especially grateful to Cara Simone Bader, Vermont Commons School; Michael Bertsch, Butte Community College; Jeannie Boniecki, Naugatuck Valley Community College; Deborah Bush, Copiah-Lincoln Community College; Brian K. Carter, Fresno City College; Judith K. Casey, University of Puerto Rico, Mayagüez; Thomas Clawson, Stone Bridge High School; Pamela Emigh-Murphy, Monroe Community College; K. Scott Forman, Weber State University; Sherilyn Hashemzadeh, Bluefield State College; Rita Higgins, Essex County College; Richard Johnson, Kirkwood Community College; Thomas Juvan, Vermont Commons School; Jennifer L. Kirchoff, California State University, San Bernardino; Alisa Klinger, Cuesta College; Denise C. Lagos, Union County College; Brad O'Brien, Francis Marion University; Joey Poole, Francis Marion University; June Roque, Milwaukee Area Technical College; Natalie Serianni, Lees-McRae College; Linda M. Smith, Winston Churchill High School; Tondalaya VanLear, Dabney S. Lancaster Community College; Carolyn Vogel, Northern New Mexico Community College; and Justin Williamson, Pearl River Community College.

It has been our good fortune to have the editorial guidance and good cheer of Greg Johnson, our developmental editor on this book; our longtime colleague and mentor Nancy Perry; and the rest of the excellent team at Bedford/St. Martin's as we worked on this new edition.

Thanks also to Sarah Federman, who authored the new material for the Instructor's Manual, and to Brian Kent, Cara Simone Bader, Tom Juvan, the late Susan Wanner, Dick Sweterlitsch, and Betsy Eschholz, who have shared their experiences using *Models for Writers* in the classroom. Our greatest debt is, as always, to our students—especially Lisa Driver, Susan Francis, Jake Jamieson, Zoe Ockenga, and Jeffrey Olesky, whose essays appear in this text—for all they have taught us over the years. Finally, we thank each other, partners in this writing and teaching venture for more than thirty-five years.

Alfred Rosa
Paul Eschholz

Contents

Preface v
Thematic Clusters xxi
Introduction for Students 1

part one **On Reading and Writing Well**

1 The Writing Process 7

Prewriting 7
- Understand Your Assignment 8
- Choose a Subject Area, and Focus on a Topic 9
- Get Ideas and Collect Information 10
- Establish Your Thesis 12
- Know Your Audience 14
- Determine Your Method of Development 15
- Map Your Organization 17

Writing the First Draft 18
- Create a Title 19
- Focus on Beginnings and Endings 19

Revising 20

Editing 21
- Run-ons: Fused Sentences and Comma Splices 21
- Sentence Fragments 22
- Subject-Verb Agreement 23
- Pronoun-Antecedent Agreement 24
- Verb Tense Shifts 25
- Misplaced and Dangling Modifiers 26

Faulty Parallelism 27
Weak Nouns and Verbs 28
ESL Concerns (Articles and Nouns) 28

Proofreading 30

Writing an Expository Essay: A Student Essay in Progress 31
Jeffrey Olesky, Golf: A Character Builder (student essay) 36

2 From Reading to Writing 41

Getting the Most Out of Your Reading 41
Prereading: Preparing Yourself 42
The First Reading: Getting an Overview of the Selection 45
The Second Reading: Coming to an Understanding of the Selection 45
Responding to Your Reading: Making Marginal Notes 45
Analyzing: Asking Yourself Questions as You Read 46
An Example: Annotating Isaac Asimov's "Intelligence" 47
Practice: Reading and Annotating Rachel Carson's "Fable for Tomorrow" 49
Rachel Carson, Fable for Tomorrow 50

Using Your Reading in the Writing Process 54
Reading as a Writer 55

Writing from Reading: Three Sample Student Essays 57
A Narrative Essay: *Lisa V. Driver,* The Strong Arm of a Sixth-Grade Teacher (student essay) 57
A Response Essay: *Zoe Ockenga,* The Excuse "Not To" (student essay) 59
An Analytical Essay: *Susan Francis,* The Disgrace of Man (student essay) 64

part two The Elements of the Essay

3 Thesis 71

Helen Keller, The Most Important Day 74
The celebrated blind and deaf writer recalls her discovery of language.

James Lincoln Collier, Anxiety: Challenge by Another Name 80
A writer asserts that we can "accomplish wonders" if we "accept anxiety as another name for challenge."

Etta Kralovec, No More Pep Rallies! 86
An educator argues that "learning the basics is often only a by-product of our public education system."

4 Unity **90**

Sandra Cisneros, My Name 94
A Chicana writer explores the many facets of her inherited name.

Anthony Komaroff, Technology's Limits 98
A doctor talks about the special relationship he had with one of his patients.

Gloria Naylor, The Meanings of a Word 103
In "meeting the word [nigger] head on," blacks have "rendered it impotent," according to a prominent African American novelist.

5 Organization **109**

Cherokee Paul McDonald, A View from the Bridge 114
An encounter with a young fisherman teaches the author a lesson in what it means to see.

Eudora Welty, The Corner Store 121
A novelist describes a cherished place from her childhood.

William Lutz, Doubts about Doublespeak 126
A professor and language consultant discusses "language that pretends to communicate but doesn't."

6 Beginnings and Endings **133**

Michael T. Kaufman, Of My Friend Hector and My Achilles Heel 140
A journalist reveals his "prejudice and stupidity" in this essay about his relationship with a childhood friend.

Robin Marantz Henig, Something's Off 146
A journalist writes about losing and then regaining her sense of smell.

Ruth Russell, The Wounds That Can't Be Stitched Up 151
A student writer reflects on a life-changing automobile accident involving her mother.

Carl T. Rowan, Unforgettable Miss Bessie 157
A newspaper columnist remembers an influential teacher in the segregated South.

7 Paragraphs 164

William Zinsser, Simplicity 168
"The secret of good writing," according to this expert, "is to strip every sentence to its cleanest components."

Robyn Marks, Raising a Son—With Men on the Fringes 175
An African American journalist writes about the challenges of being a single mother.

Mike Rose, "I Just Wanna Be Average" 182
A former student pays tribute to a high school teacher who inspired him and encouraged him to continue his studies.

8 Transitions 188

David Raymond, On Being 17, Bright, and Unable to Read 192
A dyslexic high school student describes his experiences.

Russell Baker, Becoming a Writer 199
The author remembers his joy at the discovery that his "words had the power to make people laugh."

David McCullough, Why History? 205
According to this historian and Pulitzer Prize–winning author, "history . . . enlarges and intensifies the experience of being alive."

9 Effective Sentences 210

Annie Dillard, *From* An American Childhood 215
The wonder of seeing through a microscope ignites a naturalist's lifelong curiosity.

Langston Hughes, Salvation 220
A famous poet remembers a church revival meeting at which he pretended to be "saved from sin."

Caroline Hwang, The Good Daughter 225
When the author mispronounces her own name in Korean, she questions her national—and personal—identities.

Martin Gansberg, 38 Who Saw Murder Didn't Call Police 230
A reporter's account of a notorious case of urban apathy causes us to reflect on our responsibilities to one another.

part three **The Language of the Essay**

10 Diction and Tone **239**

Dick Gregory, Shame 245
A civil rights advocate recalls a painful childhood incident.

David Sedaris, Me Talk Pretty One Day 251
A popular American essayist recounts his experience of trying to learn French in Paris.

Sarah Vowell, Pop-A-Shot 259
There are merits to "goofing off," argues this writer and cultural observer.

Merrill Markoe, Who Am I? 264
A comedy writer tries to learn about herself by filling in online personality surveys.

11 Figurative Language **270**

Robert Ramirez, The Barrio 272
A Hispanic writer paints a vivid and sensuous picture of the district called the barrio.

Gary Soto, The Jacket 279
A poet and author describes his bitter relationship with an ugly jacket from his childhood.

George Orwell, A Hanging 285
In this classic essay, the novelist and essayist argues for the value of life.

part four **Types of Essays**

12 Illustration **295**

Barbara Huttmann, A Crime of Compassion 299
A nurse pleads for new legislation that would permit terminally ill patients to choose death with dignity.

Natalie Goldberg, Be Specific 306
The challenge and joy of writing, says this verbal guru, are in the details.

Richard Lederer, The Case for Short Words 310
This English teacher and language expert argues that "short words are as good as long ones."

Christie Scotty, Can I Get You Some Manners with That? 316
A recent college graduate recounts her experiences as a waitress.

13 Narration **321**

Henry Louis Gates Jr., What's in a Name? 325
A prominent African American scholar remembers a childhood encounter with racism.

Steve Brody, How I Got Smart 330
A high school crush led this writer to become addicted to learning.

Maya Angelou, Momma, the Dentist, and Me 337
A celebrated African American writer recounts how a toothache led to a confrontation with racism.

Kate Chopin, The Story of an Hour 346
The short-story writer captures the truth of a marriage in the events of an hour.

14 Description **351**

Gilbert Highet, Subway Station 353
A writer and translator finds beauty in a subway station.

Verlyn Klinkenborg, Wyoming Clouds 357
This farmer-essayist reflects on the clouds that form in the sky above his Wyoming home.

Pete Hamill, City of Islands 361
A journalist and author describes the "archipelago of New York."

Thomas L. Friedman, My Favorite Teacher 365
A Pulitzer Prize–winning columnist describes the high school teacher who had the most influence on his career as a journalist.

15 Process Analysis **370**

Garrison Keillor, How to Write a Personal Letter 374
A teller of homespun tales offers dos and don'ts on the art of letter writing.

Bill Husted, Here's How to Revive a Computer Even after an Evil Wizard Kills the Beast 379
A computer and technology columnist tells how he brought his stepson's computer back to life.

Lars Eighner, On Dumpster Diving 385
A formerly homeless man reveals the finer points of scavenging and the lessons that can be learned along the way.

16 Definition **391**

Lawrence M. Friedman, What Is Crime? 394
A law professor explains what it takes for something to be considered criminal.

William Raspberry, The Handicap of Definition 398
An African American columnist concludes that real "harm . . . comes from too narrow a definition of what is black."

Ellen Goodman, The Company Man 403
A columnist denounces the workaholic lifestyle with a disturbing example.

17 Division and Classification **408**

Martin Luther King Jr., The Ways of Meeting Oppression 412
In this classic essay, the civil rights leader makes a case for nonviolent resistance.

Judith Viorst, Friends, Good Friends—and Such Good Friends 417
A magazine writer considers the varieties of friendship.

James David Barber, Four Types of President 426
A political scientist identifies four basic character types among U.S. presidents.

18 Comparison and Contrast **433**

Mark Twain, Two Ways of Seeing a River 438
This popular author makes his classic observation that sometimes knowledge can be blinding.

Del Miller, Mac or PC: There Is Simply No Comparison! 443
An engineer and computer expert asks, "Why don't more people buy Macintosh?"

K. Connie Kang, A Battle of Cultures 451
Conflict between Koreans and African Americans in New York yields insights into race relations.

Bruce Catton, Grant and Lee: A Study in Contrasts 456
A renowned historian compares the two Civil War generals, noting that they may have more in common than would appear at first glance.

19 Cause and Effect **462**

Stephen King, Why We Crave Horror Movies 465
The king of macabre explains the appeal of horror movies and why he thinks "we're all mentally ill."

Myriam Marquez, Why and When We Speak Spanish in Public 472
A Hispanic columnist explains why she speaks Spanish in public.

Anna Quindlen, Mom Quixote 476
This Pulitzer Prize–winning columnist chronicles her attempt to find her son the perfect toy for Christmas.

Norman Mailer, One Idea 480
A two-time Pulitzer Prize–winning author explores why today's students don't read as much as those of the generation before.

20 Argument 484

Thomas Jefferson, The Declaration of Independence 492
A country seeks to justify its action to its people and the world in this classic argument.

Martin Luther King Jr., I Have a Dream 498
In this revered speech, the celebrated civil rights leader imparts his vision of freedom and equality.

Laura Rowley, As They Say, Drugs Kill 505
A college student witnesses a fatal overdose and shares a tragic lesson.

Mary Sherry, In Praise of the F Word 510
An educator argues that schools should consider using the "trump card of failure" to motivate students.

The Obesity Epidemic: Who's to Blame?

Greg Critser, Don't Eat the Flan 515
A writer and cultural observer suggests that "gluttony . . . has become the first media non-sin."

Alison Motluk, Supersize Me: It's Time to Stop Blaming Fat People for Their Size 520
A science writer argues that environment plays a large role in the problem of obesity in the United States.

Shame: Is It an Effective Punishment?

June Tangney, Condemn the Crime, Not the Person 524
"Shame often makes a bad situation worse," suggests a psychology professor.

Dan M. Kahan, Shame Is Worth a Try 530
A law professor asserts that "shaming punishments . . . are extraordinarily effective."

Childhood Vaccinations: Should They Be Mandatory?

Barbara Loe Fisher, Parents Should Be Allowed to Opt Out of Vaccinating Their Children 535

A mother and activist argues that parents, not the government, should make healthcare decisions for their children.

Steven P. Shelov, Parents Should Not Be Allowed to Opt Out of Vaccinating Their Children 543

A doctor asserts that "allowing parents to opt out of vaccinating their children would endanger public health."

Appendix: Writing a Research Paper 551

Using Print and Online Sources 552

Developing a Working Bibliography 556

Internet Research: Subject Directories and Keyword Searches 557

Taking Notes 564

Integrating Borrowed Material into Your Text 569

A Note on Plagiarism 571

Documenting Sources 575

An Annotated Student Research Paper 584

Glossary of Useful Terms 591

Index 607

Thematic Clusters

The essay clusters that follow focus on themes that students can pursue in their own compositions. The essays themselves provide ideas and information to stimulate students' thinking as well as provide source material for writing. These clusters are suggestive rather than comprehensive and fairly narrow in scope rather than far-ranging. Instructors and students are, of course, free to develop their own thematic clusters on which to base written work and are not limited by our groupings.

Teachers and Students

Helen Keller, The Most Important Day 74
Carl T. Rowan, Unforgettable Miss Bessie 157
Mike Rose, "I Just Wanna Be Average" 182
Russell Baker, Becoming a Writer 199
David Sedaris, Me Talk Pretty One Day 251
Steve Brody, How I Got Smart 330
Thomas L. Friedman, My Favorite Teacher 365

Education Policy

Etta Kralovec, No More Pep Rallies! 86
David McCullough, Why History? 205
Norman Mailer, One Idea 480
Mary Sherry, In Praise of the F Word 510

Parenting

Robyn Marks, Raising a Son—With Men on the Fringes 175
Annie Dillard, From An American Childhood 215
Maya Angelou, Momma, the Dentist, and Me 337
Anna Quindlen, Mom Quixote 476

Heroes/Role Models

Carl T. Rowan, Unforgettable Miss Bessie 157
Mike Rose, "I Just Wanna Be Average" 182
Thomas L. Friedman, My Favorite Teacher 365

Personal Dilemmas

James Lincoln Collier, Anxiety: Challenge by Another Name 80
Robin Marantz Henig, Something's Off 146
Robyn Marks, Raising a Son—With Men on the Fringes 175
Langston Hughes, Salvation 220
Dick Gregory, Shame 245

Growing Up

Michael T. Kaufman, Of My Friend Hector and My Achilles Heel 140
David Raymond, On Being 17, Bright, and Unable to Read 192
Langston Hughes, Salvation 220
Gary Soto, The Jacket 279
Christie Scotty, Can I Get You Some Manners with That? 316
Judith Viorst, Friends, Good Friends—and Such Good Friends 417

Nature

Rachel Carson, Fable for Tomorrow 50
Annie Dillard, From An American Childhood 215
Verlyn Klinkenborg, Wyoming Clouds 357
Mark Twain, Two Ways of Seeing a River 438

The Power of Language

Sandra Cisneros, My Name 94
Gloria Naylor, The Meanings of a Word 103
William Lutz, Doubts about Doublespeak 126
Richard Lederer, The Case for Short Words 310
Henry Louis Gates Jr., What's in a Name? 325
William Raspberry, The Handicap of Definition 398

Crime and Punishment

Martin Gansberg, 38 Who Saw Murder Didn't Call Police 230
George Orwell, A Hanging 285
Lawrence M. Friedman, What Is Crime? 394
June Tangney, Condemn the Crime, Not the Person 524
Dan M. Kahan, Shame Is Worth a Try 530

Humor

David Sedaris, Me Talk Pretty One Day 251
Sarah Vowell, Pop-A-Shot 259
Merrill Markoe, Who Am I? 264
Steve Brody, How I Got Smart 330
Garrison Keillor, How to Write a Personal Letter 374
Bill Husted, Here's How to Revive a Computer Even after an Evil Wizard Kills the Beast 379
Anna Quindlen, Mom Quixote 476

Computers

Bill Husted, Here's How to Revive a Computer Even after an Evil Wizard Kills the Beast 379
Del Miller, Mac or PC: There Is Simply No Comparison! 443

The Sensual World

Helen Keller, The Most Important Day 74
Cherokee Paul McDonald, A View from the Bridge 114
Robin Marantz Henig, Something's Off 146
Verlyn Klinkenborg, Wyoming Clouds 357
Mark Twain, Two Ways of Seeing a River 438

Doctors and Patients

Anthony Komaroff, Technology's Limits 98
Barbara Huttmann, A Crime of Compassion 299
Maya Angelou, Momma, the Dentist, and Me 337
Barbara Loe Fisher, Parents Should Be Allowed to Opt Out of Vaccinating Their Children 535
Steven P. Shelov, Parents Should Not Be Allowed to Opt Out of Vaccinating Their Children 543

Writing about Writing

William Lutz, Doubts about Doublespeak 126
William Zinsser, Simplicity 168
Russell Baker, Becoming a Writer 199
Natalie Goldberg, Be Specific 306
Richard Lederer, The Case for Short Words 310
Garrison Keillor, How to Write a Personal Letter 374

Work

Natalie Goldberg, Be Specific 306
Christie Scotty, Can I Get You Some Manners with That? 316
Ellen Goodman, The Company Man 403

Recreation

Annie Dillard, From An American Childhood 215
Sarah Vowell, Pop-A-Shot 259
Garrison Keillor, How to Write a Personal Letter 374
Stephen King, Why We Crave Horror Movies 465

Discoveries/Epiphanies

Helen Keller, The Most Important Day 74
James Lincoln Collier, Anxiety: Challenge by Another Name 80
Cherokee Paul McDonald, A View from the Bridge 114
Annie Dillard, From An American Childhood 215
Langston Hughes, Salvation 220
Kate Chopin, The Story of an Hour 346

Moral Values

Martin Gansberg, 38 Who Saw Murder Didn't Call Police 230
George Orwell, A Hanging 285
Barbara Huttmann, A Crime of Compassion 299
Lawrence M. Friedman, What Is Crime? 394
Martin Luther King Jr., The Ways of Meeting Oppression 412

Social Values

Etta Kralovec, No More Pep Rallies! 86
Ruth Russell, The Wounds That Can't Be Stitched Up 151
Christie Scotty, Can I Get You Some Manners with That? 316
Lars Eighner, On Dumpster Diving 385
Laura Rowley, As They Say, Drugs Kill 505
Mary Sherry, In Praise of the F Word 510
June Tangney, Condemn the Crime, Not the Person 524
Dan M. Kahan, Shame Is Worth a Try 530

Consumerism

Eudora Welty, The Corner Store 121
Gary Soto, The Jacket 279
Lars Eighner, On Dumpster Diving 385
Del Miller, Mac or PC: There Is Simply No Comparison! 443
Anna Quindlen, Mom Quixote 476
Greg Critser, Don't Eat the Flan 515
Alison Motluk, Supersize Me: It's Time to Stop Blaming Fat People for Their Size 520

Pop Culture

Sarah Vowell, Pop-A-Shot 259
Merrill Markoe, Who Am I? 264
Bill Husted, Here's How to Revive a Computer Even after an Evil Wizard Kills the Beast 379
Del Miller, Mac or PC: There Is Simply No Comparison! 443
Stephen King, Why We Crave Horror Movies 465
Anna Quindlen, Mom Quixote 476
Norman Mailer, One Idea 480

The Immigrant Experience

Caroline Hwang, The Good Daughter 225
David Sedaris, Me Talk Pretty One Day 251
Robert Ramirez, The Barrio 272
K. Connie Kang, A Battle of Cultures 451
Myriam Marquez, Why and When We Speak Spanish in Public 472

Places and Scenes

Eudora Welty, The Corner Store 121
Robert Ramirez, The Barrio 272
Gilbert Highet, Subway Station 353
Verlyn Klinkenborg, Wyoming Clouds 357
Pete Hamill, City of Islands 361
Mark Twain, Two Ways of Seeing a River 438

Leaders

David McCullough, Why History? 205
James David Barber, Four Types of President 426
Bruce Catton, Grant and Lee: A Study in Contrasts 456

American History

David McCullough, Why History? 205
James David Barber, Four Types of President 426
Bruce Catton, Grant and Lee: A Study in Contrasts 456
Thomas Jefferson, The Declaration of Independence 492
Martin Luther King Jr., I Have a Dream 498

Drugs and Their Effects

Ruth Russell, The Wounds That Can't Be Stitched Up 151
Laura Rowley, As They Say, Drugs Kill 505

The Obesity Epidemic

Greg Critser, Don't Eat the Flan 515
Alison Motluk, Supersize Me: It's Time to Stop Blaming Fat People for Their Size 520

The City and the Country

Rachel Carson, Fable for Tomorrow 50
Robert Ramirez, The Barrio 272
Gilbert Highet, Subway Station 353
Verlyn Klinkenborg, Wyoming Clouds 357
Pete Hamill, City of Islands 361

Sense of Self

Sandra Cisneros, My Name 94
David Raymond, On Being 17, Bright, and Unable to Read 192
Caroline Hwang, The Good Daughter 225
Dick Gregory, Shame 245
Sarah Vowell, Pop-A-Shot 259
Merrill Markoe, Who Am I? 264
Gary Soto, The Jacket 279

Friends and Family

Michael T. Kaufman, Of My Friend Hector and My Achilles Heel 140
Robyn Marks, Raising a Son—With Men on the Fringes 175
Caroline Hwang, The Good Daughter 225

Kate Chopin, The Story of an Hour 346
Ellen Goodman, The Company Man 403
Judith Viorst, Friends, Good Friends—and Such Good Friends 417

Racism in America

Gloria Naylor, The Meanings of a Word 103
Henry Louis Gates Jr., What's in a Name? 325
Maya Angelou, Momma, the Dentist, and Me 337
William Raspberry, The Handicap of Definition 398
Martin Luther King Jr., The Ways of Meeting Oppression 412
K. Connie Kang, A Battle of Cultures 451
Myriam Marquez, Why and When We Speak Spanish in Public 472
Martin Luther King Jr., I Have a Dream 498

Models for Writers

Short Essays for Composition

Introduction for Students

Models for Writers is designed to help you learn to write by providing you with a collection of model essays—that is, essays that are examples of good writing. Good writing is direct and purposeful and communicates its message without confusing the reader. It doesn't wander from the topic, and it answers the reader's questions. While good writing is well developed and detailed, it also accomplishes its task with the fewest possible words and with the simplest language appropriate to the writer's topic and thesis.

We know that one of the best ways to learn to write and to improve our writing is to read. By reading we can begin to see how other writers have communicated their experiences, ideas, thoughts, and feelings. We can study how they have used the various elements of the essay—words, sentences, paragraphs, organizational patterns, transitions, examples, evidence, and so forth—and thus learn how we might effectively do the same. When we see, for example, how a writer like James Lincoln Collier develops an essay from a strong thesis statement, we can better appreciate the importance of having a clear thesis statement in our own writing. When we see the way Russell Baker uses transitions to link key phrases and important ideas so that readers can recognize clearly how the parts of his essay are meant to fit together, we have a better idea of how to achieve such coherence in our own writing.

But we do not learn only by observing, by reading. We also learn by doing—that is, by writing, and in the best of all situations, we engage in these two activities in conjunction with one another. *Models for Writers* encourages you, therefore, to practice what you are learning, to move from reading to writing.

Part One of *Models for Writers* provides you with strategies to do just that. Chapter 1 introduces you to the writing process, gives you guidelines for writing, and illustrates the writing process with a student essay. Chapter 2 shows you how to use what you learn from the essays that you will read to generate your own essays. You will soon see that an effective essay has a clear purpose, often provides useful information, has an effect on the reader's thoughts and feelings, and is usually a pleasure to read.

Those essays that you will read in *Models for Writers* were chosen because they are effective essays.

All well-written essays also share a number of structural and stylistic features that are illustrated by the various essays in *Models for Writers*. One good way to learn what these features are and how you can incorporate them into your own writing is to look at each of them in isolation. For this reason, we have divided the readings in *Models for Writers* into three major sections and, within these sections, into eighteen chapters, each with its own particular focus and emphasis.

Part Two, "The Elements of the Essay," includes chapters on the following subjects: thesis, unity, organization, beginnings and endings, paragraphs, transitions, and effective sentences. All of these elements are essential to a well-written essay, but the concepts of thesis, unity, and organization underlie all the others and so come first in our sequence. "Thesis" shows how authors put forth or state the main ideas of their essays and how they use such statements to develop and control content. "Unity" shows how authors achieve a sense of wholeness in their essays, and "Organization" illustrates some important patterns that authors use to organize their thinking and writing. The next chapter, "Beginnings and Endings," offers advice and models of ways to begin and conclude essays, while "Paragraphs" concentrates on the importance of well-developed paragraphs and what is necessary to achieve them. "Transitions" concerns the various devices that writers use to move from one idea or section of an essay to the next. Finally, "Effective Sentences" focuses on techniques to make sentences powerful and to create stylistic variety.

Part Three, "The Language of the Essay," includes a chapter on diction and tone and one on figurative language. "Diction and Tone" shows how carefully writers choose words either to convey exact meanings or to be purposely suggestive. In addition, this chapter shows how the words a writer uses can create a particular tone or relationship between the writer and reader—one of irony, for example, or humor or great seriousness. "Figurative Language" concentrates on the usefulness of the special devices of language—such as simile, metaphor, and personification—that add richness and depth to writing.

Part Four of *Models for Writers*, "Types of Essays," includes chapters on the various types of writing most often required of college writing students: illustration (how to use examples to illustrate a point or idea); narration (how to tell a story or give an account of an event); description (how to present a verbal picture); process analysis (how to explain how something is done or happens); definition (how to explain what something is); division and classification (how to divide a subject into its parts and place items into appropriate categories); comparison and contrast (how to explain the similarities and/or differences between two or more items); cause and effect (how to explain the causes of an event or the effects of an action); and argument (how to use reason and logic to persuade someone to your way of thinking). These types of writing are referred to as *organizational patterns* or *rhetorical modes.*

Studying the organizational patterns and practicing them are very important in any effort to broaden one's writing skills. In *Models for Writers*, we look at each pattern separately; we believe this is the simplest and most effective way to introduce them. However, this does not mean that a well-written essay is necessarily one that chooses a single pattern and sticks to it exclusively and rigidly. Confining oneself to comparison and contrast throughout an entire essay, for instance, might prove impractical and may yield a strained, unnatural piece of writing. In fact, it is often best to use a single pattern to organize your essay and then to use other patterns as your material dictates. As you read the model essays in this text, you will find that in the service of the dominant pattern, a good many of them utilize a combination of other patterns.

Combining organizational patterns is probably not something you want to plan or even think about when you first tackle a writing assignment. Rather, such combinations of patterns will develop naturally as you organize, draft, and revise your materials. Such combinations of patterns will also enhance the interest and impact of your writing. See Chapter 1 for a discussion of combining patterns.

Chapters 3–20 are organized in the same way. Each opens with an explanation of the element or principle under discussion. These introductions are intended to be brief, clear, and practical. Here you will also usually find one or more short examples of the feature or principle being studied, including examples from students such as yourself.

Following the introduction, we present three or four model essays (Chapter 20, with ten essays, is an exception), each with a brief introduction of its own, providing information about the author and directing your attention to the way the essay demonstrates the featured technique. A For Your Journal activity precedes each reading and prompts you to explore your own ideas and experiences regarding some facet of the issues presented in the reading. Each essay is followed by study materials in four parts: Thinking Critically about This Reading, Questions for Study and Discussion, Classroom Activity, and Suggested Writing Assignments. Read Chapter 2 for help on using the materials that accompany the readings to aid your own writing.

Models for Writers provides information, instruction, and practice in writing essays. By reading carefully and thoughtfully and by applying what you learn, you can gain more control over your writing.

part ■ one

On Reading and Writing Well

chapter **1**

The Writing Process

The essays in this book will help you understand the elements of good writing and provide ample opportunity to practice writing in response to the model essays. As you write your own essays, pay attention to your writing process. This chapter focuses on the stages of the writing process—prewriting, writing the first draft, revising, editing, and proofreading. It concludes with a sample student process that you can model your own writing after, from start to finish. The strategies suggested in this chapter for each stage of the writing process will help you overcome many of the problems you may face while writing your own essays.

■ PREWRITING

Writers rarely rely on inspiration alone to produce an effective piece of writing. Good writers prewrite or plan, write the first draft, revise, edit, and proofread. It is worth remembering, however, that the writing process is rarely as simple and as straightforward as this. Often the process is recursive, moving back and forth among the five stages. Moreover, writing is personal; no two people go about it exactly the same way. Still, it is possible to learn the steps in the process and thereby have a reassuring and reliable method for undertaking a writing task and producing a good composition.

Your reading can give you ideas and information, of course. But reading also helps expand your knowledge of the organizational patterns available to you, and, consequently, it can help direct all your prewriting activities. In *prewriting,* you select your subject and topic, gather ideas and information, and determine the thesis and organizational pattern or patterns you will use. Once you have worked through the prewriting process, you will be ready to start on your first draft. Let's explore how this works.

Understand Your Assignment

When you first receive an assignment, read it over several times. Focus on each word and each phrase to make sure you understand what you are being asked to do. Try restating the assignment in your own words to make sure you understand it. For example, consider the following assignments:

1. Narrate an experience that taught you that every situation has at least two sides.
2. Explain what is meant by *theoretical modeling* in the social sciences.
3. Write a persuasive essay in which you support or refute the following proposition: "Violence in the media is in large part responsible for an increase in violence in American society today."

Each of these assignments asks you to write in different ways. The first assignment asks you to tell the story of an event that showed you that every situation has more than one perspective. To complete the assignment, you might choose simply to narrate the event, or you might choose to analyze it in depth. In either case, you have to explain to your reader how you came to this new understanding of multiple perspectives and why it was important to you. The second assignment asks you to explain what theoretical modeling is and why it is used. To accomplish this assignment, you first need to read about the concept to gain a thorough understanding of it, and then you'll need to define it in your own words and explain its purpose and usefulness to your readers. You will also want to demonstrate the abstract concept with concrete examples to help your readers understand it. Finally, the third assignment asks you to take a position on a controversial issue for which there are many studies on both sides of the question. You will need to research the studies, consider the evidence they present, and then take a stand of your own. Your argument will necessarily have to draw on the sources and evidence you have researched, and you will need to refute the arguments and evidence presented by those experts who take an opposing position.

If, after reading the assignment several times, you are still unsure about what is being asked of you or about any additional requirements of the assignment, such as length or format, be sure to consult with your instructor. He or she should be willing to clear up any confusion before you start writing.

Choose a Subject Area, and Focus on a Topic

Although you will usually be given specific assignments in your writing course, you may sometimes have the freedom to write on any subject that interests you. In such a case, you may already have a specific idea in mind. For example, if you are interested in sports, you might argue against the use of performance-enhancing drugs by athletes. What happens, however, when you are free to choose your own subject and cannot think of anything to write about? If you find yourself in this situation, begin by determining a broad subject that you like to think about and might enjoy writing about—a general subject like virtual reality, medical ethics, amateur sports, or foreign travel. Also consider what you've recently read—essays in *Models for Writers,* for example—or your career ambitions when choosing a subject. Select several likely subjects, and let your mind explore their potential for interesting topics. Your goal is to arrive at an appropriately narrowed topic.

A topic is the specific part of a subject on which a writer focuses. Subjects such as the environment, literature, and sports are too broad to be dealt with adequately in a single essay. Entire books are written about these and other subjects. Start with your broad subject, and make it more specific. Thus if your subject is sports, you might choose as your topic rule violations in college recruiting, violence in ice hockey, types of fan behavior, the psychology of marathon runners, or the growth of sports medicine.

Suppose, for example, you select farming and advertising as possible subject areas. The examples in the following page illustrate how to narrow these broad subjects into manageable topics. Notice how each successive topic is more narrowed than the one before it. Moving from the general to the specific, the topics become appropriate for essay-length writing.

In moving from a broad subject to a particular topic, you should take into account any assigned constraints on length or format. You will also want to consider the amount of time you have to write. These practical considerations will affect the scope of your topic. For example, you couldn't adequately address subjects such as farming or

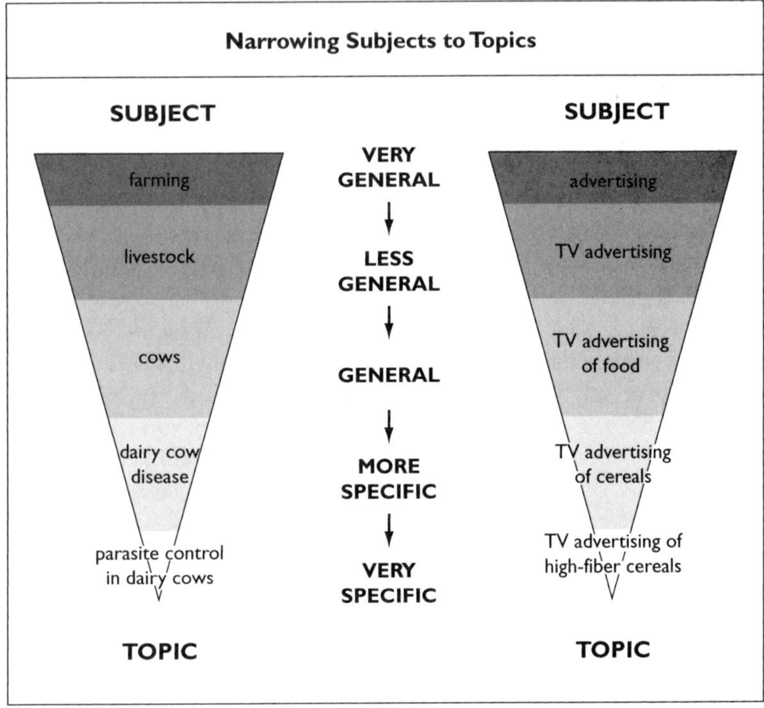

advertising in a five- to ten-page composition. These subjects are usually taken up in book-length publications.

Get Ideas and Collect Information

Once you have found your topic, you will need to determine what you want to say about it. The best way to do this is to gather information. Your ideas about a topic must be supported by information, such as facts and examples. The information you gather about a topic will influence your ideas about the topic and what you want to say. Here are some of the ways you can gather information:

1. *Ask questions about your topic.* If you were assigned the topic of theoretical modeling, for example, you could ask, what is *theoretical modeling*? Why, where, and by whom is theoretical modeling

used? What are the benefits of using it? Is it taught in school? Is it difficult to learn to use? Once the questioning starts, one question will lead to another, and the answers to these questions will be the stuff of your writing. Like a newspaper reporter going after a story, asking questions and getting answers are essential ways to understand a topic before trying to explain it to others.

2. *Brainstorm.* Jot down the things you know about a topic, freely associating ideas and information as a way to explore the topic and its possibilities. (See p. 32 for an example.) Don't censor or edit your notes, and don't worry about spelling or punctuation. Don't write your notes in list form because such an organization will imply a hierarchy of ideas, which may hamper your creativity and the free-flow of your thoughts. The objective of *brainstorming* is to free up your thinking before you start to write. You may want to set aside your notes and return to them over several days. Once you generate a substantial amount of brainstormed material, you will want to study the items, attempt to see relationships among them, or sort and group the entries by using different colored highlighters.
3. *Cluster.* Another strategy for stimulating your thinking about a topic is *clustering*. Place your topic in a circle, and draw lines from that circle to other circles in which you write related key words or phrases. Around each of these key words, generate more circles representing the various aspects of the key word that come to mind. (See p. 33 for an example.) The value of clustering over brainstorming is that you are generating ideas and organizing them at the same time. Both techniques work very well, but you may prefer one over the other or may find that one works better with one topic than another.
4. *Research.* You may want to add to what you already know about your topic with research. Research can take many forms beyond formal research carried out in your library. For example, first-hand observations and interviews with people knowledgeable about your topic can provide up-to-date information. Whatever your form of research, take careful notes so you can accurately paraphrase an author or quote an interviewee. The appendix to this book will help you research a topic.
5. *Think creatively.* To push an idea one step further, to make a connection not easily recognized by others, to step to one side of your topic and see it in a new light, to ask a question no one else would,

to arrive at a fresh insight is to be creative. Don't be afraid to step outside conventional wisdom and ask a basic or unorthodox question. Take risks. Such bravery adds creativity to your writing.

Establish Your Thesis

Once you have generated ideas and information, you are ready to begin the important task of establishing a controlling idea, or *thesis.* The thesis of an essay is its main idea, the point the writer is trying to make. The thesis is often expressed in one or two sentences called a *thesis statement.* Here's an example:

> The so-called serious news programs are becoming too much like tabloid news shows in both their content and their presentation.

The thesis statement should not be confused with your purpose for writing. While a thesis statement makes an assertion about your topic and actually appears in your essay as such, your purpose is what you are trying to do in the essay—to express, to explain, or to argue. For example, the purpose behind the preceding thesis statement might be expressed as follows:

> By comparing the transcripts of news shows like the *CBS Evening News* and tabloid shows like *Entertainment Tonight,* I will show troubling parallels in what the two genres of programs find "newsworthy."

This type of purpose statement should not appear in your essay. In other words, it's not a good idea to tell your readers what you are going to do in an essay. Just do it.

A thesis statement should be

- The most important point you make about a topic
- More general than the ideas and facts used to support it
- Focused enough to be covered in the space allotted for the essay

A thesis statement should not be a question, but rather an assertion. If you find yourself writing a question for a thesis statement, answer the question first, and then write your statement.

How to Write a Thesis Statement

An effective method for developing a thesis statement is to begin by writing, "What I want to say is that . . ."

> What I want to say is that unless language barriers between patients and healthcare providers are overcome, the lives of many patients in our more culturally diverse cities will be endangered.

Later, when you delete the formulaic opening, you will be left with a thesis statement:

> Unless language barriers between patients and healthcare providers are overcome, many patients' lives in our more culturally diverse cities will be endangered.

A good way to determine whether your thesis is too general or too specific is to consider how easy it will be to present information and examples to support it. If you stray too far in either direction, your task will become much more difficult. A thesis statement that is too general will leave you overwhelmed by the number of issues you must address. For example, the statement, "Malls have ruined the fabric of American life" would lead to the question "How?" To answer it, you would probably have to include information about traffic patterns, urban decay, environmental damage, economic studies, and so on. You would obviously have to take shortcuts, and your paper would be ineffective. On the other hand, too specific a thesis statement will leave you with too little information to present. "The Big City Mall should not have been built because it reduced retail sales at the existing Big City stores by 21.4 percent" does not leave you with any opportunities to develop an argument.

The thesis statement is usually set forth near the beginning of the essay, although writers sometimes begin with a few sentences that establish a context for the piece. One common strategy is to position the thesis as the final sentence of the first paragraph. In the opening paragraph of an essay on the harmful effects of quick weight-loss diets, student Marcie Turple builds a context for her thesis statement, which she presents in her last sentence:

> Americans are obsessed with thinness—even at the risk of dying. In the 1930s, people took dinitrophenol, an industrial poison, to lose weight. It boosted metabolism but caused blindness and some deaths. Since then dieters have used hormone injections, amphetamines, liquid protein diets, and, more recently, the controversial fen-phen. What most dieters need to realize is that there is no magic way to lose weight—no pill, no crash diet plan. *The only way to permanent weight loss is through sensible eating and exercise.*
>
> –Marcie Turple, student

Will Your Thesis Hold Water?

Once you have selected a possible thesis for an essay, ask yourself the following questions:

1. Does my thesis statement take a clear stance on an issue? And if so, what is that stance?
2. Is my thesis too general?
3. Is my thesis too specific?
4. Does my thesis apply to a larger audience than myself? If so, who is that audience?

For more on the various ways to build an effective thesis, see Chapter 3, "Thesis."

Know Your Audience

While it is not always possible to know who your readers are, you nevertheless need to consider your intended audience. Your attitude toward your topic, your tone, your sentence structure, and your choice of words are just some of the important considerations that rely on your awareness of audience. For a list of questions to help you determine your audience, see the box below.

Audience Questions

1. Who are my readers?
2. Is my audience specialized (for example, all those in my geology lab) or more general (college students)?
3. What do I know about my audience's age, gender, education, religious affiliation, socioeconomic status, and political attitudes?
4. What do my readers need to know that I can tell them?
5. Will my audience be interested, open-minded, resistant, objective, or hostile to what I am saying?
6. Is there any specialized language that my audience must have to understand my subject or that I should avoid?
7. What do I want my audience to do as a result of reading my essay?

Determine Your Method of Development

Part Four of *Models for Writers* includes chapters on the various types of writing most often required of college students. These types of writing are referred to as *methods of development, rhetorical patterns*, or *organizational patterns.*

Studying the organizational patterns and practicing the use of them are very important in any effort to broaden your writing skills. In *Models for Writers,* we look at each pattern separately because we believe this is the most effective way to introduce them. However, this does not necessarily mean that a well-written essay adheres exclusively and rigidly to a single pattern of development. Confining yourself exclusively to comparison and contrast throughout an entire essay, for instance, might prove impractical and might yield a strained, unnatural piece of writing. In fact, it is often best to use a single pattern to organize and develop your essay and then use the other patterns as your material dictates. For a description of what each method of development involves, see the box below. As you read the model essays in this text, you will find that many of them utilize a combination of patterns to support the dominant pattern.

Methods of Development

Illustration	Using examples to illustrate a point or idea
Narration	Telling a story or giving an account of an event
Description	Presenting a picture with words
Process Analysis	Explaining how something is done or happens
Definition	Explaining what something is
Division and Classification	Dividing a subject into its parts and placing them in appropriate categories
Comparison and Contrast	Demonstrating likenesses and differences
Cause and Effect	Explaining the causes of an event or the effects of an action
Argument	Using reason and logic to persuade someone to your way of thinking

Combining organizational patterns is probably not something you want to plan or even think about when you first tackle a writing assignment. Instead, let these patterns develop naturally as you organize, draft, and revise your materials. The combination of patterns will enhance the interest and impact of your writing.

If you're still undecided or concerned about combining patterns, try the following steps:

1. Summarize the point you want to make in a single phrase or sentence.
2. Restate the point as a question (in effect, the question your essay will answer).
3. Look closely at both the summary and the question for key words or concepts that suggest a particular pattern.
4. Consider other strategies that could support your primary pattern.

Here are some examples:

SUMMARY: Venus and Serena Williams are among the best women tennis players in the history of the game.

QUESTION: How do Venus and Serena Williams compare with other tennis players?

PATTERN: Comparison and contrast. The writer must compare the Williams sisters with other women players and provide evidence to support the claim that they are "among the best."

SUPPORTING PATTERNS: Illustration and description. Good evidence includes examples of their superior ability and accomplishments and descriptions of their athletic feats.

SUMMARY: How to build a personal Web site.

QUESTION: How do you build a personal Web site?

PATTERN: Process analysis. The word *how,* especially in the phrase *how to,* implies a procedure that can be explained in steps or stages.

SUPPORTING PATTERNS: Description. It will be necessary to describe the Web site at various points in the process, especially the look and design of the site.

SUMMARY: Petroleum and natural gas prices should be federally controlled.

QUESTION: What should be done about petroleum and natural gas prices?

PATTERN: Argument. The word *should* signals an argument, calling for evidence and reasoning in support of the conclusion.

SUPPORTING PATTERNS: Comparison and contrast and cause-and-effect analysis. The writer should present evidence from a comparison of federally controlled pricing with deregulated pricing as well as from a discussion of the effects of deregulation.

These are just a few examples showing how to decide on a pattern of development and supporting patterns that are suitable for your topic and what you want to say about it. In every case, your reading can guide you in recognizing the best plan to follow.

Map Your Organization

Once you decide what you want to write about and you come up with some ideas about what you might like to say, your next task is to jot down the main ideas for your essay in an order that seems both natural and logical to you. In other words, make a scratch outline. In constructing this outline, if you discover that one of the organizational patterns will help you in generating ideas, you might consider using that as your overall organizing principle.

Whether you write a formal outline, simply set down a rough sequence of the major points of your thesis, or take a middle ground between those two strategies, you need to think about the overall organization of your paper. Some writers make a detailed outline and fill it out point by point, while others follow a general plan and let the writing take them where it will, making any necessary adjustments to the plan when they revise.

Here are some major patterns of organization you may want to use for your outline:

- Chronological (oldest to newest, or the reverse)
- Spatial (top to bottom, left to right, inside to outside, and so forth)
- Least familiar to most familiar
- Easiest to most difficult to comprehend
- Easiest to most difficult to accept
- According to similarities or differences

Notice that some of these organizational patterns correspond to the rhetorical patterns in Part Four of this book. For example, a narrative essay generally follows a chronological organization. If you are having trouble developing or mapping an effective organization, refer to the introduction and readings in Chapter 5, "Organization." Once you have settled on an organizational pattern you are ready to write a first draft.

WRITING THE FIRST DRAFT

Your goal in writing a first draft is to get your ideas down on paper. Write quickly, and let the writing follow your thinking. Do not be overly concerned about spelling, word choice, or grammar because such concerns will break the flow of your ideas. After you have completed your first draft, you will go over your essay to revise and edit it.

As you write your draft, pay attention to your outline, but do not be a slave to it. It is there to help you, not restrict you. Often, when writing, you discover something new about your subject; follow that idea freely. Wherever you deviate from your plan, place an X in the margin to remind yourself of the change. When you revise, you can return to that part of your writing and reconsider the change you made, either developing it further or abandoning it.

It may happen that while writing your first draft, you run into difficulty that prevents you from moving forward. For example, suppose you want to tell the story of something that happened to you, but you aren't certain whether you should be using the pronoun *I* so often. Turn to the essays in Chapters 10 and 13 to see how the authors use diction and tone and how other narrative essays handle this problem. You will find that the frequent use of *I* isn't necessarily a problem at all. For an account of a personal experience, it's perfectly acceptable to use *I* as often as you need to. Or suppose that after writing several pages describing someone you think is quite a character, you find that your draft seems flat and doesn't express how lively and funny the person really is. If you read the introduction to Chapter 12, you will learn that descriptions need lots of factual, concrete detail; the selections in that chapter give further proof of this. You can use those guidelines to add details that are missing from your draft.

If you run into difficulties writing your first draft, don't worry or get upset. Even experienced writers run into problems at the beginning. Just try to keep going, and take the pressure off yourself. Think about your topic, and consider your details and what you want to say. You might even want to go back and look over the ideas and information you've gathered.

Create a Title

What makes a good title? There are no hard-and-fast rules, but most writers would agree that an effective title attracts attention and hooks the reader into reading the essay, either because the title is unusual or colorful and intrigues the reader or because it asks a question and the reader is curious to know the answer. A good title announces your subject and prepares your reader for the approach you take. You can create a title while writing your first draft or after you have seen how your ideas develop. Either way, the important thing is to brainstorm for titles and not simply use the first one that comes to mind. With at least a half dozen to choose from, preferably more, you will have a much better sense of how to pick an effective title, one that does important work explaining your subject to the reader and that is lively and inviting. Spend several minutes reviewing the titles of the essays in *Models for Writers* (see the table of contents, pp. xi–xx). You'll like some better than others, but reflecting on the effectiveness of each one will help you strengthen your own titles.

Focus on Beginnings and Endings

The beginning of your essay is vitally important to its success. Indeed, if your opening doesn't attract and hold your readers' attention, they may be less than enthusiastic about proceeding.

Your ending is almost always as equally important as your beginning. An effective conclusion does more than end your essay. It wraps up your thoughts and leaves readers satisfied with the presentation of your ideas and information. Your ending should be a natural outgrowth of the development of your ideas. Avoid trick endings, mechanical summaries, and cutesy comments, and never introduce new concepts or information in the ending. Just as with the writing of titles, the writing of beginnings and endings is perhaps best done by generating several alternatives and then selecting from among them. Review the box on page 20 and Chapter 6 for more help developing your beginnings and endings.

Notes on Beginnings and Endings

Beginnings and endings are very important to the effectiveness of an essay, but they can be difficult to write. Inexperienced writers often feel that they must write their essays sequentially when, in fact, it is better to write both the beginning and the ending after you have completed most of the rest of your essay. Pay particular attention to both parts during revision. Ask yourself the following questions:

1. Does my introduction grab the reader's attention?
2. Is my introduction confusing in any way? How well does it relate to the rest of the essay?
3. If I state my thesis in the introduction, how effectively is it presented?
4. Does my essay come to a logical conclusion, or does it just stop short?
5. How well does the conclusion relate to the rest of the essay? Am I careful not to introduce new topics or issues that I did not address in the body of the essay?
6. Does the conclusion help to underscore or illuminate important aspects of the body of the essay, or is it just another version of what I wrote earlier?

REVISING

Once you have completed a first draft, set it aside for a few hours or even until the next day. Removed from the process of drafting, you can approach the revision of your draft with a clear mind. When you revise, consider the most important elements of your draft first. You should focus on your thesis, purpose, content, organization, and paragraph structure. You will have a chance to look at grammar, punctuation, and mechanics after you revise. This way you will make sure that your essay is fundamentally solid and says what you want it to say before dealing with the task of editing.

It is very helpful to have someone—your roommate or member of your writing class—listen to your essay as you read it aloud. The process of reading aloud allows you to determine if your writing sounds clear and natural. If you have to strain your voice to provide emphasis, try rephrasing the idea to make it clearer. Whether you revise your work on your own or have someone assist you, the questions in the accompanying box will help you focus on the largest, most important elements of your essay early in the revision process.

Questions for Revising

1. Have I focused on my topic?
2. Does my thesis make a clear statement about my topic?
3. Is the organizational pattern I have used the best one, given my purpose?
4. Does the topic sentence of each paragraph relate to my thesis? Does each paragraph support its topic sentence?
5. Do I have enough supporting details, and are my examples the best ones that I can develop?
6. How effective are my beginning and my ending? Can I improve them?
7. Do I have a good title? Does it indicate what my subject is and hint at my thesis?

EDITING

Once you are sure that the large elements of your essay are in place and that you have said what you intended, you are ready to begin editing your essay. At this stage, it's important to correct any mistakes in grammar, punctuation, mechanics, and spelling because a series of small errors can add up and distract readers. More importantly, such errors can cause readers to doubt the important points you are trying to make.

The following section contains brief editing guidelines for the problems instructors around the country told us trouble their students most. For more guidance with these or other editing or grammar concerns, be sure to refer to your grammar handbook or ask your instructor for help. To practice finding and correcting these and many other problems, go to **bedfordstmartins.com/models** and click on "Exercise Central."

Run-ons: Fused Sentences and Comma Splices

Writers can become so absorbed in getting their ideas down on paper that they often combine two independent clauses (complete sentences that can stand alone when punctuated with a period) incorrectly, creating a *run-on sentence*. A run-on sentence fails to show where one thought ends and where another begins and can confuse readers. There are two types of run-on sentences: the fused sentence and the comma splice.

A *fused sentence* occurs when a writer combines two independent clauses with no punctuation at all. To correct a fused sentence, divide the independent clauses into separate sentences or join them by adding words and/or punctuation.

INCORRECT	Jen loves Harry Potter she was the first in line to buy the latest book.
EDITED	Jen loves Harry Potter ~~she~~ . She was the first in line to buy the latest book.
EDITED	Jen loves Harry Potter ; in fact, she was the first in line to buy the latest book.

A *comma splice* occurs when writers use only a comma to combine two independent clauses. To correct a comma splice, divide the independent clauses into separate sentences or join them by adding words and/or punctuation.

INCORRECT	The e-mail looked like spam, Marty deleted it.
EDITED	The e-mail looked like spam; Marty deleted it.
EDITED	The e-mail looked like spam, so Marty deleted it.

Sentence Fragments

A *sentence fragment* is a word group that cannot stand alone as a complete sentence. Even if a word group begins with a capital letter and ends with punctuation, it is not a sentence unless it has a subject (the person, place, or thing the sentence is about) and a verb (a word that tells what the subject does) and expresses a complete thought. Word groups that do not express complete thoughts often begin with a subordinating conjunction such as *although*, *because*, *since*, or *unless*.

To correct a fragment, add a subject or a verb or integrate the fragment into a nearby sentence to complete the thought.

INCORRECT	Divided my time between work and school last semester.
EDITED	~~Divided~~ I divided my time between work and school last semester.
INCORRECT	Terry's essay was really interesting. Because it brought up good points about energy conservation.
EDITED	Terry's essay was really interesting/ ~~Because~~ because it brought up good points about energy conservation.

Creative use of intentional sentence fragments is occasionally acceptable—in narration essays, for example—when writers are trying to establish a particular mood or tone.

> I asked him about his recent trip. He asked me about work. Short questions. One-word answers. Then an awkward pause.
>
> –David P. Bardeen

Subject-Verb Agreement

Subjects and verbs must agree in number—that is, a singular subject (one person, place, or thing) must take a singular verb, and a plural subject (more than one person, place, or thing) must take a plural verb. Most native speakers of English use proper subject-verb agreement in their writing without conscious awareness. Even so, some sentence constructions can be troublesome.

When a prepositional phrase (a phrase that includes a preposition such as *on, of, in, at,* or *between*) falls between a subject and a verb, it can obscure their relationship. To make sure the subject agrees with its verb in a sentence with an intervening prepositional phrase, mentally cross out the phrase (*of basic training* in the following example) to isolate the subject and verb and determine if they agree.

INCORRECT The first three weeks of basic training is the worst.

EDITED The first three weeks of basic training ~~is~~ are the worst.

Writers often have difficulty with subject-verb agreement in sentences with compound subjects (two or more subjects joined together with the word *and*). As a general rule, compound subjects take plural verbs.

INCORRECT My mother, sister, and cousin is visiting me next month.

EDITED My mother, sister, and cousin ~~is~~ are visiting me next month.

However, in sentences with subjects joined by *either . . . or, neither . . . nor,* or *not only . . . but also,* the verb must agree with the subject closest to it.

INCORRECT Neither the mechanics nor the salesperson know what's wrong with my car.

EDITED Neither the mechanics nor the salesperson ~~know~~ knows what's wrong with my car.

While editing your essay, be sure to identify the subjects and verbs in your sentences and to check their agreement.

Pronoun-Antecedent Agreement

A *pronoun* is a word that takes the place of a noun in a sentence. To avoid repeating nouns in our speech and writing, we use pronouns as noun substitutes. The noun to which a pronoun refers is called its *antecedent.* A pronoun and its antecedent are said to *agree* when the relationship between them is clear. Pronouns must agree with their antecedents in both *person* and *number.*

There are three types of pronouns: first person (*I* and *we*), second person (*you*), and third person (*he, she, they,* and *it*). First-person pronouns refer to first-person antecedents, second-person pronouns refer to second-person antecedents, and third-person pronouns refer to third-person antecedents.

INCORRECT	House hunters should review their finances carefully before you make an offer.
EDITED	House hunters should review their finances carefully before ~~you~~ they make an offer.

A pronoun must agree in number with its antecedent; that is, a singular pronoun must refer to a singular antecedent, and a plural pronoun must refer to a plural antecedent. When two or more antecedents are joined by the word *and*, the pronoun must be plural.

INCORRECT	Gina, Kim, and Katie took her vacations in August.
EDITED	Gina, Kim, and Katie took ~~her~~ their vacations in August.

When the subject of a sentence is an indefinite pronoun such as *everyone, each, everybody, anyone, anybody, everything, either, one, neither, someone,* or *something,* use a singular pronoun to refer to it or recast the sentence to eliminate the agreement problem.

INCORRECT	Each of the women submitted their resumé.
EDITED	Each of the women submitted ~~their~~ her resumé.
EDITED	~~Each~~ Both of the women submitted their ~~resume~~ resumés.

Verb Tense Shifts

A verb's tense indicates when an action takes place—sometime in the past, right now, or in the future. Using verb tense consistently helps your readers understand time changes in your writing. Inconsistent verb tenses, or *shifts,* within a sentence confuse readers and are especially noticeable in narration and process analysis writing, which are sequence and time oriented. Generally, you should write in the past or present tense and maintain that tense throughout your sentence.

INCORRECT	The painter studied the scene and pulls a fan brush decisively from her cup.
EDITED	The painter studied the scene and ~~pulls~~ pulled a fan brush decisively from her cup.

Misplaced and Dangling Modifiers

A *modifier* is a word or words that describes or gives additional information about other words in a sentence. Always place modifiers as close as possible to the words you want to modify. An error in modifier placement could be unintentionally confusing—or amusing—to your reader. Two common problems arise with modifiers: the misplaced modifier and the dangling modifier.

A *misplaced modifier* unintentionally modifies the wrong word in a sentence because it is placed incorrectly.

INCORRECT	The waiter brought a steak to the man covered with onions.
EDITED	The waiter brought a steak covered with onions to the man. ~~covered with onions.~~

A *dangling modifier* appears at the beginning or end of a sentence and modifies a word that does not appear in the sentence—often an unstated subject.

INCORRECT	Staring into the distance, large rain clouds form.
EDITED	Staring into the distance, Jon saw large rain clouds form.

While editing your essay, make sure you have positioned your modifiers as close as possible to the words you want to modify and that each sentence has a clear subject that is modified correctly.

Faulty Parallelism

Parallelism means using similar grammatical forms to show that ideas in a sentence are of equal importance. Faulty parallelism can interrupt the flow of your writing and confuse your readers. Writers have trouble with parallelism in three kinds of sentence constructions.

In sentences that include items in a pair or series, make sure the elements of the pair or series are parallel in form. Delete any unnecessary or repeated words.

INCORRECT	Nina likes snowboarding, roller skating, and to hike.
EDITED	Nina likes snowboarding, roller skating, and hiking ~~to hike~~.

In sentences that include connecting words such as *both . . . and, either . . . or, neither . . . nor, rather . . . than,* and *not only . . . but also,* make sure the elements being connected are parallel in form. Delete any unnecessary or repeated words.

INCORRECT	The lecture was both enjoyable and it was a form of education.
EDITED	The lecture was both enjoyable and educational. ~~it was a form of education.~~

In sentences that include the comparison word *as* or *than,* make sure the elements of the comparison are parallel in form. Delete any unnecessary or repeated words.

INCORRECT	It would be better to study now than waiting until the night before the exam.
EDITED	It would be better to study now than to wait ~~waiting~~ until the night before the exam.

Weak Nouns and Verbs

Inexperienced writers often believe that adjectives and adverbs are the stuff of effective writing. They're right in one sense, but not wholly so. Although strong adjectives and adverbs are crucial, good writing depends on well-chosen, strong nouns and verbs. *Vehicle* is not nearly as descriptive as *Jeep, snowmobile, pick-up truck,* or *SUV,* for example. Why use the weak verb *look* when your meaning would be more precisely conveyed with *glance, stare, spy, gaze, peek, examine,* or *witness*? Instead of the weak verb *run,* use *fly, gallop, hustle, jog, race, rush, scamper, scoot, scramble,* or *trot.*

While editing your essay, look for instances of weak nouns and verbs. If you can't form a clear picture in your mind of what a noun looks like or what a verb's action is, your nouns and verbs are likely weak. The more specific and strong you make your nouns and verbs, the more lively and descriptive your writing will be.

WEAK	The flowers moved toward the bright light of the sun.
EDITED	The ~~flowers moved~~ ^tulips stretched toward the bright light of the sun.

When you have difficulty thinking of strong, specific nouns and verbs, reach for a thesaurus—but only if you are sure you can discern the best word for your purpose. Thesauruses are available free online and in inexpensive paperback editions; most word processing programs include a thesaurus as well. A thesaurus will help you avoid redundancy in your writing and will be invaluable when you need to find a specific word with just the right meaning.

ESL Concerns (Articles and Nouns)

Two areas of English grammar that can be especially problematic for nonnative speakers of English are articles and nouns. In English, correct use of articles and nouns is necessary for sentences to make sense.

There are two kinds of articles in English: *indefinite* (*a* and *an*) and *definite* (*the*). Use *a* before words beginning with a consonant sound and *an* before words beginning with a vowel sound. Note, too, that *a* is used before an *h* with a consonant sound (*happy*), and *an* is used before a silent *h* (*hour*).

There are two kinds of nouns in English: count and noncount. *Count nouns* name individual things or units that can be counted or separated out from a whole, such as *students* and *pencils*. *Noncount nouns* name things that cannot be counted because they are considered wholes in themselves and cannot be divided, such as *work* and *furniture*.

Use the indefinite article (*a* or *an*) before a singular count noun when you do not specify which one.

> I would like to borrow *a* colored pencil.

Plural count nouns take *the*.

> I would like to borrow *the* colored pencils.

If a plural count noun is used in a general sense, it does not take an article at all.

> I brought colored pencils to class today.

Noncount nouns are always singular and never take an indefinite article.

> We need new living room furniture.

The is sometimes used with noncount nouns to refer to a specific idea or thing.

> *The* furniture will be delivered tomorrow.

While editing your essay, be sure that you have used articles and nouns correctly.

INCORRECT I love an aroma of freshly baked cookies.

EDITED I love ~~an~~ the aroma of freshly baked cookies.

INCORRECT	I have never had the chicken pox.
EDITED	I have never had ~~the~~ chicken pox.

Questions for Editing Sentences

1. Do I include any fused sentences or comma splices?
2. Do I include any unintentional sentence fragments?
3. Do my verbs agree with their subjects?
4. Do my pronouns agree with their antecedents?
5. Do I make any unnecessary shifts in verb tense?
6. Do I have any misplaced or dangling modifiers?
7. Are my sentences parallel?
8. Do I use strong nouns and active verbs?
9. Do I pair articles and nouns correctly?

PROOFREADING

Do not assume that because you made edits and corrections to your essay electronically in your word processor that all of your changes were saved or that your essay will print out correctly. Also do not assume that because you used your word processor's spell-check or grammar-check function that you've found and corrected every spelling and grammatical error; in fact, such checkers often allow incorrect or misspelled words to pass while flagging correct grammatical constructions as incorrect. Although your word processor's spell-checker and grammar-checker are a good "first line of defense" against certain types of errors, there is no replacement for a human proofreader—you.

Print out your essay and carefully proofread it manually. Check to make sure you do not use *your* where you intend *you're*, *its* where you mean *it's*, or *to* where you want *too*. Spell-checkers *never* catch these types of errors. If you know that you are prone to certain mistakes, go once through your essay looking for those particular problems. For example, if you often have trouble with placing commas or other punctuation marks with quotations, proofread your essay for that specific problem.

Proofread a hard copy of your essay to make sure that all of your electronic changes appear on it and that you have caught and corrected any grammatical problems. (Be sure to refer to the Questions for Editing Sentences box on p. 30, and to the Questions for Proofreading Essays box that follows.) Check to be certain you have followed your instructor's formatting guidelines. Above all, give your hard-copy essay one final read-through before submitting it to your instructor.

Questions for Proofreading Essays

1. Have I printed a hard copy of my essay for proofreading?
2. Have I misspelled or incorrectly typed any words? Has my spell-checker inadvertently approved commonly confused words like *its* and *it's*, or *their, there,* and *they're*?
3. Have I checked my essay for errors I make often?
4. Do all of my edits and corrections appear in my hard copy?
5. Have I formatted my essay according to my instructor's directions?
6. Have I given the hard copy of my final draft a thorough review before turning it in?

WRITING AN EXPOSITORY ESSAY: A STUDENT ESSAY IN PROGRESS

While he was a student in a writing class at the University of Vermont, Jeffrey Olesky was asked to write an essay on any topic using a suitable method of development. After making a brief list of the subjects that interested him, he chose to write about golf. Golf has been a part of Olesky's life since he was a youngster, so he figured he would have enough material for an essay.

First, he needed to focus on a specific topic within the broad subject area of golf. Having considered a number of aspects of the game—how it's played, its recent popularity because of Tiger Woods, the controversies of private clubs excluding women and minorities—he kept coming back to how much golf meant to him. Focusing on his love of golf, he then established his tentative thesis: Golf has taught me a lot.

Olesky needed to develop a number of examples to support his thesis, so he brainstormed for ideas, examples, and anecdotes—anything that came to mind that would help him develop his essay. These are his notes:

Brainstorming Notes

Golf is my life—I can't imagine being who I am without it.

I love to be out on the course early in the morning.

It's been embarrassing and stressful sometimes.

There's so much to know and remember about the game, even before you try to hit the ball.

The story about what my father taught me—felt badly and needed to apologize.

"You know better than that, Jeffrey."

I have pictures of me on the greens with a cut-down golf putter.

All kinds of character building goes on.

It's all about rules and playing fairly.

Wanted to be like my father.

The frustration is awesome, but you can learn to deal with it.

Golf is methodical.

I use golf to clear my head.

Golf teaches life's lessons.

Golf teaches you manners, to be respectful of others.

Golf teaches you to abide by the rules.

Golf is an internal tool.

When he thought that he had gathered enough information, he began to sort it out. He needed an organizational plan, some way to present his information that was not random but rather showed a logical progression. He realized that the character-building benefits of golf that he included in his brainstorming notes clustered around some key subtopics. He decided to do some clustering and drew circles that included his ideas about golf: the physical and mental demands of the game, the social values and morals it teaches, and the reflective benefits of golf. He then sorted out his related ideas and examples and added them, mapping their relationship in the diagram. Here is his clustering diagram:

Clustering Diagram

Before beginning to write the first draft of his paper, Olesky thought it would be a good idea to list in an informal outline the major points he wanted to make. Here is his informal outline:

Informal Outline

1. Brief introductory paragraph announcing the topic
2. An expansion of the introductory paragraph and the <u>thesis statement:</u> Golf has taught me a lot
3. A discussion of how, above all, golf teaches one to control one's emotions

4. A discussion of how much one needs to know and remember to play golf well
5. The values that golf teaches
6. A multiparagraph example illustrating a valuable lesson taught through golf
7. Golf provides an opportunity to reflect
8. Reflection, in turn, leads to a deeper appreciation of nature

With his outline before him, Olesky felt ready to try a rough draft of his paper. He wrote quickly, keeping his organizational plan in mind but striving to keep the writing going and get his thoughts down on paper. He knew that once he had a draft, he could determine how to improve it. Olesky wrote some fairly solid paragraphs, but he sensed that they were on different aspects of his topic and that the logical order of the points he was making was not quite right. He needed an organizational plan, some way to present his information that was not random but rather showed a logical progression.

Reviewing his outline, Olesky could see that there was a natural progression from the physical lessons of the sport to the social and moral lessons to the psychological, emotional, and even spiritual benefits that one could derive. He decided therefore to move item 3 ("A discussion of how, above all, golf teaches one to control one's emotions") in his original organization and make it item 6 in the revision. Here is his reordered outline:

Reordered Outline

1. Brief introductory paragraph announcing the topic
2. An expansion of the introductory paragraph and the thesis statement: Golf has taught me a lot
3. A discussion of how much one needs to know and remember to play golf well
4. The social values that golf teaches
5. A multiparagraph example illustrating a valuable lesson taught through golf
6. A discussion of how, above all, golf teaches one to control one's emotions
7. Golf provides an opportunity to reflect
8. Reflection, in turn, leads to a deeper appreciation of nature

Olesky was satisfied that his essay now had a natural and logical organization. In short, it moved from matters of lesser to greater importance to him personally. However, he now needed to revise his thesis to better suit the argument he had established. He wanted his revised thesis to be more focused and specific and to include the idea that the lessons and values golf taught him could not be as easily learned in other ways. Here is his revised thesis statement:

Revised Thesis Statement

In its simplicity, golf has taught me many lessons and values other people have trouble learning elsewhere.

After revising the organization, he was now ready to edit his essay and to correct those smaller but equally important errors in word choice, wordiness, punctuation, and mechanics. He had put aside these errors to make sure his essay had the appropriate content. Now he needed to make sure it was grammatically correct. Here are several sample paragraphs showing the editing that Olesky did on his essay:

Edited Paragraphs

	Ever since I was a little boy, no older than two or three, I
Addition for clarity	have had a golf club in my hand. My mother has pictures of me ^as a toddler
Elimination of unessential information	with my father on the putting green of the golf course. ~~that my father belonged to.~~ With a cut-down putter, the shaft ~~had been~~ reduced in length so that it would fit me, I would spend hours trying to place the small white ball into the little round hole. I'm
Change of period to colon to eliminate sentence fragment and introduce appositive phrase	sure at first that I took to the game to be like my father: ~~T~~to act like him, play like him, and hit the ball as far as he did. However, it is not what I have learned about the mechanics of the golf swing, or ~~all~~ ^about the facts ~~and figures~~ of the game that have caused golf to mean so much to me, but rather ^it is the things golf has taught me
Correction of it's *to* its	about everyday life ^in general. In it~~'~~s simplicity, golf has taught me many lessons and values other people have trouble learning elsewhere.

Elimination of wordiness

Golf is a good teacher because there ~~Along the same lines, tThere~~ are many variables and aspects to the game. ~~of golf.~~ You ~~are~~ constantly have ~~having~~ to think, analyze, and evaluate your position and strategy. ~~That is the difficulty of the game of golf.~~ Unlike many sports that rely on ~~once you~~ committing ~~committed the~~ actions to muscle memory, golf requires ~~there is no guarantee you will still perform well. There is~~ a phenomenal amount of information to think about and keys to remember. Legs shoulder-width apart, knees flexed, fingers interlocked, body loose . . . and you haven't even tried to hit the ball yet. But having to go about things so methodically in golf has enabled me to apply the skills of patience and analysis ~~the methods of golf~~ to many other parts of my life. I don't believe I would have nearly the same personality if golf had not played such an integral ~~intricate~~ role in my development.

Addition of specific information for clarity

Improved dicton

In addition to editing his revised paper, Olesky reexamined his title, "Character Builder." Olesky considered a half-dozen alternatives. He finally settled on the use of "Golf" as a main title because it was such a key word for his topic and thesis; he used "A Character Builder" as his subtitle. He also thought about his conclusion, wondering whether it was forceful enough. After considerable thought, and having sought the advice of his classmates, Olesky decided to end with the rather low-key but significantly meaningful final paragraphs he generated in his original draft. Here is the final version of his essay:

Final Essay

Title: suggests what the essay will be about

Golf: A Character Builder

Jeffrey Olesky

Golf is what I love. It is what I do, and it is who I am. In many respects it has defined and shaped my character and personality. I couldn't possibly imagine my life without golf and what it has meant for me.

Beginning: effective opening paragraph sets the context for the essay

Ever since I was a little boy, no older than two or three, I have had a golf club in my hand. My mother has pictures of me as a toddler with my father on the putting green of the golf course. With a cut-down putter, the shaft reduced in length so that it would fit me, I would spend hours trying to place the small white ball in the little round hole. I'm sure at first that I took to the game to be like my father: to act like him, play like him, and hit the ball as far as he did. However, it is not what I have learned about the mechanics of the golf swing or about the facts of the game that have caused golf to mean so much to me, but rather it is the things golf has taught me about everyday life in general. In its simplicity, golf has taught me many lessons and values other people have trouble learning elsewhere.

Thesis statement: sets clear expectation in the reader's mind

Golf is a good teacher because there are many variables and aspects to the game. You constantly have to think, analyze, and evaluate your position and strategy. Unlike many sports that rely on committing actions to muscle memory, golf requires a phenomenal amount of information to think about and keys to remember. Legs shoulder-width apart, knees flexed, fingers interlocked, body loose . . . and you haven't even tried to hit the ball yet. But having to go about things so methodically in golf has enabled me to apply the skills of patience and analysis to many other parts of my life. I don't believe I would have nearly the same personality if golf had not played such an integral role in my development.

Golf requires lots of information, both physical and mental.

Transition: discussion moves to how the game influences personality

Golf has also changed and shaped my personality by repeatedly reinforcing many of the lessons of life. You know the ones I'm referring to, the rules you learn in kindergarten: Treat others as you would like to be treated; respect other people and their property . . . the list goes on. Golf may not blare them out as obviously as my kindergarten teacher, but in its own subtle, respectful tone, golf has imbued me with many of the values and morals I have today. Simply by learning the rules of such a

Golf teaches life lessons, too.

prestigious, honest, and respected game, you gradually learn the reasoning behind them and how they relate to life.

Illustration: extended example in narrative form of some of the lessons golf teaches

A good example of such a life lesson comes from the first time my father ever took me out on an actual golf course. I had been waiting for this day for quite some time and was so excited when he finally gave me the chance. He had gone out to play with a few of his friends early one Saturday morning in one of the larger tournaments. I was caddying for my father. Although I was too young to actually carry his bag, I would clean his golf ball, rake the bunkers for him, and do the other minor tasks that caddies do. But the fact that I was actually out "with the big boys," watching them play golf, was enough to make me happy. Besides, none of the other gentlemen my father was playing with seemed to mind that I was along for the ride.

Narrative example continues

The lesson I learned that day appears rather simple now. It came on the putting green of the second hole. My father had finished putting out, and I was holding the flagstick off to the side of the green while the other players finished. Generally my father would come stand next to me and give me a hand, but due to circumstances we ended up on opposite sides of the green. During the next player's putt my father lowered his eyebrows at me and nodded his head to one side a few times. Curious as to what he wanted me to do, I almost let the question slip out of my mouth. But I knew better. I had already learned the rules of not talking or moving while other golfers were hitting. I quietly stood my ground until everyone was finished, then placed the flagstick back in the hole. While walking towards the next tee box, I neared my father. Regardless of what he had wanted me to do I thought he would commend me for not talking or moving during the ordeal.

Dialogue: "shows rather than tells," and puts the reader in the scene

"You know better than that, Jeffrey," he said.

"What?" I asked curiously, disappointed that he had not praised me on a job well done.

"You never stand so that your shadow is in someone's line."

How could I be so stupid? He had reminded me a thousand times before. You never allow your shadow to fall in the line of someone's putt because it is distracting to the person putting. I rationalized to my father that maybe the man hadn't noticed or that it didn't bother him. Unfortunately my father wasn't going to take that as an excuse. After explaining to me what I had done wrong, he suggested that I go over and apologize to the gentleman. I was still a young boy, and the figure of the older man was somewhat intimidating. This task was no easy chore because I was obviously very scared, and this is perhaps what made the lesson sink in a little deeper. I remember gradually approaching my father's friend and periodically looking back to my father for help. Once I realized I was on my own, I bashfully gave him my apologies and assured him that it wouldn't happen again. As you can probably guess, the repercussions were not as dramatic as I had envisioned them to be. Once my father had pointed out my mistake, I begged him to reconcile with the gentleman for me. However, in apologizing for myself, I learned a valuable lesson. Golf is important because it has taught me many social values such as this, but it can also be a personal, internal tool.

Transition: Golf can also be a personal, internal tool.

Organization: continues to move from concrete practical concerns to those that are more abstract

Golf has taught me how to deal with frustration and to control myself mentally in difficult and strenuous situations. Golf is about mastering your emotions in stressful times and prevailing with a methodical, calm mind. I have dealt with the disappointment of missing a two-foot putt on the last hole to break eighty and the embarrassment of shanking my drive off the first hole in front of dozens of people. In dealing with these circumstances and continuing with my game, I have learned how to control my emotions. Granted, golf is not the most physically strenuous sport, but it is the mental challenge of complete and utter concentration that makes it difficult. People who are not able to control their temper or to take command of their emotions generally do not end up playing this game for very long.

Organization: Olesky moves to more philosophic influences.

Golf gives me the opportunity to be reflective--time to myself when I can debate and organize the thoughts in my head. There are few places where you can find the peace and tranquility like that of a golf course in the early morning or late afternoon. When I am playing by myself, which I make an effort to do when I need to "get away," I am able to reflect and work out some of the difficulties I am facing. I can think in complete quietness, but at the same time I have something to do while I am thinking. There are few places in the world offering this type of sanctuary that are easily accessible.

Organization: Olesky discusses finally golf's ability to bring him close to nature.

It is in these morning reflections that I also gain an appreciation of my surroundings. I often like to get up early on a Saturday or Sunday and be the first one on the course. There are many things I love about the scenery of a golf course during the morning hours. I love the smell of the freshly cut grass as the groundskeepers crisscross their patterns onto the fairways and greens. I love looking back on my progress toward the tee box on the first hole to witness my solitary foot tracks in the morning dew. I love the chirp of the yellow finches as they signal the break of dawn. All these conditions help to create the feeling I perceive as I walk down the first fairway. Thinking back to those days on the putting green with my father, I realize how dear golf is to me. Golf has created my values, taught me my lessons, and been my outlet. I love the game for all these reasons.

Ending: a quiet but appropriate conclusion

chapter **2**

From Reading to Writing

To move from reading to writing, you need to read actively, in a thoughtful spirit, and with an alert, inquiring mind. Reading actively means learning how to analyze what you read. You must be able to discover what is going on in an essay, to figure out the writer's reasons for shaping the essay in a particular way, to decide whether the result works well or poorly—and why. At first, such digging may seem odd, and for good reason. After all, we all know how to read. But do we know how to read *actively*?

Active reading is a skill that takes time to acquire. By becoming more familiar with different types of writing, you will sharpen your critical thinking skills and learn how good writers make decisions in their writing. After reading an essay, most people feel more confident talking about the content of the piece than about the writer's style. Content is more tangible than style, which always seems so elusive. In large part, this discrepancy results from our schooling. Most of us have been taught to read for ideas. Not many of us, however, have been trained to read actively, to engage a writer and his or her writing, to ask why we like one piece of writing and not another. Similarly, most of us do not ask ourselves why one piece of writing is more convincing than another. When you learn to read actively, you begin to answer these important questions and come to appreciate the craftsmanship involved in writing. Active reading, then, is a skill you need if you are truly to engage and understand the content of a piece of writing as well as the craft that shapes the writer's ideas into a presentable form. Active reading will repay your efforts by helping you read more effectively and grow as a writer.

■ GETTING THE MOST OUT OF YOUR READING

Active reading requires, first of all, that you commit time and effort. Second, try to take a positive interest in what you are reading, even if the subject matter is not immediately appealing. Remember, you are not reading for content alone but also to understand a writer's methods—to see firsthand the kinds of choices writers make while they write.

To help you get the most out of your reading, here are some guidelines for

1. Preparing yourself to read a selection
2. Reading the selection the first time
3. Rereading the selection
4. Annotating the text with marginal notes
5. Analyzing the text with questions

Prereading: Preparing Yourself

Instead of diving right into any given selection in *Models for Writers* or any other book, there are a few things that you can do first that will prepare you to get the most out of what you will be reading. It's helpful, for example, to get a context for what it is you'll be reading. What's the essay about? What do you know about the writer's background and reputation? Where was the essay first published? Who was the intended audience for the essay? And, finally, how much do you already know about the subject of the reading selection? We encourage you to consider carefully the materials that precede each selection in this book.

Each selection begins with a *title,* a *headnote,* and a *journal prompt.* From the *title,* you often discover the writer's position on an issue or attitude toward the topic. On occasion, the title provides clues about the intended audience and the writer's purpose in writing the piece. The *headnote* contains three essential elements: a *biographical note* about the author, *publication information,* and *rhetorical highlights* of the selection. In addition to information on the person's life and work, you'll find out something about his or her reputation and authority to write on the subject of the piece. The *publication information* tells you when the essay was published and in what book or magazine it appeared. This information, in turn, gives you insight about the intended audience and the historical context. The *rhetorical highlights* direct your attention to one or more of the model features of the selection. Finally, the *journal prompt* encourages you to collect your own thoughts and opinions about the topic or related subjects before you commence reading. The journal prompt makes it easy for you to keep a record of your own knowledge or thinking about a topic before you see what the writer has to offer in the essay.

To demonstrate how these context-building materials can work for you, carefully review the following materials that accompany Isaac Asimov's "Intelligence." The essay itself appears later in this chapter.

Intelligence

Title

Isaac Asimov

Headnote

1. Biographical note

Born in the Soviet Union, Isaac Asimov immigrated to the United States in 1923. His death in 1992 ended a long, prolific career as a science-fiction and nonfiction writer. Asimov was uniquely talented at making a diverse range of topics, from Shakespeare to atomic physics, not only comprehensible but also entertaining to the general reader. Asimov earned three degrees at Columbia University and later taught biochemistry at Boston University. At the time of his death, he had published more than five hundred books. It's Been a Good Life, *published in 2002, was compiled from selections made from Asimov's three previous autobiographical volumes:* In Memory Yet Green *(1979),* In Joy Still Felt *(1980), and* I. Asimov: A Memoir *(1994). Edited by Janet Jeppson Asimov, the book also features "A Way of Thinking," Asimov's four hundredth essay for the* Magazine of Fantasy and Science Fiction.

2. Publication information

In the following essay, which first appeared in Please Explain *(1973), Asimov, an intellectually gifted man, ponders the nature of intelligence. His academic brilliance, he concedes, would mean little or nothing if like-minded intellectuals had not*

3. Rhetorical highlights

established the standards for intelligence in our society. Notice how he uses personal experience and the example of his auto mechanic to develop his definition of intelligence.

For Your Journal

Journal prompt

Our society defines the academically gifted as intelligent, but perhaps *book smart* would be a better term. IQ tests don't take into account common sense or experience, attributes that the academically gifted sometimes lack outside of a scholarly setting. Who's the smartest person you know? Is he or she academically gifted or smart in some way that would not be readily recognized as a form of intelligence?

From these preliminary materials, what expectations do you have for the selection itself? And how does this knowledge equip you to engage the selection before you read it? Asimov's title suggests the question "What is intelligence?" You can reasonably infer that Asimov will discuss the nature of intelligence. His purpose clearly seems to be to explore the subject with his readers. The short biographical note reveals that Asimov, a scientist, teacher, and prolific author, is no longer living, that he enjoyed a reputation as a renaissance man, and that he wrote with an ease and understanding that make difficult subjects readily accessible to the general public. This background material suggests that in the essay you'll get a thoughtful, easy-to-comprehend discussion of intelligence. The rhetorical highlights advise you to pay particular attention to how Asimov uses the examples of himself and his auto mechanic to think about the meaning of intelligence. Finally, the journal prompt asks you to consider how society defines the term *intelligence,* first by identifying the smartest person in your life and then by thinking about whether that person is more academically gifted (book smart) or experientially gifted (street smart). After reading the essay, you can compare your thoughts about the nature of intelligence with Asimov's.

The First Reading: Getting an Overview of the Selection

Always read the selection at least twice, no matter how long it is. The first reading gives you a chance to get acquainted with the essay and to form your first impressions of it. With the first reading, you want to get an overall sense of what the writer is saying, keeping in mind the essay's title and what you know about the writer from the essay's headnote. The essay will offer you information, ideas, and arguments—some you may have expected, some you may not have expected. As you read, you may find yourself modifying your sense of the writer's message and purpose. If there are any words that you do not recognize, circle them so that you can look them up later in a dictionary. Put question marks alongside any passages that are not immediately clear. You may, in fact, want to delay most of your annotating until a second reading so that your first reading can be fast and free.

The Second Reading: Coming to an Understanding of the Selection

Your second reading should be quite different from the first. You will know what the essay is about, where it is going, and how it gets there; now you can relate the parts of the essay more accurately to the whole. Use your second reading to test your first impressions against the words on the page, developing and deepening your sense of how the essay is written, and how well. Because you now have a general understanding of the essay, you can pay special attention to the author's purpose and means of achieving that purpose. You can look for features of organization and style that you can learn from and adapt to your own work.

Responding to Your Reading: Making Marginal Notes

When you annotate a text, you should do more than simply underline or highlight important points to remember. It is easy to underline so much that the notations become almost meaningless because you forget why you underlined the passages in the first place. Instead, as you read, write down your thoughts in the margins or on a separate piece of paper. (See pages 47–49 for Asimov's "Intelligence" with student annotations.) Mark the selection's main point when you find it stated directly. Look for the pattern or patterns of development the author uses to explore and support that point, and jot the information down. If you disagree with a statement or conclusion, object in the margin: "No!" If you feel skeptical, indicate that response: "Why?" or "Explain." If you are impressed by an argument or turn of phrase, compliment the writer: "Good point!" Place vertical lines or stars in the margin to indicate important points.

Jot down whatever marginal notes come to mind. Most readers combine brief responses written in the margins with underlining, circling, highlighting, stars, or question marks. Here are some suggestions of elements you may want to mark to help you keep a record of your responses as you read:

What to Annotate in a Text

- Memorable statements of important points
- Key terms or concepts
- Central issues or themes
- Examples that support a main point
- Unfamiliar words
- Questions you have about a point or passage
- Your responses to a specific point or passage

Remember that there are no hard-and-fast rules for which elements you annotate. Choose a method of annotation that works best for you and that will make sense when you go back to recollect your thoughts and responses to the essay. When annotating a text, don't be timid. Mark up your book as much as you like, or jot down as many responses in your notebook as you think will be helpful. Don't let annotating become burdensome. A word or phrase is usually as good as a sentence. One helpful way to focus your annotations is to ask yourself questions as you read the selection a second time.

Analyzing: Asking Yourself Questions as You Read

As you read the essay a second time, probing for a deeper understanding of and appreciation for what the writer has done, focus your attention by asking yourself some basic questions about its content and its form. Here are some questions you may find useful:

Questions to Ask Yourself as You Read
1. What does the writer want to say? What is the writer's main point or thesis? 2. Why does the writer want to make this point? What is the writer's purpose? 3. What pattern or patterns of development does the writer use? 4. How does the writer's pattern of development suit his or her subject and purpose? 5. What, if anything, is noteworthy about the writer's use of this pattern? 6. How effective is the essay? Does the writer make his or her points clearly?

Each essay in *Models for Writers* is followed by study questions similar to the ones suggested here, but more specific to the essay. These questions help you analyze both the content of the essay and the writer's craft. As you read the essay a second time, look for details that will support your answers to these questions, and then answer the questions as fully as you can.

An Example: Annotating Isaac Asimov's "Intelligence"

Notice how one of our students, guided by the six preceding questions, recorded her responses to Asimov's text with marginal notes.

Asks questions central to the essay and relates army experience

What is intelligence, anyway? When I was in the army I received a kind of aptitude test that soldiers took and, against a norm of 100, scored 160. No one at the base had ever seen a figure like that, and for two hours they made a big fuss over me. (It didn't mean anything. The next day I was still a buck private with KP as my highest duty.)

All my life I've been registering scores like that, so that I have the complacent feeling that I'm highly intelligent, and I expect other people to think so, too.

Actually, though, don't such scores simply mean that I am very good at answering the type of academic questions that are considered worthy of answers by the people who make up the intelligence tests—people with intellectual bents similar to mine?

Questions the meaning of high test scores, what do I think they mean?

Auto repair example. Any relationship between test scores and ability to fix cars?

For instance, I had an auto-repair man once, who, on these intelligence tests, could not possibly have scored more than 80, by my estimate. I always took it for granted that I was far more intelligent than he was. Yet, when anything went wrong with my car I hastened to him with it, watched him anxiously as he explored its vitals, and listened to his pronouncements as though they were divine oracles—and he always fixed my car.

Well, then, suppose my auto-repair man devised questions for an intelligence test. Or suppose a carpenter did, or a farmer, or, indeed, almost anyone but an academician. By every one of those tests, I'd prove myself a moron. And I'd *be* a moron, too. In a world where I could not use my academic training and my verbal talents but had to do something intricate or hard, working with my hands, I would do poorly. My intelligence, then, is not absolute but is a function of the society I live in and of the fact that a small subsection of that society has managed to foist itself on the rest as an arbiter of such matters.

Sees intelligence as function of roles in society. Good point!

Consider my auto-repair man, again. He had a habit of telling me jokes whenever he saw me. One time he raised his head from under the automobile hood to say. "Doc, a deaf-and-dumb guy went into a hardware store to ask for some nails. He put two fingers together on the counter and made hammering motions with the other hand. The clerk brought him a hammer. He shook his head and pointed to the two fingers he was hammering. The clerk brought him nails. He picked out the sizes he wanted, and left. Well doc, the next guy who came in was a blind man. He wanted scissors. How do you suppose he asked for them?"

Mechanic's joke about "deaf-and-dumb carpenter."

Indulgently, I lifted my right hand and made scissoring motions with my first two fingers. Whereupon my auto-repair man laughed raucously and said, "Why you dumb jerk, he used his *voice* and asked for them." Then he said, smugly, "I've been trying

Traps Asimov with question about blind customer.

What point did mechanic have?

that on all my customers today." "Did you catch many?" I asked. "Quite a few," he said, "but I knew for sure I'd catch *you*." "Why is that?" I asked, "Because you're so goddamned educated, doc, I *knew* you couldn't be very smart."

And I have an uneasy feeling he had something there.

Brings up question "Are all educated people smart?" Not in my experience!

Practice: Reading and Annotating Rachel Carson's "Fable for Tomorrow"

Before you read the following essay, think about its title, the biographical and rhetorical information in the headnote, and the journal prompt. Make some marginal notes of your expectations for the essay, and write out a response to the journal prompt. Then, as you read the essay itself for the first time, try not to stop; take it all in as if in one breath. The second time, however, pause to annotate key points in the text, using the marginal fill-in lines provided alongside each paragraph. As you read, remember the six basic questions mentioned earlier:

1. What does Carson want to say? What is her main point or thesis?
2. Why does she want to make this point? What is her purpose?
3. What pattern or patterns of development does Carson use?
4. How does Carson's pattern of development suit her subject and purpose?
5. What, if anything, is noteworthy about Carson's use of this pattern?
6. How effective is Carson's essay? Does Carson make her points clearly?

Fable for Tomorrow

Title:

Rachel Carson

Headnote:

1. Biographical note:

Naturalist Rachel Carson (1907–1964) majored in biology at the Pennsylvania College for Women (which later became Chatham College) in the mid-1920s and earned a master's degree in marine zoology from Johns Hopkins University. Later she worked as an aquatic biologist for the U.S. Bureau of Fisheries in Washington, D.C. She wrote Under the Sea Wind *(1941),* The Sea around Us *(1951), and* The Edge of the Sea *(1955)—all sensitive investigations of marine life. But it was* Silent Spring *(1962), her study of herbicides and insecticides, that made Carson a controversial figure. Once denounced as an alarmist, she is now regarded as an early prophet of the ecology movement.*

2. Publication information:

In the following fable (a short tale teaching a moral) taken from Silent Spring, *Carson uses contrast to show her readers the devastating effects of the indiscriminate use of pesticides.*

3. Rhetorical highlights:

For Your Journal

Journal prompt:

Hardly a week goes by that we don't hear a news story about the poisoning of the environment. Popular magazines have run cover stories about Americans' growing interest in organic foods. Where do you stand on the issue of using chemical fertilizers, herbicides, and pesticides to grow our nation's food? Do you seek out organic products when you shop? Why or why not?

Annotations:

1 There was once a town in the heart of America where all life seemed to live in harmony with its surroundings. The town lay in the midst of a checkerboard of prosperous farms, with fields of grain and

hillsides of orchards where, in spring, white clouds of bloom drifted above the green fields. In autumn, oak and maple and birch set up a blaze of color that flamed and flickered across a backdrop of pines. Then foxes barked in the hills and deer silently crossed the fields, half hidden in the mists of the fall mornings.

2 Along the roads, laurels, viburnum and alder, great ferns and wildflowers delighted the traveler's eye through much of the year. Even in winter the roadsides were places of beauty, where countless birds came to feed on the berries and on the seed heads of the dried weeds rising above the snow. The countryside was, in fact, famous for the abundance and variety of its bird life, and when the flood of migrants was pouring through in spring and fall people traveled from great distances to observe them. Others came to fish the streams, which flowed clear and cold out of the hills and contained shady pools where trout lay. So it had been from the days many years ago when the first settlers raised their houses, sank their wells, and built their barns.

3 Then a strange blight crept over the area and everything began to change. Some evil spell had settled on the community: mysterious maladies swept the flocks of chickens; the cattle and sheep sickened and died. Everywhere was a shadow of death. The farmers spoke of much illness among their families. In the town the doctors had become more and more puzzled by new kinds of sickness appearing among their patients. There had been several sudden and unexplained deaths, not only among adults but even among children, who would be stricken suddenly while at play and die within a few hours.

4 There was a strange stillness. The birds, for example—where had they gone? Many people spoke of them, puzzled and disturbed. The feeding stations in the backyards were deserted. The few birds seen anywhere were moribund; they trembled violently and could not fly. It was a spring without voices. On the

mornings that had once throbbed with the dawn chorus of robins, catbirds, doves, jays, wrens, and scores of other bird voices there was now no sound; only silence lay over the fields and woods and marsh.

On the farms the hens brooded, but no chicks 5
hatched. The farmers complained that they were unable to raise any pigs—the litters were small and the young survived only a few days. The apple trees were coming into bloom but no bees droned among the blossoms, so there was no pollination and there would be no fruit.

The roadsides, once so attractive, were now lined 6
with browned and withered vegetation as though swept by fire. These, too, were silent, deserted by all living things. Even the streams were now lifeless. Anglers no longer visited them, for all the fish had died.

In the gutters under the eaves and between the 7
shingles of the roofs, a white granular powder still showed a few patches; some weeks before it had fallen like snow upon the roofs and the lawns, the fields and streams.

No witchcraft, no enemy action had silenced 8
the rebirth of new life in this stricken world. The people had done it themselves.

This town does not actually exist, but it might 9
easily have a thousand counterparts in America or elsewhere in the world. I know of no community that has experienced all the misfortunes I describe. Yet every one of these disasters has actually happened somewhere, and many real communities have already suffered a substantial number of them. A grim specter has crept upon us almost unnoticed, and this imagined tragedy may easily become a stark reality we all shall know.

Once you have read and reread Carson's essay and annotated the text, write your own answers to the six basic questions listed on page 49. Then compare your answers with the set of answers that follows.

1. *What does Carson want to say? What is her main point or thesis?* Carson wants to tell her readers a fable, a short narrative

that makes an edifying or cautionary point. Carson draws the "moral" of her fable in the final paragraph. She believes that we have in our power the ability to upset the balance of nature, to turn what is an idyllic countryside into a wasteland. As she states in paragraph 8, "The people had done it [silenced the landscape] themselves." Human beings need to take heed and understand their role in environmental stewardship.

2. *Why does she want to make this point? What is her purpose?* Carson's purpose is to alert us to the clear danger of pesticides (the "white granular powder," paragraph 7) to the environment. Even though the composite environmental disaster she describes has not occurred yet, she feels compelled to inform her readers that each of the individual disasters has happened somewhere in a real community. Although Carson does not make specific recommendations for what each of us can do, her message is clear: To do nothing about pesticides is to invite environmental destruction.

3. *What pattern or patterns of development does Carson use?* Carson's dominant pattern of development is comparison and contrast. In paragraphs 1 and 2, she describes the mythical town before the blight ("all life seemed to live in harmony with its surroundings"); in paragraphs 3–7, she portrays the same town after the blight ("some evil spell had settled on the community"). Carson seems less interested in making specific contrasts than in drawing a total picture of the town before and after the blight. In this way, she makes the change dramatic and powerful. Carson enhances her contrast by using vivid descriptive details that appeal to our senses to paint her pictures of the town before and after the "strange blight." The countryside before the blight is full of life; the countryside after, barren and silent.

4. *How does Carson's pattern of development suit her subject and purpose?* Carson selects comparison and contrast as her method of development because she wants to shock her readers into seeing what happens when humans use pesticides indiscriminately. By contrasting a mythical American town before the blight with the same town after the blight, Carson is able to *show* us the differences, not merely tell us about them. The descriptive details enhance this contrast: for example, "checkerboard of prosperous farms," "white clouds of bloom," "foxes barked," "seed heads of the dried weeds," "cattle and sheep sickened," "they trembled

violently," "no bees droned," and "browned and withered vegetation." Perhaps the most striking detail is the "white granular powder" that "had fallen like snow upon the roofs and the lawns, the fields and streams" (7). The powder is the residue of the pervasive use of insecticides and herbicides in farming. Carson waits to introduce the powder for dramatic impact. Readers absorb the horror of the changing scene, wonder at its cause, and then suddenly realize it is not an unseen, uncontrollable force, but human beings who have caused the devastation.

5. *What, if anything, is noteworthy about Carson's use of this pattern?* In her final paragraph, Carson says, "A grim specter has crept upon us almost unnoticed." And this is exactly what happens in her essay. By starting with a two-paragraph description of "a town in the heart of America where all life seemed to live in harmony with its surroundings," Carson lulls her readers into thinking that all is well. But then at the beginning of paragraph 3, she introduces change: "a strange blight crept over the area." By opting to describe the preblight town in its entirety first and then to contrast it with the blighted town, she makes the change more dramatic and thus enhances its impact on readers.
6. *How effective is Carson's essay? Does Carson make her points clearly?* Instead of writing a strident argument against the indiscriminate use of pesticides, Carson chooses to engage her readers in a fable with an educational message. In reading her story of this American town, we witness what happens when farmers blanket the landscape with pesticides. When we learn in the last paragraph that "this town does not actually exist," we are given cause for hope. In spite of the fact that "every one of these disasters has actually happened somewhere," we are led to believe that there is still time to act before "this imagined tragedy" becomes "a stark reality we all shall know." Interestingly, Carson was considered an alarmist when she wrote *Silent Spring* in 1962, and now almost daily we read reports of water pollution, oil spills, hazardous waste removal, toxic waste dumps, and global warming. Her warning is as appropriate today as it was when she first wrote it more than four decades ago.

USING YOUR READING IN THE WRITING PROCESS

Reading and writing are the two sides of the same coin. Many people view writing as the making of reading. But the connection does not end there. Active reading is a means to help you become a better writer. We know that one of the best ways to learn to write and to improve our writing is to read. By reading we can begin to see how other writers have communicated their experiences, ideas, thoughts, and feelings in their writing. We can study how they have effectively used the various elements of the essay—thesis, unity, organization, beginnings and endings, paragraphs, transitions, effective sentences, diction and tone, and figurative language—to say what they wanted to say. By studying the style, technique, and rhetorical strategies of other writers, we learn how we might effectively do the same. The more we read and write, the more we begin to read as writers and, in turn, to write knowing what readers expect.

Reading as a Writer

What does it mean to read as a writer? As mentioned earlier, most of us have not been taught to read with a writer's eye, to ask why we like one piece of writing and not another. Similarly, most of us do not ask ourselves why one piece of writing is more convincing than another. When you learn to read with a writer's eye, you begin to answer these important questions. You read beyond the content to see how certain aspects of the writing itself impacts you. You come to appreciate what is involved in selecting and focusing a subject as well as the craftsmanship involved in writing—how a writer selects descriptive details, uses an unobtrusive organizational pattern, opts for fresh and lively language, chooses representative and persuasive examples, and emphasizes important points with sentence variety. You come to see writing as a series of choices or decisions the writer makes.

On one level, reading stimulates your thinking by providing you with subjects to write about. For example, after reading Annie Dillard's essay from *An American Childhood* or Helen Keller's "The Most Important Day," you might take up your pen to write about a turning point in your life. Or, by reading Mike Rose's "I Just Wanna Be Average," Carl T. Rowan's "Unforgettable Miss Bessie," and Thomas L. Friedman's "My Favorite Teacher," you might see how each writer creates a dominant impression of an influential person in his life and write about an influential person in your own life.

On a second level, reading provides you with information, ideas, and perspectives for developing your own paper. In this way, you respond to what you read, using material from what you've read in your essay. For example, after reading Christie Scotty's essay "Can I Get You Some Manners with That?" you might want to elaborate on what she has written and either agree with her examples or generate better ones of your own. You could also qualify her argument or take issue against it. Similarly, if you want to write about the effects of new technologies and medical practices on our health and well being, you will find Anthony Komaroff's "Technology's Limits" and Barbara Huttmann's "A Crime of Compassion" invaluable resources.

On a third level, active reading can increase your awareness of how others' writing affects you, thus making you more sensitive to how your own writing will affect your readers. For example, if you have ever been impressed by an author who uses convincing evidence to support each of his or her claims, you might be more likely to back up your own claims carefully. If you have been impressed by an apt turn of phrase or absorbed by a writer's new idea, you may be less inclined to feed your readers dull, worn-out, and trite phrases.

More to the point, however, the active reading that you are encouraged to do in *Models for Writers* will help you recognize and analyze the essential elements of the essay. When you see, for example, how a writer like Etta Kralovec uses a strong thesis statement to control the parts of her essay on privatizing extracurricular activities in public schools, you can better appreciate what a clear thesis statement is and see the importance of having one in your essay. When you see the way Steve Brody uses transitions to link key phrases and important ideas so that readers can recognize clearly how the parts of his essay are meant to flow together, you have a better idea of how to achieve such coherence in your own writing. And when you see how Martin Luther King Jr. divides the ways in which people characteristically respond to oppression into three distinct categories, you witness a powerful way in which you too can organize an essay using division and classification.

Another important reason, then, to master the skills of active reading is that, for everything you write, you will be your own first reader and critic. How well you are able to scrutinize your own drafts will powerfully affect how well you revise them, and revising well is crucial to writing well. So reading others' writing with a critical eye is a useful and important practice; the more you read, the more practice you will have in sharpening your skills.

Remember, writing is the making of reading. The more sensitive you become to the content and style decisions made by the writers in

Models for Writers, the more skilled you will be at seeing the rhetorical options available to you and making conscious choices in your own writing.

WRITING FROM READING: THREE SAMPLE STUDENT ESSAYS

A Narrative Essay

Reading often triggers memories of experiences that we have had. After reading several personal narratives about growing up—Steve Brody's "How I Got Smart" and Dick Gregory's "Shame," in particular—student Lisa Driver found herself thinking about what it was like growing up in rural Vermont. When her classmates asked her to share with them a childhood experience that they wouldn't be able to forget, Driver told them of an experience that she'd had in the sixth grade. She confided that as a sixth grader the experience felt very traumatic. In retrospect, however, she was able to appreciate the humor in the uncomfortable situation. Encouraged by her classmates, Driver wrote the following narrative in which she tells of her memorable encounter with Mrs. Armstrong, her teacher. Notice that she uses chronological order and descriptive details to capture both the drama and the humor of the incident.

Title: introduces subject and provides focus

The Strong Arm of a Sixth-Grade Teacher

Lisa V. Driver

Point of view: first-person narration

Context: description of self, classroom setting, and another student

Sometimes experiences that we have had in a classroom leave an indelible imprint on our lives. For me, it was one experience that I had with Mrs. Armstrong, a powerful, overbearing teacher. I was a scrawny, sixth-grade girl. I sat in the back of the classroom in the third row behind Todd, the class troublemaker. There was a little bit of safety in sitting behind Todd. Usually Mrs. Armstrong targeted him and not anyone close by. Todd was the type of kid who loved to get into trouble. He had a heart of gold but had absolutely no use for school. He was not at all intimidated by Mrs. Armstrong and her academic credentials, her perfect children, her world travel, and, most of all, her condescending manner to her rural farm students.

Context: description of teacher foreshadows later action

Mrs. Armstrong was a very large, domineering, and commanding figure. She loved jelly donuts, and it showed. Her hands, desk, and papers always had globs of sticky jam on them. She's the only person I've ever known who could make almost a whole donut disappear in one bite. The bright, red jam would ooze out the sides of the donut and get all over her face. My classmates and I all drooled at the thought of having such a treat ourselves. Most days she managed to devour a half-dozen Koffee Kup jelly donuts.

Narrative begins: antonym/synonym drill

Description: dominant impression of teacher as "drill sergeant"

On one particular dull and dreary day, Mrs. Armstrong was droning on about antonyms and synonyms. She loved to use her knowledge to evoke fear and terror in her sixth-grade students, and none of us was immune to her reign of terror. She was the type of teacher who expected the right answer right away. The drill sergeant strutted around the room that day, snapping her pudgy, sticky fingers in our faces and expecting answers on the spot. If a student did not deliver immediately, then she would yell at and humiliate that student in front of his or her classmates. Many of my classmates had suffered her snapping fingers and been left embarrassed and defeated. But I was safe--I was behind Todd.

Organization: chronological sequence of events

Descriptive details

Dramatic short sentence

Climactic moment

The class dragged on as Mrs. Armstrong delighted in her antonym game. She'd march down each aisle and point to two different things, expecting us to quickly state the correct antonyms. For example, if she pointed to the ceiling and the floor, we were supposed to respond "up and down." Or, if she pointed to the classroom and the window, the answer would be "inside and outside." As she neared my desk, I was feeling pretty safe, hidden as I was behind Todd. But then Todd cleverly knocked his pencil to the floor and leaned over to retrieve it. Well, there I was totally exposed to Mrs. Armstrong. I froze. Suddenly, she pointed to herself and then pointed at me and snapped those fingers, demanding an answer. Before I realized what I was saying, I blurted out, "fat and skinny"!

Mrs. Armstrong exploded. She started yelling and then grabbed hold of my shirt, dragged me to the door, and marched me down the hallway, screaming at me all the way. She stormed into the principal's office and deposited me in a hard wooden chair. In a loud voice she told Mr. Alderman, the principal, that I was not to come back to her class for an entire week. She slammed the door on her way out, leaving me with the principal. By now I was shaking and crying because I'd never ever been sent to the principal's office.

Descriptive details

Mr. Alderman sat in his old swivel chair and behind him on the wall hung a wooden paddle with the words "Board of Education" etched in large letters. Todd often bragged that he had firsthand knowledge of the purpose of that paddle. All that kept going through my head was that my parents were going to kill me after I'd been spanked by this man.

Conclusion: realizes mistakes and reflects on the incident

Mr. Alderman was a huge man with a short crew cut. Everyone except Todd was afraid of him. With steely eyes peering out over his glasses straight at me, the principal raised his eyebrows and demanded an explanation for my visit. I choked out the story to him between crying spells. When I told him that I had said "fat and skinny" in response to Mrs. Armstrong's antonym problem, he leaned back in his chair and started laughing as hard as I'd ever seen a person laugh. When he finished laughing and drying his eyes, he told me that the correct response should have been "teacher and student." Slowly it dawned on me that I had mistakenly given the wrong antonym to Mrs. Armstrong, and I started to giggle with the principal. I spent the entire week in Mr. Alderman's office, answering the phone and being his secretary. I think he was afraid of that teacher also.

A Response Essay

For an assignment following James Lincoln Collier's essay "Anxiety: Challenge by Another Name," Zoe Ockenga tackled the topic of anxiety. In her first draft, she explored the anxiety she felt the night before her first speech in a public speaking class and how in confronting that anxiety she benefited from the course. Ockenga read her paper aloud in class, and other students had an opportunity to ask her questions and to offer constructive criticism. Several students suggested that she might want to relate her experiences to those that Collier recounts in his essay. Another asked if she could include other examples to bolster the point she wanted to make. At this point in the discussion, Ockenga recalled a phone conversation she had had with her mother regarding her mother's indecision about accepting a new job. The thought of working outside the home for the first time in more than twenty years brought out her mother's worst fears and threatened to keep her from accepting the challenge. Armed with these valuable suggestions and ideas, Ockenga began revising. In subsequent drafts, she worked on the Collier connection, actually citing his essay on several occasions, and developed the example of the anxiety surrounding her mother's decision. What follows is the final draft of her essay, which incorporates the changes she made based on the peer evaluation of her first draft.

Title: indicates main idea of the essay

The Excuse "Not To"

Zoe Ockenga

Beginning: captures reader's attention with personal experience most college students can relate to

I cannot imagine anything worse than the nervous, anxious feeling I got the night before my first speech in public speaking class last spring semester. The knots in my stomach were so fierce that I racked my brain for an excuse to give the teacher so that I would not have to go through with the dreaded assignment. Once in bed, I lay awake thinking of all the mistakes that I might make while standing alone in front of my classmates. I spent the rest of the night tossing and turning, frustrated that now, on top of my panic, I would have to give my speech with huge bags under my eyes.

Anxiety is an intense emotion that can strike at any time or place, before a simple daily activity or a life-changing decision. For some people, anxiety is only a minor interference in the process of achieving a goal. For others, it can be a force that is impossible to overcome. In these instances, anxiety can prevent the accomplishment of lifelong hopes and dreams. Avoiding the causes of stress or fear can make us feel secure and safe. Avoiding anxiety, however, may mean forfeiting a once-in-a-lifetime opportunity. Confronting anxiety can make for a richer, more fulfilling existence.

Thesis

First example: continues story introduced in opening paragraph to support thesis

The next day I trudged to class and sat on the edge of my seat until I could not stand the tension any longer. At this point, I forced myself to raise my hand to volunteer to go next simply to end my suffering. As I walked to the front of the room and assumed my position at the podium, the faces of the twenty-five classmates I had been sitting beside a minute ago suddenly seemed like fifty. I probably fumbled over a word or two as I discussed the harmful aspects of animal testing, but my mistakes were not nearly as severe as I had imagined the night before. Less than five minutes later the whole nightmare was over, and it had been much less painful than I had anticipated. As I sat down with a huge sigh of relief to listen to the next victim stumble repeatedly over how to milk dairy cows, I realized that I had not been half bad.

Although I still dreaded giving the next series of speeches, I eventually became more accustomed to speaking in front of my peers. I would still have to force myself to volunteer, secretly hoping the teacher would forget about me, but the audience that once seemed large and forbidding eventually became much more human. A speech class is something that I would never have taken if it had not been a requirement, but I can honestly say that I am better off because of it. I was forced to grapple with my anxiety and in the process become a stronger, more self-confident individual. Before this class I had been able to hide out in large lectures, never offering any comments or insights. For the first time at college I was forced to participate, and I realized that I could speak effectively in front of strangers and, more importantly, that I had something to say.

Second example: cites essay from Models for Writers *to support thesis*

The insomnia-inducing anticipation of giving a speech was a type of anxiety that I had to overcome to meet my distribution requirements for graduation. In the essay "Anxiety: Challenge by Another Name" by James Lincoln Collier, the author tells of his own struggles with anxiety. He tells of one particular event that happened between his sophomore and junior years in college when he was asked to spend a summer in Argentina with a good friend. He writes about how he felt after he made his decision not to go:

> I had turned down something I wanted to do because I was scared, and had ended up feeling depressed. I stayed that way for a long time. And it didn't help when I went back to college in the fall to discover that Ted and his friend had had a terrific time. (81)

The proposition of going to Argentina was an extremely difficult choice for Collier as it meant abandoning the comfortable routine of the past and venturing completely out of his element. Although the idea of the trip was exciting, the author could not bring himself to choose the summer in Argentina because of his uncertainties.

The summer abroad that Collier denied himself in his early twenties left him with such a feeling of regret that he vowed to change his approach to life. From then on, he faced challenges that made him uncomfortable and was able to accomplish feats he would never have dreamed possible: interviewing celebrities, traveling extensively throughout Europe, parachuting, and even learning to ski at age forty. Collier emphasizes that he was able to make his life fulfilling and exciting by adhering to his belief that anxiety cannot be stifled by avoidance; it can only be stifled by confrontation (82).

Third example: introduces mother's dilemma

Anxiety prevents many individuals from accepting life's challenges and changes. My own mother is currently struggling with such a dilemma. At age fifty-three, having never had a career outside the home, my mother has been recommended to manage a new art gallery. The River Gallery, as it will be called, will be opening in our town of Ipswich, Massachusetts, this spring. An avid collector and art lover as well as a budding potter, my mother would, I believe, be exceptional at this job.

Anticipating this new opportunity and responsibility has caused my mother great anxiety. Reentering the workforce after over twenty years is as frightening for my mother as the trip to Argentina was for Collier. When I recently discussed the job prospect with my mother, she was negative and full of doubt. "There's no way I could ever handle such a responsibility," she commented. "I have no business experience. I would look like a fool if I actually tried to pull something like this off. Besides, I'm sure the artists would never take me seriously." Just as my mother focused on all the possible negative aspects of the opportunity in front of her, Collier questioned the value of his opportunity to spend a summer abroad. He describes having second thoughts about just how exciting the trip would be:

Quotation: quotes Collier to help explain mother's indecision

Block quote in MLA Style

> I had never been very far from New England, and I had been homesick my first few weeks at college. What would it be like in a strange country? What about the language? And besides, I had promised to teach my younger brother to sail that summer. (80–81)

Focusing on all the possible problems accompanying a new opportunity can arouse such a sense of fear that it can overpower the ability to take a risk. Both my mother and Collier found out that dwelling on possible negative outcomes allowed them to ignore the benefits of a new experience and thus maintain their safe current situations.

Currently my mother is using anxiety as an excuse "not to" act. To confront her anxiety and take an opportunity in which there is a possibility of failure as well as success is a true risk. Regardless of the outcome, to even contemplate a new challenge has changed her life. The summer forgone by Collier roused him to never again pass up an exciting opportunity and thus to live his life to the fullest. Just the thought of taking the gallery position has prompted my mother to contemplate taking evening classes so that if she refuses the offer she may be better prepared for a similar challenge in the future. Although her decision is unresolved, her anxiety has made her realize the possibilities that may be opening for her, whether or not she chooses to take them. If in the end her answer is no, I believe that a lingering "What if?" feeling will cause her to reevaluate her expectations and goals for the future.

Conclusion: includes strong statement about anxiety that echoes optimism of thesis

Anxiety can create confidence and optimism or depression, low self-esteem, and regret. The outcome of anxiety is entirely dependent on whether the individual runs from it or embraces it. Some forms of anxiety can be conquered merely by repeating the activity that causes them, such as giving speeches in a public speaking class. Anxiety brought on by unique opportunities or life-changing decisions, such as a summer in a foreign country or a new career, must be harnessed. Opportunities forgone due to anxiety and fear could be the chances of a lifetime. Although the unpleasant feelings that may accompany anxiety may make it initially easier to do nothing, the road not taken will never be forgotten. Anxiety is essentially a blessing in disguise. It is a physical and emotional trigger that tells us when and where there is an opportunity for us to grow and become stronger human beings.

MLA-style works cited list

Works Cited

Collier, James Lincoln. "Anxiety: Challenge by Another Name." Models for Writers. Eds. Alfred Rosa and Paul Eschholz. 9th ed. Boston: Bedford, 2007. 80–83.

An Analytical Essay

When student Susan Francis wrote an analysis of George Orwell's "A Hanging," her purpose was both to show that she understood the essay and to help her readers increase their understanding of it. She started by thinking about aspects of the work's meaning, structure, and style that are important but not obvious. Her analysis grew directly out of her reading and, more specifically, out of the notes she made during her first and subsequent readings of Orwell's text.

From the start, Francis knew that she had to decide what point she most wanted to make—what her thesis would be. With a little thought, she developed a list of four theses that she could use in her analytical paper:

1. In "A Hanging," George Orwell carefully selects details to persuade readers that capital punishment is wrong.
2. "A Hanging" reveals how thoroughly the British had imposed their laws, customs, and values on colonial Burma.
3. Though "A Hanging" appeals powerfully to the emotions, it does not make a reasoned argument against capital punishment.
4. In "A Hanging," George Orwell employs simile and metaphor, personification, and dialogue to express people's inhumanity to other people.

After considering the merits of each of her four choices, Francis chose thesis 4 to use in her paper. She thought she could support this thesis strongly and effectively using evidence from Orwell's essay.

Following is the final draft of her analytical paper. Her discussion is clear and coherent, and it is firmly based on Orwell's text. She cites many details from the essay that capture Orwell's attitude toward the hanging and toward his imperial colleagues, and she interprets them so that her readers can plainly see how those details contribute to the total effect of "A Hanging."

The Disgrace of Man

Susan Francis

Thesis: statement of central idea and order

George Orwell's "A Hanging" graphically depicts the execution of a prisoner in a way that expresses a universal tragedy. He artfully employs simile and metaphor, personification, *in which evidence is to be presented*

and dialogue to indicate people's inhumanity toward other people regardless of nationality and to prompt readers' sympathy and self-examination.

Point 1: examples of simile and metaphor

Orwell uses simile and metaphor to show that the prisoner is treated more like an animal than like a human being. The cells of the condemned men, "a row of sheds . . . quite bare within," are "like small animal cages" (285). The warders grip the prisoner "like men handling a fish" (286). Though they refer to the prisoner as "this man" (287) or "our friend" (289), the other characters view him as less than human. Even his cry resounds like "the tolling of a bell" rather than a human "prayer or a cry for help" (288), and after he is dead, the superintendent pokes at the body with a stick. These details direct readers' attention to the lack of human concern for the condemned prisoner.

Documentation: parenthetical citations in MLA style

Point 2: examples of personification—prisoner's body parts

In contrast, Orwell emphasizes the "wrongness . . . of cutting a life short" (287) by representing the parts of the prisoner's body as taking on human behavior. He describes how "the lock of hair . . . danced" on the man's scalp, how "his feet printed themselves on the wet gravel," and how all his organs were "toiling away" (287) like a team of laborers at some collective project. In personifying these bodily features, Orwell forces readers to confront the prisoner's vitality, his humanity. Readers, in turn, associate each body part with themselves; they become highly aware of the fragility of life. As the author focuses on how easily these actions can be stopped in any human being "with a sudden snap" (287), readers feel the "unspeakable wrongness" of the hanging as if their own lives were threatened.

Personification: example of dog

In addition to creating this sense of unmistakable life, Orwell uses the dog as a standard for evaluating the characters' appreciation of human life. The dog loves people--he is "wild with glee at finding so many human beings together" (286)--and the person he loves the most is the prisoner, who has been treated as less than human by the jail attendants. When the prisoner starts to pray, the other people are silent, but the dog "answer[s] . . . with a whine" (288). Even after the hanging, the dog runs directly to the gallows to see the prisoner again. Readers are forced to reflect on their own reactions: Which is more shocking, the dog's actions or the observers' cold response?

Point 3: insensitive dialogue regardless of nationality

Finally, Orwell refers to the characters' nationalities to stress that this insensitivity extends to all nationalities and races. The hanging takes place in Burma, in a jail run by a European army doctor and a native of southern India. The warders are also Indians, and the hangman is actually a fellow prisoner. The author calls attention to each of these participants and implies that each one of them might have halted the brutal proceeding. He was there, too, and could have intervened when he suddenly realized that killing the prisoner would be wrong. Yet the formality of the hanging goes on.

As he reflects on the meaning of suddenly destroying human life, Orwell emphasizes the similarities among all men, regardless of nationality. Before the hanging, they are "seeing, hearing, feeling, understanding the same world," and afterward there would be "one mind less, one world less" (287). Such insights do not affect the other characters, who think of the hanging not as a killing but as a job to be done, a job made unpleasant by those reminders (the incident of the dog, the prisoner's praying) that they are dealing with a human being. Orwell uses dialogue to show how selfish and callous the observers are. Though they have different accents--the superintendent's "for God's sake hurry up" (286), the Dravidian's "all hass passed off with the utmost satisfactoriness" (289)--they think and feel the same. Their words, such as "He's all right" (289), show that they are more concerned about their own lives than the one they are destroying.

Conclusion: value of human life stressed

Although George Orwell sets his story in Burma, his point is universal; although he deals with capital punishment, he implies other questions about life and death. We are all faced with issues such as capital punishment, abortion, and euthanasia, and sometimes we find ourselves directly involved, as Orwell was in

Burma. "A Hanging" confronts us with a situation that won't go away and urges us to take very seriously the value of human life.

MLA-style works cited list

Works Cited

Orwell, George. "A Hanging." Models for Writers. Eds. Alfred Rosa and Paul Eschholz. 9th ed. Boston: Bedford, 2007. 285–91.

part two

The Elements of the Essay

chapter **3**

Thesis

The **thesis** of an essay is its main or controlling idea, the point the writer is trying to make. The thesis is often expressed in a one- or two-sentence statement, although sometimes it is implied or suggested rather than stated directly. The thesis statement determines the content of the essay: Everything the writer says must be logically related to the thesis statement.

Because everything you say in your composition must be logically related to your thesis, the thesis statement controls and directs the choices you make about the content of your essay. This does not mean that your thesis statement is a straitjacket. As your essay develops, you may want to modify your thesis statement to accommodate your new thinking. This urge is not only acceptable, it is normal.

One way to develop a working thesis is to determine a question that you are trying to answer in your essay. A one- or two-sentence answer to this question often produces a tentative thesis statement. For example, a student wanted to answer the following question in her essay:

> Do men and women have different conversational speaking styles?

Her preliminary answer to this question was this:

> Men and women appear to have different objectives when they converse.

After writing two drafts, she modified her thesis to better fit the examples she had gathered:

> Very often, conversations between men and women become situations in which the man gives a mini-lecture and the woman unwittingly turns into a captive audience.

A thesis statement should be

- The most important point you make about your topic
- More general than the ideas and facts used to support it
- Appropriately focused for the length of your paper

A thesis statement should not be a question, but an assertion—a claim made about a debatable issue that can be supported with evidence.

Another effective strategy for developing a thesis statement is to begin by writing "What I want to say is that. . . ."

> What I want to say is that unless the university administration enforces its strong anti-hazing policy, the well-being of many of its student-athletes will be endangered.

Later, when you delete the formulaic opening, you will be left with a thesis statement:

> Unless the university administration enforces its strong anti-hazing policy, the well-being of many of its student-athletes will be endangered.

Usually the thesis is presented early in the essay, sometimes in the first sentence. Here are some thesis statements that begin essays:

> One of the most potent elements in body language is eye behavior.
>
> –Flora Davis

> Americans can be divided into three groups—smokers, nonsmokers, and that expanding pack of us who have quit.
>
> –Franklin E. Zimring

> Over the past ten to fifteen years it has become apparent that eating disorders have reached epidemic proportions among adolescents.
>
> –Helen A. Guthrie

> Clutter is the disease of American writing. We are a society strangling in unnecessary words, circular construction, pompous frills, and meaningless jargon.
>
> –William Zinsser

Each of these sentences does what a good thesis statement should do: It identifies the topic and makes an assertion about it.

Often writers prepare readers for the thesis statement with one or several sentences that establish a context. Notice in the following example how the author eases the reader into his thesis about television instead of presenting it abruptly in the first sentence:

> With the advent of television, for the first time in history, all aspects of animal and human life and death, of societal and individual behavior have been condensed on the average to a 19-inch diagonal screen and a 30-minute time slot. Television, a unique medium, claiming to be neither a reality nor art, has become reality for many of us, particularly for our children who are growing up in front of it.
>
> –Jerzy Kosinski

On occasion a writer may even purposely delay the presentation of a thesis until the middle or the end of an essay. If the thesis is controversial or needs extended discussion and illustration, the writer might present it later to make it easier for the reader to understand and accept it. Appearing near or at the end of an essay, a thesis also gains prominence. For example, after an involved discussion about why various groups put pressure on school libraries to ban books, a student ended an essay with her thesis:

> The effort to censor what our children are reading can turn into a potentially explosive situation and cause misunderstanding and hurt feelings within our schools and communities. If we can gain an understanding of why people have sought to censor children's books, we will be better prepared to respond in a sensitive and reasonable manner. More importantly, we will be able to provide the best educational opportunity for our children through a sensible approach, one that neither overly restricts the range of their reading nor allows them to read all books, no matter how inappropriate. *Thesis*
>
> –Tara Ketch, student

Some kinds of writing do not need thesis statements. These include descriptions, narratives, and personal writing such as letters and diaries. But any essay that seeks to explain or prove a point has a thesis that is usually set forth in a formal thesis statement.

The Most Important Day

Helen Keller

Helen Keller (1880–1968) was afflicted by a disease that left her blind and deaf at the age of eighteen months. With the aid of her teacher, Anne Mansfield Sullivan, she was able to overcome her severe handicaps, to graduate from Radcliffe College, and to lead a productive and challenging adult life. In the following selection from her autobiography, The Story of My Life *(1902), Keller tells of the day she first met Anne Sullivan, a day she regarded as the most important in her life.*

As you read, note that Keller states her thesis in the first paragraph and that the remaining paragraphs maintain unity by emphasizing the importance of the day her teacher arrived, even though they deal with the days and weeks following.

For Your Journal

Reflect on the events of what you consider "the most important day" of your life. Briefly describe what happened. Why was that particular day so significant?

The most important day I remember in all my life is the one on which my teacher, Anne Mansfield Sullivan, came to me. I am filled with wonder when I consider the immeasurable contrast between the two lives which it connects. It was the third of March, 1887, three months before I was seven years old. 1

On the afternoon of that eventful day, I stood on the porch, dumb,[1] expectant. I guessed vaguely from my mother's signs and from the hurrying to and fro in the house that something unusual was about to happen, so I went to the door and waited on the steps. The afternoon sun penetrated the mass of honeysuckle that covered the porch and fell on my upturned face. My fingers lingered almost unconsciously on the familiar leaves and blossoms which had just come forth to greet the sweet southern spring. I did not know what the future held of marvel or 2

[1]*dumb:* unable to speak; mute.

surprise for me. Anger and bitterness had preyed upon me continually for weeks and a deep languor[2] had succeeded this passionate struggle.

Have you ever been at sea in a dense fog, when it seemed as if a 3
tangible white darkness shut you in, and the great ship, tense and anxious, groped her way toward the shore with plummet and sounding-line,[3] and you waited with beating heart for something to happen? I was like that ship before my education began, only I was without compass or sounding-line, and had no way of knowing how near the harbor was. "Light! give me light!" was the wordless cry of my soul, and the light of love shone on me in that very hour.

I felt approaching footsteps. I stretched out my hand as I supposed 4
to my mother. Someone took it, and I was caught up and held close in the arms of her who had come to reveal all things to me, and, more than all things else, to love me.

The morning after my teacher came she led me into her room and 5
gave me a doll. The little blind children at the Perkins Institution[4] had sent it and Laura Bridgman[5] had dressed it; but I did not know this until afterward. When I had played with it a little while, Miss Sullivan slowly spelled into my hand the word "d-o-l-l." I was at once interested in this finger play and tried to imitate it. When I finally succeeded in making the letters correctly I was flushed with childish pleasure and pride. Running downstairs to my mother I held up my hand and made the letters for doll. I did not know that I was spelling a word or even that words existed; I was simply making my fingers go in monkeylike imitation. In the days that followed I learned to spell in this uncomprehending way a great many words, among them *pin, hat, cup* and a few verbs like *sit, stand,* and *walk*. But my teacher had been with me several weeks before I understood that everything has a name.

One day, while I was playing with my new doll, Miss Sullivan put 6
my big rag doll into my lap also, spelled "d-o-l-l" and tried to make me understand that "d-o-l-l" applied to both. Earlier in the day we had had a tussle over the words "m-u-g" and "w-a-t-e-r." Miss Sullivan had tried to impress it upon me that "m-u-g" is *mug* and that

---

[2]*languor:* sluggishness.

[3]*plummet . . . line:* a weight tied to a line that is used to measure the depth of the ocean.

[4]*Perkins Institution:* the first school for blind children in the United States.

[5]*Laura Bridgman* (1829–1889): a deaf-blind girl who was educated at the Perkins Institution in the 1840s.

"w-a-t-e-r" is *water,* but I persisted in confounding the two. In despair she had dropped the subject for the time, only to renew it at the first opportunity. I became impatient at her repeated attempts and, seizing the new doll, I dashed it upon the floor. I was keenly delighted when I felt the fragments of the broken doll at my feet. Neither sorrow nor regret followed my passionate outburst. I had not loved the doll. In the still, dark world in which I lived there was no strong sentiment or tenderness. I felt my teacher sweep the fragments to one side of the hearth, and I had a sense of satisfaction that the cause of my discomfort was removed. She brought me my hat, and I knew I was going out into the warm sunshine. This thought, if a wordless sensation may be called a thought, made me hop and skip with pleasure.

We walked down the path to the well-house, attracted by the fra- 7
grance of the honeysuckle with which it was covered. Someone was drawing water and my teacher placed my hand under the spout. As the cool stream gushed over one hand she spelled into the other the word *water,* first slowly, then rapidly. I stood still, my whole attention fixed upon the motions of her fingers. Suddenly I felt a misty consciousness as of something forgotten—a thrill of returning thought; and somehow the mystery of language was revealed to me. I knew then that "w-a-t-e-r" meant the wonderful cool something that was flowing over my hand. The living word awakened my soul, gave it light, hope, joy, set it free! There were barriers still, it is true, but barriers that could in time be swept away.

I left the well-house eager to learn. Everything had a name, and 8
each name gave birth to a new thought. As we returned to the house every object which I touched seemed to quiver with life. That was because I saw everything with the strange, new sight that had come to me. On entering the door I remembered the doll I had broken. I felt my way to the hearth and picked up the pieces. I tried vainly to put them together. Then my eyes filled with tears; for I realized what I had done, and for the first time I felt repentance and sorrow.

I learned a great many new words that day. I do not remember 9
what they all were; but I do know that *mother, father, sister, teacher* were among them—words that were to make the world blossom for me, "like Aaron's rod,[6] with flowers." It would have been difficult to find a happier child than I was as I lay in my crib at the close of that

[6]*Aaron's rod:* in Jewish and Christian traditions, a rod similar to Moses's staff that, in the high priest Aaron's hands, had miraculous power.

eventful day and lived over the joys it had brought me, and for the first time longed for a new day to come.

Thinking Critically about This Reading

Keller writes that " 'Light! give me light!' was the wordless cry of [her] soul" (paragraph 3). What was the "light" Keller longed for, and how did receiving it change her life?

Questions for Study and Discussion

1. What is Keller's thesis? What question do you think Keller is trying to answer? Does her thesis answer her question?
2. What is Keller's purpose? (Glossary: *Purpose*)
3. What was Keller's state of mind before Anne Sullivan arrived to help her? To what does she compare herself? (Glossary: *Analogy*) How effective is this comparison? Explain.
4. Why was the realization that everything has a name important to Keller?
5. How was the "mystery of language" (7) revealed to Keller? What were the consequences for her of this new understanding of the nature of language?
6. Keller narrates the events of the day Sullivan arrived (2–4), the morning after she arrived (5), and one day several weeks after her arrival (6–9). (Glossary: *Narration*) Describe what happens on each day, and explain how these separate incidents support Keller's thesis.

Classroom Activity Using Thesis

One effective way of focusing on your subject is to develop a list of specific questions about it at the start. This strategy has a number of advantages. Each question narrows the general subject area, suggesting a more manageable essay. Also, simply phrasing your topic as a question gives you a starting point; your work has focus and direction from the outset. Finally, a one- or two-sentence answer to your question often provides you with a preliminary thesis statement.

To test this strategy, develop a list of five questions about the subject "recycling paper waste on campus." To get you started, here is one possible question: Should students be required to recycle paper waste?

1. ______________________________
2. ______________________________
3. ______________________________
4. ______________________________
5. ______________________________

Suggested Writing Assignments

1. Think about an important day in your own life. Using the thesis statement "The most important day of my life was ______," write an essay in which you show the significance of that day by recounting and explaining the events that took place, as Keller does in her essay. Before you write, you might find it helpful to reflect on your journal entry for this reading.
2. For many people around the world, the life of Helen Keller symbolizes what a person can achieve despite seemingly insurmountable obstacles. Her achievements have inspired people with and without disabilities, leading them to believe they can accomplish more than they ever thought possible. Consider the role of people with disabilities in our society, develop an appropriate thesis, and write an essay on the topic.
3. Keller was visually and hearing impaired from the age of 18 months, which meant she could neither read nor hear people speak. She was eventually able to read and write using braille, a system of "touchable symbols" invented by Louis Braille. In the accompanying photograph taken at the Sorbonne in Paris, France, upon the one-hundredth anniversary of Braille's death, Keller demonstrates how to use the system. Write an essay in which you put forth the thesis that the invention of braille has liberated countless numbers of people who have shared Keller's impairment.

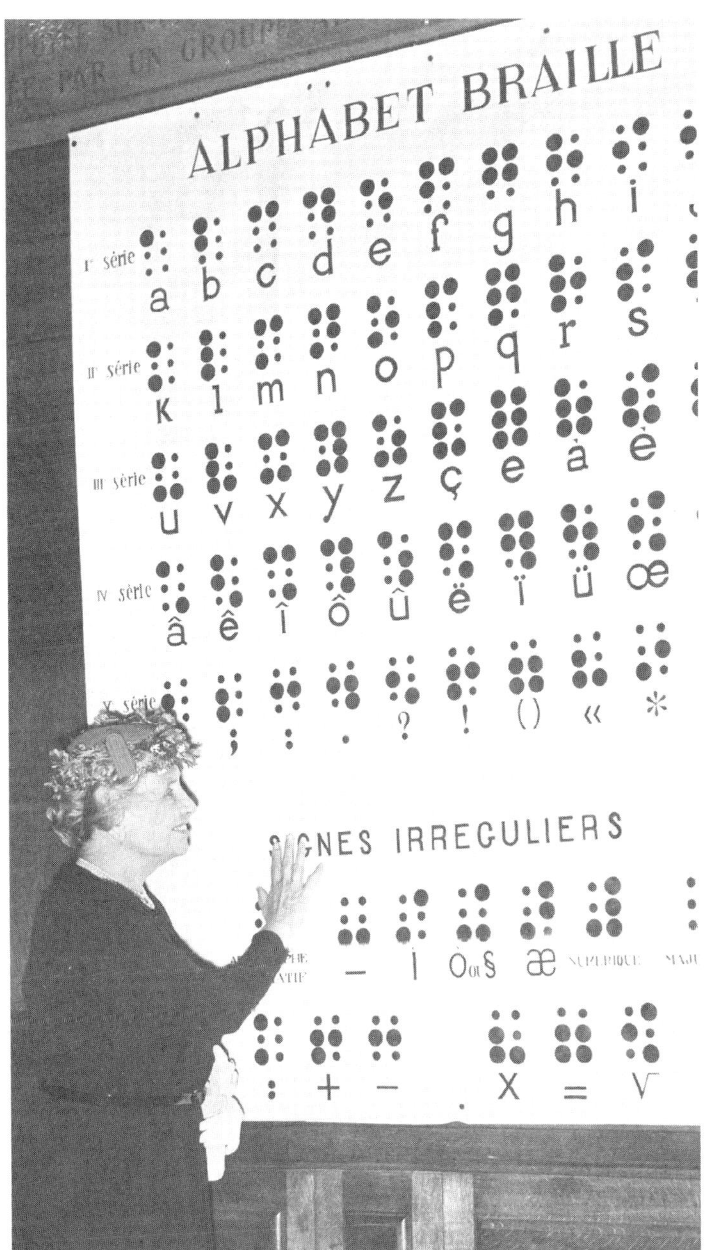
ALPHABET BRAILLE
Ir série
a b c d e f g h i
IIe série
k l m n o p q r s
IIIe série
u v x y z ç é à è
IVe série
â ê î ô û ë ï ü œ
Ve série
? ! ( ) « *
IRREGULIERS
: + − . X = √

Anxiety: Challenge by Another Name

James Lincoln Collier

James Lincoln Collier is a freelance writer with more than six hundred articles to his credit. He was born in New York in 1928 and graduated from Hamilton College in 1950. Among his published books are many works of fiction, including novels for young adults. His nonfiction writing has often focused on American music. His best-known book is The Making of Jazz: A Comprehensive History *(1978). With his son Christopher he has written a number of history books, including* A Century of Immigration: 1820–1924 *(2000),* The Civil War *(2000),* The Changing Face of American Society: 1945–2000 *(2001), and a series of biographies for young readers covering major figures in American history.*

As you read the following essay, which first appeared in Reader's Digest *in 1986, pay particular attention to where Collier places his thesis. Note also how his thesis statement identifies the topic (anxiety) and makes an assertion about it (that it can have a positive impact on our lives).*

For Your Journal

Many people tend to associate anxiety with stress and to think of it as a negative thing. Are there good kinds of anxiety, too? Provide an example of anxiety that has been beneficial to you or to someone you know.

Between my sophomore and junior years at college, a chance came up for me to spend the summer vacation working on a ranch in Argentina. My roommate's father was in the cattle business, and he wanted Ted to see something of it. Ted said he would go if he could take a friend, and he chose me. 1

The idea of spending two months on the fabled Argentine Pampas[1] was exciting. Then I began having second thoughts. I had never 2

[1]*Pampas:* a vast plain in central Argentina.

been very far from New England, and I had been homesick my first few weeks at college. What would it be like in a strange country? What about the language? And besides, I had promised to teach my younger brother to sail that summer. The more I thought about it, the more the prospect daunted[2] me. I began waking up nights in a sweat.

In the end I turned down the proposition. As soon as Ted asked somebody else to go, I began kicking myself. A couple of weeks later I went home to my old summer job, unpacking cartons at the local supermarket, feeling very low. I had turned down something I wanted to do because I was scared, and had ended up feeling depressed. I stayed that way for a long time. And it didn't help when I went back to college in the fall to discover that Ted and his friend had had a terrific time. 3

In the long run that unhappy summer taught me a valuable lesson out of which I developed a rule for myself: *do what makes you anxious; don't do what makes you depressed.* 4

I am not, of course, talking about severe states of anxiety or depression, which require medical attention. What I mean is that kind of anxiety we call stage fright, butterflies in the stomach, a case of nerves—the feelings we have at a job interview, when we're giving a big party, when we have to make an important presentation at the office. And the kind of depression I am referring to is that downhearted feeling of the blues, when we don't seem to be interested in anything, when we can't get going and seem to have no energy. 5

I was confronted by this sort of situation toward the end of my senior year. As graduation approached, I began to think about taking a crack at making my living as a writer. But one of my professors was urging me to apply to graduate school and aim at a teaching career. 6

I wavered. The idea of trying to live by writing was scary—a lot more scary than spending a summer on the Pampas, I thought. Back and forth I went, making my decision, unmaking it. Suddenly, I realized that every time I gave up the idea of writing, that sinking feeling went through me; it gave me the blues. 7

The thought of graduate school wasn't what depressed me. It was giving up on what deep in my gut I really wanted to do. Right then I learned another lesson. To avoid that kind of depression meant, inevitably, having to endure a certain amount of worry and concern. 8

The great Danish philosopher Søren Kierkegaard believed that anxiety always arises when we confront the possibility of our own 9

[2]*daunted:* discouraged.

development. It seems to be a rule of life that you can't advance without getting that old, familiar, jittery feeling.

Even as children we discover this when we try to expand our- 10
selves by, say, learning to ride a bike or going out for the school play. Later in life we get butterflies when we think about having that first child, or uprooting the family from the old hometown to find a better opportunity halfway across the country. Any time, it seems, that we set out aggressively to get something we want, we meet up with anxiety. And it's going to be our traveling companion, at least part of the way, into any new venture.

When I first began writing magazine articles, I was frequently 11
required to interview big names—people like Richard Burton,[3] Joan Rivers,[4] sex authority William Masters, baseball-great Dizzy Dean. Before each interview I would get butterflies and my hands would shake.

At the time, I was doing some writing about music. And one per- 12
son I particularly admired was the great composer Duke Ellington. Onstage and on television, he seemed the very model of the confident, sophisticated man of the world. Then I learned that Ellington still got stage fright. If the highly honored Duke Ellington, who had appeared on the bandstand some 10,000 times over 30 years, had anxiety attacks, who was I to think I could avoid them?

I went on doing those frightening interviews, and one day, as I 13
was getting onto a plane for Washington to interview columnist Joseph Alsop, I suddenly realized to my astonishment that I was looking forward to the meeting. What had happened to those butterflies?

Well, in truth, they were still there, but there were fewer of them. 14
I had benefited, I discovered, from a process psychologists call "extinction." If you put an individual in an anxiety-provoking situation often enough, he will eventually learn that there isn't anything to be worried about.

Which brings us to a corollary[5] to my basic rule: *you'll never* 15
eliminate anxiety by avoiding the things that caused it. I remember how my son Jeff was when I first began to teach him to swim at the lake cottage where we spent our summer vacations. He resisted, and when I got him into the water he sank and sputtered and wanted to

[3]*Richard Burton* (1925–1984): a well-known British stage and Hollywood movie actor.
[4]*Joan Rivers* (b. 1933): a stand-up comedian and talk-show host.
[5]*corollary:* analogy; another example.

quit. But I was insistent. And by summer's end he was splashing around like a puppy. He had "extinguished" his anxiety the only way he could—by confronting it.

The problem, of course, is that it is one thing to urge somebody else to take on those anxiety-producing challenges; it is quite another to get ourselves to do it. 16

Some years ago I was offered a writing assignment that would require three months of travel through Europe. I had been abroad a couple of times on the usual "If it's Tuesday this must be Belgium" trips, but I hardly could claim to know my way around the continent. Moreover, my knowledge of foreign languages was limited to a little college French. 17

I hesitated. How would I, unable to speak the language, totally unfamiliar with local geography or transportation systems, set up interviews and do research? It seemed impossible, and with considerable regret I sat down to write a letter begging off. Halfway through, a thought—which I subsequently made into another corollary to my basic rule—ran through my mind: *you can't learn if you don't try.* So I accepted the assignment. 18

There were some bad moments. But by the time I had finished the trip I was an experienced traveler. And ever since, I have never hesitated to head for even the most exotic of places, without guides or even advanced bookings, confident that somehow I will manage. 19

The point is that the new, the different, is almost by definition scary. But each time you try something, you learn, and as the learning piles up, the world opens to you. 20

I've made parachute jumps, learned to ski at 40, flown up the Rhine[6] in a balloon. And I know I'm going to go on doing such things. It's not because I'm braver or more daring than others. I'm not. But I don't let the butterflies stop me from doing what I want. Accept anxiety as another name for challenge and you can accomplish wonders. 21

Thinking Critically about This Reading

Collier writes that "Kierkegaard believed that anxiety always arises when we confront the possibility of our own development" (paragraph 9). How do Collier's own experiences and growth substantiate Kierkegaard's belief in the value of anxiety?

[6]*Rhine:* a major river and waterway of western Europe.

Questions for Study and Discussion

1. What is Collier's thesis? Based on your own experiences, do you think Collier's thesis is valid? Explain.
2. What is the process known to psychologists as "extinction"?
3. What causes Collier to come up with his basic rule for himself: "Do what makes you anxious; don't do what makes you depressed" (4)? (Glossary: *Cause and Effect*) How does he develop the two corollaries to his basic rule? How do the basic rule and the two corollaries prepare you for his thesis?
4. What is Collier's purpose? (Glossary: *Purpose*)
5. What figure of speech does Collier use toward the end of paragraph 10? (Glossary: *Figure of Speech*)
6. What function do paragraphs 17–19 serve in Collier's essay?

Classroom Activity Using Thesis

A good thesis statement identifies the topic and makes an assertion about it. Evaluate each of the following sentences, and explain why each one either works or doesn't work as a thesis statement.

1. Americans are suffering from overwork.
2. Life is indeed precious, and I believe the death penalty helps to affirm this fact.
3. Birthday parties are loads of fun.
4. New York is a city of sounds: muted sounds and shrill sounds; shattering sounds and soothing sounds; urgent sounds and aimless sounds.
5. Everyone is talking about the level of violence in American society.
6. Neighborhoods are often assigned human characteristics, one of which is a life cycle: They have a birth, a youth, a middle age, and an old age.

Suggested Writing Assignments

1. Building on your own experiences and the reading you have done, write an essay in which you use as your thesis either Collier's basic rule or one of his corollaries to that basic rule.

2. Write an essay in which you use any one of the following as your thesis:

   Good manners are a thing of the past.
   We need rituals in our lives.
   To tell a joke well is an art.
   We are a drug-dependent society.
   A regular low-dosage regimen of aspirin can be therapeutic.
   Regular exercise offers many benefits.

No More Pep Rallies!

■ Etta Kralovec

Born in 1949, Etta Kralovec is currently director of teacher education at Pepperdine University. She earned her BS from Lewis & Clark College and her PhD from Teachers College at Columbia University. After graduate school Kralovec taught at the College of the Atlantic in Bar Harbor, Maine, where she was professor of human studies, director of teacher education, and associate academic dean. She also taught high school in Laguna Beach, California. In 1996, she received a Fulbright Fellowship to assist in the establishment of a teacher preparation program at Africa University in Zimbabwe. Her popular book The End of Homework: How Homework Disrupts Families, Overburdens Children and Limits Learning *(2000) was widely read and not surprisingly both praised and criticized by professionals and parents across the educational spectrum.*

In the following essay, which first appeared in the February 17, 2003, issue of Forbes *magazine, Kralovec puts forth the same thesis that lies at the heart of her more recent book* Schools That Do Too Much: Wasting Time and Money and What We Can Do about It *(2003). Notice how Kralovec supports her thesis with cogent examples drawn from her own experiences in the classroom.*

For Your Journal

Reflect on your high school experience. What extracurricular activity—for example, a sport or a club—do you wish you had participated in but didn't? Why? What do you think you could have gained educationally and emotionally from the activity?

Everyone agrees that we've got to improve academic achievement in America's public schools. So why is it that school districts distract students from core academics with a barrage of activities—everything from field hockey to music, drama, debating and chess teams? And there's more: Drug education and fundraising eat away 1 at classroom time. All manner of holidays, including Valentine's Day, get celebrated during the school day, as well as children's birthdays. These diversions are costly. They consume money and time.

Here's a bold proposition: Privatize school sports and other extracurricular activities, and remove all but basic academic studies from the classroom. Sound like sacrilege?[1] Look at what these extras really cost. 2

School budgets include a section that appears to cover the costs of all extracurricular activities. But when a school board member and I did a full analysis of the $4.8 million budget of our public high school on Mount Desert Island, Maine, we found that the listed costs were the tip of the iceberg. 3

Embedded in other line items were the maintenance of the field and gym, insurance for sports teams, transportation to away games, the school doctor's salary, the standby ambulance mandated for home games and compensation for teachers who double as sports coaches. (Not to mention that teachers who coach often hold only morning classes and spend the rest of their days on sports.) Our study revealed that while 5% of the school budget officially falls in the nonacademic section, when we factored in all of the real costs, the number was closer to 10%, or $480,000. 4

At a recent school board meeting in Searsport, Maine, parents were astonished to learn that the school spent $50,000 fixing the ball field because game officials said they wouldn't officiate there if the field wasn't repaired. Parents reminded the board that the previous year the school had sent seven members of the golf team in a 72-passenger bus to a golf tournament 100 miles away. Last year 70% of the students at that school barely met standards in math and reading. 5

The culture of sports that exists in many American high schools has a cost that can't be measured in budget numbers. Time off for pep rallies, homecoming week and travel to away games are all supported, if not encouraged, by teachers, principals and peers. There's no question that this focus on sports saps the time, attention and energy that students should put into academics. 6

The United States is the only industrialized country where competitive athletics and extensive extracurricular offerings are sponsored and paid for by the public school system. What would happen if we held all school programs to a simple standard—that they must 7

[1]*sacrilege:* misuse of something sacred.

contribute to reading, writing, mathematics, science and history, as defined by state learning standards?

The extracurricular activities, now deemed central to the mission of public schools, would have to be sponsored by other institutions and organizations. Get businesses, religious organizations, the YMCA and the Scouts to take responsibility for competitive sports and other extracurricular activities. 8

Moving these programs out of public schools and into the community would not reduce their positive impact. Rather, extracurricular activities could play a larger role in the life of our towns and neighborhoods. 9

Schools are asked to do too much and end up doing too little. We have all heard about how difficult it is to find leaders to run the nation's schools. It's not surprising. We ask principals to raise standards in mathematics, literacy and science, even while they must manage an elaborate physical plant that serves as a community theater, sports arena and orchestra hall. Learning the basics is often only a by-product of our public education system. 10

Thinking Critically about This Reading

Kralovec states that "schools are asked to do too much and end up doing too little" (paragraph 10). What evidence does she use to support her claim? (Glossary: *Evidence*) Does your own experience support Kralovec's claim?

Questions for Study and Discussion

1. What is Kralovec's thesis? What solution does she offer to the problem that is at the heart of her thesis?
2. What is Kralovec's purpose? (Glossary: *Purpose*)
3. Do you think privatizing extracurricular activities can work? Why or why not? What problems do you see with Kralovec's proposition?
4. What did Kralovec discover when she investigated the budget for the public high school on Mount Desert Island, Maine?
5. Kralovec writes, "Our study revealed that while 5% of the school budget officially falls in the nonacademic section, when we

factored in all of the real costs, the number was closer to 10%, or $480,000" (4). Is that too much to spend on the nonacademic portion of a public school's budget, in your opinion?

6. What evidence does Kralovec give to show the causal link between too much money and time spent on extracurricular activities and poor scores in math and reading? (Glossary: *Evidence; Cause and Effect*)

Classroom Activity Using Thesis

Based on your reading of Kralovec's essay, write at least one thesis statement for each of the following questions:

1. What is the importance of extracurricular activities?
2. What do music, chess, drama, or field hockey teach students?
3. What percentage of a public school's budget should be spent on extracurricular activities?
4. What's wrong with raising funds in the private sector to help pay for extracurricular activities in the public schools?

Suggested Writing Assignments

1. Kralovec believes that the core academic curriculum—reading, writing, science, math, history—should be the focus of a public school education. Using the thesis "Extracurricular activities drain precious resources from public schools," write an essay in which you support Kralovec's position.
2. In paragraph 6 Kralovec states, the "focus on sports saps the time, attention and energy that students should put into academics." Write an essay in which you argue just the opposite—that students who participate in sports often budget their time more wisely, have higher levels of energy, are more team spirited, and exhibit a greater sense of community within their school and beyond than students who do not participate in sports. (Glossary: *Argumentation*)

chapter **4**

Unity

Unity is an essential quality in a well-written essay. The principle of **unity** requires that every element in a piece of writing—whether a paragraph or an essay—be related to the main idea. Sentences that stray from the subject, even though they might be related to it or provide additional information, can weaken an otherwise strong piece of writing. Note how the italicized segments in the following paragraph undermine its unity and divert our attention from its main idea:

> When I was growing up, one of the places I enjoyed most was the cherry tree in the backyard. *Behind the yard was an alley and then more houses.* Every summer when the cherries began to ripen, I used to spend hours high up in the tree, picking and eating the sweet, sun-warmed cherries. *My mother always worried about my falling out of the tree, but I never did.* But I had some competition for the cherries—flocks of birds that enjoyed them as much as I did and would perch all over the tree, devouring the fruit whenever I wasn't there. I used to wonder why the grown-ups never ate any of the cherries—*my father loved all kinds of fruit*—but actually, when the birds and I had finished, there weren't many left.
>
> –Betty Burns, student

When the italicized sentences are eliminated, the paragraph is unified and reads smoothly.

Now consider another paragraph, this one from an essay about family photographs and how they allow the author to learn about her past and to stay connected with her family in the present.

> Photographs have taken me to places I have never been and have shown me people alive before I was born. I can visit my grandmother's childhood home in Vienna, Austria, and walk down the high-ceilinged, iron staircase by looking through the small,

white album my grandma treasures. I also know of the tomboy she once was, wearing lederhosen instead of the dirndls worn by her friends. And I have seen her as a beautiful young woman who traveled with the Red Cross during the war, uncertain of her future. The photograph that rests in a red leather frame on my grandma's nightstand has allowed me to meet the man she would later marry. He died before I was born. I have been told that I would have loved his calm manner, and I can see for myself his gentle smile and tranquil expression.

–Carrie White, student

Did you notice that the first sentence gives focus and direction to the paragraph and that all of the subsequent sentences are directly related to it?

A well-written essay should be unified both within and between paragraphs; that is, everything in it should be related to its **thesis,** the main idea of the essay. The first requirement for unity is that the thesis itself be clear, either through a direct statement, called the *thesis statement,* or by implication. The second requirement is that there be no digressions, no discussion or information that is not shown to be logically related to the thesis. A unified essay stays within the limits of its thesis.

Here, for example, is a short essay by Stuart Chase about the dangers of making generalizations. As you read, notice how carefully Chase sticks to his point.

Over-Generalizing

One swallow does not make a summer, nor can two or three cases often support a dependable generalization. Yet all of us, including the most polished eggheads, are constantly falling into this mental peopletrap. It is the most common, probably the most seductive, and potentially the most dangerous, of all the fallacies. 1

You drive through a town and see a drunken man on the sidewalk. A few blocks further on you see another. You turn to your companion: "Nothing but drunks in this town!" Soon you are out in the country, bowling along at fifty. A car passes you as if you were parked. On a curve a second whizzes by. Your companion turns to you: "All the drivers in this state are crazy!" Two thumping generalizations, each built on two cases. If we stop to think, we 2 usually recognize the exaggeration and the unfairness of such generalizations. Trouble comes when we do not stop to think—or when we build them on a prejudice.

This kind of reasoning has been around for a long time. Aristotle was aware of its dangers and called it "reasoning by example," meaning too few examples. What it boils down to is failing to count your swallows before announcing that summer is here. Driving from my home to New Haven the other day, a distance of about forty miles, I caught myself saying: "Every time I look around I see a new ranch-type house going up." So on the return trip I counted them; there were exactly five under construction. And how many times had I "looked around"? I suppose I had glanced to right and left—as one must at side roads and so forth in driving—several hundred times. 3

In this fallacy we do not make the error of neglecting facts altogether and rushing immediately to the level of opinion. We start at the fact level properly enough, but *we do not stay there.* A case of two and up we go to a rousing over-simplification about drunks, speeders, ranch-style houses—or, more seriously, about foreigners, African Americans, labor leaders, teen-agers. 4

Why do we over-generalize so often and sometimes so disastrously? One reason is that the human mind is a generalizing machine. We would not be people without this power. The old academic crack: "All generalizations are false, including this one," is only a play on words. We *must* generalize to communicate and to live. But we should beware of beating the gun; of not waiting until enough facts are in to say something useful. Meanwhile it is a plain waste of time to listen to arguments based on a few handpicked examples. 5

–Stuart Chase

Everything in the essay relates to Chase's thesis statement, which is included in the essay's first sentence: ". . . nor can two or three cases often support a dependable generalization." Paragraphs 2 and 3 document the thesis with examples; paragraph 4 explains how overgeneralizing occurs; paragraph 5 analyzes why people overgeneralize; and, for a conclusion, Chase restates his thesis in different words. An essay may be longer, more complex, and more wide-ranging than this one, but to be effective it must also avoid digressions and remain close to the author's main idea.

A good way to check that your essay is indeed unified is to underline your thesis and then to explain to yourself how each paragraph in your essay is related to the thesis. If you find a paragraph that does not appear to be logically connected, you can revise it so that the relationship is clear. Similarly, it is useful to make sure that each sentence in a paragraph is related to the topic sentence. (See pages 164–66 for a discussion of topic sentences.)

My Name

■ **Sandra Cisneros**

Sandra Cisneros was born in Chicago in 1954. After graduating from Loyola University in Chicago and attending the Iowa Writers' Workshop in the late 1970s, she moved to the Southwest and now lives in San Antonio, Texas. Cisneros has had numerous occupations within the fields of education and the arts and has been a visiting writer at various universities. Although she has written two well-received books of poetry, My Wicked, Wicked Ways *(1987) and* Loose Woman *(1994), she is better known for the autobiographical fiction of* The House on Mango Street *(1984)—from which the following selection is taken—and for* Woman Hollering Creek and Other Stories *(1991). In 1995 she was awarded a grant from the prestigious MacArthur Foundation. In 2002 she published a novel,* Caramelo.

As you read "My Name," pay particular attention to how tightly Cisneros unifies her paragraphs by intertwining the meanings of her name (originally Esperanza) and her feelings about the great-grandmother with whom she shares that name.

For Your Journal

Who chose your name, and why was it given to you? Does your name have a special meaning for the person who gave it to you? Are you happy with your name?

In English my name means hope. In Spanish it means too many letters. It means sadness, it means waiting. It is like the number nine. A muddy color. It is the Mexican records my father plays on Sunday mornings when he is shaving, songs like sobbing. 1

It was my great-grandmother's name and now it is mine. She was a horse woman too, born like me in the Chinese year of the horse—which is supposed to be bad luck if you're born female—but I think this is a Chinese lie because the Chinese, like the Mexicans, don't like their women strong. 2

My great-grandmother. I would've liked to have known her, a wild horse of a woman, so wild she wouldn't marry until my great-grandfather threw a sack over her head and carried her off. Just like that, as if she were a fancy chandelier. That's the way he did it. 3

And the story goes she never forgave him. She looked out the window all her life, the way so many women sit their sadness on an elbow. I wonder if she made the best with what she got or was she sorry because she couldn't be all the things she wanted to be. Esperanza. I have inherited her name, but I don't want to inherit her place by the window. 4

At school they say my name funny as if the syllables were made out of tin and hurt the roof of your mouth. But in Spanish my name is made out of a softer something like silver, not quite as thick as my sister's name Magdalena which is uglier than mine. Magdalena who at least can come home and become Nenny. But I am always Esperanza. 5

I would like to baptize[1] myself under a new name, a name more like the real me, the one nobody sees. Esperanza as Lisandra or Maritza or Zeze the X. Yes. Something like Zeze the X will do. 6

Thinking Critically about This Reading

What does Cisneros mean when she says of her great-grandmother, "I have inherited her name, but I don't want to inherit her place by the window" (paragraph 4)? What about her great-grandmother does she admire and respect?

Questions for Study and Discussion

1. What is Cisneros's thesis? (Glossary: *Thesis*)
2. Are there any digressions, discussions, or information in this essay that do not logically connect to Cisneros's thesis? (Glossary: *Thesis*) Explain how each paragraph in the essay relates to her thesis.
3. What is Cisneros's purpose? (Glossary: *Purpose*)
4. In what way do you think a name can be "like the number nine"? Like "a muddy color" (1)? What is your impression of the author's name, based on these similes? (Glossary: *Figure of Speech*)

---

[1] *baptize:* to give a first or Christian name to.

5. What is Cisneros's tone? (Glossary: *Tone*) How does she establish the tone? What does it tell the reader about how she feels about her name?
6. Why do you think Cisneros waits until the end of paragraph 4 to reveal her given name?
7. Why do you think Cisneros chose "Zeze the X" as a name that better represents her inner self?

Classroom Activity Using Unity

Take a paragraph from a draft of an essay you have been working on, and test it for unity. Be prepared to read the paragraph in class and explain why it is unified, or why it is not, and what you need to do to make it unified.

Suggested Writing Assignments

1. If you, like Cisneros, wished to choose a different name for yourself, what would it be? Write an essay that reveals your choice of a new name and explains why you like it or why it might be particularly appropriate for you. Make sure the essay is unified and that every paragraph directly supports your name choice.
2. Choose a grandparent or other relative at least two generations older than you about whom you know an interesting story. What impact has the relative, or the stories about him or her, had on your life? Write a unified narrative essay about the relative and what is interesting about him or her. (Glossary: *Narration*)
3. In your opinion, what statement does the following cartoon make about the nature of names? What insight does the cartoon give you into Cisneros's desire to have "a name more like the real me" (6)—a name other than her great-grandmother's? After exploring the questions about names raised in "My Name" and the cartoon, write a unified essay in which you present your thinking about names. Be sure to state your position in a strong thesis and to use examples and personal experiences that directly relate to your thesis. (Glossary: *Thesis; Example*)

I really thought name-tags
would help in telling us apart...

Technology's Limits

Anthony Komaroff

Anthony Komaroff was born in 1941 in Milwaukee, Wisconsin, and graduated from Stanford University in 1963. After graduating from the University of Washington's College of Medicine in 1967 and serving a two-year stint in the U.S. Public Health Service, he took a position at Beth Israel Hospital in Boston, Massachusetts. Later he served as chief of the division of general medicine at Boston's Brigham and Women's Hospital. An internationally known expert on chronic fatigue syndrome, Komaroff is currently professor of medicine at Harvard Medical School, senior physician at Brigham and Women's, and editor-in-chief at Harvard Health Publications. He has authored more than two hundred journal articles and book chapters, as well as the book Harvard Medical School Family Health Guide *(2004).*

In the following essay, first published in a special issue of Newsweek *on medical science in June 2005, Komaroff narrates the unified story of his relationship with one of his patients. Notice how he uses each narrative detail to support his central idea about technology and patient care.*

For Your Journal

Briefly describe what you would consider the ideal doctor-patient relationship. How closely have your experiences with doctors or other healthcare providers mirrored your ideal? Explain.

In the spring of 1972, a woman I'll call Jessie walked into my office with her daughter. She was 52, born and raised in Jamaica, left school after the fifth grade and took in work as a seamstress. She had come to Boston two years earlier to live with her daughter. In lilting[1] cadences she told me that she had been suffering from bad headaches for the past two weeks. I asked her about the headaches, then pulled the curtain to give her privacy while she undressed for the physical 1

[1] *lilting:* gently rising and falling in a way that is pleasant to hear.

examination. As I did so, her daughter whispered: "She is very scared. She has never gone to see a doctor before."

Even in the hospital gown, there was something regal about her. 2
As I inflated the blood-pressure cuff, there was a flash of fear in her eyes. This was the first medical technology she had ever experienced and, briefly, it hurt. I deflated the cuff, and then peered into her eyes with my ophthalmoscope. Pressing my stethoscope to her back, I listened to her lungs. Then she lay down on the table, and I placed the palm of my right hand over her heart. At that moment, her look of apprehension melted into an expression of serenity.

When she had dressed, I explained that very high blood pressure 3
was causing her headaches and putting a strain on her heart. I prescribed two medicines that normalized her blood pressure and relieved her headaches. Neither medicine had been available even 25 years before. Technology had allowed me to make the diagnosis and prescribe effective treatment. But it was not only technology that earned her trust. I had asked about her suffering, explained its cause and answered her questions. And I had touched her.

For many years, Jessie remained quite healthy. When she came for 4
her checkups, we had time to talk. She began to ask about my life—and became free with advice. Once, she asked if I had ever been on Boston's Duck Tour, a ride around the city's streets and on its ponds. When I said I hadn't, she said sternly, "You should take your wife on the Duck Tour."

Then, in the late 1980s, Jessie's daughter died, leaving her with 5
no family in Boston. She never stopped mourning for her daughter, though she was nourished by the affection of members of her church. Her body, however, began to deteriorate. Blood vessels in the wall of her large intestine intermittently would rupture, causing massive bleeding. By this time, rather than requiring major surgery, the condition could be treated by passing a colonoscope to the point of the bleeding, and cauterizing[2] the bleeding vessel. Then Jessie developed pains in her neck and arms. An MRI revealed that the bones that surrounded and protected the spinal cord had decayed and were encroaching on the cord, threatening her with paralysis. Bone-fusion surgery protected her from that fate. Then arthritis damaged her knees. Knee-replacement surgery allowed her to walk down the aisle with other church elders.

---

[2]*cauterizing:* to seal off by burning or searing.

By 2000, I had been Jessie's doctor for nearly 30 years. What had she needed from me? She needed me to know, or find, whatever was required to diagnose and treat her suffering. We had been lucky. Technology provided me with solutions—colonoscopes, MRI scans, joint-replacement surgery—that were not available on the day we first met. She also was lucky to be living in the developed world: for most people on this planet, none of the technology would have been available. But Jessie and I were also unlucky. Even by 2000, medical science remained fundamentally ignorant about what had spiked her blood pressure, why the blood vessels in her gut ruptured and why the bones of her spine and knees had started falling apart. If we were doctor-and-patient perhaps 30 years from now, maybe I would have those answers and could prevent her suffering. Jessie also needed to trust my judgment, as I recommended tests and treatments that put her at some risk. She needed my help in navigating our complicated health-care system. Above all, she needed to know that I cared about her. 6

In December 2000, I arrived home from a trip to learn that Jessie had suffered a heart attack and was in intensive care. Her lungs were filling with fluid, and her kidneys were failing. We had run out of technologies. I went to her bedside and called her name, but she did not respond. I bent down and rested my hand on her shoulder. Suddenly she opened her eyes, looked at me and smiled. "Don't forget the Duck Tour," she whispered. She closed her eyes, her face as serene as when I first saw it 30 years before. A moment later, she left us to join her daughter. 7

Thinking Critically about This Reading

In describing his first encounter with "Jessie," Komaroff states "I had asked her about her suffering, explained its cause and answered her questions. And I had touched her" (paragraph 3). What effect did Komaroff's physical contact with Jessie have on their relationship? Why?

Questions for Study and Discussion

1. What is Komaroff's thesis? (Glossary: *Thesis*)
2. In what ways does the extended example of Jessie serve to illustrate Komaroff's thesis?
3. What effect, if any, would additional examples of Komaroff's patients have on the unity of the essay? Explain.

4. What medical technology did Komaroff use to diagnose and treat Jessie's suffering over the years? At what point did Jessie's medical problems push technology beyond its limits?
5. In the end, it's obvious that Komaroff really cares about Jessie. What details in the essay show that he both cares for and respects his patient?

Classroom Activity Using Unity

Mark Wanner, a student, wrote the following paragraphs for an essay using this thesis statement:

> In order to provide a good learning environment in school, the teachers and administrators need to be strong leaders.

Unfortunately, some of the sentences disrupt the unity of the essay. Find these sentences, eliminate them, and reread the essay.

Strong School Leaders

School administrators and teachers must do more than simply supply students with information and a school building. They must also provide students with an atmosphere that allows them to focus on learning within the walls of the school. Whether the walls are brick, steel, or cement, they are only walls, and they do not help to create an appropriate atmosphere. Strong leadership both inside and outside the classroom yields a school in which students are able to excel in their studies, because they know how to conduct themselves in their relationships with their teachers and fellow students. 1

A recent change in the administration of Eastside High School demonstrated how important strong leadership is to learning. Under the previous administration, parents and students complained that not enough emphasis was placed on studies. Most of the students lived in an impoverished neighborhood that had only one park for several thousand residents. Students were allowed to leave school at any time of the day, and little was done to curb the growing substance abuse problem. "What's the point of trying to teach algebra to students who are just going to get jobs as part-time sales clerks, anyway?" Vice Principal Iggy Norant said when questioned about 2 his school's poor academic standards. Mr. Norant was known to students as Twiggy Iggy because of his tall, thin frame. Standardized test scores at the school lagged well behind the state average, and only 16% of the graduates attended college within two years.

Five years ago, the school board hired Mary Peña, former chair of the state educational standards committee, as principal. A cheerleader in college, Ms. Peña got her B.A. in recreation science before getting her masters in education. She immediately emphasized the importance of learning, replacing any faculty members who did not share her high expectations of the students. Among those she fired was Mr. Norant; she also replaced two social studies teachers, one math teacher, four English teachers, and a lab instructor who let students play Gameboy in lab. She also established a code of conduct, which clearly stated the rules all students had to follow. Students were allowed second chances, but those who continued to conduct themselves in a way that interfered with the other students' ability to learn were dealt with quickly and severely. "The attitude at Eastside has changed so much since Mary Peña arrived," said math teacher Jeremy Rifkin after Peña's second year. "Students come to class much more relaxed and ready to learn. I feel like I can teach again." Test scores at Eastside are now well above state averages, and 68% of the most recent graduating class went straight to college. 3

–Mark Wanner, student

Suggested Writing Assignments

1. Using Komaroff's essay as a model, write an essay in which you describe the relationship you have with a person you trust—a parent, doctor, teacher, coach, clergy, or other adult figure. How long have you known this person? How was the bond of trust first established? What influence has this person had on your life? How has your relationship with this person changed over time?
2. With all the advances in medical technology that we've witnessed in the last decade alone, Americans have come to expect "miracles" every time they visit a doctor's office. Are such expectations fair to doctors? To patients? Should we rely on medical technology alone? In a unified essay explore your thoughts about the importance of a human connection in the doctor-patient relationship.

The Meanings of a Word

Gloria Naylor

American novelist, essayist, and screenwriter Gloria Naylor was born in 1950 in New York City, where she lives today. She worked first as a missionary for the Jehovah's Witnesses in 1967–1975, and then as a telephone operator until 1981. That year she graduated from Brooklyn College of the City University of New York. She also holds a graduate degree in African American studies from Yale University. Naylor has taught writing and literature at George Washington University, New York University, and Cornell University, in addition to publishing several novels: The Women of Brewster Place *(1982),* Linden Hills *(1985),* Mama Day *(1988),* Bailey's Cafe *(1992), and* The Men of Brewster Place *(1998).*

The following essay first appeared in the New York Times *in 1986. In it Naylor examines the ways in which words can take on meaning, depending on who uses them and for what purpose. Notice how the paragraphs describing her experiences with the word* nigger *relate back to a clearly stated thesis at the end of paragraph 2.*

For Your Journal

Have you ever been called a derogatory name? What was the name, and how did you feel about it?

Language is the subject. It is the written form with which I've managed to keep the wolf away from the door and, in diaries, to keep my sanity. In spite of this, I consider the written word inferior to the spoken, and much of the frustration experienced by novelists is the awareness that whatever we manage to capture in even the most transcendent[1] passages falls far short of the richness of life. Dialogue achieves its power in the dynamics of a fleeting moment of sight, sound, smell, and touch. 1

I'm not going to enter the debate here about whether it is language that shapes reality or vice versa. That battle is doomed to be waged 2

[1]*transcendent:* preeminent; above all others.

whenever we seek intermittent reprieve from the chicken and egg dispute. I will simply take the position that the spoken word, like the written word, amounts to a nonsensical arrangement of sounds or letters without a consensus that assigns "meaning." And building from the meanings of what we hear, we order reality. Words themselves are innocuous[2]; it is the consensus that gives them true power.

I remember the first time I heard the word *nigger*. In my third-grade class, our math tests were being passed down the rows, and as I handed the papers to a little boy in back of me, I remarked that once again he had received a much lower mark than I did. He snatched his test from me and spit out that word. Had he called me a nymphomaniac or a necrophiliac, I couldn't have been more puzzled. I didn't know what a nigger was, but I knew that whatever it meant, it was something he shouldn't have called me. This was verified when I raised my hand, and in a loud voice repeated what he had said and watched the teacher scold him for using a "bad" word. I was later to go home and ask the inevitable question that every black parent must face—"Mommy, what does *nigger* mean?" 3

And what exactly did it mean? Thinking back, I realize that this could not have been the first time the word was used in my presence. I was part of a large extended family that had migrated from the rural South after World War II and formed a close-knit network that gravitated around my maternal grandparents. Their ground-floor apartment in one of the buildings they owned in Harlem[3] was a weekend mecca for my immediate family, along with countless aunts, uncles, and cousins who brought along assorted friends. It was a bustling and open house with assorted neighbors and tenants popping in and out to exchange bits of gossip, pick up an old quarrel, or referee the ongoing checkers game in which my grandmother cheated shamelessly. They were all there to let down their hair and put up their feet after a week of labor in the factories, laundries, and shipyards of New York. 4

Amid the clamor, which could reach deafening proportions—two or three conversations going on simultaneously, punctuated by the sound of a baby's crying somewhere in the back rooms or out on the street—there was still a rigid set of rules about what was said and how. Older children were sent out of the living room when it was time to get into the juicy details about "you-know-who" up on the third 5

[2]*innocuous:* harmless; lacking significance or impact.
[3]*Harlem:* a predominantly African American neighborhood located in New York City.

floor who had gone and gotten herself "p-r-e-g-n-a-n-t!" But my parents, knowing that I could spell well beyond my years, always demanded that I follow the others out to play. Beyond sexual misconduct and death, everything else was considered harmless for our young ears. And so among the anecdotes[4] of the triumphs and disappointments in the various workings of their lives, the word *nigger* was used in my presence, but it was set within contexts and inflections[5] that caused it to register in my mind as something else.

In the singular, the word was always applied to a man who had 6
distinguished himself in some situation that brought their approval for his strength, intelligence, or drive:

"Did Johnny *really* do that?" 7

"I'm telling you, that nigger pulled in $6,000 of overtime last 8
year. Said he got enough for a down payment on a house."

When used with a possessive adjective by a woman—"my nigger"— 9
it became a term of endearment for her husband or boyfriend. But it could be more than just a term applied to a man. In their mouths it became the pure essence of manhood—a disembodied force that channeled their past history of struggle and present survival against the odds into a victorious statement of being: "Yeah, that old foreman found out quick enough—you don't mess with a nigger."

In the plural, it became a description of some group within the 10
community that had overstepped the bounds of decency as my family defined it. Parents who neglected their children, a drunken couple who fought in public, people who simply refused to look for work, those with excessively dirty mouths or unkempt households were all "trifling niggers." This particular circle could forgive hard times, unemployment, the occasional bout of depression—they had gone through all of that themselves—but the unforgivable sin was a lack of self-respect.

A woman could never be a "nigger" in the singular, with its con- 11
notation of confirming worth. The noun *girl* was its closest equivalent in that sense, but only when used in direct address and regardless of the gender doing the addressing. *Girl* was a token of respect for a woman. The one-syllable word was drawn out to sound like three in recognition of the extra ounce of wit, nerve, or daring that the woman had shown in the situation under discussion.

---

[4]*anecdotes:* short accounts or stories of life experiences.

[5]*inflections:* alterations in pitch or tone of voice.

"G-i-r-l, stop. You mean you said that to his face?" 12

But if the word was used in a third-person reference or shortened 13 so that it almost snapped out of the mouth, it always involved some element of communal disapproval. And age became an important factor in these exchanges. It was only between individuals of the same generation, or from any older person to a younger (but never the other way around), that *girl* would be considered a compliment.

I don't agree with the argument that use of the word *nigger* at this 14 social stratum of the black community was an internalization of racism. The dynamics were the exact opposite: the people in my grandmother's living room took a word that whites used to signify worthlessness or degradation and rendered it impotent.[6] Gathering there together, they transformed *nigger* to signify the varied and complex human beings they knew themselves to be. If the word was to disappear totally from the mouths of even the most liberal of white society, no one in that room was naive enough to believe it would disappear from white minds. Meeting the word head-on, they proved it had absolutely nothing to do with the way they were determined to live their lives.

So there must have been dozens of times that *nigger* was spoken 15 in front of me before I reached the third grade. But I didn't "hear" it until it was said by a small pair of lips that had already learned it could be a way to humiliate me. That was the word I went home and asked my mother about. And since she knew that I had to grow up in America, she took me in her lap and explained.

Thinking Critically about This Reading

What does Naylor mean when she states that "words themselves are innocuous; it is the consensus that gives them true power" (paragraph 2)? How does she use the two meanings of the word *nigger* to illustrate her point?

Questions for Study and Discussion

1. Naylor states her thesis in the last sentence of paragraph 2. (Glossary: *Thesis*) How does what she says in the first two paragraphs build unity by connecting to her thesis statement?

---

[6]*impotent:* weak; powerless.

2. What are the two meanings of the word *nigger* as Naylor uses it in her essay? Where is the clearest definition of each use of the word presented? (Glossary: *Definition*)
3. Naylor says she must have heard the word *nigger* many times while she was growing up; yet she "heard" it for the first time when she was in the third grade. How does she explain this seeming contradiction?
4. Naylor gives a detailed narration of her family and its lifestyle in paragraphs 4 and 5. (Glossary: *Narration*) What kinds of details does she include in her brief story? (Glossary: *Details*) How does this narration contribute to your understanding of the word *nigger* as used by her family? Why do you suppose she offers so little in the way of a definition of the other use of the word *nigger*? (Glossary: *Definition*) Explain.
5. Would you characterize Naylor's tone as angry, objective, cynical, or something else? (Glossary: *Tone*) Cite examples of her diction to support your answer. (Glossary: *Diction*)
6. What is the meaning of Naylor's last sentence? How well does it work as an ending for her essay? (Glossary: *Beginnings and Endings*)

Classroom Activity Using Unity

Carefully read the following five-paragraph sequence, paying special attention to how each paragraph relates to the writer's thesis. Identify the paragraph that disrupts the unity of the sequence, and explain why it doesn't belong.

How to Build a Fire in a Fireplace

1 Though "experts" differ as to the best technique to follow when building a fire, one generally accepted method consists of first laying a generous amount of crumpled newspaper on the hearth between the andirons. Kindling wood is then spread generously over this layer of newspaper and one of the thickest logs is placed across the back of the andirons. This should be as close to the back of the fireplace as possible, but not quite touching it. A second log is then placed an inch or so in front of this, and a few additional sticks of kindling are laid across these two. A third log

is then placed on top to form a sort of pyramid with air space between all logs so that flames can lick freely up between them.

Roaring fireplace fires are particularly welcome during the win- 2
ter months, especially after hearty outdoor activities. To avoid any mid-winter tragedies, care should be taken to have a professional inspect and clean the chimney before starting to use the fireplace in the fall. Also, be sure to clean out the fireplace after each use.

A mistake frequently made is building the fire too far for- 3
ward so that the rear wall of the fireplace does not get properly heated. A heated back wall helps increase the draft and tends to suck smoke and flames rearward with less chance of sparks or smoke spurting out into the room.

Another common mistake often made by the inexperienced 4
fire-tender is to try to build a fire with only one or two logs, instead of using at least three. A single log is difficult to ignite properly, and even two logs do not provide an efficient bed with adequate fuel-burning capacity.

Use of too many logs, on the other hand, is also a common 5
fault and can prove hazardous. Building too big a fire can create more smoke and draft than the chimney can safely handle, increasing the possibility of sparks or smoke being thrown out into the room. For best results, the homeowner should start with three medium-size logs as described above, then add additional logs as needed if the fire is to be kept burning.

The five paragraphs on "How to Build a Fire in a Fireplace" are taken from Bernard Gladstone's book *The New York Times Complete Manual of Home Repair.*

Suggested Writing Assignments

1. Naylor disagrees with the notion that use of the word *nigger* in the African American community can be taken as an "internalization of racism"(14). Reexamine her essay, and discuss in what ways her definition of the word *nigger* affirms or denies her position. (Glossary: *Definition*) Draw on your own experiences, observations, and reading to support your answer.
2. Write a short essay in which you define a word—for example, *wife, macho, liberal, success,* or *marriage*—that has more than one meaning, depending on one's point of view.

chapter **5**

Organization

In an essay, ideas and information cannot be presented all at once; they have to be arranged in some order. That order is the essay's **organization.**

The pattern of organization in an essay should be suited to the writer's subject and **purpose.** For example, if you are writing about your experience working in a fast-food restaurant and your purpose is to tell about the activities of a typical day, you might present those activities in chronological order. If, on the other hand, you wish to argue that working in a bank is an ideal summer job, you might proceed from the least rewarding to the most rewarding aspect of this job; this is called *climactic order.*

Some common patterns of organization are time order, space order, and logical order. Time order, or chronological order, is used to present a sequence of events as they occurred. A personal narrative, a report of a campus incident, or an account of a historical event can be most naturally and easily related in chronological order. In the following paragraph, the author uses chronological order to recount a disturbing childhood memory:

> I clearly remember my sixth birthday because Dad was in the hospital with pneumonia. He was working so hard he paid very little attention to his health. As a result, he spent almost the entire summer before I entered the first grade in the hospital. Mom visited him nightly. On my birthday I was allowed to see him. I have memories of sitting happily in the lobby of the hospital talking to the nurses, telling them with a big smile that I was going to see my dad because it was my birthday. I couldn't wait to see him because children under 12 were not allowed to visit patients, so I had not seen him in a long time. When I entered the hospital room, I saw tubes inserted into his nose and needles stuck in his arm. He was very, very thin. I was frightened and wanted to cry, but I was determined to

> have a good visit. So I stayed for a while, and he wished me a happy birthday. When it was time to go, I kissed him good-bye and waited until I left his room to cry.
>
> –Grace Ming-Yee Wai

Of course, the order of events can sometimes be rearranged for special effect. For, example, an account of an auto accident may begin with the collision itself and then flash back in time to the events leading up to it. The description of a process—such as framing a poster, constructing a bookcase with cinder blocks and boards, or serving a tennis ball—almost always calls for a chronological organization.

When analyzing a causally related series of events, writers often use a chronological organization to clarify for readers the exact sequence of events. In the following example, the writer examines sequentially the series of malfunctions that led to the near disaster at the Three Mile Island nuclear facility in Harrisburg, Pennsylvania, showing clearly how each one led to the next:

> On March 28, 1979, at 3:53 A.M., a pump at the Harrisburg plant failed. Because the pump failed, the reactor's heat was not drawn off in the heat exchanger and the very hot water in the primary loop overheated. The pressure in the loop increased, opening a release valve that was supposed to counteract such an event. But the valve stuck open and the primary loop system lost so much water (which ended up as a highly radioactive pool, six feet deep, on the floor of the reactor building) that it was unable to carry off all the heat generated within the reactor core. Under these circumstances, the intense heat held within the reactor could, in theory, melt its fuel rods, and the resulting "meltdown" could then carry a hugely radioactive mass through the floor of the reactor. The reactor's emergency cooling system, which is designed to prevent this disaster, was then automatically activated, but when it was, apparently, turned off too soon, some of the fuel rods overheated. This produced a bubble of hydrogen gas at the top of the reactor. (The hydrogen is dissolved in the water in order to react with oxygen that is produced when the intense reactor radiation splits water molecules into their atomic constituents. When heated, the dissolved hydrogen bubbles out of the solution.) This bubble blocked the flow of cooling water so that despite the action of the emergency cooling system the reactor core was again in danger of melting down. Another danger was that the gas might contain enough oxygen to cause an explosion that could rupture the huge containers that surround the reactor and release a

deadly cloud of radioactive material into the surrounding countryside. Working desperately, technicians were able to gradually reduce the size of the gas bubble using a special apparatus brought in from the atomic laboratory at Oak Ridge, Tennessee, and the danger of a catastrophic release of radioactive materials subsided. But the sealed-off plant was now so radioactive that no one could enter it for many months—or, according to some observers, for years—without being exposed to a lethal dose of radiation.

–Barry Commoner

Space order is used when describing a person, place, or thing. This organizational pattern begins at a particular point and moves in some direction, such as left to right, top to bottom, east to west, outside to inside, front to back, near to far, around, or over. In describing a house, for example, a writer could move from top to bottom, from outside to inside, or in a circle around the outside.

In the following paragraph, the subject is a baseball, and the writer describes it from the inside out, moving from its "composition-cork nucleus" to the print on its stitched cowhide cover:

> It weighs just over five ounces and measures between 2.86 and 2.94 inches in diameter. It is made of a composition-cork nucleus encased in two thin layers of rubber, one black and one red, surrounded by 121 yards of tightly wrapped blue-gray wool yarn, 45 yards of white wool yarn, 54 more yards of blue-gray wool yarn, 150 yards of fine cotton yarn, a coat of rubber cement, and a cowhide (formerly horsehide) exterior, which is held together with 216 slightly raised red cotton stitches. Printed certifications, endorsements, and outdoor advertising spherically attest to its authenticity.
>
> –Roger Angell

Logical order can take many forms, depending on the writer's purpose. Often used patterns include general to specific, most familiar to least familiar, and smallest to biggest. Perhaps the most common type of logical order is order of importance. Notice how the writer uses this order in the following paragraph:

> The Egyptians have taught us many things. They were excellent farmers. They knew all about irrigation. They built temples which were afterwards copied by the Greeks and which served as the earliest models for the churches in which we worship nowadays. They invented a calendar which proved such a useful instrument for the

purpose of measuring time that it has survived with few changes until today. But most important of all, the Egyptians learned how to preserve speech for the benefit of future generations. They invented the art of writing.

By organizing the material according to the order of increasing importance, the writer places special emphasis on the final sentence.

A student essay on outdoor education provides another example of logical order. In the paragraph that follows, the writer describes some of the special problems students have during the traditionally difficult high school years. She then explains the benefits of involving such students in an outdoor education curriculum as a possible remedy, offers a quotation from a noteworthy text on outdoor education to support her views, and presents her thesis statement in the final sentence of the paragraph—all logical steps in her writing.

Statement of problem

For many students, the normally difficult time of high school is especially troublesome. These students may have learning disabilities, emotional-behavioral disorders, or low self-esteem, or they may be labeled "at-risk" because of socioeconomic background, delinquency, or drug and alcohol abuse. Any combination of these factors contributes negatively to students' success in school. Often the traditional public or private high school may not be the ideal environment in which these students can thrive and live up to their highest potential. Outdoor Education can benefit these high schoolers and provide them with the means necessary to overcome their personal issues and develop skills, knowledge, and self-esteem that will enable them to become successful, self-aware, emotionally stable, and functional adults. In their book *Outdoor Education*, authors Smith, Carlson, Donaldson, and Masters state poignantly that Outdoor Education "can be one of the most effective forces in the community to prevent human erosion as well as land erosion; it can be one of the means of saving youngsters from the education scrap heap" (49). Outdoor Education builds a relationship between students and the natural environment that might not be formed otherwise and gives students a respect for the world in which they live.

Possible remedy is offered and explained.

Authorities are quoted to support suggested solution.

Thesis is given after preliminary discussion to increase its acceptability.

> Aspects of Outdoor Education should be implemented in the curriculums of high schools in order to achieve these results in all students.
>
> –Jinsie Ward, student

Although logical order can take many different forms, the exact rationale is always dependent upon the topic of the writing. For example, in writing a descriptive essay about a place you visited, you can move from the least striking to the most striking detail, so as to keep your readers interested and involved in the description. In an essay explaining how to pick individual stocks for investment, you can start with the point that readers will find least difficult to understand and move on to the most difficult. (That's how teachers organize many courses.) Or, in writing an essay arguing for more internships and service learning courses, you can move from your least controversial point to the most controversial, preparing your reader gradually to accept your argument.

A simple way to check the organization of an essay is to outline it once you have a draft. Does the outline represent the organizational pattern—chronological, spatial, or logical—that you set out to use? Problems in outlining will naturally indicate sections that you need to revise.

A View from the Bridge

Cherokee Paul McDonald

A fiction writer, memoirist, and journalist, Cherokee Paul McDonald was raised and schooled in Fort Lauderdale, Florida. In 1970 he returned home from a tour of duty in Vietnam and joined the Fort Lauderdale Police Department, where he rose to the rank of sergeant. In 1980, after receiving a degree in criminal science from Broward Community College, McDonald left the police department to become a writer. He worked a number of odd jobs before publishing his first book, The Patch, *in 1986. In 1991, he published* Blue Truth, *a memoir. His novel,* Summer's Reason, *was released in 1994, and his most recent book, a memoir of the Vietnam War titled* Into the Green: A Reconnaissance by Fire, *was published in 2001. "A View from the Bridge" was originally published in* Sunshine *magazine in 1990.*

As you read, notice how McDonald organizes his narrative. He tells us what the narrator and the boy are doing, but he also relies heavily on their dialogue to structure his story, which unfolds as the two talk. McDonald makes the story come alive by showing us, rather than by simply telling us, what happens.

For Your Journal

Make a list of your interests, focusing on those to which you devote a significant amount of time. Do you share any of these interests with people you know? What does a shared interest do for a relationship between two people?

I was coming up on the little bridge in the Rio Vista neighborhood of Fort Lauderdale, deepening my stride and my breathing to negotiate the slight incline without altering my pace. And then, as I neared the crest, I saw the kid. 1

He was a lumpy little guy with baggy shorts, a faded T-shirt and heavy sweat socks falling down over old sneakers. 2

Partially covering his shaggy blond hair was one of those blue baseball caps with gold braid on the bill and a sailfish patch sewn 3 onto the peak. Covering his eyes and part of his face was a pair of those stupid-looking '50s-style wrap-around sunglasses.

He was fumbling with a beat-up rod and reel, and he had a little bait bucket by his feet. I puffed on by, glancing down into the empty bucket as I passed. 4

"Hey mister! Would you help me, please?" 5

The shrill voice penetrated my jogger's concentration, and I was determined to ignore it. But for some reason, I stopped. 6

With my hands on my hips and the sweat dripping from my nose I asked, "What do you want, kid?" 7

"Would you please help me find my shrimp? It's my last one and I've been getting bites and I know I can catch a fish if I can just find that shrimp. He jumped outta my hand as I was getting him from the bucket." 8

Exasperated, I walked slowly back to the kid, and pointed. 9

"There's the damn shrimp by your left foot. You stopped me for *that?*" 10

As I said it, the kid reached down and trapped the shrimp. 11

"Thanks a lot, mister," he said. 12

I watched as the kid dropped the baited hook down into the canal. Then I turned to start back down the bridge. 13

That's when the kid let out a "Hey! Hey!" and the prettiest tarpon[1] I'd ever seen came almost six feet out of the water, twisting and turning as he fell through the air. 14

"I got one!" the kid yelled as the fish hit the water with a loud splash and took off down the canal. 15

I watched the line being burned off the reel at an alarming rate. The kid's left hand held the crank while the extended fingers felt for the drag setting. 16

"No, kid!" I shouted. "Leave the drag alone . . . just keep that damn rod tip up!" 17

Then I glanced at the reel and saw there were just a few loops of line left on the spool. 18

"Why don't you get yourself some decent equipment?" I said, but before the kid could answer I saw the line go slack. 19

"Ohhh, I lost him," the kid said. I saw the flash of silver as the fish turned. 20

[1]*tarpon:* a large silvery fish.

"Crank, kid, crank! You didn't lose him. He's coming back toward you. Bring in the slack!" 21

The kid cranked like mad, and a beautiful grin spread across his face. 22

"He's heading in for the pilings,"[2] I said. "Keep him out of those pilings!" 23

The kid played it perfectly. When the fish made its play for the pilings, he kept just enough pressure on to force the fish out. When the water exploded and the silver missile hurled into the air, the kid kept the rod tip up and the line tight. 24

As the fish came to the surface and began a slow circle in the middle of the canal, I said, "Whooee, is that a nice fish or what?" 25

The kid didn't say anything, so I said, "Okay, move to the edge of the bridge and I'll climb down to the seawall and pull him out." 26

When I reached the seawall I pulled in the leader, leaving the fish lying on its side in the water. 27

"How's that?" I said. 28

"Hey, mister, tell me what it looks like." 29

"Look down here and check him out," I said. "He's beautiful." 30

But then I looked up into those stupid-looking sunglasses and it hit me. The kid was blind. 31

"Could you tell me what he looks like, mister?" he said again. 32

"Well, he's just under three, uh, he's about as long as one of your arms," I said. "I'd guess he goes about 15, 20 pounds. He's mostly silver, but the silver is somehow made up of *all* the colors, if you know what I mean." I stopped. "Do you know what I mean by colors?" 33

The kid nodded. 34

"Okay. He has all these big scales, like armor all over his body. They're silver too, and when he moves they sparkle. He has a strong body and a large powerful tail. He has big round eyes, bigger than a quarter, and a lower jaw that sticks out past the upper one and is very tough. His belly is almost white and his back is a gunmetal gray. When he jumped he came out of the water about six feet, and his scales caught the sun and flashed it all over the place." 35

By now the fish had righted itself, and I could see the bright-red gills as the gill plates opened and closed. I explained this to the kid, and then said, more to myself, "He's a beauty." 36

[2]*pilings:* support columns driven vertically into the ground or ocean floor.

"Can you get him off the hook?" the kid asked. "I don't want to kill him." 37

I watched as the tarpon began to slowly swim away, tired but still alive. 38

By the time I got back up to the top of the bridge the kid had his line secured and his bait bucket in one hand. 39

He grinned and said, "Just in time. My mom drops me off here, and she'll be back to pick me up any minute." 40

He used the back of one hand to wipe his nose. 41

"Thanks for helping me catch that tarpon," he said, "and for helping me to see it." 42

I looked at him, shook my head, and said, "No, my friend, thank you for letting *me* see that fish." 43

I took off, but before I got far the kid yelled again. 44

"Hey, mister!" 45

I stopped. 46

"Someday I'm gonna catch a sailfish and a blue marlin and a giant tuna and *all* those big sportfish!" 47

As I looked into those sunglasses I knew he probably would. I wished I could be there when it happened. 48

Thinking Critically about This Reading

Near the end of the story, why does the narrator say to the boy, "No, my friend, thank you for letting *me* see that fish" (paragraph 43). What happens to the narrator's attitude as a result of his encounter with the boy? What lesson do you think the narrator learns?

Questions for Study and Discussion

1. How does McDonald organize his essay? What period of time would you estimate is covered in this essay?
2. What clues lead up to the revelation that the boy is blind? Why does it take McDonald so long to realize it?
3. Notice the way McDonald chooses and adjusts some of the words he uses to describe the fish to the boy in paragraphs 33–36. Why does he do this? How does he organize his description of the fish so that the boy can visualize it better?

4. By the end of the essay, we know much more about the boy than the fact that he is blind, but after the initial description, McDonald characterizes him only indirectly. As the essay unfolds, what do we learn about the boy, and how does the author convey this knowledge?
5. McDonald tells much of his experience through dialogue. (Glossary: *Dialogue*) What does this dialogue add to the narration? (Glossary: *Narration*) What would have been lost had McDonald not used dialogue?
6. What is the connotation of the word *view* in the title? (Glossary: *Connotation/Denotation*) Of the word *bridge?*

Classroom Activity Using Organization

Consider the ways in which you might organize a discussion of the seven states listed below. For each state, we have provided some basic information: the date it entered the Union, population (2000 census), land area, and number of electoral votes in a presidential election.

ALASKA
January 3, 1959
626,932 people
570,374 square miles
3 electoral votes

ARIZONA
February 14, 1912
5,130,632 people
113,642 square miles
10 electoral votes

FLORIDA
March 3, 1845
16,396,515 people
53,937 square miles
27 electoral votes

MAINE
March 15, 1820
1,274,923 people
30,865 square miles
4 electoral votes

MISSOURI
August 10, 1821
5,595,211 people
69,709 square miles
11 electoral votes

MONTANA
November 8, 1889
902,195 people
145,556 square miles
3 electoral votes

OREGON
February 14, 1859
3,472,867 people
98,386 square miles
7 electoral votes

Suggested Writing Assignments

1. In groups of two or three, take turns describing a specific beautiful or remarkable thing to the others as if they were blind. You may want to actually bring an object to observe while your classmates cover their eyes. Help each other find the best words to create a vivid verbal picture. Using McDonald's paragraphs 33–36 as a model, write a brief description of your object, retaining the informal style of your speaking voice.
2. Recall a time when you and one other person held a conversation that helped you see something more clearly—visually, in terms of understanding, or both. Using McDonald's narrative as an organizational model, tell the story of that moment, re-creating the dialogue exactly as you remember it.
3. McDonald's "A View from the Bridge" and the *Calvin and Hobbes* cartoon on page 120 are just two "fish stories" in the long and rich tradition of that genre. In their own ways, both the essay and the cartoon play on the ironic notion that fishing is a quiet sport but one in which participants come to expect the unexpected. (Glossary: *Irony*) For the narrator in McDonald's story, there is a lesson in not merely looking but truly seeing, in describing the fish so that the blind boy can "see" it. For Calvin, there is the story of "latchin' on to the big one." It is interesting that a sport in which "nothing happens" can be the source of so much storytelling. Write an essay in which you tell a "fish story" of your own, one that reveals a larger, significant truth or life lesson. Pay particular attention to the pattern of organization you choose, and be sure to revise your essay to tighten up your use of that pattern. If possible, incorporate some elements of surprise as well.

FISHING IS THE MOST BORING SPORT IN THE WORLD.

The Corner Store

■ Eudora Welty

One of the most honored and respected writers of the twentieth century, Eudora Welty was born in 1909 in Jackson, Mississippi, where she lived most of her life and where she died in 2001. Her first book, A Curtain of Green *(1941), is a collection of short stories. Although she went on to become a successful writer of novels, essays, and book reviews, among other genres (as well as a published photographer), she is most often remembered as a master of the short story.* The Collected Stories of Eudora Welty *was published in 1980. Her other best-known works include a collection of essays,* The Eye of the Story *(1975); her autobiography,* One Writer's Beginnings *(1984); and a collection of book reviews and essays,* The Writer's Eye *(1994). Welty's novel* The Optimist's Daughter *won the Pulitzer Prize for Fiction in 1973, and in 1999 the Library of Congress published two collections of her work:* Welty: Collected Novels *and* Welty: Collected Essays and Memoirs.

Welty's description of the corner store, taken from an essay in The Eye of the Story *about growing up in Jackson, recalls for many readers the neighborhood store in the town or city where they grew up. As you read, pay particular attention to the effect Welty's spatial arrangement of descriptive details has on the dominant impression of the store.*

For Your Journal

Write about a store you frequented as a child. Maybe it was the local supermarket, the hardware store, or the corner convenience store. Using your five senses (sight, smell, taste, touch, and hearing), describe what you remember about the place.

Our Little Store rose right up from the sidewalk; standing in a street of family houses, it alone hadn't any yard in front, any tree or flower bed. It was a plain frame building covered over with brick. Above the door, a little railed porch ran across on an upstairs 1 level and four windows with shades were looking out. But I didn't catch on to those.

Running in out of the sun, you met what seemed total obscurity inside. There were almost tangible smells—licorice recently sucked in a child's cheek, dill pickle brine[1] that had leaked through a paper sack in a fresh trail across the wooden floor, ammonia-loaded ice that had been hoisted from wet croker sacks[2] and slammed into the icebox[3] with its sweet butter at the door, and perhaps the smell of still untrapped mice. 2

Then through the motes of cracker dust, cornmeal dust, the Gold Dust of the Gold Dust Twins that the floor had been swept out with, the realities emerged. Shelves climbed to high reach all the way around, set out with not too much of any one thing but a lot of things—lard, molasses, vinegar, starch, matches, kerosene, Octagon soap (about a year's worth of octagon-shaped coupons cut out and saved brought a signet ring[4] addressed to you in the mail). It was up to you to remember what you came for, while your eye traveled from cans of sardines to tin whistles to ice-cream salt to harmonicas to flypaper (over your head, batting around on a thread beneath the blades of the ceiling fan, stuck with its testimonial catch). 3

Its confusion may have been in the eye of its beholder. Enchantment is cast upon you by all those things you weren't supposed to have need for, to lure you close to wooden tops you'd outgrown, boys' marbles and agates in little net pouches, small rubber balls that wouldn't bounce straight, frail, frazzly kite string, clay bubble pipes that would snap off in your teeth, the stiffest scissors. You could contemplate those long narrow boxes of sparklers gathering dust while you waited for it to be the Fourth of July or Christmas, and noisemakers in the shape of tin frogs for somebody's birthday party you hadn't been invited to yet, and see that they were all marvelous. 4

You might not have even looked for Mr. Sessions when he came around his store cheese (as big as a doll's house) and in front of the counter looking for you. When you'd finally asked him for, and received from him in its paper bag, whatever single thing it was that 5

---

[1]*brine:* salty water used to preserve or pickle food.

[2]*croker sacks:* sacks or bags made of burlap, a coarse woven fabric.

[3]*icebox:* a wooden box or cupboard that held ice in a lower compartment to cool a second compartment above it, which was used for storing perishable food.

[4]*signet ring:* a ring bearing an official-looking seal.

you had been sent for, the nickel that was left over was yours to spend.

Down at a child's eye level, inside those glass jars with mouths in their sides through which the grocer could run his scoop or a child's hand might be invited to reach for a choice, were wineballs, all-day suckers, gumdrops, peppermints. Making a row under the glass of a counter were the Tootsie Rolls, Hershey bars, Goo Goo Clusters, Baby Ruths. And whatever was the name of those pastilles that came stacked in a cardboard cylinder with a cardboard lid? They were thin and dry, about the size of tiddledy-winks,[5] and in the shape of twisted rosettes. A kind of chocolate dust came out with them when you shook them out in your hand. Were they chocolate? I'd say, rather, they were brown. They didn't taste of anything at all, unless it was wood. Their attraction was the number you got for a nickel. 6

Making up your mind, you circled the store around and around, around the pickle barrel, around the tower of Crackerjack boxes; Mr. Sessions had built it for us himself on top of a packing case like a house of cards. 7

If it seemed too hot for Crackerjacks, I might get a cold drink. Mr. Sessions might have already stationed himself by the cold-drinks barrel, like a mind reader. Deep in ice water that looked black as ink, murky shapes—that would come up as Coca-Colas, Orange Crushes, and various flavors of pop—were all swimming around together. When you gave the word, Mr. Sessions plunged his bare arm in to the elbow and fished out your choice, first try. I favored a locally bottled concoction called Lake's Celery. (What else could it be called? It was made by a Mr. Lake out of celery. It was a popular drink here for years but was not known universally, as I found out when I arrived in New York and ordered one in the Astor bar.) You drank on the premises, with feet set wide apart to miss the drip, and gave him back his bottle and your nickel. 8

But he didn't hurry you off. A standing scale was by the door, with a stack of iron weights and a brass slide on the balance arm, that would weigh you up to three hundred pounds. Mr. Sessions, whose hands were gentle and smelled of carbolic,[6] would lift you up and set your feet on the platform, hold your loaf of bread for you, 9

[5]*tiddledy-winks:* playing pieces from the game Tiddledy-Winks, flat and round in shape, the size of quarters (tiddledies) and dimes (winks).

[6]*carbolic:* a sweet, musky-smelling chemical once used in soap.

and taking his time while you stood still for him, he would make certain of what you weighed today. He could even remember what you weighed the last time, so you could subtract and announce how much you'd gained. That was goodbye.

Thinking Critically about This Reading

What does Mr. Sessions himself contribute to the overall experience of Welty's store? What does Welty's store contribute to the community?

Questions for Study and Discussion

1. Which of the three patterns of organization does Welty use in this essay: chronological, spatial, or logical? If she uses more than one, where precisely does she use each type?
2. In paragraph 2, Welty describes the smells that a person encountered when entering the corner store. Why do you think she presents these smells before giving any visual details of the inside of the store?
3. What dominant impression does Welty create in her description of the corner store? (Glossary: *Dominant Impression*) How does she create this dominant impression?
4. What impression of Mr. Sessions does Welty create? What details contribute to this impression? (Glossary: *Details*)
5. Why does Welty place certain pieces of information in parentheses? What, if anything, does this information add to your understanding of the corner store? Might this information be left out? Explain.
6. Comment on Welty's ending. (Glossary: *Beginnings and Endings*) Is it too abrupt? Why or why not?

Classroom Activity Using Organization

While cleaning out the center drawer of his desk, a student found the following items:

2 no. 2 pencils	2 pairs of scissors
3 rubber bands	1 book mailing bag

1 roll of adhesive tape	1 mechanical pencil
1 plastic comb	3 first-class postage stamps
25 3 × 5-inch cards	5 postcards
3 ballpoint pens	2 clasps
1 eraser	2 8 × 10-inch manila envelopes
6 paper clips	7 thumbtacks
1 nail clipper	1 bottle of correction fluid
1 highlighting marker	1 nail file
1 bottle of glue	1 toothbrush
3 business envelopes	1 felt-tip pen
6 postcard stamps	2 airmail stamps

To organize the student's drawer, into what categories would you divide these items? Explain which items you would place in each category, and suggest an order you might use to discuss the categories in an essay. (Glossary: *Division and Classification*)

Suggested Writing Assignments

1. Using Welty's essay as a model, describe your neighborhood store or supermarket. Gather a large quantity of detailed information from memory and from an actual visit to the store if that is still possible. You may find it helpful to reread what you wrote in response to the journal prompt. Once you have gathered your information, try to select those details that will help you create a dominant impression of the store. Finally, organize your examples and illustrations according to some clear organizational pattern.
2. Write an essay on one of the following topics:

   Local restaurants
   Reading materials
   Television shows
   Ways of financing a college education
   Types of summer employment

Be sure to use an organizational pattern that is well thought out and suited to both your material and your purpose.

Doubts about Doublespeak

■ William Lutz

William Lutz is a professor of English at Rutgers University–Camden and was the editor of the Quarterly Review of Doublespeak *for fourteen years. Born in Racine, Wisconsin, in 1940, Lutz is best known for his important works* Doublespeak: From Revenue Enhancement to Terminal Living *(1990) and* The New Doublespeak: Why No One Knows What Anyone's Saying Anymore *(1996). His most recent book,* Doublespeak Defined: Cut through the Bull**** and Get to the Point, *was published in 1999. (The term* doublespeak *comes from the Newspeak vocabulary of George Orwell's novel* Nineteen Eighty-Four. *It refers to speech or writing that presents two or more contradictory ideas in such a way that an unsuspecting audience is not consciously aware of the contradiction and is likely to be deceived.) As chair of the National Council of Teachers of English's Committee on Public Doublespeak, Lutz has been a watchdog of public officials who use language to "mislead, distort, deceive, inflate, circumvent, and obfuscate." Each year the committee presents the Orwell Awards, recognizing the most outrageous uses of doublespeak in government and business.*

The following essay first appeared in the July 1993 issue of State Government News. *As you read notice how Lutz organizes his essay by first naming and defining the four types of doublespeak, describing each one's function or consequences, and then giving examples of each type. This organizational pattern is simple, practical, and very easy to follow.*

For Your Journal

Imagine that you work for a manufacturing plant in your town and that your boss has just told you that you are on the list of people who will be "dehired" or that you are part of a program of "negative employee retention." What would you think was happening to you? Would you be happy about it? What would you think of the language your boss used to describe your situation?

During the past year, we learned that we can shop at a "unique retail biosphere" instead of a farmers' market, where we can buy items made of "synthetic glass" instead of plastic, or purchase a "high velocity, multipurpose air circulator," or electric fan. A "waste-water conveyance facility" may "exceed the odor threshold" from time to time due to the presence of "regulated human nutrients," but that is not to be confused with a sewage plant that stinks up the neighborhood with sewage sludge. Nor should we confuse a "resource development park" with a dump. Thus does doublespeak continue to spread. 1

Doublespeak is language which pretends to communicate but doesn't. It is language which makes the bad seem good, the negative seem positive, the unpleasant seem attractive, or at least tolerable. It is language which avoids, shifts, or denies responsibility; language which is at variance with its real or purported meaning. It is language which conceals or prevents thought. 2

Doublespeak is all around us. We are asked to check our packages at the desk "for our convenience" when it's not for our convenience at all but for someone else's convenience. We see advertisements for "preowned," "experienced," or "previously distinguished" cars, not used cars and for "genuine imitation leather," "virgin vinyl," or "real counterfeit diamonds." Television offers not reruns but "encore telecasts." There are no slums or ghettos, just the "inner city" or "substandard housing" where the "disadvantaged" or "economically nonaffluent" live and where there might be a problem with "substance abuse." Nonprofit organizations don't make a profit, they have "negative deficits" or experience "revenue excesses." With doublespeak it's not dying but "terminal living" or "negative patient care outcome." 3

There are four kinds of doublespeak. The first kind is the euphemism, a word or phrase designed to avoid a harsh or distasteful reality. Used to mislead or deceive, the euphemism becomes doublespeak. In 1984 the U.S. State Department's annual reports on the status of human rights around the world ceased using the word "killing." Instead the State Department used the phrase "unlawful or arbitrary deprivation of life," thus avoiding the embarrassing situation of government-sanctioned killing in countries supported by the United States. 4

A second kind of doublespeak is jargon, the specialized language of a trade, profession, or similar group, such as doctors, lawyers, plumbers, or car mechanics. Legitimately used, jargon allows members of a group to communicate with each other clearly, efficiently, and quickly. Lawyers and tax accountants speak to each other of an 5 "involuntary conversion" of property, a legal term that means the loss or destruction of property through theft, accident, or condemnation. But when lawyers or tax accountants use unfamiliar terms to speak to others, then the jargon becomes doublespeak.

In 1978 a commercial 727 crashed on takeoff, killing three passengers, injuring 21 others and destroying the airplane. The insured value of the airplane was greater than its book value, so the airline made a profit of $1.7 million, creating two problems: the airline didn't want to talk about one of its airplanes crashing, yet it had to account for that $1.7 million profit in its annual report to its stockholders. The airline solved both problems by inserting a footnote in its annual report which explained that the $1.7 million was due to "the involuntary conversion of a 727." 6

A third kind of doublespeak is gobbledygook or bureaucratese. Such doublespeak is simply a matter of overwhelming the audience with words—the more the better. Alan Greenspan, a polished practitioner of bureaucratese, once testified before a Senate committee that "it is a tricky problem to find the particular calibration in timing that would be appropriate to stem the acceleration in risk premiums created by falling incomes without prematurely aborting the decline in the inflation-generated risk premiums." 7

The fourth kind of doublespeak is inflated language, which is designed to make the ordinary seem extraordinary, to make everyday things seem impressive, to give an air of importance to people or situations, to make the simple seem complex. Thus do car mechanics become "automotive internists," elevator operators become "members of the vertical transportation corps," grocery store checkout clerks become "career associate scanning professionals," and smelling something becomes "organoleptic analysis." 8

Doublespeak is not the product of careless language or sloppy thinking. Quite the opposite. Doublespeak is language carefully designed and constructed to appear to communicate when in fact it doesn't. It is language designed not to lead but mislead. Thus, it's not a tax increase but "revenue enhancement" or "tax-base broadening." So how can you complain about higher taxes? Those aren't useless, billion dollar pork barrel projects; they're really "congressional projects of national significance," so don't complain about wasteful government spending. That isn't the Mafia in Atlantic City; those are just "members of a career-offender cartel," so don't worry about the influence of organized crime in the city. 9

New doublespeak is created every day. The Environmental Protection Agency once called acid rain "poorly-buffered precipitation" then dropped that term in favor of "atmospheric deposition of anthropogenically-derived acidic substances," but recently decided that acid rain should be called "wet deposition." The Pentagon, which has in the past given us such classic doublespeak as "hexiform rotatable surface compression unit" for steel nut, just published a pamphlet warning soldiers that exposure to nerve gas will lead to "immediate permanent incapacitation." That's almost as good as the Pentagon's official term "servicing the target," meaning to kill the enemy. Meanwhile, the Department of Energy wants to establish a "monitored retrievable storage site," a place once known as a dump for spent nuclear fuel. 10

Bad economic times give rise to lots of new doublespeak designed to avoid some very unpleasant economic realities. As the "contained depression" continues so does the corporate policy of making up even more new terms to avoid the simple, and easily understandable, term "layoff." So it is that corporations "reposition," "restructure," "reshape," or "realign" the company and "reduce duplication" through "release of resources" that involves a "permanent downsizing" or a "payroll adjustment" that results in a number of employees being "involuntarily terminated." 11

Other countries regularly contribute to doublespeak. In Japan, where baldness is called "hair disadvantaged," the economy is undergoing a "severe adjustment process," while in Canada there is an "involuntary downward development" of the work force. For some government agencies in Canada, wastepaper baskets have become "user friendly, space effective, flexible, deskside sortation units." Politicians in Canada may engage in "reality augmentation," but they never lie. As part of their new freedom, the people of Moscow can visit "intimacy salons," or sex shops as they're known in other countries. When dealing with the bureaucracy in Russia, people know that they should show officials "normal gratitude," or give them a bribe. 12

The worst doublespeak is the doublespeak of death. It is the language, wrote George Orwell in 1946, that is "largely the defense of the indefensible . . . designed to make lies sound truthful and murder respectable, and to give an appearance of solidity to pure wind." In the doublespeak of death, Orwell continued, "defenseless villages are bombarded from the air, the inhabitants driven out into the countryside, the cattle machine-gunned, the huts set on fire with incendiary bullets. This is called pacification. Millions of peasants are robbed of 13 their farms and sent trudging along the roads with no more than they can carry. This is called transfer of population or rectification of frontiers." Today, in a country once called Yugoslavia, this is called "ethnic cleansing."[1]

14 It's easy to laugh off doublespeak. After all, we all know what's going on, so what's the harm? But we don't always know what's going on, and when that happens, doublespeak accomplishes its ends. It alters our perception of reality. It deprives us of the tools we need to develop, advance, and preserve our society, our culture, our civilization. It breeds suspicion, cynicism, distrust, and, ultimately, hostility. It delivers us into the hands of those who do not have our interests at heart. As Samuel Johnson[2] noted in 18th century England, even the devils in hell do not lie to one another, since the society of hell could not subsist without the truth, any more than any other society.

Thinking Critically about This Reading

According to Lutz, doublespeak "alters our perception of reality. . . . It breeds suspicion, cynicism, distrust, and, ultimately, hostility" (paragraph 14). What is Lutz's plan for combating doublespeak and its negative effects?

Questions for Study and Discussion

1. What is Lutz's thesis? (Glossary: *Thesis*)
2. Lutz addresses four kinds of doublespeak. Why do you suppose he arranges his discussion of each type of doublespeak in the manner that he does?
3. After reading Lutz's discussion of jargon, the second type of doublespeak, what advice would you give someone about when to use jargon? (Glossary: *Jargon*)
4. Lutz's use of illustrative examples is all but mandatory. (Glossary: *Examples*) Are his examples good ones? Why or why not? Should he have used fewer examples? More examples? Explain.

---

[1] *"ethnic cleansing":* Lutz is referring to the breakup of the Federal Republic of Yugoslavia in the Balkan region of southeastern Europe in the early 1990s and the 1992–1995 genocide centered in the cities of Sarajevo and Srebrenica.
[2] *Samuel Johnson* (1709–1784): an important English literary figure.

5. Could the order of Lutz's first two paragraphs be reversed? (Glossary: *Beginnings and Endings*) What would be gained or lost if they were?
6. Reread Lutz's last paragraph, where he makes some serious claims about the importance of doublespeak. Is such seriousness on his part justified by what he has written about doublespeak in the body of his essay? Why or why not?

Classroom Activity Using Organization

Carefully read the following paragraph from William Least Heat Moon's *Blue Highways*, and identify the organizational pattern he uses to structure his description.

> The old store, lighted only by three fifty-watt bulbs, smelled of coal and baking bread. In the middle of the rectangular room, where the oak floor sagged a little, stood an iron stove. To the right was a wooden table with an unfinished game of checkers and a stool made from an apple tree stump. On the shelves around the walls sat earthen jugs with corncob stoppers . . . , a few canned goods, and some of the two-thousand old clocks and clockworks Thurmond Watts owned. Only one was ticking; the others he just looked at. I asked how long he had been in the store.
>
> –William Least Heat Moon

Based on Least Heat Moon's description, sketch the inside of Thurmond Watts's store. Compare your sketch with those of your classmates, and discuss how the paragraph's organization influenced the relative prominence of various objects in your sketch.

Suggested Writing Assignments

1. Write an essay in which you consider the effects of doublespeak. Is it always a form of lying? Is it harmful to our society, and if so, how? How can we measure its effects? Be sure to cite instances of doublespeak that are not included in Lutz's essay, examples that you uncover yourself through your reading, Web browsing, or library research.

2. Think of a commonplace subject that people might take for granted but that you find interesting. Write an essay on that subject, using one of the following types of logical order:

   Least important to most important
   Most familiar to least familiar
   Smallest to biggest
   Oldest to newest
   Easiest to understand to most difficult to understand
   Good news to bad news
   General to specific

chapter **6**

Beginnings and Endings

"Begin at the beginning and go on till you come to the end: then stop," advised the King of Hearts in *Alice in Wonderland.* "Good advice, but more easily said than done," you might be tempted to reply. Certainly, no part of writing essays can be more daunting than coming up with effective **beginnings and endings.** In fact, many writers feel these are the most important parts of any piece of writing regardless of its length. Even before coming to your introduction, your readers will usually know something about your intentions from your title. Titles such as "The Case against Euthanasia," "How to Buy a Used Car," and "What Is a Migraine Headache?" indicate both your subject and approach and prepare your readers for what follows.

BEGINNINGS

What makes for an effective beginning? Not unlike a personal greeting, a good beginning should catch a reader's interest and then hold it. The experienced writer realizes that many readers would rather do almost anything than make a commitment to read, so the opening or "lead," as journalists refer to it, requires a lot of thought and much revising to make it right and to keep the reader's attention from straying. The inexperienced writer, on the other hand, knows that the beginning is important but tries to write it first and to perfect it before moving on to the rest of the essay. Although there are no "rules" for writing introductions, we can offer one bit of general advice: Wait until the writing process is well under way or almost completed before focusing on your lead. Following this advice will keep you from spending too much time on an introduction that you will undoubtedly revise. More important, once you actually see how your essay develops, you will know better how to introduce it to your reader.

In addition to capturing your reader's attention, a good beginning usually introduces your thesis and either suggests or actually reveals the structure of the composition. Keep in mind that the best beginning is not necessarily the most catchy or the most shocking but the one most appropriate for the job you are trying to do.

There are many effective ways of beginning an essay. Consider using one of the following.

Anecdote

Introducing your essay with an anecdote, a brief narrative drawn from current news events, history, or your personal experience, can be an effective way to capture your reader's interest. In the following example, the writer introduces an essay on the topic of integrity by recounting a surprising experience he had as a public speaker.

> A couple of years ago I began a university commencement address by telling the audience that I was going to talk about integrity. The crowd broke into applause. Applause! Just because they had heard the word "integrity": that's how starved for it they were. They had no idea how I was using the word, or what I was going to say about integrity, or, indeed, whether I was for it or against it. But they knew they liked the idea of talking about it.
>
> –Stephen L. Carter

Analogy/Comparison

An analogy or comparison can be useful in getting readers to contemplate a topic they might otherwise reject as unfamiliar or uninteresting. In the following multiparagraph example, Roger Garrison introduces a subject few would consider engrossing—writing—with an analogy to stone wall building. By pairing these two seemingly unrelated concepts, he both introduces and vividly illustrates the idea he will develop in his essay: that writing is a difficult, demanding craft with specific skills to be learned.

> In northern New England, where I live, stone walls mark boundaries, border meadows, and march through the woods that grew up around them long ago. Flank-high, the walls are made of

granite rocks stripped from fields when pastures were cleared and are used to fence in cattle. These are dry walls, made without mortar, and the stones in them, all shapes and sizes, are fitted to one another with such care that a wall, built a hundred years ago, still runs as straight and solid as it did when people cleared the land.

Writing is much like wall building. The writer fits together separate chunks of meaning to make an understandable statement. Like the old Yankee wall builders, anyone who wants to write well must learn some basic skills, one at a time, to build soundly. This [essay] describes these skills and shows you how to develop them and put them together. You can learn them.

Building a stone wall is not easy: It is gut-wrenching labor. Writing is not easy either. It is a complex skill, mainly because it demands a commitment of our own complicated selves. But it is worth learning how to do well—something true of any skill. Solid walls do get built, and good writing does get done. We will clear alway some underbrush and get at the job.

–Roger Garrison

Dialogue/Quotation

Although relying heavily on the ideas of others can weaken an effective introduction, opening your essay with a quotation or a brief dialogue can attract a reader's attention and can succinctly illustrate a particular attitude or point that you want to discuss. In the following example, the writer introduces an essay about the three main types of stress in our lives by recounting a brief dialogue with one of her roommates.

My roommate, Megan, pushes open the front door, throws her keys on the counter, and flops down on the couch.

"Hey, Megan, how are you?" I yell from the kitchen.

"I don't know what's wrong with me. I sleep all the time, but I'm still tired. No matter what I do, I just don't feel well."

"What did the doctor say?"

"She said it sounds like chronic fatigue syndrome."

"Do you think it might be caused by stress?" I ask.

"Nah, stress doesn't affect me very much. I like keeping busy and running around. This must be something else."

Like most Americans, Megan doesn't recognize the numerous factors in her life that cause her stress.

–Sarah Federman

Facts and Statistics

For the most part, you should support your argument with facts and statistics rather than letting them speak for you, but a brief and startling fact or statistic can be an effective way to engage readers in your essay.

> Charles Darwin and Abraham Lincoln were born on the same day—February 12, 1809. They are also linked in another curious way—for both must simultaneously play, and for similar reasons, the role of man and legend.
>
> –Stephen Jay Gould

Irony or Humor

It is often effective to introduce an essay with irony or humor. Humor, especially, signals to the reader that your essay will be entertaining to read, and irony can indicate an unexpected approach to a topic. In his essay "Shooting an Elephant," George Orwell begins by simultaneously establishing a wry tone and indicating to the reader that he, the narrator, occupies the position of outsider in the events he is about to relate.

> In Moulmein, in lower Burma, I was hated by large numbers of people—the only time in my life that I have been important enough for this to happen to me.
>
> –George Orwell

There are several other good ways to begin an essay; the following opening sentences illustrate each approach.

Short Generalization

> It is a miracle that New York works at all.
>
> –E. B. White

Startling Claim

> It is possible to stop most drug addiction in the United States within a very short time.
>
> –Gore Vidal

Rhetorical Questions

> Just how interconnected *is* the animal world? Is it true that if we change any part of that world we risk unduly damaging life in other, larger parts of it?
>
> –Matthew Douglas

Following are some examples of how *not* to begin an essay. You should always *avoid* using beginnings such as these in your writing.

Beginnings to Avoid
Apology I am a college student and do not consider myself an expert on intellectual property, but I think file sharing and MP3 downloads should be legal.
Complaint I'd rather write about a topic of my own choice than the one that is assigned, but here goes.
Webster's Dictionary *Webster's New Collegiate Dictionary* defines the verb *to snore* as follows: "to breathe during sleep with a rough hoarse noise due to vibration of the soft palate."
Platitude America is the land of opportunity, and no one knows that better than Martha Stewart.
Reference to Title As you can see from my title, this essay is about why we should continue to experiment with embryonic stem cells.

ENDINGS

An effective ending does more than simply indicate where the writer stopped writing. A conclusion may summarize; may inspire the reader to further thought or even action; may return to the beginning by repeating key words, phrases, or ideas; or may surprise the reader by providing a particularly convincing example to support a thesis. Indeed, there are many ways to write a conclusion, but the effectiveness of any choice must be measured by how appropriately it fits what comes before it. You might consider concluding with a restatement of your thesis, with a prediction, or with a recommendation.

In an essay contrasting the traditional Hispanic understanding of the word *macho* with the meaning it has developed in mainstream American culture, Rose Del Castillo Guilbault begins her essay with a succinct, two-sentence paragraph offering her thesis:

> What is macho? That depends which side of the border you come from.

She concludes her essay by restating her thesis, but in a manner that reflects the detailed examination she has given the concept of macho in her essay:

> The impact of language in our society is undeniable. And the misuse of macho hints at a deeper cultural misunderstanding that extends beyond mere word definitions.
>
> –Rose Del Castillo Guilbault

In the following conclusion to a long chapter on weasel words, a form of deceptive advertising language, the writer summarizes the points that he has made, ending with a recommendation to the reader:

> A weasel word is a word that's used to imply a meaning that cannot be truthfully stated. Some weasels imply meanings that are not the same as their actual definition, such as "help," "like," or "fortified." They can act as qualifiers and/or comparatives. Other weasels, such as "taste" and "flavor," have no definite meanings, and are simply subjective opinions offered by the manufacturer. A weasel of omission is one that implies a claim so strongly that it forces you to supply the bogus fact. Adjectives are weasels used to convey feelings and emotions to a greater extent than the product itself can.
>
> In dealing with weasels, you must strip away the innuendos and try to ascertain the facts, if any. To do this, you need to ask questions such as: How? Why? How many? How much? Stick to basic definitions of words. Look them up if you have to. Then, apply the strict definition to the text of the advertisement or commercial. "Like" means similar to, but not the same as. "Virtually" means the same in essence, but not in fact.
>
> Above all, never underestimate the devious qualities of a weasel. Weasels twist and turn and hide in dark shadows. You must come to grips with them, or advertising will rule you forever.

> My advice to you is: Beware of weasels. They are nasty and untrainable, and they attack pocketbooks.
>
> –Paul Stevens

In the following conclusion to a composition titled "Title IX Just Makes Sense," the writer offers an overview of her argument and concludes by predicting the outcome of the solution she advocates:

> There have undeniably been major improvements in the treatment of female college athletes since the enactment of Title IX. But most colleges and universities still don't measure up to the actual regulation standards, and many have quite a ways to go. The Title IX fight for equality is not a radical feminist movement, nor is it intended to take away the privileges of male athletes. It is, rather, a demand for fairness, for women to receive the same opportunities that men have always had. When colleges and universities stop viewing Title IX budget requirements as an inconvenience and start complying with the spirit and not merely the letter of the law, collegiate female athletes will finally reach the parity they deserve.
>
> –Jen Jarjosa, student

If you are having trouble with your conclusion—and this is not an uncommon occurrence—it may be because of problems with your essay itself. Frequently, writers do not know when to end because they are not sure about their overall purpose. For example, if you are taking a trip and your purpose is to go to Chicago, you'll know when you get there and will stop. But if you don't really know where you are going, it's very difficult to know when to stop.

It's usually a good idea in your conclusion to avoid such overworked expressions as "In conclusion," "In summary," "I hope I have shown," or "Finally." Your conclusion should also do more than simply repeat what you've said in your opening paragraph. The most satisfying essays are those in which the conclusion provides an interesting way of wrapping up ideas introduced in the beginning and developed throughout so that your reader has the feeling of coming full circle.

You might find it revealing as your course progresses to read with special attention the beginnings and endings of the essays throughout *Models for Writers*. Take special note of the varieties of beginnings and endings, the possible relationship between a beginning and an ending, and the general appropriateness of these elements to the writer's subject and purpose.

Of My Friend Hector and My Achilles Heel

Michael T. Kaufman

The former writer of the "About New York" column for the New York Times, *Michael T. Kaufman was born in 1938 in Paris and grew up in the United States. He studied at the Bronx High School of Science, City College of New York, and Columbia University. He began his career at the* New York Times *as a reporter and feature writer, and before assuming his position as columnist, he served as bureau chief in Ottawa and Warsaw. The experience in Warsaw is evident in his book about Poland,* Mad Dreams, Saving Graces, *published in 1989. Kaufman is also a past winner of the George Polk Award for International Reporting. His most recent book is* Soros: The Life and Times of a Messianic Billionaire *(2002).*

In the following selection, which appeared in the New York Times *in 1992, Kaufman uses the story of his childhood friend Hector Elizondo to reflect on his own "prejudice and stupidity." Take note of how the two very brief sentences at the beginning establish the chronological and narrative structure of what follows.*

For Your Journal

Many schools "track" students by intellectual ability into such categories as "honors," "college bound," "vocational," "remedial," or "terminal." Did you go to a high school that tracked its students? How did you feel about your placement? What did you think about classmates who were on tracks higher or lower than yours?

This story is about prejudice and stupidity. My own. 1

It begins in 1945 when I was a 7-year-old living on the fifth floor of a tenement walkup on 107th Street between Columbus and Manhattan Avenues in New York City. The block was almost entirely Irish and Italian, and I believe my family was the only Jewish one around. 2

One day a Spanish-speaking family moved into one of the four apartments on our landing. They were the first Puerto Ricans I had met. They had a son who was about my age named Hector, and the two of us became friends. We played with toy soldiers and I particularly remember how, using rubber bands and wood from orange crates, we made toy pistols that shot off little squares we cut from old linoleum. 3

We visited each other's homes and I know that at the time I liked Hector and I think he liked me. I may even have eaten my first avocado at his house. 4

About a year after we met, my family moved to another part of Manhattan's West Side and I did not see Hector again until I entered Booker T. Washington Junior High School as an 11-year-old. 5

The Special Class

The class I was in was called 7SP-1; the SP was for special. Earlier, I recall, I had been in the IGC class, for "intellectually gifted children." The SP class was to complete the seventh, eighth and ninth grades in two years and almost all of us would then go to schools like Bronx Science, Stuyvesant or Music and Art, where admission was based on competitive exams. I knew I was in the SP class and the IGC class. I guess I also knew that other people were not. 6

Hector was not. He was in some other class, maybe even 7-2, the class that was held to be the next-brightest, or maybe 7-8. I remember I was happy to see him whenever we would meet, and sometimes we played punchball during lunch period. Mostly, of course, I stayed with my own classmates, with other Intellectually Gifted Children. 7

Sometimes children from other classes, those presumably not so intellectually gifted, would tease and taunt us. At such times I was particularly proud to have Hector as a friend. I assumed that he was tougher than I and my classmates and I guess I thought that if necessary he would come to my defense. 8

Different High Schools

For high school, I went uptown to Bronx Science. Hector, I think, went downtown to Commerce. Sometimes I would see him in Riverside 9

Park, where I played basketball and he worked out on the parallel bars. We would acknowledge each other, but by this time the conversations we held were perfunctory[1]—sports, families, weather.

After I finished college, I would see him around the neighborhood pushing a baby carriage. He was the first of my contemporaries to marry and to have a child. 10

A few years later, in the 60's, married and with children of my own, I was once more living on the West Side, working until late at night as a reporter. Some nights as I took the train home I would see Hector in the car. A few times we exchanged nods, but more often I would pretend that I didn't see him, and maybe he also pretended he didn't see me. Usually he would be wearing a knitted watch cap, and from that I deduced that he was probably working on the docks as a longshoreman. 11

I remember quite distinctly how I would sit on the train and think about how strange and unfair fate had been with regard to the two of us who had once been playmates. Just because I had become an intellectually gifted adult or whatever and he had become a longshoreman or whatever, was that any reason for us to have been left with nothing to say to each other? I thought it was wrong and unfair, but I also thought that conversation would be a chore or a burden. That is pretty much what I thought about Hector, if I thought about him at all, until one Sunday in the mid-70's, when I read in the drama section of this newspaper that my childhood friend, Hector Elizondo, was replacing Peter Falk[2] in the leading role in *The Prisoner of Second Avenue.*[3] 12

Since then, every time I have seen this versatile and acclaimed actor in movies or on television I have blushed for my assumptions. I have replayed the subway rides in my head and tried to fathom why my thoughts had led me where they did. 13

In retrospect it seems far more logical that the man I saw on the train, the man who had been my friend as a boy, was coming home from an Off Broadway theater or perhaps from a job as a waiter 14

[1]*perfunctory:* a routine act done with little interest or care.

[2]*Peter Falk* (b. 1927): a well-known stage, television, and movie actor who starred as the rumpled television detective Columbo.

[3]*The Prisoner of Second Avenue:* a play by Neil Simon, which premiered at the Eugene O'Neill Theatre in New York City in 1971. The Broadway hit was made into a movie released in 1975.

while taking acting classes. So why did I think he was a longshoreman? Was it just the cap? Could it be that his being Puerto Rican had something to do with it? Maybe that reinforced the stereotype I concocted, but it wasn't the root of it.

When It Got Started

No, the foundation was laid when I was 11, when I was in 7SP-1 and he was not, when I was in the IGC class and he was not. 15

I have not seen him since I recognized how I had idiotically kept tracking him for years and decades after the school system had tracked both of us. I wonder now if my experience was that unusual, whether social categories conveyed and absorbed before puberty do not generally tend to linger beyond middle age. And I wonder, too, that if they affected the behavior of someone like myself who had been placed on the upper track, how much more damaging it must have been for someone consigned to the lower. 16

I have at times thought of calling him, but kept from doing it because how exactly does one apologize for thoughts that were never expressed? And there was still the problem of what to say. "What have you been up to for the last 40 years?" Or "Wow, was I wrong about you!" Or maybe just, "Want to come over and help me make a linoleum gun?" 17

Thinking Critically about This Reading

What "thoughts that were never expressed" (paragraph 17) does Kaufman feel the need to apologize for? In retrospect, how do you suppose Kaufman feels about his treatment of Hector?

Questions for Study and Discussion

1. How do Kaufman's first two sentences affect how the reader views the rest of the essay? Did they catch your attention? Why or why not?
2. If you are unfamiliar with the Greek myth of Hector and Achilles, look it up in a book on mythology. Why does Kaufman allude to Hector and Achilles in his title? (Glossary: *Allusion*)

3. How does Kaufman organize his essay? (Glossary: *Organization*)
4. What is Kaufman's purpose? (Glossary: *Purpose*) How does his organization help him express his purpose?
5. Why did Kaufman ignore Hector after graduating from college? What does this tell him about society in general?
6. Why is Kaufman's ending effective? What point does he emphasize with his ending?

Classroom Activity Using Beginnings and Endings

Carefully read the following three possible beginnings for an essay on the world's most famous practical joker, Hugh Troy. What are the advantages and disadvantages of each? Which one would you select as an opening paragraph? Why?

> Whether questioning the values of American society or simply relieving the monotony of daily life, Hugh Troy always managed to put a little of himself into each of his stunts. One day he attached a plaster hand to his shirt sleeve and took a trip through the Holland Tunnel. As he approached the tollbooth, with his toll ticket between the fingers of the artificial hand, Troy left both ticket and hand in the grasp of the stunned tollbooth attendant and sped away.

> Nothing seemed unusual. In fact, it was a rather common occurrence in New York City. Five men dressed in overalls roped off a section of busy Fifth Avenue in front of the old Rockefeller residence, hung out MEN WORKING signs, and began ripping up the pavement. By the time they stopped for lunch, they had dug quite a hole in the street. This crew was different, however, from all the others that had descended upon the streets of the city. It was led by Hugh Troy—the world's greatest practical joker.

> Hugh Troy was born in Ithaca, New York, where his father was a professor at Cornell University. After graduating from Cornell, Troy left for New York City, where he became a successful illustrator of children's books.When World War II broke out, he went into the army and eventually became a captain in the 21st Bomber Command, 20th Air Force, under General Curtis LeMay. After the war he made his home in Garrison, New York, for a short while before finally settling in Washington, D.C., where he lived until his death.

Suggested Writing Assignments

1. Kaufman's essay is a deeply personal one. Use it as a model to write an essay about a time or an action in your life that you are not proud of. What happened? Why did it happen? What would you do differently if you could? Be sure to catch the reader's attention in the beginning and to end your essay with a thought-provoking conclusion.
2. Everyone has childhood friends that we either have lost track of or don't communicate with as often as we would like. Choose an old friend whom you have lost track of and would like to see again. Write an essay about your relationship. What made your friend special to you as a child? Why did you lose touch? What does the future hold? Organize your essay chronologically.

Something's Off

■ Robin Marantz Henig

Robin Marantz Henig was born in Brooklyn, New York, in 1953. After graduating from Cornell University in 1973 and Northwestern's School of Journalism in 1974, she worked as an editor for a number of medical magazines, including Comprehensive Therapy, New Physician, The Blue Sheet, *and* BioScience. *As a freelance writer she has written widely on a variety of medical and scientific topics since 1980. In 1981 she published* The Myth of Senility: Misconceptions about the Brain and Aging, *a book for which she received the National Media Award from the American Psychological Association. Her other nonfiction works include* A Dancing Matrix: How Science Confronts Emerging Viruses *(1993),* The Monk in the Garden: The Lost and Found Genius of Gregor Mendel, the Father of Genetics *(2000), and* Pandora's Baby: How the First Test-Tube Babies Sparked the Reproductive Revolution *(2004). Henig frequently contributes articles to* Women's Day, SciQuest, *and* New York Times Magazine.

In the following essay, a personal story with a scientific focus that first appeared in the October 17, 2004, issue of New York Times Magazine, *Henig discovers just how much she valued her sense of smell as a result of losing it for almost two years. Notice how she begins with the revelation of what it took to convince her husband that she had indeed lost her sense of smell and ends with a confession of what it felt like to smell familiar fragrances once again.*

For Your Journal

How important is your sense of smell to you? In what kinds of situations do you depend on your sense of smell? What do think it would be like to live without it if you suddenly lost your ability to smell?

A stinky old conch shell is what finally convinced my husband that I had lost my sense of smell. He was horrified to watch me stick my nose right into the opening of the shell festering on our friends' 1 back porch, something he couldn't bring himself to do because the rotting stuff inside was so revolting. Jeff had been listening for months to my complaints about not being able to smell, and I think he found the whole thing mystifying—and maybe slightly annoying. The conch shell showed him.

I felt vindicated, sort of. But mostly I felt vulnerable. Smelling is what told me not to eat spoiled egg salad and to stay clear of skunks. Without it, how could I know where the dangers lay? 2

Smell is the stepchild of the senses, the one that many think they could do without. But when I couldn't smell things, I couldn't fully inhabit the world, and my movements in it were somehow, almost imperceptibly, more clumsy. This month, when the Nobel Prize was awarded to two researchers for investigating the science of smell, it brought back my mixed feelings about my own sense of smell's protracted[1] disappearance. 3

It vanished in 2002, a result of a bad fall. As my neurosurgeon explained, when my head hit the ground, my brain sloshed around, which smashed delicate nerve endings in my olfactory[2] system. Maybe they'll repair themselves, she said (in what struck me as much too casual a tone), and maybe they won't. If I had to lose something, it might as well have been smell; at least nothing about my personality or my memory had changed, as can happen with head trauma. So it seemed almost churlish[3] to feel, as the months went on, so devastated by this particular loss. 4

But I was heartbroken. My sense of smell was always something I took pleasure in. I could tell, by smelling him, if Jeff was troubled, excited or sad. I could fall in love with him all over again—or with a passing stranger—with one good whiff. And one of my favorite parts of mothering has been smelling my daughters, those deep sweet smells in the crooks of their necks and at the shaggy tops of their heads. Without scent, I felt as if I were walking around the city without my contact lenses, dealing with people while wearing earplugs, moving through something sticky and thick. The sharpness of things, their specificity, diminished. 5

I couldn't even tell when the milk had gone bad. Oddly, my sense of taste remained perfectly fine, but I was still nervous about opening a 6

[1]*protracted:* drawn out or prolonged.
[2]*olfactory:* relating to the sense of smell.
[3]*churlish:* rude; ill-mannered.

carton of yogurt without having someone nearby to sniff it for me. I had been stripped of the sense we all use, often without realizing it, to negotiate the world, to know which things are safe and which are dangerous.

After nearly a year, I talked to a colleague savvy about neuroscience, who suggested I try to retrain my sense of smell on the assumption that the nerve endings *had* repaired themselves but that something was still broken along the pathway from nose to brain, where odor molecules activate olfactory receptors (the subject of this year's Nobel-winning research). Her advice was to expose myself to strong, distinctive fragrances, asking the person I was with to tell me exactly what I was smelling even if I wasn't conscious of smelling anything at all. 7

I began sticking my nose into everything that seemed likely to have a scent—the cumin in the spice cabinet, freshly ground coffee, red wine. I interrupted friends midsentence if we happened to be walking past a pizza place or a garbage truck and asked, stupidly, "What are you smelling now?" 8

Slowly, the smell therapy started to work. At first, distressingly, all I could smell were unnatural scents: dandruff shampoo, furniture polish, a cloud of after-shave from a stocky young man. And there was something troubling and unpleasant about the artificial fragrances, even those that were supposed to be appealing. I kept changing laundry detergents because even clean sheets smelled sour. When I passed a hot-dog vendor on the street, I caught a breath of rank, soggy fur, and soon that soggy-fur scent was all I could smell: in the park, out my window, coming from my own body and from the bodies of everyone I loved. 9

But I kept at it. I stood at the Nuts-4-Nuts cart outside my subway stop, telling myself that this is what honey-roasted peanuts smell like. I went into natural-food stores where the spices are sold from communal jars and bent my face toward the cloves and the curry powder. Usually I smelled nothing. But occasionally, something got through. 10

The first time I smelled cut grass again, in the small park near the American Museum of Natural History, was almost exactly two years after my fall. It made me cry. The tears embarrassed me, but cut grass is one of those fragrances, like my father's oil paints or my mother's L'Air du Temps, that transport me directly to the landscape of childhood. And that's what I had been missing, really, and why getting back my sense of smell was so precious: a visceral[4] connection to the person I used to be. 11

[4]*visceral:* profound; real.

Thinking Critically about This Reading

What does Henig mean when she states that for many people "smell is the stepchild of the senses" (paragraph 3)? If smell is the "stepchild," what does that make the other four senses?

Questions for Study and Discussion

1. Which of the strategies described in the introduction to this chapter does Henig use to begin her essay? How effective do you find Henig's beginning? How does her ending work with this beginning? Explain.
2. Why do you think losing her sense of smell left Henig feeling "vulnerable" (2)?
3. Soon after she lost her sense of smell, Henig confesses to feeling "heartbroken" (5). What pleasures associated with smell did she miss?
4. On the advice of a colleague, Henig decided to retrain her sense of smell. What assumption did she need to accept before proceeding? Describe the steps or stages in the retraining process.
5. Nearly two years passed between the time Henig first lost her sense of smell and when she could smell fresh-cut grass once again. What did the cut grass remind her of? Why do you think it brought her to tears?

Classroom Activity Using Beginnings and Endings

Henig opens her essay with a brief story about "a stinky old conch shell," an incident that convinced her husband Jeff that she had indeed lost her sense of smell. She then goes on to tell about the serious fall that damaged her olfactory system and the year-long process of regaining her sense of smell. Reread Henig's essay, and write an alternative beginning. Discuss your alternative beginning with your classmates, and determine the kinds of changes you would have to make to the essay to accommodate your alternative beginning.

Suggested Writing Assignments

1. Imagine that you have suddenly lost one of your senses—sight, hearing, touch, smell, or taste. Using Henig's essay as a model,

write an essay in which you describe the experience. How would you feel about losing a sense you may have taken for granted? How would you cope with the loss? Function in the world? Include sufficient detail so that your readers will know how you feel about your loss. Pay particular attention to how you use your first and last paragraphs to grab your readers' attention by focusing on the emotions associated with the loss.

2. Every day we're exposed to images on billboards, computers, televisions, cell phones, and movie screens, as well as in newspapers, magazines, and books, but how much of this visual clutter do we really *see?* We have all met people who will report that they've seen "nothing in particular" after taking a walk in a park, visiting a friend, or attending a concert or sporting event. Have you ever been in a situation when others see more in an object or a situation than you do? Have you ever wondered what makes some people more observant than others? Using examples from your own experiences, write an essay exploring why people have difficulty really "seeing" the world around them. What must people do to train themselves to see beyond the superficial?

The Wounds That Can't Be Stitched Up

■ **Ruth Russell**

Ruth Russell was born in Greenfield, Massachusetts, and graduated from Greenfield Community College. When we selected Russell's essay for inclusion in Models for Writers, *we had no idea that she had used the sixth edition as the textbook in her college composition course. Russell said of her experience with* Models, *"The book was tremendously helpful to me in learning to write. I would do a lot of the exercises at the end of the essays, even when they were not assigned, as a way of deconstructing them, of finding out how they were written, what their essential parts were. I was really interested in improving my writing." After writing the following essay for her course, she submitted it to the "My Turn" column in* Newsweek, *where it appeared in December 1999, without much editing by the column's editor, Pam Hammer. "Her suggestions helped to make it a little shorter and stronger," recalls Russell, who feels very proud to have made so much progress with her writing. "At one point I had entitled the piece 'Full Circle,' but I much prefer the present title. I often think how amazing it is that the incident that caused me to write the essay occurred on about the twentieth anniversary of my mother's accident."*

As you read notice how Russell ties her ending to her beginning, bringing the essay full circle. Although the first sentence of her final paragraph harkens back to her opening sentence, it in no way prepares you for the painfully ironic conclusion.

For Your Journal

Everyone has childhood fears that are often associated with a particular event or experience, fears that can last for years. What particular fear or fears did you have as a child? Were they caused by a specific incident that you can recall? How have they affected your life as a teenager and young adult?

It was a mild December night. Christmas was only two weeks away. The evening sky was overcast, but the roads were dry. All was quiet in our small town as I drove to my grandmother's house. 1

I heard the sirens first. Red lights and blue lights strobed in tandem. Ambulances with their interiors lit like television screens in a dark room flew by, escorted by police cruisers on the way to the hospital. 2

When I arrived at my gram's, she was on the porch steps struggling to put on her coat. "Come on," she said breathlessly, "your mother has been in an accident." I was 17 then, and it would take a long time before sirens lost their power to reduce me to tears. 3

Twenty-three years have passed, but only recently have I realized how deeply affected I was by events caused by a drunk driver so long ago. 4

When the accident occurred, my youngest brother was 8. He was sitting in the back seat of our family's large, sturdy sedan. The force of the crash sent him flying headlong into the back of the front seat, leaving him with a grossly swollen black eye. He was admitted to the hospital for observation. He didn't talk much when I visited him that night. He just sat in the bed, a lonely little figure in a darkened hospital room. 5

My sister, who was 12, was sitting in the front seat. She confided to me later how much she missed the beautiful blue coat she'd been wearing at the time. It was an early Christmas present, and it was destroyed beyond repair by the medical personnel who cut it off her body as they worked to save her life. She had a severely fractured skull that required immediate surgery. The resulting facial scar became for our family a permanent reminder of how close she came to dying that night. 6

My mother was admitted to the intensive-care unit to be stabilized before her multiple facial cuts could be stitched up. Dad tried to prepare me before we went in to see her by telling me that she looked and sounded worse than she was. One eye was temporarily held in place by a bandage wrapped around her head. Her lower lip hideously gaped,[1] exposing a mouthful of broken teeth. Delirious, she cried out for her children and apologized for an accident she neither caused nor could have avoided. An accident that happened when her car was hit head-on by a drunk driver speeding down the wrong side of the road in a half-ton truck with no headlights. 7

[1]*gaped:* opened wide.

My dad, my brothers, my sister and I spent Christmas at the hospital visiting my mother. Sometimes she was so out of it from medication that she barely recognized us. We celebrated two of my brothers' birthdays—one only days after Christmas and the other in early January—there too. 8

I remember watching the police escort the drunk driver out of the hospital the night of the accident. He looked about 35 years old, but his face was so distorted by rage and alcohol that I could only guess. A bandaged wrist was his only visible injury. He kept repeating that he'd done nothing wrong as several officers tried to get him into the cruiser waiting outside the emergency-room exit. 9

The man was jailed over the weekend and lost his license for 30 days for driving while intoxicated. I don't know if that was his first alcohol-related traffic violation, but I know it wasn't the last. Now and then I'd see his name in the court log of our local paper for another DWI, and wonder how he could still be behind the wheel. 10

Sometimes when I tell this story, I'd be asked in an accusatory[2] tone if my mom and siblings were wearing seat belts. I think that's a lot like asking a rape victim how she was dressed. The answer is no. This all happened before seat-belt-awareness campaigns began. In fact, if they had been in a smaller car, seat belts or not, I believe my mother and sister would have died. 11

Many local people who know the driver are surprised when they hear about the accident, and they are quick to defend him. They tell me he was a war hero. His parents aren't well. He's an alcoholic. Or my favorite: "He's a good guy when he doesn't drink." 12

Two years ago I discovered this man had moved into my apartment building. I felt vaguely apprehensive, but I believed the accident was ancient history. Nothing could have prepared me for what happened next. 13

It was a mild afternoon, just a few days before Christmas. I had started down the back staircase of the building, on my way to visit my son, when I recognized my neighbor's new pickup truck as it roared down the street. The driver missed the entrance to our shared parking lot. He reversed crookedly in the road, slammed the transmission into forward, then quickly pulled into his parking space. Gravel and sand flew as he stomped on the brakes to halt his truck 14

[2]*accusatory:* implying error or misdeed.

just inches from where I stood frozen on the staircase. As he staggered from his vehicle, he looked at me and asked drunkenly, "Did I scare you?"

Thinking Critically about This Reading

In paragraph 11 Russell relates a story about how people asked whether her family members were wearing seat belts at the time of the accident, and in paragraph 12 she tells of how people who knew the drunk driver responsible for the accident were quick to defend or make excuses for him. What is Russell's point in mentioning these incidents?

Questions for Study and Discussion

1. Russell begins her essay with a somewhat generic description—season, weather, road conditions—of the day of her mother's accident. Why are such details important in her memory? How does her first paragraph work with her title to draw the reader in?
2. Russell provides the reader with an image of her little brother—the least injured of the three in the car—before discussing her sister and mother. What is the image? Why is it an effective introduction to the scene at the hospital?
3. What is Russell's tone in her essay? (Glossary: *Tone*) How does she establish it? Cite specific examples from the text.
4. Russell ironically describes the platitude " 'He's a good guy when he doesn't drink' " as her "favorite" (12). Why is the statement ironic? (Glossary: *Irony*) Why do you think Russell emphasizes it as her favorite excuse for the man's behavior?
5. Russell's ending does not offer a neat conclusion to her situation and makes no concrete statement about her own feelings. Why does she leave the interaction between the drunk driver and herself so open-ended? How does her ending tie in with her purpose for writing the essay? (Glossary: *Purpose*)

Classroom Activity Using Beginnings and Endings

Choose one of the essays you have been writing for your course, and write at least two different beginnings for it. If you are having trouble coming up with two, check to see whether one of the paragraphs in the body of your essay would be appropriate, or consult the list of effective beginnings in the introduction to this chapter. After you have finished, have several classmates read your beginnings and select their favorite. Do any of your new beginnings suggest ways that you can improve the focus, the organization, or the ending of your essay? Explain these revision possibilities to your partners.

Suggested Writing Assignments

1. Russell's essay says a lot about how our society reacts to drunk drivers, but she never directly argues a point. Her experiences alone speak to the problem very clearly. Write an essay in which you present an indirect argument about a topic that is important to you, using your experiences and observations to lead the reader to the desired conclusion. (Glossary: *Argumentation*) Construct your beginning and ending with care so that the reader immediately understands how your experiences are relevant to the issue and is left with a strong image or statement that supports your point of view.
2. Write a short essay about an ongoing conflict or situation that you are either working to resolve or hoping will be resolved in the near future. For example, you can use a test you are studying for, an up-and-down relationship, or a search for employment. Have a clear purpose in mind regarding how you want the reader to react—with anger, sympathy, amusement, and so on—and craft your essay to accomplish your goal. Pay particular attention to the conclusion, which will be open-ended but should clearly communicate your purpose to the reader.
3. Carefully review the public service advertisement from Mothers against Drunk Driving (MADD) on page 156. Certainly it's sad to learn that five-year-old Carlie, pictured here hugging her dog, was killed by a drunk driver, but what did you think when you learned that Carlie's father, who wrote the letter, is a lieutenant in the police department? How did you react when you discovered that the drunk driver in question was Carlie's own mother? What is this ad's message, and what can be done to protect people from drunk drivers? Using Russell's essay, the MADD advertisement, and your own experiences and observations, write an essay in which you argue for more stringent punishments for people who drink and drive. (Glossary: *Argumentation*)

This is my precious little girl, Carlie. I always told her, "I will love you as long as there are stars in the sky." She would always smile, look up at me and say, "I love you more than there are stars in the universe." Those words are now inscribed on her tombstone. At the tender age of five, she was killed by a drunk driver – her mother.

If you think it can't happen to you – think again. Please don't drink and drive.

–Lieutenant Carl McDonald

Mothers Against Drunk Driving needs your support this holiday season to assist victims and help keep our roadways safe.
Visit www.madd.org to find out how you can volunteer or make a charitable donation.

Unforgettable Miss Bessie

■ Carl T. Rowan

In addition to being a popular syndicated newspaper columnist, Carl T. Rowan (1925–2000) was a former ambassador to Finland and director of the U.S. Information Agency. Born in Ravenscroft, Tennessee, he received degrees from Oberlin College and the University of Minnesota. He worked as a columnist for the Minneapolis Tribune *and the* Chicago Sun-Times *before moving to Washington, D.C. In 1996, Washington College awarded Rowan an honorary Doctor of Letters degree in recognition not only of his achievements as a writer, but also for his many contributions to minority youth, most notably through the organization he founded in 1987, Project Excellence. In 1991, Rowan published* Breaking Barriers: A Memoir. *He is also the author of two biographies, one of baseball great Jackie Robinson, the other of former Supreme Court Justice Thurgood Marshall. His last book,* The Coming Race War in America, *was published in 1996.*

In the following essay, first published in the March 1985 issue of Reader's Digest, *Rowan describes one of his high school teachers whose lessons went far beyond the subjects she taught. Through telling details about Miss Bessie's background, behavior, and appearance, Rowan creates a dominant impression of her—the one he wants to leave readers with. Notice how he begins with some factual information about Miss Bessie and concludes by showing why she was "so vital to the minds, hearts, and souls" of her students.*

For Your Journal

Perhaps you have at some time taught a friend or younger brother or sister how to do something—tie a shoe, hit a ball, read, solve a puzzle, drive a car—but you never thought of yourself as a teacher. Did you enjoy the experience of sharing what you know with someone else? Would you consider becoming a teacher someday?

She was only about five feet tall and probably never weighed more than 110 pounds, but Miss Bessie was a towering presence in the classroom. She was the only woman tough enough to make me read *Beowulf*[1] and think for a few foolish days that I liked it. From 1938 to 1942, when I attended Bernard High School in McMinnville, Tennessee, she taught me English, history, civics—and a lot more than I realized. 1

I shall never forget the day she scolded me into reading *Beowulf*. 2

"But Miss Bessie," I complained, "I ain't much interested in it." 3

Her large brown eyes became daggerish slits. "Boy," she said, "how dare you say 'ain't' to me! I've taught you better than that." 4

"Miss Bessie," I pleaded, "I'm trying to make first-string end on the football team, and if I go around saying 'it isn't' and 'they aren't,' the guys are gonna laugh me off the squad." 5

"Boy," she responded, "you'll play football because you have guts. But do you know what *really* takes guts? Refusing to lower your standards to those of the crowd. It takes guts to say you've got to live and be somebody fifty years after all the football games are over." 6

I started saying "it isn't" and "they aren't," and I still made first-string end—and class valedictorian—without losing my buddies' respect. 7

During her remarkable 44-year career, Mrs. Bessie Taylor Gwynn taught hundreds of economically deprived black youngsters—including my mother, my brother, my sisters, and me. I remember her now with gratitude and affection—especially in this era when Americans are so wrought-up about a "rising tide of mediocrity"[2] in public education and the problems of finding competent, caring teachers. Miss Bessie was an example of an informed, dedicated teacher, a blessing to children, and an asset to the nation. 8

Born in 1895, in poverty, she grew up in Athens, Alabama, where there was no public school for blacks. She attended Trinity School, a private institution for blacks run by the American Missionary Association, and in 1911 graduated from the Normal School (a "super" high school) at Fisk University in Nashville. Mrs. Gwynn, the essence of pride and privacy, never talked about her years in Athens; only in the 9

[1]*Beowulf:* an epic poem written in Old English by an anonymous author in the early eighth century.

[2]*mediocrity:* state of being second rate; not outstanding.

months before her death did she reveal that she had never attended Fisk University itself because she could not afford the four-year course.

At Normal School she learned a lot about Shakespeare, but most of all about the profound importance of education—especially, for a people trying to move up from slavery. "What you put in your head, boy," she once said, "can never be pulled out by the Ku Klux Klan,[3] the Congress, or anybody." 10

Miss Bessie's bearing of dignity told anyone who met her that she was "educated" in the best sense of the word. There was never a discipline problem in her classes. We didn't dare mess with a woman who knew about the Battle of Hastings, the Magna Carta, and the Bill of Rights—and who could also play the piano. 11

This frail-looking woman could make sense of Shakespeare, Milton, Voltaire, and bring to life Booker T. Washington and W. E. B. Du Bois. Believing that it was important to know who the officials were that spent taxpayers' money and made public policy, she made us memorize the names of everyone on the Supreme Court and in the President's Cabinet. It could be embarrassing to be unprepared when Miss Bessie said, "Get up and tell the class who Frances Perkins[4] is and what you think about her." 12

Miss Bessie knew that my family, like so many others during the Depression,[5] couldn't afford to subscribe to a newspaper. She knew we didn't even own a radio. Still, she prodded me to "look out for your future and find some way to keep up with what's going on in the world." So I became a delivery boy for the Chattanooga *Times.* I rarely made a dollar a week, but I got to read a newspaper every day. 13

Miss Bessie noticed things that had nothing to do with schoolwork, but were vital to a youngster's development. Once a few classmates made fun of my frayed, hand-me-down overcoat, calling me "Strings." As I was leaving school, Miss Bessie patted me on the back of that old overcoat and said, "Carl, never fret about what you *don't* have. Just make the most of what you *do* have—a brain." 14

[3]*Ku Klux Klan:* a secret organization in the United States hostile toward African Americans (eventually other groups as well), founded in 1915 and continuing to the present.

[4]*Frances Perkins:* the U.S. secretary of labor during the presidency of Franklin D. Roosevelt and the first woman appointed to a cabinet post.

[5]*Depression:* the longest and most severe economic slump in North America, Europe, and other industrialized areas of the world, which began in 1929 and ended around 1939. Also called the *Great Depression.*

Among the things that I did not have was electricity in the little frame house that my father had built for $400 with his World War I bonus. But because of her inspiration, I spent many hours squinting beside a kerosene lamp reading Shakespeare and Thoreau, Samuel Pepys and William Cullen Bryant. 15

No one in my family had ever graduated from high school, so there was no tradition of commitment to learning for me to lean on. Like millions of youngsters in today's ghettos and barrios, I needed the push and stimulation of a teacher who truly cared. Miss Bessie gave plenty of both, as she immersed me in a wonderful world of similes, metaphors and even onomatopoeia. She led me to believe that I could write sonnets as well as Shakespeare, or iambic-pentameter verse to put Alexander Pope to shame. 16

In those days the McMinnville school system was rigidly "Jim Crow,"[6] and poor black children had to struggle to put anything in their heads. Our high school was only slightly larger than the once-typical little red schoolhouse, and its library was outrageously inadequate—so small, I like to say, that if two students were in it and one wanted to turn a page, the other one had to step outside. 17

Negroes, as we were called then, were not allowed in the town library, except to mop floors or dust tables. But through one of those secret Old South arrangements between whites of conscience and blacks of stature, Miss Bessie kept getting books smuggled out of the white library. That is how she introduced me to the Brontës, Byron, Coleridge, Keats and Tennyson. "If you don't read, you can't write, and if you can't write, you might as well stop dreaming," Miss Bessie once told me. 18

So I read whatever Miss Bessie told me to, and tried to remember the things she insisted that I store away. Forty-five years later, I can still recite her "truths to live by," such as Henry Wadsworth Longfellow's lines from "The Ladder of St. Augustine": 19

> The heights by great men reached and kept
> Were not attained by sudden flight.
> But they, while their companions slept,
> Were toiling upward in the night.

---

[6] *"Jim Crow":* a term referring to the racial segregation laws in the U.S. South between the late 1800s and the mid-1900s.

Years later, her inspiration, prodding, anger, cajoling, and almost 20
osmotic infusion of learning finally led to that lovely day when Miss Bessie dropped me a note saying, "I'm so proud to read your column in the Nashville *Tennessean.*"

Miss Bessie was a spry 80 when I went back to McMinnville and 21
visited her in a senior citizens' apartment building. Pointing out proudly that her building was racially integrated, she reached for two glasses and a pint of bourbon. I was momentarily shocked, because it would have been scandalous in the 1930s and '40s for word to get out that a teacher drank, and nobody had ever raised a rumor that Miss Bessie did.

I felt a new sense of equality as she lifted her glass to mine. Then 22
she revealed a softness and compassion that I had never known as a student.

"I've never forgotten that examination day," she said, "when 23
Buster Martin held up seven fingers, obviously asking you for help with question number seven, 'Name a common carrier.' I can still picture you looking at your exam paper and humming a few bars of 'Chattanooga Choo Choo.' I was so tickled, I couldn't punish either of you."

Miss Bessie was telling me, with bourbon-laced grace, that I never 24
fooled her for a moment.

When Miss Bessie died in 1980, at age 85, hundreds of her for- 25
mer students mourned. They knew the measure of a great teacher: love and motivation. Her wisdom and influence had rippled out across generations.

Some of her students who might normally have been doomed to 26
poverty went on to become doctors, dentists, and college professors. Many, guided by Miss Bessie's example, became public-school teachers.

"The memory of Miss Bessie and how she conducted her class- 27
room did more for me than anything I learned in college," recalls Gladys Wood of Knoxville, Tennessee, a highly respected English teacher who spent 43 years in the state's school system. "So many times, when I faced a difficult classroom problem, I asked myself, *How would Miss Bessie deal with this?* And I'd remember that she would handle it with laughter and love."

No child can get all the necessary support at home, and millions 28
of poor children get *no* support at all. This is what makes a wise, educated, warm-hearted teacher like Miss Bessie so vital to the minds, hearts, and souls of this country's children.

Thinking Critically about This Reading

Rowan states that Miss Bessie "taught me English, history, civics—and a lot more than I realized" (paragraph 1). Aside from the standard school subjects, what did Miss Bessie teach Rowan? What role did she play in his life?

Questions for Study and Discussion

1. Do you think Rowan's first few paragraphs make for an effective introduction? Explain.
2. At what point in the essay does Rowan give us the details of Miss Bessie's background? Why do you suppose he delays giving us this important information?
3. Throughout the essay Rowan offers details of Miss Bessie's physical appearance. What specific details does he give, and in what context does he give them? (Glossary: *Details*) Do Miss Bessie's physical characteristics match the quality of her character? Explain.
4. Does Miss Bessie's drinking influence your opinion of her? Why or why not? Why do you think Rowan includes this part of her behavior in his essay?
5. How does dialogue serve Rowan's purpose? (Glossary: *Dialogue; Purpose*)
6. How would you sum up the character of Miss Bessie? Make a list of the key words that Rowan uses that you feel best describe her.

Classroom Activity Using Beginnings and Endings

Rowan uses a series of facts about his teacher, the "unforgettable" Miss Bessie, to begin his essay. Pick two from among the seven other methods for beginning essays discussed in the introduction to this chapter, and use them to write alternative openings for Rowan's essay. Share your beginnings with others in the class, and discuss their effectiveness.

Suggested Writing Assignments

1. In paragraph 18, Rowan writes the following: "'If you don't read, you can't write, and if you can't write, you might as well

stop dreaming,' Miss Bessie once told me." Write an essay in which you explore this theme (which, in essence, is also the theme of *Models for Writers*).

2. Think of all the teachers you have had, and write a description of the one who has had the greatest influence on you. (Glossary: *Description*) Remember to give some consideration to the balance you want to achieve between physical attributes and personality traits.

chapter **7**

Paragraphs

Within an essay, the **paragraph** is the most important unit of thought. Like the essay, it has its own main idea, often stated directly in a topic sentence. Like a good essay, a good paragraph is unified: It avoids digressions and develops its main idea. Paragraphs use many of the rhetorical strategies that essays use, strategies like classification, comparison and contrast, and cause and effect. As you read the following three paragraphs, notice how each writer develops his or her topic sentence with explanations, concrete details and statistics, or vivid examples. The topic sentence in each paragraph is italicized.

> *I've learned from experience that good friendships are based on a delicate balance.* When friends are on a par, professionally and personally, it's easier for them to root for one another. It's taken me a long time to realize that not all my "friends" wish me well. Someone who wants what you have may not be able to handle your good fortune: If you find yourself apologizing for your hard-earned raise or soft-pedaling your long-awaited promotion, it's a sure sign that the friendship is off balance. Real friends are secure enough in their own lives to share each other's successes—not begrudge them.
>
> –Stephanie Mansfield

> The problem of substance abuse is far more complex and far more pervasive than any of us really knows or is willing to admit. *Most stories of illegal drugs overshadow Americans' struggles with alcohol, tobacco, food, and nonprescription drugs—our so-called legal addictions.* In 2000, for example, 17,000 deaths were attributed to cocaine and heroin. In that same year, 435,000 deaths were attributed to tobacco and 85,000 to alcohol. It's not surprising, then, that many sociologists believe we are a nation of substance abusers—drinkers, smokers, overeaters, and pill poppers. Although the statistics are alarming, they do not begin to suggest the heavy

toll of substance abuse on Americans and their families. Loved ones die, relationships are fractured, children are abandoned, job productivity falters, and the dreams of young people are extinguished.

–Alfred Rosa and Paul Eschholz

Photographs have let me know my parents before I was born, as the carefree college students they were, in love and awaiting the rest of their lives. I have seen the light blue Volkswagen van my dad used to take surfing down the coast of California and the silver dress my mom wore to her senior prom. Through pictures I was able to witness their wedding, which showed me that there is much in their relationship that goes beyond their children. I saw the look in their eyes as they held their first, newborn daughter, as well as the jealous expressions of my sister when I was born a few years later. There is something almost magical about viewing images of yourself and your family that you were too young to remember.

–Carrie White, student

Many writers find it helpful to think of the paragraph as a very small, compact essay. Here is a paragraph from an essay on testing:

Multiple-choice questions distort the purposes of education. Picking one answer among four is very different from thinking a question through to an answer of one's own, and far less useful in life. Recognition of vocabulary and isolated facts makes the best kind of multiple-choice questions, so these dominate the tests, rather than questions that test the use of knowledge. Because schools want their children to perform well, they are often tempted to teach the limited sorts of knowledge most useful on the tests.

This paragraph, like all well-written paragraphs, has several distinguishing characteristics: It is unified, coherent, and adequately developed. It is unified in that every sentence and every idea relate to the main idea, stated in the topic sentence, "Multiple-choice questions distort the purposes of education." It is coherent in that the sentences and ideas are arranged logically and the relationships among them are made clear by the use of effective transitions. Finally, the paragraph is adequately developed in that it presents a short but persuasive argument supporting its main idea.

How much development is "adequate" development? The answer depends on many things: how complicated or controversial the main idea is; what readers already know and believe; how much space the writer is permitted. Everyone, or nearly everyone, agrees that the earth circles around the sun; a single sentence would be enough to make that point. A writer trying to argue that affirmative action has outlived its usefulness, however, would need many sentences, indeed many paragraphs, to develop that idea convincingly.

Here is another model of an effective paragraph. As you read this paragraph about the resourcefulness of pigeons in evading attempts to control them, pay particular attention to its main idea, unity, development, and coherence.

> Pigeons (and their human friends) have proved remarkably resourceful in evading nearly all the controls, from birth-control pellets to carbide shells to pigeon apartment complexes, that pigeon-haters have devised. One of New York's leading museums once put large black rubber owls on its wide ledges to discourage the large number of pigeons that roosted there. Within the day the pigeons had gotten over their fear of owls and were back perched on the owls' heads. A few years ago San Francisco put a sticky coating on the ledges of some public buildings, but the pigeons got used to the goop and came back to roost. The city then tried trapping, using electric owls, and periodically exploding carbide shells outside a city building, hoping the noise would scare the pigeons away. It did, but not for long, and the program was abandoned. More frequent explosions probably would have distressed the humans in the area more than the birds. Philadelphia tried a feed that makes pigeons vomit, and then, they hoped, go away. A New York firm claimed it had a feed that made a pigeon's nervous system send "danger signals" to the other members of its flock.

The main idea is stated at the beginning in a topic sentence. Other sentences in the paragraph support this idea with examples. Since all the separate examples illustrate how pigeons have evaded attempts to control them, the paragraph is unified. Since there are enough examples to convince the reader of the truth of the topic statement, the paragraph is adequately developed. Finally, the regular use of transitional words and phrases like *once, within the day, a few years ago,* and *then* lends the paragraph coherence.

How long should a paragraph be? In modern essays, most paragraphs range from 50 to 250 words, but some run a full page or more, and others may be only a few words long. The best answer is that a paragraph should be long enough to develop its main idea adequately.

Some writers, when they find a paragraph running very long, break it into two or more paragraphs so that readers can pause and catch their breath. Other writers forge ahead, relying on the unity and coherence of their paragraph to keep their readers from getting lost.

Articles and essays that appear in magazines and newspapers often have relatively short paragraphs, some of only one or two sentences. Short paragraphs are a convention in journalism because of the narrow columns, which make paragraphs of average length appear very long. But often you will find that these journalistic "paragraphs" could be joined together into a few longer paragraphs. Longer, adequately developed paragraphs are the kind you should use in all but journalistic writing.

Simplicity

■ William Zinsser

William Zinsser was born in New York City in 1922. After graduating from Princeton University, he worked for the New York Herald Tribune, *first as a feature writer and later as its drama editor and film critic. During the 1970s he taught writing at Yale University. A former executive editor of the Book-of-the-Month Club, Zinsser has also served on the Usage Panel of the* American Heritage Dictionary. *Currently, he is the series editor for the Writer's Craft Series, which publishes talks by writers, and teaches writing at the New School University in New York. Zinsser's own published works cover many aspects of contemporary American culture, but he is best known as the author of lucid and accessible books about writing, including* Writing to Learn *(1988),* Inventing the Truth: The Art and Craft of Memoir *(1998), with Russell Baker and Jill Ker Conway,* Writing about Your Life: A Journey into the Past *(2005), and* On Writing Well, *a perennial favorite for college writing courses, published in a twenty-fifth anniversary edition in 2001.*

In the following piece from On Writing Well, *Zinsser reminds us, as did Henry David Thoreau before him, to "simplify, simplify." As you read each paragraph, notice the clarity with which Zinsser presents its main idea, and observe how he develops that idea with adequate and logically related supporting information. You should also note that he follows his own advice about simplicity.*

For Your Journal

Sometimes we get so caught up in what's going on around us that we start to feel frantic, and we lose sight of what is really important or meaningful to us. At such times it's a good idea to take stock of what we are doing and to simplify our lives by dropping activities that are no longer rewarding. Write about a time when you've felt the need to simplify your life.

Clutter is the disease of American writing. We are a society strangling in unnecessary words, circular constructions, pompous frills, and meaningless jargon. 1

Who can understand the clotted language of everyday American commerce: the memo, the corporation report, the business letter, the notice from the bank explaining its latest "simplified" statement? What member of an insurance or medical plan can decipher the brochure explaining his costs and benefits? What father or mother can put together a child's toy from the instructions on the box? Our national tendency is to inflate and thereby sound important. The airline pilot who announces that he is presently anticipating experiencing considerable precipitation wouldn't think of saying it may rain. The sentence is too simple—there must be something wrong with it. 2

But the secret of good writing is to strip every sentence to its cleanest components. Every word that serves no function, every long word that could be a short word, every adverb that carries the same meaning that's already in the verb, every passive construction that leaves the reader unsure of who is doing what—these are the thousand and one adulterants[1] that weaken the strength of a sentence. And they usually occur in proportion to education and rank. 3

During the 1960s the president of my university wrote a letter to mollify[2] the alumni after a spell of campus unrest. "You are probably aware," he began, "that we have been experiencing very considerable potentially explosive expressions of dissatisfaction on issues only partially related." He meant the students had been hassling them about different things. I was far more upset by the president's English than by the students' potentially explosive expressions of dissatisfaction. I would have preferred the presidential approach taken by Franklin D. Roosevelt when he tried to convert into English his own government's memos, such as this blackout order of 1942: 4

> Such preparations shall be made as will completely obscure all Federal buildings and non-Federal buildings occupied by the Federal government during an air raid for any period of time from visibility by reason of internal or external illumination.

"Tell them," Roosevelt said, "that in buildings where they have to keep the work going to put something across the windows." 5

---

[1]*adulterants:* unnecessary ingredients that taint the purity of something.
[2]*mollify:* to soothe in temper; appease.

Simplify, simplify. Thoreau[3] said it, as we are so often reminded, and no American writer more consistently practiced what he preached. Open *Walden* to any page and you will find a man saying in a plain and orderly way what is on his mind: 6

> I went to the woods because I wished to live deliberately, to front only the essential facts of life, and see if I could not learn what it had to teach, and not, when I came to die, discover that I had not lived.

How can the rest of us achieve such enviable freedom from clutter? The answer is to clear our heads of clutter. Clear thinking becomes clear writing; one can't exist without the other. It's impossible for a muddy thinker to write good English. He may get away with it for a paragraph or two, but soon the reader will be lost, and there's no sin so grave, for the reader will not easily be lured back. 7

Who is this elusive creature, the reader? The reader is someone with an attention span of about 30 seconds—a person assailed by other forces competing for attention. At one time those forces were relatively few: newspapers, magazines, radio, spouse, children, pets. Today they also include a "home entertainment center" (television, VCR, tapes, CDs), e-mail, the Internet, the cellular phone, the fax machine, a fitness program, a pool, a lawn, and that most potent of competitors, sleep. The man or woman snoozing in a chair with a magazine or a book is a person who was being given too much unnecessary trouble by the writer. 8

It won't do to say that the reader is too dumb or too lazy to keep pace with the train of thought. If the reader is lost, it's usually because the writer hasn't been careful enough. The carelessness can take any number of forms. Perhaps a sentence is so excessively cluttered that the reader, hacking through the verbiage, simply doesn't know what it means. Perhaps a sentence has been so shoddily constructed that the reader could read it in several ways. Perhaps the writer has switched pronouns in midsentence, or has switched tenses, so the reader loses track of who is talking or when the action took place. Perhaps Sentence B is not a logical sequel to Sentence A; the writer, in whose head the connection is clear, hasn't bothered to provide the missing link. Perhaps the writer has used a word incorrectly by not taking the 9

[3]*Henry David Thoreau* (1817–1862): American essayist, poet, and philosopher activist. *Walden,* his masterwork, was published in 1854.

trouble to look it up. He or she may think "sanguine" and "sanguinary" mean the same thing, but the difference is a bloody big one. The reader can only infer (speaking of big differences) what the writer is trying to imply.

Faced with such obstacles, readers are at first tenacious. They blame themselves—they obviously missed something, and they go back over the mystifying sentence, or over the whole paragraph, piecing it out like an ancient rune, making guesses and moving on. But they won't do this for long. The writer is making them work too hard, and they will look for one who is better at the craft. 10

Writers must therefore constantly ask: what am I trying to say? Surprisingly often they don't know. Then they must look at what they have written and ask: have I said it? Is it clear to someone encountering the subject for the first time? If it's not, some fuzz has worked its way into the machinery. The clear writer is someone clearheaded enough to see this stuff for what it is: fuzz. 11

I don't mean that some people are born clearheaded and are therefore natural writers, whereas others are naturally fuzzy and will never write well. Thinking clearly is a conscious act that writers must force upon themselves, as if they were working on any other project that requires logic: making a shopping list or doing an algebra problem. Good writing doesn't come naturally, though most people obviously think it does. Professional writers are constantly bearded[4] by people who say they'd like to "try a little writing sometime"—meaning when they retire from their real profession, like insurance or real estate, which is hard. Or they say, "I could write a book about that." I doubt it. 12

Writing is hard work. A clear sentence is no accident. Very few sentences come out right the first time, or even the third time. Remember this in moments of despair. If you find that writing is hard, it's because it *is* hard. 13

Thinking Critically about This Reading

How does Zinsser support his claim that "we are a society strangling in unnecessary words, circular constructions, pompous frills, and meaningless jargon" (paragraph 1)? What are the implications of his claim for writers in general and for you in particular?

[4]*bearded:* confronted boldly.

Questions for Study and Discussion

1. What exactly does Zinsser mean by "clutter" (1)? How does he believe we can free ourselves of clutter?
2. Identify the main idea in each of the thirteen paragraphs. How is each paragraph related to Zinsser's topic and purpose?
3. In what ways do paragraphs 4–6 serve to illustrate the main idea of paragraph 3? (Glossary: *Illustration*)
4. In paragraph 11, Zinsser says that writers must constantly ask themselves some questions. What are these questions, and why are they important?
5. How do Zinsser's first and last paragraphs serve to introduce and conclude his essay? (Glossary: *Beginnings and Endings*)
6. What is the relationship between thinking and writing for Zinsser?

Classroom Activity Using Paragraphs

Below you will find a passage from Zinsser's final manuscript of this chapter from the first edition of *On Writing Well.* Zinsser has included these manuscript pages showing his editing for clutter in every edition of his book because he believes they are instructive. He says, "Although they look like a first draft, they had already been rewritten and retyped—like almost every other page—four or five times. With each rewrite I try to make what I have written tighter, stronger, and more precise, eliminating every element that's not doing useful work. Then I go over it once more, reading it aloud, and am always amazed at how much clutter can still be cut. (In later editions I eliminated the sexist pronoun 'he' denoting 'the writer' and 'the reader.')"

Carefully study these manuscript pages and Zinsser's editing, and be prepared to discuss how the changes enhance his paragraphs' unity, coherence, and logical development.

is too dumb or too lazy to keep pace with the ~~writer's~~ train of thought. My sympathies are ~~entirely~~ with him. ~~He's not so dumb.~~ If the reader is lost, it is generally because the writer ~~of the article~~ has not been careful enough to keep him on the ~~proper~~ path.

This carelessness can take any number of ~~different~~ forms. Perhaps a sentence is so excessively ~~long and~~ cluttered that the reader, hacking his way through ~~all~~ the verbiage, simply doesn't know what it ~~the writer~~ means. Perhaps a sentence has been so shoddily constructed that the reader could read it in any of several ~~two or three different~~ ways. ~~He thinks he knows what the writer is trying to say, but he's not sure.~~ Perhaps the writer has switched pronouns in midsentence, or ~~perhaps he~~ has switched tenses, so the reader loses track of who is talking ~~to whom~~ or ~~exactly~~ when the action took place. Perhaps Sentence B is not a logical sequel to Sentence A -- the writer, in whose head the connection is ~~perfectly~~ clear, has not bothered to provide ~~given enough thought to providing~~ the missing link. Perhaps the writer has used an important word incorrectly by not taking the trouble to look it up. ~~and make sure.~~ He may think that "sanguine" and "sanguinary" mean the same thing, but ~~I can assure you that~~ the difference is a bloody big one. ~~to the reader.~~ The reader ~~He~~ can only ~~try to~~ infer ~~xxxx~~ (speaking of big differences) what the writer is trying to imply.

Faced with these ~~such a variety of~~ obstacles, the reader is at first a remarkably tenacious bird. He ~~tends to~~ blames himself. He obviously missed something, ~~he thinks,~~ and he goes back over the mystifying sentence, or over the whole paragraph, piecing it out like an ancient rune, making guesses and moving on. But he won't do this for long. ~~He will soon run out of patience.~~ The writer is making him work too hard, ~~harder than he should have to work --~~ and the reader will look for one ~~a writer~~ who is better at his craft.

The writer must therefore constantly ask himself: What am I trying to say? ~~in this sentence?~~ Surprisingly often, he doesn't know. ~~And~~ Then he must look at what he has ~~just~~ written and ask: Have I said it? Is it clear to someone encountering ~~who is coming upon~~ the subject for the first time? If it's not, ~~clear,~~ it is because some fuzz has worked its way into the machinery. The clear writer is a person ~~who is~~ clear-headed enough to see this stuff for what it is: fuzz.

I don't mean ~~to suggest~~ that some people are born clear-headed and are therefore natural writers, whereas ~~other people~~ others are naturally fuzzy and will ~~therefore~~ never write well. Thinking clearly is ~~an entirely~~ a conscious act that the writer must ~~keep forcing~~ force upon himself, just as if he were ~~starting out~~ embarking on any other ~~kind of~~ project that ~~calls for~~ requires logic: adding up a laundry list or doing an algebra problem. ~~or playing chess.~~ Good writing doesn't ~~just~~ come naturally, though most people obviously think ~~it's as easy as walking.~~ it does.

Suggested Writing Assignments

1. If what Zinsser writes about clutter is an accurate assessment, we should easily be able to find numerous examples of clutter all around us. During the next few days, make a point of looking for clutter in the written materials you come across. Choose one example that you find—an article, an essay, a form letter, or a section from a textbook, for example—and write an extended analysis explaining how it might have been written more simply. Develop your paragraphs well, make sure they are coherent, and try not to "clutter" your own writing.
2. Using some of the ideas you explored in your journal entry for this selection, write a brief essay analyzing your need to simplify some aspect of your life. For example, are you involved in too many extracurricular activities, taking too many courses, working too many hours at an off-campus job, or not making sensible choices with regard to your social life?

Raising a Son—With Men on the Fringes

■ **Robyn Marks**

Robyn Marks was born in 1974 in Baltimore, Maryland, and attended public schools in Baltimore and Los Angeles. After graduating from Morgan State University in Baltimore in 1996 with a degree in communications, she worked in radio and television as a sports reporter and news anchor for public radio and for WGAL, the NBC affiliate in the York/Harrisburg, Pennsylvania, area. She has written for numerous publications, including Vibe Magazine, Dime Magazine, *and* Street and Smiths, *and has been written about by such publications as the* Baltimore Sun, New York Post, *and* Atlanta Journal-Constitution. *When asked to give some advice to beginning writers, Marks said, "Believe in getting everything right but not to the point of losing your voice." Marks is now at work on a book tentatively titled* Hoodrat, *a collection of personal essays by successful young women who have come from "humble urban beginnings" to make names for themselves. She believes that teenage girls who dream of becoming successful will be inspired by the book's stories to build careers for themselves.*

The following essay was first published in the July 19, 2004, issue of Newsweek. *Marks says the essay not only generated "lots of mail" but also won the 2004 New York Association of Black Journalists Award for Personal Commentary. Notice how Marks builds paragraphs that are clear, unified, and coherent, and how she effectively but subtly links those paragraphs.*

For Your Journal

For a variety of reasons many children are reared in a household headed by a single parent, most often a single mother. Based on your own experience as well as the experiences of your friends and relatives, reflect on the potential implications of single-parent child rearing. What are the benefits, as well as the shortcomings, of such circumstances on a child's later life?

Despite my best efforts, I am a single mother. It's a title I'm 1
not too fond of, a repeat of my urban family's legacy of strong black women raising a black boy with men on the fringes. My grandmother eventually became a single mother, as did my mother and now me.

My son, a gigantic 4-year-old with big, bright eyes, doesn't 2
even yet realize that he's a future "black man" and, before that, a "black male teenager," but I do. I am so panicked at the thought that every single solitary thing has to be *just so* over these next 20 years in order for me to produce a solid, productive adult who understands the world in which he lives, both the realities and the possibilities.

Studies show that African-American women have been outpacing 3
our men in education and corporate America for two generations now. Almost half of black boys wind up a grade behind in school, and only a third of 20-year-old black men are enrolled in college. All the more daunting is the fact that the majority of these boys and men were just like Jason, raised in a home by a single black mother. I have a lot of work to do to ensure that my child clears these hurdles, but they are hurdles that are so elusive, I have yet to get a firm grip on where exactly they lie.

I am a journalist who has covered crime and urban blight, and I 4
love my job. My background, I believe, allows me a certain compassion and sensibility toward the subjects of my articles. But that doesn't mean that when I head home into suburbia, I am not completely awestruck at the fact that my son is only a couple of generations and a few miles away from poverty, crime and abject desperation. He has no idea. Do I tell him? Show him? How? How much? He has to know eventually, for his own good.

I remember my brother, who is a few years younger than me, 5
not being aware of the subtle snubs and racist attitudes he occasionally faced while attending a prestigious private school, and being dumbfounded when he and a pack of friends were all taken in by the police for drinking in a public park and he (the only black kid) was the only one not just released to his parents. How do you explain that?

The plan for Jason, of course, is private school, at a cost of close to 6
$20,000 a year. But then I owe it to him to balance that with a hefty dose of African-American culture—the culture he will surely miss out on at an elite boarding or country day school. Added to the mix is the

fact that I am a Generation-X[1] child of hip-hop who embraces rap music and identifies with the likes of Allen Iverson.[2] How do I balance all that? I imagine conversations that will go something like, "OK, Jason, *general* bling-bling is fine and has its place if you work hard for it . . . but not watching videos of booty-shaking objectified women!"

He comes from an athletic background, so naturally everybody is attempting to put a basketball or football in his hands and get him signed to Reebok tomorrow, but I shun the pressure, until I realize that I have put my own pressures on him, too. I could read at the age of 2, and called his pediatrician when he couldn't (she laughed at me). I skipped grades and breezed through school, and want him to do the same. All he wants right now, the summer before pre-K, is Thomas the Tank Engine. 7

I talk to my mom all the time about raising a black man, and there's good and bad news. The good news is she did a pretty good job; the bad news is she's far from done, and my brother is 25. We worry that he moved to a bad neighborhood and may become a victim of crime or, worse yet, accused of one; that he isn't assertive enough at a job where he may be hindered by his race; that black women intimidate him, and that he'll be profiled by police because his pants are baggy. Times are ever changing, so even my mom's experience is slightly different from what mine will be. 8

Blessedly, there are great men all over the place who love and nurture Jason: my uncle, who drives 40 miles round trip out of his way each Tuesday to take Jason to the barbershop; my dad, who relishes getting it right with his only grandchild. And there are even books intended to coach me on issues like black male masculinity, peer pressure, academic achievement, the lack of fathers and goal setting. I appreciate and seek out all of it. But I still realize that at the end of the day, everything Jason is, everything he trusts about who and what he can become, will come from me. So at night—especially when I have just returned from a long work trip that has taken me away for days—I peek in at him, asleep in his room surrounded by trains and DVDs and basketballs, and I think about all the things I know I have to do for him. And then I get to the real work: I pray. 9

---

[1]*Generation-X:* a term sometimes used to describe the generation of Americans born between 1961 and 1981.

[2]*Allen Iverson* (b. 1975): a professional American basketball player.

Thinking Critically about This Reading

What does Marks mean when she states, "I am so panicked at the thought that every single solitary thing has to be *just so* over these next 20 years in order for me to produce a solid, productive adult" (paragraph 2)? What experiences have instilled such anxiety in Marks?

Questions for Study and Discussion

1. What is Marks's purpose? (Glossary: *Purpose*) Does she want only to share her concerns about her son, or does she wish to raise larger social questions? Explain.
2. Choose any two of Marks's paragraphs, and examine each one for paragraph integrity by asking the following questions (consult the Glossary for definitions of any unfamiliar terms):

   - Does the paragraph have a clear topic sentence?
   - Does the author develop the paragraph clearly and effectively?
   - Is the paragraph unified?
   - Is the paragraph coherent?

   Be prepared to discuss your evaluation of the two paragraphs.
3. Marks is a black single mother who has fears about how her son will turn out in the years ahead. Why does the fact that she is also a journalist add to those fears?
4. Marks begins her essay by expressing self-criticism for being a single mother. How does such a beginning further her purpose? (Glossary: *Beginnings and Endings; Purpose*)
5. In paragraph 2 Marks puts the terms "black man" and "black male teenager" in quotation marks. Why do you suppose she wishes to call attention to these terms? What does she imply by calling attention to them? (Glossary: *Emphasis*)
6. In your estimation, does Marks exhibit too much, not enough, or just about the right amount of concern for how her son might turn out? Explain.

Classroom Activity Using Paragraphs

Rearrange the following sentences to create an effective paragraph. Be ready to explain why you chose the order that you did.

1. PGA golfer Fred Divot learned the hard way what overtraining could do.
2. Divot's case is typical, and most researchers believe that too much repetition makes it difficult for the athlete to reduce left-hemisphere brain activity.
3. Athletes who overtrain find it very difficult to get in the flow.
4. "Two weeks later, all I could think about was mechanics, and I couldn't hit a fairway to save my life!"
5. Athletes think about mechanics (left hemisphere) rather than feel (right hemisphere), and they lose the ability to achieve peak performance.
6. "I was playing well, so I thought with a bit more practice, I could start winning on tour," Divot recalled.

Suggested Writing Assignments

1. Write a letter to Marks, supporting her effort "to produce a solid, productive adult who understands the world in which he lives, both the realities and the possibilities" (2). What special talents does Marks bring to her role as parent? What critical insights has she demonstrated? What encouragement and advice would you give her? Make sure your letter has well-developed, substantive paragraphs that carry your special voice, as Marks herself advises in the headnote.
2. If you intend to have a family someday or if you are already a parent, what are your hopes and aspirations for your children? What rewards, obstacles, dangers, and triumphs do you see ahead? Write an essay in which you explore both your hopes and fears about parenting and how you might approach them in the future. Pay particular attention to how the topic sentences in your paragraphs develop your thesis and how the sentences in those paragraphs flow into one another.
3. Marks focuses her attention on the problems black single mothers face in raising their sons. The public service advertisement sponsored by the Ad Council, 100 Black Men of America, and the National Fatherhood Initiative on p. 181 is aimed at fathers who are not involved in their children's lives. Write an essay in which you examine the effectiveness of this ad. Do you think the ad

minimizes the work of single mothers? Why or why not? Do you think the ad would inspire absentee fathers to take an active role in their children's lives? Why or why not? Build your essay on a strong thesis, and be sure your paragraphs are solidly constructed, linked by strong transitions, and clearly related to your thesis. (Glossary: *Transitions; Thesis*)

Dear Daddy,
My Mommy
Can't Be
My Daddy Too.

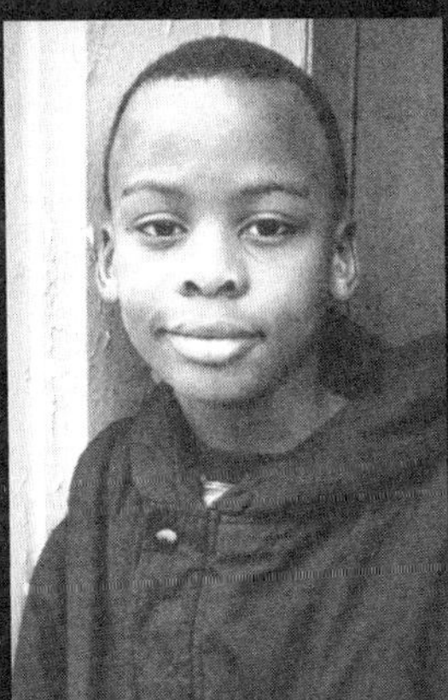

For Free Helpful Information Call 1·800·790·DADS.

www.fatherhood.org

100
BLACK MEN
OF AMERICA, INC.

"I Just Wanna Be Average"

■ **Mike Rose**

Born in Altoona, Pennsylvania, to Italian American parents, Mike Rose moved to California in the early 1950s. A graduate of Loyola University in Los Angeles, Rose is now a professor at the UCLA Graduate School of Education and Information Studies. He has written a number of books and articles on language and literacy. His best-known book, Lives on the Boundary: The Struggles and Achievements of America's Underprepared, *was recognized by the National Council of Teachers of English with its highest award in 1989. More recently he published* Possible Lives: The Promise of Public Education *(1995) and* The Mind at Work: Valuing the Intelligence of the American Worker *(2004).*

In the following selection from Lives on the Boundary, *Rose explains how his high school English teacher, Jack MacFarland, picked him up out of the doldrums of "scholastic indifference." As you read, notice that although his paragraphs are fairly lengthy, Rose never digresses from the main point of each.*

For Your Journal

Often our desire to get more out of high school and to go on to college can be traced back to the influence of a single teacher. Which teacher turned you on to learning? Describe what that person did to stimulate change in you.

Jack MacFarland couldn't have come into my life at a better time. My father was dead, and I had logged up too many years of scholastic indifference. Mr. MacFarland had a master's degree from Columbia and decided, at twenty-six, to find a little school and teach his heart out. He never took any credentialing courses, couldn't bear to, he said, so he had to find employment in a private system. He ended up at Our Lady of Mercy teaching five sections of senior English. He was a beatnik[1] who was born too late. His teeth were stained, he tucked his sorry 1

[1]*beatnik:* a person whose behavior, views, and style of dress are unconventional.

tie in between the third and fourth buttons of his shirt, and his pants were chronically wrinkled. At first, we couldn't believe this guy, thought he slept in his car. But within no time, he had us so startled with work that we didn't much worry about where he slept or if he slept at all. We wrote three or four essays a month. We read a book every two to three weeks, starting with the *Iliad*[2] and ending up with Hemingway. He gave us a quiz on the reading every other day. He brought a prep school curriculum to Mercy High.

MacFarland's lectures were crafted, and as he delivered them he would pace the room jiggling a piece of chalk in his cupped hand, using it to scribble on the board the names of all the writers and philosophers and plays and novels he was weaving into his discussion. He asked questions often, raised everything from Zeno's paradox to the repeated last line of Frost's "Stopping by Woods on a Snowy Evening." He slowly and carefully built up our knowledge of Western intellectual history—with facts, with connections, with speculations. We learned about Greek philosophy, about Dante, the Elizabethan world view, the Age of Reason, existentialism. He analyzed poems with us, had us reading sections from John Ciardi's *How Does a Poem Mean?*, making a potentially difficult book accessible with his own explanations. We gave oral reports on poems Ciardi didn't cover. We imitated the styles of Conrad, Hemingway, and *Time* magazine. We wrote and talked, wrote and talked. The man immersed us in language. 2

Even MacFarland's barbs were literary. If Jim Fitzsimmons, hung over and irritable, tried to smart-ass him, he'd rejoin[3] with a flourish that would spark the indomitable[4] Skip Madison—who'd lost his front teeth in a hapless tackle—to flick his tongue through the gap and opine, "good chop," drawing out the single "o" in stinging indictment. Jack MacFarland, this tobacco-stained intellectual, brandished linguistic weapons of a kind I hadn't encountered before. Here was this *egghead*, for God's sake, keeping some pretty difficult people in line. And from what I heard, Mike Dweetz and Steve Fusco and all the notorious Voc. Ed.[5] crowd settled down as well when MacFarland took the podium. Though a lot of guys groused in the schoolyard, it just seemed that giving trouble to this particular teacher was a silly thing to do. 3

[2]*Iliad:* an ancient Greek epic poem attributed to Homer.
[3]*rejoin:* respond sharply; counterattack.
[4]*indomitable:* impossible to subdue.
[5]*Voc. Ed.:* vocational education, training for a specific industry or trade.

Tomfoolery, not to mention assault, had no place in the world he was trying to create for us, and instinctively everyone knew that. If nothing else, we all recognized MacFarland's considerable intelligence and respected the hours he put into his work. It came to this: The troublemaker would look foolish rather than daring. Even Jim Fitzsimmons was reading *On the Road* and turning his incipient[6] alcoholism to literary ends.

There were some lives that were already beyond Jack MacFarland's ministrations,[7] but mine was not. I started reading again as I hadn't since elementary school. I would go into our gloomy little bedroom or sit at the dinner table while, on the television, Danny McShane was paralyzing Mr. Moto with the atomic drop, and work slowly back through *Heart of Darkness,* trying to catch the words in Conrad's sentences. I certainly was not MacFarland's best student; most of the other guys in College Prep, even my fellow slackers, had better backgrounds than I did. But I worked very hard, for MacFarland had hooked me. He tapped my old interest in reading and creating stories. He gave me a way to feel special by using my mind. And he provided a role model that wasn't shaped on physical prowess alone, and something inside me that I wasn't quite aware of responded to that. Jack MacFarland established a literacy club, to borrow a phrase of Frank Smith's, and invited me—invited all of us—to join. 4

There's been a good deal of research and speculation suggesting that the acknowledgment of school performance with extrinsic rewards—smiling faces, stars, numbers, grades—diminishes the intrinsic satisfaction children experience by engaging in reading or writing or problem solving. While it's certainly true that we've created an educational system that encourages our best and brightest to become cynical grade collectors and, in general, have developed an obsession with evaluation and assessment, I must tell you that venal[8] though it may have been, I loved getting good grades from MacFarland. I now know how subjective grades can be, but then they came tucked in the back of essays like bits of scientific data, some sort of spectroscopic readout that said, objectively and publicly, that I had made something of value. I suppose I'd been mediocre for too long and 5

---

[6]*incipient:* developing; starting to appear.
[7]*ministrations:* help; service.
[8]*venal:* unprincipled.

enjoyed a public redefinition. And I suppose the workings of my mind, such as they were, had been private for too long. My linguistic play moved into the world; like the intergalactic stories I told years before on Frank's berry-splattered truck bed, these papers with their circled, red B-pluses and A-minuses linked my mind to something outside it. I carried them around like a club emblem.

One day in the December of my senior year, Mr. MacFarland asked me where I was going to go to college. I hadn't thought much about it. Many of the students I teach today spent their last year in high school with a physics text in one hand and the Stanford catalog in the other, but I wasn't even aware of what "entrance requirements" were. My folks would say that they wanted me to go to college and be a doctor, but I don't know how seriously I ever took that; it seemed a sweet thing to say, a bit of supportive family chatter, like telling a gangly[9] daughter she's graceful. The reality of higher education wasn't in my scheme of things: No one in the family had gone to college; only two of my uncles had completed high school. I figured I'd get a night job and go to the local junior college because I knew that Snyder and Company were going there to play ball. But I hadn't even prepared for that. When I finally said, "I don't know," MacFarland looked down at me—I was seated in his office—and said, "Listen, you can write." 6

My grades stank. I had A's in biology and a handful of B's in a few English and social science classes. All the rest were C's—or worse. MacFarland said I would do well in his class and laid down the law about doing well in the others. Still, the record for my first three years wouldn't have been acceptable to any four-year school. To nobody's surprise, I was turned down flat by USC and UCLA. But Jack MacFarland was on the case. He had received his bachelor's degree from Loyola University, so he made calls to old professors and talked to somebody in admissions and wrote me a strong letter. Loyola finally accepted me as a probationary student. I would be on trial for the first year, and if I did okay, I would be granted regular status. MacFarland also intervened to get me a loan, for I could never have afforded a private college without it. Four more years of religion classes and four more years of boys at one school, girls at another. But at least I was going to college. Amazing. 7

[9]*gangly:* ungracefully tall and thin.

Thinking Critically about This Reading

Rose writes, "While it's certainly true that we've created an educational system that encourages our best and brightest to become cynical grade collectors and, in general, have developed an obsession with evaluation and assessment, I must tell you that venal though it may have been, I loved getting good grades from MacFarland" (paragraph 5). Why did Rose love getting good grades from his English teacher? Why did those grades mean something different coming from MacFarland?

Questions for Study and Discussion

1. Why do you think Rose chose the title "I Just Wanna Be Average"? (Glossary: *Title*) How does it relate to the essay?
2. Describe Jack MacFarland. How does his appearance contrast with his ability as a teacher?
3. Rose's paragraphs are long and full of information, but they are very coherent. Summarize the topic of each of the seven paragraphs in separate sentences.
4. How does Rose organize paragraph 2? How does he prepare the reader for the concluding sentence: "The man [MacFarland] immersed us in language"?
5. Analyze the transitions between paragraphs 2 and 3 and between paragraphs 3 and 4. (Glossary: *Transition*) What techniques does Rose use to smoothly introduce the reader to different aspects of his relationship with MacFarland?
6. Rose introduces the reader to some of his classmates, quickly establishes their personalities, and names them in full: Jim Fitzsimmons, Skip Madison, Mike Dweetz, Steve Fusco (3). Why does he do this? How does it help him describe MacFarland?
7. Why does Rose have difficulty getting into college? How does he finally make it?

Classroom Activity Using Paragraphs

Write a unified, coherent, and adequately developed paragraph using one of the following topic sentences. Be sure to select details that clearly demonstrate or support the general statement you choose. In a classroom discussion students should compare and discuss those paragraphs developed from the same topic sentences as a way to understand the potential for variety in developing a topic sentence.

1. It was the noisiest place I had ever visited.
2. I was terribly frightened.
3. Signs of the sanitation strike were evident everywhere.
4. It was the best meal I've ever eaten.
5. Even though we lost, our team earned an "A" for effort.

Suggested Writing Assignments

1. Describe how one of your teachers has influenced your life. Write an essay about the teacher using Rose's essay as a model. Make sure that each paragraph accomplishes a specific purpose and is coherent enough to be readily summarized.
2. Write an essay about the process you went through to get into college. Did you visit different schools? Did a parent or relative pressure you to go? Had you always wanted to go to college, or did you make the decision in high school, like Rose, or after high school? Did a particular teacher help you? Make sure to develop your paragraphs fully and to include effective transitions between paragraphs.

chapter **8**

Transitions

Transitions are words and phrases that are used to signal the relationships among ideas in an essay and to join the various parts of an essay together. Writers use transitions to relate ideas within sentences, between sentences, and between paragraphs. Perhaps the most common type of transition is the so-called transitional expression. Following is a list of transitional expressions categorized according to their functions.

Transitional Expressions
Addition and, again, too, also, in addition, further, furthermore, moreover, besides
Cause and Effect therefore, consequently, thus, accordingly, as a result, hence, then, so
Comparison similarly, likewise, by comparison
Concession to be sure, granted, of course, it is true, to tell the truth, certainly, with the exception of, although this may be true, even though, naturally
Contrast but, however, in contrast, on the contrary, on the other hand, yet, nevertheless, after all, in spite of
Example for example, for instance

Place
elsewhere, here, above, below, farther on, there, beyond, nearby, opposite to, around

Restatement
that is, as I have said, in other words, in simpler terms, to put it differently, simply stated

Sequence
first, second, third, next, finally

Summary
in conclusion, to conclude, to summarize, in brief, in short

Time
afterward, later, earlier, subsequently, at the same time, simultaneously, immediately, this time, until now, before, meanwhile, shortly, soon, currently, when, lately, in the meantime, formerly

Besides transitional expressions, there are two other important ways to make transitions: by using pronoun references and by repeating key words, phrases, and ideas. This paragraph begins with the phrase "Besides transitional expressions": The phrase contains the transitional word *besides* and also repeats wording from the last sentence of the previous paragraph. Thus the reader knows that this discussion is moving toward a new but related idea. Repetition can also give a word or idea emphasis: "Foreigners look to America as a land of freedom. Freedom, however, is not something all Americans enjoy."

Pronoun references avoid monotonous repetition of nouns and phrases. Without pronouns, these two sentences are wordy and tiring to read: "Jim went to the concert, where he heard Beethoven's Ninth Symphony. Afterward, Jim bought a recording of the Ninth Symphony." A more graceful and readable passage results if two pronouns are substituted in the second sentence: "Afterward, he bought a recording of it." The second version has another advantage in that it is now more tightly related to the first sentence. The transition between the two sentences is smoother.

In the following example, notice how Rachel Carson uses transitional expressions, repetition of words and ideas, and pronoun references:

> Under primitive agricultural conditions the farmer had few insect problems. *These* arose with the intensification of agriculture—the devotion of immense acreages to a single crop. *Such a system* set the stage for explosive increases in specific insect populations. Single-crop farming does not take advantage of the principles by which nature works; *it* is agriculture as an engineer might conceive it to be. Nature has introduced great variety into the landscape, but man has displayed a passion for simplifying *it*. *Thus he* undoes the built-in checks and balances by which nature holds the species within bounds. One important natural *check* is a limit on the amount of suitable habitat for each species. *Obviously then*, an insect that lives on wheat can build up its population to much higher levels on a farm devoted to wheat than on one in which wheat is intermingled with other crops to which the insect is not adapted.
>
> *The same thing* happens in other situations. A generation or more ago, the towns of large areas of the United States lined their streets with the noble elm tree. *Now* the beauty *they* hopefully created is threatened with complete destruction as disease sweeps through the elms, carried by a beetle that would have only limited chance to build up large populations and to spread from tree to tree if the elms were only occasional trees in a richly diversified planting.
>
> –Rachel Carson

Pronoun reference (These) · *Repeated key idea* (Such a system) · *Pronoun reference* (it) · *Pronoun reference* (it) · *Transitional expression; pronoun reference* (Thus he) · *Repeated key word* (check) · *Transitional expression* (Obviously then) · *Repeated key idea* (The same thing) · *Transitional expression; pronoun reference* (Now, they)

Carson's transitions in this passage enhance its **coherence**—that quality of good writing that results when all sentences and paragraphs of an essay are effectively and naturally connected.

In the following four-paragraph sequence about a vegetarian's ordeal with her family at Thanksgiving each year, the writer uses transitions effectively to link one paragraph to another.

> The holiday that I dread the most is fast approaching. The relatives will gather to gossip and

bicker, the house will be filled with the smells of turkey, onions, giblets, and allspice, and I will be pursuing trivial conversations in the hope of avoiding any commentaries upon the state of my plate.

Reference to key idea in previous paragraph

Do not misunderstand me: I am not a scrooge. I enjoy the idea of Thanksgiving—the giving of thanks for blessings received in the past year and the opportunity to share an unhurried day with family and friends. The problem for me is that I am one of those freaky, misunderstood people who—as my family jokingly reminds me—eats "rabbit food." Because all traditional Western holidays revolve around food and more specifically around ham, turkey, lamb, or roast beef and their respective starchy accompaniments, it is no picnic for us vegetarians.

Repeated key word

The mention of the word *vegetarian* has, at various family get-togethers, caused my Great-Aunt Bertha to rant and rave for what seems like hours about those "liberal conspirators." Other relations cough or groan or simply stare, change the subject or reminisce about somebody they used to know who was "into that," and some proceed either to demand that I defend my position or try to talk me out of it. That is why I try to avoid the subject, but especially during the holidays.

Transitional time reference

Repeated key idea

In years past I have had about as many *successes as failures in steering comments about my food toward other topics.* Politics and religion are the easiest outs, guaranteed to immerse the family in a heated debate lasting until the loudest shouter has been abandoned amidst empty pie plates, wine corks, and rumpled linen napkins. I prefer, however, to use this tactic as a last resort. Holidays are supposed to be for relaxing.

–Mundy Wilson-Libby, student

On Being 17, Bright, and Unable to Read

David Raymond

When the following article appeared in the New York Times *in 1976, David Raymond was a high school student in Connecticut. In 1981, Raymond graduated from Curry College outside of Boston, one of the few colleges with learning-disability programs at the time. He and his family now live in Fairfield, Connecticut, where he works as a builder.*

In his essay, Raymond poignantly discusses the great difficulties he had with reading because of his dyslexia and the many problems he experienced in school as a result. As you read, pay attention to the simple and unassuming quality of the words he uses to convey his ideas and how that naturalness of diction contributes to the essay's informal yet sincere tone. Notice how he transitions from one paragraph to the next with repeated words, repeated key ideas, and pronoun references.

For Your Journal

One of the fundamental skills that we are supposed to learn in school is how to read. How would you rate yourself as a reader? Would you like to be able to read better? How important is reading in your everyday life?

One day a substitute teacher picked me to read aloud from the textbook. When I told her "No, thank you," she came unhinged. She thought I was acting smart, and told me so. I kept calm, and that got her madder and madder. We must have spent 10 minutes trying to solve the problem, and finally she got so red in the face I thought she'd blow up. She told me she'd see me after class. 1

Maybe someone like me was a new thing for that teacher. But she wasn't new to me. I've been through scenes like that all my life. You see, even though I'm 17 and a junior in high school, I can't read because I 2 have dyslexia.[1] I'm told I read "at a fourth-grade level," but from where I sit, that's not reading. You can't know what that means unless you've been there. It's not easy to tell how it feels when you can't read your homework assignments or the newspaper or a menu in a restaurant or even notes from your own friends.

My family began to suspect I was having problems almost from the first day I started school. My father says my early years in school were the worst years of his life. They weren't so good for me, either. As I look back on it now, I can't find the words to express how bad it really was. I wanted to die. I'd come home from school screaming, "I'm dumb. I'm dumb—I wish I were dead!" 3

I guess I couldn't read anything at all then—not even my own name—and they tell me I didn't talk as good as other kids. But what I remember about those days is that I couldn't throw a ball where it was supposed to go, I couldn't learn to swim, and I wouldn't learn to ride a bike, because no matter what anyone told me, I knew I'd fail. 4

Sometimes my teachers would try to be encouraging. When I couldn't read the words on the board they'd say, "Come on, David, you know that word." Only I didn't. And it was embarrassing. I just felt dumb. And dumb was how the kids treated me. They'd make fun of me every chance they got, asking me to spell "cat" or something like that. Even if I knew how to spell it, I wouldn't; they'd only give me another word. Anyway, it was awful, because more than anything I wanted friends. On my birthday when I blew out the candles I didn't wish I could learn to read; what I wished for was that the kids would like me. 5

With the bad reports coming from school, and with me moaning about wanting to die and how everybody hated me, my parents began looking for help. That's when the testing started. The school tested me, the child-guidance center tested me, private psychiatrists tested me. Everybody knew something was wrong—especially me. 6

It didn't help much when they stuck a fancy name onto it. I couldn't pronounce it then—I was only in second grade—and I was ashamed to talk about it. Now it rolls off my tongue, because I've been living with it for a lot of years—dyslexia. 7

All through elementary school it wasn't easy. I was always having to do things that were "different," things the other kids didn't have to do. I had to go to a child psychiatrist, for instance. 8

---

[1]*dyslexia:* a learning disorder that impairs the ability to read.

One summer my family forced me to go to a camp for children 9
with reading problems. I hated the idea, but the camp turned out pretty good, and I had a good time. I met a lot of kids who couldn't read and somehow that helped. The director of the camp said I had a higher I.Q. than 90 percent of the population. I didn't believe him.

About the worst thing I had to do in fifth and sixth grade was go 10
to a special education class in another school in our town. A bus picked me up, and I didn't like that at all. The bus also picked up emotionally disturbed kids and retarded kids. It was like going to a school for the retarded. I always worried that someone I knew would see me on that bus. It was a relief to go to the regular junior high school.

Life began to change a little for me then, because I began to feel 11
better about myself. I found the teachers cared; they had meetings about me and I worked harder for them for a while. I began to work on the potter's wheel, making vases and pots that the teachers said were pretty good. Also, I got a letter for being on the track team. I could always run pretty fast.

At high school the teachers are good and everyone is trying to help 12
me. I've gotten honors some marking periods and I've won a letter on the cross-country team. Next quarter I think the school might hold a show of my pottery. I've got some friends. But there are still some embarrassing times. For instance, every time there is writing in the class, I get up and go to the special education room. Kids ask me where I go all the time. Sometimes I say, "to Mars."

Homework is a real problem. During free periods in school I go 13
into the special ed room and staff members read assignments to me. When I get home my mother reads to me. Sometimes she reads an assignment into a tape recorder, and then I go into my room and listen to it. If we have a novel or something like that to read, she reads it out loud to me. Then I sit down with her and we do the assignment. She'll write, while I talk my answers to her. Lately I've taken to dictating into a tape recorder, and then someone—my father, a private tutor or my mother—types up what I've dictated. Whatever homework I do takes someone else's time, too. That makes me feel bad.

We had a big meeting in school the other day—eight of us, four 14
from the guidance department, my private tutor, my parents and me. The subject was me. I said I wanted to go to college, and they told me about colleges that have facilities and staff to handle people like me. That's nice to hear.

As for what happens after college, I don't know and I'm worried about that. How can I make a living if I can't read? Who will hire me? How will I fill out the application form? The only thing that gives me any courage is the fact that I've learned about well-known people who couldn't read or had other problems and still made it. Like Albert Einstein,[2] who didn't talk until he was 4 and flunked math. Like Leonardo da Vinci,[3] who everyone seems to think had dyslexia. 15

I've told this story because maybe some teacher will read it and go easy on a kid in the classroom who has what I've got. Or, maybe some parent will stop nagging his kid, and stop calling him lazy. Maybe he's not lazy or dumb. Maybe he just can't read and doesn't know what's wrong. Maybe he's scared, like I was. 16

Thinking Critically about This Reading

Raymond writes about having to take a bus to another school in his town in order to attend special education classes: "I always worried that someone I knew would see me on that bus" (paragraph 10). Why doesn't Raymond want his classmates to know that he attends special education classes? What does he do to keep his learning disability a secret?

Questions for Study and Discussion

1. Writers often use repeated words and phrases, transitional expressions, pronouns that refer to a specific antecedent, and repeated key ideas to connect one paragraph to another. What types of transitional devices does Raymond use in his essay? Cite specific examples.
2. Raymond uses many colloquial and idiomatic expressions, such as "she came unhinged" and "she got so red in the face I thought she'd blow up" (1). (Glossary: *Colloquial Expression*) Identify other examples of such diction, and tell how they affect your reaction to the essay.
3. How would you describe Raymond's tone?

---

[2]*Albert Einstein* (1879–1955): German American physicist.

[3]*Leonardo da Vinci* (1452–1519): Italian painter, draftsman, sculptor, architect, and engineer.

4. What is dyslexia? Is it essential for an understanding of the essay that we know more about dyslexia than Raymond tells us? Explain.
5. What is Raymond's purpose? (Glossary: *Purpose*)
6. What does Raymond's story tell us about the importance of our early childhood experiences?

Classroom Activity Using Transitions

In *The New York Times Complete Manual of Home Repair,* Bernard Gladstone gives directions for applying blacktop sealer to a driveway. His directions appear below in scrambled order. First read all of Gladstone's 12 sentences carefully. Next, arrange the sentences in what seems to you to be the logical sequence. Finally, identify places where Gladstone has used transitional expressions, the repetition of words and ideas, and pronoun reference to give coherence to his paragraph.

1. A long-handled pushbroom or roofing brush is used to spread the coating evenly over the entire area.
2. Care should be taken to make certain the entire surface is uniformly wet, though puddles should be swept away if water collects in low spots.
3. Greasy areas and oil slicks should be scraped up, then scrubbed thoroughly with a detergent solution.
4. With most brands there are just three steps to follow.
5. In most cases one coat of sealer will be sufficient.
6. The application of blacktop sealer is best done on a day when the weather is dry and warm, preferably while the sun is shining on the surface.
7. This should not be applied until the first coat is completely dry.
8. First sweep the surface absolutely clean to remove all dust, dirt, and foreign material.
9. To simplify spreading and to ensure a good bond, the surface of the driveway should be wet down thoroughly by sprinkling with a hose.
10. However, for surfaces in poor condition a second coat may be required.
11. The blacktop sealer is next stirred thoroughly and poured on while the surface is still damp.

12. The sealer should be allowed to dry overnight (or longer if recommended by the manufacturer) before normal traffic is resumed.

Suggested Writing Assignments

1. After explaining his learning disability and how he plans to deal with it in college, Raymond goes on to say, "As for what happens after college, I don't know and I'm worried about that" (15). Write an essay in which you explain what worries you about life after college. Are you concerned about finding a job, paying off student loans, or moving away from friends and family, for example? Are you looking forward to living in "the real world," as so many college students call the post-graduation world? Why or why not?
2. Imagine that you and your friends have plans to go to a concert next weekend. However, you will not be able to attend because you have a research paper due the following Monday, and you haven't even chosen a topic yet. Write an e-mail in which you apologize to your friends and explain how you procrastinated. Make sure your e-mail is coherent and flows well by using transitional expressions to help readers follow what you did instead of working on your paper.
3. On July 28, 2003, the editors of *Time* magazine chose dyslexia for their cover story. How do you "read" the cover on p. 198 with the photograph of a boy with dyslexia? What do the two letters on the slate he's holding suggest? Do you think he looks worried, depressed, or hopeful? Why? Research dyslexia at the library and on the Internet. Then write an essay reporting on any important improvements in the diagnosis and treatment of dyslexia since Raymond wrote his essay.

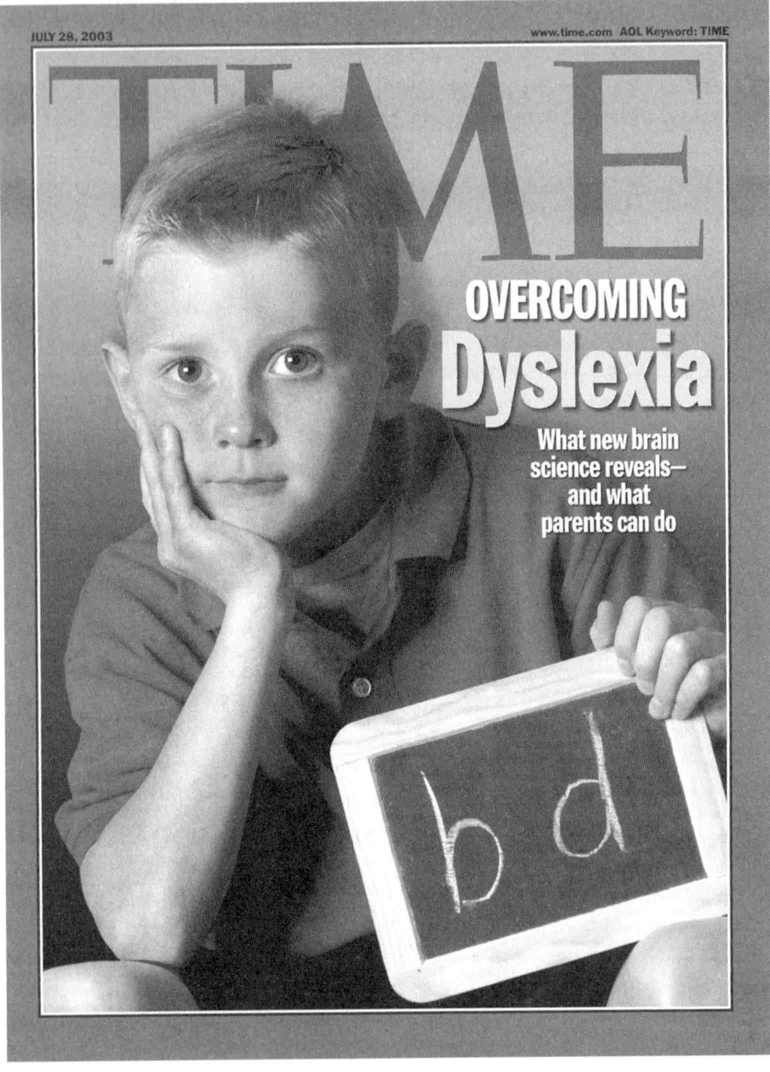
JULY 28, 2003
www.time.com AOL Keyword: TIME
TIME
OVERCOMING
Dyslexia
What new brain
science reveals—
and what
parents can do
b d

Becoming a Writer

Russell Baker

Russell Baker has had a long and distinguished career as a newspaper reporter and columnist. He was born in Morrisonville, Virginia, in 1925 and enlisted in the navy in 1943 after graduating from Johns Hopkins University. In 1947, he got his first newspaper job with the Baltimore Sun, *then moved to the* New York Times *in 1954, where he wrote the "Observer" column from 1962 to 1998. His columns have been collected in numerous books over the years. In 1979, he was awarded the Pulitzer Prize, journalism's highest award, as well as the George Polk Award for Commentary. Baker's memoir,* Growing Up *(1983) also received a Pulitzer. His autobiographical follow-up,* The Good Times, *appeared in 1989. His other works include* Russell Baker's Book of American Humor *(1993);* Inventing the Truth: The Art and Craft of Memoir, *with William Zinsser and Jill Ker Conway (revised in 1998); and* Looking Back *(2002), a collection of Baker's essays for the* New York Review of Books. *Since 1993 he has been hosting the distinguished PBS television series* Exxon-Mobil Masterpiece Theater.

The following selection is from Growing Up. *As you read Baker's account of how he discovered his abilities as a writer, note how effectively he uses repetition of key words and ideas to achieve coherence and to emphasize his emotional responses to the events he describes.*

For Your Journal

Life is full of moments that change us, for better or worse, in major and minor ways. We decide what hobbies we like and dislike, whom we want to date and perhaps eventually marry, what we want to study in school, what career we eventually pursue. Identify an event that changed your life or helped you make an important decision. How did it clarify your situation? How might your life be different if the event had never happened?

The notion of becoming a writer had flickered off and on in my head . . . but it wasn't until my third year in high school that the possibility took hold. Until then I'd been bored by everything associated with English courses. I found English grammar dull and baffling. I hated the assignments to turn out "compositions," and went at them like heavy labor, turning out laden, lackluster paragraphs that were agonies for teachers to read and for me to write. The classics thrust on me to read seemed as deadening as chloroform.[1] 1

When our class was assigned to Mr. Fleagle for third-year English I anticipated another grim year in that dreariest of subjects. Mr. Fleagle was notorious among City students for dullness and inability to inspire. He was said to be stuffy, dull, and hopelessly out of date. To me he looked to be sixty or seventy and prim to a fault. He wore primly severe eyeglasses, his wavy hair was primly cut and primly combed. He wore prim vested suits with neckties blocked primly against the collar buttons of his primly starched white shirts. He had a primly pointed jaw, a primly straight nose, and a prim manner of speaking that was so correct, so gentlemanly, that he seemed a comic antique. 2

I anticipated a listless, unfruitful year with Mr. Fleagle and for a long time was not disappointed. We read *Macbeth*. Mr. Fleagle loved *Macbeth* and wanted us to love it too, but he lacked the gift of infecting others with his own passion. He tried to convey the murderous ferocity of Lady Macbeth one day by reading aloud the passage that concludes 3

> . . . I have given suck, and know
> How tender 'tis to love the babe that milks me.
> I would, while it was smiling in my face,
> Have plucked my nipple from his boneless gums . . .

The idea of prim Mr. Fleagle plucking his nipple from boneless gums was too much for the class. We burst into gasps of irrepressible[2] snickering. Mr. Fleagle stopped.

"There is nothing funny, boys, about giving suck to a babe. It is the—the very essence of motherhood, don't you see." 4

He constantly sprinkled his sentences with "don't you see." It wasn't a question but an exclamation of mild surprise at our ignorance. "Your pronoun needs an antecedent, don't you see," he would say, 5

[1]*chloroform:* a chemical that puts one to sleep.
[2]*irrepressible:* unable to be restrained or controlled.

very primly. "The purpose of the Porter's scene, boys, is to provide comic relief from the horror, don't you see."

Late in the year we tackled the informal essay. "The essay, don't you see, is the . . ." My mind went numb. Of all forms of writing, none seemed so boring as the essay. Naturally we would have to write informal essays. Mr. Fleagle distributed a homework sheet offering us a choice of topics. None was quite so simpleminded as "What I Did on My Summer Vacation," but most seemed to be almost as dull. I took the list home and dawdled until the night before the essay was due. Sprawled on the sofa, I finally faced up to the grim task, took the list out of my notebook, and scanned it. The topic on which my eye stopped was "The Art of Eating Spaghetti." 6

This title produced an extraordinary sequence of mental images. Surging up from the depths of memory came a vivid recollection of a night in Belleville when all of us were seated around the supper table—Uncle Allen, my mother, Uncle Charlie, Doris, Uncle Hal—and Aunt Pat served spaghetti for supper. Spaghetti was an exotic treat in those days. Neither Doris nor I had ever eaten spaghetti, and none of the adults had enough experience to be good at it. All the good humor of Uncle Allen's house reawoke in my mind as I recalled the laughing arguments we had that night about the socially respectable method for moving spaghetti from plate to mouth. 7

Suddenly I wanted to write about that, about the warmth and good feeling of it, but I wanted to put it down simply for my own joy, not for Mr. Fleagle. It was a moment I wanted to recapture and hold for myself. I wanted to relive the pleasure of an evening at New Street. To write it as I wanted, however, would violate all the rules of formal composition I'd learned in school, and Mr. Fleagle would surely give it a failing grade. Never mind. I would write something else for Mr. Fleagle after I had written this thing for myself. 8

When I finished it the night was half gone and there was no time left to compose a proper, respectable essay for Mr. Fleagle. There was no choice next morning but to turn in my private reminiscence of Belleville. Two days passed before Mr. Fleagle returned the graded papers, and he returned everyone's but mine. I was bracing myself for a command to report to Mr. Fleagle immediately after school for discipline when I saw him lift my paper from his desk and rap for the class's attention. 9

"Now, boys," he said, "I want to read you an essay. This is titled 'The Art of Eating Spaghetti.' " 10

And he started to read. My words! He was reading *my words* out loud to the entire class. What's more, the entire class was listening. Listening attentively. Then somebody laughed, then the entire class was laughing, and not in contempt and ridicule, but with open-hearted enjoyment. Even Mr. Fleagle stopped two or three times to repress a small prim smile. 11

I did my best to avoid showing pleasure, but what I was feeling was pure ecstasy at this startling demonstration that my words had the power to make people laugh. In the eleventh grade, at the eleventh hour as it were, I had discovered a calling. It was the happiest moment of my entire school career. When Mr. Fleagle finished he put the final seal on my happiness by saying, "Now that, boys, is an essay, don't you see. It's—don't you see—it's of the very essence of the essay, don't you see. Congratulations, Mr. Baker." 12

For the first time, light shone on a possibility. It wasn't a very heartening possibility, to be sure. Writing couldn't lead to a job after high school, and it was hardly honest work, but Mr. Fleagle had opened a door for me. After that I ranked Mr. Fleagle among the finest teachers in the school. 13

Thinking Critically about This Reading

In paragraph 11 Baker states, "And he started to read. My words! He was reading *my words* out loud to the entire class. What's more, the entire class was listening. Listening attentively." Why was this episode so key to Baker's decision to become a writer? Why did it lead him to rank "Mr. Fleagle among the finest teachers in the school" (13)?

Questions for Study and Discussion

1. Baker makes good use of transitional expressions, repetition of words and ideas, and pronoun references in paragraphs 1 and 2. Carefully reread the paragraphs, and identify where he employs these techniques, using the analysis of Carson's essay in the introduction to this chapter as a model.
2. Examine the transitions Baker uses between paragraphs from paragraph 4 to the end of the essay. Explain how these transitions work to make the paragraphs flow smoothly from one to another.

3. How does Baker describe his English teacher, Mr. Fleagle, in the second paragraph? (Glossary: *Description*) Why does he repeat the word *prim* throughout the paragraph? Why is the vivid description important to the essay as a whole? (Glossary: *Dominant Impression*)
4. Baker gives Mr. Fleagle an identifiable voice. What is ironic about what Mr. Fleagle says? (Glossary: *Irony*) In what way does this irony contribute to Baker's purpose? (Glossary: *Purpose*)
5. What does Baker write about in his informal essay for Mr. Fleagle? Why does he write about this subject? Why doesn't he want to turn the essay in?
6. What door does Mr. Fleagle open for Baker? Why is Baker reluctant to pursue the opportunity?

Classroom Activity Using Transitions

Read the following three paragraphs. Provide transitions between paragraphs so that the narrative flows smoothly.

> In the late 1950s, I got lost on a camping trip in the Canadian wilderness. My only thought was to head south, towards warmth and civilization. My perilous journey was exhausting—the cold sapped my strength, and there were few places to find shelter and rest.
>
> There I found friendly faces and a warm fire. As I built my strength, I tried to communicate with the villagers, but they did not understand me. I came to the conclusion that I could stay in the village and wait—perhaps forever—for help to come, or I could strike out on my own again.
>
> I heard a gurgling sound. It was running water. Running water! Spring was here at last. Perhaps I would survive after all. I picked up my pack, squared my shoulders, and marched, the afternoon sun a beautiful sight, still ahead, but starting to drift to my right.

Suggested Writing Assignments

1. Using as a model Baker's effort to write about eating spaghetti, write something from your own experience that you would like to record for yourself, not necessarily for the teacher. Don't worry about writing a formal essay; simply use language with which

you are comfortable to convey why the event or experience is important to you.

2. Write an essay in which you describe how your perception of someone important in your life changed. How did you feel about the person at first? How do you feel now? What brought about the change? What impact did the transition have on you? Make sure your essay is coherent and flows well—use transitional expressions to help the reader follow the story of *your* transition.

Why History?

■ David McCullough

Pulitzer Prize–winning historian David McCullough was born in Pittsburgh, Pennsylvania, in 1933 and graduated from Yale University. He has enjoyed a full and varied career as a writer, teacher, and lecturer. He has taught at Cornell University, Dartmouth College, and Wesleyan University and has spoken as part of the White House Presidential Lecture Series. Critics call McCullough "a master of the art of narrative history," and his many books show that he is deserving of the acclaim. His presidential biographies Truman *(1992) and* John Adams *(2001) each earned him a Pulitzer Prize. He is a familiar presence on public television, hosting the popular* Smithsonian World *and* The American Experience *and narrating documentaries like* The Civil War. *In 2005, McCullough published* 1976, *the story of the turbulent beginning of the American Revolution. He writes of this period in our nation's history with the insight and gripping narrative that readers have come to expect from him.*

The following essay, based on McCullough's 1995 acceptance speech for the National Book Foundation Medal for Distinguished Contribution to American Letters, first appeared in the December 2002 issue of Reader's Digest. *In his title McCullough asks the question that becomes the focus of the essay.*

For Your Journal

What are your experiences with American history? Describe any courses you have taken on the subject, field trips to historic sites you have gone on, or movies based on historical events you have viewed. Based on your experience, do you think it is important for Americans to know about American history? Why or why not?

On a winter morning on the campus of one of our finest colleges, in a lovely Ivy League setting with snow falling outside, I sat with a seminar of 25 students, all seniors majoring in history, all honors students—supposedly the best of the best. "How many of you know 1 who George Marshall[1] was?" I asked. No one knew. Not one. At a large university in the Midwest, a young undergraduate told me how glad she was to have attended my lecture, because until then, she said, she never realized that the original 13 Colonies were all on the Eastern Seaboard. This was said, in all seriousness, by a university student.

Who are we, we Americans? How did we get where we are? What is our story and what can it teach us? Our story is our history, and if ever we should be taking steps to see that we have the best prepared, most aware citizens ever, that time is now. 2

Yet the truth is that we are raising a generation that is to an alarming degree historically illiterate. The problem has been coming on for a long time, like a disease, eating away at the national memory. While the popular culture races loudly on, the American past is slipping away. We are losing our story, forgetting who we are and what it's taken to come this far. 3

Warnings of this development have been sounded again and again. In 1995, the Department of Education reported that more than half of all high school seniors hadn't even the most basic understanding of American history. 4

Two years ago, a study by the American Council of Trustees and Alumni showed that four out of five seniors from leading colleges and universities were unable to pass a basic high school history test. To the question "Who was the American general at Yorktown?" more of these students answered Ulysses S. Grant than George Washington. 5

And there's been no improvement. This year the American Council of Trustees and Alumni reported that none of the nation's top 50 colleges and universities now require American history as part of the curriculum. In fact, one can go forth into the world today as the proud product of all but a handful of our 50 top institutions of higher learning without ever having taken a single course in history of any kind. 6

But why bother about history anyway? "That's history"—that's done with, junk for the trash heap. Why history? Because it shows us how to behave. History teaches and reinforces what we believe in, what we stand for, and what we ought to be willing to stand up for. History is about life—human nature and the human condition and all its trials and failings and noblest achievements. History is about cause and effect, 7

[1]*George Marshall* (1880–1959): American general, statesman, and Nobel Peace Prize winner who developed the Marshall Plan to rebuild Europe after World War II (1939–1945).

about the simplest of everyday things—and the mysteries of chance and genius.

History shows us what choices there are. History teaches with specific examples the evils of injustice, ignorance or demagoguery,[2] just as it shows how potent is plain courage, or one simple illuminating idea. History is—or should be—the bedrock of patriotism, not the chest-pounding kind of patriotism but the real thing, love of country. 8

At their core, the lessons of history are lessons of appreciation. Everything we have, all our great institutions, our laws, our music, art and poetry, our freedoms, everything is because somebody went before us and did the hard work, provided the creative energy, faced the storms, made the sacrifices, kept the faith. 9

Indifference to history isn't just ignorant; it's a form of ingratitude. And the scale of our ignorance seems especially shameful in the face of our unprecedented good fortune. What's so worrisome about the college student who doesn't know that George Washington was the commanding American general at Yorktown is that he also, therefore, has no idea that it was Washington who commanded the Continental Army through eight long years in the struggle for independence. I'm convinced that history encourages, as nothing else does, a sense of proportion about life, gives us a sense of how brief is our time on earth and thus how valuable that time is. 10

We live in an era of momentous change, creating great pressures and tensions. But history shows that times of tumult[3] are the times when we are most likely to learn. This nation was founded on change. We should embrace the possibilities inherent in such times and hold to a steady course, because we have a sense of navigation, a sense of what we've been through and who we are. 11

In the aftermath of September 11, 2001, history can be a source of strength and of renewed commitment to the ideals upon which the nation was founded. As unsettling as events may be, others before us have known worse. Think of what our predecessors endured and accomplished. Think of the dangerous times they knew! Churchill, in the darkest hours of World War II, reminded us that "we have not journeyed all this way because we are made of sugar candy." 12

[2]*demagoguery:* the practice of appealing to the crowd's emotions and prejudices.
[3]*tumult:* a commotion, disturbance, or uprising.

I passionately believe that history isn't just good for you in a civic way. History, really, is an extension of life. It enlarges and intensifies the experience of being alive, like poetry and art or music. And there's no great secret to making history come alive. Historian Barbara Tuchman said it perfectly in two words, "Tell stories." Part of what that means is that history is ours to enjoy. If we deny our children that enjoyment, that adventure in the larger time among the greater part of the human experience, then we're cheating them out of a full life. 13

Thinking Critically about This Reading

Why does McCullough believe that "in the aftermath of September 11, 2001, history can be a source of strength and of renewed commitment to the ideals upon which the nation was founded" (paragraph 12)? According to the writer, what do "times of tumult" (11) do to a nation?

Questions for Study and Discussion

1. What is McCullough's attitude toward American history? (Glossary: *Attitude*) What in his diction reveals this attitude to you? (Glossary: *Diction*)
2. Identify the strategies that McCullough uses to transition between paragraphs 2 and 3, 3 and 4, 4 and 5, and 6 and 7. How does each transitional strategy work? Explain.
3. McCullough starts paragraphs 2 and 7 with a series of questions. (Glossary: *Rhetorical Question*) How do these questions function in the context of his essay?
4. What does McCullough mean when he says that "the lessons of history are lessons of appreciation" (9)? Do you agree when he goes on to argue that "indifference to history isn't just ignorant; it's a form of ingratitude" (10)? Why or why not?
5. How does McCullough answer the question in his title? How would you answer the same question?

Classroom Activity Using Transitions

The following sentences, which make up the first paragraph of E. B. White's essay "Once More to the Lake," have been rearranged.

Place the sentences in what seems to you to be a coherent sequence by relying on language signals like transitions, repeated words, pronouns, and temporal references. Be prepared to explain your reasons for the placement of each sentence.

1. I have since become a salt-water man, but sometimes in summer there are days when the restlessness of the tides and the fearful cold of the sea water and the incessant wind which blows across the afternoon and into the evening make me wish for the placidity of a lake in the woods.
2. We all got ringworm from some kittens and had to rub Pond's Extract on our arms and legs night and morning, and my father rolled over in a canoe with all his clothes on; but outside of that the vacation was a success and from then on none of us ever thought there was any place in the world like that lake in Maine.
3. A few weeks ago this feeling got so strong I bought myself a couple of bass hooks and a spinner and returned to the lake where we used to go for a week's fishing and to revisit old haunts.
4. One summer, along about 1904, my father rented a camp on a lake in Maine and took us all there for the month of August.
5. We returned there summer after summer—always on August 1st for one month.

Suggested Writing Assignments

1. In paragraph 13 McCullough states, "History, really, is an extension of life. It enlarges and intensifies the experience of being alive, like poetry and art or music." On a personal level, how could knowledge of your own history be considered "an extension of life"? Using the McCullough quotation as a starting point, write an essay in which you explore both your family's story and why knowledge of your family's history impacts decisions you make in the present.
2. McCullough is not alone among historians in believing that "our story is our history" (2). Do you think our society values its history and encourages young people to study it? Write an essay in which you argue for or against the proposition that a year-long course in American history should be required of all high school students. (Glossary: *Argumentation*) What would be the potential benefits of such a requirement? The potential detriments?

chapter **9**

Effective Sentences

Each of the following paragraphs describes the city of Vancouver. Although the content of both paragraphs is essentially the same, the first paragraph is written in sentences of nearly the same length and pattern, and the second paragraph in sentences of varying length and pattern.

Unvaried Sentences

Water surrounds Vancouver on three sides. The snow-crowned Coast Mountains ring the city on the northeast. Vancouver has a floating quality of natural loveliness. There is a curved beach at English Bay. This beach is in the shape of a half moon. Residential high rises stand behind the beach. They are in pale tones of beige, blue, and ice-cream pink. Turn-of-the-century houses of painted wood frown upward at the glitter of office towers. Any urban glare is softened by folds of green lawns, flowers, fountains, and trees. Such landscaping appears to be unplanned. It links Vancouver to her ultimate treasure of greenness. That treasure is thousand-acre Stanley Park. Surrounding stretches of water dominate. They have image-evoking names like False Creek and Lost Lagoon. Sailboats and pleasure craft skim blithely across Burrard Inlet. Foreign freighters are out in English Bay. They await their turn to take on cargoes of grain.

Varied Sentences

Surrounded by water on three sides and ringed to the northeast by the snow-crowned Coast Mountains, Vancouver has a floating quality of natural loveliness. At English Bay, the half-moon curve of beach is backed by high rises in pale tones of beige, blue, and ice-cream pink. Turn-of-the-century houses of painted wood frown upward at the glitter of office towers. Yet any urban glare is quickly softened by folds of green lawns, flowers, fountains, and trees that

> in a seemingly unplanned fashion link Vancouver to her ultimate treasure of greenness—thousand-acre Stanley Park. And always it is the surrounding stretches of water that dominate, with their image-evoking names like False Creek and Lost Lagoon. Sailboats and pleasure craft skim blithely across Burrard Inlet, while out in English Bay foreign freighters await their turn to take on cargoes of grain.

The difference between these two paragraphs is dramatic. The first is monotonous because of the sameness of the sentences and because the ideas are not related to one another in a meaningful way. The second paragraph is much more interesting and readable; its sentences vary in length and are structured to clarify the relationships among the ideas. Sentence variety, an important aspect of all good writing, should not be used for its own sake, but rather to express ideas precisely and to emphasize the most important ideas within each sentence. Sentence variety includes the use of subordination, periodic and loose sentences, dramatically short sentences, active and passive voice, coordination, and parallelism.

SENTENCE VARIETY

Subordination

Subordination, the process of giving one idea less emphasis than another in a sentence, is one of the most important characteristics of an effective sentence and a mature prose style. Writers subordinate ideas by introducing them either with subordinating conjunctions (*because, if, as though, while, when, after, in order that*) or with relative pronouns (*that, which, who, whomever, what*). Subordination not only deemphasizes some ideas, but also highlights others that the writer feels are more important.

Of course, there is nothing about an idea—*any* idea—that automatically makes it primary or secondary in importance. The writer decides what to emphasize, and he or she may choose to emphasize the less profound or noteworthy of two ideas. Consider, for example, the following sentence: "Melissa was reading a detective story while the national election results were televised." Everyone, including the author of the sentence, knows that the national election is a more noteworthy event than Melissa's reading the detective story. But the sentence concerns Melissa, not the election, and so the fact that she was reading is stated in the main clause, while the election news is subordinated in a dependent clause.

Generally, writers place the ideas they consider important in main clauses, and other ideas go into dependent clauses. For example:

> When she was thirty years old, she made her first solo flight across the Atlantic.

> When she made her first solo flight across the Atlantic, she was thirty years old.

The first sentence emphasizes the solo flight; in the second, the emphasis is on the pilot's age.

Periodic and Loose Sentences

Another way to achieve emphasis is to place the most important words, phrases, and clauses at the beginning or end of a sentence. The ending is the most emphatic part of a sentence; the beginning is less emphatic; and the middle is the least emphatic of all. The two sentences about the pilot put the main clause at the end, achieving special emphasis. The same thing occurs in a much longer kind of sentence, called a *periodic sentence,* in which the main idea is placed at the end, closest to the period. Here is an example:

> On the afternoon of the first day of spring, when the gutters were still heaped high with Monday's snow but the sky itself had been swept clean, we put on our galoshes and walked up the sunny side of Fifth Avenue to Central Park.
>
> –John Updike

By holding the main clause back, Updike keeps his readers in suspense and so puts the most emphasis possible on his main idea.

A *loose sentence,* on the other hand, states its main idea at the beginning and then adds details in subsequent phrases and clauses. Rewritten as a loose sentence, Updike's sentence might read like this:

> We put on our galoshes and walked up the sunny side of Fifth Avenue to Central Park on the afternoon of the first day of spring, when the gutters were still heaped high with Monday's snow but the sky itself had been swept clean.

The main idea still gets plenty of emphasis, since it is contained in a main clause at the beginning of the sentence. A loose sentence resembles the way people talk: It flows naturally and is easy to understand.

Dramatically Short Sentences

Another way to create emphasis is to use a *dramatically short sentence*. Especially following a long and involved sentence, a short declarative sentence helps drive a point home. Here are two examples:

> The qualities that Barbie promotes (slimness, youth, and beauty) allow no tolerance of gray hair, wrinkles, sloping posture, or failing eyesight and hearing. Barbie's perfect body is eternal.
>
> –Danielle Kuykendall, student

> The executive suite on the thirty-fifth floor of the Columbia Broadcasting System skyscraper in Manhattan is a tasteful blend of dark wood paneling, expensive abstract paintings, thick carpets, and pleasing colors. It has the quiet look of power.
>
> –David Wise

Active and Passive Voice

Finally, since the subject of a sentence is automatically emphasized, writers may choose to use the *active voice* when they want to emphasize the doer of an action and the *passive voice* when they want to downplay or omit the doer completely. Here are two examples:

> High winds pushed our sailboat onto the rocks, where the force of the waves tore it to pieces.
>
> Our sailboat was pushed by high winds onto the rocks, where it was torn to pieces by the force of the waves.
>
> –Liz Coughlan, student

The first sentence emphasizes the natural forces that destroyed the boat, while the second sentence focuses attention on the boat itself. The passive voice may be useful in placing emphasis, but it has important disadvantages. As the examples show, and as the terms suggest, active-voice verbs are more vigorous and vivid than the same verbs in the passive voice. Then, too, some writers use the passive voice to hide or evade responsibility. "It has been decided" conceals who did the deciding, whereas "I have decided" makes all clear. So the passive voice should be used only when necessary—as it is in this sentence.

SENTENCE EMPHASIS

Coordination

Often a writer wants to place equal emphasis on several facts or ideas. One way to do this is to give each its own sentence. For example, consider these three sentences about golfer Nancy Lopez.

> Nancy Lopez selected her club. She lined up her shot. She chipped the ball to within a foot of the pin.

But a long series of short, simple sentences quickly becomes tedious. Many writers would combine these three sentences by using **coordination.** The coordinating conjunctions *and, but, or, nor, for, so,* and *yet* connect words, phrases, and clauses of equal importance:

> Nancy Lopez selected her club, lined up her shot, *and* chipped the ball to within a foot of the pin.
>
> –Will Briggs, student

By coordinating three sentences into one, the writer not only makes the same words easier to read, but also shows that Lopez's three actions are equally important parts of a single process.

Parallelism

When parts of a sentence are not only coordinated but also grammatically the same, they are parallel. **Parallelism** in a sentence is created by balancing a word with a word, a phrase with a phrase, or a clause with a clause. Here is a humorous example from the beginning of Mark Twain's *Adventures of Huckleberry Finn:*

> Persons attempting to find a motive in this narrative will be prosecuted; persons attempting to find a moral in it will be banished; persons attempting to find a plot in it will be shot.
>
> –Mark Twain

Parallelism is also often found in speeches. For example, in the last sentence of the Gettysburg Address, Lincoln proclaims his hope that "government of the people, by the people, for the people, shall not perish from the earth."

From *An American Childhood*

Annie Dillard

Annie Dillard was born in 1945 in Pennsylvania and attended Hollins College in Virginia. Although she is known primarily as an essayist for such works as Pilgrim at Tinker Creek *(1974), which won a Pulitzer Prize,* Teaching a Stone to Talk *(1982), and* For the Time Being *(2000), she has demonstrated an impressive versatility in her publications:* Tickets for a Prayer Wheel *(1974) and* Mornings Like This: Found Poems *(1995), poetry;* Holy the Firm *(1977), a prose narrative;* Living by Fiction *(1982), literary theory;* An American Childhood *(1987), autobiography; and* The Living *(1992), a novel. In* The Writing Life *(1989), Dillard explores the processes of writing itself. She is currently Adjunct Professor of English and Writer in Residence at Wesleyan University.*

As you read the following selection, taken from An American Childhood, *pay particular attention to the way Dillard's active verbs give her sentences strength and emphasis. A good example of parallel sentence structure is in paragraph 5.*

For Your Journal

What was your favorite possession in your preteen years? How did you get it? Why was it special to you?

After I read *The Field Book of Ponds and Streams* several times, I longed for a microscope. Everybody needed a microscope. Detectives used microscopes, both for the FBI and at Scotland Yard. Although usually I had to save my tiny allowance for things I wanted, that year for Christmas my parents gave me a microscope kit. 1

In a dark basement corner, on a white enamel table, I set up the microscope kit. I supplied a chair, a lamp, a batch of jars, a candle, and a pile of library books. The microscope kit supplied a blunt black three-speed microscope, a booklet, a scalpel, a dropper, an ingenious device for cutting thin segments of fragile tissue, a pile of clean slides and cover slips, and a dandy array of corked test tubes. 2

One of the test tubes contained "hay infusion." Hay infusion was a wee brown chip of grass blade. You added water to it, and after a 3 week it became a jungle in a drop, full of one-celled animals. This did not work for me. All I saw in the microscope after a week was a wet chip of dried grass, much enlarged.

Another test tube contained "diatomaceous earth." This was, I believed, an actual pinch of the white cliffs of Dover.[1] On my palm it was an airy, friable[2] chalk. The booklet said it was composed of the siliceous[3] bodies of diatoms—one-celled creatures that lived in, as it were, small glass jewelry boxes with fitted lids. Diatoms, I read, come in a variety of transparent geometrical shapes. Broken and dead and dug out of geological deposits, they made chalk, and a fine abrasive used in silver polish and toothpaste. What I saw in the microscope must have been the fine abrasive—grit enlarged. It was years before I saw a recognizable, whole diatom. The kit's diatomaceous earth was a bust. 4

All that winter I played with the microscope. I prepared slides from things at hand, as the books suggested. I looked at the transparent membrane inside an onion's skin and saw the cell. I looked at a section of cork and saw the cells, and at scrapings from the inside of my cheek, ditto. I looked at my blood and saw not much; I looked at my urine and saw a long iridescent crystal, for the drop had dried. 5

All this was very well, but I wanted to see the wildlife I had read about. I wanted especially to see the famous amoeba, who had eluded me. He was supposed to live in the hay infusion, but I hadn't found him there. He lived outside in warm ponds and streams, too, but I lived in Pittsburgh, and it had been a cold winter. 6

Finally late that spring I saw an amoeba. The week before, I had gathered puddle water from Frick Park; it had been festering in a jar in the basement. This June night after dinner I figured I had waited long enough. In the basement at my microscope table I spread a scummy drop of Frick Park puddle water on a slide, peeked in, and lo, there was the famous amoeba. He was as blobby and grainy as his picture; I would have known him anywhere. 7

Before I had watched him at all, I ran upstairs. My parents were still at the table, drinking coffee. They, too, could see the famous amoeba. I told them, bursting, that he was all set up, that they should hurry before his water dried. It was the chance of a lifetime. 8

---

[1]*Dover:* harbor city on the southeast coast of England, known for its fabled White Cliffs.
[2]*friable:* easily crumbled.
[3]*siliceous:* composed of silica, a crystalline compound.

Father had stretched out his long legs and was tilting back in his chair. Mother sat with her knees crossed, in blue slacks, smoking a Chesterfield. The dessert dishes were still on the table. My sisters were nowhere in evidence. It was a warm evening; the big dining-room windows gave onto blooming rhododendrons. 9

Mother regarded me warmly. She gave me to understand that she was glad I had found what I had been looking for, but that she and Father were happy to sit with their coffee, and would not be coming down. 10

She did not say, but I understood at once, that they had their pursuits (coffee?) and I had mine. She did not say, but I began to understand then, that you do what you do out of your private passion for the thing itself. 11

I had essentially been handed my own life. In subsequent years my parents would praise my drawings and poems, and supply me with books, art supplies, and sports equipment, and listen to my troubles and enthusiasms, and supervise my hours, and discuss and inform, but they would not get involved with my detective work, nor hear about my reading, nor inquire about my homework or term papers or exams, nor visit the salamanders I caught, nor listen to me play the piano, nor attend my field hockey games, nor fuss over my insect collection with me, or my poetry collection or stamp collection or rock collection. My days and nights were my own to plan and fill. 12

When I left the dining room that evening and started down the dark basement stairs, I had a life. I sat down to my wonderful amoeba, and there he was, rolling his grains more slowly now, extending an arc of his edge for a foot and drawing himself along by that foot, and absorbing it again and rolling on. I gave him some more pond water. 13

I had hit pay dirt. For all I knew, there were paramecia, too, in that pond water, or daphniae, or stentors, or any of the many other creatures I had read about and never seen: volvox, the spherical algal colony; euglena with its one red eye; the elusive, glassy diatom; hydra, rotifers, water bears, worms. Anything was possible. The sky was the limit. 14

Thinking Critically about This Reading

How does Dillard come to the realization that "you do what you do out of your private passion for the thing itself" (paragraph 11)? Why do Dillard's parents not involve themselves in their daughter's activities and interests?

Questions for Study and Discussion

1. In her second sentence, Dillard states, "Everybody needed a microscope." This confident yet naive statement indicates that she is writing from the point of view of herself as a child. (Glossary: *Point of View*) Why does she write from this point of view?
2. Analyze the sentences in the first four paragraphs. How would you describe Dillard's use of sentence variety? Identify her very short sentences—those with eight or fewer words. What does each contribute to the essay?
3. Why does the microscope appeal to Dillard? How does she react to her early disappointments?
4. Is Dillard's diction appropriate for the essay's content and point of view? (Glossary: *Diction; Point of View*) Defend your answer with specific examples from the essay.
5. Reread paragraph 12, noting Dillard's sentence constructions. In what way does their construction reinforce Dillard's content? Explain.
6. Three of the four sentences in Dillard's concluding paragraph are five words or less. What impact do these short sentences have on readers? Explain.

Classroom Activity Using Effective Sentences

Rewrite the following paragraph, presenting the information in any order you choose. Use sentence variety and subordination, as discussed in the chapter introduction, to make the paragraph more interesting to read.

> When Billy saw the crime, he was in a grocery store buying hot dog buns for the barbecue he had scheduled for the next weekend. The crime was a burglary, and the criminal was someone you would never expect to see commit a crime. His basketball shoes squeaked as he ran away, and he looked no more than fifteen years old with a fresh, eager face that was the picture of innocence. Billy watched the youth steal a purse right off a woman's shoulder, and

the bright sun reflected off the thief's forehead as he ran away, although the weather was quite chilly and had been for a week. The police officer who caught the thief tripped him and handcuffed him as Billy paid for the hot dog buns, got in his car, and drove away.

Suggested Writing Assignments

1. Dillard learned an important life lesson from her parents' reaction to her news of the amoeba. How would you describe that lesson? Use your description as the basis for a brief essay in which you discuss the role of parents in fostering children's creativity and desire for knowledge. (Glossary: *Description*) Pay close attention to your sentences, and use them to emphasize the most important parts of your discussion.
2. Write a brief essay using one of the following sentences to focus and control the descriptive details you select. Place the sentence in the essay wherever it will have the greatest emphasis.

   The music stopped.
   It was broken glass.
   I started to sweat.
   She had convinced me.
   It was my turn to step forward.
   Now I understood.

Salvation

Langston Hughes

Born in Joplin, Missouri, Langston Hughes (1902–1967) became an important figure in the African American cultural movement of the 1920s known as the Harlem Renaissance. He wrote poetry, fiction, and plays and contributed columns to the New York Post *and an African American weekly, the* Chicago Defender. *He is best known for* The Weary Blues *(1926) and other books of poetry that express his racial pride, his familiarity with African American traditions, and his understanding of blues and jazz rhythms. In his memory, New York City designated his residence at 20 East 127th Street in Harlem as a landmark, and his street was renamed "Langston Hughes Place."*

In the following selection from his autobiography, The Big Sea *(1940), note how, for the sake of emphasis, Hughes varies the length and types of sentences he uses. The impact of the dramatically short sentence in paragraph 12, for instance, derives from the variety of sentences preceding it.*

For Your Journal

What role does religion play in your family? Do you consider yourself a religious person? Have you ever felt pressure from others to participate in religious activities? How did that make you feel?

I was saved from sin when I was going on thirteen. But not really 1
saved. It happened like this. There was a big revival at my Auntie Reed's church. Every night for weeks there had been much preaching, singing, praying, and shouting, and some very hardened sinners had been brought to Christ, and the membership of the church had grown by leaps and bounds. Then just before the revival ended, they held a special meeting for children, "to bring the young lambs to the fold." My aunt spoke of it for days ahead. That night I was escorted to the front row and placed on the mourners' bench with all the other young sinners, who had not yet been brought to Jesus.

My aunt told me that when you were saved you saw a light, and something happened to you inside! And Jesus came into your life! And God was with you from then on! She said you could see and hear and feel Jesus in your soul. I believed her. I had heard a great many old people say the same thing and it seemed to me they ought to know. So I sat there calmly in the hot, crowded church, waiting for Jesus to come to me. 2

The preacher preached a wonderful rhythmical sermon, all moans and shouts and lonely cries and dire pictures of hell, and then he sang a song about the ninety and nine safe in the fold, but one little lamb was left out in the cold. Then he said: "Won't you come? Won't you come to Jesus? Young lambs, won't you come?" And he held out his arms to all us young sinners there on the mourners' bench. And the little girls cried. And some of them jumped up and went to Jesus right away. But most of us just sat there. 3

A great many old people came and knelt around us and prayed, old women with jet-black faces and braided hair, old men with work-gnarled hands. And the church sang a song about the lower lights are burning, some poor sinners to be saved. And the whole building rocked with prayer and song. 4

Still I kept waiting to *see* Jesus. 5

Finally all the young people had gone to the altar and were saved, but one boy and me. He was a rounder's son named Westley. Westley and I were surrounded by sisters and deacons praying. It was very hot in the church, and getting late now. Finally Westley said to me in a whisper: "God damn! I'm tired o' sitting here. Let's get up and be saved." So he got up and was saved. 6

Then I was left all alone on the mourners' bench. My aunt came and knelt at my knees and cried, while prayers and songs swirled all around me in the little church. The whole congregation prayed for me alone, in a mighty wail of moans and voices. And I kept waiting serenely for Jesus, waiting, waiting—but he didn't come. I wanted to see him, but nothing happened to me. Nothing! I wanted something to happen to me, but nothing happened. 7

I heard the songs and the minister saying: "Why don't you come? My dear child, why don't you come to Jesus? Jesus is waiting for you. He wants you. Why don't you come? Sister Reed, what is this child's name?" 8

"Langston," my aunt sobbed. 9

"Langston, why don't you come? Why don't you come and be saved? Oh, Lamb of God! Why don't you come?" 10

Now it was really getting late. I began to be ashamed of myself, holding everything up so long. I began to wonder what God thought about Westley, who certainly hadn't seen Jesus either, but who was now sitting proudly on the platform, swinging his knickerbockered legs and grinning down at me, surrounded by deacons and old women on their knees praying. God had not struck Westley dead for taking his name in vain or for lying in the temple. So I decided that maybe to save further trouble, I'd better lie, too, and say that Jesus had come, and get up and be saved. 11

So I got up. 12

Suddenly the whole room broke into a sea of shouting, as they saw me rise. Waves of rejoicing swept the place. Women leaped in the air. My aunt threw her arms around me. The minister took me by the hand and led me to the platform. 13

When things quieted down, in a hushed silence, punctuated by a few ecstatic "Amens," all the new young lambs were blessed in the name of God. Then joyous singing filled the room. 14

That night, for the last time in my life but one—for I was a big boy twelve years old—I cried. I cried, in bed alone, and couldn't stop. I buried my head under the quilts, but my aunt heard me. She woke up and told my uncle I was crying because the Holy Ghost had come into my life, and because I had seen Jesus. But I was really crying because I couldn't bear to tell her that I had lied, that I had deceived everybody in the church, that I hadn't seen Jesus, and that now I didn't believe there was a Jesus any more, since he didn't come to help me. 15

Thinking Critically about This Reading

Why does Hughes cry on the night of his being "saved"? What makes the story of his being saved so ironic?

Questions for Study and Discussion

1. What is salvation? Is it important to young Hughes that he be saved? Why does he expect to be saved at the revival meeting?
2. Hughes varies the length and structure of his sentences throughout the essay. How does this variety capture and reinforce the rhythms and drama of the evening's events? Explain.

3. What would be gained or lost if the essay began with the first two sentences combined as follows: "I was saved from sin when I was going on thirteen, but I was not really saved"?
4. Identify the coordinating conjunctions in paragraph 3. (Glossary: *Coordination*) Rewrite the paragraph without them. Compare your paragraph with the original, and explain what Hughes gains by using coordinating conjunctions.
5. Identify the subordinating conjunctions in paragraph 15. (Glossary: *Subordination*) What is it about the ideas in this last paragraph that makes it necessary for Hughes to use subordinating conjunctions?
6. How does Hughes's choice of words, or diction, help to establish a realistic atmosphere for a religious revival meeting? (Glossary: *Diction*)

Classroom Activity Using Effective Sentences

Using coordination or subordination, rewrite each set of short sentences as a single sentence. Here is an example:

ORIGINAL: This snow is good for Colorado's economy. Tourists are now flocking to ski resorts.

REVISED: This snow is good for Colorado's economy because tourists are now flocking to ski resorts.

1. I can take the 6:30 express train. I can catch the 7:00 bus.
2. Miriam worked on her research paper. She interviewed five people for the paper. She worked all weekend. She was tired.
3. Juan's new job kept him busy every day. He did not have time to work out at the gym for over a month.
4. The Statue of Liberty welcomes newcomers to America. It was a gift of the French government. It was completely restored for the nation's two hundredth birthday. It is over 120 years old.
5. Carla is tall. She is strong. She is a team player. She was the starting center on the basketball team.
6. Betsy loves Bach's music. She also likes Scott Joplin.

Suggested Writing Assignments

1. Like the young Hughes, we sometimes find ourselves in situations in which, for the sake of conformity, we do things we do not believe in. Consider one such experience you have had, and write an essay about it. What is it about human nature that makes us act occasionally in ways that contradict our inner feelings? As you write, pay particular attention to your sentence variety.
2. Reread the introduction to this chapter. Then review one of the essays that you have written, paying particular attention to sentence structure. Recast sentences as necessary to make your writing more interesting and effective.

The Good Daughter

Caroline Hwang

Freelance writer and editor Caroline Hwang was born in Milwaukee, Wisconsin. After graduating from the University of Pennsylvania in 1991, she entered the world of popular magazines, holding editorial positions at Glamour, Mademoiselle, *and* Redbook. *She later earned an M.F.A. from New York University. She recently published her first novel,* In Full Bloom *(2003), and was a featured reader during the Asian American Writers' Workshop event series in New York City.*

In the following essay, which first appeared in Newsweek *in 1998, Hwang illuminates the difficulty of growing up as the daughter of Korean immigrant parents. Notice how Hwang uses sentence variety for emphasis and dramatic effect in recounting how she has been torn between her parents' dreams for her and her own dreams.*

For Your Journal

What is your cultural identity? Do you consider yourself an American, or do you identify with another culture? How comfortable do you feel with this identity? Explain why you feel as you do.

The moment I walked into the dry-cleaning store, I knew the woman behind the counter was from Korea, like my parents. To show her that we shared a heritage, and possibly get a fellow countryman's discount, I tilted my head forward, in shy imitation of a traditional bow. 1

"Name?" she asked, not noticing my attempted obeisance.[1] 2

"Hwang," I answered. 3

"Hwang? Are you Chinese?" 4

Her question caught me off-guard. I was used to hearing such queries from non-Asians who think Asians all look alike, but never from one of my own people. Of course, the only Koreans I knew were 5

[1] *obeisance:* a gesture or movement that expresses respect or deference.

my parents and their friends, people who've never asked me where I came from, since they knew better than I.

I ransacked my mind for the Korean words that would tell her who I was. It's always struck me as funny (in a mirthless sort of way) that I can more readily say "I am Korean" in Spanish, German, and even Latin than I can in the language of my ancestry. In the end, I told her in English. 6

The dry-cleaning woman squinted as though trying to see past the glare of my strangeness, repeating my surname under her breath. "Oh, *Fxuang*," she said, doubling over with laughter. "You don't know how to speak your name." 7

I flinched. Perhaps I was particularly sensitive at the time, having just dropped out of graduate school. I had torn up my map for the future, the one that said not only where I was going but who I was. My sense of identity was already disintegrating. 8

When I got home, I called my parents to ask why they had never bothered to correct me. "Big deal," my mother said, sounding more flippant than I knew she intended. (Like many people who learn English in a classroom, she uses idioms that don't always fit the occasion.) "So what if you can't pronounce your name? You are American," she said. 9

Though I didn't challenge her explanation, it left me unsatisfied. The fact is, my cultural identity is hardly that clear-cut. 10

My parents immigrated to this country 30 years ago, two years before I was born. They told me often, while I was growing up, that, if I wanted to, I could be president someday, that here my grasp would be as long as my reach. 11

To ensure that I reaped all the advantages of this country, my parents saw to it that I became fully assimilated. So, like any American of my generation, I whiled away my youth strolling malls and talking on the phone, rhapsodizing over Andrew McCarthy's blue eyes, or analyzing the meaning of a certain upperclassman's offer of a ride to the Homecoming football game. 12

To my parents, I am all American, and the sacrifices they made in leaving Korea—including my mispronounced name—pale in comparison to the opportunities those sacrifices gave me. They do not see that I straddle two cultures, nor that I feel displaced in the only country I know. I identify with Americans, but Americans do not identify with me. I've never known what it's like to belong to a community—neither one at large, nor of an extended family. I know more about Europe 13 than the continent my ancestors unmistakably come from. I sometimes wonder, as I did that day in the dry cleaner's, if I would be a happier person had my parents stayed in Korea.

I first began to consider this thought around the time I decided to go to graduate school. It had been a compromise: my parents wanted me to go to law school; I wanted to skip the starched-collar track and be a writer—the hungrier the better. But after 20-some years of following their wishes and meeting all of their expectations, I couldn't bring myself to disobey or disappoint. A writing career is riskier than law, I remember thinking. If I'm a failure and my life is a washout, then what does that make my parents' lives? 14

I know that many of my friends had to choose between pleasing their parents and being true to themselves. But for the children of immigrants, the choice seems more complicated, a happy outcome impossible. By making the biggest move of their lives for me, my parents indentured me to the largest debt imaginable—I owe them the fulfillment of their hopes for me. 15

It tore me up inside to suppress my dream, but I went to school for a Ph.D. in English literature, thinking I had found the perfect compromise. I would be able to write at least about books while pursuing a graduate degree. Predictably, it didn't work out. How could I labor for five years in a program I had no passion for? When I finally left school, my parents were disappointed, but since it wasn't what they wanted me to do, they weren't devastated. I, on the other hand, felt I was staring at the bottom of the abyss. I had seen the flaw in my life of halfwayness, in my planned life of compromises. 16

I hadn't thought about my love life, but I had a vague plan to make concessions there, too. Though they raised me as an American, my parents expect me to marry someone Korean and give them grandchildren who look like them. This didn't seem like such a huge request when I was 14, but now I don't know what I'm going to do. I've never been in love with someone I dated, or dated someone I loved. (Since I can't bring myself even to entertain the thought of marrying the non-Korean men I'm attracted to, I've been dating only those I know I can stay clearheaded about.) And as I near that age when the question of marriage stalks every relationship, I can't help but wonder if my parents' expectations are responsible for the lack of passion in my life. 17

My parents didn't want their daughter to be Korean, but they don't want her fully American, either. Children of immigrants are living paradoxes. We are the first generation and the last. We are in this country 18 for its opportunities, yet filial[2] duty binds us. When my parents boarded the plane, they knew they were embarking on a rough trip. I don't think they imagined the rocks in the path of their daughter who can't even pronounce her own name.

Thinking Critically about This Reading

What does Hwang mean when she writes, "Children of immigrants are living paradoxes. We are the first generation and the last" (paragraph 18)?

Questions for Study and Discussion

1. What is Hwang's thesis? (Glossary: *Thesis*)
2. Hwang begins by recounting an unsettling incident in a dry-cleaning store. (Glossary: *Beginnings and Endings*) How effective is her opening? What contribution does dialogue make to her telling of this story? (Glossary: *Dialogue*) Where else does she use dialogue in her essay?
3. Hwang starts paragraphs 5 and 8 with short sentences. How does each of these sentences enhance the drama between Hwang and the Korean woman at the dry cleaner's?
4. Analyze the sentences in paragraph 13. In what ways does the structure of these sentences reinforce Hwang's uncertainty about her own identity? Explain.

Classroom Activity Using Effective Sentences

Rewrite the following sets of sentences to combine short, simple sentences and to reduce repetition wherever possible. Here is an example:

ORIGINAL: Angelo's team won the championship. He pitched a two-hitter. He struck out ten batters. He hit a home run.

REVISED: Angelo's team won the championship because he pitched a two-hitter, struck out ten batters, and hit a home run.

[2] *filial:* the relationship of child to parent.

1. Bonnie wore shorts. The shorts were red. The shorts had pockets.
2. The deer hunter awoke at 5 A.M. He ate a quick breakfast. The breakfast consisted of coffee, juice, and cereal. He was in the woods before the sun came up.
3. My grandparents played golf every weekend for years. Last year they stopped playing. They miss the game now.
4. Fly over any major city. Look out the airplane's window. You will be appalled at the number of tall smokestacks you will see.
5. It did not rain for over three months. Most crops in the region failed. Some farmers were on the brink of declaring bankruptcy.
6. Every weekday I go to work. I exercise. I shower and relax. I eat a light, low-fat dinner.

Suggested Writing Assignments

1. Hwang reveals that her passion is to become a writer. In deciding to go to graduate school for a doctorate in English literature, she thought she had "found the perfect compromise"(16) between her dream to be a writer and her parents' dream for her to become a lawyer. Write an essay describing your own dream, if you have one, and explain what you will need to do to fulfill it. Does your family support you in this pursuit?
2. Choose a country that you have studied, visited, or at least read about. Compare who you are now with who you think you would be if you had been born in that country. How would you be different? Why?

38 Who Saw Murder Didn't Call Police

Martin Gansberg

Reporter Martin Gansberg (1920–1995) was born in Brooklyn, New York, and graduated from St. John's University. Gansberg was an experienced copy editor completing one of his first reporting assignments when he wrote the following essay for the New York Times *in 1964, two weeks after the events he so poignantly narrates. Once you've finished reading the essay, you will understand why it has been reprinted so often and why the name Kitty Genovese is still invoked whenever questions of public apathy arise.*

Notice how Gansberg uses dialogue effectively in this essay to emphasize his point. Pay particular attention to how he constructs the sentences that incorporate dialogue and to how subordination and coordination often determine where quoted material appears.

For Your Journal

Have you ever witnessed an accident or a crime? How did you react to the situation—did you come forward and testify, or did you choose not to get involved? Why do you think you reacted the way you did? How do you feel about your behavior?

For more than half an hour 38 respectable, law-abiding citizens in Queens[1] watched a killer stalk and stab a woman in three separate attacks in Kew Gardens. 1

Twice their chatter and the sudden glow of their bedroom lights interrupted him and frightened him off. Each time he returned, sought her out, and stabbed her again. Not one person telephoned the police during the assault; one witness called after the woman was dead. 2

That was two weeks ago today. 3

Still shocked is Assistant Chief Inspector Frederick M. Lussen, in charge of the borough's detectives and a veteran of 25 years of homicide investigations. He can give a matter-of-fact recitation on many murders. 4

[1]*Queens:* one of New York City's five boroughs.

But the Kew Gardens slaying baffles him—not because it is a murder, but because the "good people" failed to call the police.

"As we have reconstructed the crime," he said, "the assailant had 5
three chances to kill this woman during a 35-minute period. He returned twice to complete the job. If we had been called when he first attacked, the woman might not be dead now."

This is what the police say happened beginning at 3:20 A.M. in 6
the staid, middle-class, tree-lined Austin Street area:

Twenty-eight-year-old Catherine Genovese, who was called Kitty 7
by almost everyone in the neighborhood, was returning home from her job as manager of a bar in Hollis. She parked her red Fiat in a lot adjacent to the Kew Gardens Long Island Rail Road Station, facing Mowbray Place. Like many residents of the neighborhood, she had parked there day after day since her arrival from Connecticut a year ago, although the railroad frowns on the practice.

She turned off the lights of her car, locked the door, and started 8
to walk the 100 feet to the entrance of her apartment at 82-70 Austin Street, which is in a Tudor building, with stores in the first floor and apartments on the second.

The entrance to the apartment is in the rear of the building because 9
the front is rented to retail stores. At night the quiet neighborhood is shrouded in the slumbering darkness that marks most residential areas.

Miss Genovese noticed a man at the far end of the lot, near a 10
seven-story apartment house at 82-40 Austin Street. She halted. Then, nervously, she headed up Austin Street toward Lefferts Boulevard, where there is a call box to the 102nd Police Precinct in nearby Richmond Hill.

She got as far as a street light in front of a bookstore before 11
the man grabbed her. She screamed. Lights went on in the 10-story apartment house at 82-67 Austin Street, which faces the bookstore. Windows slid open and voices punctuated the early-morning stillness.

Miss Genovese screamed: "Oh, my God, he stabbed me! Please 12
help me! Please help me!"

From one of the upper windows in the apartment house, a man 13
called down: "Let that girl alone!"

The assailant looked up at him, shrugged, and walked down Austin 14
Street toward a white sedan parked a short distance away. Miss Genovese struggled to her feet.

Lights went out. The killer returned to Miss Genovese, now trying to make her way around the side of the building by the parking lot to get to her apartment. The assailant stabbed her again. 15

"I'm dying!" she shrieked. "I'm dying!" 16

Windows were opened again, and lights went on in many apartments. The assailant got into his car and drove away. Miss Genovese staggered to her feet. A city bus, O-10, the Lefferts Boulevard line to Kennedy International Airport, passed. It was 3:35 A.M. 17

The assailant returned. By then, Miss Genovese had crawled to the back of the building, where the freshly painted brown doors to the apartment house held out hope for safety. The killer tried the first door; she wasn't there. At the second door, 82-62 Austin Street, he saw her slumped on the floor at the foot of the stairs. He stabbed her a third time—fatally. 18

It was 3:50 by the time the police received their first call, from a man who was a neighbor of Miss Genovese. In two minutes they were at the scene. The neighbor, a 70-year-old woman, and another woman were the only persons on the street. Nobody else came forward. 19

The man explained that he had called the police after much deliberation. He had phoned a friend in Nassau County for advice and then he had crossed the roof of the building to the apartment of the elderly woman to get her to make the call. 20

"I didn't want to get involved," he sheepishly told the police. 21

Six days later, the police arrested Winston Moseley, a 29-year-old business-machine operator, and charged him with homicide. Moseley had no previous record. He is married, has two children and owns a home at 133-19 Sutter Avenue, South Ozone Park, Queens. On Wednesday, a court committed him to Kings County Hospital for psychiatric observation. 22

When questioned by the police, Moseley also said that he had slain Mrs. Annie May Johnson, 24, of 146-12 133d Avenue, Jamaica, on February 29 and Barbara Kralik, 15, of 174-17 140th Avenue, Springfield Gardens, last July. In the Kralik case, the police are holding Alvin L. Mitchell, who is said to have confessed to that slaying. 23

The police stressed how simple it would have been to have gotten in touch with them. "A phone call," said one of the detectives, "would have done it." The police may be reached by dialing "O" for operator or SPring 7-3100.[2] 24

---

[2]*SPring 7-3100:* a mid-twentieth century phone number that used a combination of both letters (the *SP* of *spring*) and numbers.

Today witnesses from the neighborhood, which is made up of one-family homes in the $35,000 to $60,000 range with the exception of the two apartment houses near the railroad station, find it difficult to explain why they didn't call the police. 25

A housewife, knowingly if quite casually, said, "We thought it was a lovers' quarrel." A husband and wife both said, "Frankly, we were afraid." They seemed aware of the fact that events might have been different. A distraught woman, wiping her hands in her apron, said, "I didn't want my husband to get involved." 26

One couple, now willing to talk about that night, said they heard the first screams. The husband looked thoughtfully at the bookstore where the killer first grabbed Miss Genovese. 27

"We went to the window to see what was happening," he said, "but the light from our bedroom made it difficult to see the street." The wife, still apprehensive, added: "I put out the light and we were able to see better." 28

Asked why they hadn't called the police, she shrugged and replied: "I don't know." 29

A man peeked out from a slight opening in the doorway to his apartment and rattled off an account of the killer's second attack. Why hadn't he called the police at the time? "I was tired," he said without emotion. "I went back to bed." 30

It was 4:25 A.M. when the ambulance arrived to take the body of Miss Genovese. It drove off. "Then," a solemn police detective said, "the people came out." 31

Thinking Critically about This Reading

How does Gansberg reveal his attitude about the lack of response to the attack on Kitty Genovese, even though he writes in the third-person point of view and interjects no opinions of his own?

Questions for Study and Discussion

1. What is Gansberg's purpose? (Glossary: *Purpose*) What are the advantages or disadvantages in using narration to accomplish this purpose? Explain.
2. Where does the narrative actually begin? What is the function of the material that precedes the beginning of the narrative?

3. Analyze Gansberg's sentences in paragraphs 7–9. How does he use subordination to highlight what he believes is essential information? (Glossary: *Subordination*)
4. Gansberg uses a number of two- and three-word sentences in his narrative. Identify several of these sentences, and explain how they serve to punctuate and add drama to this story. Which short sentences have the greatest impact on you? Why?
5. Gansberg uses dialogue throughout his essay. (Glossary: *Dialogue*) How many people does he quote? What does he accomplish by using dialogue?
6. How would you describe Gansberg's tone? (Glossary: *Tone*) Is it appropriate for the story he narrates? Explain.
7. Reflect on Gansberg's ending. (Glossary: *Beginnings and Endings*) What would be lost or gained by adding a paragraph that analyzes the meaning of the narrative for readers?

Classroom Activity Using Effective Sentences

Repetition can be an effective writing device to emphasize important points and to enhance coherence. Unless it is handled carefully, however, it can often result in a tedious piece of writing. Rewrite the following paragraph, either eliminating repetition or reworking the repetitions to improve coherence and to emphasize important information.

> Daycare centers should be available to all women who work and have no one to care for their children. Daycare centers should not be available only to women who are raising their children alone or to families whose income is below the poverty level. All women who work should have available to them care for their children that is reliable, responsible, convenient, and does not cost an exorbitant amount. Women who work need and must demand more daycare centers. No woman should be prevented from working because of the lack of convenient and reliable facilities for child care.

Suggested Writing Assignments

1. Gansberg's essay is about public apathy and fear. What reasons did Kitty Genovese's neighbors give for not calling the police when they first heard her calls for help? How do these reasons reflect on human nature, particularly as it manifests itself in contemporary American society? Modeling your essay after Gansberg's, narrate another event or series of events you know about that

demonstrates either public involvement or public apathy. (Glossary: *Narration*)

2. It is common when using narration to tell about firsthand experience and to tell the story in the first person. (Glossary: *Narration; Point of View*) It is good practice, however, to try writing a narrative essay on something you don't know about firsthand but must learn about, much as a newspaper reporter gathers information for a story. For several days, be attentive to events occurring around you—in your neighborhood, school, community, region—events that would be appropriate for a narrative essay. Interview the principal characters involved in your story, take detailed notes, and then write your narration.
3. Both Gansberg's essay and the following cartoon illustrate how people often choose to let someone else take care of a situation instead of taking action themselves. Reflect on the essay and the cartoon, and write an essay in which you explore the reasons some people in dangerous or life-threatening situations choose to act while so many others do not. In your opinion, when should a bystander involve him- or herself in a situation such as the attack on Kitty Genovese? How involved should a bystander become? What advice do you think Gansberg would give? Why?

part ■ three

The Language of the Essay

chapter 10

Diction and Tone

DICTION

Diction refers to a writer's choice and use of words. Good diction is precise and appropriate—the words mean exactly what the writer intends, and the words are well suited to the writer's subject, purpose, and intended audience.

For careful writers it is not enough merely to come close to saying what they want to say; they select words that convey their exact meaning. Perhaps Mark Twain put this best when he said, "The difference between the right word and the almost right word is the difference between lightning and the lightning bug." Inaccurate, imprecise, or inappropriate diction not only fails to convey the writer's intended meaning but also may cause confusion and misunderstanding for the reader.

Connotation and Denotation

Both **connotation** and **denotation** refer to the meanings of words. Denotation is the dictionary meaning of a word, the literal meaning. Connotative meanings are the associations or emotional overtones that words have acquired. For example, the word *home* denotes a place where someone lives, but it connotes warmth, security, family, comfort, affection, and other more private thoughts and images. The word *residence* also denotes a place where someone lives, but its connotations are colder and more formal.

Many words in English have synonyms, words with very similar denotations—for example, *mob, crowd, multitude,* and *bunch.* Deciding which to use depends largely on the connotations that each synonym has and the context in which the word is to be used. For example, you might say, "There was a crowd at the lecture," but not "There was a mob at the lecture." Good writers are sensitive to both the denotations and the connotations of words.

Abstract and Concrete Words

Abstract words name ideas, conditions, emotions—things nobody can touch, see, or hear. Some abstract words are *love, wisdom, cowardice, beauty, fear,* and *liberty.* People often disagree about abstract things. You may find a forest beautiful, while someone else might find it frightening, and neither of you would be wrong. Beauty and fear are abstract ideas; they exist in your mind, not in the forest along with the trees and the owls. **Concrete** words refer to things we can touch, see, hear, smell, and taste, such as *sandpaper, soda, birch tree, smog, cow, sailboat, rocking chair,* and *pancake.* If you disagree with someone on a concrete issue—say, you claim that the forest is mostly birch trees, while the other person says it is mostly pine—only one of you can be right, and both of you can be wrong; the kinds of trees that grow in the forest is a concrete fact, not an abstract idea.

Good writing balances ideas and facts, and it also balances abstract and concrete diction. If the writing is too abstract, with too few concrete facts and details, it will be unconvincing and tiresome. If the writing is too concrete, devoid of abstract ideas and emotions, it can seem mundane and dry.

General and Specific Words

General and **specific** do not necessarily refer to opposites. The same word can often be either general or specific, depending on the context: *Dessert* is more specific than *food,* but more general than *chocolate cream pie.* Being very specific is like being concrete: Chocolate cream pie is something you can see and taste. Being general, on the other hand, is like being abstract. Food, dessert, and even pie are large classes of things that bring only very general tastes or images to mind.

Good writing moves back and forth from the general to the specific. Without specific words, generalities can be unconvincing and even confusing: The writer's idea of "good food" may be very different from the reader's. But writing that does not relate specifics to each other by generalization often lacks focus and direction.

Clichés

Words, phrases, and expressions that have become trite through overuse are called **clichés.** Let's assume your roommate has just returned from an evening out. You ask her, "How was the concert?" She responds, "The concert was okay, but they had us *packed in* there *like sardines.* How was your evening?" And you reply, "Well, I finished my term paper, but the noise here is enough to *drive me crazy.* The dorm is a real *zoo.*" At one time the italicized expressions were vivid and colorful, but through constant use they have grown stale and ineffective. Experienced writers always try to avoid such clichés as *believe it or not, doomed to failure, hit the spot, let's face it, sneaking suspicion, step in the right direction*, and *went to great lengths.* They strive to use fresh language.

Jargon

Jargon, or technical language, is the special vocabulary of a trade or profession. Writers who use jargon do so with an awareness of their audience. If their audience is a group of co-workers or professionals, jargon may be used freely. If the audience is more general, jargon should be used sparingly and carefully so that readers can understand it. Jargon becomes inappropriate when it is overused, used out of context, or used pretentiously. For example, computer terms like *input, output,* and *feedback* are sometimes used in place of *contribution, result,* and *response* in other fields, especially in business. If you think about it, the terms suggest that people are machines, receiving and processing information according to a program imposed by someone else.

Formal and Informal Diction

Diction is appropriate when it suits the occasion for which it is intended. If the situation is informal—a friendly letter, for example—the writing may be colloquial; that is, its words may be chosen to suggest the way people talk with each other. If, on the other hand, the situation is formal—a term paper or a research report, for example—then the words should reflect this formality. Informal writing tends to be characterized by slang, contractions, references to the reader, and concrete nouns. Formal writing tends to be impersonal, abstract, and free of contractions and references to the reader. Formal writing and informal writing are, of course, the extremes. Most writing falls between these two extremes and is a blend of those formal and informal elements that best fit the context.

TONE

Tone is the attitude a writer takes toward the subject and the audience. The tone may be friendly or hostile, serious or humorous, intimate or distant, enthusiastic or skeptical.

As you read the following paragraphs, notice how each writer creates a different tone and how that tone is supported by the diction—the writer's particular choice and use of words.

Nostalgic

> When I was six years old, I thought I knew a lot. How to jump rope, how to skip a rock across a pond, and how to color and stay between the lines—these were all things I took great pride in. Nothing was difficult, and my days were carefree. That is, until the summer when everything became complicated and I suddenly realized I didn't know that much.
>
> –Heather C. Blue, Student

Angry

> Cans. Beer cans. Glinting on the verges of a million miles of roadways, lying in scrub, grass, dirt, leaves, sand, mud, but never hidden. Piels, Rheingold, Ballantine, Schaefer, Schlitz, shining in the sun or picked by moon or the beams of headlights at night; washed by rain or flattened by wheels, but never dulled, never buried, never destroyed. Here is the mark of savages, the testament of wasters, the stain of prosperity.
>
> –Marya Mannes

Humorous

> In perpetrating a revolution, there are two requirements: someone or something to revolt against and someone to actually show up and do the revolting. Dress is usually casual and both parties may be flexible about time and place but if either faction fails to attend the whole enterprise is likely to come off badly. In the

Chinese Revolution of 1650 neither party showed up and the deposit on the hall was forfeited.

–Woody Allen

Resigned

I make my living humping cargo for Seaboard World Airlines, one of the big international airlines at Kennedy Airport. They handle strictly all cargo. I was once told that one of the Rockefellers is the major stockholder for the airline, but I don't really think about that too much. I don't get paid to think. The big thing is to beat that race with the time clock every morning of your life so the airline will be happy. The worst thing a man could ever do is to make suggestions about building a better airline. They pay people $40,000 a year to come up with better ideas. It doesn't matter that these ideas never work; it's just that they get nervous when a guy from South Brooklyn or Ozone Park acts like he has a brain.

–Patrick Fenton

Ironic

Once upon a time there was a small, beautiful, green and graceful country called Vietnam. It needed to be saved. (In later years no one could remember exactly what it needed to be saved from, but that is another story.) For many years Vietnam was in the process of being saved by France, but the French eventually tired of their labors and left. Then America took on the job. America was well equipped for country-saving. It was the richest and most powerful nation on earth. It had, for example, nuclear explosives on hand and ready to use equal to six tons of TNT for every man, woman, and child in the world. It had huge and very efficient factories, brilliant and dedicated scientists, and most (but not everybody) would agree, it had good intentions. Sadly, America had one fatal flaw—its inhabitants were in love with technology and thought it could do no wrong. A visitor to America during the time of this story would probably have guessed its outcome after seeing how its inhabitants were treating their own country. The air was mostly foul, the water putrid, and most of the land was either covered with concrete or garbage. But Americans were never much on introspection, and they didn't foresee the result of their loving embrace on the small country. They set out to save Vietnam with the same enthusiasm and determination their forefathers had displayed in conquering the frontier.

–The Sierra Club

The diction and tone of an essay are subtle forces, but they exert a tremendous influence on readers. They are instrumental in determining how we will feel while reading the essay and what attitude we will have toward its argument or the points that it makes. Of course, readers react in a variety of ways. An essay written informally but with a largely angry tone may make one reader defensive and unsympathetic; another may feel that the author is being unusually honest and courageous and may admire these qualities and feel moved by them. Either way, the diction and tone of the piece have made a strong emotional impression. As you read the essays in this chapter and throughout this book, see if you can analyze how the diction and tone shape your reactions.

Shame

Dick Gregory

Dick Gregory, activist, comedian, and nutrition expert, was born in St. Louis, Missouri, in 1932. While attending Southern Illinois University on an athletic scholarship Gregory excelled in track, winning the university's Outstanding Athlete Award in 1953. In 1954 he was drafted into the army. After his discharge, he immediately became active in the civil rights movement led by Martin Luther King Jr. In the 1960s, Gregory was an outspoken critic of America's involvement in Vietnam. This in turn led to his run for the presidency in 1968 as a write-in candidate for the Freedom and Peace Party. Throughout his life he has been a tireless crusader for economic reform, anti-drug issues, and minority rights. In 2000 he published Callus on My Soul, *the second volume of his autobiography. In recent years Gregory has been active in the diet and health food industry.*

In the following episode from Nigger *(1964), the first volume of his autobiography, Gregory narrates the story of a childhood experience that taught him the meaning of shame. Through his use of dialog, he dramatically re-creates the experience for readers. Notice in particular how his concrete nouns and strong action verbs give vividness to the scene he describes and substance to the emotional impact of the experience.*

For Your Journal

We all learn many things in school beyond the lessons we study formally. Some of the extracurricular truths we learn stay with us for the rest of our lives. Write about something you learned in school that you still find very useful—something that has made life easier or more understandable for you.

I never learned hate at home, or shame. I had to go to school for that. I was about seven years old when I got my first big lesson. I was in love with a little girl named Helene Tucker, a light-complexioned little 1 girl with pigtails and nice manners. She was always clean and she was smart in school. I think I went to school then mostly to look at her. I brushed my hair and even got me a little old handkerchief. It was a lady's handkerchief, but I didn't want Helene to see me wipe my nose on my hand. The pipes were frozen again, there was no water in the house, but I washed my socks and shirt every night. I'd get a pot, and go over to Mister Ben's grocery store, and stick my pot down into his soda machine. Scoop out some chopped ice. By evening the ice melted to water for washing. I got sick a lot that winter because the fire would go out at night before the clothes were dry. In the morning I'd put them on, wet or dry, because they were the only clothes I had.

Everybody's got a Helene Tucker, a symbol of everything you want. 2 I loved her for her goodness, her cleanness, her popularity. She'd walk down my street and my brothers and sisters would yell, "Here comes Helene," and I'd rub my tennis sneakers on the back of my pants and wish my hair wasn't so nappy[1] and the white folks' shirt fit me better. I'd run out on the street. If I knew my place and didn't come too close, she'd wink at me and say hello. That was a good feeling. Sometimes I'd follow her all the way home, and shovel the snow off her walk and try to make friends with her Momma and her aunts. I'd drop money on her stoop late at night on my way back from shining shoes in the taverns. And she had a Daddy, and he had a good job. He was a paper hanger.

I guess I would have gotten over Helene by summertime, but 3 something happened in that classroom that made her face hang in front of me for the next twenty-two years. When I played the drums in high school it was for Helene and when I broke track records in college it was for Helene and when I started standing behind microphones and heard applause I wished Helene could hear it, too. It wasn't until I was twenty-nine years old and married and making money that I finally got her out of my system. Helene was sitting in that classroom when I learned to be ashamed of myself.

It was on a Thursday. I was sitting in the back of the room, in a 4 seat with a chalk circle drawn around it. The idiot's seat, the troublemaker's seat.

The teacher thought I was stupid. Couldn't spell, couldn't read, 5 couldn't do arithmetic. Just stupid. Teachers were never interested in finding out that you couldn't concentrate because you were so hungry,

[1]*nappy:* shaggy or fuzzy.

because you hadn't had any breakfast. All you could think about was noontime, would it ever come? Maybe you could sneak into the cloakroom and steal a bite of some kid's lunch out of a coat pocket. A bite of something. Paste. You can't really make a meal of paste, or put it on bread for a sandwich, but sometimes I'd scoop a few spoonfuls out of the paste jar in the back of the room. Pregnant people get strange tastes. I was pregnant with poverty. Pregnant with dirt and pregnant with smells that made people turn away, pregnant with cold and pregnant with shoes that were never bought for me, pregnant with five other people in my bed and no Daddy in the next room, and pregnant with hunger. Paste doesn't taste too bad when you're hungry.

The teacher thought I was a troublemaker. All she saw from the front of the room was a little black boy who squirmed in his idiot's seat and made noises and poked the kids around him. I guess she couldn't see a kid who made noises because he wanted someone to know he was there. 6

It was on a Thursday, the day before the Negro payday. The eagle always flew on Friday. The teacher was asking each student how much his father would give to the Community Chest. On Friday night, each kid would get the money from his father, and on Monday he would bring it to the school. I decided I was going to buy me a Daddy right then. I had money in my pocket from shining shoes and selling papers, and whatever Helene Tucker pledged for her Daddy I was going to top it. And I'd hand the money right in. I wasn't going to wait until Monday to buy me a Daddy. 7

I was shaking, scared to death. The teacher opened her book and started calling out names alphabetically. 8

"Helene Tucker?" 9

"My daddy said he'd give two dollars and fifty cents." 10

"That's very nice, Helene. Very, very nice indeed." 11

That made me feel pretty good. It wouldn't take too much to top that. I had almost three dollars in dimes and quarters in my pocket. I stuck my hand in my pocket and held onto the money, waiting for her to call my name. But the teacher closed her book after she called everybody else in the class. 12

I stood up and raised my hand. 13

"What is it now?" 14

"You forgot me." 15

She turned toward the blackboard. "I don't have time to be playing with you, Richard." 16

"My Daddy said he'd . . ." 17

"Sit down, Richard, you're disturbing the class." 18

"My Daddy said he'd give . . . fifteen dollars." 19

She turned around and looked mad. "We are collecting this money for you and your kind, Richard Gregory. If your Daddy can give fifteen dollars you have no business being on relief." 20

"I got it right now, I got it right now, my Daddy gave it to me to turn in today, my Daddy said . . ." 21

"And furthermore," she said, looking right at me, her nostrils getting big and her lips getting thin and her eyes opening wide, "we know you don't have a Daddy." 22

Helene Tucker turned around, her eyes full of tears. She felt sorry for me. Then I couldn't see her too well because I was crying, too. 23

"Sit down, Richard." 24

And I always thought the teacher kind of liked me. She always picked me to wash the blackboard on Friday, after school. That was a big thrill, it made me feel important. If I didn't wash it, come Monday the school might not function right. 25

"Where are you going, Richard?" 26

I walked out of school that day, and for a long time I didn't go back very often. There was shame there. 27

Now there was shame everywhere. It seemed like the whole world had been inside that classroom, everyone had heard what the teacher had said, everyone had turned around and felt sorry for me. There was shame in going to the Worthy Boys Annual Christmas Dinner for you and your kind, because everybody knew what a worthy boy was. Why couldn't they just call it the Boys Annual Dinner; why'd they have to give it a name? There was shame in wearing the brown and orange and white plaid mackinaw[2] the welfare gave to three thousand boys. Why'd it have to be the same for everybody so when you walked down the street the people could see you were on relief? It was a nice warm mackinaw and it had a hood, and my Momma beat me and called me a little rat when she found out I stuffed it in the bottom of a pail full of garbage way over on Cottage Street. There was shame in running over to Mister Ben's at the end of the day and asking for his rotten peaches, there was shame in asking Mrs. Simmons for a spoonful of sugar, there was shame in running out to meet the relief truck. 28

[2]*mackinaw:* a short, double-breasted wool coat.

I hated that truck, full of food for you and your kind. I ran into the house and hid when it came. And then I started to sneak through alleys, to take the long way home so the people going into White's Eat Shop wouldn't see me. Yeah, the whole world heard the teacher that day, we all know you don't have a Daddy.

Thinking Critically about This Reading

In paragraph 28 Gregory states, "Now there was shame everywhere. It seemed like the whole world had been inside that classroom, everyone had heard what the teacher had said, everyone had turned around and felt sorry for me." What did Gregory's teacher say, and why did it hurt him so greatly?

Questions for Study and Discussion

1. How do the first three paragraphs of the essay help to establish a context for the narrative that follows? (Glossary: *Narration*)
2. What does Gregory mean by "shame"? What precisely was he ashamed of, and what in particular did he learn from the incident? (Glossary: *Definition*)
3. In a word or phrase, how would you describe Gregory's tone? What specific words or phrases in his essay lead you to this conclusion?
4. What is the teacher's attitude toward Gregory? In arriving at your answer, consider her own words and actions as well as Gregory's opinion.
5. What role does money play in Gregory's experience? How does money relate to his sense of shame?
6. Specific details can enhance the reader's understanding and appreciation of a subject. (Glossary: *Details*) Gregory's description of Helene Tucker's manners or the plaid of his mackinaw, for example, makes his account vivid and interesting. Cite several other specific details he gives, and consider how the essay would be different without them.
7. Reread this essay's first and last paragraphs, and compare how much each one emphasizes shame. (Glossary: *Beginnings and Endings*) Which emotion other than shame does Gregory reveal in the first paragraph, and does it play a role in the last one? Is the last paragraph an effective ending? Explain.

Classroom Activity Using Diction and Tone

Good writers rely on strong verbs—verbs that contribute significantly to what is being said. Because they must repeatedly describe similar situations, sportswriters, for example, are acutely aware of the need for strong action verbs. It is not enough for them to say that a team wins or loses; they must describe the type of win or loss more precisely. As a result, such verbs as *beat, bury, edge, shock,* and *trounce* are common in the headlines on the sports page. In addition to describing the act of winning, each of these verbs makes a statement about the quality of the victory. Like sportswriters, all of us write about actions that are performed daily. If we were restricted only to the verbs *eat, drink, sleep,* and *work* for each of these activities, our writing would be repetitious, monotonous, and most likely wordy. List as many verbs as you can that you could use in place of these four. What connotative differences do you find in your lists of alternatives? What is the importance of these connotative differences for you as a writer?

Suggested Writing Assignments

1. Using Gregory's essay as a model, write an essay narrating an experience that made you especially afraid, angry, surprised, embarrassed, or proud. Include sufficient detail so that your readers will know exactly what happened and pay particular attention to how you use your first and last paragraphs to present the emotion your essay focuses on.
2. Most of us grow up with some sense of the socioeconomic class that our family belongs to, and often we are aware of how we are, or believe we are, different from people of other classes. Write an essay in which you describe a possession or activity that you thought revealed your socioeconomic standing and made you self-conscious about how you were different from others. Be sure to recount an experience that seemed to confirm your belief, and discuss why it did. Pay particular attention to your essay's first and last paragraphs so that they serve your purpose.

Me Talk Pretty One Day

David Sedaris

David Sedaris was born in 1956 in Johnson City, New York, and grew up in North Carolina. He attended Kent State University but ultimately graduated from the Art Institute of Chicago in 1987. Before becoming a writer, Sedaris worked as a mover, an office temp, a housekeeper, and—famously—an elf in a department store Christmas display, an experience he wrote about in his celebrated essay "Santaland Diaries." He is a regular contributor to National Public Radio, Harper's, Details, *the* New Yorker, *and* Esquire *and has won several awards, including the James Thurber Prize for American Humor. Sedaris often writes about his quirky Greek family and his travels with his partner Hugh, with whom he currently lives in London. His essays and stories have been collected in several best-selling books, including* Barrel Fever *(1994),* Holidays on Ice *(1997),* Naked *(1997), and* Dress Your Family in Corduroy and Denim *(2004).*

The following essay about taking French language lessons in Paris first appeared in Esquire *in March 1999 and later became the title piece for Sedaris's fourth book,* Me Talk Pretty One Day *(2000). As you read, pay particular attention to how he uses his words to play with the ideas of language, understanding, and belonging.*

For Your Journal

Have you ever been in a situation where you did not speak the prevalent language—for example, in a foreign country, a language class, or a group of people who spoke a language other than yours? How did you feel about not being able to communicate? How, if at all, did you get your thoughts across to others?

At the age of forty-one, I am returning to school and having to think of myself as what my French textbook calls "a true debutant." After paying my tuition, I was issued a student ID, which allows me a discounted entry fee at movie theaters, puppet shows, 1 and Festyland, a far-flung amusement park that advertises with billboards picturing a cartoon stegosaurus sitting in a canoe and eating what appears to be a ham sandwich.

I've moved to Paris in order to learn the language. My school is the Alliance Française, and on the first day of class, I arrived early, watching as the returning students greeted one another in the school lobby. Vacations were recounted, and questions were raised concerning mutual friends with names like Kang and Vlatnya. Regardless of their nationalities, everyone spoke what sounded to me like excellent French. Some accents were better than others, but the students exhibited an ease and confidence I found intimidating. As an added discomfort, they were all young, attractive, and well dressed, causing me to feel not unlike Pa Kettle[1] trapped backstage after a fashion show. 2

I remind myself that I am now a full-grown man. No one will ever again card me for a drink or demand that I weave a floor mat out of newspapers. At my age, a reasonable person should have completed his sentence in the prison of the nervous and the insecure—isn't that the great promise of adulthood? I can't help but think that, somewhere along the way, I made a wrong turn. My fears have not vanished. Rather, they have seasoned and multiplied with age. I am now twice as frightened as I was when, at the age of twenty, I allowed a failed nursing student to inject me with a horse tranquilizer, and eight times more anxious than I was the day my kindergarten teacher pried my fingers off my mother's ankle and led me screaming toward my desk. "You'll get used to it," the woman had said. 3

I'm still waiting. 4

The first day of class was nerve-racking because I knew I'd be expected to perform. That's the way they do it here—everyone into the language pool, sink or swim. The teacher marched in, deeply tanned from a recent vacation, and rattled off a series of administrative announcements. I've spent some time in Normandy,[2] and I took a monthlong French class last summer in New York. I'm not completely in the dark, yet I understood only half of what this teacher was saying. 5

"If you have not *meismslsxp* by this time, you should not be in this room. Has everybody *apzkiubjxow*? Everyone? Good, we shall 6

---

[1]*Pa Kettle:* someone who is simple or unsophisticated; the name of a character in a series of comic movies popular in the 1950s.

[2]*Normandy:* a province in northwestern France.

proceed." She spread out her lesson plan and sighed, saying, "All right, then, who knows the alphabet?"

It was startling because a) I hadn't been asked that question in a while, and b) I realized, while laughing, that I myself did not know the alphabet. They're the same letters, but they're pronounced differently. 7

"Ahh." The teacher went to the board and sketched the letter *A*. "Do we have anyone in the room whose first name commences with an ahh?" 8

Two Polish Annas raised their hands, and the teacher instructed them to present themselves, giving their names, nationalities, occupations, and a list of things they liked and disliked in this world. The first Anna hailed from an industrial town outside of Warsaw and had front teeth the size of tombstones. She worked as a seamstress, enjoyed quiet times with friends, and hated the mosquito. 9

"Oh, really," the teacher said. "How very interesting. I thought that everyone loved the mosquito, but here, in front of all the world, you claim to detest him. How is it that we've been blessed with someone as unique and original as you? Tell us, please." 10

The seamstress did not understand what was being said, but she knew that this was an occasion for shame. Her rabbity mouth huffed for breath, and she stared down at her lap as though the appropriate comeback were stitched somewhere alongside the zipper of her slacks. 11

The second Anna learned from the first and claimed to love sunshine and detest lies. It sounded like a translation of one of those Playmate of the Month data sheets, the answers always written in the same loopy handwriting: "Turn-ons: Mom's famous five-alarm chili! Turnoffs: Insincerity and guys who come on too strong!!!" 12

The two Polish women surely had clear notions of what they liked and disliked, but, like the rest of us, they were limited in terms of vocabulary, and this made them appear less than sophisticated. The teacher forged on, and we learned that Carlos, the Argentine bandoneon[3] player, loved wine, music, and, in his words, "Making sex with the women of the world." Next came a beautiful young Yugoslavian who identified herself as an optimist, saying that she loved everything life had to offer. 13

The teacher licked her lips, revealing a hint of the sadist[4] we would later come to know. She crouched low for her attack, placed her hands 14

[3]*bandoneon:* a small accordion popular in Latin America.
[4]*sadist:* one who finds pleasure in being cruel to others.

on the young woman's desk, and said, "Oh, yeah? And do you love your little war?"[5]

While the optimist struggled to defend herself, I scrambled to think 15
of an answer to what had obviously become a trick question. How often are you asked what you love in this world? More important, how often are you asked and then publicly ridiculed for your answer? I recalled my mother, flushed with wine, pounding the table late one night, saying, "Love? I love a good steak cooked rare. I love my cat, and I love . . ." My sisters and I leaned forward, waiting to hear our names. "Tums," our mother said. "I love Tums." The teacher killed some time accusing the Yugoslavian girl of masterminding a program of genocide, and I jotted frantic notes in the margins of my pad. While I can honestly say that I love leafing through medical textbooks devoted to severe dermatological conditions, it is beyond the reach of my French vocabulary, and acting it out would only have invited unwanted attention.

When called upon, I delivered an effortless list of things I detest: 16
blood sausage, intestinal paté, brain pudding. I'd learned these words the hard way. Having given it some thought, I then declared my love for IBM typewriters, the French word for "bruise," and my electric floor waxer. It was a short list, but still I managed to mispronounce IBM and afford the wrong gender to both the floor waxer and the typewriter. Her reaction led me to believe that these mistakes were capital crimes in the country of France.

"Were you always this *palicmkrexjs*?" she asked. "Even a 17
fiuscrzsws tociwegixp knows that a typewriter is feminine."

I absorbed as much of her abuse as I could understand, thinking, 18
but not saying, that I find it ridiculous to assign a gender to an inanimate object incapable of disrobing and making an occasional fool of itself. Why refer to Lady Flesh Wound or Good Sir Dishrag when these things could never deliver in the sack?

The teacher proceeded to belittle everyone from German Eva, who 19
hated laziness, to Japanese Yukari, who loved paintbrushes and soap. Italian, Thai, Dutch, Korean, Chinese—we all left class foolishly believing that the worst was over. We didn't know it then, but the coming months would teach us what it is like to spend time in the presence of a wild animal. We soon learned to dodge chalk and to

[5]". . . *your little war*": the Balkan War (1991–2001), armed conflict and genocide in the territory of the former Yugoslavia.

cover our heads and stomachs whenever she approached us with a question. She hadn't yet punched anyone, but it seemed wise to prepare ourselves against the inevitable.

Though we were forbidden to speak anything but French, the 20
teacher would occasionally use us to practice any of her five fluent languages.

"I hate you," she said to me one afternoon. Her English was 21
flawless. "I really, really hate you." Call me sensitive, but I couldn't help taking it personally.

Learning French is a lot like joining a gang in that it involves a 22
long and intensive period of hazing. And it wasn't just my teacher; the entire population seemed to be in on it. Following brutal encounters with my local butcher and the concierge[6] of my building, I'd head off to class, where the teacher would hold my corrected paperwork high above her head, shouting, "Here's proof that *David* is an ignorant and uninspired *ensigiejsokhjx*."

Refusing to stand convicted on the teacher's charges of laziness, 23
I'd spend four hours a night on my homework, working even longer whenever we were assigned an essay. I suppose I could have gotten by with less, but I was determined to create some sort of an identity for myself. We'd have one of those "complete the sentence" exercises, and I'd fool with the thing for hours, invariably settling on something like, "A quick run around the lake? I'd love to. Just give me a minute to strap on my wooden leg." The teacher, through word and action, conveyed the message that, if this was my idea of an identity, she wanted nothing to do with it.

My fear and discomfort crept beyond the borders of my class- 24
room and accompanied me out onto the wide boulevards, where, no matter how hard I tried, there was no escaping the feeling of terror I felt whenever anyone asked me a question. I was safe in any kind of a store, as, at least in my neighborhood, one can stand beside the cash register for hours on end without being asked something so trivial as, "May I help you?" or "How would you like to pay for that?"

My only comfort was the knowledge that I was not alone. Hud- 25
dled in the smoky hallways and making the most of our pathetic French, my fellow students and I engaged in the sort of conversation commonly overheard in refugee camps.

---

[6]*concierge:* a doorman in a French apartment building.

"Sometimes me cry alone at night." 26

"That is common for me also, but be more strong, you. Much 27 work, and someday you talk pretty. People stop hate you soon. Maybe tomorrow, okay?"

Unlike other classes I have taken, here there was no sense of com- 28 petition. When the teacher poked a shy Korean woman in the eyelid with a freshly sharpened pencil, we took no comfort in the fact that, unlike Hyeyoon Cho, we all knew the irregular past tense of the verb "to defeat." In all fairness, the teacher hadn't meant to hurt the woman, but neither did she spend much time apologizing, saying only, "Well, you should have been paying more attention."

Over time, it became impossible to believe that any of us would 29 ever improve. Fall arrived, and it rained every day. It was mid-October when the teacher singled me out, saying, "Every day spent with you is like having a cesarean section." And it struck me that, for the first time since arriving in France, I could understand every word that someone was saying.

Understanding doesn't mean that you can suddenly speak the 30 language. Far from it. It's a small step, nothing more, yet its rewards are intoxicating and deceptive. The teacher continued her diatribe, and I settled back, bathing in the subtle beauty of each new curse and insult.

"You exhaust me with your foolishness and reward my efforts 31 with nothing but pain, do you understand me?"

The world opened up, and it was with great joy that I responded, 32 "I know the thing what you speak exact now. Talk me more, plus, please, plus."

Thinking Critically about This Reading

Sedaris's French teacher tells him that "every day spent with you is like having a cesarean section" (paragraph 29). Why is Sedaris's ability to recount this insult significant? What does the teacher's "cesarean section" metaphor mean?

Questions for Study and Discussion

1. Sedaris's tone is humorous. (Glossary: *Tone*) What words in particular help him create this tone? Did you find yourself smiling or

laughing out loud as you read his essay? If so, what specific passages affected you this way?

2. What is your impression of Sedaris and his classmates? What words and phrases does he use to describe himself and them?
3. Why do you think Sedaris uses nonsense jumbles of letters—*meismslsxp* and *palicmkrexjs,* for example—in several places? How would his essay be different had he used the real words instead?
4. What does Sedaris realize in the final three paragraphs? What evidence does he provide of his realization?

Classroom Activity Using Diction and Tone

Many restaurant menus use connotative language in an attempt to persuade patrons that they are about to have an exceptional dining experience: "skillfully seasoned," "festive and spicy," "fresh from the garden," "grilled to perfection," "freshly ground." Imagine that you are charged with the task of creating such a menu. Use connotative language to describe the following basic foods, making them sound as attractive and inviting as possible.

tomato juice	peas	pasta
onion soup	potatoes	ice cream
ground beef	salad	tea
chicken	bread and butter	cake

Suggested Writing Assignments

1. Write a narrative essay recounting a humorous incident in your life. (Glossary: *Narration*) Use the following questions to start thinking about the incident: Where were you? What happened? Who witnessed the incident? Did you think it was humorous at the time? Do you view it differently now? Why or why not? Choose words and phrases for your narrative that convey a humorous tone. (Glossary: *Tone*)
2. "Refusing to stand convicted on the teacher's charge of laziness," Sedaris explains, "I'd spend four hours a night on my homework, working even longer whenever we were assigned an essay" (23). Write an essay in which you evaluate Sedaris's teacher. Given that

she inspired Sedaris to apply himself to his work, do you think she was an effective teacher? Would her methods have the same effect on you? Why or why not? (Glossary: *Cause and Effect*)

3. As Sedaris's essay and the following cartoon illustrate, fitting in often depends on our ability to communicate with authenticity—using the appropriate pronunciation, terminology, or slang—to a particular audience. (Glossary: *Audience; Slang*) Have you ever felt alienated by a group because you didn't use its lingo appropriately, or have you ever alienated someone else for the same reason? Write a narrative essay in which you recount one such event. (Glossary: *Narration*) Be sure to use diction and tone creatively to convey your meaning. Before you begin, you might find it helpful to refer to your journal response for this selection.

Pop-A-Shot

Sarah Vowell

Author and cultural observer, Sarah Vowell was born in Oklahoma in 1969. She graduated from Montana State University in 1993 and earned her MA from the Art Institute of Chicago in 1996. She is perhaps best known for the witty and sometimes quirky monologues and documentaries that she's done for National Public Radio's This American Life *since 1996. Vowell has performed her comic routines at the Aspen Comedy Festival, Amsterdam's Crossing Borders Festival, and Seattle's Foolproof Comedy Festival. Vowell's essays have appeared in* Esquire, *the* Los Angeles Times, *the* Village Voice, Spin, *and* Salon. *Her books include* Radio On: A Listener's Diary *(1997),* Take the Cannoli: Stories from the New World *(2000),* The Partly Cloudy Patriot *(2002), and* Assassination Vacation *(2005). In 2004 she voiced the character Violet for the animated movie* The Incredibles.

In the following essay, taken from The Partly Cloudy Patriot, *Vowell reflects on her own fascination with the arcade game Pop-A-Shot. As you read, notice how she uses her humorous, offbeat perspective to make a point about what she does to find happiness.*

For Your Journal

What does it mean to "goof off"? What kinds of things do you and your friends do when goofing off? For example, do you play arcade games or video games when you want to escape the stresses of everyday life? What, for you, are the benefits of goofing off?

Along with voting, jury duty, and paying taxes, goofing off is one of the central obligations of American citizenship. So when my friends Joel and Stephen and I play hooky from our jobs in the middle of the afternoon to play Pop-A-Shot in a room full of children, I like to think we are not procrastinators[1]; we are patriots pursuing happiness. 1

[1]*procrastinators:* people who delay doing something unpleasant or burdensome.

Pop-A-Shot is not a video game. It involves shooting real, if miniature, basketballs for forty seconds. It's embarrassing how giddy the three of us get when it's our turn to put money into the machine. (Often, we have to stand behind some six-year-old girl who bogarts[2] the game and whose father keeps dropping in quarters even though the kid makes only about 4 points if she's lucky and we are forced to glare at the back of her pigtailed head, waiting just long enough to start questioning our adulthood and how by the time our parents were our age they were beholden to mortgages and PTA meetings and here we are, stuck in an episode of *Friends*.) 2

Finally it's my turn. A wave of balls slide toward me and I shoot, making my first basket. I'm good at this. I'm not great. The machine I usually play on has a high score of 72, and my highest score is 56. But considering that I am five foot four, that I used to get C's in gym, and that I campaigned for Dukakis,[3] the fact that I am capable of scoring 56 points in forty seconds is a source of no small amount of pride. Plus, even though these modern men won't admit it, it really bugs Joel and Steve to get topped by a girl. 3

There are two reasons I can shoot a basketball: black-eyed peas and Uncle Hoy. I was a forward on my elementary school team. This was in Oklahoma, back when girls played half-court basketball, which meant I never crossed over to the other team's side, which meant all I ever had to do was shoot, a bonus considering that I cannot run, pass, or dribble. Blessed with one solitary athletic skill, I was going to make the most of it. I shot baskets in the backyard every night after dinner. We lived out in the country, and my backboard was nailed to an oak tree that grew on top of a hill. If I missed a shot, the ball would roll downhill into the drainage ditch for the kitchen sink, a muddy rivulet[4] flecked with corn and black-eyed peas. So if the ball bounced willy-nilly off the rim, I had to run after it, retrieve it from the gross black-eyed pea mud, then hose it off. So I learned not to miss. 4

My mother's brother, Hoy, was a girls' basketball coach. Once he saw I had a knack for shooting, he used to drill me on free throws, standing under the hoop at my grandmother's house, where he 5

[2]*bogarts:* being selfish; taking more than one's share of something.

[3]*Michael Dukakis* (b. 1933): former governor of Massachusetts who lost the 1988 presidential election.

[4]*rivulet:* brook or little stream.

himself learned to play. And Hoy, who was also a math teacher—he had gone to college on a dual math-basketball scholarship—revered the geometrical arc of the swish. Hoy hated the backboard, and thought players who used it to make anything other than layups lacked elegance. And so, if I made a free throw that bounced off the backboard before gliding through the basket, he'd yell, "Doesn't count." Sometimes, trash-talking at Pop-A-Shot, I bark that at Joel and Stephen when they score their messy bank shots. "Doesn't count!" The electronic scoreboard, unfortunately, makes no distinction for grace and beauty.

I watch the NBA. I lived in Chicago during the heyday of the Bulls. 6
And I have noticed that in, as I like to call it, the moving-around-basketball, the players spend the whole game trying to shoot. There's all that wasted running and throwing and falling down on cameramen in between baskets. But Pop-A-Shot is basketball concentrate. I've made 56 points in forty seconds. Michael Jordan never did that. When Michael Jordan would make even 40 points in a game it was the lead in the eleven o'clock news. It takes a couple of hours to play a moving-around-basketball game. Pop-A-Shot distills this down to less than a minute. It is the crack cocaine of basketball. I can make twenty-eight baskets at a rate of less than two seconds per.

Joel, an excellent shot, also appreciates this about Pop-A-Shot. 7
He likes the way it feels, but he's embarrassed by how it sounds stupid when he describes it to other people. (He spent part of last year working in Canada, and I think it rubbed off on him, diminishing his innate American ability to celebrate the civic virtue of idiocy.) Joel plays in a fairly serious adult basketball league in New York. One night, he left Stephen and me in the arcade and rushed off to a—this hurt my feelings—"real" game. That night, he missed a foul shot by two feet and made the mistake of admitting to the other players that his arms were tired from throwing miniature balls at a shortened hoop all afternoon. They laughed and laughed. "In the second overtime," Joel told me, "when the opposing team fouled me with four seconds left and gave me the opportunity to shoot from the line for the game, they looked mighty smug as they took their positions along the key. Oh, Pop-A-Shot guy, I could hear them thinking to their smug selves. He'll never make a foul shot. He plays baby games. Wa-wa-wa, little Pop-A-Shot baby, would you like a zwieback biscuit? But you know what? I made those shots, and those sons of bitches had to wipe their smug grins off their smug faces and go home thinking that maybe Pop-A-Shot wasn't just a baby game after all."

I think Pop-A-Shot's a baby game. That's why I love it. Unlike the game of basketball itself, Pop-A-Shot has no standard socially redeeming value whatsoever. Pop-A-Shot is not about teamwork or getting along or working together. Pop-A-Shot is not about getting exercise or fresh air. It takes place in fluorescent-lit bowling alleys or darkened bars. It costs money. At the end of a game, one does not swig Gatorade. One sips bourbon or margaritas or munches cupcakes. Unless one is playing the Super Shot version at the ESPN Zone in Times Square,[5] in which case, one orders the greatest appetizer ever invented on this continent—a plate of cheeseburgers. 8

In other words, Pop-A-Shot has no point at all. And that, for me, is the point. My life is full of points—the deadlines and bills and recycling and phone calls. I have come to appreciate, to depend on, this one dumb-ass little passion. Because every time a basketball slides off my fingertips and drops perfectly, flawlessly, into that hole, well, swish, happiness found. 9

Thinking Critically about This Reading

At various points in her essay Vowell compares and contrasts the arcade game Pop-A-Shot to the game of basketball. How are the two games similar? How are they different? What conclusions about Pop-A-Shot does this comparison enable Vowell to draw?

Questions for Study and Discussion

1. In the opening paragraph, Vowell announces that "goofing off is one of the central obligations of American citizenship." How serious do you think she is in making this claim? How does she support this claim?
2. How does Vowell account for her success at Pop-A-Shot?
3. How would you describe Vowell's tone in this essay? How does her choice of words lead you to this conclusion?
4. What does Vowell mean when she says that "Pop-A-Shot is basketball concentrate" (paragraph 6)?

---

[5]*Times Square:* a major entertainment district in New York City.

5. In paragraph 7, Vowell relates a story about her friend Joel's experience in a "real" basketball game. How is this paragraph about Joel related to Vowell's main idea, or is this paragraph a digression in the essay? (Glossary: *Unity*)
6. What do you know about the writer as a result of reading this essay? How would you describe her?
7. What, for Vowell, is the point of Pop-A-Shot? Why does she love this game?

Classroom Activity Using Diction and Tone

Writers use different levels of diction to communicate with different audiences of readers. For example, a writer might use the formal label *police officer* in an article for law enforcement professionals and the more informal word *cop* in a humorous piece for a general audience. Recall a fairground activity, an amusement park ride, or a video game that you have enjoyed. Write a paragraph in which you describe this activity, ride, or game to an older relative. Then rewrite the paragraph to appeal to a ten-year-old.

Suggested Writing Assignments

1. Vowell states that Americans like her friend Joel have the "innate . . . ability to celebrate the civic virtue of idiocy" (7). What do you think? Has the world gotten so serious and stressful that we all need "one dumb-ass little passion" (9) like Pop-A-Shot to make life tolerable? Write an essay in which you present your views on mindless or pointless games in our culture.
2. What makes you happy? For example, do you find happiness when you are with other people or while you are doing a particular activity? Write an essay in which you explain what makes you happy.

Who Am I?

Merrill Markoe

Writer, performer, and stand-up comic, Merrill Markoe was born in New York City in 1950. She earned her MFA in 1974 from the University of California–Berkeley and subsequently taught art at the University of Southern California. Markoe's specialty is comedy, and she has received numerous awards including Emmys for her work as head writer for The David Letterman Show *and* Late Night with David Letterman. *She was a writer for a number of television series and a contributor and performer for* Not Necessarily the News *and* TV Nation. *Starting in the early 1990s, Markoe turned her comedic hand to writing books, including* What the Dogs Have Taught Me and Other Amazing Things I've Learned *(1992),* How to Be Hap-Hap-Happy like Me *(1994), and* Merrill Markoe's Guide to Love *(1997). She has also written a book for children,* The Day My Dogs Became Guys *(1999), and the novel* It's My F—ing Birthday! *(2002).*

The following essay first appeared in ON Magazine *in March 2001. As you read Markoe's very funny monologue-like answer to the age-old question in her title, notice how her frank, often sarcastic language, her choice of a situation readers can relate to, and her sense of timing come together to create her humorous tone.*

For Your Journal

If someone were to ask you who you were, how would you answer them? Are there aspects of your personality or character that might come as a surprise to others, even those close to you? Name one aspect of yourself that you think others might find surprising, and write about it.

Having spent a fair amount of time and money in therapy, debating my every move with a licensed and supposedly caring professional, I was under the impression that I had a pretty good idea of 1 what I was all about. At least until I started taking personality quizzes on the Internet. As any reader of cheesy women's magazines will tell you, this quiz-taking business can be both time-consuming and pointless in terms of gaining meaningful advice. But it can also be as utterly seductive as the horoscope pages. For about a minute and a half, the quiz glistens like a beacon of knowledge before you, offering answers to all the important questions in life. Five minutes later, awash in self loathing,[1] you can't even remember what it said or why you ever buy that magazine.

As it turns out, the Internet is so full of this kind of self-improvement quiz that it could be argued that the only thing that separates the Net from an average issue of *Cosmopolitan* is that Cosmo offers only one quiz at a time. And the Internet seems to have fewer ads for panty liners. 2

I came to know of this one day when, quite by accident, I encountered a quiz at a handy site called QuizBox.com that promised to tell me how "attractive" I was. I guess I needed a little reassurance (with emphasis on the word *little*—if the quiz couldn't see me, how reassuring could it be?). I willingly submitted to seemingly irrelevant questions like "Which city would you like to visit?" (I chose Paris over Tokyo or Beijing because, in the montage[2] in my imagination, I thought I looked more attractive in Paris.) I also selected a peck over a big kiss as my first-date kissing style because a rash of unappealing recent first dates was still fresh in my mind, and this quiz didn't specify whether the guy I was allegedly going on this first date with had any sex appeal. 3

After my scores were tallied, the quiz passed judgment. It said, in no uncertain terms, that I needed to improve my personality. I also needed to be more optimistic and smile more. I could be attractive if I would try, it sighed, but clearly it didn't think I was trying hard enough. 4

So there I was, alone in my house and suddenly a lot less attractive than I had been a few minutes earlier. I wasn't going to take this lying down. To recoup my losses, like a woman feverishly playing the slot machines, I continued to take more quizzes. 5

Instantly I was able to wrest myself from the jaws of low self-esteem via the "What kind of personality do you have?" quiz. This time, when asked to answer the question "If you could wish for anything 6

[1]*self loathing:* extreme dislike of oneself.

[2]*montage:* an image made up of many arranged or superimposed pictures or designs.

what would it be?" I chose "Become a beauty queen." (After all, my health was already pretty good, my eyes are already pretty nice, and being clever was apparently getting me nowhere.) Much to my delight, the quiz was favorably impressed. "People with your kind of character are few and far between," it informed me. "Everybody likes to be around people with your personality."

Feeling a bit more confident, I was also getting genuinely curious about the possibility of learning something new about myself this way. So I went on taking quizzes. Which is how I came to find out that every single thing I did defined my personality. 7

There was an egg test that revealed that because I eat fried eggs white-part first, instead of yolk first, I am "logical, smart and inventive . . . though sometimes too cold and selfish." That I only eat egg whites, period, didn't seem to factor in one way or another. 8

Next, by picking toilet stall No. 2 out of a drawing of three empty stalls ("The Toilet Test"), I learned I was "an efficient person" yet also "a romantic person" who can be "too hasty making decisions in love." I guess it serves me right for being so cavalier[3] about my toilet-stall selections. 9

On "The Eating Test," I made the mistake of picking eggs and toast over cereal for breakfast, while also admitting to sometimes skipping lunch entirely because of worry about my weight. Now I had inadvertently shown myself to be "jealous of people who are smarter and better looking" than I am. A harsh evaluation, I felt, for someone "with my kind of character." 10

So I left QuizBox.com's petty judgments behind and typed "personality quiz" into the Yahoo! search engine. This led me to "The Ultimate Personality Test." Three cups of coffee later (and still in my pajamas at one in the afternoon), I was saddened to learn that I was a "secret agent" who "professionally, likes to work in a cubicle and eat lunch at the desk." 11

But my mood improved considerably once I clicked on the next test I could find, and my choice of an abstract pattern from an assortment of designs offered me a complete reevaluation. Now, thank heavens, I was "dynamic, active, extroverted"[4] and "willing to accept certain risks 12

---

[3]*cavalier:* nonchalant disregard for what is important; disdainful.

[4]*extroverted:* to be interested and actively engaged with others and the surrounding environment.

and to make a strong commitment in exchange for interesting and varied work."

So which was it? Was I a cubicle worker or a risk-taker? Hoping to get off this emotional roller coaster, I wandered over to TheSpark. com, where yet another personality test branded me "an accountant. Reserved. Meticulous. Dependable." And this despite the fact that on the very same page "The Sexy Test" said I was 75 percent sexier than their average quiz-taker! Because this puzzling new image of "sexy accountant" didn't provide me with anything except an idea for a horrible new sitcom, I took a deep, cleansing breath and dived into the elaborate "How Others See You" quiz, where I emerged "extroverted, agreeable but neurotic[5] and not very conscientious." I found this confusing because a quiz at a women's financial site insisted that I was "thorough, meticulous and calm" only a few minutes later. 13

By the end of a long day, I also learned that my taste in room decor is "middle class" ("What Class Are You?"), despite the fact that my "plant personality" is "woodland natural." My "workout personality" is "40% inspirational, 30% spontaneous and 30% analytical (sailing, training for a triathlon and softball recommended)." And my religious beliefs are Unitarian Universalist, neopagan, or Malayan Buddhist. 14

Although the Ayurvedic Foundations's site tells me I have a Pitta constitution, meaning I am "hot, sharp, liquid and oily," an insurance company's longevity quiz says that I will live to be 95. 15

So there it is: I am extroverted and reserved, passive and active, risk-taking and afraid of change. I am also calm, neurotic and meticulous, dependable and not very conscientious. So what if my workout program of alternating the gym with yoga does not fit my personality? Who cares if I should belong to a religion I have never heard of? All things considered, I have to say that it feels great to really get to know myself at last. 16

Thinking Critically about This Reading

What does Markoe mean when she describes the appeal of online personality quizzes as being "as utterly seductive as the horoscope pages" (paragraph 1)? What need, according to Markoe, do personality quizzes and horoscopes fulfill?

[5]*neurotic:* emotionally unstable.

Questions for Study and Discussion

1. What is Markoe's attitude toward Internet and magazine personality quizzes? (Glossary: *Attitude*)
2. What is Markoe's purpose? (Glossary: *Purpose*) Do you think she's really interested in coming to grips with who she is, or do you think she's poking fun at personality quizzes and the people who take them? Explain.
3. Markoe explains that she happened to take the quiz on QuizBox.com's site "quite by accident" (3). After hearing the results of that quiz, why does she continue to take more quizzes? Does she seem at all interested in what the other quizzes reveal?
4. Describe Markoe's tone. Is she being humorous, angry, depressed, satiric, sarcastic, or serious?
5. Identify three similes in Markoe's essay, and explain how each one works. (Glossary: *Figurative Language*)
6. Markoe employs a number of transitional expressions and strategies to move her essay along from one paragraph to the next. (Glossary: *Transition*) Identify examples of where she uses (a) transitional expressions, (b) repeated key words, and (c) repeated key ideas. Which transitions do you find most effective? Why?

Classroom Activity Using Diction and Tone

Writers create and control tone in their writing in part through the words they choose. For example, the words *laugh, cheery, dance,* and *melody* help create a tone of celebration. Make a list of the words that come to mind for each of the following tones:

humorous	authoritative	tentative
angry	triumphant	repentant

Compare your lists of words with those of others in the class. What generalizations can you make about the connotations associated with each of these tones?

Suggested Writing Assignments

1. How would you describe yourself? What elements of your heritage, upbringing, and experience have played the strongest roles

in forming your identity? Write an essay in which you take a serious look at the question "Who am I?" Before writing, review your response to the journal prompt for this selection.

2. A recent poll revealed the not-too-startling fact that Americans are "close to being obsessed with their physical appearance." How do you like your own physical appearance? Would you consider yourself obsessed with your appearance? Ask your friends whether they have self-doubts about the way they look. Write an essay in which you discuss your feelings about the way you imagine you appear to others. What about yourself would you keep just the way it is? What would you change?

chapter **11**

Figurative Language

Figurative language is language used in an imaginative rather than a literal sense. Although it is most often associated with poetry, figurative language is used widely in our daily speech and in our writing. Prose writers have long known that figurative language not only brings freshness and color to writing, but also helps to clarify ideas. For example, when asked by his teacher to explain the concept of brainstorming, one student replied, "Well, brainstorming is like having a tornado in your head." This figurative language helps others imagine the whirl of ideas in this young writer's head as he brainstorms a topic for writing.

The two most common **figures of speech** are the simile and the metaphor. A **simile** is an explicit comparison between two essentially different ideas or things that uses the word *like* or *as* to link them.

> Canada geese sweep across the hills and valleys like a formation of strategic bombers.
>
> –Benjamin B. Bachman

> I walked toward her and hailed her as a visitor to the moon might salute a survivor of a previous expedition.
>
> –John Updike

A **metaphor** makes an implicit comparison between dissimilar ideas or things without using *like* or *as.*

> She was very old and small and she walked slowly in the dark pine shadows, moving a little from side to side in her steps, with the balanced heaviness and lightness of a pendulum in a grandfather clock.
>
> –Eudora Welty

> Charm is the ultimate weapon, the supreme seduction, against which there are few defenses.
>
> –Laurie Lee

To take full advantage of the richness of a particular comparison, writers sometimes use several sentences or even a whole paragraph to develop a metaphor. Such a comparison is called an *extended metaphor*.

> The point is that you have to strip down your writing before you can build it back up. You must know what the essential tools are and what job they were designed to do. If I may belabor the metaphor on carpentry, it is first necessary to be able to saw wood neatly and to drive nails. Later you can bevel the edges or add elegant finials, if that is your taste. But you can never forget that you are practicing a craft that is based on certain principles. If the nails are weak, your house will collapse. If your verbs are weak and your syntax is rickety, your sentences will fall apart.
>
> –William Zinsser

Another frequently used figure of speech is **personification.** In personification, the writer attributes human qualities to ideas or objects.

> The moon bathed the valley in a soft, golden light.
>
> –Corey Davis, student

> Blond October comes striding over the hills wearing a crimson shirt and faded green trousers.
>
> –Hal Borland

> Indeed, haste can be the assassin of elegance.
>
> –T. H. White

In all of the preceding examples, note how the writers' use of figurative language enlivens their prose and emphasizes their ideas. Each vividly communicates an idea or the essence of an object by comparing it to something concrete and familiar. In each case, too, the figurative language grows out of the writer's thinking, reflecting the way he or she sees the material. Be similarly honest in your use of figurative language, keeping in mind that figures of speech should never be used merely to "dress up" writing. Above all, use them to develop your ideas and clarify your meaning for the reader.

The Barrio

■ **Robert Ramirez**

Robert Ramirez was born in Edinburg, Texas, in 1949. After graduating from the University of Texas–Pan American, he taught writing and worked as a cameraman, reporter, anchor, and producer for the local news on KGBT-TV, the CBS affiliate in Harlingen, Texas. He currently works as an alumni fund-raiser for the University of Texas–Pan American.

The following essay first appeared in Pain and Promise: The Chicano Today *(1972), edited by Edward Simmens. Notice how Ramirez uses figurative language, particularly metaphors, to awaken the reader's senses to the sights, sounds, and smells that are the essence of the barrio.*

For Your Journal

Where did you grow up? What do you remember most about your childhood neighborhood? How did it feel as a young person to live in this world? Do you still call this neighborhood "home"? Explain.

The train, its metal wheels squealing as they spin along the silvery tracks, rolls slower now. Through the gaps between the cars blinks a streetlamp, and this pulsing light on a barrio streetcorner beats slower, like a weary heartbeat, until the train shudders to a halt, the light goes out, and the barrio is deep asleep. 1

Throughout Aztlán[1] (the Nahuatl term meaning "land to the north"), trains grumble along the edges of a sleeping people. From Lower California, through the blistering Southwest, down the Rio Grande[2] to the muddy Gulf, the darkness and mystery of dreams engulf communities fenced off by railroads, canals, and expressways. Paradoxical[3] 2

[1]*Aztlán:* the mythical place of origin of the Aztec peoples.
[2]*Rio Grande:* a river flowing from southwest Colorado to Texas and Mexico and into the Gulf of Mexico.
[3]*paradoxical:* seemingly contradictory.

communities, isolated from the rest of the town by concrete columned monuments of progress, and yet stranded in the past. They are surrounded by change. It eludes their reach, in their own backyards, and the people, unable and unwilling to see the future, or even touch the present, perpetuate the past.

Leaning from the expressway or jolting across the tracks, one enters a different physical world permeated by a different attitude. The physical dimensions are impressive. It is a large section of town which extends for fifteen blocks north and south along the tracks, and then advances eastward, thinning into nothingness beyond the city limits. Within the invisible (yet sensible) walls of the barrio are many, many people living in too few houses. The homes, however, are much more numerous than on the outside. 3

Members of the barrio describe the entire area as their home. It is a home, but it is more than this. The barrio is a refuge from the harshness and the coldness of the Anglo world. It is a forced refuge. The leprous people are isolated from the rest of the community and contained in their section of town. The stoical pariahs of the barrio accept their fate, and from the angry seeds of rejection grow the flowers of closeness between outcasts, not the thorns of bitterness and the mad desire to flee. There is no want to escape, for the feeling of the barrio is known only to its inhabitants, and the material needs of life can also be found here. 4

The *tortillería* [tortilla factory] fires up its machinery three times a day, producing steaming, round, flat slices of barrio bread. In the winter, the warmth of the tortilla factory is a wool *sarape* [blanket] in the chilly morning hours, but in the summer, it unbearably toasts every noontime customer. 5

The *panadería* [bakery] sends its sweet messenger aroma down the dimly lit street, announcing the arrival of fresh, hot sugary *pan dulce* [sweet rolls]. 6

The small corner grocery serves the meal-to-meal needs of customers, and the owner, a part of the neighborhood, willingly gives credit to people unable to pay cash for foodstuffs. 7

The barbershop is a living room with hydraulic chairs, radio, and television, where old friends meet and speak of life as their salted hair falls aimlessly about them. 8

The pool hall is a junior level country club where *'chucos* [young men], strangers in their own land, get together to shoot pool and rap, while veterans, unaware of the cracking, popping balls on the green 9 felt, complacently play dominoes beneath rudely hung *Playboy* foldouts.

The *cantina* [canteen or snackbar] is the night spot of the barrio. 10
It is the country club and the den where the rites of puberty are enacted. Here the young become men. It is in the taverns that a young dude shows his *machismo* through the quantity of beer he can hold, the stories of *rucas* [women] he has had, and his willingness and ability to defend his image against hardened and scarred old lions.

No, there is no frantic wish to flee. It would be absurd to leave 11
the familiar and nervously step into the strange and cold Anglo community when the needs of the Chicano[4] can be met in the barrio.

The barrio is closeness. From the family living unit, familial rela- 12
tionships stretch out to immediate neighbors, down the block, around the corner, and to all parts of the barrio. The feeling of family, a rare and treasurable sentiment, pervades and accounts for the inability of the people to leave. The barrio is this attitude manifested on the countenances[5] of the people, on the faces of their homes, and in the gaiety of their gardens.

The color-splashed homes arrest your eyes, arouse your curiosity, 13
and make you wonder what life scenes are being played out in them. The flimsy, brightly colored, wood-frame houses ignore no neon-brilliant color. Houses trimmed in orange, chartreuse, lime-green, yellow, and mixtures of these and other hues beckon the beholder to reflect on the peculiarity of each home. Passing through this land is refreshing like Brubeck,[6] not narcoticizing like revolting rows of similar houses, which neither offend nor please.

In the evenings, the porches and front yards are occupied with 14
men calmly talking over the noise of children playing baseball in the unpaved extension of the living room, while the women cook supper or gossip with female neighbors as they water the *jardines* [gardens]. The gardens mutely echo the expressive verses of the colorful houses. The denseness of multicolored plants and trees gives the house the appearance of an oasis or a tropical island hideaway, sheltered from the rest of the world.

Fences are common in the barrio, but they are fences and not the 15
walls of the Anglo community. On the western side of town, the high

[4]*Chicano:* an American of Mexican descent.
[5]*countenances:* facial expressions that indicate mood or character.
[6]*Dave Brubeck* (b. 1920): pianist, composer, and conductor of "cool" modern jazz.

wooden fences between houses are thick, impenetrable walls, built to keep the neighbors at bay. In the barrio, the fences may be rusty, wire contraptions or thick green shrubs. In either case you can see through them and feel no sense of intrusion when you cross them.

Many lower-income families of the barrio manage to maintain a comfortable standard of living through the communal action of family members who contribute their wages to the head of the family. Economic need creates interdependence and closeness. Small bare-footed boys sell papers on cool, dark Sunday mornings, deny themselves pleasantries, and give their earnings to *mamá*. The older the child, the greater the responsibility to help the head of the household provide for the rest of the family. 16

There are those, too, who for a number of reasons have not achieved a relative sense of financial security. Perhaps it results from too many children too soon, but it is the homes of these people and their situation that numbs rather than charms. Their houses, aged and bent, oozing children, are fissures[7] in the horn of plenty. Their wooden homes may have brick-pattern asbestos tile on the outer walls, but the tile is not convincing. 17

Unable to pay city taxes or incapable of influencing the city to live up to its duty to serve all the citizens, the poorer barrio families remain trapped in the nineteenth century and survive as best they can. The backyards have well-worn paths to the outhouses, which sit near the alley. Running water is considered a luxury in some parts of the barrio. Decent drainage is usually unknown, and when it rains, the water stands for days, an incubator of health hazards and an avoidable nuisance. Streets, costly to pave, remain rough, rocky trails. Tires do not last long, and the constant rattling and shaking grind away a car's life and spread dust through screen windows. 18

The houses and their *jardines*, the jollity of the people in an adverse world, the brightly feathered alarm clock pecking away at supper and cautiously eyeing the children playing nearby, produce a mystifying sensation at finding the noble savage[8] alive in the twentieth century. It is easy to look at the positive qualities of life in the barrio, and look at them with a distantly envious feeling. One wishes to experience the feelings of the barrio and not the hardships. Remembering the illness, the hunger, the feeling of time running out on you, the walls, both 19

[7]*fissures:* narrow openings or cracks.
[8]*noble savage:* in literature, an idealized concept of uncivilized man.

real and imagined, reflecting on living in the past, one finds his envy becoming more elusive, until it has vanished altogether.

Back now beyond the tracks, the train creaks and groans, the cars 20
jostle each other down the track, and as the light begins its pulsing, the barrio, with all its meanings, greets a new dawn with yawns and restless stretchings.

Thinking Critically about This Reading

What evidence does Ramirez give to support the following claim: "Members of the barrio describe the whole area as their home. It is a home, but it is more than this" (paragraph 4)?

Questions for Study and Discussion

1. What is the barrio? Where is it? What does Ramirez mean when he states, "There is no want to escape, for the feeling of the barrio is known only to its inhabitants, and the material needs of life can also be found here" (4)?
2. Ramirez uses Spanish phrases throughout his essay. Why do you suppose he uses them? What is their effect on the reader? He also uses the words *home, refuge, family*, and *closeness*. What do they connote in the context of this essay? (Glossary: *Connotation/Denotation*) In what ways, if any, are they essential to the writer's purpose? (Glossary: *Purpose*)
3. Identify several metaphors and similes that Ramirez uses in his essay, and explain why they are particularly appropriate.
4. In paragraph 6, Ramirez uses personification when he calls the aroma of freshly baked sweet rolls a "messenger" who announces the arrival of the baked goods. Cite other words or phrases that Ramirez uses to give human characteristics to the barrio.
5. Explain Ramirez's use of the imagery of walls and fences to describe a sense of cultural isolation. What might this imagery symbolize? (Glossary: *Symbol*)
6. Ramirez begins with a relatively positive picture of the barrio, but ends on a more disheartening note. (Glossary: *Beginnings and Endings*) Why does he organize his essay in this way? What might the effect have been if he had reversed these images?

Classroom Activity Using Figurative Language

Create a metaphor or simile that would be helpful in describing each item in the following list. The first one has been completed for you to illustrate the process.

1. Skyscraper: The skyscraper sparkled like a huge glass needle.
2. Sound of an explosion
3. Intelligent student
4. Crowded bus
5. Slow-moving car
6. Pillow
7. Narrow alley
8. Greasy french fries
9. Hot sun
10. Dull knife

Compare your metaphors and similes with those written by other members of your class. Which metaphors and similes for each item on the list seem to work best? Why? Do any seem tired or clichéd?

Suggested Writing Assignments

1. In paragraph 19 Ramirez states, "One wishes to experience the feelings of the barrio and not the hardships." Explore his meaning in light of what you have just read and of other experience or knowledge you may have of "ghetto" living. In what way can it be said that the hardships of such living are a necessary part of its "feelings"? How might barrio life change, for better or for worse, if the city were to "live up to its duty to serve all the citizens" (18)?
2. Write a brief essay in which you describe your own neighborhood. (Glossary: *Description*) You may find it helpful to review what you wrote in response to the journal prompt for this selection.
3. The photograph on p. 278 shows a Hispanic woman in San Diego, California, carrying her groceries past a striking mural honoring Hispanic heroes and revolutionaries. Prominently featured are such figures as Cesar Chavez, an American who led migrant farmworkers' protests against poor working conditions in California in the 1950s–1970s, and Che Guevara, a Cuban revolutionary leader

who helped Fidel Castro come to power in the late 1950s. What details about the San Diego community can you glean from the mural? Which details tell you about the neighborhood? About the socioeconomic struggles of the barrio? Write an essay about life in the barrio as it is depicted in the mural, incorporating the visual details you see and inferences you draw from them. Be creative—use as many figures of speech as you can in your essay.

The Jacket

■ **Gary Soto**

*Born in Fresno, California, in 1952 to working-class Mexican American parents, Gary Soto is an award-winning author of poetry and fiction for readers of all ages, as well as an opera librettist and film producer. After laboring as a migrant farmworker in the San Joaquin Valley during the 1960s, he studied geography at California State University-Fresno and at the University of California-Irvine before turning his hand to poetry. In his first two collections of poetry—*The Elements of San Joaquin *(1977) and* The Tale of Sunlight *(1978)—Soto draws heavily on his childhood experiences as a Mexican American growing up in the central valley of California. To date he has published four other volumes of poetry, a collection of short stories, and four works of nonfiction, including* Living up the Street: Narrative Recollections *(1985) and* A Summer Life *(1991). His latest novel,* Amnesia in a Republican County *(2003), is a satire on political correctness.*

"The Jacket" is taken from Soto's popular collection of essays, The Effects of Knut Hamsun on a Fresno Boy *(2000). As you read, notice how Soto makes the intensity of his feelings for his jacket known through his extensive use of figurative language—simile, personification, and metaphor.*

For Your Journal

Do you remember an article of clothing that took on special significance for you as you were growing up? It might have been a pair of beautiful cowboy boots, a dress that made you feel like a princess, or a T-shirt you couldn't bear to be without. Recall the emotions that arose when you wore that special article of clothing. Reflect on the relationship between clothes and one's identity.

My clothes have failed me. I remember the green coat that I wore in fifth and sixth grades when you either danced like a champ or pressed yourself against a greasy wall, bitter as a penny toward the happy couples. 1

When I needed a new jacket and my mother asked what kind I wanted, I described something like bikers wear: black leather and silver studs with enough belts to hold down a small town. We were in the kitchen, steam on the windows from her cooking. She listened so long while stirring dinner that I thought she understood for sure the kind I wanted. The next day when I got home from school, I discovered draped on my bedpost a jacket the color of day-old guacamole. I threw my books on the bed and approached the jacket slowly, as if it were a stranger whose hand I had to shake. I touched the vinyl sleeve, the collar, and peeked at the mustard-colored lining. 2

From the kitchen mother yelled that my jacket was in the closet. I closed the door to her voice and pulled at the rack of clothes in the closet, hoping the jacket on the bedpost wasn't for me but my mean brother. No luck. I gave up. From my bed, I stared at the jacket. I wanted to cry because it was so ugly and so big that I knew I'd have to wear it a long time. I was a small kid, thin as a young tree, and it would be years before I'd have a new one. I stared at the jacket, like an enemy, thinking bad things before I took off my old jacket whose sleeves climbed halfway to my elbow. 3

I put the big jacket on. I zipped it up and down several times, and rolled the cuffs up so they didn't cover my hands. I put my hands in the pockets and flapped the jacket like a bird's wings. I stood in front of the mirror, full face, then profile, and then looked over my shoulder as if someone had called me. I sat on the bed, stood against the bed, and combed my hair to see what I would look like doing something natural. I looked ugly. I threw it on my brother's bed and looked at it for a long time before I slipped it on and went out to the backyard, smiling a "thank you" to my mom as I passed her in the kitchen. With my hands in my pockets I kicked a ball against the fence, and then climbed it to sit looking into the alley. I hurled orange peels at the mouth of an open garbage can and when the peels were gone I watched the white puffs of my breath thin to nothing. 4

I jumped down, hands in my pockets, and in the backyard on my knees I teased my dog, Brownie, by swooping my arms while making bird calls. He jumped at me and missed. He jumped again and again, until a tooth sunk deep, ripping an L-shaped tear on my left sleeve. I pushed Brownie away to study the tear as I would a cut on my arm. There was no blood, only a few loose pieces of fuzz. Damn dog, I thought, and pushed him away hard when he tried to bite again. I got 5 up from my knees and went to my bedroom to sit with my jacket on my lap, with the lights out.

That was the first afternoon with my new jacket. The next day I wore it to sixth grade and got a D on a math quiz. During the morning recess Frankie T., the playground terrorist, pushed me to the ground and told me to stay there until recess was over. My best friend, Steve Negrete, ate an apple while looking at me, and the girls turned away to whisper on the monkey bars. The teachers were no help: they looked my way and talked about how foolish I looked in my new jacket. I saw their heads bob with laughter, their hands half-covering their mouths. 6

Even though it was cold, I took off the jacket during lunch and played kickball in a thin shirt, my arm feeling like braille[1] from the goose bumps. But when I returned to class I slipped the jacket on and shivered until I was warm. I sat on my hands, heating them up, while my teeth chattered like a cup of crooked dice. Finally warm, I slid out of the jacket but a few minutes later put it back on when the fire bell rang. We paraded out into the yard where we, the sixth graders, walked past all the other grades to stand against the back fence. Everybody saw me. Although they didn't say out loud, "Man, that's ugly," I heard the buzz-buzz of gossip and even laughter that I knew was meant for me. 7

And so I went, in my guacamole-colored jacket. So embarrassed, so hurt, I couldn't even do my homework. I received Cs on quizzes, and forgot the state capitals and rivers of South America, our friendly neighbor. Even the girls who had been friendly blew away like loose flowers to follow the boys in neat jackets. 8

I wore that thing for three years until the sleeves grew short and my forearms stuck out like the necks of turtles. All during that time no love came to me—no little dark girl in a Sunday dress she wore on Monday. At lunchtime I stayed with the ugly boys who leaned against the chainlink fence and looked around with propellers of grass spinning in our mouths. We saw girls walk by alone, saw couples, hand in hand, their heads like bookends pressing air together. We saw them and spun our propellers so fast our faces were blurs. 9

I blame that jacket for those bad years. I blame my mother for her bad taste and her cheap ways. It was a sad time for the heart. With a friend I spent my sixth-grade year in a tree in the alley, waiting for something good to happen to me in that jacket, which had become 10

[1]*braille:* a system of writing for the blind in which characters are formed with patterns of raised dots that can be felt with the fingers.

the ugly brother who tagged along wherever I went. And it was about that time that I began to grow. My chest puffed up with muscle and, strangely, a few more ribs. Even my hands, those fleshy hammers, showed bravely through the cuffs, the fingers already hardening for the coming fights. But that L-shaped rip on the left sleeve got bigger, bits of stuffing coughed out from its wound after a hard day of play. I finally Scotch-taped it closed, but in rain or cold weather the tape peeled off like a scab and more stuffing fell out until that sleeve shriveled into a palsied arm. That winter the elbows began to crack and whole chunks of green began to fall off. I showed the cracks to my mother, who always seemed to be at the stove with steamed-up glasses, and she said that there were children in Mexico who would love that jacket. I told her that this was America and yelled that Debbie, my sister, didn't have a jacket like mine. I ran outside, ready to cry, and climbed the tree by the alley to think bad thoughts and watch my breath puff white and disappear.

But whole pieces still casually flew off my jacket when I played 11
hard, read quietly, or took vicious spelling tests at school. When it became so spotted that my brother began to call me "camouflage," I flung it over the fence into the alley. Later, however, I swiped the jacket off the ground and went inside to drape it across my lap and mope.

I was called to dinner: steam silvered my mother's glasses as she 12
said grace; my brother and sister with their heads bowed made ugly faces at their glasses of powdered milk. I gagged too, but eagerly ate big rips of buttered tortilla that held scooped-up beans. Finished, I went outside with my jacket across my arm. It was a cold sky. The faces of clouds were piled up, hurting. I climbed the fence, jumping down with a grunt. I started up the alley and soon slipped into my jacket, that green ugly brother who breathed over my shoulder that day and ever since.

Thinking Critically about This Reading

Does Soto's embarrassment come from what people around him say about his jacket or from another source? Would his sense of embarrassment have been relieved if his mother had bought him the leather jacket he wanted? Explain.

Questions for Study and Discussion

1. Explain the relationship between Soto and the jacket. What does the jacket symbolize for him? (Glossary: *Symbol*) In what sense

might the jacket be something more than the cause of his failures and embarrassments? What is the jacket's role in Soto's essay? Explain.

2. What does the tree in the backyard symbolize? (Glossary: *Symbol*)
3. Why do you suppose that Soto's mother did not buy him the black leather jacket he wanted so badly? Was she trying to embarrass him or punish him in some way? What other reason might explain her decision to buy a jacket that was the color of "day-old guacamole" (paragraph 2)?
4. Soto includes a rich range of figurative language in his narrative. Identify at least six figures of speech. What purpose does each one serve? What effect does each one have on you as a reader? Would his story have been as effective had he not used these figures of speech? Explain.
5. Soto refers to his brother when explaining how much he disliked the new jacket. What is the relationship between the new jacket and the brother?
6. Did Soto's new jacket cause his grades to suffer? Explain. (Glossary: *Cause and Effect*) Did the jacket cause Soto to miss out on any friendships with girls? Explain.

Classroom Activity Using Figurative Language

Soto makes use of a variety of figures of speech, including personification. For example, the essay begins with "My clothes have failed me" (1), and it ends with Soto referring to his jacket as "that green ugly brother who breathed over my shoulder that day and ever since" (12). Select an article of your own clothing, and personify it in a brief description or narrative.

Suggested Writing Assignments

1. It might be argued that in times of crisis everything becomes symbolic. So it is with this essay. Soto is going through a rough period in his life as he tries to negotiate the stresses of approaching adolescence. The jacket becomes symbolic of all the difficulties he is having, or perceives himself to be having, with his circumstances and everyone around him. (Glossary: *Symbol*) His situation

is not unlike our own at times. That Soto is able to make us understand and feel for the narrator is the product of his expertise as a writer. Write an essay about a dilemma or crisis, real or perceived, in your life that is similar to what the narrator experiences in "The Jacket." Try to include as many figures of speech as you can but only if they are natural and occasioned by the context of your narrative.

2. In an interview in *Esquire* magazine, Hollywood producer Bob Evans said the following: "Background makes foreground. This goes for the movies, it goes for dressing, it goes for living. Here's an example: If I go to a party and eight different people come over and say, 'Gee, that's a great-looking tie,' as soon as I get home, I take the tie off and put it in the shredder. Screw the tie! I'm not there to make the *tie* look good. The tie is there to make *me* look good. That's what I mean by background makes foreground." Write an essay on the relationship between people and clothes. Do clothes make the person? If not, why are so many people clothes-conscious? Use as many types of figurative language as you can to enliven your prose and make your point.

A Hanging

George Orwell

Although probably best known for his novels Animal Farm *(1945) and* 1984 *(1949), George Orwell (1903–1950) was also a renowned essayist on language and politics. Two of his most famous essays, "Shooting an Elephant" and "Politics and the English Language," are among the most frequently reprinted. Orwell was born in Bengal, India, and was educated in England. He traveled a great deal during his life and spent five years serving with the British colonial police in Burma.*

The following essay is a product of his experience in Burma, and first appeared in Shooting an Elephant and Other Essays *(1950). Notice how Orwell relies consistently on similes to help convey and emphasize his attitude about the events he describes, events in which he is both an observer and a participant.*

For Your Journal

Throughout history, people have gone out of their way to witness events in which someone was certain to be killed, such as fights between gladiators, jousting tournaments, and public executions. Why do you think such events fascinate people?

It was in Burma,[1] a sodden morning of the rains. A sickly light, like yellow tinfoil, was slanting over the high walls into the jail yard. We were waiting outside the condemned cells, a row of sheds fronted with double bars, like small animal cages. Each cell measured about ten feet by ten and was quite bare within except for a plank bed and a pot of drinking water. In some of them brown silent men were squatting at the inner bars, with their blankets draped round them. These were the condemned men, due to be hanged within the next week or two. 1

[1]*Burma:* a country in Southeast Asia, formerly part of Britain's Indian Empire, now known as Myanmar.

One prisoner had been brought out of his cell. He was a Hindu,[2] a puny wisp of a man, with a shaven head and vague liquid eyes. He had a thick, sprouting moustache, absurdly too big for his body, rather like the moustache of a comic man in the films. Six tall Indian warders were guarding him and getting him ready for the gallows. Two of them stood by with rifles with fixed bayonets, while the others handcuffed him, passed a chain through his handcuffs and fixed it to their belts, and lashed his arms tight to his sides. They crowded very close about him, with their hands always on him in a careful, caressing grip, as though all the while feeling him to make sure he was there. It was like men handling a fish which is still alive and may jump back into the water. But he stood quite unresisting, yielding his arms limply to the ropes, as though he hardly noticed what was happening. 2

Eight o'clock struck and a bugle call, desolately thin in the wet air, floated from the distant barracks. The superintendent of the jail, who was standing apart from the rest of us, moodily prodding the gravel with his stick, raised his head at the sound. He was an army doctor, with a gray toothbrush moustache and a gruff voice. "For God's sake hurry up, Francis," he said irritably. "The man ought to have been dead by this time. Aren't you ready yet?" 3

Francis, the head jailer, a fat Dravidian[3] in a white drill suit and gold spectacles, waved his black hand. "Yes sir, yes sir," he bubbled. "All iss satisfactorily prepared. The hangman iss waiting. We shall proceed." 4

"Well, quick march, then. The prisoners can't get their breakfast till this job's over." 5

We set out for the gallows. Two warders marched on either side of the prisoner, with their files at the slope; two others marched close against him, gripping him by arm and shoulder, as though at once pushing and supporting him. The rest of us, magistrates and the like, followed behind. Suddenly, when we had gone ten yards, the procession stopped short without any order or warning. A dreadful thing had happened—a dog, come goodness knows whence, had appeared in the yard. It came bounding among us with a loud volley of barks, and leapt round us wagging its whole body, wild with glee at finding so many human beings together. It was a large woolly dog, half Airedale, 6

[2]*Hindu:* a person whose beliefs and practices are rooted in the philosophical and religious tenets of Hinduism, which originated in India.

[3]*Dravidian:* someone who speaks one of the twenty-three languages belonging to the family of languages known as Dravidian, which is spoken in South Asia.

half pariah.[4] For a moment it pranced round us, and then, before anyone could stop it, it had made a dash for the prisoner, and jumping up tried to lick his face. Everyone stood aghast, too taken aback even to grab at the dog.

"Who let that bloody brute in here?" said the superintendent angrily. "Catch it, someone!" 7

A warder, detached from the escort, charged clumsily after the dog, 8 but it danced and gamboled[5] just out of his reach, taking everything as part of the game. A young Eurasian jailer picked up a handful of gravel and tried to stone the dog away, but it dodged the stones and came after us again. Its yaps echoed from the jail walls. The prisoner, in the grasp of the two warders, looked on incuriously, as though this was another formality of the hanging. It was several minutes before someone managed to catch the dog. Then we put my handkerchief through its collar and moved off once more, with the dog still straining and whimpering.

It was about forty yards to the gallows. I watched the bare brown 9 back of the prisoner marching in front of me. He walked clumsily with his bound arms, but quite steadily, with that bobbing gait of the Indian who never straightens his knees. At each step his muscles slid neatly into place, the lock of hair on his scalp danced up and down, his feet printed themselves on the wet gravel. And once, in spite of the men who gripped him by each shoulder, he stepped slightly aside to avoid a puddle on the path.

It is curious, but till that moment I had never realized what it 10 means to destroy a healthy, conscious man. When I saw the prisoner step aside to avoid the puddle, I saw the mystery, the unspeakable wrongness, of cutting a life short when it is in full tide. This man was not dying, he was alive just as we were alive. All the organs of his body were working—bowels digesting food, skin renewing itself, nails growing, tissues forming—all toiling away in solemn foolery. His nails would still be growing when he stood on the drop, when he was falling through the air with a tenth of a second to live. His eyes saw the yellow gravel and the gray walls, and his brain still remembered, foresaw, reasoned—reasoned even about puddles. He and we were a party of men walking together, seeing, hearing, feeling, understanding the same world; and in two minutes, with a sudden snap, one of us would be gone—one mind less, one world less.

---

[4]*pariah:* social outcast.
[5]*gamboled:* leaped about playfully; frolicked.

The gallows stood in a small yard, separate from the main grounds of the prison, and overgrown with tall prickly weeds. It was a brick erection like three sides of a shed, with planking on top, and above that two beams and a crossbar with the rope dangling. The hangman, a gray-haired convict in the white uniform of the prison, was waiting beside his machine. He greeted us with a servile crouch as we entered. At a word from Francis the two warders, gripping the prisoner more closely than ever, half led, half pushed him to the gallows and helped him clumsily up the ladder. Then the hangman climbed up and fixed the rope round the prisoner's neck. 11

We stood waiting, five yards away. The warders had formed in a rough circle round the gallows. And then, when the noose was fixed, the prisoner began crying out to his god. It was a high, reiterated cry of "Ram! Ram! Ram! Ram!," not urgent and fearful like a prayer or a cry for help, but steady, rhythmical, almost like the tolling of a bell. The dog answered the sound with a whine. The hangman, still standing on the gallows, produced a small cotton bag like a flour bag and drew it down over the prisoner's face. But the sound, muffled by the cloth, still persisted, over and over again: "Ram! Ram! Ram! Ram! Ram!" 12

The hangman climbed down and stood ready, holding the lever. Minutes seemed to pass. The steady, muffled crying from the prisoner went on and on, "Ram! Ram! Ram!" never faltering for an instant. The superintendent, his head on his chest, was slowly poking the ground with his stick; perhaps he was counting the cries, allowing the prisoner a fixed number—fifty, perhaps, or a hundred. Everyone had changed color. The Indians had gone gray like bad coffee, and one or two of the bayonets were wavering. We looked at the lashed, hooded man on the drop, and listened to his cries—each cry another second of life; the same thought was in all our minds: oh, kill him quickly, get it over, stop that abominable noise! 13

Suddenly the superintendent made up his mind. Throwing up his head he made a swift motion with his stick. "Chalo!" he shouted almost fiercely. 14

There was a clanking noise, and then dead silence. The prisoner had vanished, and the rope was twisting on itself. I let go of the dog, and it galloped immediately to the back of the gallows; but when it got there it stopped short, barked, and then retreated into the corner of the yard, where it stood among the weeds, looking timorously[6] out at us. We went round the gallows to inspect the prisoner's body. He 15

[6]*timorously:* timidly; fearfully.

was dangling with his toes pointed straight downwards, very slowly revolving, as dead as a stone.

The superintendent reached out with his stick and poked the bare body; it oscillated,[7] slightly. "*He's* all right," said the superintendent. He backed out from under the gallows, and blew out a deep breath. The moody look had gone out of his face quite suddenly. He glanced at his wristwatch. "Eight minutes past eight. Well, that's all for this morning, thank God." 16

The warders unfixed bayonets and marched away. The dog, sobered and conscious of having misbehaved itself, slipped after them. We walked out of the gallows yard, past the condemned cells with their waiting prisoners, into the big central yard of the prison. The convicts, under the command of warders armed with lathis,[8] were already receiving their breakfast. They squatted in long rows, each man holding a tin pannikin, while two warders with buckets marched round ladling out rice; it seemed quite a homely, jolly scene, after the hanging. An enormous relief had come upon us now that the job was done. One felt an impulse to sing, to break into a run, to snigger. All at once everyone began chattering gaily. 17

The Eurasian boy walking beside me nodded towards the way we had come, with a knowing smile: "Do you know, sir, our friend (he meant the dead man), when he heard his appeal had been dismissed, he pissed on the floor of his cell. From fright.—Kindly take one of my cigarettes, sir. Do you not admire my new silver case, sir? From the boxwallah,[9] two rupees eight annas. Classy European style." 18

Several people laughed—at what, nobody seemed certain. 19

Francis was walking by the superintendent, talking garrulously[10]: "Well, sir, all hass passed off with the utmost satisfactoriness. It wass all finished—flick! like that. It iss not always so—oah, no! I have known cases where the doctor wass obliged to go beneath the gallows and pull the prisoner's legs to ensure decease. Most disagreeable!" 20

"Wriggling about, eh? That's bad," said the superintendent. 21

"Ach, sir, it iss worse when they become refractory![11] One man, I recall, clung to the bars of hiss cage when we went to take him out. You will scarcely credit, sir, that it took six warders to dislodge him, 22

[7]*oscillated:* swung back and forth.
[8]*lathis:* a wooden or metal baton.
[9]*boxwallah:* a trader or peddler.
[10]*garrulously:* annoyingly talkative and loud.
[11]*refractory:* resistant to authority; unruly.

three pulling at each leg. We reasoned with him. 'My dear fellow,' we said, 'think of all the pain and trouble you are causing to us!' But no, he would not listen! Ach, he wass very troublesome!"

I found that I was laughing quite loudly. Everyone was laughing. Even the superintendent grinned in a tolerant way. "You'd better all come out and have a drink," he said quite genially. "I've got a bottle of whisky in the car. We could do with it." 23

We went through the big double gates of the prison, into the road. "Pulling at his legs!" exclaimed a Burmese magistrate suddenly, and burst into a loud chuckling. We all began laughing again. At that moment Francis's anecdote seemed extraordinarily funny. We all had a drink together, native and European alike, quite amicably. The dead man was a hundred yards away. 24

Thinking Critically about This Reading

Orwell goes to some pains to identify the multicultural nature—Hindu, Dravidian, Eurasian, European, Burmese—of the group participating in the hanging scene. Why is the variety of the participants' backgrounds important to the central idea of the essay?

Questions for Study and Discussion

1. In paragraph 6, why is the appearance of the dog "a dreadful thing"? From whose point of view is it dreadful?
2. The role of the narrator of this essay is never clearly defined, nor is the nature of the prisoner's transgression. (Glossary: *Narration*) Why does Orwell deliberately withhold this information?
3. In paragraphs 9 and 10, the prisoner steps aside to avoid a puddle, and Orwell considers the implications of this action. What understanding does he reach? In paragraph 10, what is the meaning of the phrase "one mind less, one world less"?
4. In paragraph 22, what is ironic about Francis's story of the "troublesome" prisoner? (Glossary: *Irony*)
5. Throughout this essay, Orwell uses figurative language, primarily similes, to bring a foreign experience closer to the reader's understanding. Find and explain three or four similes that clarify the event for a modern American reader.

6. What words would you use to describe the mood of the group that observed the hanging before the event? Afterward? Cite specific details to support your word choice. Why are the moods so extreme?

Classroom Activity Using Figurative Language

Think of a time when you were one of a group of people assembled to do something most or all of you didn't really want to do. People in such a situation behave in various ways, showing their discomfort. One might stare steadily at the ground, for example. A writer describing the scene could use a metaphor to make it more vivid for the reader: "With his gaze he drilled a hole in the ground between his feet." Other people in an uncomfortable situation might fidget, lace their fingers together, breathe rapidly, squirm, or tap an object, such as a pen or a key. Create a simile or a metaphor to describe each of these behaviors.

Suggested Writing Assignments

1. Are the men who carry out the hanging in Orwell's essay cruel? Are they justified in their actions, following orders from others better able to judge? Or should they question their assigned roles as executioners? Who has the right to take the life of another? Write an essay in which you either condemn or support Orwell's role in the hanging. Was it appropriate for him to have participated, even as a spectator? What, if anything, should or could he have done when he "saw the mystery, the unspeakable wrongness, of cutting a life short when it is in full tide" (10)?
2. Recall and narrate an event in your life when you or someone you know underwent some sort of punishment. (Glossary: *Narration*) You may have been a participant or a spectator in the event. How did you react when you learned what the punishment was to be? When it was administered? After it was over? Use figurative language to make vivid the scene during which the punishment was imposed.

part ■ four

Types of Essays

chapter **12**

Illustration

Illustration is the use of **examples**—facts, opinions, samples, and anecdotes or stories—to make ideas more concrete and to make generalizations more specific and detailed. Examples enable writers not just to tell, but also to show what they mean. The more specific the example, the more effective it is. For instance, in an essay about alternative sources of energy, a writer might offer an example of how a local architecture firm designed a home heated by solar collectors instead of a conventional oil, gas, or electric system.

A writer uses examples to clarify or support the thesis in an essay and the main ideas in paragraphs. Sometimes a single striking example suffices; at other times a whole series of related examples is necessary. The following paragraph presents a single extended example—an anecdote that illustrates the writer's point about cultural differences:

> Whenever there is a great cultural distance between two people, there are bound to be problems arising from differences in behavior and expectations. An example is the American couple who consulted a psychiatrist about their marital problems. The husband was from New England and had been brought up by reserved parents who taught him to control his emotions and to respect the need for privacy. His wife was from an Italian family and had been brought up in close contact with all the members of her large family, who were extremely warm, volatile, and demonstrative. When the husband came home after a hard day at the office, dragging his feet and longing for peace and quiet, his wife would rush to him and smother him. Clasping his hands, rubbing his brow, crooning over his weary head, she never left him alone. But when the wife was upset or anxious about her day, the husband's response was to withdraw completely and leave her alone. No comforting, no affectionate embrace, no attention—just solitude. The woman became convinced her husband didn't love her and, in desperation,

she consulted a psychiatrist. Their problem wasn't basically psychological but cultural.

–Edward T. Hall

This single example is effective because it is *representative*—that is, essentially similar to other such problems Hall might have described and familiar to many readers. Hall tells the story with enough detail that readers can understand the couple's feelings and so better understand the point he is trying to make.

In contrast, another writer supports his topic sentence about superstitions with ten examples:

> In the folklore of the country, numerous superstitions relate to winter weather. Back-country farmers examine their corn husks—the thicker the husk, the colder the winter. They watch the acorn crop—the more acorns, the more severe the season. They observe where white-faced hornets place their paper nests—the higher they are, the deeper will be the snow. They examine the size and shape and color of the spleens of butchered hogs for clues to the severity of the season. They keep track of the blooming of dogwood in the spring—the more abundant the blooms, the more bitter the cold in January. When chipmunks carry their tails high and squirrels have heavier fur and mice come into country houses early in the fall, the superstitious gird themselves for a long, hard winter. Without any scientific basis, a wider-than-usual black band on a woolly-bear caterpillar is accepted as a sign that winter will arrive early and stay late. Even the way a cat sits beside the stove carries its message to the credulous. According to a belief once widely held in the Ozarks, a cat sitting with its tail to the fire indicates very cold weather is on the way.
>
> –Edwin Way Teale

Teale uses numerous examples because he is writing about various superstitions. Also, putting all those strange beliefs side by side in a kind of catalog makes the paragraph fun to read as well as convincing and informative.

To use illustration effectively, begin by thinking of ideas and generalizations about your topic that you can make clearer and more persuasive by illustrating them with facts, anecdotes, or specific details. You should focus primarily on your main point, the central generalization that you will develop in your essay. Also be alert for other statements or references that may benefit from illustration. Points that are already clear and uncontroversial, that your readers will understand and immediately agree with, can stand on their own as you pass along quickly to your next idea; belaboring the obvious wastes your time and energy, as well as your reader's. Often, however, you will find that examples add clarity, color, and weight to what you say.

Consider the following generalization:

> Americans are a pain-conscious people who would rather get rid of pain than seek and cure its root causes.

This assertion is broad and general; it raises the following questions: How so? What does this mean exactly? Why does the writer think so? The statement could be the topic sentence of a paragraph or perhaps even the thesis of an essay or of an entire book. As a writer, you could make the generalization stronger and more meaningful through illustration. You might support this statement by citing specific situations or specific cases in which Americans have gone to the drugstore instead of to a doctor, as well as by supplying sales figures per capita of painkillers in the United States as compared with other countries.

Illustration is so useful and versatile a strategy that it is found in all kinds of writing. It is essential, for example, in writing a successful argument essay. In an essay arguing that non-English-speaking students starting school in the United States should be taught English as a second language, one writer supports her argument with the following illustration, drawn from her own experience as a Spanish-speaking child in an English-only school:

> Without the use of Spanish, unable to communicate with the teacher or students, for six long weeks we guessed at everything we did. When we lined up to go anywhere, neither my sister nor I knew what to expect. Once, the teacher took the class on a bathroom break, and I mistakenly thought we were on our way to the cafeteria for lunch. Before we left, I grabbed our lunch money, and one of the girls in line began sneering and pointing. Somehow she figured out my mistake before I did. When I realized why she was laughing, I became embarrassed and threw the money into my sister's desk as we walked out of the classroom.
>
> –Hilda Alvarado, student

Alvarado could have summarized her point in the preceding paragraph in fewer words:

> Not only are non-English-speaking students in English-only schools unable to understand the information they are supposed to be learning, but they are also subject to frequent embarrassment and teasing from their classmates.

By offering an illustration, however, Alvarado makes her point more vividly and effectively.

A Crime of Compassion

Barbara Huttmann

Barbara Huttmann, who lives in the San Francisco Bay Area, received her nursing degree in 1976. After obtaining a master's degree in nursing administration, she cofounded a healthcare consulting firm for hospitals, nursing organizations, and consumers. Her interest in patients' rights is clearly evident in her two books, The Patient's Advocate *(1981) and* Code Blue *(1982).*

In the following essay, which first appeared in Newsweek *in 1983, Huttmann narrates the final months of the life of Mac, one of her favorite patients. By using emotional and graphic detail, Huttmann hopes Mac's example will convince her audience of the need for new legislation that would permit terminally ill patients to choose to die rather than suffer great pain and indignity. As you read about Mac, consider the degree to which his experience seems representative of what patients often endure because medical technology is now able to keep them alive longer than they would be able to survive on their own.*

For Your Journal

For most people, being sick is at best an unpleasant experience. Reflect on an illness you have had, whether you were sick with a simple common cold or with an affliction that required you to be hospitalized for a time. What were your concerns and fears? For what were you most thankful?

"Murderer," a man shouted. "God help patients who get *you* for a nurse." 1

"What gives you the right to play God?" another one asked. 2

It was the *Phil Donahue Show*[1] where the guest is a fatted calf and the audience a 200-strong flock of vultures hungering to pick at the bones. I had told them about Mac, one of my favorite cancer 3

[1]*Phil Donahue Show:* the first daytime TV talk show that got the audience involved, airing from 1970 to 1996.

patients. "We resuscitated him 52 times in just one month. I refused to resuscitate him again. I simply sat there and held his hand while he died."

There wasn't time to explain that Mac was a young, witty, macho cop who walked into the hospital with 32 pounds of attack equipment, looking as if he could single-handedly protect the whole city, if not the entire state. "Can't get rid of this cough," he said. Otherwise, he felt great. 4

Before the day was over, tests confirmed that he had lung cancer. And before the year was over, I loved him, his wife, Maura, and their three kids as if they were my own. All the nurses loved him. And we all battled his disease for six months without ever giving death a thought. Six months isn't such a long time in the whole scheme of things, but it was long enough to see him lose his youth, his wit, his macho, his hair, his bowel and bladder control, his sense of taste and smell, and his ability to do the slightest thing for himself. It was also long enough to watch Maura's transformation from a young woman into a haggard, beaten old lady. 5

When Mac had wasted away to a 60-pound skeleton kept alive by liquid food we poured down a tube, IV solutions we dripped into his veins, and oxygen we piped to a mask on his face, he begged us: "Mercy . . . for God's sake, please just let me go." 6

The first time he stopped breathing, the nurse pushed the button that calls a "code blue" throughout the hospital and sends a team rushing to resuscitate the patient. Each time he stopped breathing, sometimes two or three times in one day, the code team came again. The doctors and technicians worked their miracles and walked away. The nurses stayed to wipe the saliva that drooled from his mouth, irrigate the big craters of bedsores that covered his hips, suction the lung fluids that threatened to drown him, clean the feces that burned his skin like lye,[2] pour the liquid food down the tube attached to his stomach, put pillows between his knees to ease the bone-on-bone pain, turn him every hour to keep the bedsores from getting worse, and change his gown and linen every two hours to keep him from being soaked in perspiration. 7

At night I went home and tried to scrub away the smell of decaying flesh that seemed woven into the fabric of my uniform. It was in my hair, the upholstery of my car—there was no washing it away. 8

[2]*lye:* a chemical used in cleaning products that can burn skin.

And every night I prayed that Mac would die, that his agonized eyes would never again plead with me to let him die.

Every morning I asked his doctor for a "no-code" order. Without 9
that order, we had to resuscitate every patient who stopped breathing. His doctor was one of several who believe we must extend life as long as we have the means and knowledge to do it. To not do it is to be liable for negligence, at least in the eyes of many people, including some nurses. I thought about what it would be like to stand before a judge, accused of murder, if Mac stopped breathing and I didn't call a code.

And after the fifty-second code, when Mac was still lucid enough 10
to beg for death again, and Maura was crumbled in my arms again, and when no amount of pain medication stilled his moaning and agony, I wondered about a spiritual judge. Was all this misery and suffering supposed to be building character or infusing us all with the sense of humility that comes from impotence?

Had we, the whole medical community, become so arrogant that 11
we believed in the illusion of salvation through science? Had we become so self-righteous that we thought meddling in God's work was our duty, our moral imperative, and our legal obligation? Did we really believe that we had the right to force "life" on a suffering man who had begged for the right to die?

Such questions haunted me more than ever early one morning 12
when Maura went home to change her clothes and I was bathing Mac. He had been still for so long, I thought he at last had the blessed relief of coma. Then he opened his eyes and moaned, "Pain . . . no more . . . Barbara . . . do something . . . God, let me go."

The desperation in his eyes and voice riddled me with guilt. "I'll 13
stop," I told him as I injected the pain medication.

I sat on the bed and held Mac's hands in mine. He pressed his 14
bony fingers against my hand and muttered, "Thanks." Then there was one soft sigh and I felt his hands go cold in mine. "Mac?" I whispered, as I waited for his chest to rise and fall again.

A clutch of panic banded my chest, drew my finger to the code 15
button, urged me to do something, anything . . . but sit there alone with death. I kept one finger on the button, without pressing it, as a waxen pallor[3] slowly transformed his face from person to empty shell. Nothing I've ever done in my 47 years has taken so much effort as it took *not* to press that code button.

---

[3]*pallor:* extreme paleness.

Eventually, when I was as sure as I could be that the code team would fail to bring him back, I entered the legal twilight zone and pushed the button. The team tried. And while they were trying, Maura walked into the room and shrieked, "No . . . don't let them do this to him . . . for God's sake . . . please, no more." 16

Cradling her in my arms was like cradling myself, Mac, and all those patients and nurses who had been in this place before, who do the best they can in a death-denying society. 17

So a TV audience accused me of murder. Perhaps I am guilty. If a doctor had written a no-code order, which is the only *legal* alternative, would he have felt any less guilty? Until there is legislation making it a criminal act to code a patient who has requested the right to die, we will all of us risk the same fate as Mac. For whatever reason, we developed the means to prolong life, and now we are forced to use it. We do not have the right to die. 18

Thinking Critically about This Reading

In the rhetorical question "Did we really believe that we had the right to force 'life' on a suffering man who had begged for the right to die?" (paragraph 11), why do you think Huttmann places the word *life* in quotation marks?

Questions for Study and Discussion

1. Why do people in the audience of the *Phil Donahue Show* call Huttmann a "murderer"? Is their accusation justified? In what ways do you think Huttmann might agree with them?
2. In paragraph 15, Huttmann states, "Nothing I've ever done in my 47 years has taken so much effort as it took *not* to press that code button." How effectively does she describe her struggle against pressing the button? What steps led to her ultimate decision not to press the code button?
3. What, according to Huttmann, is "the only *legal* alternative" (18) to her action? What does she find hypocritical about that choice?
4. Huttmann makes a powerfully emotional appeal for a patient's right to die. Some readers might even find some of her story shocking or offensive. Cite examples of some of the graphic scenes

Huttmann describes, and discuss their impact on you as a reader. (Glossary: *Example*) Do they help persuade you to Huttmann's point of view, or do you find them overly unnerving? What would have been gained or lost had she left them out?

5. Huttmann's story covers a period of six months. In paragraphs 4–6, she describes the first five months of Mac's illness; in paragraphs 7–10, the sixth month; and in paragraphs 12–17, the final morning. What important point about narration does her use of time in this sequence demonstrate? (Glossary: *Narration*)
6. Huttmann concludes her essay with the statement "We do not have the right to die" (18). What does she mean by this? In your opinion, is she exaggerating or simply stating the facts? Does her example of Mac adequately illustrate Huttmann's concluding point? Explain.

Classroom Activity Using Illustration

Huttmann illustrates her thesis by using the single example of Mac's experience in the hospital. Using the first statement as a model, find a single example that might be used to best illustrate each of the following potential thesis statements:

Seat belts save lives. (*Possible answer:* an automobile accident in which a relative's life was saved because she was wearing her seat belt.)

Friends can be very handy.
Having good study skills can improve a student's grades.
Loud music can damage your hearing.
Reading the directions for a new product you have just purchased can save time and aggravation.
Humor can often make a bad situation more tolerable.
American manufacturers can make their products safer.

Suggested Writing Assignments

1. Write a letter to the editor of *Newsweek* in response to Huttmann's essay. Are you for or against legislation that would give terminally ill patients the right to die? Give examples from your personal experience or from your reading to support your opinion.

2. Using one of the following sentences as your thesis statement, write an essay giving examples from your personal experience or from your reading to support your opinion.

   Consumers have more power than they realize.

   Most products do (or do not) measure up to the claims of their advertisements.

   Religion is (or is not) alive and well in America.

   Our government works far better than its critics claim.

   Being able to write well is more than a basic skill.

   The seasons for professional sports are too long.

   Today's college students are (or are not) serious minded when it comes to academics.

3. In the photograph on page 305, taken on March 29, 2005, a young protester holds a poster in front of the Woodside Hospice in Pinellas Park, Florida, where Terri Schiavo was being cared for. You may remember images like this from news coverage as America intently witnessed the long and often bitter legal battle to prolong the Florida woman's life after several courts ordered her feeding tube removed. The Schiavo case served to galvanize public opinion on the issues of the right to die and who makes end-of-life decisions for an incapacitated person. Are you surprised to see such a young boy at a protest like this one? Why or why not? What does the message on his poster mean to you? Do you think the boy understands his sign? Why or why not? Write an essay in which you present your position on the issue of children and protests. At what age, if at all, should children participate in demonstrations on life-and-death issues?

AMURDERICA

Be Specific

■ **Natalie Goldberg**

Born in 1948, Natalie Goldberg has made a specialty of writing about writing. Her first and best-known work, Writing Down the Bones: Freeing the Writer Within, *was published in 1986. Goldberg's advice to would-be writers is, on the one hand, practical and pithy; on the other, it is almost mystical in its call to know and appreciate the world. Her other books about writing include* Wild Mind: Living the Writer's Life *(1990),* Living Color *(1996), and* Thunder and Lightning: Cracking Open the Writer's Craft *(2000). Goldberg has also written fiction. Her first novel,* Banana Rose, *was published in 1994. She is also a painter whose work is exhibited in Taos, New Mexico.* Living Color: A Writer Paints Her World *(1997) is about painting as her second art form, and* Top of My Lungs *(2002) is a collection of poetry and paintings.*

In "Be Specific," a chapter from Writing Down the Bones, *notice how Goldberg demonstrates her advice to be specific.*

For Your Journal

Suppose someone says to you, "I walked in the woods." What do you envision? Write down what you see in your mind's eye. Now suppose someone says, "I walked in the redwood forest." Again, write what you see. How are the two descriptions different, and why?

Be specific. Don't say "fruit." Tell what kind of fruit—"It is a pomegranate." Give things the dignity of their names. Just as with human beings, it is rude to say, "Hey, girl, get in line." That "girl" has a name. (As a matter of fact, if she's at least twenty years old, she's a woman, not a "girl" at all.) Things, too, have names. It is much better to say "the geranium in the window" than "the flower in the window." "Geranium"—that one word gives us a much more specific picture. It penetrates more deeply into the beingness of that flower. It immediately gives us the scene by the window—red petals, green circular leaves, all straining toward sunlight. 1

About ten years ago I decided I had to learn the names of plants and flowers in my environment. I bought a book on them and walked down the tree-lined streets of Boulder,[1] examining leaf, bark, and seed, trying to match them up with their descriptions and names in the book. Maple, elm, oak, locust. I usually tried to cheat by asking people working in their yards the names of the flowers and trees growing there. I was amazed how few people had any idea of the names of the live beings inhabiting their little plot of land. 2

When we know the name of something, it brings us closer to the ground. It takes the blur out of our mind; it connects us to the earth. If I walk down the street and see "dogwood," "forsythia," I feel more friendly toward the environment. I am noticing what is around me and can name it. It makes me more awake. 3

If you read the poems of William Carlos Williams,[2] you will see how specific he is about plants, trees, flowers—chicory, daisy, locust, poplar, quince, primrose, black-eyed Susan, lilacs—each has its own integrity. Williams says, "Write what's in front of your nose." It's good for us to know what is in front of our nose. Not just "daisy," but how the flower is in the season we are looking at it—"The days-eye hugging the earth / in August . . . brownedged, / green and pointed scales / armor his yellow."* Continue to hone your awareness: to the name, to the month, to the day, and finally to the moment. 4

Williams also says: "No idea, but in things." Study what is "in front of your nose." By saying "geranium" instead of "flower," you are penetrating more deeply into the present and being there. The closer we can get to what's in front of our nose, the more it can teach us everything. "To see the World in a Grain of Sand, and a heaven in a Wild Flower . . ."** 5

In writing groups and classes too, it is good to quickly learn the names of all the other group members. It helps to ground you in the group and make you more attentive to each other's work. 6

Learn the names of everything: birds, cheese, tractors, cars, buildings. A writer is all at once everything—an architect, French cook, farmer—and at the same time, a writer is none of these things. 7

---

[1]*Boulder:* a city in Colorado.

[2]*William Carlos Williams* (1883–1963): American poet.

* William Carlos Williams, "Daisy," in *The Collected Earlier Poems* (New York: New Directions, 1938). [Goldberg's note]

** William Blake, "The Auguries of Innocence." [Goldberg's note]

Thinking Critically about This Reading

What does Goldberg mean when she states, "Give things the dignity of their names" (paragraph 1)? Why, according to Goldberg, should writers refer to things by their specific names?

Questions for Study and Discussion

1. How does Goldberg "specifically" follow the advice she gives writers in this essay?
2. Goldberg makes several lists of the names of things. What purpose do these lists serve? (Glossary: *Purpose*)
3. Throughout the essay, Goldberg instructs the reader to be specific and to be aware of the physical world. Of what besides names is the reader advised to be aware? Why?
4. In paragraphs 3, 5, and 6, Goldberg cites a number of advantages to be gained by knowing the names of things. What are these advantages? Do they ring true to you?
5. What specific audience does Goldberg address? (Glossary: *Audience*) How do you know?

Classroom Activity Using Illustration

A useful exercise in learning to be specific is to see the words we use for people, places, things, and ideas as being positioned somewhere on a "ladder of abstraction." In the following chart, notice how the words progress from more general to more specific.

More General	*General*	*Specific*	*More Specific*
Organism	Plant	Flower	Alstrumaria
Vehicle	Car	Chevrolet	1958 Chevrolet Impala

Try to fill in the missing parts of the following ladder of abstraction:

More General	*General*	*Specific*	*More Specific*
Writing instrument	________	Fountain pen	Waterman fountain pen
________	Sandwich	Corned beef sandwich	Reuben

American	___________	Navaho	Laguna Pueblo
Book	Reference book	Dictionary	___________
School	High school	Technical high school	___________
Medicine	Oral medicine	Gel capsule	___________

Suggested Writing Assignments

1. Goldberg likes William Carlos Williams's statement, "No idea, but in things" (5). Using this line as both a title and a thesis, write your own argument for the use of the specific over the general in a certain field—news reporting, poetry, or baking, for example. (Glossary: *Argumentation*) Be sure to support your argument with examples.
2. Write a brief essay advising your readers of something they should do. Title your essay, as Goldberg does, with a directive ("Be Specific"). Tell your readers how they can improve their lives by taking your advice, and give strong examples of the behavior you are recommending.

The Case for Short Words

Richard Lederer

Born in 1938, Richard Lederer holds degrees from Haverford College, Harvard, and the University of New Hampshire. He has been a prolific and popular writer about language. A former high school English teacher, he is vice president of SPELL, the Society for the Preservation of English Language and Literature. Lederer has written numerous books about how Americans use language, including Anguished English *(1987),* Crazy English: The Ultimate Joy Ride through Our Language *(1989),* The Play of Words *(1990),* The Miracle of Language *(1991),* More Anguished English *(1993),* Adventures of a Verbivore *(1994), and* Fractured English *(1996). In addition to writing books, Lederer pens a weekly column called "Looking at Language" for newspapers and magazines across the United States. He is also the Grammar Grappler for* Writer's Digest, *the language commentator for National Public Radio, and an award-winning public speaker who makes approximately two hundred appearances each year.*

In the following essay, taken from The Miracle of Language, *pay particular attention to the different ways Lederer uses examples to illustrate. The title and first four paragraphs serve as an extended example of his point about small words, while later in the essay he incorporates examples from his students' writing to illustrate that point more deliberately.*

For Your Journal

We all carry with us a vocabulary of short, simple-looking words that possess a special personal meaning. For example, to some the word *rose* represents not just a flower, but a whole array of gardens, ceremonies, and romantic occasions. What little words have special meaning for you? What images do they bring to mind?

When you speak and write, there is no law that says you have to use big words. Short words are as good as long ones, and short, old words—like *sun* and *grass* and *home*—are best of all. A lot 1 of small words, more than you might think, can meet your needs with a strength, grace, and charm that large words do not have.

Big words can make the way dark for those who read what you write and hear what you say. Small words cast their clear light on big things—night and day, love and hate, war and peace, and life and death. Big words at times seem strange to the eye and the ear and the mind and the heart. Small words are the ones we seem to have known from the time we were born, like the hearth fire that warms the home. 2

Short words are bright like sparks that glow in the night, prompt like the dawn that greets the day, sharp like the blade of a knife, hot like salt tears that scald the cheek, quick like moths that flit from flame to flame, and terse like the dart and sting of a bee. 3

Here is a sound rule: Use small, old words where you can. If a long word says just what you want to say, do not fear to use it. But know that our tongue is rich in crisp, brisk, swift, short words. Make them the spine and the heart of what you speak and write. Short words are like fast friends. They will not let you down. 4

The title of this [essay] and the four paragraphs that you have just read are wrought entirely of words of one syllable. In setting myself this task, I did not feel especially cabined, cribbed, or confined. In fact, the structure helped me to focus on the power of the message I was trying to put across. 5

One study shows that twenty words account for twenty-five percent of all spoken English words, and all twenty are monosyllabic. In order of frequency they are: *I, you, the, a, to, is, it, that, of, and, in, what, he, this, have, do, she, not, on,* and *they*. Other studies indicate that the fifty most common words in written English are each made of a single syllable. 6

For centuries our finest poets and orators have recognized and employed the power of small words to make a straight point between two minds. A great many of our proverbs punch home their points with pithy monosyllables: "Where there's a will, there's a way," "A stitch in time saves nine," "Spare the rod and spoil the child," "A bird in the hand is worth two in the bush." 7

Nobody used the short word more skillfully than William Shakespeare, whose dying King Lear laments: 8

And my poor fool is hang'd! No, no, no life!
Why should a dog, a horse, a rat have life,
And thou no breath at all? . . .
Do you see this? Look on her, look, her lips.
Look there, look there!

9 Shakespeare's contemporaries made the King James Bible a centerpiece of short words—"And God said, Let there be light: and there was light. And God saw the light, that it was good." The descendants of such mighty lines live on in the twentieth century. When asked to explain his policy to Parliament, Winston Churchill[1] responded with these ringing monosyllables: "I will say: it is to wage war, by sea, land, and air, with all our might and with all the strength that God can give us." In his "Death of the Hired Man" Robert Frost[2] observes that "Home is the place where, when you have to go there, / They have to take you in." And William H. Johnson[3] uses ten two-letter words to explain his secret of success: "If it is to be, / It is up to me."

10 You don't have to be a great author, statesman, or philosopher to tap the energy and eloquence of small words. Each winter I ask my ninth graders at St. Paul's School to write a composition composed entirely of one-syllable words. My students greet my request with obligatory moans and groans, but, when they return to class with their essays, most feel that, with the pressure to produce high-sounding polysyllables relieved, they have created some of their most powerful and luminous prose. Here are submissions from two of my ninth graders:

> What can you say to a boy who has left home? You can say that he has done wrong, but he does not care. He has left home so that he will not have to deal with what you say. He wants to go as far as he can. He will do what he wants to do.
>
> This boy does not want to be forced to go to church, to comb his hair, or to be on time. A good time for this boy does not lie in your reach, for what you have he does not want. He dreams of ripped jeans, shorts with no starch, and old socks.
>
> So now this boy is on a bus to a place he dreams of, a place with no rules. This boy now walks a strange street, his long hair blown back by the wind. He wears no coat or tie, just jeans and an old shirt. He hates your world, and he has left it.
>
> –Charles Shaffer

[1]*Sir Winston Churchill* (1874–1965): British orator, author, and statesman.
[2]*Robert Frost* (1874–1963): American poet.
[3]*William H. Johnson* (1771–1834): associate justice of the U.S. Supreme Court, 1804–1834.

> For a long time we cruised by the coast and at last came to a wide bay past the curve of a hill, at the end of which lay a small town. Our long boat ride at an end, we all stretched and stood up to watch as the boat nosed its way in.
>
> The town climbed up the hill that rose from the shore, a space in front of it left bare for the port. Each house was a clean white with sky blue or gray trim; in front of each one was a small yard, edged by a white stone wall strewn with green vines.
>
> As the town basked in the heat of noon, not a thing stirred in the streets or by the shore. The sun beat down on the sea, the land, and the back of our necks, so that, in spite of the breeze that made the vines sway, we all wished we could hide from the glare in a cool, white house. But, as there was no one to help dock the boat, we had to stand and wait.
>
> At last the head of the crew leaped from the side and strode to a large house on the right. He shoved the door wide, poked his head through the gloom, and roared with a fierce voice. Five or six men came out, and soon the port was loud with the clank of chains and creak of planks as the men caught ropes thrown by the crew, pulled them taut, and tied them to posts. Then they set up a rough plank so we could cross from the deck to the shore. We all made for the large house while the crew watched, glad to be rid of us.
>
> –Celia Wren

You too can tap into the vitality and vigor of compact expres- 11
sion. Take a suggestion from the highway department. At the boundaries of your speech and prose place a sign that reads "Caution: Small Words at Work."

Thinking Critically about This Reading

Lederer states that "short, old words—like *sun* and *grass* and *home*—are best of all" (paragraph 1). What attributes make these words the "best"? Why are they superior to short, new words?

Questions for Study and Discussion

1. In this essay, written to encourage the use of short words, Lederer himself employs many polysyllabic words, especially in paragraphs 5–9. What is his purpose in doing so? (Glossary: *Purpose*)

2. Lederer quotes a wide variety of passages to illustrate the effectiveness of short words. For example, he quotes from famous, universally familiar sources such as Shakespeare and the King James Bible, and from unknown contemporary sources such as his own ninth-grade students. How does the variety of his illustrations serve to inform his readers? How does each example gain impact from the inclusion of the others?
3. To make clear to the reader why short words are effective, Lederer relies heavily on metaphors and similes, especially in the first four paragraphs. (Glossary: *Figure of Speech*) Choose at least one metaphor and one simile from these paragraphs, and explain the comparison implicit in each.
4. In paragraph 10, Lederer refers to the relief his students feel when released from "the pressure to produce high-sounding polysyllables." Where does this pressure come from? How does it relate to the central purpose of this essay?
5. How does the final paragraph serve to close the essay effectively? (Glossary: *Beginnings and Endings*)
6. This essay abounds with examples of striking sentences and passages consisting entirely of words of one syllable. Choose four of the single-sentence examples or a section of several sentences from one of the longer examples, and rewrite them, using primarily words of two or more syllables. Notice how the revision differs from the original.

Classroom Activity Using Illustration

In your opinion, what is the finest sort of present to give or receive? Why? Define the ideal gift. Illustrate by describing one or more of the best gifts you have received or given, making it clear how each fits the ideal.

Suggested Writing Assignments

1. Follow the assignment Lederer gives his own students, and write a composition composed entirely of one-syllable words. Make your piece about the length of his student examples or of his own four-paragraph opening.

2. A chief strength of Lederer's essay is his use of a broad variety of examples to illustrate his thesis that short words are the most effective. Choose a subject about which you are knowledgeable, and find as wide a range of examples as you can to illustrate its appeal. For example, if you are enthusiastic about water, you could explore the relative attractions of puddles, ponds, lakes, and oceans; if you are a music lover, you might consider why Bach or the Beatles remain popular today.

Can I Get You Some Manners with That?

■ **Christie Scotty**

Christie Scotty graduated from the University of Rochester in 2000 with a degree in journalism. As an undergraduate she was a member of the women's cross-country running team and, in the summers, she waited tables in local restaurants. Scotty moved to Newberg, Oregon, in 2001, to work as a reporter for the Newberg Graphic, *a small-town newspaper, where she wrote about local and state politics and the arts.*

In the following essay, first published in Newsweek *on October 18, 2004, Scotty comments on the surprising lack of civility she discovered in the workplace. She supports her thesis about the rude behavior of "professionals" with striking examples of how they treated her when she worked at a local restaurant and, by contrast, as a newspaper reporter.*

For Your Journal

Have you ever worked as a waiter, sales clerk, babysitter, housekeeper, landscaper, truck driver, or receptionist? Describe your interaction with the public. Did you feel that customers were interested in you as a person, or did you feel looked down on or even invisible? Describe one memorable incident.

Like most people, I've long understood that I will be judged by my occupation. It's obvious that people care what others do for a living: head into any social setting and introductions of "Hi, my name is . . ." are quickly followed by the ubiquitous[1] "And what do you do?" I long ago realized my profession is a gauge that people use to see how smart or talented I am. Recently, however, I was disappointed to see that it also decides how I'm treated as a person. 1

[1] *ubiquitous:* seeming to always be there.

Last year I left a professional position as a small-town reporter 2 and took a job waiting tables while I figured out what I wanted to do next. As someone paid to serve food to people, I had customers say and do things to me I suspect they'd never say or do to their most casual acquaintances. Some people would stare at the menu and mumble drink orders—"Bring me a water, extra lemon, no ice"—while refusing to meet my eyes. Some would interrupt me midsentence to say the air conditioning was too cold or the sun was too bright through the windows. One night a man talking on his cell phone waved me away, then beckoned me back with his finger a minute later, complaining he was ready to order and asking where I'd been.

I had waited tables during summers in college and was treated 3 like a peon[2] by plenty of people. But at 19 years old, I sort of believed I deserved inferior treatment from professional adults who didn't blink at handing over $24 for a seven-ounce fillet. Besides, people responded to me differently after I told them I was in college. Customers would joke that one day I'd be sitting at their table, waiting to be served. They could imagine me as their college-age daughter or future co-worker.

Once I graduated I took a job at a community newspaper. From 4 my first day, I heard a respectful tone from most everyone who called me, whether they were readers or someone I was hoping to interview. I assumed this was the way the professional world worked—cordially.

I soon found out differently. I sat several feet away from an 5 advertising sales representative with a similar name. Our calls would often get mixed up and someone asking for Kristen would be transferred to Christie. The mistake was immediately evident. Perhaps it was because their relationship centered on "gimme," perhaps it was because money was involved, but people used a tone with Kristen that they never used with me.

"I called yesterday and you still haven't faxed—" 6

"Hi, this is so-and-so over at the real-estate office. I need—" 7

"I just got into the office and I don't like—" 8

"Hi, Kristen. Why did—" 9

I was just a fledgling[3] reporter, but the governor's press secretary 10 returned my calls far more politely than Kristen's accounts did hers, even though she had worked with many of her clients for years.

---

[2]*peon:* an unskilled laborer who often isn't respected.

[3]*fledgling:* young and inexperienced.

11 My job title made people chat me up and express their concerns and complaints with courtesy. I came to expect friendliness from perfect strangers. So it was a shock to return to the restaurant industry. Sure, the majority of customers were pleasant, some even a delight to wait on, but all too often someone shattered that scene.

12 I often saw my co-workers storm into the kitchen in tears or with a mouthful of expletives after a customer had interrupted, degraded or ignored them. In the eight months I worked there, I heard my friends muttering phrases like "You just don't treat people like that!" on an almost daily basis.

13 It's no secret that there's a lot to put up with when waiting tables, and fortunately, much of it can be easily forgotten when you pocket the tips. The service industry, by definition, exists to cater to others' needs. Still, it seemed that many of my customers didn't get the difference between *server* and *servant.*

14 Some days I tried to force good manners. When a customer said hello but continued staring at his menu without glancing up at me, I'd make it a point to say, "Hi, my name is Christie," and then pause and wait for him to make eye contact. I'd stand silent an awkwardly long time waiting for a little respect. It was my way of saying "I am a person, too."

15 I knew I wouldn't wait tables forever, so most days I just shook my head and laughed, pitying the people whose lives were so miserable they treated strangers shabbily in order to feel better about themselves.

16 Three months ago I left the restaurant world and took an office job where some modicum[4] of civility exists. I'm now applying to graduate school, which means someday I'll return to a profession where people need to be nice to me in order to get what they want. I think I'll take them to dinner first, and see how they treat someone whose only job is to serve them.

Thinking Critically about This Reading

Scotty ends her essay with the revelation that she is applying to graduate school and one day fully intends to return to the professional

[4]*modicum:* a small amount or quantity.

world. Why does Scotty state that in the future she plans to take her business associates out to dinner? What does she hope to learn about them from the experience?

Questions for Study and Discussion

1. Scotty begins by describing a situation we can all relate to: "And what do you do?" If you reply "I'm a student" or "I'm in college," the response then is often, "And what are you studying to be?" Why do you think people want to know what we do or what we are studying to be?
2. What examples does Scotty use to illustrate her claim, "I had customers say and do things to me I suspect they'd never say or do to their most casual acquaintances" (paragraph 2)? How do her examples differ?
3. Scotty explains that she waited on tables both during summers while she was in college and again after leaving her job at the small-town newspaper. How does she compare and contrast the two jobs waiting tables? (Glossary: *Comparison and Contrast*) How did Scotty herself change during that time?
4. Scotty confesses that she expected professional people to act "cordially" (4). What example does she use to show that this was not always the case? Do you find the example convincing? Why or why not?
5. Why do you think Scotty feels so strongly about her customers making eye contact with her?

Classroom Activity Using Illustration

To present a good example you need to provide details that appeal to the senses, and to do this you must be observant. To test your powers of observation, try listing the features of an ordinary object—a water bottle, a ballpoint pen, a backpack—something everyone in class has access to. Compare your list of characteristics with those of other members of the class. Discuss whether having a name for the object is a help or a hindrance in describing it.

Suggested Writing Assignments

1. Many Americans believe that we live in an increasingly hostile and uncivil society. Write an essay in which you agree or disagree with this statement, using examples from your own experience, observation, or reading to support your position.
2. Do you value courtesy, civility, good manners? Why? In what types of situations are good manners essential? Have you ever been treated rudely by a peer? By an adult? Write an essay in which you defend the place of good manners in today's world.

chapter **13**

Narration

To *narrate* is to tell a story or to recount a series of events. Whenever you relate an incident or use an **anecdote** (a very brief story) to make a point, you use narration. In its broadest sense, **narration** is any account of any event or series of events. We all love to hear stories; some people believe that sharing stories is a part of what defines us as human beings. Good stories are interesting, sometimes suspenseful, and always instructive because they give us insights into the human condition. Although most often associated with fiction, narration is effective and useful in all kinds of writing. For example, in "How I Got Smart" (p. 330), retired high school English teacher Steve Brody narrates the humorous story of how an infatuation with a classmate, Debbie, motivated him to hit the books. In "As They Say, Drugs Kill" (p. 505), Laura Rowley recounts a particularly poignant experience to argue against substance abuse.

Good narration has five essential features: a clear context; well-chosen and thoughtfully emphasized details; a logical, often chronological organization; an appropriate and consistent point of view; and a meaningful point or purpose. Consider, for example, the following narrative, titled "Is Your Jar Full?"

> One day, an expert in time management was speaking to a group of business students and, to drive home a point, used an illustration those students will never forget. As he stood in front of the group of high-powered overachievers he said, "Okay, time for a quiz" and he pulled out a one-gallon mason jar and set it on the table in front of him. He also produced about a dozen fist-sized rocks and carefully placed them, one at a time, into the jar. When the jar was filled to the top and no more rocks would fit inside, he asked, "Is this jar full?"
>
> Everyone in the class yelled, "Yes."
>
> The time management expert replied, "Really?" He reached under the table and pulled out a bucket of gravel. He dumped some

gravel in and shook the jar causing pieces of gravel to work themselves down into the spaces between the big rocks. He then asked the group once more, "Is the jar full?" By this time the class was on to him.

"Probably not," one of them answered.

"Good!" he replied. He reached under the table and brought out a bucket of sand. He started dumping the sand in the jar and it went into all of the spaces left between the rocks and the gravel.

Once more he asked the question, "Is this jar full?"

"No!" the class shouted.

Once again he said, "Good." Then he grabbed a pitcher of water and began to pour it in until the jar was filled to the brim. Then he looked at the class and asked, "What is the point of this illustration?"

One eager beaver raised his hand and said, "The point is, no matter how full your schedule is, if you try really hard you can always fit some more things in it!"

"No," the speaker replied, "that's not the point. The truth this illustration teaches us is: If you don't put the big rocks in first, you'll never get them in at all. What are the 'big rocks' in your life—time with your loved ones, your faith, your education, your dreams, a worthy cause, teaching or mentoring others? Remember to put these BIG ROCKS in first or you'll never get them in at all."

So, tonight, or in the morning, when you are reflecting on this short story, ask yourself this question: What are the "big rocks" in my life? Then, put those in your jar first.

This story contains all the elements of good narration. The writer begins by establishing a clear context for her narrative, telling when, where, and to whom the action happened. She has chosen details well, including enough detail so that we know what is happening but not so much that we become overwhelmed, confused, or bored. The writer organizes her narration logically, with a beginning that sets the scene, a middle that relates the exchange between the time-management expert and the students, and an end that makes her point, all arranged chronologically. She tells the story from the third-person point of view. Finally, she reveals the point of her narration: People need to think about what's important in their lives and put these activities first.

The writer could have told her story from the first-person point of view. In this point of view, the narrator is a participant in the action and uses the pronoun *I*. In the following example, Willie Morris tells a story of how the comfortably well-off respond coolly to the tragedies of the ghetto. We experience the event directly through the writer's eyes and ears, as if we too had been on the scene of the action.

> One afternoon in late August, as the summer's sun streamed into the [railroad] car and made little jumping shadows on the windows, I sat gazing out at the tenement-dwellers, who were themselves looking out of their windows from the gray crumbling buildings along the tracks of upper Manhattan. As we crossed into the Bronx, the train unexpectedly slowed down for a few miles. Suddenly from out of my window I saw a large crowd near the tracks, held back by two policemen. Then, on the other side from my window, I saw a sight I would never be able to forget: a little boy almost severed in halves, lying at an incredible angle near the track. The ground was covered with blood, and the boy's eyes were opened wide, strained and disbelieving in his sudden oblivion. A policeman stood next to him, his arms folded, staring straight ahead at the windows of our train. In the orange glow of late afternoon the policemen, the crowd, the corpse of the boy were for a brief moment immobile, motionless, a small tableau to violence and death in the city. Behind me, in the next row of seats, there was a game of bridge. I heard one of the four men say as he looked out at the sight, "God, that's horrible." Another said, in a whisper, "Terrible, terrible." There was a momentary silence, punctuated only by the clicking of the wheels on the track. Then, after the pause, I heard the first man say: "Two hearts."
>
> –Willie Morris

As you begin to write your own narration, take time to ask yourself why you are telling your story. Your purpose in writing will influence which events and details you include and which you leave out. You should include enough detail about the action and its context so that your readers can understand what's going on. You should not get so carried away with details that your readers become confused or bored by an excess of information, however. In good storytelling, deciding what to leave out is as important as deciding what to include.

Be sure to give some thought to the organization of your narrative. While chronological organization is natural in narration because it is a reconstruction of the original order of events, it is not always the most interesting. To add interest to your storytelling, try using a technique common in the movies and theater called *flashback*. Begin your narration midway through the story with an important or exciting event and then use flashback to fill in what happened earlier. Notice how one of our students uses this very technique. She disrupts the chronological organization of her narrative by beginning in the recent past and then uses a flashback to take us back to when she was a youngster:

> It was a Monday afternoon, and I was finally home from track practice. The coach had just told me that I had a negative attitude and should contemplate why I was on the team. My father greeted me in the living room.
>
> *Essay opens in recent past*
>
> "Hi, honey. How was practice?"
>
> *Dialogue creates historical present*
>
> "Not good, Dad. Listen, I don't want to do this anymore. I hate the track team."
>
> "What do you mean *hate*?"
>
> "The constant pressure is making me crazy."
>
> "How so?"
>
> "It's just not fun anymore."
>
> "Well, I'll have to talk to the coach—"
>
> "No! You're supposed to be my father, not my coach."
>
> "I am your father, but I'm sure . . ."
>
> "Just let me do what I want. You've had your turn."
>
> He just let out a sigh and left the room. Later he told me that I was wasting my "God-given abilities." The funny part was that none of my father's anger hit me at first. All I knew was that I was free.
>
> *Essay returns in time to when troubles began*
>
> My troubles began the summer I was five years old. It was late June. . . .
>
> –Trena Isley, student

What's in a Name?

Henry Louis Gates Jr.

The preeminent African American scholar of our time, Henry Louis Gates Jr. is the W. E. B. Du Bois Professor of the Humanities, chair of Afro-American Studies, and director of the W. E. B. Du Bois Institute of Afro-American Research at Harvard University. Among his impressive list of publications are Figures in Black: Words, Signs and the "Racial" Self *(1987),* The Signifying Monkey: A Theory of Afro-American Literary Criticism *(1988),* Loose Canons: Notes on Culture Wars *(1992),* The Future of the Race *(1997),* Thirteen Ways of Looking at a Black Man *(1999), and* Mr. Jefferson and Miss Wheatley *(2003). His* Colored People: A Memoir *(1994) recollects in a wonderful prose style his youth growing up in Piedmont, West Virginia, and his emerging sexual and racial awareness. Born in 1950, Gates graduated from Yale and took his advanced degrees at Clare College at the University of Cambridge. He has been honored with a MacArthur Foundation Fellowship, inclusion in* Time *magazine's "25 Most Influential Americans" list, a National Humanities Medal, and election to the American Academy of Arts and Letters.*

"What's in a Name?," excerpted from a longer article published in the fall 1989 issue of Dissent *magazine, tells the story of Gates's first encounter with one of the "bynames" used by white people to refer to African Americans.*

For Your Journal

Reflect on the use of racially charged language. For example, has anyone ever used a racial epithet or name to refer to you? When did you first become aware that such names existed? How do you feel about being characterized by your race? If you yourself have ever used such names, what was your intent in using them? What was the response of others?

The question of color takes up much space in these pages, but the question of color, especially in this country, operates to hide the graver questions of the self.

—JAMES BALDWIN, 1961

. . . blood, darky, Tar Baby, Kaffir, shine . . . moor, blackamoor, Jim Crow, spook . . . quadroon, meriney, red bone, high yellow . . . Mammy, porch monkey, home, homeboy, George . . . spearchucker, schwarze, Leroy, Smokey . . . mouli, buck, Ethiopian, brother, sistah. . . .

–TREY ELLIS, 1989

I had forgotten the incident completely, until I read Trey Ellis's essay, "Remember My Name," in a recent issue of the *Village Voice*[1] (June 13, 1989). But there, in the middle of an extended italicized list of the bynames of "the race" ("the race" or "our people" being the terms my parents used in polite or reverential discourse, "jigaboo" or "nigger" more commonly used in anger, jest, or pure disgust) it was: "George." Now the events of that very brief exchange return to mind so vividly that I wonder why I had forgotten it. 1

My father and I were walking home at dusk from his second job. He "moonlighted" as a janitor in the evenings for the telephone company. Every day but Saturday, he would come home at 3:30 from his regular job at the paper mill, wash up, eat supper, then at 4:30 head downtown to his second job. He used to make jokes frequently about a union official who moonlighted. I never got the joke, but he and his friends thought it was hilarious. All I knew was that my family always ate well, that my brother and I had new clothes to wear, and that all of the white people in Piedmont, West Virginia, treated my parents with an odd mixture of resentment and respect that even we understood at the time had something directly to do with a small but certain measure of financial security. 2

He had left a little early that evening because I was with him and I had to be in bed early. I could not have been more than five or six, and we had stopped off at the Cut-Rate Drug Store (where no black person in town but my father could sit down to eat, and eat off real plates with real silverware) so that I could buy some caramel ice cream, two scoops in a wafer cone, please, which I was busy licking when Mr. Wilson walked by. 3

Mr. Wilson was a very quiet man, whose stony, brooding, silent manner seemed designed to scare off any overtures of friendship, even from white people. He was Irish, as was one-third of our village (another third being Italian), the more affluent among whom sent their children to "Catholic School" across the bridge in Maryland. He 4

[1]*Village Voice:* a nationally distributed weekly newspaper published in New York City.

had white straight hair, like my Uncle Joe, whom he uncannily resembled, and he carried a back worn metal lunch pail, the kind that Riley[2] carried on the television show. My father always spoke to him, and for reasons that we never did understand, he always spoke to my father.

"Hello, Mr. Wilson," I heard my father say. 5

"Hello, George." 6

I stopped licking my ice cream cone, and asked my Dad in a loud 7
voice why Mr. Wilson had called him "George."

"Doesn't he know your name, Daddy? Why don't you tell him 8
your name? Your name isn't George."

For a moment I tried to think of who Mr. Wilson was mixing 9
Pop up with. But we didn't have any Georges among the colored people in Piedmont; nor were there colored Georges living in the neighboring towns and working at the mill.

"Tell him your name, Daddy." 10

"He knows my name, boy," my father said after a long pause. 11
"He calls all colored people George."

A long silence ensued. It was "one of those things," as my Mom 12
would put it. Even then, that early, I knew when I was in the presence of "one of those things," one of those things that provided a glimpse, through a rent[3] curtain, at another world that we could not affect but that affected us. There would be a painful moment of silence, and you would wait for it to give way to a discussion of a black superstar such as Sugar Ray[4] or Jackie Robinson.[5]

"Nobody hits better in a clutch than Jackie Robinson." 13

"That's right. Nobody." 14

I never again looked Mr. Wilson in the eye. 15

Thinking Critically about This Reading

What is "one of those things," as Gates's mom put it (paragraph 12)? In what ways is "one of those things" really Gates's purpose in telling this story?

---

[2]*Riley:* a character on the U.S. television show *The Life of Riley,* a blue-collar, ethnic sitcom popular in the 1950s.

[3]*rent:* torn.

[4]*Sugar Ray:* Walker Smith Jr. (1921–1989), American professional boxer and six-time world champion.

[5]*Jackie Robinson* (1919–1972): the first black baseball player in the National Baseball League.

Questions for Study and Discussion

1. Gates prefaces his essay with two quotations. What is the meaning of each quotation? Why do you suppose Gates uses both quotations? How does each relate to his purpose? (Glossary: *Purpose*)
2. Gates begins by explaining where he got the idea for his essay. How well does this approach work? Is it an approach that you could see yourself using often? Explain.
3. Gates sets the context for his narrative in his first paragraph. He also reveals that his parents used terms of racial abuse among themselves. Why does Gates make so much of Mr. Wilson's use of *George* when his own parents used words so much more obviously offensive?
4. Gates describes and provides some background information about Mr. Wilson in paragraph 4. (Glossary: *Description*) What is Gates's purpose in providing this information? (Glossary: *Purpose*)

Classroom Activity Using Narration

Beginning at the beginning and ending at the end is not the only way to tell a story. Think of the events in a story that you would like to tell. Don't write the story, but simply list the events that need to be included. Be sure to include at least ten major events in your story. Now play with the arrangement of those events so as to avoid the chronological sequencing of them that would naturally come to mind. Try to develop as many patterns as you can, but be careful that you have a purpose in developing each sequence and that you create nothing that might confuse a listener or reader. Discuss your results with your classmates.

Suggested Writing Assignments

1. Using Gates's essay as a model, identify something that you have recently read that triggers in you a story from the past. Perhaps a newspaper article about how local high school students helped the community reminds you of a community project you and your classmates were involved in. Or perhaps reading about some act of heroism reminds you of a situation in which you performed (or failed to perform) a similar deed. Make sure that you

have a purpose in telling the story, that you establish a clear context for it, and that you have enough supporting details to enrich your story. (Glossary: *Purpose*; *Details*) Think, as well, about how to begin and end your story and which narrative sequence you will use. (Glossary: *Beginnings and Endings*)

2. How do you feel about your name? Do you like it? Does it sound pleasant? Do you think your name shapes your self-identity in a positive or negative way, or do you think it has no effect on your sense of who you are? Write an essay about your name and the way it helps or fails to help you present yourself to the world. Be sure to develop your essay using narration by including several anecdotes or a longer story involving your name. (Glossary: *Anecdote*)

How I Got Smart

■ Steve Brody

Steve Brody is a retired high school English teacher who enjoys writing about the lighter side of teaching. He was born in Chicago in 1915 and received his bachelor's degree in English from Columbia University. In addition to his articles in educational publications, Brody has published many newspaper articles on travel and a humorous book about golf, How to Break Ninety before You Reach It *(1979).*

As you read his account of how love made him smart, an essay that first appeared in the New York Times *in September 1986, notice his well-chosen and thoughtfully emphasized details.*

For Your Journal

Motivation is a difficult topic about which to generalize. What motivates one person to act often will not work on another person. How do you get motivated to work, to join extracurricular activities, or to take care of yourself? Are you able to motivate yourself, or do you need someone else to give you a push?

A common misconception among youngsters attending school is that their teachers were child prodigies.[1] Who else but a bookworm, prowling the libraries and disdaining the normal youngster's propensity for play rather than study, would grow up to be a teacher anyway? 1

I tried desperately to explain to my students that the image they had of me as an ardent devotee of books and homework during my adolescence was a bit out of focus. Au contraire! I hated compulsory education with a passion. I could never quite accept the notion of having to go to school while the fish were biting. 2

Consequently, my grades were somewhat bearish.[2] That's how my father, who dabbled in the stock market, described them. Presenting 3

[1]*prodigies:* people with exceptional talents.
[2]*bearish:* trending downward; a term used to describe the stock market.

my report card for my father to sign was like serving him a subpoena. At midterm and other sensitive periods, my father kept a low profile.

But in my sophomore year, something beautiful and exciting happened. Cupid aimed his arrow and struck me squarely in the heart. All at once, I enjoyed going to school, if only to gaze at the lovely face beneath the raven tresses in English II. My princess sat near the pencil sharpener, and that year I ground up enough pencils to fuel a campfire. 4

Alas, Debbie was far beyond my wildest dreams. We were separated not only by five rows of desks, but by about 50 I.Q. points. She was the top student in English II, the apple of Mrs. Larrivee's eye. I envisioned how eagerly Debbie's father awaited her report card. 5

Occasionally, Debbie would catch me staring at her, and she would flash a smile—an angelic smile that radiated enlightenment and quickened my heartbeat. It was a smile that signaled hope and made me temporarily forget the intellectual gulf that separated us. 6

I schemed desperately to bridge that gulf. And one day, as I was passing the supermarket, an idea came to me. 7

A sign in the window announced that the store was offering the first volume of a set of encyclopedias at the introductory price of 29 cents. The remaining volumes would cost $2.49 each, but it was no time to be cynical. 8

I purchased Volume I—Aardvark to Asteroid—and began my venture into the world of knowledge. I would henceforth become a seeker of facts. I would become chief egghead in English II and sweep the princess off her feet with a surge of erudition.[3] I had it all planned. 9

My first opportunity came one day in the cafeteria line. I looked behind me and there she was. 10

"Hi," she said. 11

After a pause, I wet my lips and said, "Know where anchovies come from?" 12

She seemed surprised. "No, I don't." 13

I breathed a sigh of relief. "The anchovy lives in salt water and is rarely found in fresh water." I had to talk fast, so that I could get all the facts in before we reached the cash register. "Fishermen catch anchovies in the Mediterranean Sea and along the Atlantic coast near Spain and Portugal." 14

"How fascinating," said Debbie. 15

[3]*erudition:* extensive knowledge gained from books.

"The anchovy is closely related to the herring. It is thin and silvery in color. It has a long snout and a very large mouth." 16

"Incredible." 17

"Anchovies are good in salads, mixed with eggs, and are often used as appetizers before dinner, but they are salty and cannot be digested too rapidly." 18

Debbie shook her head in disbelief. It was obvious that I had made quite an impression. 19

A few days later, during a fire drill, I sidled[4] up to her and asked, "Ever been to the Aleutian Islands?" 20

"Never have," she replied. 21

"Might be a nice place to visit, but I certainly wouldn't want to live there," I said. 22

"Why not?" said Debbie, playing right into my hands. 23

"Well, the climate is forbidding. There are no trees on any of the 100 or more islands in the group. The ground is rocky and very little plant life can grow on it." 24

"I don't think I'd even care to visit," she said. 25

The fire drill was over and we began to file into the building, so I had to step it up to get the natives in. "The Aleuts are short and sturdy and have dark skin and black hair. They subsist on fish, and they trap blue fox, seal, and otter for their valuable fur." 26

Debbie's hazel eyes widened in amazement. She was undoubtedly beginning to realize that she wasn't dealing with an ordinary lunkhead. She was gaining new and valuable insights instead of engaging in the routine small talk one would expect from most sophomores. 27

Luck was on my side, too. One day I was browsing through the library during my study period. I spotted Debbie sitting at a table, absorbed in a crossword puzzle. She was frowning, apparently stumped on a word. I leaned over and asked if I could help. 28

"Four-letter word for Oriental female servant," Debbie said. 29

"Try *amah,*" I said, quick as a flash. 30

Debbie filled in the blanks, then turned to stare at me in amazement. "I don't believe it," she said. "I just don't believe it." 31

And so it went, that glorious, amorous, joyous sophomore year. Debbie seemed to relish our little conversations and hung on my every word. Naturally, the more I read, the more my confidence 32

---

[4]*sidled:* approached sideways or in a stealthy manner.

grew. I expatiated[5] freely on such topics as adenoids,[6] air brakes, and arthritis.

In the classroom, too, I was gradually making my presence felt. Among my classmates, I was developing a reputation as a wheeler-dealer in data. One day, during a discussion of Coleridge's "The Ancient Mariner," we came across the word *albatross*. 33

"Can anyone tell us what an albatross is?" asked Mrs. Larrivee. 34

My hand shot up. "The albatross is a large bird that lives mostly in the ocean regions below the equator, but may be found in the north Pacific as well. The albatross measures as long as four feet and has the greatest wingspread of any bird. It feeds on the surface of the ocean, where it catches shellfish. The albatross is a very voracious[7] eater. When it is full it has trouble getting into the air again." 35

There was a long silence in the room. Mrs. Larrivee couldn't quite believe what she had just heard. I sneaked a peek at Debbie and gave her a big wink. She beamed proudly and winked back. 36

It was a great feeling, having Debbie and Mrs. Larrivee and my peers according me respect and paying attention when I spoke. 37

My grades edged upward and my father no longer tried to avoid me when I brought home my report card. I continued reading the encyclopedia diligently, packing more and more into my brain. 38

What I failed to perceive was that Debbie all this while was going steady with a junior from a neighboring school—a hockey player with a C+ average. The revelation hit me hard, and for a while I felt like disgorging[8] and forgetting everything I had learned. I had saved enough money to buy Volume II—Asthma to Bullfinch—but was strongly tempted to invest in a hockey stick instead. 39

How could she lead me on like that—smiling and concurring and giving me the impression that I was important? 40

I felt not only hurt, but betrayed. Like Agamemnon, but with less dire consequences, thank God. 41

In time I recovered from my wounds. The next year Debbie moved from the neighborhood and transferred to another school. Soon she became no more than a fleeting memory. 42

[5]*expatiated:* to speak or write at length.
[6]*adenoids:* masses of tissue that obstruct nasal and ear passages into the throat.
[7]*voracious:* excessively eager.
[8]*disgorging:* discharging violently; vomiting.

Although the original incentive was gone, I continued poring over the encyclopedias, as well as an increasing number of other books. Having savored the heady wine of knowledge, I could not now alter my course. For: 43

> "A little knowledge is a dangerous thing:
> Drink deep, or taste not the Pierian spring."

So wrote Alexander Pope, Volume XIV, Paprika to Pterodactyl. 44

Thinking Critically about This Reading

In paragraph 43 Brody states, "Although the original incentive was gone, I continued poring over the encyclopedias, as well as an increasing number of other books." What was Brody's "original incentive"? What other incentive did Brody have to continue his quest to learn?

Questions for Study and Discussion

1. How are paragraphs 2 and 3, 3 and 4, 5 and 6, 31 and 32, and 43 and 44 linked? (Glossary: *Transitions*)
2. Brody uses dialogue to tell his story in paragraphs 10–35. (Glossary: *Dialogue*) What does the dialogue add to his narrative? What would have been lost had he simply told his readers what happened?
3. Why didn't Brody stop reading the encyclopedia when he discovered that Debbie had a steady boyfriend?
4. If you find Brody's narrative humorous, try to explain the sources of his humor. For example, what humor resides in the choice of examples Brody uses?
5. Brody refers to Coleridge's "The Ancient Mariner" in paragraph 33 and to Agamemnon in paragraph 41, and he quotes Alexander Pope in paragraph 43. Use an encyclopedia to explain Brody's allusions. (Glossary: *Allusion*)
6. Comment on the effectiveness of the beginning and ending of Brody's essay. (Glossary: *Beginnings and Endings*)

Classroom Activity Using Narration

The number of words or paragraphs a writer devotes to the retelling of an event does not usually correspond to the number of minutes or hours the event took to happen. A writer may require multiple paragraphs to recount an important or complex 10–15 minute encounter, but then pass over several hours, days, or even years in several sentences. In narration, length has less to do with chronological time than with the amount of detail the writer includes, and that's a function of the amount of emphasis the writer wants to give to a particular incident. Identify several passages in Brody's essay where he uses multiple paragraphs to retell a relatively brief encounter and where he uses only a paragraph or two to cover a long period of time. Why do you suppose Brody chose to tell his story in this manner?

Suggested Writing Assignments

1. One serious thought that arises as a result of reading Brody's essay is that perhaps we learn best when we are sufficiently motivated to do so. And once we are motivated, the desire to learn seems to feed on itself: "Having savored the heady wine of knowledge, I could not now alter my course" (43). Write an essay in which you explore this subject using your own experiences.
2. Relationships can influence our lives either positively or negatively. Even the appearance of a relationship can have an effect, as we saw in Brody's infatuation with Debbie during his sophomore year in high school. By trying to impress Debbie with his knowledge, Brody got hooked on learning and chose a career in education. Write a brief essay in which you explore the effects that a relationship has had on your life.
3. Brody's essay and the cartoon on p. 336 illustrate the lengths to which two boys will go to impress girls. What do you remember about your own first crush or experience with "puppy love"? What did you do to "impress" the other person? Did the other person do anything that particularly impressed you? Do you think boys and girls behave differently when it comes to impressing a potential love? If so, how? Using Brody's essay as a model, write an essay in which you narrate the story of one of your first loves.

"If I want to impress a woman online, what font should I use? Aristocrat Bold so she'll think I'm rich or Comic Sans so she'll think I'm funny?"

Momma, the Dentist, and Me

■ Maya Angelou

Best-selling author and poet Maya Angelou was born in 1928. She is an educator, historian, actress, playwright, civil rights activist, producer, and director. She is best known as the author of I Know Why the Caged Bird Sings *(1970), the first book in a series that constitutes her recently completed autobiography, and for "On the Pulse of the Morning," a characteristically optimistic poem on the need for personal and national renewal that she read at President Bill Clinton's inauguration in 1993. Starting with her beginnings in St. Louis in 1928, Angelou's autobiography presents a life of joyful triumph over hardships that test her courage and threaten her spirit. It includes the titles* All God's Children Need Traveling Shoes *(1986),* Wouldn't Take Nothing for My Journey Now *(1993), and* Heart of a Woman *(1997). The sixth and final book in the series,* A Song Flung Up to Heaven, *was published in 2002. Several volumes of her poetry were collected in* Complete Collected Poems of Maya Angelou *in 1994.*

In the following excerpt from I Know Why the Caged Bird Sings, *Angelou narrates what happened, and what might have happened, when her grandmother, the "Momma" of the story, took her to the local dentist. As you read, consider how vital first-person narration is to the essay's success, particularly as you gauge the effect of the italicized paragraphs.*

For Your Journal

When you were growing up, were you ever present when one or both of your parents were arguing with another adult about a matter concerning you? What were the circumstances? Narrate the events that brought about the controversy, and show how it was resolved. Were you embarrassed by your parents' actions or happy that they stood up for you?

The angel of the candy counter had found me out at last, and was 1
exacting excruciating penance for all the stolen Milky Ways,

Mounds, Mr. Goodbars and Hersheys with Almonds. I had two cavities that were rotten to the gums. The pain was beyond the bailiwick[1] of crushed aspirins or oil of cloves. Only one thing could help me, so I prayed earnestly that I'd be allowed to sit under the house and have the building collapse on my left jaw. Since there was no Negro dentist in Stamps, nor doctor either, for that matter, Momma had dealt with previous toothaches by pulling them out (a string tied to the tooth with the other end looped over her fist), pain killers and prayer. In this particular instance the medicine had proved ineffective; there wasn't enough enamel left to hook a string on, and the prayers were being ignored because the Balancing Angel was blocking their passage.

I lived a few days and nights in blinding pain, not so much toying with as seriously considering the idea of jumping in the well, and Momma decided I had to be taken to a dentist. The nearest Negro dentist was in Texarkana, twenty-five miles away, and I was certain that I'd be dead long before we reached half the distance. Momma said we'd go to Dr. Lincoln, right in Stamps, and he'd take care of me. She said he owed her a favor. 2

I knew there were a number of whitefolks in town that owed her favors. Bailey and I had seen the books which showed how she had lent money to Blacks and whites alike during the Depression, and most still owed her. But I couldn't aptly remember seeing Dr. Lincoln's name, nor had I ever heard of a Negro's going to him as a patient. However, Momma said we were going, and put water on the stove for our baths. I had never been to a doctor, so she told me that after the bath (which would make my mouth feel better) I had to put on freshly starched and ironed underclothes from inside out. The ache failed to respond to the bath, and I knew then that the pain was more serious than that which anyone had ever suffered. 3

Before we left the Store, she ordered me to brush my teeth and then wash my mouth with Listerine. The idea of even opening my clamped jaws increased the pain, but upon her explanation that when you go to a doctor you have to clean yourself all over, but most especially the part that's to be examined, I screwed up my courage and unlocked my teeth. The cool air in my mouth and the jarring of my molars dislodged what little remained of my reason. I had frozen to the pain, my family nearly had to tie me down to take the toothbrush away. It was 4

[1]*bailiwick:* a specific area of interest, skill, or authority.

no small effort to get me started on the road to the dentist. Momma spoke to all the passers-by, but didn't stop to chat. She explained over her shoulder that we were going to the doctor and she'd "pass the time of day" on our way home.

Until we reached the pond the pain was my world, an aura that 5
haloed me for three feet around. Crossing the bridge into whitefolks' country, pieces of sanity pushed themselves forward. I had to stop moaning and start walking straight. The white towel, which was drawn under my chin and tied over my head, had to be arranged. If one was dying, it had to be done in style if the dying took place in whitefolks' part of town.

On the other side of the bridge the ache seemed to lessen as if a 6
whitebreeze blew off the whitefolks and cushioned everything in their neighborhood—including my jaw. The gravel road was smoother, the stones smaller and the tree branches hung down around the path and nearly covered us. If the pain didn't diminish then, the familiar yet strange sights hypnotized me into believing that it had.

But my head continued to throb with the measured insistence of 7
a bass drum, and how could a toothache pass the calaboose,[2] hear the songs of the prisoners, their blues and laughter, and not be changed? How could one or two or even a mouthful of angry tooth roots meet a wagonload of powhitetrash children, endure their idiotic snobbery and not feel less important?

Behind the building which housed the dentist's office ran a small 8
path used by servants and those tradespeople who catered to the butcher and Stamps' one restaurant. Momma and I followed that lane to the backstairs of Dentist Lincoln's office. The sun was bright and gave the day a hard reality as we climbed up the steps to the second floor.

Momma knocked on the back door and a young white girl 9
opened it to show surprise at seeing us there. Momma said she wanted to see Dentist Lincoln and to tell him Annie was there. The girl closed the door firmly. Now the humiliation of hearing Momma describe herself as if she had no last name to the young white girl was equal to the physical pain. It seemed terribly unfair to have a toothache and a headache and have to bear at the same time the heavy burden of Blackness.

---

[2]*calaboose:* a jail.

It was always possible that the teeth would quiet down and 10
maybe drop out of their own accord. Momma said we would wait. We leaned in the harsh sunlight on the shaky railings of the dentist's back porch for over an hour.

He opened the door and looked at Momma. "Well, Annie, what 11
can I do for you?"

He didn't see the towel around my jaw or notice my swollen 12
face.

Momma said, "Dentist Lincoln. It's my grandbaby here. She got 13
two rotten teeth that's giving her a fit."

She waited for him to acknowledge the truth of her statement. 14
He made no comment, orally or facially.

"She had this toothache purt' near four days now, and today I 15
said, 'Young lady, you going to the Dentist.'"

"Annie?" 16

"Yes, sir, Dentist Lincoln." 17

He was choosing words the way people hunt for shells. "Annie, 18
you know I don't treat nigra, colored people."

"I know, Dentist Lincoln. But this here is just my little grand- 19
baby, and she ain't gone be no trouble to you . . ."

"Annie, everybody has a policy. In this world you have to have a 20
policy. Now, my policy is I don't treat colored people."

The sun had baked the oil out of Momma's skin and melted the 21
Vaseline in her hair. She shone greasily as she leaned out of the dentist's shadow.

"Seem like to me, Dentist Lincoln, you might look after her, she 22
ain't nothing but a little mite.[3] And seems like maybe you owe me a favor or two."

He reddened slightly. "Favor or no favor. The money has all 23
been repaid to you and that's the end of it. Sorry, Annie." He had his hand on the doorknob. "Sorry." His voice was a bit kinder on the second "Sorry," as if he really was.

Momma said, "I wouldn't press on you like this for myself but I 24
can't take No. Not for my grandbaby. When you come to borrow my money you didn't have to beg. You asked me, and I lent it. Now, it wasn't my policy. I ain't no moneylender, but you stood to lose this building and I tried to help you out."

[3] *mite:* a very small creature.

"It's been paid, and raising your voice won't make me change my mind. My policy . . ." He let go of the door and stepped nearer Momma. The three of us were crowded on the small landing. "Annie, my policy is I'd rather stick my hand in a dog's mouth than in a nigger's." 25

He had never once looked at me. He turned his back and went through the door into the cool beyond. Momma backed up inside herself for a few minutes. I forgot everything except her face which was almost a new one to me. She leaned over and took the doorknob, and in her everyday soft voice she said, "Sister, go on downstairs. Wait for me. I'll be there directly." 26

Under the most common of circumstances I knew it did no good to argue with Momma. So I walked down the steep stairs, afraid to look back and afraid not to do so. I turned as the door slammed, and she was gone. 27

Momma walked in that room as if she owned it. She shoved that silly nurse aside with one hand and strode into the dentist's office. He was sitting in his chair, sharpening his mean instruments and putting extra sting into his medicines. Her eyes were blazing like live coals and her arms had doubled themselves in length. He looked up at her just before she caught him by the collar of his white jacket. 28

"Stand up when you see a lady, you contemptuous scoundrel." Her tongue had thinned and the words rolled off well enunciated. Enunciated and sharp like little claps of thunder. 29

The dentist had no choice but to stand at R.O.T.C.[4] *attention. His head dropped after a minute and his voice was humble. "Yes, ma'am, Mrs. Henderson."* 30

"You knave, do you think you acted like a gentleman, speaking to me like that in front of my granddaughter?" She didn't shake him, although she had the power. She simply held him upright. 31

"No, ma'am, Mrs. Henderson." 32

"No, ma'am, Mrs. Henderson, what?" Then she did give him the tiniest of shakes, but because of her strength the action set his head and arms to shaking loose on the ends of his body. He stuttered much worse than Uncle Willie. "No, ma'am, Mrs. Henderson, I'm sorry." 33

With just an edge of her disgust showing, Momma slung him back in his dentist's chair. "Sorry is as sorry does, and you're about the sorriest 34

---

[4]*R.O.T.C.:* Reserve Officers Training Corps of the U.S. military.

dentist I ever laid my eyes on." (She could afford to slip into the vernacular[5] *because she had such eloquent command of English.)*

35 *"I didn't ask you to apologize in front of Marguerite, because I don't want her to know my power, but I order you, now and herewith. Leave Stamps by sundown."*

36 *"Mrs. Henderson, I can't get my equipment . . ." He was shaking terribly now.*

37 *"Now, that brings me to my second order. You will never again practice dentistry. Never! When you get settled in your next place, you will be a vegetarian caring for dogs with the mange, cats with the cholera and cows with the epizootic. Is that clear?"*

38 *The saliva ran down his chin and his eyes filled with tears. "Yes, ma'am. Thank you for not killing me. Thank you, Mrs. Henderson."*

39 *Momma pulled herself back from being ten feet tall with eight-foot arms and said, "You're welcome for nothing, you varlet,*[6] *I wouldn't waste a killing on the likes of you."*

40 *On her way out she waved her handkerchief at the nurse and turned her into a crocus sack of chicken feed.*

41 Momma looked tired when she came down the stairs, but who wouldn't be tired if they had gone through what she had. She came close to me and adjusted the towel under my jaw (I had forgotten the toothache; I only knew that she made her hands gentle in order not to awaken the pain). She took my hand. Her voice never changed. "Come on, Sister."

42 I reckoned we were going home where she would concoct a brew to eliminate the pain and maybe give me new teeth too. New teeth that would grow overnight out of my gums. She led me toward the drugstore, which was in the opposite direction from the Store. "I'm taking you to Dentist Baker in Texarkana."

43 I was glad after all that I had bathed and put on Mum[7] and Cashmere Bouquet talcum powder. It was a wonderful surprise. My toothache had quieted to solemn pain, Momma had obliterated the evil white man, and we were going on a trip to Texarkana, just the two of us.

44 On the Greyhound she took an inside seat in the back, and I sat beside her. I was so proud of being her granddaughter and sure that some of her magic must have come down to me. She asked if I was

---

[5]*vernacular:* the everyday language spoken by people of a particular country or region.
[6]*varlet:* a rascal; lowlife.
[7]*Mum:* a brand of deodorant.

scared. I only shook my head and leaned over on her cool brown upper arm. There was no chance that a dentist, especially a Negro dentist, would dare hurt me then. Not with Momma there. The trip was uneventful, except that she put her arm around me, which was very unusual for Momma to do.

The dentist showed me the medicine and the needle before he deadened my gums, but if he hadn't I wouldn't have worried. Momma stood right behind him. Her arms were folded and she checked on everything he did. The teeth were extracted and she bought me an ice cream cone from the side window of a drug counter. The trip back to Stamps was quiet, except that I had to spit into a very small empty snuff can which she had gotten for me and it was difficult with the bus humping and jerking on our country roads. 45

At home, I was given a warm salt solution, and when I washed out my mouth I showed Bailey the empty holes, where the clotted blood sat like filling in a pie crust. He said I was quite brave, and that was my cue to reveal our confrontation with the peckerwood dentist and Momma's incredible powers. 46

I had to admit that I didn't hear the conversation, but what else could she have said than what I said she said? What else done? He agreed with my analysis in a lukewarm way, and I happily (after all, I'd been sick) flounced into the Store. Momma was preparing our evening meal and Uncle Willie leaned on the door sill. She gave her version. 47

"Dentist Lincoln got right uppity. Said he'd rather put his hand in a dog's mouth. And when I reminded him of the favor, he brushed it off like a piece of lint. Well, I sent Sister downstairs and went inside. I hadn't never been in his office before, but I found the door to where he takes out teeth, and him and the nurse was in there thick as thieves. I just stood there till he caught sight of me." Crash bang the pots on the stove. "He jumped just like he was sitting on a pin. He said, 'Annie, I done tole you, I ain't gonna mess around in no niggah's mouth.' I said, 'Somebody's got to do it then,' and he said, 'Take her to Texarkana to the colored dentist' and that's when I said, 'If you paid me my money I could afford to take her.' He said, 'It's all been paid.' I tole him everything but the interest been paid. He said, ''Twasn't no interest.' I said, ''Tis now. I'll take ten dollars as payment in full.' You know, Willie, it wasn't no right thing to do, 'cause I lent that money without thinking about it. 48

"He tole that little snippety nurse of his'n to give me ten dollars and make me sign a 'paid in full' receipt. She gave it to me and I 49 signed the papers. Even though by rights he was paid up before, I figger, he gonna be that kind of nasty, he gonna have to pay for it."

Momma and her son laughed and laughed over the white man's 50
evilness and her retributive[8] sin.

I preferred, much preferred, my version. 51

Thinking Critically about This Reading

What does Angelou mean when she states, "On the other side of the bridge the ache seemed to lessen as if a whitebreeze blew off the whitefolks and cushioned everything in their neighborhood—including my jaw" (paragraph 6). How long did Angelou's pain relief last? Why?

Questions for Study and Discussion

1. What is Angelou's purpose? (Glossary: *Purpose*)
2. Compare and contrast the content and style of the interaction between Momma and the dentist that is given in italics with the one given at the end of the narrative. (Glossary: *Comparison and Contrast*)
3. Angelou tells her story chronologically and in the first person. (Glossary: *Point of View*) What are the advantages of first-person narration?
4. Identify three similes that Angelou uses in her narrative. (Glossary: *Figure of Speech*) Explain how each simile serves her purpose. (Glossary: *Purpose*)
5. Why do you suppose Angelou says she prefers her own version of the episode to that of her grandmother?
6. This is a story of pain—and not just the pain of a toothache. How does Angelou describe the pain of the toothache? What other pain does she tell of in this autobiographical piece?

Classroom Activity Using Narration

One of Angelou's themes in "Momma, the Dentist, and Me" is that cruelty, whether racial, social, professional, or personal, is very difficult

---

[8] *retributive:* demanding something in repayment, especially punishment.

to endure and leaves a lasting impression on a person. As a way of practicing chronological order, consider a situation in which an unthinking or insensitive person made you feel inferior. Rather than write a draft of an essay at this point, simply list the sequence of events that occurred, in chronological order. Once you have completed this step, consider whether there is a more dramatic order you might use if you were actually to write an essay.

Suggested Writing Assignments

1. Using Angelou's essay as a model, give two versions of an actual event—one the way you thought or wished it had happened, and the other the way events actually took place. You may want to refer to your journal entry for this reading before you begin writing.
2. Every person who tells a story does so by putting his or her signature on it in some way—by the sequencing of events, the amount and type of details used, and the tone the teller of the story employs. (Glossary: *Tone*) If you and a relative or friend experienced the same interesting sequence of events, try telling the story of those events from your unique perspective. (Glossary: *Point of View*) Once you have done so, try telling the story from what you imagine the other person's perspective to be. Perhaps you even heard the other person actually tell the story. What is the same in both versions? How do the renditions differ?

The Story of an Hour

■ Kate Chopin

Kate Chopin (1851–1904) was born in St. Louis, of Creole Irish descent. After her marriage she lived in Louisiana, where she acquired the intimate knowledge of Creole Cajun culture that provided the impetus for much of her work and earned her a reputation as a writer who captured the ambience of the bayou region. When her first novel, The Awakening *(1899), was published, however, it generated scorn and outrage for its explicit depiction of a southern woman's sexual awakening. Only recently has Chopin been recognized for her literary talent and originality. Besides* The Awakening, *her works include two collections of short fiction,* Bayou Folk *(1894) and* A Night in Acadie *(1897). In 1969,* The Complete Works of Kate Chopin *was published by Louisiana State University Press, and the Library of America published* Kate Chopin: Complete Novels and Stories *in 2002.*

As you read the following story, first published as "The Dream of an Hour" in Vogue *magazine in 1894, try to gauge how your reactions to Mrs. Mallard are influenced by Chopin's use of third-person narration.*

For Your Journal

How do you react to the idea of marriage—committing to someone for life? What are the advantages of such a union? What are the disadvantages?

Knowing that Mrs. Mallard was afflicted with a heart trouble, great care was taken to break to her as gently as possible the news of her husband's death. 1

It was her sister Josephine who told her, in broken sentences; veiled hints that revealed in half concealing. Her husband's friend Richards was there, too, near her. It was he who had been in the newspaper office when intelligence of the railroad disaster was received, with Brently Mallard's name leading the list of "killed." He 2 had only taken the time to assure himself of its truth by a second telegram, and had hastened to forestall any less careful, less tender friend in bearing the sad message.

She did not hear the story as many women have heard the same, with a paralyzed inability to accept its significance. She wept at once, with sudden, wild abandonment, in her sister's arms. When the storm of grief had spent itself she went away to her room alone. She would have no one follow her. 3

There stood, facing the open window, a comfortable, roomy armchair. Into this she sank, pressed down by a physical exhaustion that haunted her body and seemed to reach into her soul. 4

She could see in the open square before her house the tops of trees that were all aquiver with the new spring life. The delicious breath of rain was in the air. In the street below a peddler was crying his wares. The notes of a distant song which someone was singing reached her faintly, and countless sparrows were twittering in the eaves. 5

There were patches of blue sky showing here and there through the clouds that had met and piled one above the other in the west facing her window. 6

She sat with her head thrown back upon the cushion of the chair, quite motionless, except when a sob came up into her throat and shook her, as a child who has cried itself to sleep continues to sob in its dreams. 7

She was young, with a fair, calm face, whose lines bespoke repression and even a certain strength. But now there was a dull stare in her eyes, whose gaze was fixed away off yonder on one of those patches of blue sky. It was not a glance of reflection, but rather indicated a suspension of intelligent thought. 8

There was something coming to her and she was waiting for it, fearfully. What was it? She did not know; it was too subtle and elusive to name. But she felt it, creeping out of the sky, reaching toward her through the sounds, the scents, the color that filled the air. 9

Now her bosom rose and fell tumultuously. She was beginning to recognize this thing that was approaching to possess her, and she was striving to beat it back with her will—as powerless as her two white slender hands would have been. 10

When she abandoned herself a little whispered word escaped her slightly parted lips. She said it over and over under her breath: "free, free, free!" The vacant stare and the look of terror that had followed it went from her eyes. They stayed keen and bright. Her pulses beat 11 fast, and the coursing blood warmed and relaxed every inch of her body.

She did not stop to ask if it were or were not a monstrous joy that held her. A clear and exalted perception enabled her to dismiss the suggestion as trivial. 12

She knew that she would weep again when she saw the kind, tender hands folded in death; the face that had never looked save with love upon her, fixed and gray and dead. But she saw beyond that bitter moment a long procession of years to come that would belong to her absolutely. And she opened and spread her arms out to them in welcome. 13

There would be no one to live for her during those coming years; she would live for herself. There would be no powerful will bending hers in that blind persistence with which men and women believe they have a right to impose a private will upon a fellow-creature. A kind intention or a cruel intention made the act seem no less a crime as she looked upon it in that brief moment of illumination. 14

And yet she had loved him—sometimes. Often she had not. What did it matter! What could love, the unsolved mystery, count for in face of this possession of self-assertion which she suddenly recognized as the strongest impulse of her being! 15

"Free! Body and soul free!" she kept whispering. 16

Josephine was kneeling before the closed door with her lips to the keyhole, imploring for admission. "Louise, open the door! I beg; open the door—you will make yourself ill. What are you doing, Louise? For heaven's sake open the door." 17

"Go away. I am not making myself ill." No; she was drinking in a very elixir of life through that open window. 18

Her fancy was running riot along those days ahead of her. Spring days, and summer days, and all sorts of days that would be her own. She breathed a quick prayer that life might be long. It was only yesterday she had thought with a shudder that life might be long. 19

She arose at length and opened the door to her sister's importunities.[1] There was a feverish triumph in her eyes, and she carried herself unwittingly like a goddess of Victory. She clasped her sister's waist, and together they descended the stairs. Richards stood waiting for them at the bottom. 20

[1]*importunities:* urgent requests or demands.

Some one was opening the front door with a latchkey. It was Brently Mallard who entered, a little travel-stained, composedly carrying his grip-sack and umbrella. He had been far from the scene of the accident, and did not even know there had been one. He stood amazed at Josephine's piercing cry; at Richards' quick motion to screen him from the view of his wife. 21

But Richards was too late. 22

When the doctors came they said she had died of heart disease— 23
of joy that kills.

Thinking Critically about This Reading

Chopin describes Mrs. Mallard as "beginning to recognize this thing that was approaching to possess her, and she was striving to beat it back with her will—as powerless as her two white slender hands would have been" (paragraph 10). Why does Mrs. Mallard fight her feeling of freedom, however briefly? How does she come to accept it?

Questions for Study and Discussion

1. What assumptions do Mrs. Mallard's relatives and friends make about her feelings toward her husband? What are her true feelings?
2. Reread paragraphs 5–9. What is Chopin's purpose in this section? (Glossary: *Purpose*) Do these paragraphs add to the story's effectiveness? Explain.
3. All of the events of Chopin's story take place in an hour. Would the story be as poignant if they had taken place over the course of a day, or even several days? Explain. Why do you suppose the author selected the time frame as a title for her story? (Glossary: *Title*)
4. Chopin could have written an essay detailing the oppression of women in marriage, but she chose instead to write a fictional narrative. This allows her to show readers the type of situation that can arise in an outwardly happy marriage, rather than tell them about it. Why else do you think she chose to write a fictional narrative? What other advantages does it give her over nonfiction?
5. Why does Chopin narrate her story in the third person? (Glossary: *Point of View*)

Classroom Activity Using Narration

Using cues in the following sentences, rearrange them in chronological order.

1. The sky was gray and gloomy for as far as she could see, and sleet hissed off the glass.
2. "Oh, hi, I'm glad you called," she said happily, but her smile dimmed when she looked outside.
3. As Betty crossed the room, the phone rang, startling her.
4. "No, the weather's awful, so I don't think I'll get out to visit you today," she sighed.
5. "Hello," she said, and she wandered over to the window, dragging the phone cord behind her.

Write five sentences of your own that cover a progression of events. Try to include dialogue. (Glossary: *Dialogue*) Then scramble them, and see if a classmate can put them back in the correct order.

Suggested Writing Assignments

1. Using Chopin's story as a model, write a short piece of narrative fiction in which your main character reacts to a specific, dramatic event. Portray the character's emotional response, as well as how the character perceives his or her surroundings. What does the character see, hear, touch? How are these senses affected by the situation?
2. Write a narrative essay in which you describe your reaction to a piece of news that you once received—good or bad—that provoked a strong emotional response. What were your emotions? What did you do in the couple of hours after you received the news? How did your perceptions of the world around you change? What made the experience memorable?

chapter **14**

Description

To describe is to create a verbal picture. A person, a place, a thing—even an idea or a state of mind—can be made vividly concrete through **description.** Here, for example, is a brief description of a delicatessen:

> It was a narrow room, with a rather high ceiling, and crowded from floor to ceiling with goodies. There were rows and rows of hams and sausages of all shapes and colors—white, yellow, red, and black; fat and lean and round and long—rows of canned preserves, cocoa and tea, bright translucent glass bottles of honey, marmalade, and jam; round bottles and slender bottles, filled with liqueurs and punch—all these things crowded every inch of the shelves from top to bottom.
>
> –Thomas Mann

Writing any description requires, first of all, that the writer gather many details about a subject, relying not only on what the eyes see but on the other sense impressions—touch, taste, smell, hearing—as well. From this catalog of details the writer selects those that will most effectively create a **dominant impression**—the single quality, mood, or atmosphere that the writer wishes to emphasize. Consider, for example, the details that Mary McCarthy uses to evoke the dominant impression in the following passage, and contrast them with those in the subsequent example by student Dan Bubany:

> Whenever we children came to stay at my grandmother's house, we were put to sleep in the sewing room, a bleak, shabby, utilitarian rectangle, more office than bedroom, more attic than office, that played to the hierarchy of chambers the role of poor relation. It was a room without pride: the old sewing machine, some cast-off chairs, a shadeless lamp, rolls of wrapping paper, piles of cardboard boxes that might someday come in handy, papers of pins,

> and remnants of a material united with the iron folding cots put out for our use and the bare floor boards to give an impression of intense and ruthless temporality. Thin white spreads, of the kind used in hospitals and charity institutions, and naked blinds at the windows reminded us of our orphaned condition and of the ephemeral character of our visit; there was nothing here to encourage us to consider this our home.
>
> –Mary McCarthy

> For this particular Thursday game against Stanford, Fleming wears white gloves, a maroon sport coat with brass buttons, and gray slacks. Shiny silver-framed bifocals match the whistle pressed between the lips on his slightly wrinkled face, and he wears freshly polished black shoes so glossy that they reflect the grass he stands on. He is not fat, but his coat neatly conceals a small, round pot belly.
>
> –Dan Bubany, student

The dominant impression that McCarthy creates is one of clutter, bleakness, and shabbiness. There is nothing in the sewing room that suggests permanence or warmth. Bubany, on the other hand, creates a dominant impression of a neat, polished, kindly man.

Writers must also carefully plan the order in which to present their descriptive details. The pattern of organization must fit the subject of the description logically and naturally and must be easy to follow. For example, visual details can be arranged spatially—from left to right, top to bottom, near to far, or in any other logical order. Other patterns include smallest to largest, softest to loudest, least significant to most significant, most unusual to least unusual. McCarthy, for example, suggests a jumble of junk not only by her choice of details but by the apparently random order in which she presents them.

How much detail is enough? There is no fixed answer. A good description includes enough vivid details to create a dominant impression and to bring a scene to life, but not so many that readers are distracted, confused, or bored. In an essay that is purely descriptive, there is room for much detail. Usually, however, writers use description to create the setting for a story, to illustrate ideas, to help clarify a definition or a comparison, or to make the complexities of a process more understandable. Such descriptions should be kept short and should include just enough detail to make them clear and helpful.

Subway Station

■ Gilbert Highet

Gilbert Highet (1906–1978) was born in Scotland and became a naturalized U.S. citizen in 1951. A prolific writer and translator, distinguished scholar, and critic, Highet was for many years a professor of classics at Columbia University, as well as a popular radio essayist. His Art of Teaching *(1950), a classic in education, was reissued in paperback and is still available. Another of his books,* The Classical Tradition: Greek and Roman Influences on Western Literature, *was reissued in paperback in 1992.*

The following selection is from his book Talents and Geniuses *(1957). Take note of Highet's keen eye for detail as you read. Concrete and vivid images help him re-create the unseemly world of a subway station.*

For Your Journal

Try to remember what it is like to be in a subway station, airport, or bus station. What are the sights, sounds, and smells you recall? What do you remember most about any of these crowded, transient places? What was your overall impression of the place?

Standing in a subway station, I began to appreciate the place— 1
almost to enjoy it. First of all, I looked at the lighting: a row of meager electric bulbs, unscreened, yellow, and coated with filth, stretched toward the black mouth of the tunnel, as though it were a bolt hole in an abandoned coal mine. Then I lingered, with zest, on the walls and ceiling: lavatory tiles which had been white about fifty years ago, and were now encrusted with soot, coated with the remains of a dirty liquid which might be either atmospheric humidity mingled with smog or the result of a perfunctory[1] attempt to clean them with cold water; and, above them, gloomy vaulting from which dingy paint was peeling off like scabs from an old wound, sick black paint leaving a leprous white undersurface. Beneath my feet, the floor was

[1]*perfunctory:* hasty and without attention to detail.

a nauseating dark brown with black stains upon it which might be stale oil or dry chewing gum or some worse defilement; it looked like the hallway of a condemned slum building. Then my eye traveled to the tracks, where two lines of glittering steel—the only positively clean objects in the whole place—ran out of darkness into darkness above an unspeakable mass of congealed oil, puddles of dubious[2] liquid, and a mishmash of old cigarette packets, mutilated and filthy newspapers, and the débris that filtered down from the street above through a barred grating in the roof. As I looked up toward the sunlight, I could see more débris sifting slowly downward, and making an abominable pattern in the slanting beam of dirt-laden sunlight. I was going on to relish more features of this unique scene: such as the advertisement posters on the walls—here a text from the Bible, there a half-naked girl, here a woman wearing a hat consisting of a hen sitting on a nest full of eggs, and there a pair of girl's legs walking up the keys of a cash register—all scribbled over with unknown names and well-known obscenities in black crayon and red lipstick; but then my train came in at last, I boarded it, and began to read. The experience was over for the time.

Thinking Critically about This Reading

In his opening sentence, Highet reveals that he "began to appreciate the place—almost enjoy it." What does he mean by "appreciate"? Explain.

Questions for Study and Discussion

1. What dominant impression does Highet create in his description? (Glossary: *Dominant Impression*) List the details that help Highet create his dominant impression.
2. Why do you think Highet observes the subway station with "zest" and "relish"? What does he find appealing about the experience?
3. What similes and metaphors can you find in Highet's description? (Glossary: *Figure of Speech*) How do they help make the description vivid?

[2]*dubious:* of uncertain or questionable content.

4. What mix of advertisements does Highet observe? Based on Highet's description of what they depict, their current appearance, and the atmosphere of their surroundings, suggest what product each poster might be advertising. Explain your suggestions.
5. Highet has an eye for detail that is usually displayed by those who are seeing something for the first time. Do you think it is his first time in a subway station, or is he a regular rider who is taking time out to "relish" his physical surroundings? What in the essay leads you to your conclusion?

Classroom Activity Using Description

Make a long list of the objects and people in your classroom as well as the physical features of the room—desks, windows, chalkboard, students, professor, dirty walls, burned-out lightbulb, a clock that is always ten minutes fast, and so on. Determine a dominant impression that you would like to create in describing the classroom. Now choose from your list those items that would best illustrate the dominant impression you have chosen. Your instructor may wish to have students compare their responses.

Suggested Writing Assignments

1. Using Highet's essay as a model, write an extended one-paragraph description of a room in your house or apartment where you do not spend much time. Take your time observing the details in the room. Before you write, decide on the dominant impression you wish to communicate to the reader. (Glossary: *Dominant Impression*)
2. Write a short essay in which you describe one of the following places (or another place of your choice). Arrange the details of your description from top to bottom, left to right, near to far, or according to some other spatial organization.

closet	barbershop or beauty salon
pizza parlor	bookstore
locker room	campus dining hall

3. Consider the photograph on p. 356 of a subway station in Moscow. What is your dominant impression of the subway station? (Glossary: *Dominant Impression*) What details in the photograph create this

dominant impression for you? How does the subway station Highet describes compare to the one in the photo? (Glossary: *Comparison and Contrast*) Using Highet's essay as a model, write a description of this Moscow subway station that creates a dominant impression for your readers.

Wyoming Clouds

Verlyn Klinkenborg

Born in 1953, Verlyn Klinkenborg grew up on farms in Iowa and Minnesota, where he developed his keen observation skills. After receiving his PhD from Princeton University, he embarked on a career as a writer and farmer. His first book, Making Hay *(1986), reflects Klinkenborg's fascination with small family farms.* The Last Fine Time *(1992) is a history of immigrant life in Buffalo, New York, where his father-in-law owned a neighborhood bar. Since 1997 his column "The Rural Life" has appeared regularly on the editorial pages of the* New York Times, *and in 2002 these essays were published in the collection* The Rural Life. *Klinkenborg's essays have also appeared in* Harper's *and the* New Yorker.

The following essay is taken from a section titled "August" in The Rural Life. *Here Klinkenborg describes Wyoming's often unpredictable summer clouds. Often described as a prose poet, notice how Klinkenborg uses personification, metaphor, and simile to capture the ever-changing cloud formations.*

For Your Journal

When you hear the word *cloud,* what comes to mind? Is it an image or a feeling? Have you ever watched the summer clouds drift by and fantasized about the particular shapes some clouds take? Describe one memorable experience with clouds.

Wyoming is a metropolis[1] of clouds. Some are born in the state, some move here from other places, but they all prosper, because Wyoming is also a theater of wind. For days at a time this summer, the clouds have passed in migratory flight, complicating the sunlight. In late afternoon especially, along the northeastern rim of the Bighorn Mountains, great rafts[2] of orographic clouds—shaped by the mountains, 1

[1]*metropolis:* a densely populated city.
[2]*rafts:* large amounts.

that is—rise with the terrain and then lean out over the creek bottoms, darkening the face of the Bighorns and reabsorbing that darkness.

It's been a wet summer in Wyoming, and rich in cloud life. Hay bales have been stacked in pyramids in the fields to keep the damp off, and the barley has gone unirrigated. Often enough, when morning dawns, the dogs run up the hayfield road, inhaling and exhaling cloud, until they vanish into even grayness. 2

Those are the usual summer days, which often turn cloudless by noon. They end with lightning flickering all around the night horizon, the storms so distant that they lie beneath the constellation Scorpio, which never gets very high in the sky this far north. But along the road from Cheyenne to Sheridan a squall[3] line blew in from the open prairie to the east, an ominous, upward-thrusting shield of precipitation. The temperature dropped nearly thirty degrees, and the rain fell against the direction of the wind so heavily that drivers pulled off the road, turned off their wipers, and watched the lightning take dead aim around them. 3

Twenty miles down the road, the temperature rose as much as it had fallen. The squall line broke apart into a landscape of sky that beggared[4] the landscape of earth. Clouds congealed into innumerable shapes, each requiring its own analogy. Shards of flint and flakes of obsidian knifed through the middle atmosphere. Mammatus clouds, as smoothly pebbled as a low-water beach, clung to the underside of thunderheads, while pileus clouds—the name means skullcap—clung to their tops. 4

Some clouds had become castellated,[5] and others had been beaten into sheets of lead or folded back upon themselves again and again like Damascus steel. The galactic gas jets of the deep universe were present and so were the nebulae. So too was the tight, blue-tinted hairdo of a matron marching westward in dudgeon[6] across the sky. She canted over the sagebrush flats, hit an updraft, and was teased into nothingness. 5

Thinking Critically about This Reading

What does Klinkenborg means when he states, "Wyoming is a . . . theater of wind" (paragraph 1)? How does this metaphor establish the context of his description?

[3]*squall:* sudden, violent wind and rainstorm.
[4]*beggared:* rivaled; was beyond comparison to.
[5]*castellated:* shaped like a castle, with turrets and battlements.
[6]*in dudgeon:* in a gloomy mood; sullen.

Questions for Study and Discussion

1. Identify at least one instance of personification, metaphor, and simile in Klinkenborg's essay. (Glossary: *Figure of Speech*) What does each add to the essay as a whole?
2. How does Klinkenborg organize his essay? (Glossary: *Organization*) Is his organization effective? Explain.
3. How would you characterize Klinkenborg's description of the Wyoming clouds—scientific (objective), poetic (subjective), or some combination of the two? Where is he more scientific? More poetic?
4. In paragraph 4, Klinkenborg states that he finds analogy useful in describing the sometimes fanciful shapes the clouds take. (Glossary: *Analogy*) Do his analogies help you create mental images of the clouds' various shapes? Explain.
5. How effective are Klinkenborg's beginning and ending? (Glossary: *Beginnings and Endings*) Do you think his final image of the blue-haired matron being "teased into nothingness" (5) captures the essence of clouds? Why or why not?

Classroom Activity Using Description

The verbs you use in writing a description can themselves convey much descriptive information. Take, for example, the verb *walk*. This word actually tells us little more than "to move on foot," in the most general sense. Using more precise and descriptive alternatives—*hike*, *slink*, *saunter*, *stalk*, *step*, *stride*, *stroll*, *tramp*, *wander*—enhances your descriptive powers and enlivens your writing. For each of the following verbs, make a list of at least four descriptive alternatives. Then compare your list of descriptive alternatives with those of others in the class.

go	throw	exercise
see	take	study
say	drink	sleep

Suggested Writing Assignments

1. As Klinkenborg has done with the clouds of Wyoming, write a short composition analyzing and describing a common weather phenomenon in your area. For example, does your region of the

country get more than its share of drought, flooding, hurricanes, thunderstorms, blizzards, or ice storms? Include details that will appeal to your readers' senses of sight, sound, and smell.

2. Describe a familiar inanimate object in a way that brings out its character and makes it interesting to the reader. First, determine your purpose in describing the object. Suppose, for example, your family has had the same dining table for as long as you can remember. Think of what that table has been a part of over the years—the birthday parties, the fights, the holiday meals, the long hours of studying and doing homework. A description of such a table would give your reader a sense of the history of your family. Next, make an exhaustive list of the object's physical features, and include in your descriptive essay the features that contribute to your dominant impression and support your purpose. (Glossary: *Dominant Impression*)

City of Islands

■ Pete Hamill

Pete Hamill was born in Brooklyn, New York, in 1935. After serving in the U.S. Navy in the early 1950s, he attended Mexico City College, Pratt Institute, and the School of Visual Arts before starting his career at the New York Post *in 1960. He has been a columnist for the* New York Post, New York Daily News, *and* Village Voice, *and his articles have appeared in such magazines as* Playboy, Esquire, Conde Nast Traveler, Vanity Fair, *and* New York Times Magazine. *His distinguished journalism career includes having served as editor-in-chief of both the* New York Post *and* New York Daily News. *Currently he is on the staff of the* New Yorker. *Hamill is the author of sixteen books, including the novels* Snow in August *(1997) and* Forever *(2003), the memoir* A Drinking Life *(1995), and the nonfiction works* Why Sinatra Matters *(1998) and* Diego Rivera *(1999).*

The following essay first appeared in New York: A City of Islands *(1998), a collaboration between Hamill and photographer Jake Raj. Here Hamill gives us a bird's-eye view of the city. Imagine for a moment that you are arriving via airplane in New York City; as you read, let Hamill describe the vista outside your window. Notice, in particular, how he distinguishes each of the five boroughs of this great, historic city.*

For Your Journal

What are your impressions of New York City? Are your impressions based on firsthand experience with the city, or are they based on what you have read or seen on television or in movies? When you hear the name of this famous city mentioned, where do your thoughts go? Why?

The archipelago[1] of New York is seen most clearly from the air. 1
You are arriving from some distant place on a day bright with

[1]*archipelago:* a large group of islands.

the sparkle and clarity of October. Below you is the great harbor, its entrance guarded by the steel geometry of the Verrazano Bridge. The span ties together Brooklyn and the green pastures of Staten Island. There in the harbor, as tiny as a toy, is the Statue of Liberty and directly behind it, Ellis Island. And then, announced suddenly by its eruptions of spires and the glitter of a million windows, you see Manhattan. It is long and irregular, narrowing as it moves north, with the mighty Hudson coursing down its western coast, the East River separating it from the head of Long Island. There are dots of green visible from the sky and the long sward[2] of Central Park, but from the air, as the airplane banks to the right, it appears that every acre has been shaped by man.

Off to the left, as the airplane turns, above Manhattan, is the Bronx. 2
It is the only one of New York's five boroughs that is on the mainland and from the air it does look oddly separate, a dark painting with a scumbled[3] texture but no borders, no frame; its northern edge simply eases into the rest of America. You can see Yankee Stadium. You can see the narrowing Hudson. You can see the waters of Long Island Sound. But from the air, the Bronx seems different. It is not until you move through its streets and sense its emotional and psychic separation from the mainland that you realize that the Bronx too is one of the New York islands.

You are over Long Island now. It is shaped like an immense scaly 3
fish with sharp humps that has come aground in flight from Europe. Queens and Brooklyn are its head. Queens is at the top of the head curving around behind Brooklyn to form a jaw. Brooklyn is its immense snout, pushing at the harbor. Shea Stadium is its tiny green eye. The immense fish seems poised to gnaw at Manhattan.

From the air, Queens and Brooklyn are flatter than Manhattan, 4
more collage[4] than bas-relief.[5] Queens is brighter. The houses are newer, hundreds of thousands of them built after World War Two. They are painted white. They have shingled rooftops. They have backyards and in some you can glimpse the azure shimmer of tiny swimming pools. Brooklyn is darker, older, a place of brownstone or brick, of aging tenements and ugly housing projects. The street grids of both boroughs are less rigid than that of Manhattan; some go off at odd angles, a

[2]*sward:* a lawn or meadow.
[3]*scumbled:* covered with a film of opaque or semi-opaque color; rubbed.
[4]*collage:* an artistic composition of materials and objects pasted over a surface.
[5]*bas-relief:* a sculpture that projects very little from a flat background.

few form circles, others end abruptly. Boulevards, avenues, and highways cut through them, going west to Manhattan or east to the suburbs of Nassau and Suffolk. At the southern edge, you can sometimes see the tiny islands of Jamaica Bay and the bright white beaches of Coney Island and the Rockaways, all of them washed by the endless Atlantic.

City of Islands. Shaped by geography and history, by the great 5
harbor and the millions who entered it to build the city. Without the harbor and the rivers, the history would have been different. But it was that harbor and the emerging port that drew the millions. They lashed themselves together with bridges and miles of subway track. They built bridges and tunnels to connect them to the rest of the United States. And upon the five main islands, they evolved other islands, shaped by commerce or manufacturing, by ethnicity, by class. They can't be seen from the air.

Thinking Critically about This Reading

Hamill points to the Statue of Liberty in New York Harbor and tells us that it "is tiny as a toy" (paragraph 1). In what ways does this simple simile prepare readers to better visualize the city?

Questions for Study and Discussion

1. Hamill describes the islands that are New York City from the air because he believes that "it is seen most clearly" (1) from this perspective. What would have been lost had he tried to describe the city from the ground? Explain.
2. Hamill uses an extended metaphor to describe Long Island. (Glossary: *Figure of Speech*) Does it help you visualize Long Island itself and see its relationship to the other islands of New York? Explain.
3. Hamill is careful to give the names of places, objects, and geographical features whenever possible—Queens, Coney Island, the Verrazano Bridge, Shea Stadium, the Hudson and East Rivers. What do these names add to Hamill's description?
4. How would you characterize Hamill's diction? (Glossary: *Diction*) Is it specific and concrete or general and abstract? (Glossary: *Concrete/Abstract*; *Specific/General*)

5. What dominant impression of New York City does Hamill's description give you? (Glossary: *Dominant Impression*) What specific details create this impression for you?
6. What is Hamill's attitude toward New York City? (Glossary: *Attitude*) What details lead you to this conclusion?

Classroom Activity Using Description

Write five sentences describing the place you would most like to go. What details about the place do you want to include? Choose your words carefully so that you create the dominant impression that you have of that place—such as beautiful, dangerous, serene, fun, or relaxing.

Suggested Writing Assignments

1. What is your favorite city, and what are your favorite places in that city? For example, if Washington, D.C., is your favorite city, the capital building, White House, National Gallery, Washington Monument, Lincoln Memorial, Vietnam War Memorial, and National Zoo might be among your favorite places. Write an essay in which you describe the city you love.
2. American landscape architect Frederick Law Olmsted (1822–1903) designed Central Park in New York City. In addition to Central Park, what other public places did Olmsted design? What are the hallmarks of an Olmsted-designed landscape? Conduct some research in your library or on the Internet, and then write a brief report about Olmsted and his work. If you have ever visited a place designed by Olmsted, be sure to include your personal experiences with his landscapes.

My Favorite Teacher

■ Thomas L. Friedman

New York Times *foreign affairs columnist Thomas L. Friedman was born in Minneapolis, Minnesota, in 1953. He graduated from Brandeis University in 1975 and received a Marshall Scholarship to study Modern Middle East Studies at St. Antony's College, Oxford University, where he earned a master's degree. He has worked for the* New York Times *since 1981, first in Lebanon, then in Israel, and since 1989 in Washington, D.C. He has won three Pulitzer Prizes. His 1989 bestseller,* From Beirut to Jerusalem, *received the National Book Award for nonfiction. Friedman's most recent books are* The Lexus and the Olive Tree: Understanding Globalization *(2000),* Longitudes and Attitudes: Exploring the World after September 11 *(2002), and* The World Is Flat: A Brief History of the Twenty-First Century *(2005).*

In the following essay, which first appeared in the New York Times *on January 9, 2001, Friedman pays tribute to his tenth-grade journalism teacher. As you read Friedman's profile of Hattie M. Steinberg, note the descriptive detail he selects to create the dominant impression of "a woman of clarity in an age of uncertainty."*

For Your Journal

If you had to name your three favorite teachers to date, who would be on your list? Why do you consider each of the teachers a favorite? Which one, if any, are you likely to remember twenty-five years from now? Why?

Last Sunday's *New York Times Magazine* published its annual review of people who died last year who left a particular mark on the world. I am sure all readers have their own such list. I certainly do. Indeed, someone who made the most important difference in my life died last year—my high school journalism teacher, Hattie M. Steinberg. 1

I grew up in a small suburb of Minneapolis, and Hattie was the legendary journalism teacher at St. Louis Park High School, Room 313. I took her intro to journalism course in 10th grade, back in 1969, and have never needed, or taken, another course in journalism since. She was that good. 2

Hattie was a woman who believed that the secret for success in life was getting the fundamentals right. And boy, she pounded the fundamentals of journalism into her students—not simply how to write a lead or accurately transcribe a quote, but, more important, how to comport yourself in a professional way and to always do quality work. To this day, when I forget to wear a tie on assignment, I think of Hattie scolding me. I once interviewed an ad exec for our high school paper who used a four-letter word. We debated whether to run it. Hattie ruled yes. That ad man almost lost his job when it appeared. She wanted to teach us about consequences. 3

Hattie was the toughest teacher I ever had. After you took her journalism course in 10th grade, you tried out for the paper, *The Echo,* which she supervised. Competition was fierce. In 11th grade, I didn't quite come up to her writing standards, so she made me business manager, selling ads to the local pizza parlors. That year, though, she let me write one story. It was about an Israeli general who had been a hero in the Six-Day War[1], who was giving a lecture at the University of Minnesota. I covered his lecture and interviewed him briefly. His name was Ariel Sharon[2]. First story I ever got published. 4

Those of us on the paper, and the yearbook that she also supervised, lived in Hattie's classroom. We hung out there before and after school. Now, you have to understand, Hattie was a single woman, nearing 60 at the time, and this was the 1960's. She was the polar opposite of "cool," but we hung around her classroom like it was a malt shop and she was Wolfman Jack[3]. None of us could have articulated it then, but it was because we enjoyed being harangued[4] by her, disciplined by her, and taught by her. She was a woman of clarity in an age of uncertainty. 5

---

[1]*Six-Day War:* the short but pivotal war in June 1967 between Israel and the allied countries of Egypt, Syria and Jordan.

[2]*Ariel Sharon* (b. 1928): Israeli general and politician, elected prime minister of Israel in 2001.

[3]*Wolfman Jack:* pseudonym of Robert Weston Smith (1938–1995), a famous American rock-and-roll radio disc jockey.

[4]*harangued:* given a long, scolding lecture.

We remained friends for 30 years, and she followed, bragged about, and critiqued every twist in my career. After she died, her friends sent me a pile of my stories that she had saved over the years. Indeed, her students were her family—only closer. Judy Harrington, one of Hattie's former students, remarked about other friends who were on Hattie's newspapers and yearbooks: "We all graduated 41 years ago; and yet nearly each day in our lives something comes up—some mental image, some admonition[5] that makes us think of Hattie." 6

Judy also told the story of one of Hattie's last birthday parties, when one man said he had to leave early to take his daughter somewhere. "Sit down," said Hattie. "You're not leaving yet. She can just be a little late." 7

That was my teacher! I sit up straight just thinkin' about her. 8

Among the fundamentals Hattie introduced me to was *The New York Times*. Every morning it was delivered to Room 313. I had never seen it before then. Real journalists, she taught us, start their day by reading *The Times* and columnists like Anthony Lewis and James Reston. 9

I have been thinking about Hattie a lot this year, not just because she died on July 31, but because the lessons she imparted seem so relevant now. We've just gone through this huge dot-com-Internet-globalization bubble—during which a lot of smart people got carried away and forgot the fundamentals of how you build a profitable company, a lasting portfolio, a nation state, or a thriving student. It turns out that the real secret of success in the information age is what it always was: fundamentals—reading, writing and arithmetic, church, synagogue and mosque, the rule of law, and good governance. 10

The Internet can make you smarter, but it can't make you smart. It can extend your reach, but it will never tell you what to say at a P.T.A. meeting. These fundamentals cannot be downloaded. You can only upload them, the old-fashioned way, one by one, in places like Room 313 at St. Louis Park High. I only regret that I didn't write this column when the woman who taught me all that was still alive. 11

Thinking Critically about This Reading

What do you think Friedman means when he states, "The Internet can make you smarter, but it can't make you smart" (paragraph 11)?

[5]*admonition:* cautionary advice or warning.

Questions for Study and Discussion

1. Friedman claims that his high school journalism teacher, Hattie M. Steinberg, was "someone who made the most important difference in my life" (1). What descriptive details does Friedman use to support this thesis? (Glossary: *Thesis*)
2. Hattie Steinberg taught her students the fundamentals of journalism—"not simply how to write a lead or accurately transcribe a quote, but, more important, how to comport yourself in a professional way and to always do quality work" (3). According to Friedman, what other fundamentals did she introduce to her students? Why do you think he values these fundamentals so much?
3. Friedman punctuates his description of Steinberg's teaching with short, pithy sentences. For example, he ends paragraph 2 with the sentence "She was that good" and paragraph 3 with "She wanted to teach us about consequences." Identify several other short sentences Friedman uses. What do these sentences have in common? How do short sentences like these affect you as a reader? Explain.
4. Why do you think Friedman tells us three times that Hattie's classroom was number 313 at St. Louis Park High School?
5. What details in Friedman's portrait of his teacher stand out for you? Why do you suppose Friedman chose the details that he did? What dominant impression of Hattie M. Steinberg do they collectively create? (Glossary: *Dominant Impression*)
6. According to Friedman, what went wrong when the "huge dot-com-Internet-globalization bubble" (10) of the late 1990s burst? Do you agree?

Classroom Activity Using Description

Important advice for writing well is to show rather than tell. Let's assume that your task is to reveal a person's character. What activities might you show the person doing to give your readers the correct impression of his or her character? For example, to indicate that someone is concerned about current events without coming out and saying so, you might show her reading the morning newspaper. Or you might show a character's degree of formality by including his typical greeting: *How ya doing?* In other words, the things a person says and does are often important indicators of personality. Choose one of the following traits, and make a list of at least four ways to show that someone possesses that trait. Share your list with the class, and discuss the "show-not-tell" strategies you have used.

simple but good	thoughtful	independent
reckless	politically involved	quick-witted
sensitive to the arts	irresponsible	public spirited
a sports lover		

Suggested Writing Assignments

1. Friedman believes that "the real secret of success in the information age is what it always was: fundamentals—reading, writing and arithmetic, church, synagogue and mosque, the rule of law, and good governance" (10). Do you agree? What are the fundamentals that you value most? Write an essay in which you discuss what you believe to be the secret of success today.
2. Who are your favorite teachers? What important differences did these people make in your life? What characteristics do these teachers share with Hattie M. Steinberg in this essay, Miss Bessie in Carl T. Rowan's "Unforgettable Miss Bessie" (pp. 157–63), or Anne Mansfield Sullivan in Helen Keller's "The Most Important Day" (74–79)? Using examples from your own school experience as well as from one or more of the essays above, write an essay in which you explore what makes a great teacher. Be sure to choose examples that clearly illustrate each of your points.

chapter **15**

Process Analysis

When you give someone directions to your home, tell how to make ice cream, or explain how a president is elected, you are using **process analysis.**

Process analysis usually arranges a series of events in order and relates them to one another, as narration and cause and effect do, but process analysis has a different emphasis. Whereas narration tells mainly *what* happens and cause and effect focuses on *why* it happens, process analysis tries to explain—in detail—*how* it happens.

There are two types of process analysis: directional and informational. The *directional* type provides instructions on how to do something. These instructions can be as brief as the directions for making instant coffee printed on the label or as complex as the directions in a manual for assembling a new gas grill. The purpose of directional process analysis is simple: to give the reader directions to follow that will lead to the desired results.

Consider these directions for sharpening a knife:

> If you have never done any whittling or wood carving before, the first skill to learn is how to sharpen your knife. You may be surprised to learn that even a brand-new knife needs sharpening. Knives are never sold honed (finely sharpened), although some gouges and chisels are. It is essential to learn the firm stroke on the stone that will keep your blades sharp. The sharpening stone must be fixed in place on the table, so that it will not move around. You can do this by placing a piece of rubber inner tube or a thin piece of foam rubber under it. Or you can tack four strips of wood, if you have a rough worktable, to frame the stone and hold it in place. Put a generous puddle of oil on the stone—this will soon disappear into the surface of a new stone, and you will need to keep adding more oil. Press the knife blade flat against the stone in the puddle of oil, using your index finger. Whichever way the cutting edge of the

> knife faces is the side of the blade that should get a little more pressure. Move the blade around three or four times in a narrow oval about the size of your fingernail, going *counterclockwise* when the sharp edge is facing right. Now turn the blade over in the same spot on the stone, press hard, and move it around the small oval *clockwise,* with more pressure on the cutting edge that faces left. Repeat the ovals, flipping the knife blade over six or seven times, and applying lighter pressure to the blade the last two times. Wipe the blade clean with a piece of rag or tissue and rub it flat on the piece of leather strop at least twice on each side. Stroke *away* from the cutting edge to remove the little burr of metal that may be left on the blade.
>
> –Florence H. Pettit

After first establishing her context and purpose, Pettit presents step-by-step directions for sharpening a knife, selecting details that a novice would understand.

After explaining in two previous paragraphs the first two steps in his article on juggling, a student writer moves to the important third step. Notice here how he explains the third step, offers advice on what to do if things go wrong, and encourages your efforts—all useful in directional process writing:

> Step three is merely a continuum of "the exchange" with the addition of the third ball. Don't worry if you are confused—I will explain. Hold two balls in your right hand and one in your left. Make a perfect toss with one of your balls in your right hand and then an exchange with the one in your left hand. The ball coming from your left hand should now be exchanged with the, as of now, unused ball in your right hand. This process should be continued until you find yourself reaching under nearby chairs for bouncing tennis balls. It is true that many persons' backs and legs become sore when learning how to juggle because they've been picking up balls that they've inadvertently tossed around the room. Try practicing over a bed; you won't have to reach down so far. Don't get too upset if things aren't going well; you're probably keeping the same pace as everyone else at this stage.
>
> –William Peterson, student

The *informational* type of process analysis, on the other hand, tells how something works, how something is made, or how something occurs. You would use informational process analysis if you wanted to explain how the human heart functions, how an atomic bomb works, how hailstones are formed, how you selected the college you are attending, or how the polio vaccine was developed. Rather than giving specific directions, informational process analysis explains and informs.

In the illustration by Nigel Holmes on page 373, Jim Collins uses informational process analysis to explain a basic legislative procedure: how a bill becomes a law.

Clarity is crucial for successful process analysis. The most effective way to explain a process is to divide it into steps and to present those steps in a clear (usually chronological) sequence. Transitional words and phrases such as *first, next, after,* and *before* help to connect steps to one another. Naturally, you must be sure that no step is omitted or given out of order. Also, you may sometimes have to explain *why* a certain step is necessary, especially if it is not obvious. With intricate, abstract, or particularly difficult steps, you might use analogy or comparison to clarify the steps for your reader.

Illustration by Nigel Holmes.

How to Write a Personal Letter

■ **Garrison Keillor**

Writer and broadcaster Garrison Keillor was born in Anoka, Minnesota, in 1942. After graduating from the University of Minnesota, he became a successful writer of humorous stories, many of which appeared in the New Yorker. *He is perhaps best known for his radio program,* A Prairie Home Companion, *which is broadcast on National Public Radio. Keillor has written many books, including* Lake Wobegon Days *(1985),* Leaving Home: A Collection of Lake Wobegon Stories *(1987),* Me: By Jimmy (Big Boy) Valente *(1999),* A Prairie Home Companion: Pretty Good Joke Book *(2000), and* Love Me *(2003). In 2002, he published a book of poetry titled* Good Poems *that he compiled and introduces. He has also produced a wide selection of recordings featuring his stories and radio shows.*

In this selection, written as part of a popular and highly successful advertising campaign for the International Paper Company in the early 1980s, the sage of Lake Wobegon offers some sound and practical directions for writing personal letters.

For Your Journal

How do you feel when you receive a letter from a relative or friend? Do you feel the same way about telephone calls or e-mail messages? To you, what does a letter say about the person who wrote it?

We shy persons need to write a letter now and then, or else we'll dry up and blow away. It's true. And I speak as one who loves to reach for the phone and talk. The telephone is to shyness what Hawaii is to February; it's a way out of the woods. *And yet:* a letter is better. 1

Such a sweet gift—a piece of handmade writing, in an envelope that is not a bill, sitting in our friend's path when she trudges home 2 from a long day spent among wahoos[1] and savages, a day our words will help repair. They don't need to be immortal, just sincere. She can read them twice and again tomorrow: *You're someone I care about, Corinne, and think of often, and every time I do, you make me smile.*

We need to write, otherwise nobody will know who we are. They will have only a vague impression of us as A Nice Person, because, frankly, we don't shine at conversation, we lack the confidence to thrust our faces forward and say, "Hi, I'm Heather Hooten, let me tell you about my week." Mostly we say "Uh-huh" and "Oh really." People smile and look over our shoulder, looking for someone else to talk to. 3

So a shy person sits down and writes a letter. To be known by another person—to meet and talk freely on the page—to be close despite distance. To escape from anonymity and be our own sweet selves and express the music of our souls. 4

We want our dear Aunt Eleanor to know that we have fallen in love, that we quit our job, that we're moving to New York, and we want to say a few things that might not get said in casual conversation: *Thank you for what you've meant to me. I am very happy right now.* 5

The first step in writing letters is to get over the guilt of *not* writing. You don't "owe" anybody a letter. Letters are a gift. The burning shame you feel when you see unanswered mail makes it harder to pick up a pen and makes for a cheerless letter when you finally do. *I feel bad about not writing, but I've been so busy,* etc. Skip this. Few letters are obligatory, and they are *Thanks for the wonderful gift* and *I am terribly sorry to hear about George's death.* Write these promptly if you want to keep your friends. Don't worry about the others, except love letters, of course. When your true love writes *Dear Light of My Life, Joy of My Heart,* some response is called for. 6

Some of the best letters are tossed off in a burst of inspiration, so keep your writing stuff in one place where you can sit down for a few minutes and—*Dear Roy, I am in the middle of an essay but thought I'd drop you a line. Hi to your sweetie too*—dash off a note to a pal. Envelopes, stamps, address book, everything in a drawer so you can write fast when the pen is hot. 7

A blank white 8 × 11 sheet can look as big as Montana if the pen's not so hot—try a smaller page and write boldly. Get a pen that makes a sensuous line, get a comfortable typewriter, a friendly word processor—whichever feels easy to the hand. 8

[1]*wahoos:* slang for weirdos.

Sit for a few minutes with the blank sheet of paper in front of 9
you, and let your friend come in mind. Remember the last time you saw each other and how your friend looked and what you said and what perhaps was unsaid between you; when your friend becomes real to you, start to write.

Write the salutation—*Dear You*—and take a deep breath and 10
plunge in. A simple declarative sentence will do, followed by another and another. As if you were talking to us. Don't think about grammar, don't think about style, just give us your news. Where did you go, who did you see, what did they say, what do you think?

If you don't know where to begin, start with the present: *I'm sitting* 11
at the kitchen table on a rainy Saturday morning. Everyone is gone and the house is quiet. Let the letter drift along. The toughest letter to crank out is one that is meant to impress, as we all know from writing job applications; if it's hard work to slip off a letter to a friend, maybe you're trying too hard to be terrific. A letter is only a report to someone who already likes you for reasons other than your brilliance. Take it easy.

Don't worry about form. It's not a term paper. When you come 12
to the end of one episode, just start a new paragraph. You can go from a few lines about the sad state of rock 'n' roll to the fight with your mother to your fond memories of Mexico to the kitchen sink and what's in it. The more you write, the easier it gets, and when you have a True True Friend to write to, a soul sibling, then it's like driving a car; you just press on the gas.

Don't tear up the page and start over when you write a bad 13
line—try to write your way out of it. Make mistakes and plunge on. Let the letter cook along and let yourself be bold. Outrage, confusion, love—whatever is in your mind, let it find a way to the page. Writing is a means of discovery, always, and when you come to the end and write *Yours ever* or *Hugs and Kisses,* you'll know something you didn't when you wrote *Dear Pal.*

Probably your friend will put your letter away, and it'll be read 14
again a few years from now—and it will improve with age.

And forty years from now, your friend's grandkids will dig it out 15
of the attic and read it, a sweet and precious relic of the [early twenty-first century] that gives them a sudden clear glimpse of the world we old-timers knew. You will have then created an object of art. Your simple lines about where you went, who you saw, what they said, will speak to those children and they will feel in their hearts the humanity of our times.

You can't pick up a phone and call the future and tell them about our times. You have to pick up a piece of paper. 16

Thinking Critically about This Reading

What does Keillor mean when he states, "We need to write, otherwise nobody will know who we are" (paragraph 3)?

Questions for Study and Discussion

1. Keillor calls a personal letter a "gift" (2). Why do you suppose he thinks of a letter in this way?
2. What advice does Keillor have for people before they start writing? In what ways is this advice part of his process analysis? Why does he suggest small stationery instead of 8 × 11 sheets of paper?
3. Is Keillor's process analysis directional or informational? What leads you to this conclusion?
4. Keillor suggests that before starting to write a friend, you think about that friend for a while until he or she becomes real to you. At that point you're ready to write. What should happen next in the process?
5. Instead of taking us step-by-step through a personal letter in paragraphs 12–14, Keillor anticipates the problems that a letter writer is likely to encounter and offers his own advice. What are the most common problems? What solutions does Keillor offer? (Glossary: *Example*) How does he organize his advice? (Glossary: *Organization*)
6. By the time you have come to the end of a letter, what, according to Keillor, should have happened? Why?
7. Do you think Keillor would consider an e-mail message as much a "gift" as a letter? Why or why not?

Classroom Activity Using Process Analysis

Most do-it-yourself jobs require that you follow a set process to achieve the best results. Make a list of the steps involved in doing one of the following household activities:

cleaning windows	baking chocolate chip cookies
repotting a plant	changing a flat tire
doing laundry	unclogging a drain

Suggested Writing Assignments

1. What does Keillor see as the advantages of a letter over a telephone call? Can you think of times when a telephone call or e-mail message is preferable? Write an essay in which you agree or disagree with Keillor's position on the importance of personal letters. Before starting to write, you may find it helpful to review what you wrote in your journal for this selection.
2. Write an essay in which you give directions or advice for finding a summer job or part-time employment during the school year. In what ways is looking for such jobs different from looking for permanent positions? You can use Keillor's essay as a model for your own.

Here's How to Revive a Computer Even after an Evil Wizard Kills the Beast

■ Bill Husted

Bill Husted was born in Springfield, Missouri, in 1946. After earning a BS in education from Henderson State University in Arkansas in 1968, he wrote television and print advertising copy for a subsidiary of Saatchi and Saatchi, one of the biggest advertising firms in the world. He now writes the "TechnoBuddy" column for the Atlanta Journal-Constitution *in Atlanta, where he won the 2004 National Headliners First Place in the Nation for Business Writing Award for a series of articles on spam, or unsolicited e-mail. Husted says, "Many people write and ask how I come up with the ideas for my columns. I get them from life really. Something happens at home and if you consider yourself fairly typical, as I do, you realize that what you find interesting, other people will as well. So be alert to what's happening around you and you'll never have to worry about where your ideas will come from."*

In the following selection, which first appeared in the Atlanta Journal-Constitution *on March 30, 2003, Husted takes us through the process he followed to successfully restart his stepson's "dead" computer.*

For Your Journal

If your computer were to crash, would you know how to bring it back to life? If yes, make a list of the steps you would follow and explain why you chose that order of steps. If no, whom would you contact for help? Why?

My stepson is a computer wizard. An evil wizard. Computers 1
do things for him that aren't ordinary. And none of these things is good.

So I wasn't surprised when he managed to wreck his computer again. This time he really did it. The computer was dead, and, unlike most times a computer freezes up, it offered no signs of returning to life when I tried to restart it. 2

It's worth your time today to suffer through my attempts to get the computer going. 3

There are only two kinds of computer users: those who have already experienced a dead machine and those who will. I am not talking about a balky machine. These are machines that just flat don't work. 4

I'll tell you what I did to return his machine to life. I started off—as you should—with the easiest ways of restarting the machine. Even though the easy ways didn't work with his PC, you may be luckier. So pay attention. Just as is true when fixing a car, it's always smart to start with the obvious. Before you tear the engine apart, check to see if it's out of gas. 5

That's why my first effort involved turning the PC off and then on again. Sometimes a PC has the equivalent of a human hiccup. It freezes because of a one-time problem that needs no fixing at all. If you try this and the computer runs fine when it restarts, don't do anything else. More machines get messed up from unneeded "fixing" than by computer viruses or lightning. 6

Next I tried to start the machine in Safe Mode. When Windows starts up that way, it loads only the bare necessities. Even a seemingly dead machine will sometimes start in Safe Mode. 7

Once you're there, you can attempt to undo the causes of the PC's problems. In my case, Ryan had connected his digital video camera to the machine just before it died. Sometimes loading a program or adding hardware can be the cause. 8

You can also run fix-it programs like Norton SystemWorks or Windows' own defragmenting and ScanDisk utilities.[1] Let me tell you a Safe Mode secret. Sometimes just starting the machine in Safe Mode and then shutting it down will fix things. I have no idea why. But a man is not supposed to question the gods. 9

To get to Safe Mode, tap on the F8 key as Windows tries to start. That will take you to a menu that includes Safe Mode. I never got that far. All that happened with me was the appearance of a screen that was a rather nice shade of blue. So my day wasn't over yet. 10

---

[1]*defragmenting and ScanDisk utilities:* programs in Windows that make sure a computer's files are saved in the proper order and that there is no wasted space in the computer's memory.

Ryan's PC has Windows XP. With that version of Windows, as well as Windows ME, there's a really handy feature called a Restore Point. Remember the menu that included the option for Safe Mode? It also has an option called Last Known Good Configuration. If you select that, Windows will reset itself to the last time it was working correctly. 11

That seemed like a good notion to me. So I tried it. Again, I saw that same blue screen. 12

I was getting a little quivery by now. I wasn't completely sure what to do to fix things since—to repair the problem—I needed access to a semi-working computer, not a blue screen. It was getting late. 13

Luckily, there was more that could be done. I used the Windows XP CD to start the computer. On our machine, you can force it to boot up[2] from the CD by pressing the F12 key as it starts. The method may be different for your PC, so check the manual that came with it, or watch for on-screen messages as the computer starts up. Often you'll find directions there. 14

Starting the machine from the CD makes it think that you are installing Windows for the first time. But don't panic. You probably don't need to do that (although it's always a last-ditch possibility). Just sit back and watch as the CD prepares to install Windows. You'll finally arrive at a screen where you can tell it to go ahead and start the installation or select an option called Recovery Console, which will try to fix things up. 15

Once I got to Recovery Console, I was given the option of running a utility that goes all the way back to the DOS days. It's called Chkdsk (pronounced Check Disk). Chkdsk attempts to fix errors on the hard disk. When a computer refuses to start at all, that's often where the problems are. 16

Working with the Recovery Console, you won't have a fancy Windows screen. Instead of pointing and clicking with your mouse, you have to work the old fashioned way—by typing. So I typed "chkdsk/r" (without the quotation marks) to tell Windows to check things out and fix them, too. 17

After more than an hour, chkdsk finished running. 18

I restarted the machine, and good ol' Windows greeted me. By now, Ryan had lost interest in the entire process. So I left him a note saying that the computer was running again. The world was once again safe from evil wizards. 19

---

[2]*boot up:* to start a computer by loading an operating system.

Thinking Critically about This Reading

According to Husted, "There are only two kinds of computer users: those who have already experienced a dead machine and those who will" (paragraph 4). What purpose does this statement serve? (Glossary: *Purpose*)

Questions for Study and Discussion

1. On what principle has Husted organized the steps he takes in reviving the computer? (Glossary: *Organization*) If you are computer savvy, would you have followed the same process as Husted? Explain.
2. Describe Husted's tone. (Glossary: *Tone*) How does he achieve it?
3. Husted uses his stepson as the reason for writing this essay. How effective is this device, in your opinion?
4. Does Husted use too much computer jargon? (Glossary: *Jargon*) Too little? Just the right amount? Does the jargon he uses need more explanation? (Glossary: *Audience*) Explain.
5. One measure of the usefulness of a set of directions is whether or not you would consider saving them for future use or, at least, remembering how to access them again. Would you consider saving Husted's directions for reviving a "dead" computer? Why or why not?

Classroom Activity Using Process Analysis

Carefully read the directions for constructing an astro tube—a cylindrical airfoil made from a sheet of heavy writing paper—on page 383. Now construct your own astro tube, and fly it. How far, if at all, did your astro tube fly? How helpful did you find the illustrations that accompany the written instructions? Based on your results, what revisions to the instructions would you make? Why?

Suggested Writing Assignments

1. Use the illustration on page 373 as a preliminary outline of how a bill becomes law, and research the topic more thoroughly through reading and, if possible, discussing the process with a

Making an Astro Tube

Start with an 8.5-inch by 11-inch sheet of heavy writing paper. (Never use newspaper in making paper models because it isn't strongly bonded and can't hold a crease.) Follow these numbered steps, corresponding to the illustrations.

1. With the long side of the sheet toward you, fold up one third of the paper.
2. Fold the doubled section in half.
3. Fold the section in half once more and crease well.
4. Unfold preceding crease.
5. Curve the ends together to form a tube, as shown in the illustration.
6. Insert the right end inside the left end between the single outer layer and the doubled layers. Overlap the ends about an inch and a half. (This makes a tube for right-handers, to be used with an underhand throw. For an overhand tube, or an underhand version to be thrown by a lefty, reverse the directions, and insert the left end inside the right end at this step.)
7. Hold the tube at the seam with one hand, where shown by the dot in the illustration, and turn the rim inward along the crease made in step 3. Start turning in at the seam and roll the rim under, moving around the circumference in a circular manner. Then round out the rim.
8. Fold the fin to the left, as shown, then raise it so that it's perpendicular to the tube. Be careful not to tear the paper at the front.
9. Hold the tube from above, near the rim. Hold it between the thumb and fingers. The rim end should be forward, with the fin on the bottom. Throw the tube underhanded, with a motion like throwing a bowling ball, letting it spin off the fingers as it is released. The tube will float through the air, spinning as it goes. Indoor flights of 30 feet or more are easy. With practice you can achieve remarkable accuracy.

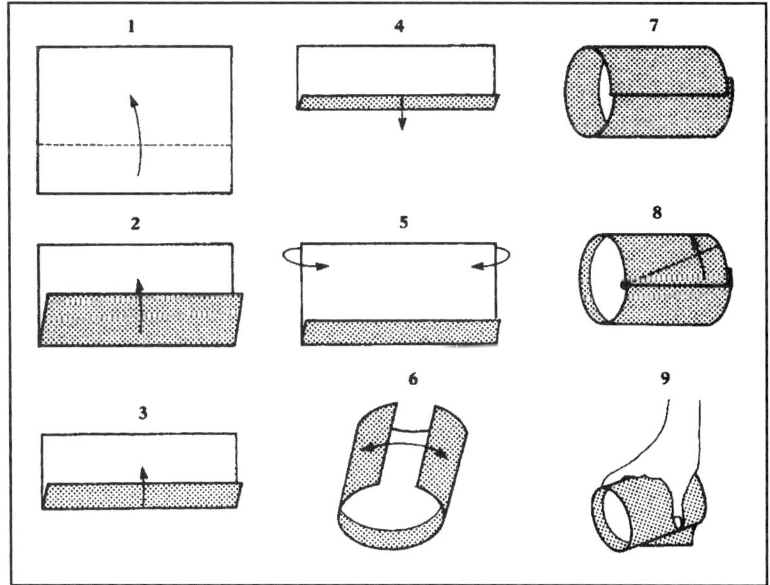

political science instructor at your school. The illustration ends with the question, "Does it *ever* go as smoothly as this?" and the answer, "Nope." What kinds of situations can and often do alter the process?

2. Think about a familiar process that you believe needs improvement. After choosing your topic, you might want to do some background research in the library. Make sure you are able to put the process into your own words, and then write a process analysis in which you argue for a revision of the existing process. (Glossary: *Argumentation*) For example, are you happy with the process for dealing with recyclables where you live, the process for registering for classes, or the way dorm rooms are assigned on campus?

On Dumpster Diving

Lars Eighner

Born in Texas in 1948, Lars Eighner attended the University of Texas at Austin. After graduation, he launched a career writing essays and fiction. A volume of his short stories, Bayou Boy and Other Stories, *was published in 1985. Eighner became homeless in 1988 when he left his job as an attendant at a mental hospital. He has written two novels,* Pawn to Queen Four *(1995) and* Whispered in the Dark *(1996), and a collection of essays,* Gay Cosmos *(1995).*

The following selection, which appeared in Utne Reader *in 1995, is an abridged version of an essay that first appeared in* Threepenny Review. *The piece eventually became part of Eighner's startling account of the three years he spent as a homeless person,* Travels with Lizbeth *(1993). Eighner uses a number of rhetorical strategies in "On Dumpster Diving," but pay particular attention to the importance of process analysis in the success of the essay overall as he delineates the "stages a person goes through in learning to scavenge."*

For Your Journal

Some people believe that acquiring material objects is what life is all about and that the measure of their own "worth" is in the inventory of their possessions. Comment on the role that material objects play in your life and on whether your view of their importance has changed as you have grown older.

I began Dumpster diving about a year before I became homeless. 1

I prefer the term *scavenging*. I have heard people, evidently 2
meaning to be polite, use the word *foraging*, but I prefer to reserve that word for gathering nuts and berries and such, which I also do, according to the season and opportunity.

I like the frankness of the word *scavenging*. I live from the refuse 3
of others. I am a scavenger. I think it a sound and honorable niche, although if I could I would naturally prefer to live the comfortable

consumer life, perhaps—and only perhaps—as a slightly less wasteful consumer owing to what I have learned as a scavenger.

Except for jeans, all my clothes come from Dumpsters. Boom boxes, candles, bedding, toilet paper, medicine, books, a typewriter, a virgin male love doll, coins sometimes amounting to many dollars: all came from Dumpsters. And, yes, I eat from Dumpsters, too. 4

There is a predictable series of stages that a person goes through in learning to scavenge. At first the new scavenger is filled with disgust and self-loathing. He is ashamed of being seen. 5

This stage passes with experience. The scavenger finds a pair of running shoes that fit and look and smell brand-new. He finds a pocket calculator in perfect working order. He finds pristine ice cream, still frozen, more than he can eat or keep. He begins to understand: people do throw away perfectly good stuff, a lot of perfectly good stuff. 6

At this stage he may become lost and never recover. All the Dumpster divers I have known come to the point of trying to acquire everything they touch. Why not take it, they reason, it is all free. This is, of course, hopeless, and most divers come to realize that they must restrict themselves to items of relatively immediate utility. 7

The finding of objects is becoming something of an urban art. Even respectable, employed people will sometimes find something tempting sticking out of a Dumpster or standing beside one. Quite a number of people, not all of them of the bohemian[1] type, are willing to brag that they found this or that piece in the trash. 8

But eating from Dumpsters is the thing that separates the dilettanti[2] from the professionals. Eating safely involves three principles: using the senses and common sense to evaluate the condition of the found materials; knowing the Dumpsters of a given area and checking them regularly; and seeking always to answer the question "Why was this discarded?" 9

Yet perfectly good food can be found in Dumpsters. Canned goods, for example, turn up fairly often in the Dumpsters I frequent. I also have few qualms about dry foods such as crackers, cookies, cereal, chips, and pasta if they are free of visible contaminants and still dry and crisp. Raw fruits and vegetables with intact skins seem perfectly 10

---

[1]*bohemian:* nonconformist; eccentric.

[2]*dilettanti:* amateurs; dabblers, not experts.

safe to me, excluding, of course, the obviously rotten. Many are discarded for minor imperfections that can be pared away.

A typical discard is a half jar of peanut butter—though non-organic peanut butter does not require refrigeration and is unlikely to spoil in any reasonable time. One of my favorite finds is yogurt—often discarded, still sealed, when the expiration date has passed—because it will keep for several days, even in warm weather. 11

No matter how careful I am I still get dysentery[3] at least once a month, oftener in warm weather. I do not want to paint too romantic a picture. Dumpster diving has serious drawbacks as a way of life. 12

I find from the experience of scavenging two rather deep lessons. The first is to take what I can use and let the rest go. I have come to think that there is no value in the abstract. A thing I cannot use or make useful, perhaps by trading, has no value, however fine or rare it may be. 13

The second lesson is the transience of material being. I do not suppose that ideas are immortal, but certainly they are longer-lived than material objects. 14

The things I find in Dumpsters, the love letters and rag dolls of so many lives, remind me of this lesson. Now I hardly pick up a thing without envisioning the time I will cast it away. This, I think, is a healthy state of mind. Almost everything I have now has already been cast out at least once, proving that what I own is valueless to someone. 15

I find that my desire to grab for the gaudy bauble has been largely sated. I think this is an attitude I share with the very wealthy—we both know there is plenty more where whatever we have came from. Between us are the rat-race millions who have confounded their selves with the objects they grasp and who nightly scavenge the cable channels for they know not what. 16

I am sorry for them. 17

Thinking Critically about This Reading

What does Eighner mean when he states that "eating from Dumpsters is the thing that separates the dilettanti from the professionals" (paragraph 9)?

[3]*dysentery:* severe diarrhea caused by an infection.

Questions for Study and Discussion

1. What is "Dumpster diving"? Why does Eighner prefer the word *scavenging* to *foraging* or *Dumpster diving*? What do these three terms mean to him? What does his discussion of these terms early in the essay tell you about Eighner himself?
2. What stages do beginning scavengers go through before they become "professionals"? What examples does Eighner use to illustrate the passage through these stages?
3. Summarize the various steps in Eighner's explanation of the process of Dumpster diving. Why do you think Eighner did not title the essay "How to Dumpster Dive"?
4. What two lessons does Eighner learn from scavenging? Why are they important to him? In what ways has scavenging benefited Eighner? In what ways has it harmed him?
5. Eighner's essay deals with both the immediate, physical aspects of Dumpster diving, such as what can be found in a typical Dumpster and the physical price one pays for eating out of them, and the larger, abstract issues that Dumpster diving raises, such as materialism and the transience of material objects. (Glossary: *Concrete/Abstract*) Why do you suppose he describes the concrete details before he discusses the abstract issues? What does he achieve by using both types of elements?
6. Writers often use process analysis in conjunction with another strategy—especially argument—to try to improve the way a process is carried out or to comment on issues exposed by the process analysis. (Glossary: *Argumentation*) For example, Eighner uses a full process analysis to present his views on American values and materialism. In what ways does his analysis support his views on society?

Classroom Activity Using Process Analysis

In her best-selling Italian memoir *Under the Tuscan Sun,* Frances Mayes shares a number of her favorite recipes, including this one for Lemon Cake. As you carefully read her directions, imagine yourself making this cake. Then answer these questions: Do you find her recipe interesting to read? How clear are her directions? Are there any parts of the recipe that need clarification? Is it necessary to be familiar with the world of baking to read or appreciate Mayes's recipe? Explain.

Lemon Cake

A family import, this Southern cake is one I've made a hundred times. Thin slices seem at home here with summer strawberries and cherries or winter pears. . . .

Cream together 1 cup of sweet butter and 2 cups of sugar. Beat in 3 eggs, one at a time. The mixture should be light. Mix together 3 cups of flour, 1 teaspoon of baking powder, 1/4 teaspoon of salt, and incorporate this with the butter mixture alternately with 1 cup buttermilk. (In Italy, I use one cup of cream since buttermilk is not available.) Begin and end with the flour mixture. Add 3 tablespoons of lemon juice and the grated zest of the lemon. Bake in a nonstick tube pan at 300° for 50 minutes. Test for doneness with a toothpick. The cake can be glazed with 1/4 cup of soft butter into which 1-1/2 cups of powdered sugar and 3 tablespoons of lemon juice have been beaten. Decorate with tiny curls of lemon rind.

Suggested Writing Assignments

1. How important are material objects to you? Eighner emphasizes the transience of material objects and thinks that all of us delude ourselves with the objects we strive to acquire. Is there anything wrong with desiring material goods? Write an essay in which you react to Eighner's position on materialism.
2. Write a process analysis in which you explain the steps you usually follow when deciding to make a purchase of some importance or expense to you. Hint: It's best to analyze your process with a specific product or products in mind. Do you compare brands, store prices, and so on? What are your priorities—that the item be stylish or durable, offer good overall value, or give high performance?
3. In paragraph 3 Eighner states that he "live[s] from the refuse of others." How do his confession and the following cartoon affect you? Do you agree with the cartoon's central idea—that "we've . . . become a throwaway society"? If so, how? How do Eighner's accounts of homelessness and Dumpster diving make you feel about your own consumerism and trash habits? Write an essay in which you examine the things you throw away in a single day. What items did you get rid of? Why? Could those items be used by someone else? Have you ever felt guilty about throwing something away? If so, what was it and why?

"We've certainly become a throwaway society."

chapter **16**

Definition

Definition allows you to communicate precisely what you want to say. At the most basic level, you will frequently need to define key words. Your reader needs to know just what you mean when you use unfamiliar words, such as *accoutrement,* or words that are open to various interpretations, such as *liberal,* or words that, while generally familiar, are used in a particular sense. Failure to define important terms, or to define them accurately, confuses readers and hampers communication.

Consider the opening paragraph from a student essay titled "Secular Mantras":

> Remember *The Little Engine That Could*? That's the story about the tiny locomotive that hauled the train over the mountain when the big, rugged locomotives wouldn't. Remember how the Little Engine strained and heaved and chugged, "I think I can—I think I can—I think I can" until she reached the top of the mountain? That's a perfect example of a secular mantra in action. You probably have used a secular mantra (pronounce it "mantruh") already today. It's any word or group of words that helps you use your energy when you consciously repeat it to yourself. You must understand two qualities about secular mantras to be able to recognize one.
>
> –Keith Eldred, student

Eldred engages his readers with the story of the Little Engine and then uses that example to lead into a definition of *secular mantras.* He concludes the paragraph with a sentence that clearly tells readers what is coming next.

There are three basic ways to define a word; each is useful in its own way. The first method is to give a *synonym,* a word that has nearly the same meaning as the word you wish to define: *face* for *countenance, nervousness* for *anxiety.* No two words have exactly the same meaning, but you can nevertheless pair an unfamiliar word with a familiar one and thereby clarify your meaning.

Another way to define a word quickly, often within a single sentence, is to give a *formal definition;* that is, to place the term to be defined in a general class and then to distinguish it from other members of that class by describing its particular characteristics. For example:

Word	*Class*	*Characteristics*
A watch	is a mechanical device	for telling time and is usually carried or worn.
Semantics	is an area of linguistics	concerned with the study of the meaning of words.

The third method is known as *extended definition.* While some extended definitions require only a single paragraph, more often than not you will need several paragraphs or even an entire essay to define a new or difficult term or to rescue a controversial word from misconceptions and associations that may obscure its meaning.

In an essay-length extended definition, you provide your readers with far more information than you would when using a synonym or a formal definition. You are, in most cases, exploring the meaning of your topic, whether it be a single word, a concept, or an object. In many cases, you must consider what your readers already know, or think they know, about your topic. Are there popular misconceptions that need to be done away with? Are there aspects of the topic that are seldom considered? Have particular experiences helped you understand the topic? You can use synonyms or formal definitions to help define your topic, but you must convince readers to accept your particular understanding of it.

In the following four-paragraph sequence, the writers provide an extended definition of *freedom,* an important but elusive concept.

> Choosing between negative alternatives often seems like no choice at all. Take the case of a woman trying to decide whether to stay married to her inconsiderate, incompetent husband, or get a divorce. She doesn't want to stay with him, but she feels divorce is a sign of failure and will stigmatize her socially. Or think of the decision faced by many young men [more than thirty] years ago, when they were forced to choose between leaving their country and family or being sent to Vietnam.

> When we face decisions involving only alternatives we see as negatives, we feel so little freedom that we twist and turn searching for another choice with some positive characteristics.
>
> Freedom is a popular word. Individuals talk about how they feel free with one person and not with another, or how their bosses encourage or discourage freedom on the job. We hear about civil wars and revolutions being fought for greater freedom, with both sides righteously making the claim. The feeling of freedom is so important that people say they're ready to die for it, and supposedly have.
>
> Still, most people have trouble coming up with a precise definition of freedom. They give answers describing specific situations—"Freedom means doing what I want to do, not what the Government wants me to do," or "Freedom means not having my mother tell me when to come home from a party"—rather than a general definition covering many situations. The idea they seem to be expressing is that freedom is associated with making decisions, and that other people sometimes limit the number of alternatives from which they can select.
>
> –Jerald M. Jellison and John H. Harvey

Another term that illustrates the need for extended definition is *obscene*. What is obscene? Books that are banned in one school system are considered perfectly acceptable in another. Movies that are shown in one town cannot be shown in a neighboring town. Clearly, the meaning of *obscene* has been clouded by contrasting personal opinions as well as by conflicting social norms. Therefore, if you use the term *obscene* (and especially if you tackle the issue of obscenity itself), you must be careful to define clearly and thoroughly what you mean by that term—that is, you have to give an extended definition. There are a number of methods you might use to develop such a definition. You could define *obscene* by explaining what it does not mean. You could also make your meaning clear by narrating an experience, by comparing and contrasting it to related terms such as *pornographic* or *exotic*, by citing specific examples, or by classifying the various types of obscenity. Any of these methods could provide an effective definition.

What Is Crime?

■ Lawrence M. Friedman

Born in 1930 in Chicago, Lawrence M. Friedman is currently the Marion Rice Kirkwood Professor of Law at Stanford University. He earned his undergraduate degree in 1948 and his law degree in 1951, both from the University of Chicago. After serving a two-year stint in the military, he practiced law in Chicago before embarking on his long and distinguished teaching and writing career. He taught law at St. Louis University and the University of Wisconsin before settling at Stanford in 1968. An expert on the history of American law, Friedman is perhaps best known for his A History of American Law *(1973) and its sequel* American Law in the Twentieth Century *(2002). His other books include* The Republic of Choice: Law, Authority, and Culture *(1990),* The Horizontal Society *(1999), and* Law in America: A Short History *(2002). Currently he is president of the American Society for Legal History.*

The following selection is taken from the introduction to Crime and Punishment in American History *(1993), a book in which Friedman traces the response to crime throughout U.S. history. Here he carefully explains what it takes for a certain behavior or act to be considered a crime.*

For Your Journal

How would you answer the question "What is crime?" For you, what makes some acts criminal and others not? Explain.

There is no real answer to the question, What is crime? There are popular ideas about crime: crime is bad behavior, antisocial behavior, blameworthy acts, and the like. But in a very basic sense, crime is a *legal* concept: what makes some conduct criminal, and other conduct not, is the fact that some, but not others, are "against the law."* 1

*Most criminologists, but not all, would agree with this general formulation; for an exception see Michael R. Gottfredson and Travis Hirschi, *A General Theory of Crime* (1990). [Friedman's note]

Crimes, then, are forbidden acts. But they are forbidden in a special way. We are not supposed to break contracts, drive carelessly, slander people, or infringe copyrights; but these are not (usually) criminal acts. The distinction between a *civil* and a *criminal* case is fundamental in our legal system. A civil case has a life cycle entirely different from that of a criminal case. If I slander somebody, I might be dragged into court, and I might have to open my checkbook and pay damages; but I cannot be put in prison or executed, and if I lose the case, I do not get a criminal "record." Also, in a slander case (or a negligence case, or a copyright-infringement case), the injured party pays for, runs, and manages the case herself. He or she makes the decisions and hires the lawyers. The case is entirely voluntary. Nobody forces anybody to sue. I can have a good claim, a valid claim, and simply forget it, if I want. 2

In a criminal case, in theory at least, society is the victim, along with the "real" victim—the person robbed or assaulted or cheated. The crime may be punished without the victim's approval (though, practically speaking, the complaining witness often has a crucial role to play). In "victimless crimes" (gambling, drug dealing, certain sex offenses), there is nobody to complain; both parties are equally guilty (or innocent). Here the machine most definitely has a mind of its own. In criminal cases, moreover, the state pays the bills. It should be pointed out, however, that the further back in history one goes, the more this pat[1] distinction between "civil" and "criminal" tends to blur. In some older cultures, the line between private vengeance and public prosecution was indistinct or completely absent. Even in our own history, we shall see some evidence that the cleavage between "public" and "private" enforcement was not always deep and pervasive. 3

All sorts of nasty acts and evil deeds are not against the law, and thus not crimes. These include most of the daily events that anger or irritate us, even those we might consider totally outrageous. Ordinary lying is not a crime; cheating on a wife or husband is not a crime in most states (at one time it was, almost everywhere); charging a huge markup at a restaurant or store is not, in general, a crime; psychological abuse is (mostly) not a crime. 4

Before some act can be isolated and labeled as a crime, there must be a special, solemn, social and *political* decision. In our society, Congress, 5

[1] *pat:* seemingly precise.

a state legislature, or a city government has to pass a law or enact an ordinance adding the behavior to the list of crimes. Then this behavior, like a bottle of poison, carries the proper label and can be turned over to the heavy artillery of law for possible enforcement.

We repeat: crime is a *legal* concept. This point, however, can lead to a misunderstanding. The law, in a sense, "creates" the crimes it punishes; but what creates criminal law? Behind the law, and above it, enveloping it, is society; before the law made the crime a crime, some aspect of social reality transformed the behavior, culturally speaking, into a crime; and it is the social context that gives the act, and the legal responses, their real meaning. Justice is supposed to be blind, which is to say impartial. This may or may not be so, but justice is blind in one fundamental sense: justice is an abstraction.[2] It cannot see or act on its own. It cannot generate its own norms, principles, and rules. Everything depends on society. Behind every *legal* judgment of criminality is a more powerful, more basic *social* judgment; a judgment that this behavior, whatever it is, deserves to be outlawed and punished. 6

Thinking Critically about This Reading

What does Friedman mean when he states, "Behind every *legal* judgment of criminality is a more powerful, more basic *social* judgment; a judgment that this behavior, whatever it is, deserves to be outlawed and punished" (paragraph 6)? According to Friedman, what must happen before any offensive behavior can be deemed criminal?

Questions for Study and Discussion

1. What general definition of *crime* do most criminologists agree on, according to Friedman?
2. What are the major differences between a criminal case and a civil case? Why is it important that Friedman makes this distinction? Explain.
3. In what sense is society the "victim" in a criminal case (3)? Do you believe that it is important for society to join with the "real victim" in prosecuting the criminal case? Explain.

[2]*abstraction:* a theoretical concept.

4. Friedman states that "all sorts of nasty acts and evil deeds are not against the law, and thus not crimes" (4). What examples does he provide to illustrate this point? (Glossary: *Example*) Do any of his examples surprise you? Explain.
5. What does Friedman mean by "crime is a *legal* concept" (1)? Why do you think he repeats that statement in paragraph 6? According to the writer, what misunderstanding can the statement lead to?

Classroom Activity Using Definition

Try formally defining one of the following terms by putting it in a class and then differentiating it from other words in the class. (See p. 392.)

potato chips	tenor saxophone	sociology	Monopoly (the game)
love	physical therapy	chickadee	Buddhism

Suggested Writing Assignments

1. Write an essay recounting a time when you were the "victim" of somebody's outrageous behavior. What were the circumstances of the incident? How did you respond at the time? What action, if any, did you take at a later time? According to Friedman's definition, was the behavior criminal?
2. Some of the most pressing social issues in American life today are further complicated by imprecise definitions of critical terms. Various medical cases, for example, have brought worldwide attention to the legal and medical definitions of the word *death*. Debates continue about the meanings of other controversial words. Using one of the following controversial terms or another of your choosing, write an essay in which you discuss not only its definition but also the problems associated with defining it.

minority (ethnic)	theft	equality
monopoly (business)	lying	success
morality	addiction	pornography
cheating	life	marriage

The Handicap of Definition

■ **William Raspberry**

William Raspberry was born in the small community of Okolona, Mississippi, in 1935. He says of his community, "we had two of everything there, one for whites and one for blacks." After graduating in 1960 from Indiana Central College with a degree in history, Raspberry served two years in the military before launching his career in journalism at the Washington Post *in 1962. As one of the most influential journalists of his time, Raspberry has won numerous journalism awards and been honored with fifteen honorary degrees. He won the Pulitzer Prize for Distinguished Commentary in 1994. As a* Washington Post *op-ed commentator since 1971, Raspberry has voiced his views on such subjects as crime, justice, drug abuse, racism, terrorism, affirmative action, prisons, and education. His column is syndicated in more than two hundred newspapers, and he has a tremendous following across the country. Currently Raspberry teaches at Duke University where he holds the Knight Chair in Communications and Journalism.*

The following essay first appeared in Raspberry's column in 1982. Here he asks readers to consider the definitions of black *and* white, *together with their positive and negative connotations. In considering what it means to be black, Raspberry concludes that real "harm . . . comes from too narrow a definition of what is black."*

For your Journal

Make a list of ten things that come to mind when you hear the word *black.* Now do the same for the word *white.* How would you characterize the words on each of your lists—generally positive, negative, or some combination of the two? How are the two lists different?

I know all about bad schools, mean politicians, economic deprivation and racism. Still, it occurs to me that one of the heaviest burdens black Americans—and black children in particular—have to 1 bear is the handicap of definition: the question of what it means to be black.

Let me explain quickly what I mean. If a basketball fan says that the Boston Celtics' Larry Bird plays "black," the fan intends it—and Bird probably accepts it—as a compliment. Tell pop singer Tom Jones he moves "black" and he might grin in appreciation. Say to Teena Marie or The Average White Band that they sound "black" and they'll thank you. 2

But name one pursuit, aside from athletics, entertainment or sexual performance in which a white practitioner will feel complimented to be told he does it "black." Tell a white broadcaster he talks "black," and he'll sign up for diction[1] lessons. Tell a white reporter he writes "black" and he'll take a writing course. Tell a white lawyer he reasons "black" and he might sue you for slander. 3

What we have here is a tragically limited definition of blackness, and it isn't only white people who buy it. 4

Think of all the ways black children can put one another down with charges of "whiteness." For many of these children, hard study and hard work are "white." Trying to please a teacher might be criticized as acting "white." Speaking correct English is "white." Scrimping today in the interest of tomorrow's goals is "white." Educational toys and games are "white." 5

An incredible array of habits and attitudes that are conducive[2] to success in business, in academia, in the nonentertainment professions are likely to be thought of as somehow "white." Even economic success, unless it involves such "black" undertakings as numbers banking, is defined as "white." 6

And the results are devastating. I wouldn't deny that blacks often are better entertainers and athletes. My point is the harm that comes from too narrow a definition of what is black. 7

One reason black youngsters tend to do better at basketball, for instance, is that they assume they can learn to do it well, and so they practice constantly to prove themselves right. 8

Wouldn't it be wonderful if we could infect black children with the notion that excellence in math is "black" rather than white, or possibly Chinese? Wouldn't it be of enormous value if we could create the myth that morality, strong families, determination, courage and love 9

---

[1]*diction:* appropriate word choice.

[2]*conducive:* lead or contribute to.

of learning are traits brought by slaves from Mother Africa and therefore quintessentially[3] black?

There is no doubt in my mind that most black youngsters could 10
develop their mathematical reasoning, their elocution[4] and their attitudes the way they develop their jump shots and their dance steps: by the combination of sustained, enthusiastic practice and the unquestioned belief that they can do it.

In one sense, what I am talking about is the importance of devel- 11
oping positive ethnic traditions. Maybe Jews have an innate talent for communication; maybe Chinese are born with a gift for mathematical reasoning; maybe blacks are naturally blessed with athletic grace. I doubt it. What is at work, I suspect, is assumption, inculcated[5] early in their lives, that this is a thing our people do well.

Unfortunately, many of the things about which blacks make this 12
assumption are things that do not contribute to their career success—except for that handful of the truly gifted who can make it as entertainers and athletes. And many of the things we concede to whites are the things that are essential to economic security.

So it is with a number of assumptions black youngsters make about 13
what it is to be a "man": physical aggressiveness, sexual prowess, the refusal to submit to authority. The prisons are full of people who, by this perverted definition, are unmistakably men.

But the real problem is not so much that the things defined as 14
"black" are negative. The problem is that the definition is much too narrow.

Somehow, we have to make our children understand that they are 15
intelligent, competent people, capable of doing whatever they put their minds to and making it in the American mainstream, not just in a black subculture.

What we seem to be doing, instead, is raising up yet another gen- 16
eration of young blacks who will be failures—by definition.

Thinking Critically about This Reading

Raspberry argues that "the real problem is not so much that the things defined as 'black' are negative. The real problem is that the definition

[3]*quintessentially:* representing a perfect example of something.
[4]*elocution:* a style or manner of speaking in public.
[5]*inculcated:* instilled; taught through repetition.

is much too narrow" (paragraph 14). What problems arise when the definition "is much too narrow"?

Questions for Study and Discussion

1. What is Raspberry's purpose? (Glossary: *Purpose*) Does he aim to inform or persuade his readers? Explain.
2. With his syndicated column appearing in over two hundred newspapers, Raspberry's audience includes large numbers of black as well as white readers. (Glossary: *Audience*) Do you think his essay is intended mainly for his black readers, his white readers, or both? What evidence in the essay leads you to this conclusion?
3. Raspberry's paragraphs are divided into four discreet sections or paragraph blocks: paragraphs 1–4, 5–7, 8–11, and 12–16. What is the central idea or assertion for each section? What examples does he use to support each assertion? (Glossary: *Example; Evidence*) Is his organizational plan effective? (Glossary: *Organization*) Why or why not?
4. In paragraph 13 Raspberry lists several assumptions that black boys make about what it takes to be a man. What point is he attempting to make with these examples? Explain why you find them convincing—or not.
5. According to Raspberry, how can ordinary citizens help broaden the definition of *black*? Has any progress been made since Raspberry wrote his essay in 1982? Explain.

Classroom Activity Using Definition

Definitions are often dependent on perspective, as Raspberry illustrates in his essay. Discuss with your classmates other words or terms—such as *competition, happiness, wealth, success, ethnicity, failure, luxury*—whose definitions are dependent on one's perspective. Choose several of these words, and write brief definitions for them from your perspective. Discuss your definitions with your classmates. What perspective differences, if any, are apparent in the definitions?

Suggested Writing Assignments

1. Write an essay in which you explore the idea that many Americans' definitions of *black* and *white* help create stereotypes and foster

prejudice. Be sure to define the key terms *stereotype* and *prejudice* and to use examples from your own experience, observation, or reading to support your position.

2. Write an essay defining one of the words listed here, telling not only what the word is, but also what it is *not* (for example, one could argue that "music is not silence, but neither is it noise.") Remember, however, that defining by negation does not relieve you of the responsibility of defining the term in other ways as well.

creativity	loyalty	patriotism
leadership	intelligence	leadership
wealth	heroism	family

The Company Man

Ellen Goodman

Ellen Goodman was born in Boston in 1941. After graduating cum laude *from Radcliffe College in 1963, she worked as a reporter and researcher for* Newsweek. *In 1967, she began working at the* Boston Globe *and, since 1974, has been a full-time columnist. Her regular column, "At Large," is syndicated by the* Washington Post*'s Writer's Group and appears in nearly four hundred newspapers across the country. In addition, her writing has appeared in* McCall's, Harper's Bazaar, *and* Family Circle, *and her commentaries have been broadcast on radio and television. Several collections of Goodman's columns have been published as books, including* Close to Home *(1979),* At Large *(1981),* Keeping in Touch *(1985),* Value Judgments *(1995),* Making Sense *(1999), and* Paper Trail: Common Sense in Uncommon Times *(2004).*

In "The Company Man," taken from Close to Home, *Goodman defines* workaholic *by offering a poignant case-in-point example.*

For Your Journal

While many jobs have regular hours, some, like journalism, medicine, and high-level management, are less predictable and may require far more time. Think about your career goals. Do you anticipate a greater emphasis on your work life or your home life? How much time beyond the standard forty hours per week are you willing to sacrifice to advance your career? Has this issue influenced your choice of career in any way, or do you anticipate that it will? Explain.

He worked himself to death, finally and precisely, at 3:00 A.M. Sunday morning. 1

The obituary didn't say that, of course. It said that he died of a coronary thrombosis—I think that was it—but everyone among his friends and acquaintances knew it instantly. He was a perfect 2

Type A, a workaholic, a classic, they said to each other and shook their heads—and thought for five or ten minutes about the way they lived.

This man who worked himself to death finally and precisely at 3:00 A.M. Sunday morning—on his day off—was fifty-one years old and a vice-president. He was, however, one of six vice-presidents, and one of three who might conceivably—if the president died or retired soon enough—have moved to the top spot. Phil knew that. 3

He worked six days a week, five of them until eight or nine at night, during a time when his own company had begun the four-day week for everyone but the executives. He worked like the Important People. He had no outside "extracurricular interests," unless, of course, you think about a monthly golf game that way. To Phil, it was work. He always ate egg salad sandwiches at his desk. He was, of course, overweight, by 20 or 25 pounds. He thought it was okay, though, because he didn't smoke. 4

On Saturdays, Phil wore a sports jacket to the office instead of a suit, because it was the weekend. 5

He had a lot of people working for him, maybe sixty, and most of them liked him most of the time. Three of them will be seriously considered for his job. The obituary didn't mention that. 6

But it did list his "survivors" quite accurately. He is survived by his wife, Helen, forty-eight years old, a good woman of no particular marketable skills, who worked in an office before marrying and mothering. She had, according to her daughter, given up trying to compete with his work years ago, when the children were small. A company friend said, "I know how much you will miss him." And she answered, "I already have." 7

"Missing him all these years," she must have given up part of herself which had cared too much for the man. She would be "well taken care of." 8

His "dearly beloved" eldest of the "dearly beloved" children is a hard-working executive in a manufacturing firm down South. In the day and a half before the funeral, he went around the neighborhood researching his father, asking the neighbors what he was like. They were embarrassed. 9

His second child is a girl, who is twenty-four and newly married. She lives near her mother and they are close, but whenever she was alone with her father, in a car driving somewhere, they had nothing to say to each other. 10

The youngest is twenty, a boy, a high-school graduate who has spent the last couple of years, like a lot of his friends, doing enough odd jobs to stay in grass and food. He was the one who tried to grab at his father, and tried to mean enough to him to keep the man at home. He was his father's favorite. Over the last two years, Phil stayed up nights worrying about the boy. 11

The boy once said, "My father and I only board here." 12

At the funeral, the sixty-year-old company president told the forty-eight-year-old widow that the fifty-one-year-old deceased had meant much to the company and would be missed and would be hard to replace. The widow didn't look him in the eye. She was afraid he would read her bitterness and, after all, she would need him to straighten out the finances—the stock options and all that. 13

Phil was overweight and nervous and worked too hard. If he wasn't at the office, he was worried about it. Phil was a Type A, a heart-attack natural. You could have picked him out in a minute from a lineup. 14

So when he finally worked himself to death, at precisely 3:00 A.M. Sunday morning, no one was really surprised. 15

By 5:00 P.M. the afternoon of the funeral, the company president had begun, discreetly of course, with care and taste, to make inquiries about his replacement. One of three men. He asked around: "Who's been working the hardest?" 16

Thinking Critically about This Reading

What is the significance of Phil's youngest son's statement, "My father and I only board here" (paragraph 12)? What does it convey about Phil's relationship with his family?

Questions for Study and Discussion

1. After reading Goodman's essay, how would you define *company man*? As you define the term, consider what such a man is not, as well as what he is. Is *company man* synonymous with *workaholic*? Explain.
2. In paragraph 4, Goodman says that Phil worked like "the Important People." How would you define that term in the context of the essay?

3. What is Goodman's purpose? (Glossary: *Purpose*) Explain.
4. Do you think Goodman's unemotional tone is appropriate for her purpose? (Glossary: *Tone; Purpose*) Why or why not?
5. Goodman repeats the day and time that Phil worked himself to death. Why are those facts important enough to bear repetition? What about them is ironic? (Glossary: *Irony*)

Classroom Activity Using Definition

The connotation of the term *workaholic* depends on the context. For Phil's employers—and at his workplace in general—the term obviously had a positive connotation. For those who knew Phil outside the workplace, it had a negative one. Choose one of the terms below, and provide two definitions, one positive and one negative, that could apply to the term in different contexts.

go-getter	overachiever
party animal	mover and shaker

Suggested Writing Assignments

1. A procrastinator—a person who continually puts off responsibilities—is very different from a workaholic. Write an essay, modeled on Goodman's, using an extended example to define this interesting personality type.
2. One issue that Goodman does not raise is how a person becomes a workaholic. Write an essay in which you speculate about how someone might develop workaholism. How does a desirable trait like hard work begin to adversely affect someone? How might workaholism be avoided?
3. The following cartoon depicts one "businessdog" talking with another about job benefits. What is your reaction to the idea of a company putting workers "to sleep at its own expense"? What insights does the cartoon give you into Goodman's essay about work in the corporate world? Write an essay in which you describe the ideal employee-management relationship. Use as support examples from Goodman's essay, the cartoon, or your own work experience and observations.

"And when the time comes the company will put you to sleep at its own expense."

chapter **17**

Division and Classification

A writer practices **division** by separating a class of things or ideas into categories following a clear principle or basis. In the following paragraph, journalist Robert MacNeil establishes categories of speech according to the level of formality:

> It fascinates me how differently we all speak in different circumstances. We have levels of formality, as in our clothing. There are very formal occasions, often requiring written English: the job application or the letter to the editor—the darksuit, serious-tie language, with everything pressed and the lint brushed off. There is our less formal out-in-the-world language—a more comfortable suit, but still respectable. There is language for close friends in the evenings, on weekends—bluejeans-and-sweat-shirt language, when it's good to get the tie off. There is family language, even more relaxed, full of grammatical short cuts, family slang, echoes of old jokes that have become intimate shorthand—the language of pajamas and uncombed hair. Finally, there is the language with no clothes on; the talk of couples—murmurs, sighs, grunts—language at its least self-conscious, open, vulnerable, and primitive.
>
> –Robert MacNeil

With **classification,** on the other hand, a writer groups individual objects or ideas into already established categories. Division and classification can operate separately but often accompany one another. Here, for example, is a passage about levers in which the writer first discusses generally how levers work. In the second paragraph, the writer uses division to establish three categories of levers and then uses classification to group individual levers into those categories:

> Every lever has one fixed point called the "fulcrum" and is acted upon by two forces—the "effort" (exertion of hand muscles) and the "weight" (object's resistance). Levers work according to a

> simple formula: the effort (how hard you push or pull) multiplied by its distance from the fulcrum (effort arm) equals the weight multiplied by its distance from the fulcrum (weight arm). Thus two pounds of effort exerted at a distance of four feet from the fulcrum will raise eight pounds located one foot from the fulcrum.
>
> There are three types of levers, conventionally called "first kind," "second kind," and "third kind." Levers of the first kind have the fulcrum located between the effort and the weight. Examples are a pump handle, an oar, a crowbar, a weighing balance, a pair of scissors, and a pair of pliers. Levers of the second kind have the weight in the middle and magnify the effort. Examples are the handcar crank and doors. Levers of the third kind, such as a power shovel or a baseball batter's forearm, have the effort in the middle and always magnify the distance.

The following paragraph introduces a classification of the kinds of buyers who purchase stereo systems:

> As stereo equipment gets better and prices go down, stereo systems are becoming household necessities rather than luxuries. People are buying stereos by the thousands. During my year as a stereo salesman, I witnessed this boom firsthand. I dealt with hundreds of customers, and it didn't take long for me to learn that people buy stereos for different reasons. Eventually, though, I was able to divide all stereo buyers into four basic categories: the looks buyer, the wattage buyer, the price buyer, and the quality buyer.
>
> –Gerald Cleary, student

In the remainder of his essay, Cleary explains in detail the distinguishing characteristics of each type of stereo system buyer.

In writing, division and classification are affected directly by the writer's practical purpose. That purpose—what the writer wants to explain or prove—determines the class of things or ideas being divided and classified. For instance, a writer might divide television programs according to their audiences—adults, families, or children—and then classify individual programs into each of these categories to show how much emphasis the television stations place on reaching each audience. A different purpose would require different categories. A writer concerned about the prevalence of violence in television programming would first divide television programs into those that include fights and murders and those that do not, and would then classify a large sample of programs into those categories.

Other writers with different purposes might divide television programs differently—by the day and time of broadcast, for example, or by the number of women featured in prominent roles—and then classify individual programs accordingly.

Another example may help clarify how division and classification work hand in hand in writing. Suppose a sociologist wants to determine whether the socioeconomic status of the people in a particular neighborhood has any influence on their voting behavior. Having decided on her purpose, the sociologist chooses as her subject the fifteen families living on Maple Street. Her goal then becomes to group these families in a way that will be relevant to her purpose. She immediately knows that she wants to divide the neighborhood in two ways: (1) according to socioeconomic status (low-income earners, middle-income earners, and high-income earners) and (2) according to voting behavior (voters and nonvoters). However, her process of division won't be complete until she can classify individual families into her various groupings.

In confidential interviews with each family, the sociologist learns first the family's income and then whether any member of the household has voted in a state or federal election during the last four years. Based on this information, she begins to classify each family according to her established categories and at the same time to divide the neighborhood into the subclasses crucial to her study. Her work leads her to construct a diagram of her divisions and classifications.

The diagram on p. 411 allows the sociologist to visualize her division and classification system and its essential components: subject, basis or principle of division, subclasses or categories, and conclusion. It is clear that her ultimate conclusion depends on her ability to work back and forth between the potential divisions or subclasses and the actual families to be classified.

The following guidelines can help you in using division and classification in your writing:

1. *Identify a clear purpose, and be sure that your principle of division is appropriate to that purpose.* If, for example, you want to examine the common characteristics of four-year athletic scholarship recipients at your college or university, you might consider the following principles of division: program of study, sport, place of origin, or gender. In this case it would not be useful to divide students on the basis of their favorite type of music because that seems irrelevant to your purpose.

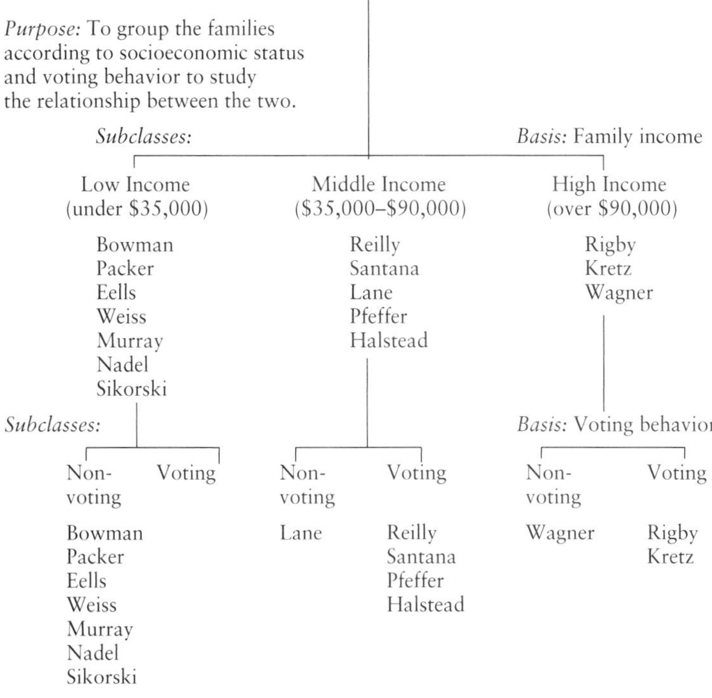

Conclusion: On Maple Street, there seems to be a relationship between socioeconomic status and voting behavior: the low-income families are nonvoters.

2. *Divide your subject into categories that are mutually exclusive.* An item can belong to only one category. For example, it would be unsatisfactory to divide students as men, women, and athletes.
3. *Make your division and classification complete.* Your categories should account for all items in a subject class. In dividing students on the basis of geographic origin, for example, it would be inappropriate to consider only the United States, for such a division would not account for foreign students. Then, for your classification to be complete, every student must be placed in one of the established categories.
4. *Be sure to state clearly the conclusion that your division and classification lead you to draw.* For example, after conducting your division and classification of athletic scholarship recipients, you might conclude that the majority of male athletes with athletic scholarships come from the western United States.

The Ways of Meeting Oppression

■ **Martin Luther King Jr.**

Martin Luther King Jr. (1929–1968) was the leading spokesman for the rights of African Americans during the 1950s and 1960s before his assassination in 1968. He established the Southern Christian Leadership Conference, organized many civil rights demonstrations, and opposed the Vietnam War and the draft. In 1964, he was awarded the Nobel Peace Prize.

In the following essay, taken from his book Strive toward Freedom *(1958), King classifies the three ways oppressed people throughout history have reacted to their oppressors. As you read, pay particular attention to how King's discussions within the categories of classification lead him to the conclusion he presents in paragraph 8.*

For Your Journal

Isaac Asimov once said, "Violence is the last resort of the incompetent." What are your thoughts on the reasons for violent behavior on either a personal or a national level? Is violence ever justified? If so, under what circumstances?

Oppressed people deal with their oppression in three characteristic ways. One way is acquiescence: the oppressed resign themselves to their doom. They tacitly adjust themselves to oppression, and thereby become conditioned to it. In every movement toward freedom some of the oppressed prefer to remain oppressed. Almost 2800 years ago Moses[1] set out to lead the children of Israel from the slavery of Egypt to the freedom of the promised land. He soon discovered that slaves do not always welcome their deliverers. They become accustomed to being slaves. They would rather bear those ills they have, as Shakespeare 1

[1]*Moses:* a Hebrew prophet, teacher, and leader of the fourteenth to thirteenth centuries B.C.E.

pointed out, than flee to others that they know not of. They prefer the "fleshpots of Egypt" to the ordeals of emancipation.

There is such a thing as the freedom of exhaustion. Some people are so worn down by the yoke of oppression that they give up. A few years ago in the slum areas of Atlanta, a Negro guitarist used to sing almost daily: "Been down so long that down don't bother me."[2] This is the type of negative freedom and resignation that often engulfs the life of the oppressed. 2

But this is not the way out. To accept passively an unjust system is to cooperate with that system; thereby the oppressed become as evil as the oppressor. Noncooperation with evil is as much a moral obligation as is cooperation with good. The oppressed must never allow the conscience of the oppressor to slumber. Religion reminds every man that he is his brother's keeper. To accept injustice or segregation passively is to say to the oppressor that his actions are morally right. It is a way of allowing his conscience to fall asleep. At this moment the oppressed fails to be his brother's keeper. So acquiescence—while often the easier way—is not the moral way. It is the way of the coward. The Negro cannot win the respect of his oppressor by acquiescing; he merely increases the oppressor's arrogance and contempt. Acquiescence is interpreted as proof of the Negro's inferiority. The Negro cannot win the respect of the white people of the South or the peoples of the world if he is willing to sell the future of his children for his personal and immediate comfort and safety. 3

A second way that oppressed people sometimes deal with oppression is to resort to physical violence and corroding hatred. Violence often brings about momentary results. Nations have frequently won their independence in battle. But in spite of temporary victories, violence never brings permanent peace. It solves no social problem; it merely creates new and more complicated ones. 4

Violence as a way of achieving racial justice is both impractical and immoral. It is impractical because it is a descending spiral ending in destruction for all. The old law of an eye for an eye leaves everybody blind. It is immoral because it seeks to humiliate the opponent rather than win his understanding; it seeks to annihilate rather than to convert. Violence is immoral because it thrives on hatred rather than love. It destroys community and makes brotherhood impossible. 5

---

[2] *"Been down . . . bother me"*: lyric possibly adapted from "Stormy Blues" by the American jazz singer Billie Holiday (1915–1959).

It leaves society in monologue rather than dialogue. Violence ends by defeating itself. It creates bitterness in the survivors and brutality in the destroyers. A voice echoes through time saying to every potential Peter, "Put up your sword."[3] History is cluttered with the wreckage of nations that failed to follow this command.

If the American Negro and other victims of oppression succumb 6 to the temptation of using violence in the struggle for freedom, future generations will be the recipients of a desolate night of bitterness, and our chief legacy to them will be an endless reign of meaningless chaos. Violence is not the way.

The third way open to oppressed people in their quest for freedom 7 is the way of nonviolent resistance. Like the synthesis in Hegelian[4] philosophy, the principle of nonviolent resistance seeks to reconcile the truths of two opposites—acquiescence and violence—while avoiding the extremes and immoralities of both. The nonviolent resister agrees with the person who acquiesces that one should not be physically aggressive toward his opponent; but he balances the equation by agreeing with the person of violence that evil must be resisted. He avoids the nonresistance of the former and the violent resistance of the latter. With nonviolent resistance, no individual or group need submit to any wrong, nor need anyone resort to violence in order to right a wrong.

It seems to me that this is the method that must guide the actions 8 of the Negro in the present crisis in race relations. Through nonviolent resistance the Negro will be able to rise to the noble height of opposing the unjust system while loving the perpetrators of the system. The Negro must work passionately and unrelentingly for full stature as a citizen, but he must not use inferior methods to gain it. He must never come to terms with falsehood, malice, hate, or destruction.

Nonviolent resistance makes it possible for the Negro to remain 9 in the South and struggle for his rights. The Negro's problem will not be solved by running away. He cannot listen to the glib suggestion of those who would urge him to migrate en masse to other sections of the country. By grasping his great opportunity in the South he can

[3]*"Put up your sword"*: the apostle Peter had drawn his sword to defend Christ from arrest; the voice was Christ's, who surrendered himself for trial and crucifixion (John 18:11).

[4]*Georg Wilhelm Friedrich Hegel* (1770–1831): German philosopher.

make a lasting contribution to the moral strength of the nation and set a sublime example of courage for generations yet unborn.

By nonviolent resistance, the Negro can also enlist all men of good 10
will in his struggle for equality. The problem is not a purely racial one, with Negroes set against whites. In the end, it is not a struggle between people at all, but a tension between justice and injustice. Nonviolent resistance is not aimed against oppressors but against oppression. Under its banner consciences, not racial groups, are enlisted.

Thinking Critically about This Reading

King states that "there is such a thing as the freedom of exhaustion" (paragraph 2). Why, according to King, is this type of freedom "negative"?

Questions for Study and Discussion

1. What is King's purpose? (Glossary: *Purpose*) How does classifying the three types of resistance to oppression serve this purpose?
2. What principle of division does King use in this essay?
3. Why do you suppose King discusses acquiescence, violence, and nonviolent resistance in that order? (Glossary: *Organization*)
4. Why, according to King, do slaves not always welcome their deliverers?
5. King states that he favors nonviolent resistance over the other two ways of meeting oppression. What are the disadvantages that King sees in meeting oppression with acquiescence or with violence? Look closely at the words he uses to describe nonviolent resistance and those he uses to describe acquiescence and violence. How does his choice of words contribute to his argument? (Glossary: *Argument*) Show examples.

Classroom Activity Using Division and Classification

Examine the following lists of hobbies, books, and buildings. Determine at least three principles that could be used to divide the items listed in each group. Finally, classify the items in each group according to one of the principles you have established.

Hobbies

watching sports on TV
stamp collecting
scuba diving
surfing the Web
hiking
dancing

Books

The Adventures of Huckleberry Finn
American Heritage Dictionary
The Joy of Cooking
Guinness Book of World Records
To Kill a Mockingbird
Gone with the Wind

Buildings

Empire State Building
White House
The Alamo
Taj Mahal
Library of Congress
Buckingham Palace

Suggested Writing Assignments

1. Using King's essay as a model, write an essay about a current social or personal problem, using division and classification to discuss various possible solutions. You might discuss something personal, such as the problem of giving up smoking, or a pressing social issue, such as gun control or gay marriage. Whatever your topic, use an appropriate principle of division to establish categories that suit the purpose of your discussion. (Glossary: *Purpose*)
2. Consider any one of the following topics for an essay of classification. You may find it helpful to review the guidelines for using division and classification on pages 410–11.

movies
college courses
sports fans
teenage lifestyles
country music
newspapers
pets
students

Friends, Good Friends—and Such Good Friends

■ **Judith Viorst**

Judith Viorst was born in Newark, New Jersey, in 1931 and attended Rutgers University. She has published several volumes of light verse and collections of prose, as well as many articles in popular magazines. Her numerous children's books include the perennial favorite Alexander and the Terrible, Horrible, No Good, Very Bad Day *(1972). Her recent books for adults include* Necessary Losses: The Loves, Illusions, Dependencies, and Impossible Expectations That All of Us Have to Give Up in Order to Grow *(1997),* Imperfect Control: Our Lifelong Struggles with Power and Surrender *(1998),* Suddenly 60: And Other Shocks of Late-Life *(2000), and* Grown-Up Marriage: What We Know, Wish We Had Known, and Still Need to Know about Being Married *(2002).*

The following selection appeared in Viorst's regular column in Redbook *in 1977. In it she analyzes and classifies the various types of friends that a person can have. As you read, assess the validity of her analysis by trying to place your own friends into her categories. Determine also whether the categories themselves are mutually exclusive.*

For Your Journal

Think about your friends. Do you regard them all in the same light? Would you group them in any way? On what basis would you group them?

Women are friends, I once would have said, when they totally love and support and trust each other, and bare to each other the secrets of their souls, and run—no questions asked—to help each other, and tell harsh truths to each other (no, you can't wear that dress unless you lose ten pounds first) when harsh truths must be told. 1

Women are friends, I once would have said, when they share the same affection for Ingmar Bergman,[1] plus train rides, cats, warm rain, charades, Camus,[2] and hate with equal ardor Newark[3] and Brussels sprouts and Lawrence Welk[4] and camping. 2

In other words, I once would have said that a friend is a friend all the way, but now I believe that's a narrow point of view. For the friendships I have and the friendships I see are conducted at many levels of intensity, serve many different functions, meet different needs, and range from those as all-the-way as the friendship of the soul sisters mentioned above to that of the most nonchalant and casual playmates. 3

Consider these varieties of friendship: 4

1. Convenience friends. These are women with whom, if our paths weren't crossing all the time, we'd have no particular reason to be friends: a next-door neighbor, a woman in our car pool, the mother of one of our children's closest friends, or maybe some mommy with whom we serve juice and cookies each week at the Glenwood Co-op Nursery. 5

Convenience friends are convenient indeed. They'll lend us their cups and silverware for a party. They'll drive our kids to soccer when we're sick. They'll take us to pick up our car when we need a lift to the garage. They'll even take our cats when we go on vacation. As we will for them. 6

But we don't, with convenience friends, ever come too close or tell too much; we maintain our public face and emotional distance. "Which means," says Elaine, "that I'll talk about being overweight but not about being depressed. Which means I'll admit being mad but not blind with rage. Which means that I might say that we're pinched this month but never that I'm worried sick over money." 7

But which doesn't mean that there isn't sufficient value to be found in these friendships of mutual aid, in convenience friends. 8

2. Special-interest friends. These friendships aren't intimate, and they needn't involve kids or silverware or cats. Their value lies in some interest jointly shared. And so we may have an office friend or a yoga friend or a tennis friend or a friend from the Women's Democratic Club. 9

[1]*Ingmar Bergman* (b. 1918): Swedish film writer and director.

[2]*Albert Camus* (1913–1960): French novelist, essayist, and playwright.

[3]*Newark:* a city in northeastern New Jersey.

[4]*Lawrence Welk* (1903–1992): American band leader and accordion player whose *The Lawrence Welk Show* aired on television in 1955–1971.

"I've got one woman friend," says Joyce, "who likes, as I do, to take psychology courses. Which makes it nice for me—and nice for her. It's fun to go with someone you know and it's fun to discuss what you've learned, driving back from the classes." And for the most part, she says, that's all they discuss. 10

"I'd say that what we're doing is *doing* together, not being together," Suzanne says of her Tuesday-doubles friends. "It's mainly a tennis relationship, but we play together well. And I guess we all need to have a couple of playmates." 11

I agree. 12

My playmate is a shopping friend, a woman of marvelous taste, a woman who knows exactly *where* to buy *what,* and furthermore is a woman who always knows beyond a doubt what one ought to be buying. I don't have the time to keep up with what's new in eyeshadow, hemlines, and shoes and whether the smock look is in or finished already. But since (oh, shame!) I care a lot about eyeshadow, hemlines, and shoes, and since I don't *want* to wear smocks if the smock look is finished, I'm very glad to have a shopping friend. 13

3. Historical friends. We all have a friend who knew us when . . . maybe way back in Miss Meltzer's second grade, when our family lived in that three-room flat in Brooklyn, when our dad was out of work for seven months, when our brother Allie got in that fight where they had to call the police, when our sister married the endodontist[5] from Yonkers,[6] and when, the morning after we lost our virginity, she was the first, the only, friend we told. 14

The years have gone by and we've gone separate ways and we've little in common now, but we're still an intimate part of each other's past. And so whenever we go to Detroit we always go to visit this friend of our girlhood. Who knows how we looked before our teeth were straightened. Who knows how we talked before our voice got un-Brooklyned. Who knows what we ate before we learned about artichokes. And who, by her presence, puts us in touch with an earlier part of ourself, a part of ourself it's important never to lose. 15

"What this friend means to me and what I mean to her," says Grace, "is having a sister without sibling rivalry. We know the texture of each other's lives. She remembers my grandmother's cabbage 16

---

[5]*endodontist:* a dentist who specializes in diseases of the teeth and gums.

[6]*Yonkers:* a city in southeastern New York, just north of New York City.

soup. I remember the way her uncle played the piano. There's simply no other friend who remembers those things."

4. Crossroads friends. Like historical friends, our crossroads friends are important for *what was*—for the friendship we shared at a crucial, now past, time of life. A time, perhaps, when we roomed in college together; or worked as eager young singles in the Big City together; or went together, as my friend Elizabeth and I did, through pregnancy, birth, and that scary first year of new motherhood. 17

Crossroads friends forge powerful links, links strong enough to endure with not much more contact than once-a-year letters at Christmas. And out of respect for those crossroad years, for those dramas and dreams we once shared, we will always be friends. 18

5. Cross-generational friends. Historical friends and crossroads friends seem to maintain a special kind of intimacy—dormant but always ready to be revived—and though we may rarely meet, whenever we do connect, it's personal and intense. Another kind of intimacy exists in the friendships that form across generations in what one woman calls her daughter–mother and her mother–daughter relationships. 19

Evelyn's friend is her mother's age—"but I share so much more than I ever could with my mother"—a woman she talks to of music, of books and of life. "What I get from her is the benefit of her experience. What she gets—and enjoys—from me is a youthful perspective. It's a pleasure for both of us." 20

I have in my own life a precious friend, a woman of 65 who has lived very hard, who is wise, who listens well; who has been where I am and can help me understand it; and who represents not only an ultimate ideal mother to me but also the person I'd like to be when I grow up. 21

In our daughter role we tend to do more than our share of self-revelation; in our mother role we tend to receive what's revealed. It's another kind of pleasure—playing wise mother to a questing younger person. It's another very lovely kind of friendship. 22

6. Part-of-a-couple friends. Some of the women we call our friends we never see alone—we see them as part of a couple at couples' parties. And though we share interests in many things and respect each other's views, we aren't moved to deepen the relationship. Whatever the reason, a lack of time or—and this is more likely—a lack of chemistry, our friendship remains in the context of a group. But the fact that our feeling on seeing each other is always, "I'm *so* glad she's 23

here" and the fact that we spend half the evening talking together says that this too, in its own way, counts as a friendship.

(Other part-of-a-couple friends are the friends that came with the marriage, and some of these are friends we could live without. But sometimes, alas, she married our husband's best friend; and sometimes, alas, she *is* our husband's best friend. And so we find ourself dealing with her, somewhat against our will, in a spirit of what I'll call *reluctant* friendship.) 24

7. Men who are friends. I wanted to write just of women friends, but the women I've talked to won't let me—they say I must mention man–woman friendships too. For these friendships can be just as close and as dear as those that we form with women. Listen to Lucy's description of one such friendship: 25

"We've found we have things to talk about that are different from what he talks about with my husband and different from what I talk about with his wife. So sometimes we call on the phone or meet for lunch. There are similar intellectual interests—we always pass on to each other the books that we love—but there's also something tender and caring too." 26

In a couple of crises, Lucy says, "he offered himself for talking and for helping. And when someone died in his family he wanted me there. The sexual, flirty part of our friendship is very small, but *some*—just enough to make it fun and different." She thinks—and I agree—that the sexual part, though small, is always *some,* is always there when a man and a woman are friends. 27

It's only in the past few years that I've made friends with men, in the sense of a friendship that's *mine,* not just part of two couples. And achieving with them the ease and the trust I've found with women friends has value indeed. Under the dryer at home last week, putting on mascara and rouge, I comfortably sat and talked with a fellow named Peter. Peter, I finally decided, could handle the shock of me minus mascara under the dryer. Because we care for each other. Because we're friends. 28

8. There are medium friends, and pretty good friends, and very good friends indeed, and these friendships are defined by their level of intimacy. And what we'll reveal at each of these levels of intimacy is calibrated with care. We might tell a medium friend, for example, that yesterday we had a fight with our husband. And we might tell a pretty good friend that this fight with our husband made us so mad that we slept on the couch. And we might tell a very good friend that 29

the reason we got so mad in that fight that we slept on the couch had something to do with that girl that works in his office. But it's only to our very best friends that we're willing to tell all, to tell what's going on with that girl in his office.

The best of friends, I still believe, totally love and support and trust each other, and bare to each other the secrets of their souls, and run—no questions asked—to help each other, and tell harsh truths to each other when they must be told. 30

But we needn't agree about everything (only 12-year-old girl friends agree about *everything*) to tolerate each other's point of view. To accept without judgment. To give and to take without ever keeping score. And to *be* there, as I am for them and as they are for me, to comfort our sorrows, to celebrate our joys. 31

Thinking Critically about This Reading

The third type of friend Viorst writes about is the "historical friend." Why is it important to have a friend who "puts us in touch with an earlier part of ourself" (paragraph 15)?

Questions for Study and Discussion

1. In her opening paragraph, Viorst explains how she once would have defined *friendship*. Why does she now think differently?
2. What is Viorst's purpose? (Glossary: *Purpose*) Why is division and classification an appropriate strategy for her to use?
3. Into what categories does Viorst divide her friends?
4. What principles of division does Viorst use to establish her categories of friends? Where does she state these principles?
5. Discuss the ways in which Viorst makes her categories distinct and memorable.
6. What is Viorst's tone? (Glossary: *Tone*) In what ways is her tone appropriate for both her audience and subject matter? (Glossary: *Audience*) Explain.

Classroom Activity Using Division and Classification

The following drawing is a basic exercise in classification. By determining the features that the figures have in common, establish the general class to which they all belong. Next, establish subclasses by

a
b
c
d
e
f
g
h
i
j
k
l
m
o
n

determining the distinctive features that distinguish one subclass from another. Finally, place each figure in an appropriate subclass within your classification system. You may wish to compare your classification system with those developed by other members of your class and to discuss any differences that exist.

Suggested Writing Assignments

1. Review the categories of friends that Viorst establishes in her essay. Do the categories apply to your friends? What new categories would you create? Write an essay in which you explain the types of friends in your life.
2. Music can be classified into many different types, such as jazz, country, pop, rock, hard rock, alternative, classical, big band, hip-hop, and so on. Each of these large classifications has a lot of variety within it. Write an essay in which you identify your favorite type of music as well as at least three subclassifications of that music. Explain the characteristics of each category, using two or three artists as examples.
3. In her essay Viorst focuses on the types of friendships between women. (Glossary: *Focus*) What about friendships between men, one of which is represented in the cartoon on page 425? What statement do you think the cartoon makes about the nature of men's friendships? In what ways do they differ from women's friendships? (Glossary: *Comparison and Contrast*) Using Viorst's essay as a model, write an essay in which you divide and classify the friendships you think men have.

A friend will give up his life for you.
A *real* friend will help you move.

Four Types of President

■ James David Barber

James David Barber (1930–2004) was born in Charleston, West Virginia, and educated at the University of Chicago and Yale University. Before his death he was a professor of political science at Duke University, the chair of his department, and a frequent lecturer at colleges and universities throughout the United States. He wrote and edited The Presidential Character: Predicting Performance in the White House *(1992),* Race for the Presidency: The Media and the Nominating Process *(1978), and* The Pulse of Politics: Electing Presidents in the Media Age *(1980), three important books in the field of political science.*

In the following selection taken from The Presidential Character, *Barber uses division and classification to identify four basic types of U.S. president.*

For Your Journal

What are the four most important character traits you think the president of the United States should possess? Make a list, and explain in a few sentences each trait and why you think it is important.

Who the president is at a given time can make a profound differ- 1
ence in the whole thrust and direction of national politics. Since we have only one president at a time, we can never prove this by comparison, but even the most superficial speculation confirms the commonsense view that the man himself weighs heavily among other historical factors. A Wilson re-elected in 1920, a Hoover in 1932, a John F. Kennedy in 1964 would, it seems very likely, have guided the body politic along rather different paths from those their actual successors chose. Or try to imagine a Theodore Roosevelt ensconced behind today's "bully pulpit"[1] of a presidency, or Lyndon Johnson as president

[1] *"bully pulpit"*: elected office that allows the holder to speak out and be listened to on any matter.

in the age of McKinley. Only someone mesmerized by the lures of historical inevitability can suppose that it would have made little or no difference to government policy had Alf Landon replaced FDR[2] in 1936, and Dewey beaten Truman in 1948, or Adlai Stevenson[3] reigned through the 1950s. Not only would these alternative presidents have advocated different policies—they would have approached the office from very different psychological angles. It stretches credibility to think that Eugene McCarthy[4] would have run the institution the way Lyndon Johnson did.

The first baseline in defining presidential types is *activity-passivity.* 2
How much energy does the man invest in his presidency? Lyndon Johnson went at his day like a human cyclone, coming to rest long after the sun went down. Calvin Coolidge often slept eleven hours a night and still needed a nap in the middle of the day. In between, the presidents array themselves on the high or low side of the activity line.

The second baseline is *positive-negative affect* toward one's 3
activity—that is, how he feels about what he does. Relatively speaking, does he seem to experience his political life as happy or sad, enjoyable or discouraging, positive or negative, in its main effect. The feeling I am after here is not grim satisfaction in a job well done, not some philosophical conclusion. The idea is this: is he someone who, on the surfaces we can see, gives forth the feeling that he has *fun* in political life? Franklin Roosevelt's Secretary of War, Henry L. Stimson, wrote that the Roosevelts "not only understood the *use* of power, they knew the *enjoyment* of power, too. . . . Whether a man is burdened by power or enjoys power; whether he is trapped by responsibility or made free by it; whether he is moved by other people and outer forces or moves them—that is the essence of leadership."

The positive negative baseline, then, is a general symptom of the fit 4
between the man and his experience, a kind of register of *felt* satisfaction.

Why might we expect these two simple dimensions to outline the 5
main character types? Because they stand for two central features of anyone's orientation toward life. In nearly every study of personality, some form of the active-passive contrast is critical; the general tendency

[2]*FDR:* Franklin D. Roosevelt (1882–1945), thirty-second U.S. president, 1933–1945.
[3]*Landon, Dewey, Stevenson:* Alf Landon (1882–1945), Thomas Dewey (1902–1971), and Adlai Stevenson (1900–1965) all lost presidential elections against incumbents.
[4]*Eugene McCarthy* (1916–2005): politician who lost to incumbent Lyndon Johnson (1908–1973) for the Democratic Party's nomination for the 1968 presidential election.

to act or be acted upon is evident in such concepts as dominance-submission, extraversion-introversion, aggression-timidity, attack-defense, fight-flight, engagement-withdrawal, approach-avoidance. In everyday life we sense quickly the general energy output of the people we deal with. Similarly we catch on fairly quickly to the affect dimension—whether the person seems to be optimistic or pessimistic, hopeful or skeptical, happy or sad. The two baselines are clear and they are also independent of one another: all of us know people who are very active but seem discouraged, others who are quite passive but seem happy, and so forth. The activity baseline refers to what one does, the affect baseline to how one feels about what he does.

Both are crude clues to character. They are leads into four basic 6
character patterns long familiar in psychological research. In summary form, these are the main configurations:

Active-positive. There is a congruence, a consistency, between 7
much activity and the enjoyment of it, indicating relatively high self-esteem and relative success in relating to the environment. The man shows an orientation toward productiveness as a value and an ability to use his styles flexibly, adaptively, suiting the dance to the music. He sees himself as developing over time toward relatively well-defined personal goals—growing toward his image of himself as he might yet be. There is an emphasis on rational mastery, on using the brain to move the feet. This may get him into trouble; he may fail to take account of the irrational in politics. Not everyone he deals with sees things his way and he may find it hard to understand why.

Active-negative. The contradiction here is between relatively 8
intense effort and relatively low emotional reward for that effort. The activity has a compulsive quality, as if the man were trying to make up for something or to escape from anxiety into hard work. He seems ambitious, striving upward, power-seeking. His stance toward the environment is aggressive and he has a persistent problem in managing his aggressive feelings. His self-image is vague and discontinuous. Life is a hard struggle to achieve and hold power, hampered by the condemnations of a perfectionistic conscience. Active-negative types pour energy into the political system, but it is an energy distorted from within.

Passive-positive. This is the receptive, compliant, other-directed 9
character whose life is a search for affection as a reward for being agreeable and cooperative rather than personally assertive. The contradiction is between low self-esteem (on grounds of being unlovable,

unattractive) and a superficial optimism. A hopeful attitude helps dispel doubt and elicits encouragement from others. Passive-positive types help soften the harsh edges of politics. But their dependence and the fragility of their hopes and enjoyments make disappointment in politics likely.

Passive-negative. The factors are consistent—but how are we to account for the man's *political* role-taking? Why is someone who does little in politics and enjoys it less there at all? The answer lies in the passive-negative's character-rooted orientation toward doing dutiful service; this compensates for low self-esteem based on a sense of uselessness. Passive-negative types are in politics because they think they ought to be. They may be well adapted to certain nonpolitical roles, but they lack the experience and flexibility to perform effectively as political leaders. Their tendency is to withdraw, to escape from the conflict and uncertainty of politics by emphasizing vague principles (especially prohibitions) and procedural arrangements. They become guardians of the right and proper way, above the sordid politicking of lesser men. 10

Active-positive presidents want most to achieve results. Active-negatives aim to get and keep power. Passive-positives are after love. Passive-negatives emphasize their civic virtue. The relation of activity to enjoyment in a president thus tends to outline a cluster of characteristics, to set apart the adapted from the compulsive, compliant, and withdrawn types. 11

The first four presidents of the United States, conveniently, ran through this gamut of character types. (Remember, we are talking about tendencies, broad directions; no individual man exactly fits a category.) George Washington—clearly the most important president in the pantheon[5]—established the fundamental legitimacy of an American government at a time when this was a matter in considerable question. Washington's dignity, judiciousness, his aloof air of reserve and dedication to duty fit the passive-negative or withdrawing type best. Washington did not seek innovation, he sought stability. He longed to retire to Mount Vernon,[6] but fortunately was persuaded to stay on through a second term, in which, by rising above the political conflict between Hamilton and Jefferson and inspiring confidence in 12

[5]*pantheon:* a highly regarded group of people in the same field.

[6]*Mount Vernon:* George Washington's estate on the Potomac River near Washington, D.C.

his own integrity, he gave the nation time to develop the organized means for peaceful change.

John Adams followed, a dour New England Puritan, much given to work and worry, an impatient and irascible man—an active-negative president, a compulsive type. Adams was far more partisan than Washington; the survival of the system through his presidency demonstrated that the nation could tolerate, for a time, domination by one of its nascent[7] political parties. As president, an angry Adams brought the United States to the brink of war with France, and presided over the new nation's first experiment in political repression: the Alien and Sedition Acts, forbidding, among other things, unlawful combinations "with intent to oppose any measure or measures of the government of the United States," or "any false, scandalous, and malicious writing or writings against the United States, or the President of the United States, with intent to defame . . . or to bring them or either of them, into contempt or disrepute." 13

Then came Jefferson. He too had his troubles and failures—in the design of national defense, for example. As for his presidential character (only one element in success or failure), Jefferson was clearly active-positive. A child of the Enlightenment,[8] he applied his reason to organizing connections with Congress aimed at strengthening the more popular forces. A man of catholic[9] interests and delightful humor, Jefferson combined a clear and open vision of what the country could be with a profound political sense, expressed in his famous phrase, "Every difference of opinion is not a difference of principle." 14

The fourth president was James Madison, "Little Jemmy," the constitutional philosopher thrown into the White House at a time of great international turmoil. Madison comes closest to the passive-positive, or compliant, type; he suffered from irresolution, tried to compromise his way out, and gave in too readily to the "warhawks" urging combat with Britain. The nation drifted into war, and Madison wound up ineptly commanding his collection of amateur generals in the streets of Washington. General Jackson's victory at New Orleans saved the Madison administration's historical reputation; but he left the presidency with the United States close to bankruptcy and secession. 15

[7] *nascent:* emerging.

[8] *Enlightenment:* an eighteenth-century philosophical movement that emphasized reason.

[9] *catholic:* of broad or liberal scope.

These four presidents—like all presidents—were persons trying to cope with the roles they had won by using the equipment they had built over a lifetime. The president is not some shapeless organism in a flood of novelties, but a man with a memory in a system with a history. Like all of us, he draws on his past to shape his future. The pathetic hope that the White House will turn a Caligula[10] into a Marcus Aurelius[11] is as naive as the fear that ultimate power inevitably corrupts. The problem is to understand—and to state understandably—what in the personal past foreshadows the presidential future. 16

Thinking Critically about This Reading

What does Barber mean when he states, "The president is not some shapeless organism in a flood of novelties, but a man with a memory in a system with a history" (paragraph 16)?

Questions for Study and Discussion

1. Barber uses the baselines "activity-passivity" (2) and "positive-negative affect" (3) to define presidential types. Briefly define what he means by each baseline. (Glossary: *Definition*) How are the two baselines related? How accurate would you say they are in defining character?
2. Identify the four basic character patterns and the defining character traits of each. According to Barber, what do presidents in each category want to achieve?
3. How does Barber organize his essay? (Glossary: *Organization*) What is the purpose of paragraphs 2–6? (Glossary: *Purpose*) How are paragraphs 12–15 related to paragraphs 7–10?
4. How does Barber classify the first four U.S. presidents? What leads him to his choices?
5. What does Barber believe is the key to predicting, or at least trying to predict, a president's performance?
6. Why does Barber admit that within his system of classification "no individual man exactly fits a category" (12)? What good are the categories then? Explain.

---

[10]*Caligula* (12–41 C.E.): Roman emperor known for his extravagance and cruelty.

[11]*Marcus Aurelius* (121–180 C.E.): Roman emperor known for his intellect and strength.

Classroom Activity Using Division and Classification

Explain how Barber's choice of words helps him characterize each of the four presidents he writes about in paragraphs 12–15. Point out specific descriptive words in each case. In a classroom discussion compare your choices and assessments with those of your classmates.

Suggested Writing Assignments

1. Use Barber's four personality categories as the basis for an essay of classification. You may choose three or four recent presidents as your subjects for classification. Or you may wish to classify teachers you've known or people you've met at work or school. Whatever your subject, be sure to use enough examples of behavior to justify or adequately explain your classification.
2. Analyze your own behavior and attitudes according to Barber's two baselines. Are you an energetic and relatively passive person? Are you basically positive and optimistic, or are you likely to be discouraged and negative? Into which of Barber's four categories would you place yourself? Write an essay in which you explain what people can learn about themselves as a result of such analysis and classification.

chapter **18**

Comparison and Contrast

A **comparison** points out the ways that two or more people, places, or things are alike. A **contrast** points out how they differ. The subjects of a comparison or contrast should be in the same class or general category; if they have nothing in common, there is no good reason for setting them side by side.

The function of any comparison or contrast is to clarify and explain. The writer's purpose may be simply to inform or to make readers aware of similarities or differences that are interesting and significant in themselves. Or the writer may explain something unfamiliar by comparing it with something very familiar, perhaps explaining the game of squash by comparing it with tennis. Finally, the writer can point out the superiority of one thing by contrasting it with another—for example, showing that one product is the best by contrasting it with all its competitors.

As a writer, you have two main options for organizing a comparison or contrast: the subject-by-subject pattern or the point-by-point pattern. For a short essay comparing and contrasting the Atlanta Braves and the Seattle Mariners, you would probably follow the *subject-by-subject* pattern of organization. With this pattern, you first discuss the points you wish to make about one team, and then go on to discuss the corresponding points for the other team. An outline of the body of your essay might look like this:

Subject-by-Subject Pattern

I. Atlanta Braves
   A. Pitching
   B. Fielding
   C. Hitting

II. Seattle Mariners
   A. Pitching
   B. Fielding
   C. Hitting

The subject-by-subject pattern presents a unified discussion of each team by placing the emphasis on the teams and not on the three points of comparison. Since these points are relatively few, readers should easily remember what was said about the Braves' pitching when you later discuss the Mariners' pitching and should be able to make the appropriate connections between them.

For a somewhat longer essay comparing and contrasting solar energy and wind energy, however, you should consider the *point-by-point* pattern of organization. With this pattern, your essay is organized according to the various points of comparison. Discussion alternates between solar and wind energy for each point of comparison. An outline of the body of your essay might look like this:

Point-by-Point Pattern

I. Installation Expenses
   A. Solar
   B. Wind
II. Efficiency
   A. Solar
   B. Wind
III. Operating Costs
   A. Solar
   B. Wind
IV. Convenience
   A. Solar
   B. Wind
V. Maintenance
   A. Solar
   B. Wind
VI. Safety
   A. Solar
   B. Wind

The point-by-point pattern allows the writer to make immediate comparisons between solar and wind energy, thus enabling readers to consider each of the similarities and differences separately.

Each organizational pattern has its advantages. In general, the subject-by-subject pattern is useful in short essays where there are few points to be considered, whereas the point-by-point pattern is preferable in long essays where there are numerous points under consideration.

A good essay of comparison and contrast tells readers something significant that they do not already know—that is, it must do more than merely point out the obvious. As a rule, therefore, writers tend to draw contrasts between things that are usually perceived as being similar or comparisons between things usually perceived as being different. In fact, comparison and contrast often go together. For example, an essay about Minneapolis and St. Paul might begin by showing how much they are alike but end with a series of contrasts revealing how much they differ. A consumer magazine might report the contrasting claims made by six car manufacturers and then go on to demonstrate that the cars all actually do much the same thing in the same way.

The following student essay about hunting and photography explores the increasing popularity of photographic safaris. After first pointing out the obvious differences between hunting with a gun and hunting with a camera, the writer focuses on the similarities between the two activities that make many hunters "willing to trade their guns for cameras." Notice how she successfully uses the subject-by-subject organizational plan in the body of her essay to explore three key similarities between hunters and photographers.

Guns and Cameras

The hunter has a deep interest in the apparatus he uses to kill his prey. He carries various types of guns, different kinds of ammunition, and special sights and telescopes to increase his chances of success. He knows the mechanics of his guns and understands how and why they work. This fascination with the hardware of his sport is practical—it helps him achieve his goal—but it frequently becomes an end, almost a hobby in itself.

Not until the very end of the long process of stalking an animal does a game hunter use his gun. First he enters into the animal's world. He studies his prey, its habitat, its daily habits, its watering holes and feeding areas, its migration patterns, its enemies and allies, its diet and food chain. Eventually the hunter himself becomes animal-like, instinctively sensing the habits and moves of his prey. Of course, this instinct gives the hunter a better chance of killing the animal; he knows where and when he will get the best shot. But it gives him more than that. Hunting is not just pulling the trigger and killing the prey. Much of it is a multifaceted and ritualistic identification with nature.

After the kill, the hunter can do a number of things with his trophy. He can sell the meat or eat it himself. He can hang the animal's head on the wall or lay its hide on the floor or even sell these objects. But any of these uses is a luxury, and its cost is high. An animal has been destroyed; a life has been eliminated.

Like the hunter, the photographer has a great interest in the tools he uses. He carries various types of cameras, lenses, and film to help him get the picture he wants. He understands the way cameras work, the uses of telephoto and micro lenses, and often the technical procedures of printing and developing. Of course, the time and interest a photographer invests in these mechanical aspects of his art allow him to capture and produce the image he wants. But as with the hunter, these mechanics can and often do become fascinating in themselves.

The wildlife photographer also needs to stalk his "prey" with knowledge and skill in order to get an accurate "shot." Like the hunter, he has to understand the animal's patterns, characteristics, and habitat; he must become animal-like in order to succeed. And like the hunter's, his pursuit is much more prolonged and complicated than the shot itself. The stalking processes are almost identical and give many of the same satisfactions.

The successful photographer also has something tangible to show for his efforts. A still picture of an animal can be displayed in a home, a gallery, a shop; it can be printed in a publication, as a postcard, or as a poster. In fact, a single photograph can be used in all these ways at once; it can be reproduced countless times. And despite all these ways of using his "trophies," the photographer continues to preserve his prey.

–Barbara Bowman, student

Analogy is a special form of comparison. When a subject is unobservable, complex, or abstract—when it is so generally unfamiliar that readers may have trouble understanding it—**analogy** can be most effective. By pointing out certain similarities between a difficult subject and a more familiar or concrete subject, writers can help their readers achieve a firmer grasp of the difficult subject. Unlike a true comparison, though, which analyzes items that belong to the same class—breeds of dogs or types of engines—analogy pairs things from different classes, things that have nothing in common except through the imagination of the writer. In addition, whereas comparison seeks to illuminate specific features of both subjects, the primary purpose of analogy is to clarify the one subject that is complex or unfamiliar. For example, an exploration of the similarities (and differences) between short stories and novels—two forms of fiction—would constitute a logical comparison; short stories and novels belong to the same class (fiction), and your purpose is to reveal something about both. If, however, your purpose is to explain the craft of fiction writing, you might note its similarities to the craft of carpentry. Then you would be drawing an analogy because the two subjects clearly belong to different classes. Carpentry is the more concrete subject and the one more people will have direct experience with. If you use your imagination, you will easily see many ways the tangible work of the carpenter can be used to help readers understand the more abstract work of the novelist.

Depending on its purpose, an analogy can be made in several paragraphs to clarify a particular aspect of the larger topic being discussed, as in the following example, or it can provide the organizational strategy for an entire essay.

> It has long struck me that the familiar metaphor of "climbing the ladder" for describing the ascent to success or fulfillment in any field is inappropriate and misleading. There are no ladders that lead to success, although there may be some escalators for those lucky enough to follow in a family's fortunes.
>
> A ladder proceeds vertically, rung by rung, with each rung evenly spaced, and with the whole apparatus leaning against a relatively flat and even surface. A child can climb a ladder as easily as an adult, and perhaps with a surer footing.
>
> Making the ascent in one's vocation or profession is far less like ladder climbing than mountain climbing, and here the analogy is a very real one. Going up a mountain requires a variety of skills, and includes a diversity of dangers, that are in no way involved in mounting a ladder.
>
> Young people starting out should be told this, both to dampen their expectations and to allay their disappointments. A mountain is rough and precipitous, with uncertain footing and a predictable number of falls and scrapes, and sometimes one has to take the long way around to reach the shortest distance.
>
> –Sydney J. Harris

Two Ways of Seeing a River

■ Mark Twain

Samuel L. Clemens (1835–1910), who wrote under the pen name of Mark Twain, was born in Florida, Missouri, and raised in Hannibal, Missouri. He wrote the novels Tom Sawyer *(1876),* The Prince and the Pauper *(1882),* Huckleberry Finn *(1884), and* A Connecticut Yankee in King Arthur's Court *(1889), as well as many other works of fiction and nonfiction. One of America's most popular writers, Twain is generally regarded as the most important practitioner of the realistic school of writing, a style that emphasizes observable details.*

The following passage is taken from Life on the Mississippi *(1883), Twain's study of the great river and his account of his early experiences learning to be a river steamboat pilot. As you read the passage, notice how Twain makes use of figurative language in describing two quite different ways of seeing the Mississippi River.*

For Your Journal

As we age and gain experience, our interpretation of the same memory—or how we view the same scene—can change. For example, the way we view our own appearance changes all the time, and photos from our childhood or teenage years may surprise us in the decades that follow. Perhaps something we found amusing in our younger days may make us feel uncomfortable or embarrassed now, or the house we grew up in later seems smaller or less appealing. Write about a memory that has changed for you over the years. How does your interpretation of it now contrast with how you experienced it at the time?

Now when I had mastered the language of this water and had come 1
to know every trifling feature that bordered the great river as familiarly as I knew the letters of the alphabet, I had made a valuable acquisition. But I had lost something, too. I had lost something which could never be restored to me while I lived. All the grace, the beauty, the poetry, had gone out of the majestic river! I still kept in mind a

certain wonderful sunset which I witnessed when steamboating was new to me. A broad expanse of the river was turned to blood; in the middle distance the red hue brightened into gold, through which a solitary log came floating, black and conspicuous; in one place a long, slanting mark lay sparkling upon the water; in another the surface was broken by boiling, tumbling rings that were as many-tinted as an opal[1]; where the ruddy flush was faintest was a smooth spot that was covered with graceful circles and radiating lines, ever so delicately traced; the shore on our left was densely wooded, and the somber shadow that fell from this forest was broken in one place by a long, ruffled trail that shone like silver; and high above the forest wall a clean-stemmed dead tree waved a single leafy bough that glowed like a flame in the unobstructed splendor that was flowing from the sun. There were graceful curves, reflected images, woody heights, soft distances, and over the whole scene, far and near, the dissolving lights drifted steadily, enriching it every passing moment with new marvels of coloring.

I stood like one bewitched. I drank it in, in a speechless rapture. The world was new to me and I had never seen anything like this at home. But as I have said, a day came when I began to cease from noting the glories and the charms which the moon and the sun and the twilight wrought upon the river's face; another day came when I ceased altogether to note them. Then, if that sunset scene had been repeated, I should have looked upon it without rapture and should have commented upon it inwardly after this fashion: "This sun means that we are going to have wind tomorrow; that floating log means that the river is rising, small thanks to it; that slanting mark on the water refers to a bluff reef which is going to kill somebody's steamboat one of these nights, if it keeps on stretching out like that; those tumbling 'boils' show a dissolving bar and a changing channel there; the lines and circles in the slick water over yonder are a warning that that troublesome place is shoaling up dangerously; that silver streak in the shadow of the forest is the 'break' from a new snag and he has located himself in the very best place he could have found to fish for steamboats; that tall dead tree, with a single living branch, is not going to last long, and then how is a body ever going to get through this blind place at night without the friendly old landmark?" 2

No, the romance and beauty were all gone from the river. All the value any feature of it had for me now was the amount of usefulness 3

[1]*opal:* a multicolored, iridescent gemstone.

it could furnish toward compassing the safe piloting of a steamboat. Since those days, I have pitied doctors from my heart. What does the lovely flush in a beauty's cheek mean to a doctor but a "break" that ripples above some deadly disease? Are not all her visible charms sown thick with what are to him the signs and symbols of hidden decay? Does he ever see her beauty at all, or doesn't he simply view her professionally and comment upon her unwholesome condition all to himself? And doesn't he sometimes wonder whether he has gained most or lost most by learning his trade?

Thinking Critically about This Reading

In the opening paragraph Twain exclaims, "All the grace, the beauty, the poetry, had gone out of the majestic river!" What is "the poetry," and why was it lost for him?

Questions for Study and Discussion

1. What method of organization does Twain use in this selection? (Glossary: *Organization*) What alternative methods might he have used? What would have been gained or lost?
2. Explain the analogy that Twain uses in paragraph 3. (Glossary: *Analogy*) What is his purpose in using this analogy?
3. Twain uses a number of similes and metaphors in this selection. (Glossary: *Figure of Speech*) Identify three of each, and explain what Twain is comparing in each case. What do these figures of speech add to Twain's writing?
4. Now that he has learned the trade of steamboating, does Twain feel he has "gained most or lost most" (3)? What has he gained, and what has he lost?
5. Twain points to a change of attitude he underwent as a result of seeing the river from a new perspective, that of a steamboat pilot. What role does knowledge play in Twain's inability to see the river as he once did?

Classroom Activity Using Comparison and Contrast

Compare two places that have the same purpose. For example, compare your college cafeteria with your dining room at home, or the classroom you are in now with another one on campus. Draw up a list of descriptive adjectives for each, and discuss them with your classmates. What do you like about each place? What do you dislike? What do you learn from comparing them? How important are your surroundings to you?

Suggested Writing Assignments

1. Twain's essay contrasts the perception of one person before and after acquiring a particular body of knowledge. Of course, different people usually do perceive the same scene or event differently, even if they are experiencing it simultaneously. To use an example from Twain's writing, a poet and a doctor might perceive a rosy-cheeked young woman in entirely different ways. Write a comparison and contrast essay in which you show how two people with different experience might perceive the same subject. It can be a case of profound difference, such as a musician and an electrician at the same pyrotechnic rock music concert, or more subtle, such as a novelist and a screenwriter seeing the same lovers' quarrel in a restaurant. Add a short postscript in which you explain your choice of subject-by-subject comparison or point-by-point comparison in your essay.
2. Learning how to drive a car may not be as involved as learning how to pilot a steamboat on the Mississippi River, but it still has a tremendous impact on how we function and on how we perceive our surroundings. Write an essay about a short trip you took as a passenger and as a driver. Compare and contrast your perceptions and actions. What is most important to you as a passenger? What is most important to you as a driver? How do your perceptions shift between the two roles? What changes in what you notice around you and in the way you notice it?
3. What perspective does the cartoon on p. 442 give you on Twain's point about his different views of the Mississippi River? Is it possible for two people to have two completely different views of something? How might experience or perspective change how they view something? Write an essay modeled on Twain's in which you offer two different views of an event. You might consider a reporter's view compared with a victim's view, a teacher's view compared with a student's view, or a customer's view compared with a salesclerk's view.

"By George, you'er right! I thought there was something familiar about it."

Mac or PC: There Is Simply No Comparison!

■ Del Miller

Del Miller was born in 1945 in Waynesville, Missouri. He earned his BS in mechanical engineering from the University of Missouri in 1977 and has spent the past twenty-five years in a variety of engineering, sales and marketing, and management positions. He lives in Southern California, and in his spare time designs sensing equipment for materials-testing applications. Miller's experiences with computers led to his writing articles about Apple's Macintosh, the computer platform he favors. Since 1998 Miller's pieces have appeared regularly in the "Difference Engine" column at MacOpinion.com and the "Abacus" column at AppleLinks.com.

In this piece, first published by MacOpinion.com on July 25, 2003, Miller uses comparison and contrast to address the question "Why don't more people buy Macintosh?" His answer might surprise you.

For Your Journal

Do you consider yourself a "Mac person" or a "PC person"—that is, have you been using your computer system long enough to establish what might be called a "relationship" with your machine? Or do you not have a preference or use whichever system is available to you? Would you ever consider using another computer system or one system over the other? Why or why not?

Why don't more people buy Macintosh? Mac fans ask this question all the time it seems, in spite of the fact that each asking prompts a cornucopia[1] of helpful and often not so helpful answers. Perhaps the old saying applies: "When you have lots of different answers, it means none of them are very good." 1

---

[1] *cornucopia:* overflowing, inexhaustible abundance.

Sure, there's probably some validity to everyone's take on the matter. If somebody says Macs are too expensive then that represents at least one data point on the chart. If another claims there is no software for the Macintosh, you can assume that at least someone couldn't find a specific program on the shelf. Others mention lack of upgradeability, the cost of replacing PC software, compatibility or some other reason—and these all likely have some basis in reality. 2

But for those of us who have been using the Macintosh for lo these many years, these reasons don't ring quite true. We inhabit the same planet as the critics, yet we have happily and productively used Apple computers and find that, whatever anyone else says, these drawbacks either don't seem to exist or else are insignificant in light of all the advantages the Macintosh returns. 3

When I look around at what the bulk of the computing public actually uses their computer for, I see absolutely no reason why a significant portion of them couldn't switch to the Macintosh tomorrow and be perfectly pleased with the results. 4

Now I'm not talking about the Slashdotters and the Arsonists and Tom's Hardwarriors and the denizens[2] of other, technical computer forums spread across the Internet. Many of these folks might actually have requirements, or at least some unrequited[3] desire, for computing specifications that disfavor the Mac. These guys and gals (OK, mostly guys) might be programmers or engineers, or at least power users grown up in a system that really doesn't lend itself to an Apple solution. For some of them the economics of web serving or system administration might cause them to conclude that the Macintosh doesn't meet their needs. Debatable points for sure. 5

But if you take all of these technically oriented people and add up their numbers, they wouldn't amount to a significant fraction of the consumer market for computers. Apple could easily grow its customer base tenfold without needing a single computer enthusiast to change his stripes. No, the enormous consumer market is composed of ordinary folks for whom a Macintosh would be a perfectly fine home computer, and many of them would actually be happier with a Mac. 6

Consumers don't care about bus topology or whether the RAM is double data rate or not. They don't know what a SPEC benchmark 7

[2]*denizens:* frequenters of a particular place.
[3]*unrequited:* unreturned or unsatisfied.

is, and I doubt most could tell you the clock rate of their CPU. What they do want is for their computer to serve their needs and not break. They want it to be a good value. For this, Macintoshes positively shine.

So Why Don't More Consumers Buy Macintosh?

The consumers that make up the pig-in-the-python part of the bell curve primarily use a web browser and an email client and they aren't terribly picky about either one. Good grief, millions use the AOL browser, so how demanding could they be? These people don't wait up for the nightly Mozilla builds to make sure they are operating with the latest browser technology, or fuss at length about some obscure email feature so that Aunt Edna knows how the kids are doing. 8

What else does the average Joe need for his computing pleasure? A word processor, of course, but Microsoft Word works just fine on a Macintosh, and even that is such extravagant overkill for most people as to be comical. The typical person doesn't need, use, or is even aware of annotations, style sheets, or ninety percent of the bells and whistles that Word offers. The functionality needed by all but a few people is available for free with Appleworks, which can open and save Word documents anyway. 9

Excel? Please. Excel is a wonderful program and I'm a bona fide power user. But the percentage of people that make use of even a fraction of Excel's features disappears into the demographic haze. Appleworks' spreadsheet would do practically everyone just fine. 10

Tax programs? The Macs got 'em. Drawing programs? The same. You can go down the list for days and the answer is nearly always identical—the Macintosh can easily do what the majority of computer users need it to do, and can do it as well as any PC and ofttimes better. 11

But wait, what about the cost of replacing all those Windows pro grams with Macintosh equivalents? Apple bundles all kinds of nifty software with each iMac, software of just the sort that a consumer needs. For most people additional software expense is not necessary because the really necessary stuff comes with the computer—for free. Specialty software is most often available for a cross-platform upgrade fee and generally speaking, if you need to upgrade your computer it's probably time to upgrade your most treasured software. Besides, the average consumer doesn't use Photoshop or AutoCad or really pricy programs anyway. There just isn't that much they need to upgrade. 12

Games

But then there's games, and we all know that the hot new games come out first and sometimes only for PCs. This is seen by many as the reason why Macintoshes can't break out of their niche. But this doesn't really make a lot of sense either. 13

Now I know that many of you might find this astoundingly difficult to believe, but there are a huge number of people who do *not* play computer games—really, it's true. These sad cases do other things with their lives besides run mazes and shoot demons. 'Tis a pity, I know, but for these people the vast arsenal of PC games holds no attraction. 14

Of the households who do play computer games close to half of them have a console for the purpose. If you have a Playstation in the house, you might as well have a Macintosh as your computer. Besides, it's not like there isn't a very large assortment of games for the Macintosh as well. 15

In other words, over half the households in the United States, and a significantly higher percentage worldwide, don't need a rip-snorting PC to play games. If even a tiny fraction of these people chose a Macintosh it could triple Apple's market share. 16

Money

And we all know that Macintoshes are more expensive than PCs. Well not exactly: It is more accurate to say that Apple machines are more competitive in some price ranges and in some configurations than in others. But for an all-purpose computer with the features and qualities that many households would find both useful and attractive, the iMac or an eMac is hard to beat. 17

Now, anyone can look up some vendor's pricelists and construct a comparison that shows whatever one wants to show. This game is constantly played on bulletin board battlegrounds all over the web, and I'll not try to settle this issue here. 18

Did your next-door neighbors buy the cheapest car on the lot? Did they buy their clothes at a thrift store? Probably not. In fact, if you look around you'll see that people will consistently pay more for a better experience—it is the rule not the exception. There's no reason to believe that consumers would avoid the Mac because of price, if they thought it would serve them better. 19

Suffice it to say that there are a vast number of consumers that have no particular need to choose a PC over a Macintosh. Going a bit further let's say there is a significant fraction that would actually be happier with a Mac if they would only give it a try. So what keeps them from choosing Apple? 20

So Why Don't More People Buy Macintosh?

The answer is simply this: People don't even look at the Macintosh as an option. 21

When the typical consumer decides to buy a new computer, the Macintosh is seldom even considered—*there is simply no comparison* performed. 22

I've seen it dozens of times: A friend or relative mentions buying a computer and describes a range of uses that almost define a Macintosh. So I ask, "Have you considered looking at a Mac?" 23

The reply is . . . well, there isn't a reply, generally. What I normally get is a slight frown and a glazed eyeball, wary expression of something like incomprehension; as if I had suggested that they smear butter all over their bodies. 24

There is seldom a definable objection and certainly not a reasoned and knowledgeable discussion of the technical merits of the Windows operating system. The decision to buy the PC has nothing to do with a purchasing matrix,[4] and even if Macintoshes were cheaper than PCs, had higher clock rates, included every piece of software the buyer would ever need, and vacuumed the rug every Saturday, the decision would still be the same. 25

No, for most people, the Macintosh is just not a consideration. In the eyes of the masses, a computer is perceived as something like what sits on their desk at work, or what their brother-in-law Elroy has. A *computer* has a **Start** button. 26

Simply No Comparison

I laugh when I hear people suggest that Apple should change its advertising to focus on features and specifications. Sure, four percent 27

[4]*purchasing matrix:* a checklist of pros and cons consumers use to narrow their choices when planning to buy something.

of the population would really care about such things, while the rest would slip into a mild coma. For the biggest chunk of the consumer market, *there is simply no comparison* performed of any kind and a technical description as long as your arm isn't going to sell computers if no one bothers to compare the data.

So how does Apple convince a non-technical, risk-averse, late-adopting, reluctant-to-compare public to seriously consider switching to a Macintosh? 28

Apple Computer's "Switch" campaign was designed to get the public's attention and to simply open their minds to the possibility of buying a Macintosh. The message is, "Buy a Mac and you'll be happy." In the final analysis, that's what people really want. 29

Those Apple retail stores weren't located in the fancy-shmancy shopping malls by accident either. Those are the venues where people shop for the finer things, and Apple is trying to make that association crystal clear. 30

"The Digital Hub" is pushed as a lifestyle enhancer, something for which people generally have a soft spot in their wallet. This, like the rest of Apple's marketing scheme, is not about competing feature for feature against PCs, it's a flank attack on the psychology of a buying public that is reluctant to compare. 31

But will it work? The latest market-share numbers seem to say no, but it's still early in the game. If the public begins to embrace Apple's suggestion that they will be happier with a Macintosh, the numbers should start to turn around within the next year. 32

If so, then Apple's marketing campaign will be taught in business schools for the next fifty years. 33

Thinking Critically about This Reading

How does Miller support his claim that "the Macintosh can easily do what the majority of computer users need it to do, and can do it as well as any PC and ofttimes better" (paragraph 11)?

Questions for Study and Discussion

1. What is Miller's purpose? (Glossary: *Purpose*) In your estimation, does he accomplish what he sets out to do? Explain.

2. Who is Miller's audience? (Glossary: *Audience*) What is his attitude toward his subject? (Glossary: *Attitude*) What in his essay leads you to these conclusions?
3. On what points does Miller compare Macs and PCs? How does he select his points of comparison, and how does he organize them? (Glossary: *Organization*)
4. According to Miller, how does the American public buy computers? What does he say is the real answer to the question "Why don't more people buy Macintosh?"
5. Miller does not provide readers with a long checklist of detailed information about comparable features and specifications for the Mac and PC. What kinds of information does he provide in his comparison? How does knowing his purpose and intended audience help you understand the strategy behind his comparison? (Glossary: *Purpose; Audience*) Explain.
6. What were your expectations when you first read Miller's title? (Glossary: *Title*) What does the title mean to you now that you have read his article? Explain.

Classroom Activity Using Comparison and Contrast

Carefully read and analyze the following paragraph from Suzanne Britt's "That Lean and Hungry Look," an essay that first appeared in *Newsweek* and later became the basis for her book *Skinny People Are Dull and Crunchy like Carrots* (1982). Then answer the questions that follow.

> Some people say the business about the jolly fat person is a myth, that all of us chubbies are neurotic, sick, sad people. I disagree. Fat people may not be chortling all day long, but they're a hell of a lot *nicer* than the wizened and shriveled. Thin people turn surly, mean, and hard at a young age because they never learn the value of a hot-fudge sundae for easing tension. Thin people don't like gooey soft things because they themselves are neither gooey nor soft. They are crunchy and dull, like carrots. They go straight to the heart of the matter while fat people let things stay all blurry and hazy and vague, the way things actually are. Thin people want to face the truth. Fat people know there is no truth. One of my thin friends is always staring at complex, unsolvable problems and saying, "The key thing is. . . ." Fat people never say that. They know there isn't any such thing as the key thing about anything.

What is the point of Britt's paragraph? How does she use comparison and contrast to make this point? How does Britt organize her paragraph?

Suggested Writing Assignments

1. What role do computers play in your daily life? Do you take class notes on a computer? Do you e-mail your friends and family? Do you access the Internet for academic purposes? Nonacademic purposes? Do you think computers are indispensable tools for today's students? Why or why not? Using examples from your own experiences and observations, write an essay in which you compare the life of a student before computers with the life of a student after computers.
2. Many educators believe that Americans have been too quick to jump on the technology bandwagon. They question whether computers, the Internet, and interactive learning toys add up to a better education and quicker access to accurate information, success, and wealth. As Thomas L. Friedman reminds us in "My Favorite Teacher" (p. 365), "The real secret of success in the information age is what it always was: fundamentals—reading, writing and arithmetic, church, synagogue and mosque, the rule of law, and good governance" (paragraph 10). Write an essay in which you argue for an educational program that would allow today's students to harness the power of computers and the Internet and not be overwhelmed by disconnected information.

A Battle of Cultures

K. Connie Kang

K. Connie Kang was born in Korea in 1942 but grew up in Japan and the United States. After graduating from the School of Journalism at the University of Missouri, Kang went on to earn a master of science degree from the Medill School of Journalism at Northwestern University. During more than three decades in journalism, this award-winning newspaperwoman has worked as a reporter, editor, foreign correspondent, columnist, and editorial writer for the San Francisco Examiner, *the* San Francisco Chronicle, *and United Press International. Currently, she is a reporter for the* Los Angeles Times. *Kang's career began in June 1964, when there were only a handful of Asians in the metropolitan newsrooms in the United States. Always mindful of her Asian heritage, she wrote about Asians and the issues affecting their communities long before they were considered newsworthy. In 1995, she published* Home Was the Land of Morning Calm: A Saga of a Korean American Family.

The following essay, which first appeared in Asian Week *in May 1990, reminds us that we need both "cultural insight" and understanding if we are to "make democracy work" in a multicultural society. Notice how Kang uses comparison and contrast when presenting aspects of Korean and African American cultures to demonstrate her point.*

For Your Journal

People of different ethnic, racial, and cultural backgrounds sometimes find it difficult to achieve a common ground of understanding. What suggestions do you have for what we can do, either personally or through our institutions, to increase understanding? Rather than composing an answer, make a list of several suggestions that you would like to contribute to a classroom discussion.

A volatile inner-city drama is taking place in New York where blacks have been boycotting[1] Korean groceries for four months. 1

[1] *boycotting:* refusing to patronize in order to express disapproval.

The recent attack on three Vietnamese men by a group of blacks who mistook them for Koreans has brought this long-simmering tension between two minority groups to the world's attention. Korean newspapers from San Francisco to Seoul have been running front-page stories. Non-Asian commentators around the country, whose knowledge of Korea may not be much more than images from the Korean War and the ridiculous television series *M.A.S.H.*,[2] are making all sorts of comments. 2

As I see it, the problem in the Flatbush area of Brooklyn started with cultural misunderstanding and was compounded by a lack of bilingual and bicultural community leaders to intervene quickly. 3

Frictions between Korean store owners in New York and blacks had been building for years. Korean merchants have been complaining about thefts. On the other hand, their black customers have been accusing immigrant store owners of making money in their neighborhoods without putting anything back into the community. They have also complained about store owners being brusque.[3] Over the past eight years, there have been sporadic boycotts but none has lasted as long as the current one, which stemmed from an accusation by a black customer in January that she had been attacked by a store employee. In defense, the store owner has said the employee caught the woman stealing. 4

The attack on the Vietnamese on May 13 wasn't the first time one group of Asians has been mistaken for another in America. But the publicity surrounding the case has made this unfortunate situation a case study in inter-ethnic tension. 5

What's missing in this inner-city drama is cultural insight. 6

What struck me more than anything was a recent remark by a black resident: "The Koreans are a very, very rude people. They don't understand you have to smile." 7

I wondered whether her reaction would have been the same, had she known that Koreans don't smile at Koreans either without a reason. To a Korean, a smile is not a facial expression he can turn on and off mechanically. Koreans have a word for it—*mu-ttuk-ttuk-hada* (stiff). In other words, the Korean demeanor is *myu-po-jung*—lack of expression. 8

[2]*M.A.S.H.* (mobile army surgical unit): a popular U.S. television series set in Korea during the Korean War (1950–1953) that aired in 1972–1983.

[3]*brusque:* rude; blunt.

It would be an easy thing for blacks who are naturally friendly and gregarious[4] to misunderstand Korean ways. 9

As a Korean American I've experienced this many times. Whenever I'm in Korea, which is often, I'm chided for smiling too much. "Why do you smile so easily? You act like a Westerner," people tell me. My inclination is to retort: "Why do you always have to look like you've got indigestion?" But I restrain myself because I know better. 10

In our culture, a smile is reserved for people we know and for a proper occasion. Herein lies a big problem when newcomers from Korea begin doing business in America's poor inner-city neighborhoods. 11

Culturally and socially, many newcomers from Korea, like other Asian immigrants, are ill-equipped to run businesses in America's inner cities. But because they are denied entry into mainstream job markets, they pool resources and open mom-and-pop operations in the only places where they can afford it. They work 14 and 15 hours a day, seven days a week, dreaming of the day when their children will graduate from prestigious schools and make their sacrifices worthwhile. 12

From the other side, inner-city African Americans must wonder how these new immigrants find the money to run their own businesses, when they themselves can't even get a small loan from a bank. Their hope of getting out of the poverty cycle is grim, yet they see newcomers living in better neighborhoods and driving new cars. 13

"They ask me, 'Where do you people get the money to buy a business?' " Bong-jae Jang, owner of one of the grocery stores being boycotted, told me. "How can I explain to my neighbors in my poor English the concept of our family system, the idea of 'kye' (uniquely Korean private money-lending system), our way of life?" 14

I think a little learning is in order on both sides. Korean immigrants, like other newcomers, need orientation before they leave their country as well as when they arrive in the United States. It's also important for Korean immigrants, like other Asians who live in the United States, to realize that they are indebted to blacks for the social gains won by their civil rights struggle. They face less discrimination today because blacks have paved the way. Instead of looking down on their culture, it would be constructive to learn their history, literature, music and values and see our African American brothers and sisters in their full humanity. 15

[4]*gregarious:* sociable.

I think it is also important to remind ourselves that while the Confucian culture[5] has taught us how to be good parents, sons, and daughters and how to behave with people we know, it has not prepared us for living in a democracy. The Confucian ethos[6] lacks the value of social conscience, which makes democracy work. 16

It isn't enough that we think of educating our children and send them to the best schools. We need to think of other peoples' children, too. Most of all, we need to be more tolerant of other peoples' cultures. We need to celebrate our similarities as well as our differences. 17

Jang, the grocer, told me this experience has been painful but he has learned an important lesson. "We Koreans must learn to participate in this society," he said. "When this is over, I'm going to reach out. I want to give part-time work to black youths." 18

He also told me that he has been keeping a journal. "I'm not a writer but I've been keeping a journal," he said. "I want to write about this experience someday. It may help someone." 19

By reaching out, we can make a difference. The Korean grocer's lesson is a reminder to us all that making democracy work in a multicultural society is difficult but we have no choice but to strive for it. 20

Thinking Critically about This Reading

Does Kang herself resort to racial stereotypes when she states, "It would be an easy thing for blacks who are naturally friendly and gregarious to misunderstand Korean ways" (paragraph 9). Explain.

Questions for Study and Discussion

1. What is the "battle of cultures" named in the title? (Glossary: *Title*) How are the contrasts between the cultures helping to cause the "battle," according to Kang? (Glossary: *Cause and Effect*) What specific differences does she identify in her comparison and contrast analysis of the situation?
2. What is Kang's thesis? (Glossary: *Thesis*) How does her use of comparison and contrast help her argue her thesis?

---

[5]*Confucian culture:* the traditions based on the ideas of Confucius (551–479 B.C.E.), China's most famous and influential teacher, philosopher, and political theorist.
[6]*ethos:* guiding beliefs of a person, group, or institution.

3. Why are the Korean grocery stores being boycotted by African American customers?
4. Why are most Asian immigrants ill-equipped to run businesses in the inner cities of the United States, according to Kang? Why are they indebted to African Americans?
5. How does Kang's point of view contribute to the effectiveness of the essay? (Glossary: *Point of View*)
6. What is it about their culture that makes it difficult for Koreans to adapt to life in a multicultural society, according to Kang?

Classroom Activity Using Comparison and Contrast

After reviewing the discussion of analogy in the introduction to this chapter (pp. 436–37), create an analogy to explain your relationship with one of your parents or with a relative.

Suggested Writing Assignments

1. Choose an ethnic group other than your own that lives in or near your home community. Using Kang's essay as a model, compare and/or contrast its culture with your own. What could you do to understand the other culture better? How would you describe relations between the two groups?
2. Choose a country that you have studied, visited, or read about. Compare who you are now with who you think you would be if you had been born and raised in that country. How do you think you would be different? Why?

Grant and Lee: A Study in Contrasts

■ Bruce Catton

Bruce Catton (1899–1978) was born in Petoskey, Michigan, and attended Oberlin College. Early in his career, Catton worked as a reporter for various newspapers, among them the Cleveland Plain Dealer. *Having an interest in history, Catton became a leading authority on the Civil War and published a number of books on this subject, including* Mr. Lincoln's Army *(1951),* Glory Road *(1952),* A Stillness at Appomattox *(1953),* The Hallowed Ground *(1956),* The Coming Fury *(1961),* Never Call Retreat *(1966), and* Gettysburg: The Final Fury *(1974). Catton was awarded both the Pulitzer Prize and the National Book Award in 1954.*

The following selection was included in The American Story: The Age of Exploration to the Age of the Atom *(1956), a collection of historical essays edited by Earl Schenk Miers. In it Catton considers "two great Americans, Grant and Lee—very different, yet under everything very much alike." As you read, pay particular attention to the way Catton organizes his essay of comparison and contrast and how this organization helps readers follow Catton's thinking.*

For Your Journal

Do a brief freewrite about the Civil War generals Ulysses S. Grant and Robert E. Lee. What do you know about each man and his respective role in the war? What images do you have, and what stories have you heard about each one?

When Ulysses S. Grant[1] and Robert E. Lee[2] met in the parlor of a modest house at Appomattox Court House, Virginia, on April 9, 1865, to work out the terms for the surrender of Lee's Army of Northern Virginia, a great chapter in American life came to a close, and a great new chapter began. 1

These men were bringing the Civil War to its virtual finish. To be sure, other armies had yet to surrender, and for a few days the fugitive Confederate government[3] would struggle desperately and vainly, trying to find some way to go on living now that its chief support was gone. But in effect it was all over when Grant and Lee signed the papers. And the little room where they wrote out the terms was the scene of one of the poignant,[4] dramatic contrasts in American history. 2

They were two strong men, these oddly different generals, and they represented the strengths of two conflicting currents that, through them, had come into final collision. 3

Back of Robert E. Lee was the notion that the old aristocratic concept might somehow survive and be dominant in American life. 4

Lee was tidewater Virginia, and in his background were family, culture, and tradition . . . the age of chivalry[5] transplanted to a New World which was making its own legends and its own myths. He embodied a way of life that had come down through the age of knighthood and the English country squire. America was a land that was beginning all over again, dedicated to nothing much more complicated than the rather hazy belief that all men had equal rights and should have an equal chance in the world. In such a land Lee stood for the feeling that it was somehow of advantage to human society to have a pronounced inequality in the social structure. There should be a leisure class, backed by ownership of land; in turn, society itself should be keyed to the land as the chief source of wealth and influence. It would bring forth (according to this ideal) a class of men with a strong sense of obligation to the 5

---

[1]*Ulysses S. Grant* (1822–1885): commander of the Union armies during the late years (1864–1865) of the American Civil War, and eighteenth president of the United States (1869–1877).

[2]*Robert E. Lee* (1807–1870): Confederate general, commander of the Army of Northern Virginia, the most successful of the Southern armies during the American Civil War (1861–1865).

[3]*Confederate government:* also called the Confederacy, the American Civil War government of 11 Southern states that seceded from the Union.

[4]*poignant:* touching; emotional.

[5]*chivalry:* values of courtesy, valor, and civility associated with medieval knights.

community; men who lived not to gain advantage for themselves, but to meet the solemn obligations which had been laid on them by the very fact that they were privileged. From them the country would get its leadership; to them it could look for the higher values—of thought, of conduct, of personal deportment—to give it strength and virtue.

Lee embodied the noblest elements of this aristocratic ideal. 6
Through him, the landed nobility justified itself. For four years, the Southern states had fought a desperate war to uphold the ideals for which Lee stood. In the end, it almost seemed as if the Confederacy fought for Lee; as if he himself was the Confederacy . . . the best thing that the way of life for which the Confederacy stood could ever have to offer. He had passed into legend before Appomattox.[6] Thousands of tired, underfed, poorly clothed Confederate soldiers, long since past the simple enthusiasm of the early days of the struggle, somehow considered Lee the symbol of everything for which they had been willing to die. But they could not quite put this feeling into words. If the Lost Cause, sanctified by so much heroism and so many deaths, had a living justification, its justification was General Lee.

Grant, the son of a tanner on the Western frontier, was everything 7
Lee was not. He had come up the hard way and embodied nothing in particular except the eternal toughness and sinewy[7] fiber of the men who grew up beyond the mountains. He was one of a body of men who owed reverence and obeisance[8] to no one, who were self-reliant to a fault, who cared hardly anything for the past but who had a sharp eye for the future.

These frontier men were the precise opposite of the tidewater aris- 8
tocrats. Back of them, in the great surge that had taken people over the Alleghenies and into the opening Western country, there was a deep, implicit dissatisfaction with a past that had settled into grooves. They stood for democracy, not from any reasoned conclusion about the proper ordering of human society, but simply because they had grown up in the middle of democracy and knew how it worked. Their society might have privileges, but they would be privileges each man had won for himself. Forms and patterns meant nothing. No man was born to anything, except perhaps to a chance to show how far he could rise. Life was competition.

[6]*Appomattox:* a town in Virginia, site of the courthouse where the Confederate forces surrendered on April 9, 1865.
[7]*sinewy:* strong; tough.
[8]*obeisance:* deference; homage.

Yet along with this feeling had come a deep sense of belonging to a national community. The Westerner who developed a farm, opened a shop, or set up in business as a trader, could hope to prosper only as his own community prospered—and his community ran from the Atlantic to the Pacific and from Canada down to Mexico. If the land was settled, with towns and highways and accessible markets, he could better himself. He saw his fate in terms of the nation's own destiny. As its horizons expanded, so did his. He had, in other words, an acute dollars-and-cents stake in the continued growth and development of his country. 9

And that, perhaps, is where the contrast between Grant and Lee becomes most striking. The Virginia aristocrat, inevitably, saw himself in relation to his own region. He lived in a static society which could endure almost anything except change. Instinctively, his first loyalty would go to the locality in which that society existed. He would fight to the limit of endurance to defend it, because in defending it he was defending everything that gave his own life its deepest meaning. 10

The Westerner, on the other hand, would fight with an equal tenacity[9] for the broader concept of society. He fought so because everything he lived by was tied to growth, expansion, and a constantly widening horizon. What he lived by would survive or fall with the nation itself. He could not possibly stand by unmoved in the face of an attempt to destroy the Union.[10] He would combat it with everything he had, because he could only see it as an effort to cut the ground out from under his feet. 11

So Grant and Lee were in complete contrast, representing two diametrically opposed elements in American life. Grant was the modern man emerging; beyond him, ready to come on the stage, was the great age of steel and machinery, of crowded cities and a restless burgeoning vitality. Lee might have ridden down from the old age of chivalry, lance in hand, silken banner fluttering over his head. Each man was the perfect champion of his cause, drawing both his strengths and his weaknesses from the people he led. 12

Yet it was not all contrast, after all. Different as they were—in background, in personality, in underlying aspiration—these two great soldiers had much in common. Under everything else, they were marvelous fighters. Furthermore, their fighting qualities were really very much alike. 13

Each man had, to begin with, the great virtue of utter tenacity and fidelity. Grant fought his way down the Mississippi Valley in spite 14

[9]*tenacity:* persistence; stubbornness.
[10]*Union:* the federal government of the United States.

of acute personal discouragement and profound military handicaps. Lee hung on in the trenches at Petersburg after hope itself had died. In each man there was an indomitable quality . . . the born fighter's refusal to give up as long as he can still remain on his feet and lift his two fists.

Daring and resourcefulness they had, too; the ability to think 15
faster and move faster than the enemy. These were the qualities which gave Lee the dazzling campaigns of Second Manassas and Chancellorsville and won Vicksburg[11] for Grant.

Lastly, and perhaps greatest of all, there was the ability, at the end, 16
to turn quickly from war to peace once the fighting was over. Out of the way these two men behaved at Appomattox came the possibility of a peace of reconciliation. It was a possibility not wholly realized, in the years to come, but which did, in the end, help the two sections to become one nation again . . . after a war whose bitterness might have seemed to make such a reunion wholly impossible. No part of either man's life became him more than the part he played in their brief meeting in the McLean house[12] at Appomattox. Their behavior there put all succeeding generations of Americans in their debt. Two great Americans, Grant and Lee—very different, yet under everything very much alike. Their encounter at Appomattox was one of the great moments of American history.

Thinking Critically about This Reading

What do you think Catton means when he claims that Grant was "the modern man emerging" (paragraph 12)? How does he support this statement?

Questions for Study and Discussion

1. In paragraphs 10–12 Catton discusses what he considers to be the most striking contrast between Grant and Lee. What is that difference?
2. List the similarities that Catton sees between Grant and Lee. What similarity does Catton believe is most important? Why?

---

[11] *Second Manassas, Chancellorsville, Vicksburg:* significant battles during the American Civil War.

[12] *McLean house:* the specific building of the Appomattox Court House in which Lee formally surrendered to Grant.

3. What would have been lost had Catton compared Grant and Lee before contrasting them? Would anything have been gained?
4. How does Catton organize the body of his essay—paragraphs 3–16? (Glossary: *Organization*) You may find it helpful in answering this question to summarize the point of comparison in each paragraph and label it as being concerned with Lee, Grant, or both.
5. What attitudes and ideas does Catton describe to support the view that tidewater Virginia was a throwback to the "age of chivalry" (5)? (Glossary: *Attitude*)
6. Catton constructs clear transitions between paragraphs. (Glossary: *Transition*) Identify the transitional devices he uses. How do they help you read the essay?

Classroom Activity Using Comparison and Contrast

In preparation for writing an essay of comparison and contrast on two world leaders (or popular singers, actors, or sports figures), write out answers to the following questions:

Who could I compare and contrast?
What is my purpose?
Are their similarities or differences more interesting?
What specific points should I discuss?
What organizational pattern will best suit my purpose: subject-by-subject or point-by-point?

Suggested Writing Assignments

1. Using your answers to the Classroom Activity as your starting point, write an essay in which you compare and contrast any two world leaders (or popular singers, actors, or sports figures).
2. Select one of the following topics, and write an essay of comparison and contrast:

two cities	two sections of the town you live in
two friends	two books by the same author
two cars	two ways to heat a home
two restaurants	two teachers
two mountains	two brands of pizza

chapter **19**

Cause and Effect

Every time you try to answer a question that asks *why*, you engage in the process of *causal analysis*—you attempt to determine a *cause* or series of causes for a particular *effect*. When you try to answer a question that asks *what if*, you attempt to determine what *effect* will result from a particular *cause*. You will have frequent opportunity to use **cause-and-effect analysis** in the writing you will do in college. For example, in history you might be asked to determine the causes for the 1991 breakup of the former Soviet Union; in political science you might be asked to determine the critical issues in the 2004 presidential election; in sociology you might be asked to analyze the effects that the AIDS epidemic has had on sexual-behavior patterns among Americans; and in economics you might be asked to predict what will happen to our country if we enact large tax cuts.

Fascinated by the effects that private real estate development was having on his neighborhood, a student writer decided to find out what was happening in the older sections of cities across the country. In his first paragraph, Kevin Cunningham describes three possible effects (or fates) of a city's aging. In his second paragraph, he singles out one effect, redevelopment, and discusses in detail the impact it has had on Hoboken, New Jersey.

Effect: decay

Effect: urban renewal

Effect: redevelopment

Effects of redevelopment

One of three fates awaits the aging neighborhood. Decay may continue until the neighborhood becomes a slum. It may face urban renewal, with old buildings being razed and ugly new apartment houses taking their place. Or it may undergo redevelopment, in which government encourages the upgrading of existing housing stock by offering low-interest loans or outright grants; thus, the original character of the neighborhood may be retained or restored, allowing the city to keep part of its identity.

> An example of redevelopment at its best is Hoboken, New Jersey. In the early 1970s Hoboken was a dying city, with rundown housing and many abandoned buildings. However, low-interest loans enabled some younger residents to refurbish their homes, and soon the area began to show signs of renewed vigor. Even outsiders moved in and rebuilt some of the abandoned houses. Today, whole blocks have been restored, and neighborhood life is active again. The city does well, too, because property values are higher and so are property taxes.
>
> –Kevin Cunningham, student

Determining causes and effects is usually thought-provoking and quite complex. One reason for this is that there are two types of causes: *immediate causes,* which are readily apparent because they are closest to the effect, and *ultimate causes,* which, being somewhat removed, are not as apparent and may perhaps even be hidden. Furthermore, ultimate causes may bring about effects which themselves become immediate causes, thus creating a *causal chain.* Consider the following causal chain: Sally, a computer salesperson, prepared extensively for a meeting with an important client (ultimate cause), impressed the client (immediate cause), and made a very large sale (effect). The chain did not stop there: The large sale caused her to be promoted by her employer (effect). For a detailed example of a causal chain, read Barry Commoner's analysis of the near disaster at the Three Mile Island nuclear facility in Chapter 5 (pp. 110–11).

A second reason causal analysis can be so complex is that an effect may have any number of possible or actual causes, and a cause may have any number of possible or actual effects. An upset stomach may be caused by eating spoiled food, but it may also be caused by overeating, flu, allergy, nervousness, pregnancy, or any combination of factors. Similarly, the high cost of electricity may have multiple effects: higher profits for utility companies, fewer sales of electrical appliances, higher prices for other products, and the development of alternative sources of energy.

Sound reasoning and logic, while present in all good writing, are central to any causal analysis. Writers of believable causal analysis examine their material objectively and develop their essays carefully. They examine methodically all causes and effects and evaluate them. They are convinced by their own examination of the material but are not afraid to admit other possible causes and effects. Above all, they do not let their own prejudices interfere with the logic of their analyses and presentations.

Because people are accustomed to thinking of causes with their effects, they sometimes commit an error in logic known as the "after this, therefore because of this" fallacy (in Latin, *post hoc, ergo propter hoc*). This **logical fallacy** leads people to believe that because one event occurred after another event, the first event somehow caused the second; that is, they sometimes make causal connections that are not proven. For example, if students began to perform better after a free breakfast program was instituted at their school, one could not assume that the improvement was caused by the breakfast program. There could, of course, be any number of other causes for this effect, and a responsible writer would analyze and consider them all before suggesting the cause.

Why We Crave Horror Movies

Stephen King

Stephen King's name is synonymous with horror stories. Born in 1947, King is a 1970 graduate of the University of Maine. He worked as a janitor in a knitting mill, a laundry worker, and a high school English teacher before he struck it big with his writing. Many consider King to be the most successful writer of modern horror fiction today. To date, he has written dozens of novels, collections of short stories and novellas, and screenplays, among other works. His books have sold well over 250 million copies worldwide, and many of his novels have been made into popular motion pictures, including Stand by Me, Misery, The Green Mile, *and* Dreamcatcher. *His books, starting with* Carrie *in 1974, include* Salem's Lot *(1975),* The Shining *(1977),* The Dead Zone *(1979),* Christine *(1983),* Pet Sematary *(1983),* The Dark Half *(1989),* The Girl Who Loved Tom Gordon *(1999),* From a Buick 8 *(2002), and* Everything's Eventual: Five Dark Tales *(2002), his first collection of short stories in nine years. Other works of his include* Danse Macabre *(1980), a nonfiction look at horror in the media, and* On Writing: A Memoir of the Craft *(2000). The widespread popularity of horror books and films attests to the fact that many people share King's fascination with the macabre.*

In the following selection, originally published in Playboy *in 1982, a variation on "The Horror Movie as Junk Food" chapter in* Danse Macabre, *King analyzes the reasons we flock to good horror movies.*

For Your Journal

What movies have you seen recently? Do you prefer watching any particular kind of movie—comedy, drama, science fiction, or horror, for example—more than others? How do you explain your preference?

I think that we're all mentally ill; those of us outside the asylums only hide it a little better—and maybe not all that much better, after all. 1

We've all known people who talk to themselves, people who sometimes squinch their faces into horrible grimaces when they believe no one is watching, people who have some hysterical fear—of snakes, the dark, the tight place, the long drop ... and, of course, those final worms and grubs that are waiting so patiently underground.

When we pay our four or five bucks and seat ourselves at tenth-row center in a theater showing a horror movie, we are daring the nightmare. 2

Why? Some of the reasons are simple and obvious. To show that we can, that we are not afraid, that we can ride this roller coaster. Which is not to say that a really good horror movie may not surprise a scream out of us at some point, the way we may scream when a roller coaster twists through a complete 360 or plows through a lake at the bottom of the drop. And horror movies, like roller coasters, have always been the special province of the young; by the time one turns 40 or 50, one's appetite for double twists or 360-degree loops may be considerably depleted. 3

We also go to re-establish our feelings of essential normality; the horror movie is innately conservative, even reactionary. Freda Jackson as the horrible melting woman in *Die, Monster, Die!* confirms for us that no matter how far we may be removed from the beauty of a Robert Redford or a Diana Ross, we are still light-years from true ugliness. 4

And we go to have fun. 5

Ah, but this is where the ground starts to slope away, isn't it? Because this is a very peculiar sort of fun, indeed. The fun comes from seeing others menaced—sometimes killed. One critic has suggested that if pro football has become the voyeur's[1] version of combat, then the horror film has become the modern version of the public lynching. 6

It is true that the mythic, "fairy-tale" horror film intends to take away the shades of gray.... It urges us to put away our more civilized and adult penchant for analysis and to become children again, seeing things in pure blacks and whites. It may be that horror movies provide psychic relief on this level because this invitation to lapse into simplicity, irrationality and even outright madness is extended so rarely. We are told we may allow our emotions a free rein ... or no rein at all. 7

[1] *voyeur:* one who observes from a distance.

If we are all insane, then sanity becomes a matter of degree. If your insanity leads you to carve up women like Jack the Ripper or the Cleveland Torso Murderer,[2] we clap you away in the funny farm (but neither of those two amateur-night surgeons was ever caught, heh-heh-heh); if, on the other hand, your insanity leads you only to talk to yourself when you're under stress or to pick your nose on your morning bus, then you are left alone to go about your business . . . though it is doubtful that you will ever be invited to the best parties. 8

The potential lyncher is in almost all of us (excluding saints, past and present; but then, most saints have been crazy in their own ways), and every now and then, he has to be let loose to scream and roll around in the grass. Our emotions and our fears form their own body, and we recognize that it demands its own exercise to maintain proper muscle tone. Certain of these emotional muscles are accepted—even exalted—in civilized society; they are, of course, the emotions that tend to maintain the status quo of civilization itself. Love, friendship, loyalty, kindness—these are all the emotions that we applaud, emotions that have been immortalized in the couplets of Hallmark cards and in the verses (I don't dare call it poetry) of Leonard Nimoy.[3] 9

When we exhibit these emotions, society showers us with positive reinforcement; we learn this even before we get out of diapers. When, as children, we hug our rotten little puke of a sister and give her a kiss, all the aunts and uncles smile and twit and cry, "Isn't he the sweetest little thing?" Such coveted treats as chocolate-covered graham crackers often follow. But if we deliberately slam the rotten little puke of a sister's fingers in the door, sanctions follow—angry remonstrance from parents, aunts, and uncles; instead of a chocolate-covered graham cracker, a spanking. 10

But anticivilization emotions don't go away, and they demand periodic exercise. We have such "sick" jokes as, "What's the difference between a truckload of bowling balls and a truckload of dead babies? (You can't unload a truckload of bowling balls with a pitchfork . . . a joke, by the way, that I heard originally from a ten-year-old). Such a joke may surprise a laugh or a grin out of us even as we recoil, a possibility that confirms the thesis: if we share a brotherhood of 11

---

[2]*Jack the Ripper, Cleveland Torso Murderer:* serial murderers who were active in the 1880s and the 1930s, respectively.

[3]*Leonard Nimoy* (b. 1931): actor famous for playing Mr. Spock on the U.S. television series *Star Trek,* which aired in 1966–1969.

man, then we also share an insanity of man. None of which is intended as a defense of either the sick joke or insanity but merely as an explanation of why the best horror films, like the best fairy tales, manage to be reactionary, anarchistic,[4] and revolutionary all at the same time.

The mythic horror movie, like the sick joke, has a dirty job to do. It deliberately appeals to all that is worst in us. It is morbidity unchained, our most base instincts let free, our nastiest fantasies realized . . . and it all happens, fittingly enough, in the dark. For those reasons, good liberals often shy away from horror films. For myself, I like to see the most aggressive of them—*Dawn of the Dead,* for instance—as lifting a trap door in the civilized forebrain and throwing a basket of raw meat to the hungry alligators swimming around in that subterranean river beneath. 12

Why bother? Because it keeps them from getting out, man. It keeps them down there and me up here. It was Lennon and McCartney who said that all you need is love, and I would agree with that. 13

As long as you keep the gators fed. 14

Thinking Critically about This Reading

What does King mean when he states that "the horror movie is innately conservative, even reactionary" (paragraph 4)?

Questions for Study and Discussion

1. What, according to King, causes people to crave horror movies? What other reasons can you add to King's list?
2. Identify the analogy King uses in paragraph 3, and explain how it works. (Glossary: *Analogy*)
3. What emotions does society applaud? Why? Which ones does King label "anticivilization emotions" (11)?
4. In what ways is a horror movie like a sick joke? What is the "dirty job" or effect that the two have in common (12)?
5. King starts his essay with the attention-grabbing sentence, "I think that we're all mentally ill." How does he develop this idea of

---

[4]*anarchistic:* against any authority; anarchy.

insanity in his essay? What does King mean when he says, "The potential lyncher is in almost all of us" (9)? How does King's last line relate to the theme of mental illness?

6. What is King's tone? (Glossary: *Tone*) Point to particular words or sentences that lead you to this conclusion.

Classroom Activity Using Cause and Effect

Use the following test, developed by William V. Haney, to determine your ability to analyze accurately evidence that is presented to you. After completing Haney's test, discuss your answers with other members of your class.

THE UNCRITICAL INFERENCE TEST

Directions

1. You will read a brief story. Assume that all of the information presented in the story is definitely accurate and true. Read the story carefully. You may refer back to the story whenever you wish.
2. You will then read statements about the story. Answer them in numerical order. *Do not go back* to fill in answers or to change answers. This will only distort your test score.
3. After you read each statement carefully, determine whether the statement is:
   a. "T"—meaning: On the basis of the information presented in the story the statement is *definitely true.*
   b. "F"—meaning: On the basis of the information presented in the story the statement is *definitely false.*
   c. "?"—The statement *may* be true (or false) but on the basis of the information presented in the story you cannot be definitely certain (If any part of the statement is doubtful, mark the statement "?".)
4. Indicate your answer by circling either "T" or "F" or "?" opposite the statement.

The Story

Babe Smith has been killed. Police have rounded up six suspects, all of whom are known gangsters. All of them are known to have been near the scene of the killing at the approximate time that it occurred. All had substantial motives for wanting Smith killed. However, one of these suspected gangsters, Slinky Sam, has positively been cleared of guilt.

Statements about the Story

1. Slinky Sam is known to have been near the scene of the killing of Babe Smith.	T	F	?
2. All six of the rounded-up gangsters were known to have been near the scene of the murder.	T	F	?
3. Only Slinky Sam has been cleared of guilt.	T	F	?
4. All six of the rounded-up suspects were near the scene of Smith's killing at the approximate time that it took place.	T	F	?
5. The police do not know who killed Smith.	T	F	?
6. All six suspects are known to have been near the scene of the foul deed.	T	F	?
7. Smith's murderer did not confess of his own free will.	T	F	?
8. Slinky Sam was not cleared of guilt.	T	F	?
9. It is known that the six suspects were in the vicinity of the cold-blooded assassination.	T	F	?

Suggested Writing Assignments

1. Write an essay in which you analyze, in light of King's remarks about the causes of our cravings for horror movies, a horror movie you've seen. In what ways did the movie satisfy your "anticivilization emotions" (11)? How did you feel before going to the theater? How did you feel when leaving?
2. Write an essay in which you analyze the most significant reasons or causes for your going to college. You may wish to discuss such matters as your high school experiences, people and events that influenced your decision, and your goals in college as well as in later life.
3. In the following screen shot from Alfred Hitchcock's 1960 thriller *Psycho*, Marion Crane (Janet Leigh) screams in terror as Norman Bates (Anthony Perkins) opens the shower curtain and she realizes he is about to kill her with a large kitchen knife. For many viewers, this scene is iconographic, an unforgettable symbol of the very essence of terror itself. Of course, for many others, different scenes of terror, actual or artistically represented, have become similarly powerful. Write an essay examining a situation or scene that terrifies you and examining the causes of your fright.

Why and When We Speak Spanish in Public

■ **Myriam Marquez**

An award-winning columnist for the Orlando Sentinel, *Myriam Marquez was born in Cuba in 1954 and grew up in South Florida. After graduating from the University of Maryland in 1983 with a degree in journalism and a minor in political science, she worked for United Press International in Washington, D.C., and in Maryland, covering the Maryland legislature as statehouse bureau chief. Marquez joined the editorial board of the* Sentinel *in 1987 and, since 1990, has been writing three weekly columns. Her commentaries focus on state and national politics, the human condition, civil liberties, and issues important to women and Hispanics. The Florida Society of Newspaper Editors awarded her its highest award for commentary in 2003.*

As a Hispanic, Marquez recognizes that English is the "common language" in America but knows that being American has little if anything to do with what language one speaks. In this article, which first appeared in the Orlando Sentinel *on July 5, 1999, Marquez explains why she and her parents, all bilingual, continue to speak Spanish when they are together, even though they have lived in the United States for forty years.*

For Your Journal

When you are in public and hear people around you speaking a foreign language, what is your immediate reaction? Are you intrigued? Do you feel uncomfortable? How do you regard people who speak a language other than English in public? Why?

When I'm shopping with my mother or standing in line with my stepdad to order fast food or anywhere else we might be together, we're going to speak to one another in Spanish. 1

That may appear rude to those who don't understand Spanish and overhear us in public places. 2

Those around us may get the impression that we're talking about them. They may wonder why we would insist on speaking in a foreign tongue, especially if they knew that my family has lived in the United States for 40 years and that my parents do understand English and speak it, albeit with difficulty and a heavy accent. 3

Let me explain why we haven't adopted English as our official family language. For me and most of the bilingual people I know, it's a matter of respect for our parents and comfort in our cultural roots. 4

It's not meant to be rude to others. It's not meant to alienate anyone or to Balkanize[1] America. 5

It's certainly not meant to be un-American—what constitutes an "American" being defined by English speakers from North America. 6

Being an American has very little to do with what language we use during our free time in a free country. From its inception,[2] this country was careful not to promote a government-mandated official language. 7

We understand that English is the common language of this country and the one most often heard in international business circles from Peru to Norway. We know that, to get ahead here, one must learn English. 8

But that ought not mean that somehow we must stop speaking in our native tongue whenever we're in a public area, as if we were ashamed of who we are, where we're from. As if talking in Spanish—or any other language, for that matter—is some sort of litmus test[3] used to gauge American patriotism. 9

Throughout this nation's history, most immigrants—whether from Poland or Finland or Italy or wherever else—kept their language through the first generation and, often, the second. I suspect that they spoke among themselves in their native tongue—in public. Pennsylvania even provided voting ballots written in German during much of the 1800s for those who weren't fluent in English. 10

In this century, Latin American immigrants and others have fought for this country in U.S.-led wars. They have participated fully in this nation's democracy by voting, holding political office, and paying taxes. And they have watched their children and grandchildren become so "American" that they resist speaking in Spanish. 11

You know what's rude? 12

[1]*Balkanize:* to divide a region or territory into small, often hostile units.
[2]*inception:* the beginning of something.
[3]*litmus test:* a test that uses a single indicator to prompt a decision.

When there are two or more people who are bilingual and another person who speaks only English and the bilingual folks all of a sudden start speaking Spanish, which effectively leaves out the English-only speaker. I don't tolerate that. 13

One thing's for sure. If I'm ever in a public place with my mom or dad and bump into an acquaintance who doesn't speak Spanish, I will switch to English and introduce that person to my parents. They will respond in English, and do so with respect. 14

Thinking Critically about This Reading

Marquez states that "being an American has very little to do with what language we use during our free time in a free country" (paragraph 7). What activities, then, does Marquez suggest truly make someone an American?

Questions for Study and Discussion

1. What is Marquez's thesis? (Glossary: *Thesis*)
2. Against what ideas does she seem to be arguing? How do you know?
3. Writers are often advised not to begin a paragraph with the word *but*. Why do you think Marquez ignores this rule in paragraph 9?
4. Is this essay one of causes, effects, or both? What details lead you to this conclusion?
5. Do you agree with Marquez that our patriotism ought not be gauged by whether or not we speak English in public? Or do you think that people living in this country ought to affirm their patriotism by speaking only English in public? Explain.

Classroom Activity Using Cause and Effect

Develop a causal chain in which you examine the ramifications of an action you took in the past. Identify each part in the chain. For example, you decided you wanted to do well in a course (ultimate cause), so you got started on a research project early (immediate cause), which enabled you to write several drafts of your paper (immediate cause), which earned you an A for the project (effect), which earned you an excellent grade for the class (effect), which enabled you to take the advanced seminar you wanted (effect).

Suggested Writing Assignments

1. Marquez's essay is set against the backdrop of a larger language-based controversy currently taking place in the United States called the English-only movement. Research the controversy in your school library or on the Internet, and write a cause-and-effect essay exploring the reasons the movement began and what is keeping it alive.
2. There is often more than one cause for an event. List at least six possible causes for one of the following events:

an upset victory in a competition	a change in your major
an injury you suffered	a quarrel with a friend

   Examine your list and identify the causes that seem most probable. Which of these are immediate causes, and which are ultimate causes? Using this material, write a short cause-and-effect essay on one of the topics.

Mom Quixote

■ **Anna Quindlen**

Anna Quindlen was born in Philadelphia in 1953. After graduating from Barnard College in 1974, she became a reporter for the New York Times *and later a columnist, winning the Pulitzer Prize for her "Public and Private" column in 1992. Quindlen left the* Times *in 1994 to concentrate on writing fiction and a new column at* Newsweek. *Quindlen's novels include* Object Lessons *(1991),* One True Thing *(1995),* Black and Blue *(1998), and* Blessings *(2003). Her most recent nonfiction books,* How Reading Changed My Life *(1998),* A Short Guide to a Happy Life *(2000),* Loud and Clear *(2004), and* Being Perfect *(2005), focus on issues of everyday life.*

In the following essay, which originally appeared in Newsweek *on December 13, 1993, Quindlen reports in journal form the guilt and suffering she endures trying to fulfill her younger son's desire for a highly sought after Christmas toy based on a popular children's television series.*

For Your Journal

Did you ever wish so fervently for a gift from your parents that you drove yourself and them to distraction? What do you think was the cause of such a strong desire? How do you regard the situation now? Why?

Day three of my search for Mighty Morphin Power Ranger toys, and I grow weary. Sneering clerks in three stores behave as though I've asked for gold bullion when I inquire whether they have these items in stock. Driving home, I wonder whom to blame: retailers, manufacturers, or the child who waited until November to articulate a need more profound than the need for food or water. Every Christmas there is one plaything everyone desires and no one can get. Sort of like the Hope diamond. I will persevere. 1

Day five: Missed by minutes the unpacking of a box of Mighty Morphin Power Ranger toys at the mall. Drat these column deadlines! 2

All were swiftly purchased by parents and (I am convinced) scalpers.[1] My quest is complicated by the fact that I have no idea what these toys look like, since I have not yet set eyes on one. I will buy first, look later.

Day seven: "If I don't get Mighty Morphin Power Rangers, I'll know there's no Santa Claus," says the eight-year-old as he plays with his spaghetti. Back to the mall tomorrow. 3

Day eight: I have a vivid dream in which the Princess of Wales and I are fighting over a Mighty Morphin Power Ranger in the aisles of (I think) Harrods. "He doesn't need this," I scream, "he'll be king someday." Using her obsessively worked pectoral muscles to shove me backward, she replies, "It's not for Wills, it's for Harry." I am arrested by her security detail and taken to the Tower of London, where my son is waiting. "You didn't get them," he wails. I awaken in a cold sweat. 4

Day eleven: I join a group of women chatting about Mighty Morphin Power Rangers in the aisle of a Toys "R" Us. Several liken this to the Teenage Mutant Ninja Turtle mania several years ago. One woman recalls driving to Delaware to buy a Donatello. The delivery truck arrives with Mighty Maxes, X-Men, Snailiens, and Street Fighters, but no Mighty Morphin Power Rangers. One woman calls the driver a vulgar name. I buy an economy-size bag of Butterfingers and return home, disconsolate. 5

Day twelve: At a cocktail party I meet a woman who personally participated in the Cabbage Patch riots of 1983, sustaining a black eye while unsuccessfully fighting for a pig-faced doll with brown braids. She says her daughter is now seventeen years old and wrote a senior English essay called "Shattered Dreams" on how she felt when she did not get a Cabbage Patch doll that Christmas. "She says that's how she knew there was no Santa Claus," the woman says. My husband asks in the cab why I am so sad. I say it's the holiday spirit. 6

Day fifteen: I briefly consider using my influence as a member of the media to acquire Mighty Morphin Power Rangers. I muse aloud about requesting Power Rangers from the manufacturer to illustrate a story on the season's toys. My husband mentions that I have consistently refused to get tickets for opening day at Yankee Stadium under somewhat similar circumstances. Men. 7

Day seventeen: Preparations for the Christmas season continue apace. I am excoriated[2] for not having a cookie cutter in the shape of Bart Simpson. Our oldest child pretends to believe in Santa Claus. His 8

[1]*scalpers:* those who sell sought-after items at highly inflated or marked-up prices.

[2]*excoriated:* reprimanded strongly; denounced.

brother asks whether Santa ever runs out of toys. "Hardly ever," he replies. "What about Mighty Morphin Power Rangers?" the younger asks. "If you want Power Rangers, he'll bring Power Rangers," his brother says. I send him upstairs to study for a spelling test.

Day nineteen: *It's a Wonderful Life* is on, and I imagine my life without Mighty Morphin Power Rangers. It's better. 9

Day twenty: The eight-year-old talks to me while I am taking a shower. "Do you know what I am going to do on Christmas morning?" he says. "What?" I shout from the shower. "I'm going to sit all day and play with my Mighty Morphin Power Rangers," he says. "What?" I shout. When I turn off the water I see that I have forgotten to rinse the shampoo from my hair. "Do you know what?" he says as soon as I have turned the water back on. "What?" I scream. "You are the best mom in the whole wide world." 10

Day twenty-one: There is a shipment of Mighty Morphin Power Rangers arriving at the mall at 10:00 A.M., or at least that is what one of the sneering salesmen was overheard to say. I will be there but I cannot stay long. Drat these column deadlines! How long does it take to drive to Delaware? I will persevere. 11

Thinking Critically about This Reading

In paragraph 6 Quindlen writes, "My husband asks in the cab why I am so sad. I say it's the holiday spirit." Why is Quindlen sad? Why is her statement ironic?

Questions for Study and Discussion

1. What are the effects of the boy's desire for a Power Ranger toy on his mother?
2. What does Quindlen think may be the causes of her son's desire for the Power Ranger toy? Are the causes important to her at the time? Why or why not?
3. Why do you suppose Quindlen doesn't report every day on her quest for the toy? What do you think happens on those days?
4. How and where does Quindlen use dialogue to make her narrative come alive? (Glossary: *Dialogue*; *Narration*)
5. How effective are the beginning and ending of Quindlen's essay? (Glossary: *Beginnings and Endings*) Why does she repeat the last sentence in paragraph 1, "I will persevere," at the end of her essay?
6. What is the significance of Quindlen's title? (Glossary: *Title*)

Classroom Activity Using Cause and Effect

Determining causes and effects requires careful thought. However, establishing a causal chain of events often brings clarity and understanding to complex issues. Consider the following example involving pollution and environmental stewardship:

ULTIMATE CAUSE	Industrial smokestack emissions
IMMEDIATE CAUSE	Smoke and acid rain damage
EFFECT	Clean air legislation
EFFECT	Improved air quality and forest growth

Develop a causal chain for each of the following cause-and-effect pairs. Then mix two of the pairs (for example, develop a causal chain for vacation/anxiety). Be prepared to discuss your answers with the class.

fire drill/fear	party/excitement
giving a speech/anxiety	vacation/relaxation

Suggested Writing Assignments

1. Quindlen doesn't spend much time on the causes of her son's desire for the Power Ranger toy. She does write in paragraph 1, however, "I wonder whom to blame: retailers, manufacturers, or the child who waited until November to articulate a need more profound than the need for food or water." Write an essay in which you examine the possible causes for her son's obsessive need—those she speculates on as well as those you consider plausible.
2. It is interesting to think of ourselves in terms of the influences that have caused us to be who we are. Write an essay in which you discuss two or three of what you consider the most important influences on your life. Following are some areas you may wish to consider in planning your essay.

parent	book or movie
clergy member	teacher
friend	hero
youth organization	coach
your neighborhood	your ethnic background

One Idea

Norman Mailer

Norman Mailer was born in Long Branch, New Jersey, in 1923 and graduated from Harvard University in 1943 with a degree in engineering. While at Harvard he made the decision to become a writer, and with the publication of The Naked and the Dead *(1948), based on his war experiences in the Pacific during World War II, Mailer established himself as a writer of note. Since then Mailer's literary interests have ranged widely, from novels to nonfiction and journalism; from politics, sports, feminism, and lunar exploration to criminality, popular culture, and ancient history. He has won two national book awards, two Pulitzer Prizes, and the Emerson-Thoreau Medal from the American Academy of Arts and Sciences for lifetime literary achievement.*

The following essay is excerpted from a longer piece published in the January 23, 2005, issue of Parade. *The question put to Mailer by the editors of* Parade *was: "If you could do one thing to change America for the better, what would it be?" Mailer explains his answer—that students need to read more—in this selection.*

For Your Journal

Reflect on your current reading habits. About how many books a year would you say you read? Has the number increased, stayed the same, or decreased over the past five years? To what would you attribute any changes that have occurred in the number of books you read a year?

If the desire to read diminishes, so does one's ability to read. The search for a culprit does not have to go far. There are confirming studies all over academia and the media that too many hours are devoted each day to the tube. Television is seen as the culprit, since the ability to read well is directly related to one's ability to learn. If it is universally understood that the power to concentrate while reading is the royal road to knowledge, what may not be perceived as clearly is how much concentration itself is a species of psychic strength. It can be 1 developed or it can go soft in much the manner that body muscle can be built up or allowed to go slack. The development of physical ability is in direct relation to use. Reading offers its analogy. When children become interested in an activity, their concentration is firm—until it is interrupted. Sixty years ago, children would read for hours. Their powers of concentration developed as naturally as breathing. Good readers became very good readers, even as men and women who go in for weight-lifting will bulk up. The connection between loving to read and doing well in school was no mystery to most students.

With the advent of television, the nature of concentration was altered. Yet children could still develop such powers by watching TV. Video and books had a common denominator then—narrative. 2

In the early years of television, it was even hoped that the attention children gave to TV would improve their interest in reading. Indeed, it might have if TV, left to itself, consisted of uninterrupted narratives. That, of course, was soon not the case. There were constant interruptions to programs—the commercials. 3

Every parent has had the experience of picking up a 2- or 3-year-old who is busy at play. All too often, a tantrum occurs. Even as adults, we have to learn to contain our annoyance when our thoughts are broken into. For a child, an interruption to one's concentration can prove as painful as a verbal rebuke.[1] 4

Yet this is what we do to our children for hours every day. On the major networks, the amount of time given to commercials and other promotional messages increased by 36 percent from 1991 to 2003. Each of the four major networks now offers 52 minutes of commercials in the three hours from 8 P.M. to 11 P.M. every day. It is equal to saying that every seven, 10 or 12 minutes, our attention to what is happening on the tube is cut into by a commercial. It is as bad for most children's shows. Soon enough, children develop a fail-safe. Since the child knows that any interesting story will soon be amputated by a kaleidoscope[2] of toys, food, dolls, clowns, new colors and the clutter of six or seven wholly different products all following one another in 10-, 20- and 30-second spots all the way through a three-minute break, the child also comes to recognize that concentration is not one's friend but is treacherous. For soon enough, attention will be turned inside out. The need to get up and move can become a frantic if routine response 5

[1] *rebuke:* sharp criticism.
[2] *kaleidoscope:* a diverse collection.

for highly keyed children. Other kids, stupefied[3] by the onslaught of a quick series of ads that have nothing to do with each other, suffer a dire spiritual product—stagnation. They sit on the couch in a stupor, they eat and drink, and alarms are sounded through the nation. Our children are becoming obese.

What then, is to be done? ... We have an economy that is stimulated by TV advertising. Yet the constant interruption of concentration it generates not only dominates much of our lives, but over the long run also is bound to bleed into our prosperity. The rest of the world is getting into position to do far better than us with future economic conditions. 6

If we want to have the best of all possible worlds, we had better recognize that we cannot have all the worlds. I believe that television commercials have got to go. Let us pay directly for what we enjoy on television rather than pass the spiritual cost on to our children and their children. 7

Thinking Critically about This Reading

Mailer writes, "If it is universally understood that the power to concentrate while reading is the royal road to knowledge, what may not be perceived as clearly is how much concentration itself is a species of psychic strength" (paragraph 1). What does Mailer mean by "species of psychic strength"?

Questions for Study and Discussion

1. What is Mailer's thesis? (Glossary: *Thesis*) What is his purpose? (Glossary: *Purpose*)
2. What is the causal relationship Mailer makes between the desire to read and the ability to read?
3. What does Mailer mean when he writes, "The development of physical ability is in direct relation to use. Reading offers its analogy" (1). (Glossary: *Analogy*) What is the analogy, and how does it work?
4. What is the causal link that Mailer makes between too many commercials on television and obesity in children? Do you think the link is valid? Why or why not?

---

[3] *stupefied:* made stupid or groggy; entranced.

5. Explain the connection that Mailer makes between the inability to concentrate and our economic future? Do you agree with this assessment? Why or why not?
6. What is Mailer's solution to the problems he examines? Where does he offer it?

Classroom Activity Using Cause and Effect

In preparation for writing a cause-and-effect essay, list two effects on society and two effects on personal behavior for one of the following items: television, cell phones, e-mail, microwave ovens, DVD technology, the Internet, or an item of your choice. For example, a car could be said to have the following effects:

SOCIETY

Development of the infrastructure based on asphalt roads

Expansion of the size and influence of the petroleum and insurance industries

PERSONAL BEHAVIOR

Convenient transportation

Freedom and independence

Be prepared to discuss your answers with the class.

Suggested Writing Assignments

1. Write a cause-and-effect essay answering the same question the editors of *Parade* asked Mailer: "If you could do one thing to change America for the better, what would it be?" As Mailer has done, be sure to give a clear articulation of the problem that needs fixing along with clear examples of what you mean. Finally, make sure your solution is intellectually sound and has some reasonable chance of being implemented.
2. Write an essay about a recent achievement—your own or someone else's—or about an important achievement in your community. Explain the causes of the success. Look at the underlying elements involved in the accomplishment, and explain how you selected the main cause of the causal chain that led to the achievement.

chapter **20**

Argument

The word **argument** probably brings to mind a verbal disagreement of the sort that everyone has at least witnessed, if not participated in directly. Such disputes are occasionally satisfying: You can take pleasure in knowing you have converted someone to your point of view. More often, though, verbal arguments are inconclusive and frustrating when you realize that you have failed to make your position understood, or enraging when you feel that your opponent has been stubborn and unreasonable. Such dissatisfaction is inevitable because verbal arguments generally arise spontaneously and so cannot be thoughtfully planned or researched; it is difficult to come up with appropriate evidence on the spur of the moment or to find the language that will make a point hard to deny. Indeed, it is often not until later that the convincing piece of evidence or the forcefully phrased assertion finally comes to mind.

Also known as **argumentation,** written arguments share common goals with spoken ones: They attempt to convince a reader to agree with a particular point of view, to make a particular decision, or to pursue a particular course of action. Written arguments, however, involve the presentation of well-chosen evidence and the artful control of language. Writers of arguments have no one around to dispute their words directly, so they must imagine their probable audience to predict the sorts of objections that may be raised. Written arguments, therefore, must be much more carefully planned—the writer must settle in advance on a specific, sufficiently detailed thesis or proposition. There is a greater need for organization, for choosing the most effective types of evidence from all that is available, for determining the strategies of rhetoric, language, and style that will best suit the argument's subject, purpose, and thesis, as well as ensure its effect on the intended audience. In the end, however, such work can be far more satisfying than spontaneous oral argument.

Most people who specialize in the study of arguments identify two essential categories: persuasion and logic. *Persuasive appeals* are directed at readers' emotions, at their subconscious, even at their biases and prejudices. These appeals involve diction, slanting, figurative language, analogy, rhythmic patterns of speech, and the establishment of a tone that will encourage a positive response. It is important to understand, as well, that persuasion very often attempts to get the audience to take action. Examples of persuasive argument are found in the exaggerated claims of advertisers and the speech making of political and social activists.

Logical appeals, on the other hand, are directed primarily at the audience's intellectual faculties, understanding, and knowledge. Such appeals depend on the reasoned movement from assertion to evidence to conclusion and on an almost mathematical system of proof and counterproof. Logical argument, unlike persuasion, does not normally impel its audience to action. Logical argument is commonly found in scientific or philosophical articles, in legal decisions, and in technical proposals.

Most arguments, however, are neither purely persuasive nor purely logical. A well-written newspaper editorial, for example, will present a logical arrangement of assertions and evidence, but it will also employ striking diction and other persuasive patterns of language to reinforce its effectiveness. Thus the kinds of appeals a writer emphasizes depend on the nature of the topic, the thesis or proposition of the argument, the writer's purpose, the various kinds of support (evidence, opinions, examples, facts, statistics) offered, and a thoughtful consideration of the audience. Knowing the differences between persuasive and logical appeals is essential in learning both to read and to write arguments.

True arguments make assertions about which there is a legitimate and recognized difference of opinion. It is unlikely that anyone will ever need to convince a reader that falling in love is a beautiful and intense experience, that crime rates should be reduced, or that computers are changing the world; most everyone would agree with such assertions. But not everyone would agree that women experience love more intensely than men, that the death penalty reduces the incidence of crime, or that computers are changing the world for the worse; these assertions are arguable and admit of differing perspectives. Similarly, a leading heart specialist might argue in a popular magazine that too many doctors are advising patients to have pacemakers implanted when the devices are not necessary; the editorial writer for a small-town newspaper could write urging that a local agency supplying food to poor families be given a larger percentage of the town's budget; in a long and complex book, a foreign-policy specialist might attempt to prove that the current administration exhibits no consistent policy in its relationship with other countries and that the Department of State needs to be overhauled. No matter what its forum or its structure, an argument has as its chief purpose the detailed setting forth of a particular point of view and the rebuttal of any opposing views.

Argumentation frequently utilizes the other rhetorical strategies covered in Chapters 12–19. In your efforts to argue convincingly, you may find it necessary to define, to compare and contrast, to analyze causes and effects, to classify, to describe, or to narrate. Nevertheless, it is the writer's attempt to convince, not explain, that is of primary importance in an argumentative essay. In this respect, it is helpful to keep in mind that there are two basic patterns of thinking and presenting our thoughts that are followed in argumentation: **induction** and **deduction.**

Inductive reasoning, the more common type of reasoning, moves from a set of specific examples to a general statement. In doing so, the writer makes an *inductive leap* from the evidence to the generalization. For example, after examining enrollment statistics, we can conclude that students do not like to take courses offered early in the morning or late in the afternoon.

Deductive reasoning, in contrast, moves from a general statement to a specific conclusion. It works on the model of the **syllogism,** a simple three-part argument that consists of a major premise, a minor premise, and a conclusion, as in the following example:

a. All women are mortal. *(Major premise)*
b. Jeanne is a woman. *(Minor premise)*
c. Jeanne is mortal. *(Conclusion)*

Obviously, a syllogism will fail to work if either of the premises is untrue:

a. All living creatures are mammals. *(Major premise)*
b. A butterfly is a living creature. *(Minor premise)*
c. A butterfly is a mammal. *(Conclusion)*

The problem is immediately apparent. The major premise is obviously false: Many living creatures are not mammals, and a butterfly happens to be one of the nonmammals. Consequently, the conclusion is invalid.

WRITING ARGUMENTS

Writing an argument is a challenging assignment but one that can be very rewarding. By nature, an argument must be carefully reasoned and thoughtfully structured to have maximum effect. Allow yourself, therefore, enough time to think about your thesis, to gather the evidence you need, and to draft, revise, edit, and proofread your essay. Fuzzy thinking, confused expression, and poor organization will be immediately evident to your reader and will diminish your chances for completing the assignment successfully. The following steps will remind you of some key features of arguments and will help you sequence your activities as you research and write.

1. Determine the Thesis or Proposition

Begin by deciding on a topic that interests you and about which there is some significant difference of opinion or about which you have a number of questions. Find out what's in the news about your topic, what people are saying about it, what authors and instructors are emphasizing as important intellectual arguments. As you pursue your research, consider what assertion or assertions you can make about the topic you choose. The more specific this thesis or proposition, the more directed your research can become and the more focused your ultimate argument will be. Don't hesitate along the way to modify or even reject an initial thesis as your continued research warrants.

A thesis can be placed anywhere in an argument, but it is probably best while learning to write arguments to place the statement of your controlling idea somewhere near the beginning of your composition. Explain the importance of the thesis, and make clear to your reader that you share a common concern or interest in this issue. You may wish to state your central assertion directly in your first or second paragraph so that your reader will have no doubt or confusion about your position. You may also wish to lead off with a particularly striking piece of evidence to capture your reader's interest.

2. Take Account of Your Audience

In no other type of writing is the question of audience more important than in argumentation. The tone you establish, the type of diction you choose, the kinds of evidence you select to buttress your assertions, and indeed the organizational pattern you follow can influence your audience to trust you and believe your assertions. If you judge the nature of your audience accurately, respect its knowledge of the subject, and correctly envision whether it is likely to be hostile, neutral, complacent, or receptive, you will be able to tailor the various aspects of your argument appropriately. (For more on audience, refer to the discussion of ethos, pathos, and logos on pp. 490–91.)

3. Gather the Necessary Supporting Evidence

For each point of your argument, be sure to provide appropriate and sufficient evidence: verifiable facts and statistics, illustrative examples and narratives, or quotations from authorities. Don't overwhelm your reader with evidence, but don't skimp either; it is important to demonstrate your command of the topic and control of the thesis by choosing carefully from all the evidence at your disposal.

4. Settle on an Organizational Pattern

Once you think you have sufficient evidence to make your assertion convincing, consider how best to organize your argument. To some extent, your organization will depend on your method of reasoning: inductive, deductive, or a combination of the two. For example, is it necessary to establish a major premise before moving on to discuss a minor premise? Should most of your evidence precede your direct statement of an assertion, or follow it? Will induction work better with the particular audience you have targeted? As you present your primary points, you may find it effective to move from least important to most important or from least familiar to most familiar. A scratch outline can help; but often a writer's most crucial revisions in an argument involve rearranging its components into a sharper, more coherent order. Very often it is difficult to tell what that order should be until the revision stage of the writing process.

5. Consider Refutations to Your Argument

As you proceed with your argument, you may wish to take into account well-known and significant opposing arguments. To ignore opposing views would be to suggest to your readers any one of the following: You don't know about the opposing views; you know about them and are obviously and unfairly weighting the arguments in your favor; or you know about them and have no reasonable answers for them. Grant the validity of opposing arguments or refute them, but respect your reader's intelligence by addressing the objections to your assertion. Your readers will in turn respect you for doing so.

6. Avoid Faulty Reasoning

Have someone read your argument for errors in judgment and for faulty reasoning. Sometimes others can see easily what you can't see because you are so intimately tied to your assertion. These errors are typically called **logical fallacies.** Review the accompanying "Logical Fallacies" box, making sure that you have not committed any of these errors in reasoning.

Logical Fallacies

Oversimplification: A drastically simple solution to what is clearly a complex problem: *We have a balance-of-trade deficit because foreigners make better products than we do.*

Hasty generalization: In inductive reasoning, a generalization that is based on too little evidence or on evidence that is not representative: *My grandparents eat bran flakes for breakfast, just as most older folks do.*

Post hoc, ergo propter hoc: "After this, therefore because of this." Confusing chance or coincidence with causation. The fact that one event comes after another does not necessarily mean that the first event caused the second: *I went to the hockey game last night. The next thing I knew I had a cold.*

Begging the question: Assuming in a premise something that needs to be proven: *Lying is wrong because people should always tell the truth.*

False analogy: Making a misleading analogy between logically unconnected ideas: *If we can clone mammals, we should be able to find a cure for cancer.*

Either/or thinking: Seeing only two alternatives when there may in fact be other possibilities: *Either you love your job, or you hate it.*

Non sequitur: "It does not follow." An inference or conclusion that is not clearly related to the established premises or evidence: *She is very sincere. She must know what she's talking about.*

7. Conclude Forcefully

In the conclusion of your essay, be sure to restate your position in new language, at least briefly. Besides persuading your reader to accept your point of view, you may also want to encourage some specific course of action. Above all, your conclusion should not introduce new information that may surprise your reader; it should seem to follow naturally, almost seamlessly, from the series of points that you have carefully established in the body of the essay. Don't overstate your case, but at the same time don't qualify your conclusion with the use of too many words or phrases like *I think, in my opinion, maybe, sometimes,* and *probably.* These words can make you sound indecisive and fuzzy-headed rather than rational and sensible.

THINKING CRITICALLY ABOUT ARGUMENT

Take a Stand

Even though you have chosen a topic, gathered information about it, and established a thesis statement or proposition, you need to take a stand, to fully commit yourself to your beliefs and ideas about the issue before you. If you attempt to work with a thesis that you have not clearly thought through or are confused about, or if you take a position you do not fully believe in or care about, your writing will show it. Your willingness to research, to dig up evidence, to find the most effective organizational pattern for your material, to construct strong paragraphs and sentences, and to find just the right diction to convey your argument, is a direct reflection of just how strongly you take a stand and how much you believe in that stand. With a strong stand you can argue vigorously and convincingly.

Consider Ethos, Pathos, and Logos

Classical thinkers believed that there are three key components in all rhetorical communication: the *speaker* (or writer) who comments on a *subject* to an *audience.* For purposes of discussion we can isolate each of these entities, but in actual rhetorical situations they are inseparable, each inextricably tied to and influencing the other two. The ancients also recognized the importance of three elements of argumentation: ethos, which is related to the speaker/writer; logos, which is related to the subject; and pathos, which is related to the audience.

Ethos (the Greek word for "character") has to do with the authority, credibility, and, to a certain extent, morals of the speaker/writer. The classical rhetoricians believed that it was important for the speaker/writer to be credible and to argue for a worthwhile cause. Putting one's argumentative skills in the service of a questionable cause was simply not acceptable. But how does one establish credibility? Sometimes it is gained through achievements outside the rhetorical arena—that is, the speaker has had experience with an issue, has argued the subject before, and has been judged to be honest and sincere. In the case of your own writing, establishing such credentials is not always possible, so you will need to be more concerned than usual with presenting your argument reasonably, sincerely, and in language untainted by excessive emotionalism. Finally, it is worth remembering that you should always respect your audience in your writing.

Logos (Greek for "word"), related as it is to the subject, is the effective presentation of the argument itself. Is the thesis or claim worthwhile? Is it logical, consistent, and well buttressed by supporting evidence? Is the evidence itself factual, reliable, and convincing? Finally, is the argument so thoughtfully organized and clearly presented that it will have an impact on the audience? Indeed, this aspect of argumentation is at once the most difficult to accomplish and the most rewarding.

Pathos (Greek for "emotion") has most to do with the audience. How does the speaker/writer present an argument to maximize its appeal for a given audience? One way, of course, is through artful and strategic use of well-crafted language. Certain buzzwords, slanted diction, or loaded language may become either rallying cries or causes of resentment in an argument. Remember, too, that audiences can range from friendly and sympathetic to hostile and resistant, with a myriad of possibilities in between. A friendly audience will welcome new information and support your position; a hostile audience will look for flaws in your logic and examples of dishonest manipulation. Caution, subtlety, and critical thinking must be applied to an uncommitted audience.

The Declaration of Independence

■ Thomas Jefferson

President, governor, statesman, lawyer, architect, philosopher, and writer, Thomas Jefferson (1743–1826) is one of the most important figures in U.S. history. He was born in Albemarle County, Virginia, in 1743 and attended the College of William and Mary. After being admitted to law practice in 1767, he began a long and illustrious career of public service to the colonies and, later, the new republic. In 1809, after two terms as president, Jefferson retired to Monticello, a home he had designed and helped build. Ten years later he founded the University of Virginia. Jefferson died at Monticello on July 4, 1826, the fiftieth anniversary of the signing of the Declaration of Independence.

Jefferson drafted the Declaration in 1776. Although it was revised by Benjamin Franklin and his colleagues at the Continental Congress, the declaration retains in its sound logic and forceful, direct style the unmistakable qualities of Jefferson's prose.

For Your Journal

In your mind, what is the meaning of democracy? Where do your ideas about democracy come from?

When in the course of human events, it becomes necessary for one people to dissolve the political bands which have connected them with another, and to assume among the Powers of the earth, the separate and equal station to which the Laws of Nature and of Nature's God entitle them, a decent respect to the opinions of mankind requires that they should declare the causes which impel them to the separation. 1

We hold these truths to be self-evident, that all men are created equal, that they are endowed by their Creator with certain unalienable Rights, that among these are Life, Liberty and the pursuit of Happiness. That to secure these rights, Governments are instituted among Men deriving their just powers from the consent of the governed. That 2 whenever any Form of Government becomes destructive of these ends, it is the Right of the People to alter or to abolish it, and to institute new Government, laying its foundation on such principles and organizing its powers in such form, as to them shall seem most likely to effect their Safety and Happiness. Prudence, indeed, will dictate that Governments long established should not be changed for light and transient[1] causes; and accordingly all experience hath shown, that mankind are more disposed to suffer, while evils are sufferable, than to right themselves by abolishing the forms to which they are accustomed. But when a long train of abuses and usurpations pursuing invariably the same Object evinces a design to reduce them under absolute Despotism, it is their right, it is their duty, to throw off such government, and to provide new Guards for their future security. Such has been the patient sufferance of these Colonies; and such is now the necessity which constrains them to alter their former Systems of Government. The history of the present King of Great Britain[2] is a history of repeated injuries and usurpations, all having in direct object the establishment of an absolute Tyranny over these States. To prove this, let Facts be submitted to a candid world.

He has refused his Assent to Laws, the most wholesome and necessary for the public good. 3

He has forbidden his Governors to pass Laws of immediate and pressing importance, unless suspended in their operation till his Assent should be obtained; and when so suspended, he has utterly neglected to attend to them. 4

He has refused to pass other Laws for the accommodation of large districts of people, unless those people would relinquish the right of Representation in the Legislature, a right inestimable to them and formidable to tyrants only. 5

He has called together legislative bodies at places unusual, uncomfortable, and distant from the depository of their Public Records, for the sole purpose of fatiguing them into compliance with his measures. 6

He has dissolved Representative Houses repeatedly, for opposing with manly firmness his invasions on the rights of the people. 7

He has refused for a long time, after such dissolutions, to cause others to be elected; whereby the Legislative Powers, incapable of 8

[1]*transient:* not lasting; not permanent.

[2]*King of Great Britain:* King George III (1738–1820), who ruled the British empire in 1760–1820.

Annihilation, have returned to the People at large for their exercise; the State remaining in the mean time exposed to all the dangers of invasion from without, and convulsions within.

He has endeavoured to prevent the population of these States; for 9
that purpose obstructing the Laws of Naturalization of Foreigners; refusing to pass others to encourage their migration hither, and raising the conditions of new Appropriations of Lands.

He has obstructed the Administration of Justice, by refusing his 10
Assent to Laws for establishing Judiciary Powers.

He has made Judges dependent on his Will alone, for the tenure of 11
their offices, and the amount and payment of their salaries.

He has erected a multitude of New Offices, and sent hither swarms 12
of Officers to harass our People, and eat out their substance.

He has kept among us, in time of peace, Standing Armies without 13
the Consent of our Legislature.

He has affected to render the Military independent of and superior 14
to the Civil Power.

He has combined with others to subject us to jurisdictions foreign 15
to our constitution, and unacknowledged by our laws; giving his Assent to their acts of pretended Legislation:

For quartering large bodies of armed troops among us: 16

For protecting them, by a mock Trial, from Punishment for 17
any Murders which they should commit on the Inhabitants of these States:

For cutting off our Trade with all parts of the world: 18

For imposing Taxes on us without our Consent: 19

For depriving us in many cases, of the benefits of Trial by Jury: 20

For transporting us beyond Seas to be tried for pretended offenses: 21

For abolishing the free System of English Laws in a Neighbouring 22
Province, establishing therein an Arbitrary government, and enlarging its boundaries so as to render it at once an example and fit instrument for introducing the same absolute rule into these Colonies:

For taking away our Charters, abolishing our most valuable Laws, 23
and altering fundamentally the Forms of our Governments:

For suspending our own Legislatures, and declaring themselves 24
invested with Power to legislate for us in all cases whatsoever.

He has abdicated Government here, by declaring us out of his 25
Protection and waging War against us.

He has plundered our seas, ravaged our Coasts, burnt our towns 26
and destroyed the Lives of our people.

He is at this time transporting large Armies of foreign Mercenaries to compleat works of death, desolation and tyranny, already begun with circumstances of Cruelty & perfidy scarcely paralleled in the most barbarous ages, and totally unworthy the Head of a civilized nation. 27

He has constrained our fellow Citizens taken Captive on the high Seas to bear Arms against their Country, to become the executioners of their friends and Brethren, or to fall themselves by their Hands. 28

He has excited domestic insurrections amongst us, and has endeavoured to bring on the inhabitants of our frontiers, the merciless Indian Savages, whose known rule of warfare, is an undistinguished destruction of all ages, sexes and conditions. 29

In every stage of these Oppressions We Have Petitioned for Redress in the most humble terms: Our repeated petitions have been answered only by repeated injury. A Prince, whose character is thus marked by every act which may define a Tyrant, is unfit to be the ruler of a free People. 30

Nor have We been wanting in attention to our British brethren. We have warned them from time to time of attempts by their legislature to extend an unwarrantable jurisdiction over us. We have reminded them of the circumstances of our emigration and settlement here. We have appealed to their native justice and magnanimity[3] and we have conjured them by the ties of our common kindred to disavow these usurpations, which would inevitably interrupt our connections and correspondence. They too have been deaf to the voice of justice and of consanguinity. We must, therefore acquiesce[4] in the necessity, which denounces our Separation, and hold them, as we hold the rest of mankind, Enemies in War, in Peace Friends. 31

We, therefore, the Representatives of the United States of America, in General Congress, Assembled, appealing to the Supreme Judge of the world for the rectitude of our intentions, do, in the Name, and by Authority of the good People of these Colonies, solemnly publish and declare, That these United Colonies are, and of Right ought to be Free and Independent States; that they are Absolved from all Allegiance to the British Crown, and that all political connection between them and the State of Great Britain, is and ought to be totally dissolved; and that as Free and Independent States, they have full power to levy War, 32

[3]*magnanimity:* quality of being calm, generous, upstanding.

[4]*acquiesce:* comply; accept.

conclude Peace, contract Alliances, establish Commerce, and to do all other Acts and Things which Independent States may of right do. And for the support of this Declaration, with a firm reliance on the protection of Divine Providence, we mutually pledge to each other our lives, our Fortunes and our sacred Honor.

Thinking Critically about This Reading

What, according to the Declaration of Independence, is the purpose of government?

Questions for Study and Discussion

1. In paragraph 2, Jefferson presents certain "self-evident" truths. What are these truths, and how are they related to his argument? Do you consider them self-evident?
2. The Declaration of Independence is a deductive argument; it can, therefore, be presented in the form of a syllogism. (Glossary: *Syllogism*) What are the major premise, the minor premise, and the conclusion of Jefferson's argument?
3. The list of charges against the king is given as evidence in support of Jefferson's minor premise. (Glossary: *Evidence*) Does he offer any evidence in support of his major premise?
4. How, specifically, does Jefferson refute the possible charge that the colonists had not tried to solve their problems by less drastic means?
5. Where in the Declaration does Jefferson use parallel structure? (Glossary: *Parallelism*) What does he achieve by using it?
6. While the basic structure of the Declaration reflects sound deductive reasoning, Jefferson's language, particularly when he lists the charges against the king, tends to be emotional. (Glossary: *Diction*) Identify as many examples of this emotional language as you can, and discuss possible reasons for why Jefferson uses this kind of language.

Classroom Activity Using Argument

Choose one of the following controversial subjects, and think about how you would write an argument for or against it. Write three sentences that summarize three important points, two based on logic and one based on persuasion/emotion. Then write one sentence that acknowledges the opposing point of view. For example, if you were to argue for stricter enforcement of a leash law and waste pickup ordinance for dog owners in your town, you might write:

Logic	Dogs allowed to run free can be a menace to joggers and local wildlife.
Logic	Dog waste poses a health risk, particularly in areas where children play.
Emotion	How would you feel if you hit an unleashed dog with your car?
Counterargument	Dogs need fresh air and exercise, too.

Gun control
Tobacco restrictions
Cutting taxes and social programs
Paying college athletes
Assisted suicide for the terminally ill
Widespread legalization of gambling

Suggested Writing Assignments

1. In recent years, the issue of human rights has been much discussed. Review the arguments for and against our country's active and outspoken promotion of the human rights issue as reported in the press. Then write an argument of your own in favor of a continued strong human rights policy on the part of our nation's leaders.
2. Using one of the subjects listed below, develop a thesis and then write an essay in which you argue in support of that thesis.

Minimum wage	Welfare
Social Security	Separation of church and state
Capital punishment	First Amendment rights
Erosion of individual rights	

I Have a Dream

■ Martin Luther King Jr.

Civil rights leader Martin Luther King Jr. (1929–1968) was the son of a Baptist minister in Atlanta, Georgia. Ordained at the age of eighteen, King went on to earn academic degrees from Morehouse College, Crozer Theological Seminary, Boston University, and Chicago Theological Seminary. He came to prominence in 1955 in Montgomery, Alabama, when he led a successful boycott against the city's segregated bus system. The first president of the Southern Christian Leadership Conference, King became the leading spokesman for the civil rights movement during the 1950s and 1960s, espousing a consistent philosophy of nonviolent resistance to racial injustice. He also championed women's rights and protested the Vietnam War. Named Time *magazine's Man of the Year in 1963, King was awarded the Nobel Peace Prize in 1964. King was assassinated in April 1968 after speaking at a rally in Memphis, Tennessee.*

"I Have a Dream," the keynote address for the March on Washington in 1963, has become one of the most renowned and recognized speeches of the past century. Note how King uses allusions and parallelism to give life to his argument.

For Your Journal

Most Americans have seen film clips of King delivering the "I Have a Dream" speech. What do you know of the speech? What do you know of the events and conditions under which King presented it over forty years ago now?

Five score years ago, a great American, in whose symbolic shadow we stand, signed the Emancipation Proclamation.[1] This momentous decree came as a great beacon light of hope to millions of Negro slaves 1

[1]*Emancipation Proclamation:* a decree enacted by Abraham Lincoln (1809–1865) in 1863 that freed the slaves in the southern states.

who had been seared in the flames of withering injustice. It came as a joyous daybreak to end the long night of captivity.

But one hundred years later, we must face the tragic fact that the Negro is still not free. One hundred years later, the life of the Negro is still sadly crippled by the manacles of segregation and the chains of discrimination. One hundred years later, the Negro lives on a lonely island of poverty in the midst of a vast ocean of material prosperity. One hundred years later, the Negro is still languishing in the corners of American society and finds himself an exile in his own land. So we have come here today to dramatize an appalling condition. 2

In a sense we have come to our nation's Capitol to cash a check. When the architects of our republic wrote the magnificent words of the Constitution and the Declaration of Independence, they were signing a promissory note to which every American was to fall heir. This note was a promise that all men would be guaranteed the unalienable rights of life, liberty, and the pursuit of happiness. 3

It is obvious today that America has defaulted on this promissory note insofar as her citizens of color are concerned. Instead of honoring this sacred obligation, America has given the Negro people a bad check; a check which has come back marked "insufficient funds." But we refuse to believe that the bank of justice is bankrupt. We refuse to believe that there are insufficient funds in the great vaults of opportunity of this nation. So we have come to cash this check—a check that will give us upon demand the riches of freedom and the security of justice. We have also come to this hallowed spot to remind America of the fierce urgency of *now*. This is no time to engage in the luxury of cooling off or to take the tranquilizing drug of gradualism. *Now* is the time to make real the promises of Democracy. *Now* is the time to rise from the dark and desolate valley of segregation to the sunlit path of racial justice. *Now* is the time to open the doors of opportunity to all of God's children. *Now* is the time to lift our nation from the quicksands of racial injustice to the solid rock of brotherhood. 4

It would be fatal for the nation to overlook the urgency of the moment and to underestimate the determination of the Negro. This sweltering summer of the Negro's legitimate discontent will not pass until there is an invigorating autumn of freedom and equality. 1963 is not an end, but a beginning. Those who hope that the Negro needed to blow off steam and will now be content will have a rude awakening if the nation returns to business as usual. There will be neither rest nor tranquility in America until the Negro is granted his citizenship rights. 5

The whirlwinds of revolt will continue to shake the foundations of our nation until the bright day of justice emerges.

But there is something I must say to my people who stand on the warm threshold which leads into the palace of justice. In the process of gaining our rightful place we must not be guilty of wrongful deeds. Let us not seek to satisfy our thirst for freedom by drinking from the cup of bitterness and hatred. We must forever conduct our struggle on the high plane of dignity and discipline. We must not allow our creative protest to degenerate into physical violence. Again and again we must rise to the majestic heights of meeting physical force with soul force. The marvelous new militancy which has engulfed the Negro community must not lead us to a distrust of all white people, for many of our white brothers, as evidenced by their presence here today, have come to realize that their destiny is tied up with our destiny and their freedom is inextricably bound to our freedom. We cannot walk alone. 6

And as we walk, we must make the pledge that we shall march ahead. We cannot turn back. There are those who are asking the devotees of civil rights, "When will you be satisfied?" We can never be satisfied as long as the Negro is the victim of the unspeakable horrors of police brutality. We can never be satisfied as long as our bodies, heavy with the fatigue of travel, cannot gain lodging in the motels of the highways and the hotels of the cities. We cannot be satisfied as long as the Negro's basic mobility is from a smaller ghetto to a larger one. We can never be satisfied as long as a Negro in Mississippi cannot vote and a Negro in New York believes he has nothing for which to vote. No, no, we are not satisfied, and we will not be satisfied until justice rolls down like waters and righteousness like a mighty stream. 7

I am not unmindful that some of you have come here out of great trials and tribulations. Some of you have come fresh from narrow jail cells. Some of you have come from areas where your quest for freedom left you battered by the storms of persecution and staggered by the winds of police brutality. You have been the veterans of creative suffering. Continue to work with the faith that unearned suffering is redemptive. 8

Go back to Mississippi, go back to Alabama, go back to South Carolina, go back to Georgia, go back to Louisiana, go back to the slums and ghettoes of our northern cities, knowing that somehow this situation can and will be changed. Let us not wallow in the valley of despair. 9

I say to you today, my friends, that in spite of the difficulties and frustrations of the moment I still have a dream. It is a dream deeply rooted in the American dream. 10

I have a dream that one day this nation will rise up and live out the true meaning of its creed: "We hold these truths to be self-evident; that all men are created equal."[2] 11

I have a dream that one day on the red hills of Georgia the sons of former slaves and the sons of former slaveowners will be able to sit down together at the table of brotherhood. 12

I have a dream that the state of Mississippi, a desert state sweltering with the heat of injustice and oppression, will be transformed into an oasis of freedom and justice. 13

I have a dream that my four little children will one day live in a nation where they will not be judged by the color of their skin but by the content of their character. 14

I have a dream today. 15

I have a dream that the state of Alabama, whose governor's[3] lips are presently dripping with the words of interposition and nullification,[4] will be transformed into a situation where little black boys and black girls will be able to join hands with little white boys and white girls and walk together as sisters and brothers. 16

I have a dream today. 17

I have a dream that one day every valley shall be exalted, every hill and mountain shall be made low, the rough places will be made plain, and the crooked places will be made straight, and the glory of the Lord shall be revealed, and all flesh shall see it together. 18

This is our hope. This is the faith with which I return to the South. With this faith we will be able to hew out of the mountain of despair a stone of hope. With this faith we will be able to transform the jangling discords of our nation into a beautiful symphony of brotherhood. With this faith we will be able to work together, to pray together, to struggle together, to go to jail together, to stand up for freedom together, knowing that we will be free one day. 19

This will be the day when all of God's children will be able to sing with new meaning. 20

---

[2]*"We hold . . . created equal":* from the Declaration of Independence by Thomas Jefferson (1743–1826); see p. 492.

[3]*Alabama . . . governor:* George Wallace (1919–1998), a segregationist in 1963 who later changed his views and received integrated political support.

[4]*nullification:* a state's refusal to recognize or enforce within its borders U.S. federal law.

> My country, 'tis of thee
> Sweet land of liberty,
> Of thee I sing:
> Land where my fathers died,
> Land of the pilgrims' pride,
> From every mountainside
> Let freedom ring.

And if America is to be a great nation this must become true. So let freedom ring from the prodigious hilltops of New Hampshire. Let freedom ring from the mighty mountains of New York. Let freedom ring from the heightening Alleghenies of Pennsylvania! 21

Let freedom ring from the snowcapped Rockies of Colorado! 22

Let freedom ring from the curvaceous peaks of California! 23

But not only that; let freedom ring from Stone Mountain of Georgia! 24

Let freedom ring from Lookout Mountain of Tennessee! 25

Let freedom ring from every hill and molehill of Mississippi. From every mountainside, let freedom ring. 26

When we let freedom ring, when we let it ring from every village and every hamlet, from every state and every city, we will be able to speed up that day when all of God's children, black men and white men, Jews and Gentiles, Protestants and Catholics, will be able to join hands and sing in the words of the old Negro spiritual, "Free at last! free at last! thank God almighty, we are free at last!" 27

Thinking Critically about This Reading

What does King mean when he says that "in the process of gaining our rightful place [in society] we must not be guilty of wrongful deeds" (paragraph 6)? Why is this issue so important to him?

Questions for Study and Discussion

1. What is King's thesis? (Glossary: *Thesis*) How has America "defaulted" on its promise?
2. King delivered his speech to two audiences: the huge audience that listened to him in person, and another, even larger audience. (Glossary: *Audience*) What is that larger audience? How does King's speech catch the audience's attention and deliver his point?

3. Examine the speech to determine how King organizes his presentation. (Glossary: *Organization*) What are the main sections of the speech, and what is the purpose of each? How does the organization serve King's overall purpose? (Glossary: *Purpose*)
4. King uses parallel constructions and repetitions throughout his speech. (Glossary: *Parallelism*) Identify the phrases and words that he emphasizes. Explain what these techniques add to the persuasiveness of his argument.
5. Explain King's choice for the title. (Glossary: *Title*) Why is the title particularly appropriate given the context in which the speech was delivered? What other titles might he have used?

Classroom Activity Using Argument

Write a paragraph that argues that people should compliment one another more. Use *one* of the following quotes to support your argument:

> "Compliments are the high point of a person's day," said self-help author Melodie Bronson. "Without compliments, anyone's life is sure to be much more difficult."
>
> "Compliments have been proven to lower blood pressure and increase endorphin production to the brain," said Dr. Ruth West of the Holistic Medicine Committee. "A compliment a day may lengthen your life span by as much as a year."
>
> "Compliments are a special way people communicate with each other," said Bill Goodbody, therapist at the Good Feeling Institute. "Ninety percent of our patients report happier relationships or marriages after they begin compliment therapy."

Explain why you chose the quote you did. How did you integrate it into your paragraph?

Suggested Writing Assignments

1. King's language is powerful, and his imagery is vivid, but the effectiveness of any speech depends partially on its delivery. If read in monotone, King's use of repetition and parallel language would sound almost redundant rather than inspiring. (Glossary: *Parallelism*) Keeping presentation in mind, write a short speech

that argues a point of view about which you feel strongly. Using King's speech as a model, incorporate imagery, repetition, and metaphor to communicate your point. (Glossary: *Figure of Speech*) Read your speech aloud to a friend to see how it flows and how effective your use of language is. Refine your presentation—both your text and how you deliver it—before presenting the speech in class.

2. Using King's assessment of the condition of African Americans in 1963 as a foundation, research the changes that have occurred in the years following King's speech. How have laws changed? How have demographics changed? Present your information in an essay that assesses what still needs to be done to fulfill King's dream for America. Where do we still fall short of the racial equality envisioned by King? What are the prospects for the future?

As They Say, Drugs Kill

■ Laura Rowley

Born in 1965, Laura Rowley is a columnist for Self *magazine and author of* On Target: How the World's Hottest Retailer Hit a Bull's-Eye *(2003). Her freelance writing has appeared in the* New York Times, Parents, *and other publications. Rowley also spent five years at CNN in New York, reporting on air for "Your Money" and "Business Unusual" and producing live programs. Before going to work for CNN, she was an editor for* United Nations Chronicle *and editor-in-chief of* Multi-Housing News, *a trade magazine for builders. She graduated from the University of Illinois at Urbana–Champaign in 1987 with a degree in journalism, and she received a master's in divinity from New York Theological Seminary in 1999.*

In the following essay, which first appeared in Newsweek on Campus *in 1987, Rowley argues against substance abuse by recounting a particularly poignant experience. Although her narrative appeals primarily to the reader's emotions, she nonethless attempts to persuade without preaching.*

For Your Journal

What is your best argument against the use of drugs? If you could tell a story that argues against drugs and that would persuade young people not to use them, what would that story be? It might be a personal story, a story about friends who were unlucky in their use of drugs, or a story that you read about or saw portrayed in the movies or on television.

The fastest way to end a party is to have someone die in the middle of it. 1

At a party last fall I watched a 22-year-old die of cardiac arrest after he had used drugs. It was a painful, undignified way to die. And I would like to think that anyone who shared the experience would feel his or her ambivalence about substance abuse dissolving. 2

This victim won't be singled out like Len Bias[1] as a bitter example for "troubled youth." He was just another ordinary guy celebrating with friends at a private house party, the kind where they roll in the keg first thing in the morning and get stupefied while watching the football games on cable all afternoon. The living room was littered with beer cans from last night's party—along with dirty socks and the stuffing from the secondhand couch. 3

And there were drugs, as at so many other college parties. The drug of choice this evening was psilocybin, hallucinogenic mushrooms. If you're cool you call them "'shrooms." 4

This wasn't a crowd huddled in the corner of a darkened room with a single red bulb, shooting needles in their arms. People played darts, made jokes, passed around a joint and listened to the Grateful Dead on the stereo. 5

Suddenly, a thin, tall, brown-haired young man began to gasp. His eyes rolled back in his head, and he hit the floor face first with a crash. Someone laughed, not appreciating the violence of his fall, thinking the afternoon's festivities had finally caught up with another guest. The laugh lasted only a second, as the brown-haired guest began to convulse and choke. The sound of the stereo and laughter evaporated. Bystanders shouted frantic suggestions: 6

"It's an epileptic fit, put something in his mouth!" 7

"Roll him over on his stomach!" 8

"Call an ambulance; God, somebody breathe into his mouth." 9

A girl kneeling next to him began to sob his name, and he seemed to moan. 10

"Wait, he's semicoherent." Four people grabbed for the telephone, to find no dial tone, and ran to use a neighbor's. One slammed the dead phone against the wall in frustration—and miraculously produced a dial tone. 11

But the body was now motionless on the kitchen floor. "He has a pulse, he has a pulse." 12

"But he's not breathing!" 13

"Well, get away—give him some f—ing air!" The three or four guests gathered around his body unbuttoned his shirt. 14

"Wait—is he OK? Should I call the damn ambulance?" 15

---

[1]*Len Bias* (1963–1986): college basketball star who died of a drug overdose after signing a contract with the Boston Celtics.

A chorus of frightened voices shouted, "Yes, yes!" 16

"Come on, come on, breathe again. Breathe!" 17

Over muffled sobs came a sudden grating, desperate breath that 18
passed through bloody lips and echoed through the kitchen and living room.

"He's had this reaction before—when he did acid at a concert last 19
spring. But he recovered in 15 seconds . . . ," one friend confided.

The rest of the guests looked uncomfortably at the floor or paced 20
purposelessly around the room. One or two whispered, "Oh, my God," over and over, like a prayer. A friend stood next to me, eyes fixed on the kitchen floor. He mumbled, just audibly, "I've seen this before. My dad died of a heart attack. He had the same look . . . ." I touched his shoulder and leaned against a wall, repeating reassurances to myself. People don't die at parties. People don't die at parties.

Eventually, no more horrible, gnashing sounds tore their way from 21
the victim's lungs. I pushed my hands deep in my jeans pockets wondering how much it costs to pump a stomach and how someone could be so careless if he had had this reaction with another drug. What would he tell his parents about the hospital bill?

Two uniformed paramedics finally arrived, lifted him onto a 22
stretcher and quickly rolled him out. His face was grayish blue, his mouth hung open, rimmed with blood, and his eyes were rolled back with a yellowish color on the rims.

The paramedics could be seen moving rhythmically forward and 23
back through the small windows of the ambulance, whose lights threw a red wash over the stunned watchers on the porch. The paramedics' hands were massaging his chest when someone said, "Did you tell them he took psilocybin? Did you tell them?"

"No, I . . ." 24

"My God, so tell them—do you want him to die?" Two people ran 25
to tell the paramedics the student had eaten mushrooms five minutes before the attack.

It seemed irreverent[2] to talk as the ambulance pulled away. My 26
friend, who still saw his father's image, muttered, "That guy's dead." I put my arms around him half to comfort him, half to stop him from saying things I couldn't believe.

[2]*irreverent:* lacking proper respect or seriousness.

The next day, when I called someone who lived in the house, I found that my friend was right. 27

My hands began to shake and my eyes filled with tears for someone I didn't know. Weeks later the pain has dulled, but I still can't unravel the knot of emotion that has moved from my stomach to my head. When I told one friend what happened, she shook her head and spoke of the stupidity of filling your body with chemical substances. People who would do drugs after seeing that didn't value their lives too highly, she said. 28

But others refused to read any universal lessons from the incident. Many of those I spoke to about the event considered him the victim of a freak accident, randomly struck down by drugs as a pedestrian might be hit by a speeding taxi. They speculated that the student must have had special physical problems; what happened to him could not happen to them. 29

Couldn't it? Now when I hear people discussing drugs I'm haunted by the image of him lying on the floor, his body straining to rid itself of substances he chose to take. Painful, undignified, unnecessary—like a wartime casualty. But in war, at least, lessons are supposed to be learned, so that old mistakes are not repeated. If this death cannot make people think and change, that will be an even greater tragedy. 30

Thinking Critically about This Reading

Based on Rowley's opening sentence—"The fastest way to end a party is to have someone die in the middle of it"—for whom do you think she is writing?

Questions for Study and Discussion

1. Rowley uses an extended narrative example to develop her argument. (Glossary: *Narration*) How does she use dialogue, diction choices, and appropriate details to make her argument more compelling? (Glossary: *Dialogue; Diction; Details*)
2. Although Rowley does not argue her point until the last sentence of the essay, her purpose is clear early on. (Glossary: *Purpose*) What does she want us to believe? What does she want us to do? How does her anecdote serve as the foundation for her argument? (Glossary: *Anecdote*)

3. What does Rowley gain by sharing this powerful experience with her readers? How did Rowley's friends react when she told them her story?
4. Why do you think Rowley chose not to name the young man who died? In what ways is this young man different from Len Bias, the talented basketball player who died of a drug overdose?
5. What in Rowley's tone particularly contributes to the persuasiveness of the essay? (Glossary: *Tone*) Cite examples from the selection that support your conclusion.
6. How does Rowley's opening paragraph affect you? (Glossary: *Beginnings and Endings*) What would have been lost had she combined the first two paragraphs?

Classroom Activity Using Argument

Choose *one* of the following position statements, and make a list of the types of information and evidence you would need to write an argumentative essay on the topic. Indicate where and how you might obtain this information.

1. More parking spaces should be provided on campus for students.
2. English should be declared the official language of the United States.
3. Performance standards in our schools should be raised.
4. The Food and Drug Administration takes too long to decide whether new drugs will be made available to consumers.
5. Job placement is not the responsibility of colleges and universities.

Suggested Writing Assignments

1. Write a persuasive essay supporting or refuting the following proposition: "Television advertising is in large part responsible for Americans' belief that over-the-counter drugs are cure-alls." Does such advertising, in fact, promote drug dependence or abuse?
2. What is the most effective way to bring about social change and influence societal attitudes? Concentrating on the sorts of changes you have witnessed over the last ten years, write an essay in which you describe how best to influence public opinion.

In Praise of the F Word

Mary Sherry

Mary Sherry was born in Bay City, Michigan, and received her bachelor's degree from Rosary College in River Forest, Illinois. She owns her own research and publishing company specializing in information for economic and development organizations. Sherry also teaches in adult-literacy programs and has written essays on educational problems for various newspapers, including the Wall Street Journal *and* Newsday.

In the following essay, originally published in Newsweek *in 1991, Sherry takes a provocative stance—that the threat of flunking is a "positive teaching tool." She believes students would all be better off if they had a "healthy fear of failure," and she marshals a series of logical appeals to both clarify and support her argument.*

For Your Journal

Comment on what you see as the relationship between learning and grades. Do teachers and students pay too much attention to grades at the expense of learning? Or are grades not seen as important enough?

Tens of thousands of 18-year-olds will graduate this year and be handed meaningless diplomas. These diplomas won't look any different from those awarded their luckier classmates. Their validity will be questioned only when their employers discover that these graduates are semiliterate. 1

Eventually a fortunate few will find their way into educational-repair shops—adult-literacy programs, such as the one where I teach basic grammar and writing. There, high-school graduates and high-school dropouts pursuing graduate-equivalency certificates will learn the skills they should have learned in school. They will also discover they have been cheated by our educational system. 2

As I teach, I learn a lot about our schools. Early in each session I ask my students to write about an unpleasant experience they had in school. No writers' block here! "I wish someone would have made me 3 stop doing drugs and made me study." "I liked to party and no one seemed to care." "I was a good kid and didn't cause any trouble, so they just passed me along even though I didn't read well and couldn't write." And so on.

I am your basic do-gooder, and prior to teaching this class I blamed 4 the poor academic skills our kids have today on drugs, divorce, and other impediments to concentration necessary for doing well in school. But, as I rediscover each time I walk into the classroom, before a teacher can expect students to concentrate, he has to get their attention, no matter what distractions may be at hand. There are many ways to do this, and they have much to do with teaching style. However, if style alone won't do it, there is another way to show who holds the winning hand in the classroom. That is to reveal the trump card[1] of failure.

I will never forget a teacher who played that card to get the atten- 5 tion of one of my children. Our youngest, a world-class charmer, did little to develop his intellectual talents but always got by. Until Mrs. Stifter.

Our son was a high-school senior when he had her for English. 6 "He sits in the back of the room talking to his friends," she told me. "Why don't you move him to the front row?" I urged, believing the embarrassment would get him to settle down. Mrs. Stifter looked at me steely-eyed over her glasses. "I don't move seniors," she said. "I flunk them." I was flustered. Our son's academic life flashed before my eyes. No teacher had ever threatened him with that before. I regained my composure and managed to say that I thought she was right. By the time I got home I was feeling pretty good about this. It was a radical approach for these times, but, well, why not? "She's going to flunk you," I told my son. I did not discuss it any further. Suddenly English became a priority in his life. He finished out the semester with an A.

I know one example doesn't make a case, but at night I see a 7 parade of students who are angry and resentful for having been passed along until they could no longer even pretend to keep up. Of average intelligence or better, they eventually quit school, concluding they were too dumb to finish. "I should have been held back" is a comment I hear frequently. Even sadder are those students who are high-school graduates who say to me after a few weeks of class, "I don't know how I ever got a high-school diploma."

---

[1]*trump card:* secret weapon; hidden advantage.

Passing students who have not mastered the work cheats them and the employers who expect graduates to have basic skills. We excuse this dishonest behavior by saying kids can't learn if they come from terrible environments. No one seems to stop to think that—no matter what environments they come from—most kids don't put school first on their list unless they perceive something is at stake. They'd rather be sailing. 8

Many students I see at night could give expert testimony on unemployment, chemical dependency, abusive relationships. In spite of these difficulties, they have decided to make education a priority. They are motivated by the desire for a better job or the need to hang on to the one they've got. They have a healthy fear of failure. 9

People of all ages can rise above their problems, but they need to have a reason to do so. Young people generally don't have the maturity to value education in the same way my adult students value it. But fear of failure, whether economic or academic, can motivate both. 10

Flunking as a regular policy has just as much merit today as it did two generations ago. We must review the threat of flunking and see it as it really is—a positive teaching tool. It is an expression of confidence by both teachers and parents that the students have the ability to learn the material presented to them. However, making it work again would take a dedicated, caring conspiracy between teachers and parents. It would mean facing the tough reality that passing kids who haven't learned the material—while it might save them grief for the short term—dooms them to long-term illiteracy. It would mean that teachers would have to follow through on their threats, and parents would have to stand behind them, knowing their children's best interests are indeed at stake. This means no more doing Scott's assignments for him because he might fail. No more passing Jodi because she's such a nice kid. 11

This is a policy that worked in the past and can work today. A wise teacher, with the support of his parents, gave our son the opportunity to succeed—or fail. It's time we return this choice to all students. 12

Thinking Critically about This Reading

According to Sherry, "We must review the threat of flunking and see it as it really is—a positive teaching tool. It is an expression of confidence by both teachers and parents that the students have the ability to learn the material presented to them" (paragraph 11). How can flunking students be "an expression of confidence" in them?

Questions for Study and Discussion

1. What is Sherry's *thesis?* (Glossary: *Thesis*) What evidence does she use to support her argument?
2. Sherry uses dismissive terms to characterize objections to flunking: *cheats* and *excuses.* In your opinion, does she do enough to acknowledge the other side of the argument? Explain.
3. What is the "F word" discussed in the essay? Does referring to it as the "F word" increase the effectiveness of the essay? Why?
4. Who is Sherry's audience? (Glossary: *Audience*) Is it receptive to the "F word"? Explain your answer.
5. In what way is Sherry qualified to comment on the potential benefits of flunking students? Do you think her induction is accurate?

Classroom Activity Using Argument

A first-year composition student, Marco Schmidt, is preparing to write an essay in which he will argue that music should be a required course for all public high school students. He has compiled the following pieces of evidence:

- Informal interviews with four classmates. Three of the classmates stated that they would have enjoyed and benefited from taking a music course in high school, and the fourth stated that she would not have been interested in taking music.
- An article from a professional journal for teachers comparing the study habits of students who were involved in music and those who were not. The author, a psychologist, found that students who play an instrument or sing regularly have better study habits than students who do not.
- A brief article from a national newsmagazine praising an inner-city high school's experimental curriculum, in which music classes play a prominent part.
- The personal Web site of a high school music teacher who posts information about the successes and achievements of her former students.

Discuss these pieces of evidence with your classmates. Which are most convincing? Which provide the least support for Marco's argument?

Why? What other types of evidence might Marco find to support his argument?

Suggested Writing Assignments

1. Write an essay in which you argue against Sherry's thesis. (Glossary: *Thesis*) In what ways is flunking bad for students? Are there techniques more positive than a "fear of failure" that can be used to motivate students?
2. Think of something that involves short-term pain or sacrifice, but can be beneficial in the long run. For example, exercising requires exertion, but it may help prevent health problems. Studying and writing papers when you'd rather be having fun or even sleeping may seem painful, but a college degree leads to personal growth and development. Even if the benefits are obvious, imagine a skeptical audience, and write an argument in favor of the short-term sacrifice over the long-term consequences of avoiding it. (Glossary: *Audience*)

Don't Eat the Flan

■ Greg Critser

Greg Critser lives in Pasadena, California, and writes regularly for USA Today *and the* Los Angeles Times *on issues of nutrition, health, and medicine. An authority on the subject of food politics, Critser has been interviewed by PBS and other media, and his writing on obesity earned him a James Beard nomination for best feature writing in 1999. Embarrassed by a passing motorist who shouted "Watch it, fatso," Critser went on a diet and lost forty pounds. In the process he discovered that in America, weight is a class issue—fat and poor often go together. In exposing the heavy truths about American obesity, Critser gives our bloated nation a wake-up call. His books include* Fat Land: How Americans Became the Fattest People in the World *(2003) and* Generation Rx: How Prescription Drugs Are Altering American Lives, Minds, and Bodies *(2005).*

In the following essay, which first appeared in the February 3, 2003, issue of Forbes, *Critser explains that in doing the research for* Fat Land *he could not find any present-day connection between the sin of gluttony and our national problem with obesity. He argues, therefore, that we should reintroduce moral authority in fighting obesity, a tactic that has worked well in our fight against unsafe sex and smoking.*

For Your Journal

Most health reports indicate that obesity continues to rise in America toward epidemic proportions. What do you think has gone wrong? What do you think needs to be done? What incentives are needed to encourage change?

By now you have likely seen nearly every imaginable headline about obesity in America. You've seen the ominous statistical 1 ones: "Nearly two-thirds of all Americans now overweight, study says." Or the sensational ones: "Two N.Y. teens sue McDonald's for making them fat." Or the medical ones: "Adult-onset diabetes now soars among children."

But one obesity headline you will not see is the one that deals with morality. Specifically, it is the one that might read like this: "Sixth deadly sin at root of obesity epidemic, researchers say." This is because gluttony,[1] perhaps alone among humanity's vices, has become the first media non-sin. 2

I first got a whiff of this transformation a few years ago while working on a book about obesity. Looking for a book about food and morality, I asked a clerk in the religious bookstore at the Fuller Seminary in Pasadena where I might find one on gluttony. 3

"Hmm," he pondered. "Maybe you'd want to look under eating disorders." 4

"But I'm not looking for a medical book. I'm looking for something about gluttony—you know, one of the seven deadly sins." I was sure he'd point me to Aquinas, Dante or at least a nice long shelf on sin. But he didn't. 5

"Oh, why didn't you say so?" the young man said, now quite serious. "If we have anything like that, it'll be over in self-help." 6

I then made inquiries about interviewing a professor who might be an expert on sin. I was told there was no one at this conservative seminary who had anything to say on the subject. 7

What might be called the "therapization" of gluttony is hardly limited to the sphere of conventional religion. Of much greater import is the legitimizing of gluttony in medicine and public health. For at least two decades any suggestion that morality—or even parental admonition[2]—be used to fight the curse of overeating has been greeted like Ted Bundy at a Girl Scout convention. Behind this lies the notion, widely propounded[3] by parenting gurus, that food should never become a dinner-table battle. 8

The operative notion here is simple: Telling people to not eat too much food is counterproductive. Worse, it leads to "stigmatization," which can lead to eating disorders, low self-esteem, and bad body image. Though the consequences of being overweight, numerous and 9

[1]*gluttony:* excessive eating or drinking.
[2]*admonition:* cautionary advice or warning.
[3]*propounded:* put forth; supported.

well documented, are dangerous, little if any evidence supports the notion that it is dangerous to stigmatize unhealthy behavior. Nevertheless, suggest to an "obesity counselor" that people should be counseled against gluttony and nine out of ten times you will be admonished as a veritable child abuser.

That's too bad, because it eliminates a fundamental—and proven— public health tactic. In the campaigns against unsafe sex and smoking, stigmatizing unhealthy behaviors proved highly effective in reducing risk. 10

Worse, this absence of moral authority in the realm of food leaves children—everyone, really—vulnerable to the one force in American life that has no problem making absolute claims: food advertisers, who spend billions teaching kids how to bug their parents into feeding them high-fat, high-sugar foods. Combine that with the lingering (albeit debunked) 1980s dogma—that "kids know when kids are full"—and you get, as one nutritionist-parent forcefully told me, the idea that "kids have the right to make bad nutritional decisions." 11

You would have a hard time selling that to the one Western nation that apparently avoided the obesity epidemic: France. The French intentionally created a culture of dietary restraint in the early 20th century, through a state-sponsored program known as *puériculture*. Reacting to early cases of childhood obesity, health activists wrote parenting manuals, conducted workshops and published books. Their advice: Parents must control the dinner table; all portions should be moderate; desserts were for holidays. Eating too much food was a bad thing. 12

And therein lies at least part of the explanation for the legendary leanness of the very confident French: They were taught as children not to overeat. And they didn't even have to look in the self-help section for the advice. 13

Thinking Critically about This Reading

What does Critser mean by "gluttony, perhaps alone among humanity's vices, has become the first media non-sin" (paragraph 2)? What evidence does he provide to support this claim?

Questions for Study and Discussion

1. What is Critser's argument in this essay? How convincing do you find it?

2. What do you think of people who sue fast-food companies such as McDonald's for making them fat? Who is most responsible in these cases—the fast-food companies or the people who choose to eat there? Explain.
3. How have the French fought off obesity, according to Critser? Are you convinced of the cause-and-effect relationship that Critser points to between the *puériculture* the French established in the early twentieth century and their "legendary leanness" (13)? (Glossary: *Cause and Effect*) Might there be other reasons for their leanness?
4. What does Critser mean by the "'therapization' of gluttony" (8)? Why do you suppose he places the word in quotation marks?
5. What are the "seven deadly sins" (5)? Are they all now as much out of favor as gluttony itself, in your estimation? Explain.
6. What is the meaning of the word *flan* in Critser's title? (Glossary: *Title*) How effective is the title in your opinion?

Classroom Activity Using Argument

Identify the fallacy in each of the following statements. (For more information on logical fallacies, see the box on p. 489.)

a. Oversimplification
b. Hasty generalization
c. *Post hoc, ergo propter hoc*
d. Begging the question
e. False analogy
f. Either/or thinking
g. *Non sequitur*

1. America: Love it or leave it! ______
2. Two of my best friends who are overweight don't exercise at all. Overweight people are simply not getting enough exercise. ______
3. If we use less gasoline, the price of gasoline will fall. ______
4. Life is precious because we want to protect it at all costs. ______
5. Randy is a good mechanic so he'll be a good race car driver.______
6. Susan drank hot lemonade and her cold went away. ______
7. Students do poorly in college because they do too much surfing on the Web. ______
8. If we can eliminate pollution, we can cure cancer. ______
9. Such actions are illegal because they are prohibited by law. ______

10. Every time I have something important to do on my computer it crashes. ______
11. We should either raise taxes or cut social programs. ______
12. Education ought to be managed just as a good business is managed. ______

Suggested Writing Assignments

1. Have you ever been criticized for being too heavy or too thin? Have you ever tried to lose or gain weight? Was it difficult? What were the ups and downs? What did you learn from the experience? Did criticism about your weight help or hinder your efforts? Write an essay, based on your own experiences, in which you argue for or against a particular approach to maintaining a healthy weight.
2. As Critser points out, "food advertisers . . . spend billions teaching kids how to bug their parents into feeding them high-fat, high sugar foods" (11). Write an essay in which you argue that food advertising has a negative influence on children and what they eat. Be sure to support your claim by offering evidence that children in general are vulnerable to advertising and, in particular, to claims made about food.
3. Write an essay in which you argue that a lack of exercise is at the root of the obesity epidemic. How have "indoor media," such as video games, the Internet, and television, contributed to children's physical inactivity? What effect has slashed physical education programs in schools had on children's health? (Glossary: *Cause and Effect*) Conduct library and Internet research to find evidence—facts, figures, and expert testimony—that supports your argument. (Glossary: *Evidence*) To begin your research online, go to **bedfordstmartins.com/models** and click on "Argument Links."

Supersize Me: It's Time to Stop Blaming Fat People for Their Size

■ **Alison Motluk**

Alison Motluk was born in Hamilton, Ontario, where she went to public school before receiving her BA from the University of Toronto. The creator of two radio documentaries, See, If You Can Hear This *and* Synaesthesia, *Motluk has written numerous articles for* New Scientist *magazine where she covers science policy.*

In the following essay, first published in New Scientist *on October 30, 2004, Motluk argues that instead of blaming people for being overweight, health officials have turned their attention to what has been termed our "obesogenic" environment, a new set of conditions that has made it much easier in the last few decades for people to gain weight.*

For Your Journal

What kind of physical activities were part of your childhood experience? In general, are you more, less, or about as active as you were as a child? What, if anything, has changed about you, your interests, or your environment to affect your activity as you have aged? Explain.

Whether it is undertakers introducing a new range of extra-large coffins or airlines planning to charge passengers by the kilo,[1] these days our expanding waistlines are rarely out of the news. It is hard to ignore the fact that body shape has changed dramatically over the past few decades. 1

In 1992 about 13 percent of Americans were clinically obese. Only 10 years later that figure had rocketed to 22 percent, and in the three fattest states, Alabama, Mississippi, and West Virginia, it was over 2

[1]*kilo:* kilogram; a metric unit of weight equal to 2.2 pounds.

25 percent. As the UK, Australia, and many other Western countries follow the U.S. lead, the epidemic of obesity is now seen as one of the developed world's biggest public-health problems.

It is tempting to blame fat people for the state they're in. But health officials have recently begun to focus on a different culprit: the so-called "obesogenic" environment. In the United States, goes the argument, the prevailing culture actually promotes obesity, making an unhealthy lifestyle the default option. 3

Take diet. "Calorie-dense foods are far more readily available than ever before," says Martin Binks, a psychologist at Duke University's Diet and Fitness Center in Durham, North Carolina. Thanks to widespread affluence and agricultural subsidies, food in the United States is cheap and plentiful. Because fewer households have a stay-at-home parent to prepare meals from scratch, families increasingly turn to highly processed convenience foods, takeouts, or fast-food restaurants. Half the average American food budget goes on food eaten outside the home, much of which is high-fat. 4

Another insidious[2] influence on the American diet has been the gradual increase in portion sizes. "You eat more," says Judith Stern, a nutritionist and physician at the University of California at Davis, "even if you don't finish it." Restaurants and processed-food manufacturers can boost their profits by ratcheting up portion size and charging a little more because the price of food ingredients is so low relative to other costs such as packaging and transport. The original 1960s McDonald's meal of a hamburger, fries, and a 12-ounce Coke contained about 590 calories. But today, a quarter-pounder with cheese and supersized fries and Coke—a meal that some kids consider an after-school snack—racks up a whopping 1550 calories. That's about three-quarters of the recommended daily calorie intake for an average woman. 5

The supersized diet is becoming the norm just as activity levels are dropping to an all-time low. "There's a great deal less access to physical activity than ever before in history," says Binks. The problem starts young. One-third of U.S. secondary-school students fail to get enough physical activity and over a tenth get none at all, according to recent figures from the Centers for Disease Control in Atlanta, Georgia. "The average child doesn't have any physical activity in school any more," says Binks. Many schools no longer even have breaks, let alone 6

[2]*insidious:* working harmfully in a subtle manner.

structured physical education, he says. "Physical activity is put on the back burner in favor of test results."

And thanks to the way that most U.S. towns and cities are designed, it is becoming increasingly difficult to get anywhere without driving. "We have suburbs without sidewalks," laments Stern. 7

Ironically, the U.S.'s obesogenic environment is one that societies through the ages have dreamed of: tasty, cheap food in abundance and barely a lick of hard work to be done. Who would have thought that it would one day hasten our demise? 8

Thinking Critically about This Reading

What does Motluk mean when she writes, "Ironically, the U.S.'s obesogenic environment is one that societies through the ages have dreamed of: tasty, cheap food in abundance and barely a lick of hard work to be done" (paragraph 8)? Explain the irony.

Questions for Study and Discussion

1. Motluk argues that health officials are beginning to blame our "obesogenic" environment for the obesity gripping our society (3). What is the "obesogenic" environment, and what are its components, according to Motluk?
2. Motluk concedes, "It is tempting to blame fat people for the state they're in" (3). Why doesn't she elaborate on this concession or put more blame on people's eating habits for their obesity?
3. What kinds of proof does Motluk offer for her claim that portion sizes have increased? (Glossary: *Evidence*)
4. Is obesity a problem that Americans alone face? Explain.
5. What solutions, if any, does Motluk propose to lessen the harmful effects of our "obesogenic" environment?

Classroom Activity Using Argument

In "Supersize Me," Motluk argues that it is "Time to Stop Blaming Fat People for Their Size." Through classroom discussion explore ways in which we can lessen the prejudice against those who are overweight by shedding light on the causes of obesity that go beyond personal eating habits.

Suggested Writing Assignments

1. Write an essay in which you argue for ways to counter the "obesogenic" environment. What can individuals, families, support groups, dietitians, schools, advertisers, food producers, and policy makers do to lessen the harmful trends that Motluk points out?
2. In an essay, argue that the federal government should make it mandatory for every school child to participate, according to his or her ability, in some form of daily exercise in school. What objections would you anticipate arising as a result of such a mandate, and what counterarguments would you offer in defense of your proposal? After sharing your argument with your classmates, considering their advice, and revising your argument accordingly, send it to your congressional representatives for their consideration.
3. Write an essay in which you argue that obesity is both a serious health problem and a major economic concern. Conduct library and Internet research on the estimated costs of obesity to the insurance and healthcare industries, employers, and individuals. What effects do these costs have on the economy? (Glossary: *Cause and Effect*) To begin your research online, go to **bedfordstmartins.com/models** and click on "Argument Links."

Condemn the Crime, Not the Person

■ **June Tangney**

*Psychology educator and researcher June Tangney was born in Buffalo, New York, in 1958. After graduating from SUNY–Buffalo in 1979, she attended the University of California–Los Angeles where she earned a master's degree in 1981 and a doctorate in 1985. Tangney taught briefly at Bryn Mawr College and held a research position at the Regional Center for Infants and Young Children in Rockville, Maryland. Since 1988 she has been a professor of psychology at George Mason University, where she was recognized with a Teaching Excellence Award. She is a co-author of two books—*Self-Conscious Emotions: The Psychology of Shame, Guilt, Embarrassment, and Pride *(1995), with Kurt W. Fisher, and* Shame and Guilt *(2002), with Rhonda L. Dearing—and an associate editor at the journal* Self and Identity.

In the following essay, first published in the Boston Globe *on August 5, 2001, Tangney argues against the use of public humiliation as punishment. She bases her position on recent scientific evidence, much of which comes from her own work on shame and guilt.*

For Your Journal

For you, what is the difference between *shame* and *guilt*? Provide an example from your own experience to illustrate your understanding of each concept.

As the costs of incarceration mount and evidence of its failure as a deterrent grows, judges understandably have begun to search for creative alternatives to traditional sentences. One recent trend is the use of "shaming" sentences—sanctions explicitly designed to induce feelings of shame. 1

Judges across the country are sentencing offenders to parade around in public carrying signs broadcasting their crimes, to post signs on their front lawns warning neighbors of their vices, and to display "drunk driver" bumper stickers on their cars. 2

A number of social commentators have urged America to embrace public shaming and stigmatization as cheaper and effective alternatives for curbing a broad range of nonviolent crimes. Punishments aimed at public humiliation certainly appeal to our sense of moral righteousness. They do indeed appear fiscally attractive when contrasted with the escalating costs of incarceration. 3

But recent scientific evidence suggests that such attempts at social control are misguided. Rather than fostering constructive change, shame often makes a bad situation worse. 4

The crux[1] of the matter lies in the distinction between shame and guilt. Recent research has shown that shame and guilt are distinct emotions with very different implications for subsequent moral and interpersonal behavior. Feelings of shame involve a painful focus on the self—the humiliating sense that "I am a bad person." 5

Such humiliation is typically accompanied by a sense of shrinking, of being small, worthless, and powerless, and by a sense of being exposed. Ironically, research has shown that such painful and debilitating feelings of shame do not motivate constructive changes in behavior. 6

Shamed individuals are no less likely to repeat their transgressions (often more so), and they are no more likely to attempt reparation[2] (often less so). Instead, because shame is so intolerable, people in the midst of the experience often resort to any one of a number of defensive tactics. 7

They may seek to hide or escape the shameful feeling, denying responsibility. They may seek to shift the blame outside, holding others responsible for their dilemma. And not infrequently, they become irrationally angry with others, sometimes resorting to overtly aggressive and destructive actions. In short, shame serves to escalate the very destructive patterns of behavior we aim to curb. 8

Contrast this with feelings of guilt which involve a focus on a specific behavior—the sense that "I did a bad thing" rather than "I am a bad person." 9

[1]*crux:* the essential or deciding point.
[2]*reparation:* a making of amends; repayment.

Feelings of guilt involve a sense of tension, remorse, and regret over 10 the "bad thing done."

Research has shown that this sense of tension and regret typically 11 motivates reparative action (confessing, apologizing, or somehow repairing the damage done) without engendering[3] all the defensive and retaliative responses that are the hallmark of shame.

Most important, feelings of guilt are much more likely to foster 12 constructive changes in future behavior because what is at issue is not a bad, defective self, but a bad, defective behavior. And, as anyone knows, it is easier to change a bad behavior (drunken driving, slumlording, thievery) than to change a bad, defective self.

How can we foster constructive feelings of guilt among America's 13 offenders? Well, one way is to force offenders to focus on the negative consequences of their behavior, particularly on the painful negative consequences for others.

Community service sentences can do much to promote constructive 14 guilt when they are tailored to the nature of the crime. What is needed are imposed activities that underscore the tangible destruction caused by the offense and that provide a path to redemption by ameliorating[4] similar human misery.

Drunk drivers, for example, could be sentenced to help clear sites 15 of road accidents and to assist with campaigns to reduce drunken driving. Slumlords could be sentenced to assist with nuts and bolts repairs in low-income housing units. In this way, offenders are forced to see, first-hand, the potential or actual destructiveness of their infractions and they become actively involved in constructive solutions.

Some critics have rejected community service as an alternative to 16 incarceration, suggesting that such community-based sentences somehow cheapen an otherwise honorable volunteer activity while at the same time not adequately underscoring the criminal's disgrace.

Scientific research, however, clearly indicates that public shaming 17 and humiliation is not the path of choice. Such efforts are doomed to provoke all sorts of unintended negative consequences.

In contrast, thoughtfully constructed guilt-oriented community ser- 18 vice sentences are more likely to foster changes in offenders' future behaviors, while contributing to the larger societal good. My guess is

[3]*engendering:* causing or producing.
[4]*ameliorating:* improving or making better.

that any honorable community service volunteer would welcome such constructive changes.

Thinking Critically about This Reading

Tangney states that "a number of social commentators have urged America to embrace public shaming and stigmatization as cheaper and effective alternatives for curbing a broad range of nonviolent crimes" (paragraph 3). What evidence does she present to counter these arguments?

Questions for Study and Discussion

1. What is a "shaming" sentence (1)? According to Tangney, why do judges use such sentences in place of more traditional ones?
2. What is Tangney's position on using sentences intended to shame offenders? Briefly state her thesis in your own words. (Glossary: *Thesis*)
3. What for Tangney is the key difference between *shame* and *guilt*? Why does she believe guilt works better than shame as a form of punishment?
4. Paragraph 13 begins with a rhetorical question: "How can we foster constructive feelings of guilt among America's offenders?" (Glossary: *Rhetorical Question*) How does Tangney answer this question? What suggestions would you add to her solution?
5. How does Tangney counter the critics of community service? Do you find her counterarguments convincing? Why or why not?

Classroom Activity Using Argument

The effectiveness of a writer's argument depends in large part on the writer's awareness of audience. For example, a writer arguing that there is too much violence portrayed on television might find it necessary to present different kinds of evidence, reasoning, and diction if the intended audience included parents, lawmakers, or television producers and writers.

Review several of the argument essays you have read in this chapter. In your opinion, for what primary audience is each essay intended? List the evidence you use to determine your answers. (Glossary: *Evidence*)

Suggested Writing Assignments

1. Write an essay in which you tell the story of a childhood punishment you received or witnessed. (Glossary: *Narration*) How did you feel about the punishment? Was it justified? Appropriate? Effective? Why or why not? In retrospect, did the punishment shame or humiliate you, or did it bring out feelings of guilt? What did you learn from this experience? Before starting to write, read or review Lisa V. Driver's "The Strong Arm of a Sixth-Grade Teacher" (pp. 57–59) and Dick Gregory's "Shame" (pp. 245–50).
2. What statement does the following cartoon make about punishment? How would Tangney respond to the cartoon? Why? Using Tangney's essay, the cartoon, and your own experience, write an argument essay in which you take a position on how people should be held accountable for bad behavior.

"What do I think is an appropriate punishment? I think an appropriate punishment would be to make me live with my guilt."

3. According to Tangney, "as the costs of incarceration mount and evidence of its failure as a deterrent grows, judges understandably have begun to search for creative alternatives to traditional sentences" (1). Ideally, knowing what the punishment will be should deter people from doing the wrong thing in the first place, but do punishments really act as deterrents? Are certain punishments more effective as deterrents than others? What are the deterrent benefits of both shame and guilt punishments? Conduct library and Internet research to answer these questions, and then report your findings and conclusions in an essay. To begin your research online, go to **bedfordstmartins.com/models** and click on "Argument Links."

Shame Is Worth a Try

■ **Dan M. Kahan**

Dan M. Kahan graduated from Middlebury College in 1986 and Harvard Law School in 1989, where he served as president of the Harvard Law Review. *He clerked for Judge Harry Edwards of the U.S. Court of Appeals for the District of Columbia circuit in 1989–1990 and for Justice Thurgood Marshall of the U.S. Supreme Court in 1990–1991. After practicing law for two years in Washington, D.C., Kahan launched his teaching career, first at the University of Chicago Law School and later at Yale Law School, where since 2003 he has been the Elizabeth K. Dollard Professor of Law. His teaching and research interests include criminal law, risk perception, punishment, and evidence. Kahan, who has written widely in legal journals on current social issues including gun control, is the co-author, with Tracey Meares, of* Urgent Times: Policing and Rights in Inner-City Communities *(1999). In 2005 he was appointed deputy dean of Yale Law School.*

In the following essay, first published in the Boston Globe *on August 5, 2001, Kahan argues in favor of the use of shame as a punishment that is "an effective, cheap, and humane alternative to imprisonment."*

For Your Journal

Think about the times you were punished as a child. Who punished you—parents, teachers, or other authority figures? What kinds of bad behavior were you punished for? What type of punishment worked best to deter you from behaving badly later on? Explain.

Is shame an appropriate criminal punishment? Many courts and legislators around the country think so. Steal from your employer in Wisconsin and you might be ordered to wear a sandwich board proclaiming your offense. Drive drunk in Florida or Texas and you might be required to place a conspicuous "DUI" bumper sticker to your car. Refuse to make your child-support payments in Virginia and you will 1 find that your vehicle has been immobilized with an appropriately colored boot (pink if the abandoned child is a girl, blue if a boy).

Many experts, however, are skeptical of these new shaming punishments. Some question their effectiveness as a deterrent. Others worry that the new punishments are demeaning and cruel. 2

Who's right? As is usually the case, both sides have their points. But what the shame proponents seem to be getting, and the critics ignoring, is the potential of shame as an effective, cheap, and humane alternative to imprisonment. 3

There's obviously no alternative to imprisonment for murderers, rapists, and other violent criminals. But they make up less than half the American prison population. 4

Liberal and conservative reformers alike have long believed that the remainder can be effectively punished with less severe "alternative sanctions," like fines and community service. These sanctions are much cheaper than jail. They also allow the offender to continue earning an income so he can compensate his victim, meet his child-support obligations, and the like. 5

Nevertheless, courts and legislators have resisted alternative sanctions—not so much because they won't work, but because they fail to express appropriate moral condemnation of crime. Fines seem to say that offenders may buy the privilege of breaking the law; and we can't very well condemn someone for purchasing what we are willing to sell. 6

Nor do we condemn offenders to educate the retarded, install smoke detectors in nursing homes, restore dilapidated low income housing, and the like. Indeed, saying that such community service is punishment for criminals insults both those who perform such services voluntarily and those whom the services are supposed to benefit. 7

There's no confusion about the law's intent to condemn, however, when judges resort to public shaming. As a result, judges, legislators, and the public at large generally do accept shame as a morally appropriate punishment for drunken driving, nonaggravated assaults, embezzlement,[1] small-scale drug distribution, larceny,[2] toxic waste dumping, perjury, and a host of other offenses that ordinarily would result in a short jail term. 8

[1]*embezzlement:* stealing money or goods entrusted to one's care.

[2]*larceny:* theft.

The critics' anxieties about shame, moreover, seem overstated. 9
Clearly, shame hurts. People value their reputations for both emotional and financial reasons. In fact, a series of studies by Harold Grasmick, a sociologist at the University of Oklahoma, suggests that the prospect of public disgrace exerts greater pressure to comply with the law than does the threat of imprisonment and other formal punishments.

There's every reason to believe, then, that shaming penalties will be 10
an effective deterrent, at least for nonviolent crimes. Indeed, preliminary reports suggest that certain shaming punishments, including those directed at dead beat dads, are extraordinarily effective.

At the same time, shame clearly doesn't hurt as much as imprison- 11
ment. Individuals who go to jail end up just as disgraced as those who are shamed, and lose their liberty to boot. Those who've served prison time are also a lot less likely to regain the respect and trust of their law-abiding neighbors—essential ingredients of rehabilitation. Given all this, it's hard to see shame as cruel.

Consider the case of a Florida mother sentenced to take out a 12
newspaper ad proclaiming "I purchased marijuana with my kids in the car."

The prospect that her neighbors would see the ad surely caused 13
her substantial embarrassment. But the alternative was a jail sentence, which would not only have humiliated her more but could also have caused her to lose custody of her children. Not surprisingly, the woman voluntarily accepted the shaming sanction in lieu of[3] jail time, as nearly all offenders do.

Shame, like any other type of criminal punishment, can definitely be 14
abused. Some forms of it, like the public floggings imposed by authoritarian states abroad, are pointlessly degrading.

In addition, using shame as a supplement rather than a substitute 15
for imprisonment only makes punishment more expensive for society and destructive for the offender. Accordingly, requiring sex offenders to register with local authorities is harder to defend than are other types of shaming punishments, which are true substitutes for jail.

These legitimate points, however, are a reason to insist that 16
shaming be carried out appropriately, not to oppose it across the board.

---

[3]*in lieu of:* in place of; instead of.

In short, shame is cheap and effective and frees up scarce prison space for the more serious offenses. Why not at least give it a try? 17

Thinking Critically about This Reading

What does Kahan mean when he states that "requiring sex offenders to register with local authorities is harder to defend than are other types of shaming punishments" (paragraph 15)?

Questions for Study and Discussion

1. What is Kahan's thesis? (Glossary: *Thesis*) Where does he state it most clearly?
2. What examples of shaming punishments does Kahan provide? For you, do these punishments seem to fit the crime? Explain.
3. How does Kahan handle the opposition argument that public shaming is cruel?
4. According to Kahan, why have courts and legislators resisted alternative punishments such as fines and community service?
5. What evidence does Kahan present to show that shaming punishments work? (Glossary: *Evidence*)
6. How convincing is Kahan's argument? What is the strongest part of his argument? The weakest part? Explain.

Classroom Activity Using Argument

Can killing ever be justified? If so, under what circumstances? Have six members of the class, three on each side of the question, volunteer to hold a debate. Team members should assign themselves different aspects of their position and then do library and Internet research to develop ideas and evidence. The teams should be allowed equal time to present their assertions and the evidence they have to support them. Finally, the rest of the class should be prepared to discuss the effectiveness of the presentations on both sides of the question.

Suggested Writing Assignments

1. Write an essay in which you argue your position on the issue of using public shaming as a punishment. Is public shaming

appropriate for some or all offenses that would otherwise result in a short jail term? Explain. Support your argument with evidence from Kahan's essay, June Tangney's "Condemn the Crime, Not the Person" (pp. 524–29), and your own experiences and observations. (Glossary: *Evidence*) You may find it helpful to review your journal response for this selection.

2. Identify several current problems at your college or university involving violations of campus rules for parking, cheating on exams, plagiarizing papers, recycling waste, using drugs or alcohol, defacing school property, and so on. Select *one* problem, and write a proposal to treat violators with a shaming punishment of your own design. Address your proposal to your school's student government organization or administration office.
3. What is your position on the issue of whether convicted sex offenders should be required to register with local authorities or not—because they have already served their sentences in prison? Should people have the right to know the identity of any sex offenders living in their neighborhoods, or is this an invasion of privacy? Conduct library and Internet research on the subject of sex offender registration, and write an essay arguing for or against such measures. To begin your research online, go to **bedfordstmartins.com/models** and click on "Argument Links."

Parents Should Be Allowed to Opt Out of Vaccinating Their Children

Barbara Loe Fisher

Barbara Loe Fisher is the cofounder and president of the National Vaccine Information Center (NVIC) in Vienna, Virginia, a non-profit advocacy group calling for safer vaccines. As NVIC's public spokesperson, Fisher has spent over twenty years giving speeches at healthcare conferences, doing radio and television interviews, organizing public workshops, offering testimony to Congress, working with parents to prevent vaccine-related deaths and injuries, and arguing for informed consent to vaccination. She has written DPT: Shot in the Dark *(1985), with Harris Coulter, the first major study of America's mass vaccination system, and* The Consumer's Guide to Childhood Vaccines *(1997). She is as well the editor of the* Vaccine Reaction, *a twice-weekly natural health newsletter. Fisher has three children, the oldest of whom Fisher claims developed multiple learning disabilities and attention-deficit disorder after receiving his fourth DPT shot in 1980 at the age of two and a half.*

In the following article, first published on April 24, 2000, in Insight, *Fisher presents her argument against indiscriminate mass vaccinations and makes a call for more government-funded research on the possible connections between vaccines and such diseases as asthma, diabetes, autism, and chronic arthritis.*

For Your Journal

What knowledge do you have of vaccinations? If you are a parent, how did you react to the need to have your child vaccinated? If you plan to be a parent someday, what would your reaction to this requirement be?

Parents do not want their children to be injured or die from a disease or a vaccination. As guardians of their children until those children are old enough to make life-and-death decisions for themselves, parents take very seriously the responsibility of making informed vaccination decisions for the children they love. That responsibility includes becoming educated about the relative risks of diseases when compared to the vaccines aimed at preventing them. 1

Like every encounter with a viral or bacterial infection, every vaccine containing lab-altered viruses or bacteria has an inherent ability to cause injury or even death. Vaccination either can produce immunity without incident or can result in mild to severe brain and immune-system damage, depending upon the vaccine or combination of vaccines given, the health of the person at the time of vaccination, and whether the individual is genetically or otherwise biologically at risk for developing complications. 2

The fact that vaccines can cause injury and death officially was acknowledged in the United States in 1986 when Congress passed the National Childhood Vaccine Injury Act, creating a no-fault federal compensation system for vaccine-injured children to protect the vaccine manufacturers and doctors from personal-injury lawsuits. Since then, the system has paid out more than $1 billion to 1,000 families, whose loved ones have died or been harmed by vaccines, even though three out of four applicants are turned away. 3

Since 1990, between 12,000 and 14,000 reports of hospitalizations, injuries, and deaths following vaccination are made to the federal Vaccine Adverse Event Reporting System, or VAERS, annually, but it is estimated that only between 1 and 10 percent of all doctors make reports to VAERS. Therefore, the number of vaccine-related health problems occurring in the United States every year may be more than 1 million. 4

In the late 1980s, the Institute of Medicine, or IOM, and the National Academy of Sciences convened committees of physicians to study existing medical knowledge about vaccines and, in 1991 and 1994, IOM issued historic reports confirming vaccines can cause death, as well as a wide spectrum of brain and immune-system damage. But the most important conclusion, which deserves greater public attention and congressional action, was: "The lack of adequate data regarding many of the [vaccine] adverse events under study was of major concern to the committee. [T]he committee encountered many gaps and limitations in knowledge bearing directly or indirectly on the safety of vaccines." 5

Because so little medical research has been conducted on vaccine side effects, no tests have been developed to identify and screen out vulnerable children. As a result, public-health officials have taken a "one-size-fits-all" approach and have aggressively implemented mandatory vaccination laws while dismissing children who are injured or die after vaccination as unfortunate but necessary sacrifices "for the greater good." This utilitarian rationale is of little comfort to the growing number of mothers and fathers who watch their once-healthy, bright children get vaccinated and then suddenly descend into mental retardation, epilepsy, learning and behavior disorders, autism, diabetes, arthritis, and asthma. Some adverse reactions are fatal. 6

As vaccination rates have approached 98 percent for children entering kindergarten in many states, there is no question that mass vaccination in the last quarter-century has suppressed infectious diseases in childhood, eradicating[1] polio in the Western hemisphere and lowering the number of cases of measles from a high of more than 400,000 cases in 1965 to only 100 in 1999. Yet, even as infectious-disease rates have fallen, rates of chronic disease and disability among children and young adults have risen dramatically. 7

A University of California study published by the U.S. Department of Education in 1996 found that "the proportion of the U.S. population with disabilities has risen markedly during the last quarter-century. [T]his recent change seems to be due not to demographics, but to greater numbers of children and young adults reported as having disabilities." The study concluded the change was due to "increases in the prevalence of asthma, mental disorders (including attention-deficit disorder), mental retardation and learning disabilities that have been noted among children in recent years." 8

Instead of epidemics of measles and polio, we have epidemics of chronic autoimmune and neurological disease: In the last 20 years rates of asthma and attention-deficit disorder have doubled, diabetes and learning disabilities have tripled, chronic arthritis now affects nearly one in five Americans, and autism has increased by 300 percent or more in many states. The larger unanswered question is: To what extent has the administration of multiple doses of multiple vaccines in early childhood—when the body's brain and immune system is developing at its most rapid rate—been a cofactor in epidemics of chronic disease? 9

[1]*eradicating:* getting rid of.

The assumption that mass-vaccination policies have played no role is as unscientific and dangerous as the assumption that an individual child's health problems following vaccination are only coincidentally related to the vaccination.

Questions about vaccination only can be answered by scientific research into the biological mechanism of vaccine injury and death so that pathological[2] profiles can be developed to distinguish between vaccine-induced health problems and those that are not. Whether the gaps in scientific knowledge about vaccines will be filled in this decade or remain unanswered in the next depends upon the funding and research priorities set by Congress, the National Institutes of Health, and industry. 10

With the understanding that medical science and the doctors who practice it are not infallible, today's better-educated healthcare consumer is demanding more information, more choices, and a more equal decision-making partnership with doctors. Young mothers, who are told that their children must be injected with 33 doses of 10 different vaccines before the age of 5, are asking questions such as: "Why does my 12-hour-old newborn infant have to be injected with hepatitis B vaccine when I am not infected with hepatitis B and my infant is not an IV-drug user or engaging in sex with multiple partners—the two highest risk groups for hepatitis B infection?" And: "Why does my 12-month-old have to get chicken-pox vaccine when chicken pox is a mild disease and once my child gets it he or she will be immune for life?" Informed parents know that hepatitis B is not like polio and that chicken pox is not like smallpox. They know the difference between taking a risk with a vaccine for an adult disease that is hard to catch, such as the blood-transmitted hepatitis B, and using a vaccine to prevent a devastating, highly contagious childhood disease such as polio. 11

All diseases and all vaccines are not the same and neither are children. Parents understand the qualitative difference between options freely taken and punishing dictates. They are calling for enlightened, humane implementation of state vaccination laws, including insertion of informed-consent protections that strengthen exemptions for sincerely held religious or conscientious beliefs. This is especially critical for parents with reason to believe that their child may be at high risk for dying or being injured by one or more vaccines but cannot find a doctor to write an exemption. 12

[2]*pathological:* relating to or caused by disease.

Informed consent has been the gold standard in the ethical practice of medicine since World War II, acknowledging the human right for individuals or their guardians to make fully informed, voluntary decisions about whether to undergo a medical procedure that could result in harm or death. To the extent that vaccination has been exempted from informed-consent protections and vaccine makers and doctors have been exempted from liability for vaccine injuries and deaths, the notion that a minority of individuals are expendable in service to the majority has prevented a real commitment of will and resources to develop ways to screen out vulnerable children and spare their lives. It is not difficult to understand why some parents resist offering up their children as sacrifices for a government policy that lacks scientific and moral integrity. 13

But even as educated healthcare consumers are asking for more information and choices, mechanisms are being set up to restrict those choices. Government-operated, electronic vaccine-tracking systems already are in place in most states, using healthcare identifier numbers to tag and track children without the parent's informed consent in order to enforce use of all government-recommended vaccines now and in the future. Health-maintenance organizations are turning down children for health insurance, and federal entitlement programs are economically punishing parents who cannot show proof their child got every state-recommended vaccine. Even children who have suffered severe vaccine reactions are being pressured to get revaccinated or be barred from getting an education. 14

Drug companies and federal agencies are developing more than 200 new vaccines, including ones for gonorrhea and herpes that will target 12-year-olds. On March 2, 2002, President Clinton joined with the international pharmaceutical industry, multinational banks, and the Bill and Melinda Gates Foundation to launch the Millennium Vaccine Initiative with several billion dollars committed to vaccinating all children in the world with existing and future vaccines, including those in accelerated development for AIDS, tuberculosis, and malaria. 15

With so many unanswered questions about the safety and necessity of giving so many vaccines to children, the right to informed consent to vaccination takes on even greater legal and ethical significance as we head into the 21st century. In a broader sense, the concept of informed consent transcends medicine and addresses the constitutional concept of individual freedom and the moral concept of individual 16 inviolability.[3] If the state can tag, track down, and force individuals into being injected with biological agents of unknown toxicity today, will there be any limit on what individual freedoms the state can take away in the name of the greater good tomorrow?

Parents, who know and love their children better than anyone else, have the right to make informed, voluntary vaccination decisions for their children without facing state-sanctioned punishment. Whether a child is hurt by a vaccine or a disease, it is the mother and father—not the pediatrician, vaccine maker, or public-health official—who will bear the lifelong grief and burden of what happens to that child. 17

Thinking Critically about This Reading

If, as Fisher writes, "there is no question that mass vaccination in the last quarter-century has suppressed infectious diseases in childhood" (paragraph 7), what is her objection to vaccination?

Questions for Study and Discussion

1. What is Fisher's purpose? (Glossary: *Purpose*) Does she achieve it? Explain.
2. What proof does Fisher present that vaccinations can cause injury and death? (Glossary: *Evidence*)
3. How does Fisher support her claim that the actual number of "hospitalizations, injuries, and deaths following vaccination" may vastly exceed the number of reports made to VAERS (4)? (Glossary: *Evidence*)
4. Fisher argues that "instead of epidemics of measles and polio, we have epidemics of chronic autoimmune and neurological disease" (9). What proof does she offer that the shift is caused by vaccinations? (Glossary: *Evidence*) What proof can you offer that it is not?
5. Vaccination has been exempted from informed-consent protections, and vaccine makers and doctors have been exempted from liability. Do you agree or disagree with these government policies? Explain.
6. What changes would Fisher like to see take place with regard to public health policy as it applies to vaccinations?

[3]*inviolability:* secure from assault or violation.

Classroom Activity Using Argument

Deductive reasoning works on the model of the syllogism. After reviewing the material on syllogisms in the chapter introduction (p. 486), analyze the following syllogisms. Which work well, and which do not?

1. All of my CDs have blue lettering on them.
   I saw the new Youssou N'Dour CD the other day.
   The new Youssou N'Dour CD has blue lettering on it.
2. I have never lost a tennis match.
   I played a tennis match yesterday.
   I won my tennis match yesterday.
3. Surfers all want to catch the perfect wave.
   Jenny is a surfer.
   Jenny wants to catch the perfect wave.
4. Writers enjoy reading books.
   Bill enjoys reading books.
   Bill is a writer.
5. Cotton candy is an incredibly sticky kind of candy.
   Amy ate some incredibly sticky candy.
   Amy ate cotton candy.

Write two effective syllogisms of your own.

Suggested Writing Assignments

1. Write an argumentative essay answering the provocative question that Fisher poses in paragraph 16: "If the state can tag, track down, and force individuals into being injected with biological agents of unknown toxicity today, will there be any limit on what individual freedoms the state can take away in the name of the greater good tomorrow?" In your opinion, does the current vaccination policy open the door to future losses of personal freedoms? Why or why not?
2. In paragraph 3, Fisher writes that the National Childhood Vaccine Injury Act of 1986 created "a no-fault federal compensation system for vaccine-injured children to protect the vaccine manufacturers and doctors from personal-injury lawsuits." Given that the government mandates vaccinations, do you think it should be solely responsible for compensating individuals harmed by vaccines? Why

or why not? Would the fear of lawsuits cause manufacturers to stop producing and developing vaccines or doctors to stop administering them? Write an essay in which you speculate about the potential effects on the healthcare system if vaccine manufactures and doctors were not protected by the 1986 act. (Glossary: *Cause and Effect*)

3. One potential terrorist threat is the weaponization of a biological agent such as smallpox or anthrax. Conduct library and Internet research on the threat of bioterrorism and methods of protecting ourselves. Write an essay in which you argue for or against preemptive vaccinations for diseases likely to be used in a biological attack. The following questions will help you focus the topic: What is the likelihood of a biological attack? How prepared are we to deal with bioterrorism if it were to occur? What risks are associated with the vaccines that might be administered? What, if any, alternative approaches to vaccination should we consider? To begin your research online, go to **bedfordstmartins.com/models** and click on "Argument Links."

Parents Should Not Be Allowed to Opt Out of Vaccinating Their Children

Steven P. Shelov

Steven P. Shelov is professor of pediatrics at Mount Sinai School of Medicine, chairman of pediatrics at Maimonides Medical Center and Lutheran Medical Center, and vice president of the Infants' and Children's Hospital of Brooklyn in New York. Born in 1944 in Honolulu, Hawaii, he earned a BS from Yale University in 1966, an MD from the Medical College of Wisconsin in 1971, and an MS from the University of Wisconsin in 1995. Shelov is editor-in-chief of a series of books for the American Academy of Pediatrics that includes Guide to Your Child's Symptoms *(1997) and* Caring for Your Baby and Young Child: Birth to Age Five *(2004). In 2002 Shelov won the Lifetime Achievement in Education Award from the American Academy of Pediatrics.*

In the following article, which was published on April 24, 2000, in Insight, *Shelov argues that allowing parents to opt out of vaccinating their children would open the door to epidemics of some deadly childhood diseases.*

For Your Journal

Do you remember being immunized against certain diseases when you were a child? What was the experience like? Did you have any reactions to the vaccines? You might want to check with some of your classmates and friends about their experiences.

Children's immunization programs should not be optional. Failure to vaccinate a child would greatly increase his or her risk of contracting dangerous infectious diseases; it would also expose other children to illness and possibly lead to a deadly epidemic. On occasion children do have mild negative reactions to vaccines, but severe adverse reactions are extremely rare. Furthermore, there is no evidence linking vaccines to disorders such as autism, sudden infant death syndrome, 1 multiple sclerosis, or asthma. The hazards associated with illnesses such as tetanus, measles, and polio are far greater than the risks posed by immunization. Allowing parents to opt out of vaccinating their children would endanger public health.

Some parents today are in a quandary regarding the need for immunizing their children. They need not be. 2

True, recent media stories about an increase in childhood autism associated with immunizations and other illnesses have led some to question the need to give their children the full range of vaccinations required by most school districts in the country. In addition, numerous others have had unfortunate experiences with their own children or relatives with respect to a bad reaction to an immunization. Yet, it is important to keep all these issues and incidents in perspective and not to erode public confidence in immunizing our children. In fact, if the U.S. population or any population regards immunizing children as optional, we risk having large numbers of children becoming vulnerable to the most deadly diseases known to man. As a practicing pediatrician, I am passionately opposed to that. The following are a few questions some skeptical parents are asking about the vaccination issue: 3

What would happen if I did not have my child immunized? Without immunizations there would be a significant possibility that your child would contract some of the diseases that are now waiting to come back. These include: whooping cough (pertussis), tetanus, polio, measles, mumps, German measles (rubella), bacterial meningitis, and diphtheria. 4

These illnesses all may injure children severely, leaving them deaf, blind, paralyzed, or they even may cause death. For example, in 1960 there were more than 1.5 million cases of measles and more than 400 deaths associated with this disease. As a result of our active immunization process in 1998 the United States had only 89 cases of measles, and there were no deaths. 5

Why should I accept any risk of immunization for my child when other children already are immunized? Won't that protect my child? It is important to understand the concept of herd immunity and public health versus individual risk. Individual risk is always a possibility with any procedure, medication, new activity, or vaccine. The key to any program or new intervention is to minimize the risk. There is no question that vaccines are the safest, most risk-free type of medication ever developed. Nevertheless, occasionally—very occasionally—children have been known to experience a bad, or adverse, reaction to a vaccine. In some cases—polio vaccine, for example—one in 1 million doses appears to 6 have been associated with vaccine-related mild polio disease. The reactions to other vaccines also have been very, very small, though nevertheless significant for the child or family who have experienced one.

It is not, however, good public policy to give those few at-risk situations priority over the goal of protecting the population as a whole from those diseases. If the pool of unimmunized children becomes large enough, then the disease itself may reemerge in those unimmunized children, possibly in epidemic proportions. This has occurred in countries where immunizations have been allowed to decrease; most recently pertussis (whooping cough) resurfaced in Europe. Failure to immunize a child not only puts that child at risk of illness but also increases the potential for harm to other children who are not able to be vaccinated because they are too young or too ill or to those who in rare cases are vaccinated but the vaccination fails to provide the expected protection. 7

Are immunizations safe? Don't they hurt? Reactions to vaccines may occur, but they usually are mild. Serious reactions are very, very rare but also may occur. Remember, the risks from these potentially dangerous childhood illnesses are far greater than any risk of serious reaction from immunization. Even though immunizations may hurt a little when they are given, and your baby may cry for a few minutes, and there might be some swelling, protecting your child's health is worth a few tears and a little temporary discomfort. 8

Isn't it better that children get a disease such as chicken pox to give them a permanent immunity? If a child gets the disease, the danger is that the child may develop serious complications from the disease. The immunity conferred[1] following the recommended immunization schedule will give excellent immunity and not place the child at risk. 9

Is it true that hepatitis B vaccine can cause autism or juvenile diabetes, sudden infant death syndrome (SIDS), multiple sclerosis, or asthma? There have been occasional reports in the media associating this vaccine with all of the above illnesses. Scientific research has not found any evidence linking the hepatitis B vaccine to autism, SIDS, multiple sclerosis, juvenile diabetes, or asthma. In fact, SIDS rates have declined during the same time period that the hepatitis B vaccine has been recommended for routine immunization. Although some media have circulated reports that health authorities in France have stopped giving the hepatitis vaccine to children, that is not true. French health 10

[1]*conferred:* gained.

officials did not stop giving the hepatitis vaccine but decided not to administer the vaccine in the schools and recommended that the vaccine be given in medical settings.

Is there a link between measles vaccine and autism? No. There is no scientifically proven link between measles vaccine and autism. Autism is a chronic developmental disorder often first identified in toddlers ages 18 months to 30 months. The MMR (mumps, measles, rubella) vaccine is administered just before the [onset] of autism that has caused some parents to assume a causal relationship, but a recent study in a British journal showed there was no association between the MMR vaccine and autism. 11

It is assumed that there has been an increase in the diagnosis of autism because the definition for who would fall under that category has changed. In addition, parents and medical professionals are more aware of this condition and are more likely to pursue that diagnosis. Though there may be an increase in the number of children who have autism, there have been many studies completed that show that the MMR does not cause autism. 12

Aren't measles, mumps, and rubella relatively harmless illnesses? Measles is a highly contagious respiratory disease. It causes a rash, high fever, cough, and runny nose. In addition, it can cause encephalitis, which leads to convulsions, deafness, or mental retardation in one to two children of every 2,000 who get it. Of every 1,000 people who get measles, one to two will die. MMR can prevent this disease. Mumps is less serious than measles but may cause fever, headache, and swelling of one or both sides of the jaw. Four to 6 percent of those who get mumps will get meningitis, which puts the child at risk for significant disability and potential retardation. In addition, inflammation of the testicles occurs in four of every 10 adult males who get mumps, and mumps may result in hearing loss that usually is permanent. The effects of rubella are mild in children and adults—causing only a minor rash—but the major reason to prevent rubella in the community is to prevent exposure of pregnant women to children who have rubella. When contracted by a pregnant woman, rubella may infect her unborn baby, leading to a significant potential for mental retardation and a host of serious defects. This devastating disease, known as congenital rubella syndrome, essentially has been eliminated with the use of rubella vaccine. 13

Given that measles, rubella, and mumps essentially have disappeared from the United States and therefore are uncommon, why should we continue to immunize? The measles virus continues to be 14 present in other countries outside the United States. Given the large number of immigrants to this country, the potential for exposure to measles remains a real potential. Just a few weeks ago [in early 2000] several young children who recently emigrated from the United Kingdom came into one of our pediatrician's offices. Due to the decrease in immunization vigilance in the United Kingdom against measles, these young children were infected with measles, and they put at risk the other infants and children in the waiting room of this busy pediatrician's office. If those other children contract measles, they will be at risk for developing [a] serious sequela[2] of the disease. And, should they develop the disease, they potentially will expose others as well. A mini-epidemic could have been caused by these infected children with measles.

Should parents be able to choose not to vaccinate their child with- 15
out being barred from enrolling that child in school? Immunizing children is a public-health issue. Public-health laws in all 50 states require immunization of children as a condition of school enrollment. This is as it should be, since public health must take precedence. Immunizations have a clear community benefit and, therefore, individual preferences should not be permitted to expose the public to the hazards of infectious diseases.

In summary, it is clear that the risk of exposing children to infec- 16
tious disease should there be a decline in immunizations is a risk to which the population of the United States should not be exposed. It always is regrettable when an individual case of an adverse event occurs no matter what might have taken place. These adverse events clearly affect the child and obviously the family as well, and there indeed is always an outcry when this does occur. However, as with all safe, proven interventions, an exception could always occur given a normal risk ratio.

It would be actual malpractice and poor public-health philosophy 17
and practice to consider not immunizing our children against the potentially deadly infectious diseases. We should be thankful to our research scientists, epidemiologists,[3] and medical and pharmaceutical industry for the skill and care with which these important vaccines have been developed and the care with which the vaccine policies have been developed and monitored. There is no question in my mind that

[2]*sequela:* an aftereffect of disease.

[3]*epidemiologists:* doctors who study the causes, distribution, and treatment of diseases.

immunizations are one of the most important ways parents can protect their children against serious diseases. Without immunizations the children of the United States would be exposed to deadly diseases that continue to occur throughout the world.

Thinking Critically about This Reading

According to Shelov, why do "public health laws in all 50 states require immunization of children as a condition of school enrollment" (paragraph 15)?

Questions for Study and Discussion

1. What is Shelov's thesis? (Glossary: *Thesis*)
2. Shelov includes a number of questions and answers in his essay. How effective are they as counterarguments?
3. What concessions does Shelov make to opponents of mass vaccination? How do his concessions help support his argument in favor of vaccinations?
4. Shelov uses comparison and contrast in paragraph 7 to argue against letting "the pool of unimmunized children" grow to dangerous proportions. (Glossary: *Comparison and Contrast*) How effective is this strategy in your opinion?
5. What evidence does Shelov give to prove that the hepatitis B vaccine does not cause an array of illnesses? (Glossary: *Evidence*) Are you convinced by his evidence? Why or why not?
6. Shelov concedes that rubella is a mild disease. Why does he say that we still need to vaccinate children against it? (Glossary: *Cause and Effect*)
7. What threats to our public health exist, according to Shelov, as a result of the public health policies of other countries? What evidence does he provide that the threat actually exists? (Glossary: *Evidence*)

Classroom Activity Using Argument

Find an editorial in a local or national newspaper that presents a view on an issue that you disagree with. Bring the editorial to class, reread and study it for a few minutes, and then write a brief letter to the editor of the newspaper arguing against its position on the issue. Your letter should be brief; short letters have a much better chance of being published than long ones. During a subsequent class, form groups of two or three students to share your letters and comment on the effectiveness of each other's arguments. Revise your letter, if necessary, and consider sending it to the newspaper for possible publication.

Suggested Writing Assignments

1. Write an essay in which you argue that people need to know more about the controversy over mass immunizations—both to be better informed about the pros and cons of the issue and to come to a better understanding of where they stand on it. What can the government and the media do to better inform the public about the risks and benefits of vaccinations? What can individuals do to better inform themselves? Explain.
2. Before mass immunization, pertussis (or whooping cough) was a worldwide killer of infants and a leading killer of children in the United States. Write an essay in which you argue, as Shelov does, in favor of continued mass inoculations for children based on the rise of pertussis in such countries as the United Kingdom, Sweden, and Japan, where inoculations were curtailed over fears of the vaccines' potentially harmful side effects.
3. The controversy over mandatory immunizations is partly a patients' rights issue. Patients' rights are widely accepted principles that guarantee informed and fair treatment by hospitals, doctors, and other healthcare professionals. Mass immunization is a patients' rights issue in that we are usually pressured to be immunized or to have our children immunized, and we may not be aware of our right to refuse immunization. Conduct library and Internet research on patients' rights issues. Write an essay in which you explain patients' rights and argue that by being more informed about them we can make better choices. To begin your research online, go to **bedfordstmartins.com/models** and click on "Argument Links."

appendix

Writing a Research Paper

The research paper is an important part of a college education—and for good reason. In writing a research paper, you acquire a number of indispensable skills that you can adapt to other college assignments and to situations after graduation.

The real value of writing a research paper, however, goes beyond acquiring basic skills; it is a unique hands-on learning experience. The purpose of a research paper is not to present a collection of quotations that show you can report what others have said about your topic. Rather, your goal is to analyze, evaluate, and synthesize the materials you research—and thereby learn how to do so with any topic. You learn how to view the results of research from your own perspective and to arrive at an informed opinion of a topic.

Writing a researched essay is not very different from the other writing you will be doing in your college writing course. You will find yourself drawing heavily on what you learned from the four student papers in the first two chapters of this text. First you determine what you want to write about. Then you decide on a purpose, consider your audience, develop a thesis, collect your evidence, write a first draft, revise and edit, and prepare a final copy. What differentiates the research paper from other kinds of papers is your use of outside sources and how you acknowledge them.

In this appendix, you will learn the steps in the research process:

- Locate and use print and Internet sources.
- Evaluate print and Internet sources.
- Develop a working bibliography.
- Conduct Internet research using directory and keyword searches.
- Take useful notes.
- Summarize, paraphrase, and quote your sources.

- Integrate your notes into your paper.
- Acknowledge your sources using MLA style.
- Avoid plagiarism.

USING PRINT AND ONLINE SOURCES

In most cases, you should use print sources (books, newspapers, journals, magazines, encyclopedias, pamphlets, brochures, and government documents) as your primary tools for research. Print sources, unlike many Internet sources, are often reviewed by experts in the field before they are published, are generally overseen by a reputable publishing company or organization, and are examined by editors and fact checkers for accuracy and reliability. Unless you are instructed otherwise, you should try to use print sources in your research.

To find print sources, search through your library's reference works, card catalog, periodical indexes, and other databases to generate a preliminary listing of books, magazine and newspaper articles, public documents and reports, and other sources that may be helpful in exploring your topic. At this early stage, it is better to err on the side of listing too many sources. Then, later on, you will not have to relocate sources you discarded too hastily.

You will find that Internet sources can be informative and valuable additions to your research. The Internet is especially useful in providing recent data, stories, and reports. For example, you might find a just-published article from a university laboratory or a news story in your local newspaper's online archives. Generally, however, Internet sources should be used alongside print sources and not as a replacement for them. Whereas print sources are generally published under the guidance of a publisher or an organization, practically anyone with access to a computer and an Internet connection can place text and pictures online; there is no governing body that checks Web sites' content for accuracy. The Internet offers a vast number of carefully maintained resources, but it also contains much unreliable information. It is your responsibility to determine whether a given Internet source should be trusted.

Preview Your Print and Online Sources

You will not have to spend much time in the library to realize that you cannot read every print and online source that appears relevant.

The key to successful research is identifying those books, articles, Web sites, and other online sources that will help you most. You must preview your potential sources to determine which materials you will read, which you will skim, and which you will simply eliminate. The following box lists previewing strategies for identifying promising sources.

Strategies for Previewing Print and Online Sources

Previewing a Book

- Read the cover or dust jacket for insights into the book's coverage and currency and the author's expertise.
- Scan the table of contents for promising chapters.
- Read the author's preface, looking for the thesis and purpose.
- Check the index for key words or phrases related to your topic.
- Read the opening and concluding paragraphs of each promising chapter; if you are still unsure about its usefulness, skim the whole chapter.
- Try to determine if the author has a discernable bias.

Previewing an Article

- Consider the journal or magazine's reputation and readership.
- Consider the title or headline of the article as well as the opening paragraphs and conclusion.
- For articles in journals, read the abstract (a summary of the main points) if there is one.
- Examine any photographs, charts, graphs, or other illustrations that accompany the article.

Previewing a Web Site

- Examine the site's home page for relevance to your research topic.
- Identify the site's author and, if possible, determine if the author's credentials are appropriate to the content.
- Scan the site to see if it has been updated within the last six months.

Evaluate Your Print and Online Sources

Before beginning to take notes, evaluate your sources for their relevance, bias, overall argument, and reliability in helping you explore your topic. Look for the writers' main ideas, key examples, strongest arguments, and conclusions. Read critically: While it is easy to become absorbed in sources that support your beliefs, always seek out several sources with opposing viewpoints, if only to test your own position. Look for information about the authors themselves—information that will help you determine their authority and perspective or bias on the issues. You should also know the reputation and special interests of book publishers and magazines because you are likely to get different views—conservative, liberal, international, feminist—on the same topic depending on the publication you read. Use the accompanying checklist to help evaluate your print and online sources.

Checklist for Evaluating Print and Online Sources

- What is the writer's thesis or claim?
- How does the writer support this thesis? Does the evidence seem reasonable and ample, or is it mainly anecdotal?
- Does the writer consider opposing viewpoints?
- Does the writer have any obvious political or religious biases? Is the writer associated with a special-interest group such as Planned Parenthood, Greenpeace, Amnesty International, or the National Rifle Association?
- Is the writer an expert on the subject? Do other writers mention this author in their work?
- Does the publisher or publication have a reputation for accuracy and objectivity?
- Is the author's purpose to inform? Or is it to argue for a particular position or action?
- Do the writer's thesis and purpose clearly relate to your topic?
- Does the source appear to be too general or too technical for your needs and audience?
- Does the source reflect current thinking and research in the field?

The quality of Internet sources varies tremendously. While most books, magazine articles, and scholarly journals are reviewed by a panel of experts and/or editors before being published, no such controls exist for most postings on the Internet. Consider the following Questions for Evaluating Web Sites as you compile online sources. For additional guidance, go to **bedfordstmartins.com/rewriting** and click on "Evaluating Online Sources Tutorial."

Questions for Evaluating Web Sites

1. **Who sponsors the site?**
   a. A corporation, university, or individual?
   b. The site's domain name indicates the sponsor of the site:

.com	Business/commercial site
.edu	Educational institution
.gov	Government site
.mil	Military site
.net	Various types of networks
.org	Nonprofit organization

2. **Who is the authority or author?**
   a. What individual or company is responsible for the site?
   b. Can you verify if the site is official, that is, actually sanctioned by the organization or company?
   c. What are the author's or company's qualifications for writing on this subject?
   d. Can you verify the legitimacy of this individual or company? Are links to a home page or resumé provided?

3. **What is the site's purpose and audience?**
   a. What appears to be the author's or sponsor's purpose or motivation?
   b. Who is the intended audience?

4. **Is the site objective?**
   a. Are advertising, opinion, and factual information clearly distinguished?
   b. What biases, if any, can you detect?

5. **How accurate is the site?**
   a. Is important information documented through links so that it can be verified or corroborated by other sources?
   b. Is the text well written and free of careless errors in spelling and grammar?

6. **Is the coverage thorough and accurate?**
   a. Is the site still under construction?
   b. For sources with print equivalents, is the Web version more or less extensive than the print version?
   c. How detailed is the site's treatment of its subject matter?
   d. How current is the site's information (the date of last update or a statement regarding frequency of updates)?

DEVELOPING A WORKING BIBLIOGRAPHY

As you discover books, journal and magazine articles, newspaper stories, and Web sites that you think might be helpful, you need to start maintaining a record of important information about each source. This record, called a *working bibliography,* will enable you to know where sources are located as well as what they are when it comes time to consult and acknowledge them in your paper and list of works cited (see pp. 577–83 and 590). In all likelihood, your working bibliography will contain more sources than you actually consult and include in your list of works cited.

You may find it easy to make a separate bibliography card, using a 4 × 6 index card, for each work that you think might be helpful to your research. As your collection of cards grows, alphabetize them by the authors' last names. By using a separate card for each book, article, or Web site, you can continually edit your working bibliography, dropping sources that do not prove helpful and adding new ones.

With the computerization of most library resources, you now have the option of printing out bibliographic information from the library computer catalog and periodical indexes or from the Internet. Be sure to check the bibliographic information on your printouts against the following Checklist for a Working Bibliography, and supply any information that is missing. One advantage of the printouts over the index card method is that the printouts ensure accuracy of spelling, punctuation, and capitalization. Whichever method you use, you will find the cards or printouts indispensable when you compile your final list of works cited.

Checklist for a Working Bibliography

For Books
- Library call number
- Names of all authors, editors, and translators
- Title and subtitle
- Publication data
  - Place of publication (city and state)
  - Publisher's name
  - Date of publication
- Edition number (if not the first) and volume number (if applicable)

For Periodical Articles

- Names of all authors
- Name and subtitle of article
- Title of journal, magazine, or newspaper
- Publication data
  - Volume number and issue number
  - Date of issue
  - Page numbers

For Internet Sources

- Names of all authors, editors, compilers, or sponsoring agents
- Title and subtitle of the document
- Title of the longer work to which the document belongs (if applicable)
- Title of the site or discussion list name
- Author, editor, or compiler of the Web site or online database
- Date of release, online posting, or latest revision
- Name and vendor of database or name of online service or network
- Medium (online, CD-ROM, etc.)
- Format of online source (Web page, e-mail, etc.)
- Date of access
- Electronic address (URL or network path)

For Other Sources

- Name of author, government agency, organization, company, recording artist, personality, etc.
- Title of the work
- Format (pamphlet, unpublished diary, interview, television broadcast, etc.)
- Publication or production data
  - Name of publisher or producer
  - Date of publication, production, or release
  - Identifying codes or numbers (if applicable)

INTERNET RESEARCH: SUBJECT DIRECTORIES AND KEYWORD SEARCHES

Beyond knowing how to identify and evaluate the Web sites that will help you most, you will need to know the best methods for finding them. This will help you save time as you do your research. Keep in mind the questions for previewing and evaluating sources as you use subject directories and keyword searches to find information.

Using Subject Directories to Refine Your Research Topic

The subject directories on the home pages of search engines make it easy to browse various subjects and topics, a big help if you are undecided about your exact research question or if you simply want to see if there is enough material online to supplement your research work with print sources. Often the most efficient approach to Web research is to start with the subject directory of a search engine. Once you choose a subject area in the directory, you can maneuver through the directory to narrow down the subject and eventually arrive at a list of sites closely related to your topic.

Suppose you want to research acupuncture in America, and you are using the search engine Google, www.google.com. You would start your search with the following "Google Directory" screen. Your first

Google Directory.

task would be to choose, from the sixteen categories listed, the one most likely to contain information about acupuncture. Remember that just as you often need to browse through tables of contents and indexes of numerous books on a given subject to uncover the three or four sources that will be most useful to you, more than one general subject category in a Web directory may seem appropriate on the surface.

The most common question students have at this stage in a directory search is, "How can I tell if I'm looking in the right place?" If several subject categories sound plausible, you will have to dig more deeply into each of their subdirectories, using logic and the process of elimination to determine which one is likely to produce the best Web site listings for your topic. In most cases, it doesn't take long—usually just one or two clicks—to figure out whether you are searching in the right subject area. If you click on a subject category and none of the topics listed in its subdirectory seems to pertain even remotely to your research topic, try a different subject area. For example, to find acupuncture links, you might be tempted to click on "Science," which

Google Directory categories for alternative health.

has a "Biology" link. If you do, you'll find that none of the biology topics listed relates to acupuncture, which is a strong sign that "Science" is the wrong subject category for your topic. The other logical possibility is "Health." Clicking on "Health" takes you to a screen that lists forty-eight more subject categories, including "Alternative," a logical place to find sites on acupuncture and other alternative medical practices. For "Alternative" alone, there are more than 7,300 Web sites listed, so chances are good that some of those sites address your subject.

When you click on "Alternative," you bring up a screen that lists categories related to alternative medicine (see p. 559). Because you are interested in acupuncture, "Acupuncture and Chinese Medicine," which lists 1,038 Web sites, is the natural next step. Clicking on this link takes you to a screen where you find a number of subdirectory categories, including one for "Acupuncture." By clicking on "Acupuncture," you arrive at the screen below that lists potentially valuable Web sites, including several sites that provide good overviews of acupuncture in America.

Google Directory listings for acupuncture.

Using Keyword Searches to Find Specific Information

When you type in a keyword in the search box on a search engine's home page, the search engine looks for Web sites that match your term. One problem with keyword searches is that they can produce tens of thousands of matches, making it difficult to locate sites of immediate value. For that reason, make your keywords as specific as you can, and make sure that you have the correct spelling. It is always a good idea to consult the help screens or advanced search instructions for the search engine you are using before initiating a keyword search. Once you start a search, you may want to narrow or broaden it depending on the number of hits, or matches, you get.

Refining Keyword Searches on the Web

While some variation in command terms and characters exists among electronic databases and popular Internet search engines, the following functions are almost universally accepted. If you have a particular question about refining your keyword search, seek assistance by clicking on the site's "Help" or "Advanced Search" links.

- Use quotation marks or parentheses to indicate that you are searching for words in exact sequence—for example, "whooping cough"; (Supreme Court).
- Use AND or a plus sign (+) between words to narrow your search by specifying that all words need to appear in a document—for example, tobacco AND cancer; Shakespeare + sonnet.
- Use NOT or a minus sign (−) between words to narrow your search by eliminating unwanted words—for example, monopoly NOT game; cowboys –Dallas.
- Use an asterisk (*) to indicate that you will accept variations of a term—for example, "food label*" for food labels, food labeling, and so forth.

When using a keyword search, you need to be careful about selecting the keywords that will yield the best results. If your keywords are too general, your results will be at best unwieldy and at worst not usable at all. During her initial search for her paper on monarchs, a butterfly indigenous to North and Central America, student Erin Elio typed in "monarch." To her surprise, this produced approximately 5,270,000 hits, mostly for products, services, or teams carrying the name.

Search results for "monarch."

After thinking about how to narrow her search, Elio decided to type in "monarch butterfly." This search yielded about 543,000 hits, still too many for her purposes. In an effort to narrow her search even more, she tried "monarch butterfly + life cycle" —a search that yielded a far more manageable 1,360 hits.

Among these hits, she located a Web page titled "Monarch butterfly life cycle" on the Lifestrands Web site, a site created by teachers who use monarch butterflies to teach scientific inquiry to young students.

This site was the perfect starting point for Elio. Here she found information about the life cycle of monarch butterflies as well as the opportunity to learn more about any particular stage of the cycle. Equipped with a basic understanding of the monarch's life cycle, Elio continued her search to discover the relationship between the butterfly's life cycle and its heralded yearly migration.

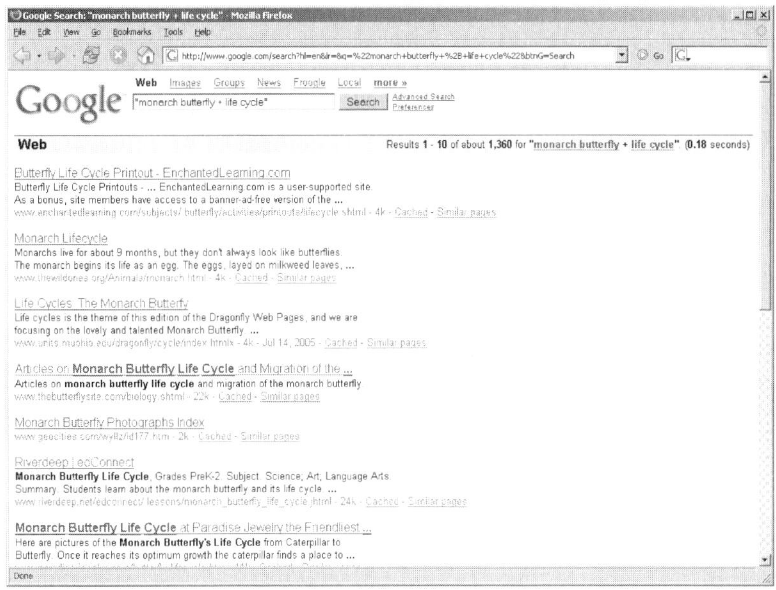

Used with permission. Courtesy of www.google.com.

Search results for "monarch butterfly + life cycle."

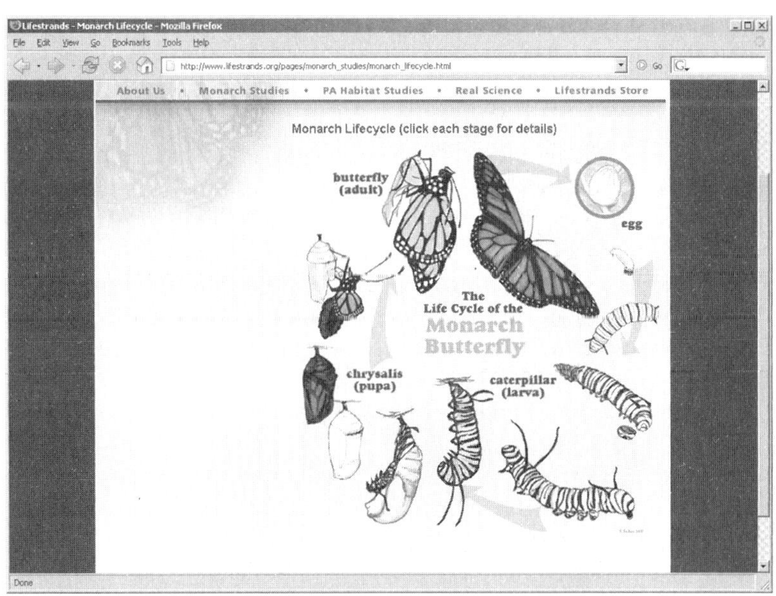

Used with permission. Courtesy of www.lifestrands.org.

The life cycle of the monarch butterfly from the Lifestrands Web site.

TAKING NOTES

As you gather and sort your source materials, you'll want to record the information that you consider most pertinent to your topic. As you read, take notes. You're looking for ideas, facts, opinions, statistics, examples, and other evidence that you think will be useful as you write your paper. As you work through books and articles, look for recurring themes, and notice where writers are in agreement and where they differ. Try to remember that the effectiveness of your paper is largely determined by the quality—not necessarily the quantity—of your notes. Your purpose is not to present a collection of quotes that show you've read all the material and know what others have said about your topic. Your goal is to analyze, evaluate, and synthesize the information you collect—in other words, to enter into the discussion of the issues and thereby take ownership of your topic. You want to view the results of your research from your own perspective and arrive at an informed opinion of your topic.

Now for some practical advice on taking notes: First, be systematic in your note taking. As a rule, write one note on a card and include the author's full name, the complete title of the source, and a page number indicating the origin of the note. Use cards of uniform size, preferably 4 × 6 cards because they are large enough to accommodate even a long note on a single card and yet small enough to be easily handled and conveniently carried. Following this system will also help you when you get to the planning and writing stage because you will be able to sequence your notes according to the plan you envision for your paper. Furthermore, should you decide to alter your organizational plan, you can easily reorder your cards to reflect your revisions. You can, of course, do note taking on your computer as well, which makes it easy for you to reorder your notes. An added advantage of the computer is that the Copy and Paste features let you move notes and their citations directly into your essay.

Second, try not to take too many notes. One good way to control your note taking is to ask yourself, "How exactly does this material help prove or disprove my thesis?" Try to envision where in your paper you could use the information. If it does not seem relevant to your thesis, don't bother to take a note.

Once you decide to take a note, you must decide whether to summarize, paraphrase, or quote directly. The approach you take should be determined by the content of the passage and the way you plan to use it in your paper.

Summary

When you *summarize* material from one of your sources, you capture in condensed form the essential idea of a passage, an article, or an entire chapter. Summaries are particularly useful when you are working with lengthy, detailed arguments or long passages of narrative or descriptive background information in which the details are not germane to the overall thrust of your paper. You simply want to capture the essence of the passage because you are confident that your readers will readily understand the point being made or do not need to be convinced about its validity. Because you are distilling information, a summary is always shorter than the original; often a chapter or more can be reduced to a paragraph, or several paragraphs to a sentence or two. Remember, in writing a summary you should use your own words.

Consider the following paragraphs, in which Richard Lederer compares big words with small words in some detail:

> When you speak and write, there is no law that says you have to use big words. Short words are as good as long ones, and short, old words—like *sun* and *grass* and *home*—are best of all. A lot of small words, more than you might think, can meet your needs with a strength, grace, and charm that large words do not have.
>
> Big words can make the way dark for those who read what you write and hear what you say. Small words cast their clear light on big things—night and day, love and hate, war and peace, and life and death. Big words at times seem strange to the eye and ear and the mind and the heart. Small words are the ones we seem to have known from the time we were born, like the hearth fire that warms the home.
>
> –Richard Lederer, "The Case for Short Words," page 310

A student wishing to capture the gist of Lederer's point without repeating his detailed contrast created the accompanying summary note card.

Summary Note Card

Short Words

Lederer favors short words for their clarity, familiarity, durability, and overall usefulness.

Lederer, "The Case for Short Words," 310

Paraphrase

When you *paraphrase* material from a source, you restate the information in your own words instead of quoting directly. Unlike a summary, which gives a brief overview of the essential information in the original, a paraphrase seeks to maintain the same level of detail as the original to aid readers in understanding or believing the information presented. A paraphrase presents the original information in approximately the same number of words, but with different wording. To put it another way, your paraphrase should closely parallel the presentation of ideas in the original, but it should not use the same words or sentence structure as the original. Even though you are using your own words in a paraphrase, it's important to remember that you are borrowing ideas and therefore must acknowledge the source of these ideas with a citation.

How would you paraphrase the following passage from "The Ways of Meeting Oppression" by Martin Luther King Jr.?

> If the American Negro and other victims of oppression succumb to the temptation of using violence in the struggle for freedom, future generations will be the recipients of a desolate night

> of bitterness, and our chief legacy to them will be an endless reign of meaningless chaos. Violence is not the way.
>
> –Martin Luther King Jr., "The Ways of Meeting Oppression," page 414

See the accompanying note card for an example of how one student paraphrased the passage.

Paraphrase Note Card

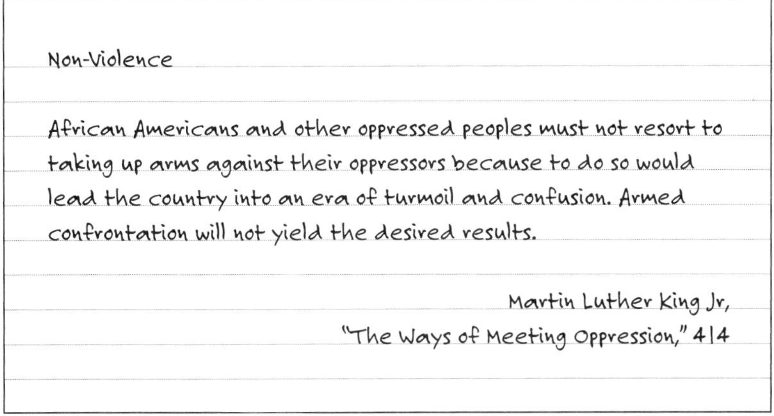

Non-Violence

African Americans and other oppressed peoples must not resort to taking up arms against their oppressors because to do so would lead the country into an era of turmoil and confusion. Armed confrontation will not yield the desired results.

Martin Luther King Jr,
"The Ways of Meeting Oppression," 414

In most cases, it is best to summarize or paraphrase material—which by definition means using your own words—instead of quoting verbatim (word for word). Capturing an idea in your own words demonstrates that you have thought about and understood what your source is saying.

Direct Quotation

When you *quote* a source directly, you copy the words of your source exactly, putting all quoted material in quotation marks. When you make a quotation note card, check the passage carefully for accuracy, including punctuation and capitalization. Be selective about what you choose to quote; reserve direct quotation for important ideas stated memorably, for especially clear explanations by authorities, and for arguments by proponents of a particular position in their own words.

Consider the accompanying direct quotation note card. It quotes a passage from William Zinsser's "Simplicity," on page 169 in this text, emphasizing the importance—and rarity—of clear, concise writing.

Direct Quotation Note Card

Wordiness

"Clutter is the disease of American writing. We are a society strangling in unnecessary words, circular constructions, pompous frills, and meaningless jargon."

William Zinsser, "Simplicity," 169

On occasion you'll find a long, useful passage with some memorable wording in it. Avoid the temptation to quote the whole passage; instead, try combining summary or paraphrase with direct quotation. Consider the third paragraph from Robyn Marks's essay "Raising a Son—With Men on the Fringes":

> Studies show that African-American women have been outpacing our men in education and corporate America for two generations now. Almost half of black boys wind up a grade behind in school, and only a third of 20-year-old black men are enrolled in college. All the more daunting is the fact that the majority of these boys and men were just like Jason, raised in a home by a single black mother. I have a lot of work to do to ensure that my child clears these hurdles, but they are hurdles that are so elusive, I have yet to get a firm grip on where exactly they lie.
>
> –Robyn Marks, "Raising a Son—With Men on the Fringes," page 176

In the accompanying quotation and summary note card, notice how the student is careful to put quotation marks around all words borrowed directly.

Quotation and Summary Note Card

Obstacles for black males

In the last forty years black women have outperformed black men in school and in the workplace. "Almost half of black boys wind up a grade behind in school, and only a third of 20-year-old black men are enrolled in college." Most of these young men were "raised in a home by a single black mother." These mothers need to be aware of the obstacles their sons face.

Robyn Marks, "Raising a Son—With Men on the Fringes," 176

Notes from Internet Sources

Working from the computer screen or from a printout, you can take notes just as you would from print sources. You will need to decide whether to summarize, paraphrase, or quote directly the information you wish to borrow. Use the same 4 × 6 index-card system that you use with print sources. The medium of the Internet, however, has an added advantage. An easy and accurate technique for capturing passages of text from the Internet is to copy the material into a separate computer file on your hard drive or diskette. For example, you can use your mouse to highlight the portion of the text you want to save and then use the Copy and Paste commands to add it to your file of research notes. You can also use the same commands to capture the bibliographic information you will need later.

■ INTEGRATING BORROWED MATERIAL INTO YOUR TEXT

Being familiar with the material in your notes will help you decide how to integrate it into your drafts. Though it is not necessary to use all of your notes, or to use them all at once in your first draft, you do need to know which ones support your thesis, extend your ideas, offer better wording of your ideas, and reveal the opinions of noted authorities. Occasionally you will want to use notes that include ideas contrary to your own so that you can rebut them in your own argument. Once you have analyzed all of your notes, you may even alter your thesis slightly in light of the information and ideas you have found.

Whenever you want to use borrowed material, be it a summary, paraphrase, or quotation, it's best to introduce the material with a *signal phrase*—a phrase that alerts the reader that borrowed information is to follow. A signal phrase usually consists of the author's name and a verb. Well-chosen signal phrases help you integrate quotations, paraphrases, and summaries into the flow of your paper. Besides, signal phrases let your reader know who is speaking and, in the case of summaries and paraphrases, exactly where your ideas end and someone else's begin. Never confuse your reader with a quotation that appears suddenly without introduction. Unannounced quotations leave your reader wondering how the quoted material relates to the point you are trying to make. Look at the following student example. The quotation is from Ruth Russell's "The Wounds That Can't Be Stitched Up," which appears on pages 151–53 in this text.

Unannounced Quotation

> America has a problem with drinking and driving. In 2004 drunk drivers killed almost 17,000 people and injured 500,000 others. While many are quick to condemn drinking and driving, they are also quick to defend or offer excuses for such behavior, especially when the offender is a friend. "Many local people who know the driver are surprised when they hear about the accident, and they are quick to defend him. They tell me he was a war hero. His parents aren't well. He's an alcoholic. Or my favorite: 'He's a good guy when he doesn't drink' " (Russell 150). When are we going to get tough with drunk drivers?

In the following revision, the student integrates the quotation into the text not only by means of a signal phrase, but in a number of other ways as well. By giving the name of the writer being quoted, referring to her authority on the subject, and noting that the writer is speaking from experience, the student provides more context so that the reader can better understand how this quotation fits into the discussion.

Integrated Quotation

> America has a problem with drinking and driving. In 2004 drunk drivers killed almost 17,000 people and injured 500,000 others.

> While many are quick to condemn drinking and driving, they are also quick to defend or offer excuses for such behavior, especially when the offender is a friend. Ruth Russell, whose family's life was shattered by a drunk driver, recalls that "many local people who know the driver are surprised when they hear about the accident, and they are quick to defend him. They tell me he was a war hero. His parents aren't well. He's an alcoholic. Or my favorite: 'He's a good guy when he doesn't drink' " (150). When are we going to get tough with drunk drivers?

How well you integrate a quote, paraphrase, or summary into your paper depends partly on varying your signal phrases and, in particular, on choosing a verb for the signal phrase that accurately conveys the tone and intent of the writer you are citing. If a writer is arguing, use the verb *argues* (or *asserts, claims,* or *contends*); if a writer is contesting a particular position or fact, use the verb *contests* (or *denies, disputes, refutes,* or *rejects*). In using verbs that are specific to the situation in your paper, you bring your readers into the intellectual debate and avoid the monotony of such all-purpose verbs as *says* or *writes.* Following are just a few examples of how you can vary signal phrases to add precision to your paper:

Ellen Goodman asserts that . . .

To summarize Judith Viorst's observations on friends, . . .

Social activist and nutrition guru Dick Gregory demonstrates that . . .

Mary Sherry explains . . .

George Orwell rejects the widely held belief that . . .

Norman Mailer exposes . . .

Other verbs that you should keep in mind when constructing signal phrases include the following:

acknowledges	compares	grants	reasons
adds	confirms	implies	reports
admits	declares	insists	responds
believes	endorses	points out	suggests

A NOTE ON PLAGIARISM

The importance of honesty and accuracy in doing library research cannot be stressed enough. Any material borrowed word for word must be placed within quotation marks and be properly cited; any idea, explanation, or argument you have paraphrased or summarized must be documented, and it must be clear where the paraphrased material begins and ends. In short, to use someone else's ideas, whether in their original form or in an altered form, without proper acknowledgment is to be guilty of *plagiarism*.

The Council of Writing Program Administrators offers the following helpful definition of *plagiarism* in academic settings for administrators, faculty, and students: "In an instructional setting, plagiarism occurs when a writer deliberately uses someone else's language, ideas, or other (not common-knowledge) material without acknowledging its source." Accusations of plagiarism can be substantiated even if plagiarism is accidental. A little attention and effort at the note-taking stage can go a long way toward eliminating inadvertent plagiarism. Check all direct quotations against the wording of the original, and double-check your paraphrases to be sure that you have not used the writer's wording or sentence structure. It is easy to forget to put quotation marks around material taken verbatim or to use the same sentence structure and most of the same words—substituting a synonym here and there—and treat it as a paraphrase. In working closely with the ideas and words of others, intellectual honesty demands that we distinguish between what we borrow—acknowledging it in a citation—and what is our own.

While writing your paper, be careful whenever you incorporate one of your notes into your paper. Make sure that you put quotation marks around material taken verbatim, and double-check your text against your note card—or, better yet, against the original if you have it on hand—to make sure that your quotation is accurate. When paraphrasing or summarizing, make sure you do not inadvertently borrow key words or sentence structures from the original.

For additional guidance, go to the St. Martin's Tutorial on Avoiding Plagiarism at **bedfordstmartins.com/plagiarismtutorial.**

Using Quotation Marks for Language Borrowed Directly

When you use another person's exact words or sentences, you must enclose the borrowed language in quotation marks. Without quotation marks, you give your reader the impression that the wording is your own. Even if you cite the source, you are guilty of plagiarism if you fail to use quotation marks. The following examples demonstrate both plagiarism and a correct citation for a direct quotation.

Original Source

> So Grant and Lee were in complete contrast, representing two diametrically opposed elements in American life. Grant was the modern man emerging; beyond him, ready to come on the stage, was the great age of steel and machinery, of crowded cities and a restless burgeoning vitality.
>
> –Bruce Catton, "Grant and Lee: A Study in Contrasts," page 459

Plagiarism

> So Grant and Lee were in complete contrast, according to Civil War historian Bruce Catton, representing two diametrically opposed elements in American life. Grant was the modern man emerging; beyond him, ready to come on the stage, was the great age of steel and machinery, of crowded cities and a restless burgeoning vitality (459).

Correct Citation of Borrowed Words in Quotation Marks

> "So Grant and Lee were in complete contrast," according to Civil War historian Bruce Catton, "representing two diametrically opposed elements in American life. Grant was the modern man emerging; beyond him, ready to come on the stage, was the great age of steel and machinery, of crowded cities and a restless burgeoning vitality" (459).

Using Your Own Words and Word Order When Summarizing and Paraphrasing

When summarizing or paraphrasing a source, you must use your own language. Pay particular attention to word choice and word order, especially if you are paraphrasing. Remember, it is not enough simply to use a synonym here or there and think you have paraphrased the source; you *must* restate the original idea in your own words, using your own style and sentence structure. In the following examples, notice how plagiarism can occur when care is not taken in the wording or sentence structure of a paraphrase. Notice that in the acceptable paraphrase, the student writer uses her own language and sentence structure.

Original Source

Worse, this absence of moral authority in the realm of food leaves children—everyone, really—vulnerable to the one force in American life that has no problem making absolute claims: food advertisers, who spend billions teaching kids how to bug their parents into feeding them high-fat, high-sugar foods. Combine that with the lingering (albeit debunked) 1980s dogma—that "kids know when kids are full"—and you get, as one nutritionist-parent forcefully told me, the idea that "kids have the right to make bad nutritional decisions."

–Greg Critser, "Don't Eat the Flan," page 517

Unacceptably Close Wording

According to Critser, when there is no moral authority guiding what we eat, children are left unprotected to the strong claims of food advertisers. Each year billions of dollars are spent persuading kids to persuade their parents into serving foods that are high-fat and high-sugar. When this is taken together with the 1980s belief that children know when children are full, the result is children not only make but they actually have the right to make unhealthy nutritional decisions, according to one informed parent (517).

Unacceptably Close Sentence Structure

Critser believes that without any objective directives when it comes to food all of us—especially children—are left defenseless to the one economic power free to make unquestioned assertions: food producers who spend huge dollars convincing children they need unhealthy foods loaded with fats and sugars. Blend that thinking with the still heard (but false) 1980s mantra—children stop eating when they're full—and the result is, as one informed adult argued, anything goes when children make their own diet choices (517).

Acceptable Paraphrase

Critser believes that Americans, especially our children, have no public directives to follow about food choices. Large advertising campaigns, costing billions of dollars, push unhealthy foods that are high in fat and sugar. Much of this advertising is aimed at impressionable children who, in turn, beg their parents to buy the advertised products. When coupled with the 1980s belief that children know their limits when it comes to food, the result is a formula for disaster—children somehow have the right to make unhealthy dietary choices (517).

Review the Avoiding Plagiarism box below as you proofread your final draft and check your citations one last time. If at any time while you are taking notes or writing your paper you have a question about plagiarism, consult your instructor for clarification and guidance before proceeding.

Avoiding Plagiarism

Questions to Ask about Direct Quotations

- Do quotation marks clearly indicate the language that I borrowed verbatim?
- Is the language of the quotation accurate, with no missing or misquoted words or phrases?
- Do the brackets or ellipsis marks clearly indicate any changes or omissions I have introduced?
- Does a signal phrase naming the author introduce each quotation?
- Does the verb in the signal phrase help establish a context for each quotation?
- Does a parenthetical page citation follow each quotation?

Questions to Ask about Summaries and Paraphrases

- Is each summary or paraphrase written in my own words and style?
- Does each summary or paraphrase accurately represent the opinion, position, or reasoning of the original writer?
- Does each summary or paraphrase start with a signal phrase so that readers know where my borrowed material begins?
- Does each summary or paraphrase conclude with a parenthetical page citation?

Questions to Ask about Facts and Statistics

- Do I use a signal phrase or some other marker to introduce each fact or statistic that is not common knowledge so that readers know where the borrowed material begins?
- Is each fact or statistic that is not common knowledge clearly documented with a parenthetical page citation?

DOCUMENTING SOURCES

Whenever you summarize, paraphrase, or quote a person's thoughts and ideas, and whenever you use facts or statistics that are not commonly known or believed, you must properly acknowledge the source of your information. If you do not properly acknowledge ideas and information created by someone else, you are guilty of *plagiarism*, of using someone else's material but making it look as if it were your own. You must document the source of your information whenever you do the following:

- Quote a source word-for-word
- Refer to information and ideas from another source that you present in your own words as either a paraphrase or a summary
- Cite statistics, tables, charts, or graphs

You do not need to document these types of information:

- Your own observations, experiences, and ideas
- Factual information available in a number of reference works (known as "common knowledge")
- Proverbs, sayings, and familiar quotations

A reference to the source of your borrowed information is called a *citation*. There are many systems for making citations, and your citations must consistently follow one of these systems. The documentation style recommended by the Modern Language Association is commonly used in English and the humanities and is the style used throughout this book. Another common system is the American Psychological Association (APA) style, which is generally used in the social sciences. Your instructor will probably tell you which style to use. For more information on documentation styles, consult the appropriate manual or handbook or go to Diana Hacker's Research and Documentation Online at **bedfordstmartins.com/resdoc.**

There are two components of documentation: *In-text citations* are placed in the body of your paper; the *list of works cited* provides complete publication data for your in-text citations and is placed at the end of your paper. Both are necessary for complete documentation.

In-Text Citations

In-text citations, also known as *parenthetical citations,* give the reader citation information immediately, at the point at which it is most meaningful. Rather than having to find a footnote or an endnote, the reader sees the citation as a part of the writer's text.

Most in-text citations consist of only the author's last name and a page reference. Usually the author's name is given in an introductory or signal phrase at the beginning of the borrowed material, and the page reference is given in parentheses at the end. If the author's name is not given at the beginning, put it in parentheses along with the page reference. When you borrow material from two or more works by the same author, you must include the title of the work in the signal phrase or parenthetically at the end. (See pages 586, 587, and 589 for examples.) The parenthetical reference signals the end of the borrowed material and directs your readers to the list of works cited should they want to pursue a particular source. Treat electronic sources as you do print sources, keeping in mind that some electronic sources use paragraph numbers instead of page numbers. Consider the following examples of in-text citations, which are from student Bonnie Sherman's paper titled "Should Shame Be Used as Punishment?"

In-Text Citations (MLA Style)

The use of "shaming" punishments as alternatives to traditional sentences of jail time has sparked a heated debate in the world of criminal justice. Many believe that such punishments—designed to humiliate offenders—are unusually cruel and should be abandoned. Psychology professor June Tangney argues that "shame serves to escalate the very destructive patterns of behavior we aim to curb" (525). In contrast, one law school professor believes that "the critics' anxieties about shame . . . seem overstated" and cites a recent study showing "that the prospect of public disgrace exerts greater pressure to comply with the law than does the threat of imprisonment" (Kahan 532).

List of Works Cited (MLA Style)

Kahan, Dan M. "Shame Is Worth a Try." Models for Writers. 9th ed. Eds. Alfred Rosa and Paul Eschholz. Boston: Bedford, 2007. 530–33.

Tangney, June. "Condemn the Crime, Not the Person." Models for Writers. 9th ed. Eds. Alfred Rosa and Paul Eschholz. Boston: Bedford, 2007. 524–27.

List of Works Cited

In this section, you will find general MLA guidelines for creating a works cited list followed by sample entries that cover the citation situations you will encounter most often. Make sure that you follow the formats as they appear on the following pages. If you would like to compile your list of works cited online, go to **bedfordstmartins.com/bibliographer.**

General Guidelines

- Begin the works cited list on a new page following the last page of text. Center the title "Works Cited" at the top of the page.
- Organize the list alphabetically by authors' last names. If a source has no author, alphabetize the entry using the first major word of the title.
- Double-space within and between entries.
- Begin each entry at the left margin. If the entry is longer than one line, indent the second and subsequent lines five spaces or one-half inch.
- Do not number entries.

Books

BOOK BY ONE AUTHOR

List the author's last name first, followed by a comma and the first name. Underline the title. Follow with the city of publication and a shortened version of the publisher's name—for example, *Houghton* for *Houghton Mifflin,* or *Cambridge UP* for *Cambridge University Press.* End with the date of publication.

Nathan, Rebekah. My Freshman Year: What a Professor Learned by Becoming a Student. Ithaca: Cornell UP, 2005.

BOOK BY TWO OR THREE AUTHORS

List the first author (following the order on the title page) in the same way as for a single-author book; list subsequent authors, first name first, in the order in which they appear on the title page.

Drew, Ned, and Paul Sternberger. By Its Cover: Modern American Book Cover Design. New York: Princeton Architectural P, 2004.

BOOK BY FOUR OR MORE AUTHORS

List the first author in the same way as for a single-author book, followed by a comma and the abbreviation *et al.* ("and others").

Beardsley, John, et al. Gee's Bend: The Women and Their Quilts. Atlanta: Tinwood, 2002.

Or you may list the first author in the same way as for a single-author book, followed by a comma and then the names of all subsequent authors, first name first, in the order in which they appear on the title page. (Note, however, that if you choose this method your in-text citations must list each author's last name, matching the corresponding entry on your works cited page.)

Beardsley, John, William Arnett, Paul Arnett, Jane Livingston, and Alvia J. Wardlaw. Gee's Bend: The Women and Their Quilts. Atlanta: Tinwood, 2002.

TWO OR MORE SOURCES BY THE SAME AUTHOR

List two or more sources by the same author in alphabetical order by title. List the first source by the author's name. After the first source, in place of the author's name substitute three unspaced hyphens followed by a period.

Quart, Alissa. Branded: The Buying and Selling of Teenagers. New York: Perseus, 2003.

---. "Welcome to (Company Name Here) High (TM)." New York Times 1 July 2003, late ed.: A19.

REVISED EDITION

Phillipson, David W. African Archeology. 3rd ed. New York: Cambridge UP, 2005.

EDITED BOOK

Wollstonecraft, Mary. The Collected Letters of Mary Wollstonecraft. Ed. Janet Todd. New York: Penguin, 2004.

TRANSLATION

Basho, Matsuo. Basho's Journey: The Literary Prose of Matsuo Basho. Trans. David Landis Barnhill. Albany: State U of New York P, 2005.

ANTHOLOGY

Eggers, Dave, ed. The Best American Nonrequired Reading, 2002. New York: Houghton, 2002.

SELECTION FROM AN ANTHOLOGY

Smith, Seaton. "'Jiving' with Your Teen." The Best American Nonrequired Reading, 2002. Ed. Dave Eggers. New York: Houghton, 2002. 88-94.

SECTION OR CHAPTER FROM A BOOK

Kurlansky, Mark. "The Hapsburg Pickle." Salt: A World History. New York: Walker, 2002. 234-310.

Periodicals

ARTICLE IN A JOURNAL WITH CONTINUOUS PAGINATION THROUGHOUT AN ANNUAL VOLUME

Some journals paginate issues continuously, by volume; that is, the page numbers in one issue pick up where the previous issue left off. For these journals, the year of publication, in parentheses, follows the volume number.

Kramer-Moore, Daniela, and Michael Moore. "Pardon Me for Breathing: Seven Types of Apology." ETC: A Review of General Semantics 60 (2003): 160-69.

ARTICLE IN A JOURNAL WITH SEPARATE PAGINATION IN EACH ISSUE

Some journals paginate by issue; that is, each issue begins with page 1. For these journals, follow the volume number with a period and the issue number. Then give the year of publication in parentheses.

McGlone, Matthew S. "Quoted Out of Context: Contextomy and Its Consequences." Journal of Communication 55.2 (2005): 330-46.

ARTICLE IN A MONTHLY MAGAZINE

List the author or authors the same way as for books. List the article's title in quotation marks, followed by the publication's title, underlined. Abbreviate all months except May, June, and July. If an article in a magazine or newspaper is not printed on consecutive pages—for example, an article might begin on page 45 and then skip to 48—include only the first page, followed by a plus sign.

Kaiser, Charles. "Civil Marriage, Civil Rights." Advocate Mar. 2004: 72.

ARTICLE IN A WEEKLY OR BIWEEKLY MAGAZINE

Kluger, Jeffrey. "When Gambling Becomes Obsessive." Time 1 Aug. 2005: 52+.

ARTICLE IN A NEWSPAPER

If the newspaper lists an edition, add a comma after the date and specify the edition.

Wheeler, Ginger. "Weighing in on Chubby Kids: Smart Strategies to Curb Obesity." Chicago Tribune 9 Mar. 2004, final ed.: C11+.

EDITORIAL (SIGNED/UNSIGNED)

Jackson, Derrick Z. "The Winner: Hypocrisy." Editorial. Boston Globe 6 Feb. 2004, late ed.: A19.

"Rescuing Education Reform." Editorial. New York Times 2 Mar. 2004, late ed.: A22.

LETTER TO THE EDITOR

Liu, Penny. Letter. New York Times 17 Jan. 2004, late ed.: A14.

Internet Sources

Citations for Internet sources follow the same rules as citations for print sources, but several additional pieces of information are required to cite an Internet source: the date of electronic publication (if available), the date you accessed the source, and the source's URL. Additionally, citations for different types of Internet sources require different types of information, so be sure to review the models that follow. (Note: When writing a citation for an Internet source, MLA style requires that you break URLs only *after* a slash.)

ENTIRE WEB SITE (SCHOLARLY PROJECT, INFORMATION DATABASE, OR PROFESSIONAL WEB SITE)

List the site's title first, underlined, followed by the editor, compiler, or person responsible for maintaining or updating the site, if known. Next, include the date of the site's last update, if known; the name of the sponsoring organization, if known; the date you accessed the site; and the URL, enclosed in angle brackets.

BBC: Religion and Ethics. British Broadcasting Corporation. 2005. 29 Sept. 2005 <http://www.bbc.co.uk/religion/ethics/index.shtml>.

The Victorian Web. Ed. George P. Landow. 1 Aug. 2005. Brown U. 10 Jan. 2006 <http://www.victorianweb.org>.

SHORT WORK FROM A WEB SITE

"Designer Babies." BBC: Religion and Ethics. British Broadcasting Corporation. 2005. 29 Sept. 2005 <http://www.bbc.co.uk/religion/ethics/issues/designer_babies/index.shtml>.

Wojtczak, Helena. "The Women's Social and Political Union." The Victorian Web. Ed. George P. Landow. 1 Aug. 2005. Brown U. 10 Jan. 2006 <http://www.victorianweb.org/gender/wojtczak/wspu.html>.

PERSONAL HOME PAGE

Rufus, Anneli. Home page. 27 July 2005. 30 Aug. 2005 <http://www.annelirufus.com>.

ONLINE BOOK

Whitman, Walt. Leaves of Grass. 1900. Bartleby.com: Great Books Online. Ed. Steven van Leeuwen. 2004. 31 Aug. 2005 <http://www.bartleby.com/142>.

SECTION OR CHAPTER FROM AN ONLINE BOOK

Whitman, Walt. "Crossing Brooklyn Ferry." Leaves of Grass. 1900. Bartleby.com: Great Books Online. Ed. Steven van Leeuwen. 2004. 1 Sept. 2005 <http://www.bartleby.com/142/86.html>.

ARTICLE IN AN ONLINE SCHOLARLY JOURNAL

Drury, Nevill. "How Can I Teach Peace When the Book Only Covers War?" Online Journal of Peace and Conflict Resolution 5.1 (2003). 18 Mar. 2006 <http://www.trinstitute.org/ojpcr/5_1finley.htm>.

ARTICLE IN AN ONLINE MAGAZINE

Engber, Daniel. "How Do You Measure Sea Level?" Slate 29 Aug. 2005. 1 Sept. 2005 <http://www.slate.com/id/2125229>.

ARTICLE IN AN ONLINE NEWSPAPER

Bhatt, Sanjay. "Got Game? Foundation Promotes Chess as Classroom Learning Tool." Seattle Times Online 15 Mar. 2004. 31 Aug. 2005 <http://seattletimes.nwsource.com/html/education/2001879251_chess15m.html>.

ARTICLE IN AN ONLINE REFERENCE WORK

"Chili Pepper." Encyclopedia Britannica. 2005. Encyclopedia Britannica Premium Service. 11 Dec. 2005 <http://www.britannica.com/eb/article?eu=24458>.

ARTICLE FROM A LIBRARY SUBSCRIPTION SERVICE

Follow the guidelines for citing an article from a print periodical. Complete the citation by providing the name of the database, underlined, if known; the name of the subscription service; the name of the library, with city and state abbreviation; date of your access; and main search page URL, enclosed in angle brackets.

Strimel, Courtney B. "The Politics of Terror: Rereading Harry Potter." Children's Literature in Education Mar. 2004: 35-53. Academic Search Premier. EBSCO. Skidmore College Lib., Saratoga Springs, NY. 22 Feb. 2006 <http://www.epnet.com>.

E-MAIL MESSAGE

Johnson, Gregory S. "Re: Schedule and Deadlines." E-mail to Alfred Rosa. 29 Aug. 2005.

ONLINE POSTING

Zarela, Scot. "Old Fat Hamlet?" Online posting. 18 Aug. 2005. Shaksper: The Global Electronic Shakespeare Conf. 15 Nov. 2005 <http://www.shaksper.net/archives/2005/1342.html>.

Other Nonprint Sources

TELEVISION OR RADIO PROGRAM

"Everyone's Waiting." Six Feet Under. Dir. Alan Ball. Perf. Peter Krause, Michael C. Hall, Frances Conroy, and Lauren Ambrose. Writ. Alan Ball. HBO. 21 Aug. 2005.

FILM OR VIDEO RECORDING

Million Dollar Baby. Dir. Clint Eastwood. Perf. Clint Eastwood, Hilary Swank, and Morgan Freeman. 2004. DVD. Warner, 2005.

PERSONAL INTERVIEW

Kozalek, Mark. Personal interview. 22 Jan. 2006.

LECTURE

England, Paula. "Gender and Inequality: Trends and Causes." President's Distinguished Lecture Series. U of Vermont Memorial Lounge, Burlington. 22 Mar. 2004.

AN ANNOTATED STUDENT RESEARCH PAPER

Jake Jamieson's assignment was to write an argument, and he was free to choose his own topic. After considering a number of possible topics and doing some preliminary research on several of them, he turned to the material he was studying in another of his courses, which focused on the study of the English language. In that course, he had become intrigued with the English-only movement. As he said, "I chose this topic to do my paper on because it is an aspect of speech that I had previously explored, and my interest was piqued. The topic absolutely intrigued me, from the prospect of banning languages other than English right down to the question of funding for bilingualism."

Jamieson began by brainstorming about his topic. He made lists of ideas, facts, issues, arguments, and opposing arguments. Once he was confident that he had amassed enough information to begin writing, he made a rough outline of an organizational pattern he felt he could follow. Keeping this pattern in mind, he wrote a first draft of his essay. Then he went back and examined it carefully, assessing how it could be improved.

After he reread his first draft, he realized that his organizational pattern could be clearer and that his examples needed to be sharper and more to the point. He also struck upon the idea of asking a series of rhetorical questions in the eighth paragraph, and he took particular delight in being able to use them in this paper: "I have always enjoyed these kinds of rhetorical questions, and I was excited when I got a chance to sneak them into this paper, lampooning the air of superiority and unwillingness to accept difference that characterize the English-only viewpoint." Most importantly, Jamieson scoured his sources for the most appropriate and memorable quotations to include in his paper, all the while being careful to keep accurate notes on where he found them.

The final draft of Jamieson's research paper illustrates that he has learned how the parts of a well-researched and well-written paper fit together and how to make the revisions that emulate some of the qualities of the model essays he has read and studied. The following is the final draft of the paper, and it demonstrates MLA format for research papers.

Jamieson 1

Jake Jamieson

Professor Rosa

English Composition

16 May 2006

The English-Only Movement: Can America Proscribe Language with a Clear Conscience?

Announces melting pot debate

A common conception among many people in this country is that the United States is a giant cultural "melting pot." For these people, the melting pot is a place where people from other places come together and bathe in the warm waters of assimilation. For many others, however, the melting pot analogy doesn't work. They see the melting pot as a giant cauldron into which immigrants are placed; here their cultures, values, and backgrounds are boiled away in the scalding waters of discrimination. One major point of contention in this debate is language: Should immigrants be pushed toward learning English or encouraged to retain their native tongues?

Asks question to be answered in paper

Those who argue that the melting pot analogy is valid believe that people who come to America do so willingly and should be expected to become a part of its culture instead of hanging on to their past. For them, the expectation that people who come to this country will celebrate this country's holidays, dress as we do, embrace our values, and most importantly speak our language is not unreasonable. They believe that assimilation offers the only way for everyone in this country to live together in harmony and the only way to dissipate the tensions that inevitably arise when cultures clash. A major problem with this argument, however, is that no one seems to be able to agree on what exactly constitutes "our way" of doing things.

Not everyone in America is of the same religious persuasion or has the same set of values, and different people affect vastly different styles of dress. There are so many sets of variables that it would be hard to defend the argument that there

Jamieson 2

is only one culture in the United States. What seems to be the most widespread constant in our country is that much of the population speaks English, and a major movement is being staged in favor of making English the official language. Making English America's official language would, according to William F. Buckley, involve making it the only language in which government business can be conducted on any level, from federal dealings right down to the local level (71). Many reasons are given to support the notion that making English the official language is a good idea and that it is exactly what this country needs, especially in the face of growing multilingualism. Indeed, one Los Angeles school recently documented sixty different languages spoken in the homes of its students (National Education Association, par. 4).

Defines English as the official language

Uses MLA citation format, including introductory signal phrase and parenthetical page number

Supporters of English-only contend that all government communication must be in English. Because communication is absolutely necessary for a democracy to survive, they believe that the only way to ensure the existence of our nation is to make sure a common language exists. Making English official would ensure that all government business, from ballots to official forms to judicial hearings, would have to be conducted in English. According to former senator and presidential candidate Bob Dole, "Promoting English as our national language is not an act of hostility but a welcoming act of inclusion." He goes on to state that while immigrants are encouraged to continue speaking their native languages, "thousands of children [are] failing to learn the language, English, that is the ticket to the 'American Dream'" (qtd. in Donegan 51). Greg Lewis echoes Dole's sentiments when he boldly states, "to succeed in America . . . it's important to speak, read, and understand English as most Americans speak it" (197).

Introduces English-only position

For those who do not subscribe to this way of thinking, however, this type of legislation is anything but the "welcoming

Jamieson 3

Introduces anti-English-only position

act of inclusion" that it is described to be. Many of them, like Myriam Marquez, readily acknowledge the importance of English but fear that "talking in Spanish—or any other language, for that matter—is some sort of litmus test used to gauge American patriotism" ("Why and When" 473). Others suggest that anyone attempting to regulate language is treading dangerously close to the First Amendment and must have a hidden agenda of some type. Why, it is asked, make a language official when it is already firmly entrenched and widely used in this country and, according to U.S. General Accounting Office statistics, 99.96 percent of all federal documents are already in English without legislation to mandate it (Underwood, "English-Only" par. 2)? According to author James Crawford, the answer is quite plain: discrimination. He states that "it is certainly more respectable to discriminate by language than by race." He points out that "most people are not sensitive to language discrimination in this nation, so it is easy to argue that you're doing someone a favor by making them speak English" (qtd. in Donegan 51). English-only legislation has been described as bigoted, anti-immigrant, mean-spirited, and steeped in nativism by those who oppose it, and some go so far as to say that this type of legislation will not foster better communication, as is the claim, but will instead encourage a "fear of being subsumed by a growing 'foreignness' in our midst" (Underwood, "At Issue" 65).

Uses an example to question English-only position that speaking Spanish in the home is abusive

For example, when a judge in Texas ruled that a mother was abusing her five-year-old girl by speaking to her only in Spanish, an uproar ensued. This ruling was accompanied by the statement that by talking to her in a language other than English, the mother was "abusing that child and . . . relegating her to the position of house maid." This statement was condemned by the National Association for Bilingual Education (NABE) for "labeling the Spanish language as abuse." The judge, Samuel C. Kiser, subsequently apologized to the housekeepers of the country, adding that he held them "in the highest esteem," but stood firm on his ruling (qtd. in Donegan 51). One might notice that he went out of his way to apologize to the housekeepers he might have offended but saw no need to apologize to the hundreds of thousands of Spanish speakers whose language had just been belittled in a nationally publicized case.

Argues against the English-only idea of multilingualism as irrational

This tendency of official-English proponents to put down other languages is one that shows up again and again, even though it is maintained that they have nothing against other languages or the people who speak them. If there is no malice toward other languages, why is the use of any language other than English tantamount to lunacy according to an almost constant barrage of literature and editorial opinions? In a recent publication of the "New Year's Resolutions" of various conservative organizations, a group called U.S. English, Inc., stated that the U.S. government was not doing its job of convincing immigrants that they "must learn English to succeed in this country." Instead, according to this publication, "in a bewildering display of irrationality, the U.S. government makes it possible to vote, file a tax return, get married, obtain a driver's license, and become a U.S. citizen in many languages" (Moore et al. 46).

Asks rhetorical questions

Now, according to this mindset, not only is speaking any language other than English abusive, but it is also irrational and bewildering. What is this world coming to when people want to speak and make transactions in their native language? Why do they refuse to change and become more like us? Why can't immigrants see that speaking English is right and anything else is wrong? These and many other questions are implied by official-English proponents as they discuss the issue.

Conservative attorney David Price argues that official-English legislation is a good idea because many English-speaking Americans prefer "out of pride and convenience to speak their native language on the job" (A13). Not only does this statement

Jamieson 5

Points to growing popularity of English-only position

imply that the pride and convenience of non-English-speaking Americans is unimportant, but that their native tongues are not as important as English. The scariest prospect of all is that this opinion is quickly gaining popularity all around the country.

Presents status report of English-only legislation

To date a number of official-English bills and one amendment to the Constitution have been proposed in the House and Senate. There are twenty-two states, including Alabama, California, and Arizona, that have made English their official language, and more are debating it every day (Donegan 52). An especially disturbing fact about this debate is that official-English laws always seem to be linked to other anti-immigrant legislation, such as proposals to "limit immigration and restrict government benefits to immigrants" ("English-Only Law Faces Test" 1).

Concludes that English-only legislation is not in our best interest

Although official-English proponents maintain that their bid for language legislation is in the best interest of immigrants, the facts tend to show otherwise. A decision has to be made in this country about what kind of message we will send to the rest of the world. Do we plan to allow everyone in this country the freedom of speech that we profess to cherish, or will we decide to reserve it only for those who speak the same language as we do? Will we hold firm to our belief that everyone is deserving of life, liberty, and the pursuit of happiness in this country? Or will we show the world that we believe in these things only when they pertain to ourselves and people like us? "The irony," as Hispanic columnist Myriam Marquez observes, "is that English-only laws directed at government have done little to change the inevitable multicultural flavor of America" ("English-Only Laws" A10).

Jamieson 6

Works Cited

Follows MLA citation guidelines

Buckley, William F. "Se Hable Ingles." National Review 9 Oct. 1995: 70-71.

Donegan, Craig. "Debate over Bilingualism: Should English Be the Nation's Official Language?" CQ Researcher 19 Jan. 1996: 51-71.

"English-Only Law Faces Test." Burlington Free Press 26 Mar. 1996: 1.

Lewis, Greg. "An Open Letter to Diversity's Victims." Language Awareness. 9th ed. Eds. Paul Eschholz, Alfred Rosa, and Virginia Clark. Boston: Bedford, 2005. 196-98.

Marquez, Myriam. "English-Only Laws Serve to Appease Those Who Fear the Inevitable." Orlando Sentinel 10 July 2000: A10.

---. "Why and When We Speak Spanish in Public." Models for Writers. 9th ed. Eds. Alfred Rosa and Paul Eschholz. Boston: Bedford, 2007. 472-74.

Moore, Stephen, et al. "New Year's Resolutions." National Review 29 Jan. 1996: 46-48.

National Education Association. "NEA Statement on the Debate over English Only." Teacher's College, U. of Nebraska, Lincoln. 27 Sept. 1999. 14 Mar. 2006 <http://www.tc.unl.edu/enemeth/biling/engonly.html>.

Price, David. "English-Only Rules: EEOC Has Gone Too Far." USA Today 28 Mar. 1996, final ed.: A13.

Underwood, Robert A. "At Issue: Should English Be the Official Language of the United States?" CQ Researcher 19 Jan. 1996: 65.

---. "English-Only Legislation." U.S. House of Representatives. 28 Nov. 1995. 14 Mar. 2006. <http://www.house.gov/underwood/speeches/english.htm>.

Glossary of Useful Terms

Abstract *See Concrete/Abstract.*

Allusion An allusion is a passing reference to a familiar person, place, or thing, often drawn from history, the Bible, mythology, or literature. An allusion is an economical way for a writer to capture the essence of an idea, atmosphere, emotion, or historical era, as in "The scandal was his Watergate" or "He saw himself as a modern Job" or "The campaign ended not with a bang but a whimper." An allusion should be familiar to the reader; if it is not, it will add nothing to the meaning.

Analogy Analogy is a special form of comparison in which the writer explains something unfamiliar by comparing it to something familiar: "A transmission line is simply a pipeline for electricity. In the case of a water pipeline, more water will flow through the pipe as water pressure increases. The same is true of electricity in a transmission line."

Anecdote An anecdote is a short narrative about an amusing or interesting event. Writers often use anecdotes to begin essays as well as to illustrate certain points.

Argumentation To argue is to attempt to persuade the reader to agree with a point of view, to make a given decision, or to pursue a particular course of action. There are two basic types of argumentation: logical and persuasive. See the introduction to Chapter 20 (pp. 484–91) for a detailed discussion of argumentation.

Attitude A writer's attitude reflects his or her opinion of a subject. The writer can think very positively or very negatively about a subject or have an attitude that falls somewhere in between. See also *Tone.*

Audience An audience is the intended readership for a piece of writing. For example, the readers of a national weekly newsmagazine come from all walks of life and have diverse interests, opinions, and educational backgrounds. In contrast, the readership for an organic chemistry journal is made up of people whose interests and education are quite similar. The essays in *Models for Writers* are intended for general readers, intelligent people who may lack specific information about the subject being discussed.

Beginnings and Endings A beginning is the sentence, group of sentences, or section that introduces an essay. Good beginnings usually identify the thesis or controlling idea, attempt to interest readers, and establish a tone.

An ending is the sentence or group of sentences that brings an essay to a close. Good endings are purposeful and well planned. They can be a summary, a concluding example, an anecdote, or a quotation. Endings satisfy readers when they are the natural outgrowths of the essays themselves and give readers a sense of finality or completion. Good essays do not simply stop; they conclude. See the introduction to Chapter 6 (pp. 133–39) for a detailed discussion of beginnings and endings.

Cause and Effect Cause-and-effect analysis explains the reasons for an occurrence or the consequences of an action. See the introduction to Chapter 19 (pp. 462–64) for a detailed discussion of cause and effect.

Classification See *Division and Classification.*

Cliché A cliché is an expression that has become ineffective through overuse. Expressions such as *quick as a flash, jump for joy,* and *slow as molasses* are clichés. Writers normally avoid such trite expressions and seek instead to express themselves in fresh and forceful language. See also *Diction.*

Coherence Coherence is a quality of good writing that results when all sentences, paragraphs, and longer divisions of an essay are naturally connected. Coherent writing is achieved through (1) a logical sequence of ideas (arranged in chronological order, spatial order, order of importance, or some other appropriate order), (2) the purposeful repetition of key words and ideas, (3) a pace suitable for your topic and your reader, and (4) the use of transitional words and expressions. Coherence should not be confused with unity. (See *Unity.*) See also *Transition.*

Colloquial Expression A colloquial expression is an expression that is characteristic of or appropriate to spoken language or to writing that seeks the effect of spoken language. Colloquial expressions are informal, as *chem, gym, come up with, be at wit's end, won't,* and *photo* illustrate. Thus, colloquial expressions are acceptable in formal writing only if they are used purposefully. See also *Diction.*

Combined Strategies By combining rhetorical strategies, writers are able to develop their ideas in interesting ways. For example, in writing a cause-and-effect essay about a major oil spill, the writer might want to describe the damage that the spill caused, as well as explain the cleanup process step by step.

Comparison and Contrast Comparison and contrast is used to point out the similarities and differences between two or more subjects in the same class or category. The function of any comparison and contrast is to clarify—to reach some conclusion about the items being compared and contrasted. See the introduction to Chapter 18 (pp. 433–37) for a detailed discussion of comparison and contrast.

Conclusions See *Beginnings and Endings.*

Concrete/Abstract A concrete word names a specific object, person, place, or action that can be directly perceived by the senses: *car, bread, building, book, John F. Kennedy, Chicago,* or *hiking.* An abstract word, in contrast, refers to general qualities, conditions, ideas, actions, or relationships that cannot be directly perceived by the senses: *bravery, dedication, excellence, anxiety, stress, thinking,* or *hatred.* See the introduction to Chapter 10 (pp. 239–44) for more on abstract and concrete words.

Connotation/Denotation Both connotation and denotation refer to the meanings of words. Denotation is the dictionary meaning of a word, the literal meaning. Connotation, on the other hand, is the implied or suggested meaning of a word. For example, the denotation of *lamb* is "a young sheep." The connotations of *lamb* are numerous: *gentle, docile, weak, peaceful, blessed, sacrificial, blood, spring, frisky, pure, innocent,* and so on. See the introduction to Chapter 10 (pp. 239–44) for more on connotation and denotation.

Controlling Idea See *Thesis.*

Coordination Coordination is the joining of grammatical constructions of the same rank (e.g., words, phrases, clauses) to indicate that they are of equal importance. For example, "*They ate hot dogs,* and *we ate hamburgers.*" See the introduction to Chapter 9 (pp. 210–14) for more on coordination. See also *Subordination.*

Deduction Deduction is the process of reasoning from stated premises to a conclusion that follows necessarily. This form of reasoning moves from the general to the specific. See the introduction to Chapter 20 (pp. 484–91) for a discussion of deductive reasoning and its role in argumentation. See also *Syllogism.*

Definition Definition is a rhetorical pattern. Definition is a statement of the meaning of a word. A definition may be either brief or extended, part of an essay or an entire essay itself. See the introduction to Chapter 16 (pp. 391–93) for a detailed discussion of definition.

Denotation See *Connotation/Denotation.*

Description Description tells how a person, place, or thing is perceived by the five senses. See the introduction to Chapter 14 (pp. 351–52) for a detailed discussion of description.

Details Details are the small elements that collectively contribute to the overall impression of a person, place, thing, or idea. For example, in the sentence "The *organic, whole-grain* dog biscuits were *reddish brown, beef flavored,* and in the *shape of a bone*" the italicized words are details.

Dialogue Dialogue is the conversation of two or more people as represented in writing. Dialogue is what people say directly to one another.

Diction Diction refers to a writer's choice and use of words. Good diction is precise and appropriate: The words mean exactly what the writer intends, and the words are well suited to the writer's subject, intended audience, and purpose in writing. The word-conscious writer knows that there are differences among *aged, old,* and *elderly; blue, navy,* and *azure;* and *disturbed, angry,* and *irritated.* Furthermore, this writer knows in which situation to use each word. See the introduction to Chapter 10 (pp. 239–44) for a detailed discussion of diction. See also *Cliché; Colloquial Expression; Connotation/Denotation; Jargon; Slang.*

Division and Classification Division and classification are rhetorical patterns used by the writer first to establish categories and then to arrange or sort people, places, or things into these categories according to their different characteristics, thus making them more manageable for the writer and more understandable and meaningful for the reader. See the introduction to Chapter 17 (pp. 408–11) for a detailed discussion of division and classification.

Dominant Impression A dominant impression is the single mood, atmosphere, or quality a writer emphasizes in a piece of descriptive writing. The dominant impression is created through the careful selection of details and is, of course, influenced by the writer's subject, audience, and purpose. See the introduction to Chapter 14 (pp. 351–52) for more on dominant impression.

Emphasis Emphasis is the placement of important ideas and words within sentences and longer units of writing so that they have the greatest impact. In general, what comes at the end has the most impact, and at the beginning nearly as much; what comes in the middle gets the least emphasis.

Endings See *Beginnings and Endings.*

Evaluation An evaluation of a piece of writing is an assessment of its effectiveness or merit. In evaluating a piece of writing, one should ask the following questions: What is the writer's purpose? Is it a worthwhile purpose? Does the writer achieve the purpose? Is the writer's information sufficient and accurate? What are the strengths of the essay? What are its weaknesses? Depending on the type of writing and the purpose, more specific questions can also be asked. For example, with an argument one could ask: Does the writer follow the principles of logical thinking? Is the writer's evidence sufficient and convincing?

Evidence Evidence is the information on which a judgment or argument is based or by which proof or probability is established. Evidence usually takes the form of statistics, facts, names, examples or illustrations, and opinions of authorities.

Example An example illustrates a larger idea or represents something of which it is a part. An example is a basic means of developing or clarifying an idea. Furthermore, examples enable writers to show and not simply to tell readers what they mean. See the introduction to Chapter 12 (pp. 295–98) for more on example.

Facts Facts are pieces of information presented as having objective reality—that is, having actual existence. For example, water boils at 212°F, Katherine Hepburn died in 2003, and the USSR no longer exists—these are all facts.

Fallacy See *Logical Fallacy.*

Figure of Speech A figure of speech is a brief, imaginative comparison that highlights the similarities between things that are basically dissimilar. Figures of speech make writing vivid, interesting, and memorable. The most common figures of speech are:

Simile: An explicit comparison introduced by *like* or *as.* "The fighter's hands were like stone."

Metaphor: An implied comparison that makes one thing the equivalent of another. "All the world's a stage."

Personification: A special kind of figure of speech in which human traits are assigned to ideas or objects. "The engine coughed and then stopped."

See the introduction to Chapter 11 (pp. 270–71) for a detailed discussion of figurative language.

Focus Focus is the limitation that a writer gives his or her subject. The writer's task is to select a manageable topic given the constraints of time, space, and purpose. For example, within the general subject of sports, a writer could focus on government support of amateur athletes or narrow the focus further to government support of Olympic athletes.

General See *Specific/General.*

Idiom An idiom is a word or phrase that is used habitually with special meaning. The meaning of an idiom is not always readily apparent to nonnative speakers of that language. For example, *catch cold, hold a job, make up your mind,* and *give them a hand* are all idioms in English.

Illustration Illustration is the use of examples to explain, elucidate, or corroborate. Writers rely heavily on illustration to make their ideas both clear and concrete. See the introduction to Chapter 12 (pp. 295–98) for a detailed discussion of illustration.

Induction Induction is the process of reasoning to a conclusion about all members of a class through an examination of only a few members of the class. This form of reasoning moves from the particular to the general. See the introduction to Chapter 20 (pp. 484–91) for a discussion of inductive reasoning and its role in argumentation.

Inductive Leap An inductive leap is the point at which a writer of an argument, having presented sufficient evidence, moves to a generalization or conclusion. See also *Induction.*

Introduction See *Beginnings and Endings.*

Irony Irony is the use of words to suggest something different from their literal meaning. For example, when Jonathan Swift suggested in "A Modest Proposal" that Ireland's problems could be solved if the people of Ireland fattened their babies and sold them to the English landlords for food, he meant that almost any other solution would be preferable. A writer can use irony to establish a special relationship with the reader and to add an extra dimension or twist to the meaning. See the introduction to Chapter 10 (pp. 239–44) for more on irony.

Jargon Jargon, or technical language, is the special vocabulary of a trade, profession, or group. Doctors, construction workers, lawyers, and teachers, for example, all have a specialized vocabulary that they use on the job. See also *Diction.*

Logical Fallacy A logical fallacy is an error in reasoning that renders an argument invalid. See the introduction to Chapter 20 (pp. 484–91) for a discussion of common logical fallacies.

Metaphor See *Figure of Speech.*

Narration To narrate is to tell a story, to tell what happened. While narration is most often used in fiction, it is also important in expository writing, either by itself or in conjunction with other types of prose. See the introduction to Chapter 13 (pp. 321–24) for a detailed discussion of narration.

Opinion An opinion is a belief or conclusion, which may or may not be substantiated by positive knowledge or proof. (If not substantiated, an opinion is a prejudice.) Even when based on evidence and sound reasoning, an opinion is personal and can be changed and is therefore less persuasive than facts and arguments.

Organization Organization is the pattern or order that the writer imposes on his or her material. Some often-used patterns of organization include time order, space order, and order of importance. See the introduction to Chapter 5 (pp. 109–13) for a detailed discussion of organization.

Paradox A paradox is a seemingly contradictory statement that is nonetheless true. For example, "We little know what we have until we lose it" is a paradoxical statement.

Paragraph The paragraph, the single most important unit of thought in an essay, is a series of closely related sentences. These sentences adequately develop the central or controlling idea of the paragraph. This central idea, usually stated in a topic sentence, is necessarily related to the purpose of the whole composition. A well-written paragraph has several distinguishing characteristics: a clearly stated or implied topic sentence, adequate development, unity, coherence, and an appropriate organizational strategy. See the introduction to Chapter 7 (pp. 164–67) for a detailed discussion of paragraphs.

Parallelism Parallel structure is the repetition of word order or grammatical form either within a single sentence or in several sentences that develop the same central idea. As a rhetorical device, parallelism can aid coherence and add emphasis. Franklin Roosevelt's statement "I see one-third of a nation ill-housed, ill-clad, and ill-nourished" illustrates effective parallelism. See the introduction to Chapter 9 (pp. 210–14) for more on parallelism.

Personification See *Figure of Speech.*

Persuasion Persuasion, or persuasive argument, is an attempt to convince readers to agree with a point of view, to make a decision, or to pursue a particular course of action. Persuasion appeals strongly to the emotions, whereas logical argument does not.

Point of View Point of view refers to the grammatical person in an essay. For example, the first-person point of view uses the pronoun *I* and is commonly found in autobiography and the personal essay; the third-person point of view uses the pronouns *he, she,* or *it* and is commonly found in objective writing. See the introduction to Chapter 13 (pp. 321–24) for a discussion of point of view in narration.

Process Analysis Process analysis is a rhetorical strategy used to explain how something works or to give step-by-step directions for doing something. See the introduction to Chapter 15 (pp. 370–73) for a detailed discussion of process analysis.

Purpose Purpose is what the writer wants to accomplish in a particular piece of writing. Purposeful writing seeks to *tell* (narration), to *describe* (description), to *explain* (process analysis, definition, classification, comparison and contrast, and cause and effect), or to *convince* (argumentation).

Rhetorical Question A rhetorical question is asked for its rhetorical effect but requires no answer from the reader. "When will nuclear proliferation end?" is such a question. Writers use rhetorical questions to introduce topics they plan to discuss or to emphasize important points. See the introduction to Chapter 6 (pp. 133–39) for another example.

Sentence A sentence is a grammatical unit that expresses a complete thought. It consists of at least a subject (a noun) and a predicate (a verb). See the introduction to Chapter 9 (pp. 210–14) for a detailed discussion of effective sentences.

Simile See *Figure of Speech.*

Slang Slang is the unconventional, informal language of particular subgroups in our culture. Slang terms, such as *bummed, sweat, dark,* and *cool,* are acceptable in formal writing only if used selectively for specific purposes.

Specific/General General words name groups or classes of objects, qualities, or actions. Specific words, on the other hand, name individual objects, qualities, or actions within a class or group. To some extent the terms *general* and *specific* are relative. For example, *clothing* is a class of things. *Shirt,* however, is more specific than *clothing* but more general than *T-shirt*. See also *Diction.*

Strategy A strategy is a means by which a writer achieves his or her purpose. Strategy includes the many rhetorical decisions that the writer makes about organization, paragraph structure, sentence structure, and diction. In terms of the whole essay, strategy refers to the principal rhetorical mode that a writer uses. If, for example, a writer wishes to explain how to make chocolate chip cookies, the most effective strategy would be process analysis. If it is the writer's purpose to analyze why sales of American cars have declined in recent years, the most effective strategy would be cause-and-effect analysis.

Style Style is the individual manner in which a writer expresses his or her ideas. Style is created by the author's particular choice of words, construction of sentences, and arrangement of ideas.

Subordination Subordination is the use of grammatical constructions to make one part of a sentence dependent on, rather than equal to, another. For example, the italicized clause in the following sentence is subordinate: "They all cheered *when I finished the race.*" See the introduction to Chapter 9 (pp. 210–14) for more on subordination. See also *Coordination.*

Supporting Evidence See *Evidence.*

Syllogism A syllogism is an argument that utilizes deductive reasoning and consists of a major premise, a minor premise, and a conclusion:

> All trees that lose leaves are deciduous. (*Major premise*)
> Maple trees lose their leaves. (*Minor premise*)
> Therefore, maple trees are deciduous. (*Conclusion*)

See pages 484–91 in Chapter 20 for more on syllogisms. See also *Deduction.*

Symbol A symbol is a person, place, or thing that represents something beyond itself. For example, the bald eagle is a symbol of the United States, and the maple leaf, a symbol of Canada.

Syntax Syntax refers to the way in which words are arranged to form phrases, clauses, and sentences, as well as to the grammatical relationship among the words themselves.

Technical Language See *Jargon.*

Thesis The thesis, also known as the controlling idea, is the main idea of an essay. It may sometimes be implied rather than stated directly. See the introduction to Chapter 3 (pp. 71–73) for more on the thesis statement.

Title A title is a word or phrase set off at the beginning of an essay to identify the subject, to state the main idea of the essay, or to attract the reader's attention. A title may be explicit or suggestive. A subtitle, when used, explains or restricts the meaning of the main title.

Tone Tone is the manner in which a writer relates to an audience, the "tone of voice" used to address readers. Tone may be friendly, serious, distant, angry, humorous, cheerful, bitter, cynical, enthusiastic, morbid, resentful, warm, playful, and so forth. A particular tone results from a writer's diction, sentence structure, purpose, and attitude toward the subject. See the introduction to Chapter 10 (pp. 239–44) for several examples that display different tones.

Topic Sentence The topic sentence states the central idea of a paragraph and thus limits the content of the paragraph. Although the topic sentence normally appears at the beginning of the paragraph, it may appear at any other point, particularly if the writer is trying to create a special effect. Not all paragraphs contain topic sentences. See also *Paragraph.*

Transition A transition is a word or phrase that links sentences, paragraphs, and larger units of a composition to achieve coherence. Transitions include parallelism, pronoun references, conjunctions, and the repetition of key ideas, as well as the many conventional transitional expressions such as *moreover, on the other hand, in addition, in contrast,* and *therefore.* See the introduction to Chapter 8 (pp. 188–91) for a detailed discussion of transitions. See also *Coherence.*

Unity Unity is that quality of oneness in an essay that results when all the words, sentences, and paragraphs contribute to the thesis. The elements of a unified essay do not distract the reader. Instead, they all harmoniously support a single idea or purpose. See the introduction to Chapter 4 (pp. 90–93) for a detailed discussion of unity.

Verb Verbs can be classified as either strong verbs (*scream, pierce, gush, ravage,* and *amble*) or weak verbs (*be, has, get,* and *do*). Writers prefer to use strong verbs to make their writing more specific, more descriptive, and more action filled.

Voice Verbs can be classified as being in either the active or the passive voice. In the *active voice,* the doer of the action is the grammatical subject. In the *passive voice,* the receiver of the action is the subject:

> *Active:* Glenda questioned all of the children.
> *Passive:* All of the children were questioned by Glenda.

Acknowledgments

Maya Angelou. "Momma, the Dentist, and Me." From *I Know Why the Caged Bird Sings* by Maya Angelou. Copyright © 1969 and renewed 1997 by Maya Angelou. Used with the permission of Random House, Inc.

Isaac Asimov. "Intelligence." Published by the permission of the Isaac Asimov Estate, C/o Ralph M. Vicinanza Ltd.

Russell Baker. "Becoming a Writer." Excerpt from Chapter 2 in *Growing Up* by Russell Baker. Copyright © 1982 by Russell Baker. Reprinted by permission of Don Congdon Associates Inc.

James David Barber. "Four Types of President." From *The Presidential Character*, 2d edition by James David Barber. Copyright © 1977, 1972 by James David Barber. Published by Prentice-Hall, Inc., Englewood Cliffs, NJ 07632. Reprinted with permission of the author.

Steve Brody. "How I Got Smart." From *The New York Times*, September 21, 1986. Copyright © 1986 by The New York Times Company. Reprinted by permission.

Rachel Carson. "Fable for Tomorrow." From *Silent Spring* by Rachel Carson. Copyright © 1962 by Rachel L. Carson. Copyright © renewed 1990 by Roger Christie. Reprinted by permission of Houghton Mifflin Company. All rights reserved.

Bruce Catton. "Grant and Lee: A Study in Contrasts." From *The American Song*, edited by Earl Schenck Miers. Reprinted by permission of the United States Capitol Historical Society.

Kate Chopin. "The Story of an Hour." From *The Complete Works of Kate Chopin*, Volume 1, edited by Per Seyersted. Copyright © 1969 by Per Seyersted. Reprinted by Louisiana State University Press.

Sandra Cisneros. "My Name." From *The House on Mango Street* by Sandra Cisneros. Copyright © 1984 by Sandra Cisneros. Published by Vintage Books, a division of Random House, Inc. and in hardcover by Alfred A. Knopf in 1994. Reprinted by permission of Susan Literary Services, New York. All rights reserved.

James Lincoln Collier. "Anxiety: Challenge by Another Name." Originally published in *Reader's Digest*, December 1986. Reprinted with permission of the author.

Greg Critser. "Don't Eat the Flan." From *Forbes*, February 3, 2003. Copyright © 2005 Forbes, Inc. Reprinted by permission of Forbes Magazine.

Annie Dillard. "From *An American Childhood*." Excerpt from pp. 147–49 in *An American Childhood* by Annie Dillard. Copyright © 1987 by Annie Dillard. Reprinted by permission of HarperCollins Publishers, Inc.

Lars Eighner. "On Dumpster Diving." From *Travels with Lizabeth* by Lars Eighner. Copyright © 1993 by the author and reprinted by permission of St. Martin's Press, LLC.

Barbara Loe Fisher. "Parents Should Be Allowed to Opt Out of Vaccinating Their Children." From *Insight*, April 24, 2000. Copyright © 2000 News World Communications, Inc. Reprinted with permission. All rights reserved.

Lawrence M. Friedman. "What Is Crime?" From *Crime and Punishment in American History* by Lawrence M. Friedman. Copyright © 1993 by Lawrence M. Friedman. Reprinted by permission of Basic Books, a member of Perseus Books LLC.

Thomas L. Friedman. "My Favorite Teacher." From *The New York Times*, January 9, 2001, Section A, p. 19. Copyright © 2001 by The New York Times Company. Reprinted by permission.

Martin Gansberg. "38 Who Saw Murder Didn't Call Police." From *The New York Times*, March 17, 1964. Copyright © 1964 by The New York Times Company. Reprinted by permission.

Henry Louis Gates Jr. "What's in a Name?" Originally published in *Dissent*, Fall 1989, Volume 36, No. 4. Reprinted with permission of the Foundation for the Study of Independent Social Ideas. Reprinted by permission.

Natalie Goldberg. "Be Specific." From *Writing Down the Bones* by Natalie Goldberg. © 1986. Reprinted by arrangement with Shambhala Publications, Inc., Boston. www.shambhala.com.

Ellen Goodman. "The Company Man." From *Value Judgments* by Ellen Goodman. © by Ellen Goodman. Reprinted with the permission of International Creative Management Inc.

Dick Gregory. "Shame." From *Nigger: An Autobiography* by Dick Gregory. Copyright © 1964 by Dick Gregory Enterprises, Inc. Used by permission of Dutton, a division of Penguin Group (USA), Inc.

Pete Hamill. "City of Islands." Copyright © 1998 by Pete Hamill. Reprinted by permission of International Creative Management, Inc.

Robin Marantz Henig. "Something's Off." From *The New York Times Magazine*, October 17, 2004, p. 110. Copyright © 2004 by The New York Times. Reprinted by permission of the author.

Gilbert Highet. "Subway Station." From *Talents and Geniuses* by Gilbert Highet. Copyright © 1957 by Gilbert Highet. Reprinted by permission of Curtis Brown, Ltd.

Langston Hughes. "Salvation." From *The Big Sea* by Langston Hughes. Copyright © 1940 by Langston Hughes. Copyright renewed 1968 by Arna Bontemps and George Houston Bass. Reprinted by permission of Hill and Wang, a division of Farrar, Straus and Giroux, LLC.

Bill Husted. "Here's How to Revive a Computer Even after an Evil Wizard Kills the Beast." Originally titled "'Evil Wizard' computer killer thwarted one more time." By Bill Husted. From the *Atlanta Journal-Constitution*, March 30, 2003. Copyright 2003 by *Atlanta Journal Constitution*. Reproduced with permission of *Atlanta Journal Constitution* in the format Textbook via Copyright Clearance Center.

Barbara Huttmann. "A Crime of Compassion." Originally published in *Newsweek*, August 8, 1983. Copyright © 1983 by Barbara Huttmann. Reprinted with the permission of the author.

Caroline Hwang. "The Good Daughter." First appeared in *Newsweek*, September 21, 1998, p. 16. Copyright © 1998 by Caroline Hwang. Reprinted by permission of the author and the Sandra Dijkstra Literary Agency.

Dan M. Kahan. "Shame Is Worth a Try." First published in *The Boston Globe*, August 5, 2001. Copyright © 2001 Dan M. Kahan. Reprinted with the permission of the author.

K. Connie Kang. "A Battle of Cultures." First published in *Asian Week*, May 25, 1990. Copyright © K. Connie Kang. Reprinted by permission of the author.

Michael T. Kaufman. "Of My Friend Hector and My Achilles Heel." From *The New York Times*, November 11, 1992. Copyright © 1992 by The New York Times Company. Reprinted with permission.

Garrison Keillor. "How to Write a Personal Letter." From *We Are Still Married* by Garrison Keillor. Originally written for *Power of the Printed Word* series by the International Paper Company. Copyright © 1987 by International Paper Company. Reprinted by permission of Garrison Keillor/Prairie Home Productions.

Helen Keller. "The Most Important Day." Originally published as "Three Days to See" in the January 1993 issue of *The Atlantic Monthly*. Copyright © 1932 by The Helen Keller Foundation. Reprinted with permission.

Martin Luther King Jr. "The Ways of Meeting Oppression." From *Stride toward Freedom* by Martin Luther King. Copyright © 1958 Dr. Martin Luther King Jr. Copyright © 1986 by Coretta Scott King. "I Have a Dream." Copyright © 1963 Dr. Martin Luther King Jr. Copyright renewed 1991 Coretta Scott King. Reprinted by arrangement with the Estate of Martin Luther King Jr., c/o Writers House as agent for the proprietor New York, NY.

Stephen King. "Why We Crave Horror Movies." Originally appeared in *Playboy* (1982). © Stephen King. All rights reserved. Reprinted with permission.

Verlyn Klinkenborg. "Wyoming Clouds." From *The Rural Life* by Verlyn Klinkenborg. Copyright © 2003 by Verlyn Klinkenborg. By permission of Little, Brown & Company, Inc.

Anthony Komaroff, M.D. "Technology's Limits." From *Newsweek*, June 20, 2005, p. 88. Copyright © 2005 by Harvard Health Publications. Reprinted by permission of Harvard Health Publications. Fellows of Harvard College.

Etta Kralovec. "No More Pep Rallies!" From *Forbes*, February 17, 2003. Copyright © 2005 Forbes, Inc. Reprinted by permission of Forbes Magazine.

Richard Lederer. "The Case for Short Words." From *The Miracle of Language* by Richard Lederer. Copyright © 1991 by Richard Lederer. Reprinted with the permission of Atria Books, an imprint of Simon & Schuster Adult Publishing Group. All rights reserved.

William Lutz. "Doubts about Doublespeak." Appeared in *State Government News*, July 1993. Copyright © 1993 by William Lutz. Reprinted with the permission of the author.

Norman Mailer. "One Idea." From *Parade*, January 23, 2005, pp. 5–6. Copyright © 2005 Norman Mailer. Reprinted with permission of Parade Publications. All rights reserved.

Merrill Markoe. "Who Am I?" From *Time*, March 3, 2001. Copyright © 2001 Time, Inc. Reprinted with permission.

Robyn Marks. "Raising a Son—With Men on the Fringes." From *Newsweek*, July 19, 2004. Copyright © 2004 Newsweek, Inc. All rights reserved. Reprinted with permission.

Myriam Marquez. "Why and When We Speak Spanish in Public." From *Orlando Sentinel*, June 28, 1999. Copyright © 1999 by the Orlando Sentinel. Reprinted with permission of the publisher.

David McCullough. "Why History?" From the December 2002 issue of *Reader's Digest*. Copyright © 2002 Reader's Digest. Reprinted with permission of the publisher.

Cherokee Paul McDonald. "A View from the Bridge." From the *Sun Sentinel*, February 12, 1989. Copyright © 1989. Reprinted by permission of Knight Ridder-Tribune Information Services.

Del Miller. "Mac or PC: There Is Simply No Comparison!" Originally appeared in "Difference Engine" at Macopinion.com, July 25, 2005. Copyright © 2003 by Del Miller. Republished by permission of the author.

Alison Motluck. "Supersize Me: It's Time to Stop Blaming Fat People for Their Size." First published in *New Scientist*, October 30, 2004. Copyright © 2004. Reprinted with permission of New Scientist.

Gloria Naylor. "The Meanings of a Word." From *What's in a Name*. Copyright © 1986 by Gloria Naylor. Reprinted by permission of Sterling Lord Literistic, Inc.

George Orwell. "A Hanging." From *Shooting an Elephant and Other Essays* by George Orwell. Copyright © 1950 by Sonia Brownell Orwell and renewed 1978 by Sonia Pitt-Rivers, reprinted by permission of Harcourt, Inc. (U.S.) Copyright © George Orwell 1931 by permission of Bill Hamilton as the Literary Executor of the Estate of the Late Sonia Brownell Orwell and Secker & Warburg Ltd.

Anna Quindlen. "Mom Quixote." From *Loud and Clear* by Anna Quindlen. Copyright © 2004. Copyright © 2004 by Anna Quindlen. Reprinted with permission of International Creative Management, Inc.

Robert Ramirez. "The Barrio." Originally titled "The Woolen Sarape" from *Pain and Promise: The Chicano Today*, edited by Edward Simmens. Published by New American Library in 1972. Reprinted by permission of the author.

William Raspberry. "The Handicap of Definition." From *The Washington Post*, 1983. Copyright © 1983 The Washington Post Writers Group. Reprinted with permission.

David Raymond. "On Being 17, Bright, and Unable to Read." From *The New York Times*, April 25, 1976. Copyright © 1976 The New York Times Company. Reprinted with permission.

Mike Rose. "I Just Wanna Be Average." From *Lives on the Boundary: The Struggles and Achievements of America's Underprepared* by Mike Rose. Copyright © 1989 by Mike Rose. Reprinted with the permission of The Free Press, a Division of Simon & Schuster Adult Publishing Group.

Carl T. Rowan. "Unforgettable Miss Bessie." Copyright © 1985 by The Reader's Digest Association, Inc. Reprinted with permission from the March 1985 Reader's Digest.

Laura Rowley. "As They Say, Drugs Kill." First published in the February 1987 issue of *Newsweek on Campus*. Reprinted by permission of the author.

Ruth Russell. "The Wounds That Can't Be Stitched Up." From *Newsweek*, December 20, 1999, p. 11. Copyright © 1999 Newsweek, Inc. Reprinted by permission. All rights reserved.

Christie Scotty. "Can I Get You Some Manners with That?" From *Newsweek*, October 18, 2004, p. 24. Copyright © 2004 by Newsweek, Inc. Reprinted with permission. All rights reserved.

David Sedaris. "Me Talk Pretty One Day." Excerpt from pp. 166–73 in *Me Talk Pretty One Day* by David Sedaris. Copyright © 2000 by David Sedaris. By permission of Little, Brown & Company, Inc.

Steven P. Shelov. "Parents Should Not Be Allowed to Opt Out of Vaccinating Their Children." From *Insight*, April 20, 2000. Copyright © 2000 News World Communications, Inc. Reprinted with permission. All rights reserved.

Mary Sherry. "In Praise of the F Word." First published in *Newsweek*, May 6, 1991. Copyright © 1991 by Mary Sherry. Reprinted by permission of the author.

Gary Soto. "The Jacket." From *The Effects of Knut Hamsun on a Fresno Boy: Recollections and Short Essays* by Gary Soto. Copyright © 1983, 2000 by Gary Soto. Reprinted by permission of Persea Books, Inc. (New York).

June Tangney. "Condemn the Crime, Not the Person." From *The Boston Globe*, August 5, 2001. Copyright © 2001 by June Tangney. Reprinted with permission of the author.

Judith Viorst. "Friends, Good Friends—and Such Good Friends." Copyright © 1977 by Judith Viorst. Originally appeared in *Redbook*. Reprinted by permission of Lescher & Lescher, Ltd. All rights reserved.

Sarah Vowell. "Pop-A-Shot." From *The Partly Cloudy Patriot* by Sarah Vowell. © 2002 by Sarah Vowell. Reprinted by permission of Simon & Schuster Adult Publishing Group. All rights reserved.

Eudora Welty. "The Corner Store." Originally titled "The Little Store," from *The Eye of the Story: Selected Essays and Reviews* by Eudora Welty. Copyright © 1975 by Eudora Welty. Used by permission of Random House, Inc.

William Zinsser. "Simplicity." Published in *On Writing Well* 6th Edition (HarperCollins). Copyright © 1976, 1980, 1985, 1988, 1990, 1994, 1998 by William K. Zinsser. Reprinted by permission of the author.

Index

abstract words, 240
active reading, 41–42
active voice, 213
"after this, therefore because of this" fallacy, 464, 489
American Childhood, An (Dillard), 215–19
analogies, 436–37
  in beginnings, 134–35
  false, 489
anecdotes, 321
  in beginnings, 134
Angelou, Maya, "Momma, the Dentist, and Me," 337–45
angry tone, 242
"Anxiety: Challenge by Another Name" (Collier), 80–85
apologies, in beginnings, 137
argument, 484–549
  classroom activities using, 496–97, 503, 509, 513, 518, 522, 527, 533, 541, 548–49
  logical appeals, 485–86
  persuasive appeals, 485
  readings
    "As They Say, Drugs Kill" (Rowley), 505–9
    "Condemn the Crime, Not the Person" (Tangney), 524–29
    "Declaration of Independence, The" (Jefferson), 492–97
    "Don't Eat the Flan" (Critser), 515–19
    "I Have a Dream" (King), 498–504
    "In Praise of the F Word" (Sherry), 510–14
    "Parents Should Be Allowed to Opt Out of Vaccinating Their Children" (Fisher), 535–42
    "Parents Should Not Be Allowed to Opt Out of Vaccinating Their Children" (Shelov), 543–49
    "Shame Is Worth a Try" (Kahan), 530–34
    "Supersize Me: It's Time to Stop Blaming Fat People for Their Size" (Motluk), 520–23
  suggested writing assignments, 497, 503–4, 509, 514, 519, 523, 528, 533, 541, 549
  thinking critically about, 490–91
  writing, 487–90
articles (parts of speech), ESL concerns, 28–30
articles (periodical), in list of works cited, 580–81
Asimov, Isaac, "Intelligence," 43–49
"As They Say, Drugs Kill" (Rowley), 505–9
audience
  knowing your, 14
  writing arguments and, 487–88

Baker, Russell, "Becoming a Writer," 199–204
Barber, James David, "Four Types of President," 426–32
"Barrio, The" (Ramirez), 272–78
"Battle of Cultures, A" (Kang), 451–55
"Becoming a Writer" (Baker), 199–204
begging the question, 489
beginnings and endings, 133–63
  beginnings, 19–20, 133–37
  classroom activities using, 144, 149, 154–55, 162
  endings, 19–20, 137–39
  readings
    "Of My Friend Hector and My Achilles Heel" (Kaufman), 140–45

beginnings and endings (*contd.*)
  readings (*contd.*)
    "Something's Off" (Henig), 146–50
    "Unforgettable Miss Bessie" (Rowan), 157–63
    "Wounds That Can't Be Stitched Up, The" (Russell), 151–56
  suggested writing assignments, 145, 149–50, 155, 162–63
"Be Specific" (Goldberg), 306–9
biographical note, 42
books
  in list of works cited, 578–80
  in working bibliography, 556
brainstorming, 11
Brody, Steve, "How I Got Smart," 330–36

"Can I Get You Some Manners with That?" (Scotty), 316–20
Carson, Rachel, "Fable for Tomorrow," 49–54
"Case for Short Words, The" (Lederer), 310–15
Catton, Bruce, "Grant and Lee: A Study in Contrasts," 456–61
cause and effect, 462–83
  classroom activities using, 469–70, 474, 479, 483
  readings
    "Mom Quixote" (Quindlen), 476–79
    "One Idea" (Mailer), 480–83
    "Why and When We Speak Spanish in Public" (Marquez), 472–75
    "Why We Crave Horror Movies" (King), 465–71
  suggested writing assignments, 470, 475, 479, 483
Chopin, Kate, "The Story of an Hour," 346–50
chronological order (time order), 109–11
Cisneros, Sandra, "My Name," 94–97
citations, 576–83
"City of Islands" (Hamill), 361–64
classification. *See* division and classification
clichés, 241
climactic order, 109
clustering, 11
coherence, transitions and, 190
Collier, James Lincoln, "Anxiety: Challenge by Another Name," 80–85
comma splice, 22
"Company Man, The" (Goodman), 403–6
comparison and contrast, 433–61
  in beginnings, 134–35
  classroom activities using, 440–41, 449, 455, 461
  readings
    "Battle of Cultures, A" (Kang), 451–55
    "Grant and Lee: A Study in Contrasts" (Catton), 456–61
    "Mac or PC: There Is Simply No Comparison!" (Miller), 443–50
    "Two Ways of Seeing a River" (Twain), 438–42
  suggested writing assignments, 441, 450, 455, 461
complaints, in beginnings, 137
concrete words, 240
"Condemn the Crime, Not the Person" (Tangney), 524–29
connotation, 239–40
coordination, 214
"Corner Store, The" (Welty), 121–25
count nouns, 29
creative thinking, 11–12
"Crime of Compassion, A" (Huttmann), 299–305
Critser, Greg, "Don't Eat the Flan," 515–19

dangling modifiers, 26–27
"Declaration of Independence, The" (Jefferson), 492–97
deductive reasoning, 486
definite article, 28–29
definition, 391–406
  in beginnings, 137
  classroom activities using, 397, 401, 406
  extended, 392

formal, 392
readings
"Company Man, The" (Goodman), 403–6
"Handicap of Definition, The" (Raspberry), 398–402
"What Is Crime?" (Friedman), 394–97
suggested writing assignments, 397, 401, 406
denotation, 239–40
description, 351–69
classroom activities using, 355, 359, 364, 368–69
readings
"City of Islands" (Hamill), 361–64
"My Favorite Teacher" (Friedman), 365–69
"Subway Station" (Highet), 353–56
"Wyoming Clouds" (Klinkenborg), 357–60
suggested writing assignments, 355–56, 359–60, 364, 369
dialogue, in beginnings, 135
diction and tone
classroom activities using, 250, 257, 263, 268
diction, 239–42
formal and informal diction, 241–42
readings
"Me Talk Pretty One Day" (Sedaris), 251–58
"Pop-A-Shot" (Vowell), 259–63
"Shame" (Gregory), 245–50
"Who Am I?" (Markoc), 264–69
suggested writing assignments, 250, 257–58, 263, 268–69
tone, 242–44
Dillard, Annie, From *An American Childhood*, 215–19
direct quotation, 567–69
division and classification, 408–32
classroom activities using, 415–16, 422, 424, 432
guidelines for using, 410–11
readings
"Four Types of President" (Barber), 426–32
"Friends, Good Friends—and Such Good Friends" (Viorst), 417–24
"Ways of Meeting Oppression, The" (King), 412–16
suggested writing assignments, 416, 424, 432
documenting sources, 575–83
dominant impression, 351
"Don't Eat the Flan" (Critser), 515–19
"Doubts about Doublespeak" (Lutz), 126–31
draft, first, 18–20
dramatically short sentences, 213

editing, 21–30
effective sentences, 210–35
classroom activities using, 218–19, 223–24, 228, 234
readings
From *An American Childhood* (Dillard), 215–19
"Good Daughter, The" (Hwang), 225–29
"Salvation" (Hughes), 220–24
"38 Who Saw Murder Didn't Call Police" (Gansberg), 230–35
suggested writing assignments, 219, 224, 229, 234–35
Eighner, Lars, "On Dumpster Diving," 385–89
either/or thinking, 489
endings, 19–20, 137–39. *See also* beginnings and endings
ESL concerns, articles and nouns, 28–30
ethos, 490–91
evaluating sources, 553–55
evidence, writing arguments and, 488
examples, 295–96
extended definition, 392
extended metaphors, 271

"Fable for Tomorrow" (Carson), 49–54
facts and statistics, in beginnings, 136
false analogy, 489
figurative language, 270–91
classroom activities using, 277, 283, 291
readings

figurative language (*contd.*)
readings (*contd.*)
"Barrio, The" (Ramirez), 272–78
"Hanging, A" (Orwell), 285–91
"Jacket, The" (Soto), 279–84
suggested writing assignments, 277–78, 283–84, 291
first draft, 18–20
Fisher, Barbara Loe, "Parents Should Be Allowed to Opt Out of Vaccinating Their Children," 535–42
flashback, 323–24
focusing on a topic, 9–10
formal definition, 392
"Four Types of President" (Barber), 426–32
Friedman, Lawrence M., "What Is Crime?" 394–97
Friedman, Thomas L., "My Favorite Teacher," 365–69
"Friends, Good Friends—and Such Good Friends" (Viorst), 417–24
fused sentences, 22

Gansberg, Martin, "38 Who Saw Murder Didn't Call Police," 230–35
Gates, Henry Louis, Jr., 325
generalization(s), 91–93
in beginnings, 136
illustration and, 296–97
general words, 240
Goldberg, Natalie, "Be Specific," 306–9
"Good Daughter, The" (Hwang), 225–29
Goodman, Ellen, "The Company Man," 403–6
"Grant and Lee: A Study in Contrasts" (Catton), 456–61
Gregory, Dick, "Shame," 245–50

Hamill, Pete, "City of Islands," 361–64
"Handicap of Definition, The" (Raspberry), 398–402
Haney, William V., 469
"Hanging, A" (Orwell), 285–91
hasty generalization, 489
headnote, 42
Henig, Robin Marantz, "Something's Off," 146–50
"Here's How to Revive a Computer Even after an Evil Wizard Kills the Beast" (Husted), 379–84
Highet, Gilbert, "Subway Station," 353–56
"How I Got Smart" (Brody), 330–36
"How to Write a Personal Letter" (Keillor), 374–78
Hughes, Langston, "Salvation," 220–24
humor, in beginnings, 136
humorous tone, 242–43
Husted, Bill, "Here's How to Revive a Computer Even after an Evil Wizard Kills the Beast," 379–84
Huttmann, Barbara, "A Crime of Compassion," 299–305
Hwang, Caroline, "The Good Daughter," 225–29

"I Have a Dream" (King), 498–504
"I Just Wanna Be Average" (Rose), 182–87
illustration, 295–320
classroom activities using, 303, 308, 314, 319
readings
"Be Specific" (Goldberg), 306–9
"Can I Get You Some Manners with That?" (Scotty), 316–20
"Case for Short Words, The" (Lederer), 310–15
"Crime of Compassion, A" (Huttmann), 299–305
suggested writing assignments, 303–4, 309, 314–15, 320
indefinite articles, 28–29
inductive leap, 486
inductive reasoning, 486
"In Praise of the F Word" (Sherry), 510–14
integrating borrowed material into your text, 569–71
"Intelligence" (Asimov), 43–49
Internet research, 557–63. *See also* sources, print and online
keyword searches, 561–63

notes from Internet sources, 569
subject directories, 558–60
in-text citations, 576–77
introductions. *See* beginnings and endings: beginnings
ironic tone, 243
irony, in beginnings, 136

"Jacket, The" (Soto), 279–84
jargon, 241
Jefferson, Thomas, "The Declaration of Independence," 492–97
journal prompt, 43

Kahan, Dan M., "Shame Is Worth a Try," 530–34
Kang, K. Connie, "A Battle of Cultures," 451–55
Kaufman, Michael T., "Of My Friend Hector and My Achilles Heel," 140–45
Keillor, Garrison, "How to Write a Personal Letter," 374–78
Keller, Helen, "The Most Important Day," 74–79
keyword searches, 561–63
King, Martin Luther, Jr.
"I Have a Dream," 498–504
"Ways of Meeting Oppression, The" (King), 412–16
King, Stephen, "Why We Crave Horror Movies," 465–71
Klinkenborg, Verlyn, "Wyoming Clouds," 357–60
Komaroff, Anthony, "Technology's Limits," 98–102
Kralovec, Etta, "No More Pep Rallies!" 86–89

Lederer, Richard, "The Case for Short Words," 310–15
list of works cited, 577–83
logical appeals, 485–86
logical fallacies, 489
logical order, 111–13
logos, 490, 491
loose sentences, 212
Lutz, William, "Doubts about Doublespeak," 126–31

"Mac or PC: There Is Simply No Comparison!" (Miller), 443–50
Mailer, Norman, "One Idea," 480–83
Markoe, Merrill, "Who Am I?" 264–69
Marks, Robyn, "Raising a Son—With Men on the Fringes," 175–81
Marquez, Myriam, "Why and When We Speak Spanish in Public," 472–75
McCullough, David, "Why History?" 205–9
McDonald, Cherokee Paul, "A View from the Bridge," 114–18
"Meanings of a Word, The" (Naylor), 103–8
"Me Talk Pretty One Day" (Sedaris), 251–58
metaphors, 270–71
methods of development. *See* organizational patterns
Miller, Del, "Mac or PC: There Is Simply No Comparison!" 443–50
misplaced modifiers, 26
MLA style
citations, 577
list of works cited, 577–83
modifiers, misplaced and dangling, 26–27
"Momma, the Dentist, and Me" (Angelou), 337–45
"Mom Quixote" (Quindlen), 476–79
"Most Important Day, The" (Keller), 74–79
Motluk, Alison, "Supersize Me: It's Time to Stop Blaming Fat People for Their Size," 520–23
"My Favorite Teacher" (Friedman), 365–69
"My Name" (Cisneros), 94–97

narration, 321–50
classroom activities using, 328, 335, 344–45, 350
readings
"How I Got Smart" (Brody), 330–36
"Momma, the Dentist, and Me" (Angelou), 337–45

narration (*contd.*)
readings (*contd.*)
"Story of an Hour, The" (Chopin), 346–50
"What's in a Name?" (Gates), 325–29
suggested writing assignments, 328–29, 335, 345, 350
narrative essay, sample student essay, 57–59
Naylor, Gloria, "The Meanings of a Word," 103–8
"No More Pep Rallies!" (Kralovec), 86–89
noncount nouns, 29
nostalgic tone, 242
note-taking, 564–69
nouns
count, 29
ESL concerns, 28–30
noncount, 29
weak, 28

"Of My Friend Hector and My Achilles Heel" (Kaufman), 140–45
"On Being 17, Bright, and Unable to Read" (Raymond), 192–98
"On Dumpster Diving" (Eighner), 385–89
"One Idea" (Mailer), 480–83
organization (organizational patterns), 15–18, 109–32
classroom activities using, 118, 124–25, 131
mapping, 17–18
readings
"Corner Store, The" (Welty), 121–25
"Doubts about Doublespeak" (Lutz), 126–31
"View from the Bridge, A" (McDonald), 114–18
suggested writing assignments, 119, 125, 131–32
writing arguments and, 488
Orwell, George, "A Hanging," 285–91
over-generalizing, 91–93
oversimplification, 489
paragraphs, 164–87
classroom activities using, 172, 178, 186–87
readings
"I Just Wanna Be Average" (Rose), 182–87
"Raising a Son—With Men on the Fringes" (Marks), 175–81
"Simplicity" (Zinsser), 168–74
suggested writing assignments, 174, 179, 187
parallelism, 214
faulty, 27
paraphrasing, 566–67
using your own words and word order when, 573–74
parenthetical citations, 576–77
"Parents Should Be Allowed to Opt Out of Vaccinating Their Children" (Fisher), 535–42
"Parents Should Not Be Allowed to Opt Out of Vaccinating Their Children" (Shelov), 543–49
passive voice, 213
pathos, 490, 491
periodical articles
in list of works cited, 580–81
in working bibliography, 557
periodic sentences, 212
personification, 271
persuasive appeals, 485
plagiarism, 571–76
platitudes, in beginnings, 137
"Pop-A-Shot" (Vowell), 259–63
post hoc, ergo propter hoc fallacy, 464, 489
prereading, 42–43
previewing sources, 552–53
prewriting, 7–18
choosing a subject area, and focusing on a topic, 9–10
establishing your thesis, 12–14
first draft, 18–20
getting ideas and collecting information, 10–12
knowing your audience, 14
organizational patterns, 15–18
understanding your assignment, 8–9

process analysis, 370–90
  classroom activities using, 377–78, 382, 388
  readings
    "Here's How to Revive a Computer Even after an Evil Wizard Kills the Beast" (Husted), 379–84
    "How to Write a Personal Letter" (Keillor), 374–78
    "On Dumpster Diving" (Eighner), 385–89
  suggested writing assignments, 378, 382, 384, 389
pronoun-antecedent agreement, 24–25
proofreading, 30–31
publication information, 42

Quindlen, Anna, "Mom Quixote," 476–79
quotation marks, for language borrowed directly, 572–73
quotations
  direct, 567–69
  integrating, 570–71

"Raising a Son—With Men on the Fringes" (Marks), 175–81
Ramirez, Robert, "The Barrio," 272–78
Raspberry, William, "The Handicap of Definition," 398–402
Raymond, David, "On Being 17, Bright, and Unable to Read," 192–98
reading
  active, 41–42
  as a writer, 55–57
refutations to arguments, 488–89
research, 11. *See also* Internet research
research papers, writing, 551–90
  annotated student research paper, 584–90
  documenting sources, 575–83
  integrating borrowed material into your text, 569–71
  plagiarism, 571–75
  sources, 552–55
resigned tone, 243
revising, 20–21
rhetorical highlights, 42–43
rhetorical patterns. *See* organizational patterns
rhetorical questions, in beginnings, 137
Rose, Mike, "I Just Wanna Be Average," 182–87
Rowan, Carl T., "Unforgettable Miss Bessie," 157–63
Rowley, Laura, "As They Say, Drugs Kill," 505–9
run-on sentences, 21–22
Russell, Ruth, "The Wounds That Can't Be Stitched Up," 151–56

"Salvation" (Hughes), 220–24
Scotty, Christie, "Can I Get You Some Manners with That?" 316–20
Sedaris, David, "Me Talk Pretty One Day," 251–58
sentence emphasis, 214
sentence fragments, 22–23
sentences, effective. *See* effective sentences
sentence variety, 211–13
"Shame" (Gregory), 245–50
"Shame Is Worth a Try" (Kahan), 530–34
Shelov, Steven P., "Parents Should Not Be Allowed to Opt Out of Vaccinating Their Children," 543–49
Sherry, Mary, "In Praise of the F Word," 510–14
similes, 270
"Simplicity" (Zinsser), 168–74
"Something's Off" (Henig), 146–50
Soto, Gary, "The Jacket," 279–84
sources, print and online
  evaluating, 553–55
  in list of works cited, 581–83
  previewing, 552–53
  for research papers, 552–55
  in working bibliography, 557
space order, 111
specific words, 240
startling claim, in beginnings, 136
"Story of an Hour, The" (Chopin), 346–50

subject, choosing a, 9–10
subject directories, 558–60
subject-verb agreement, 23–24
subordination, 211–12
"Subway Station" (Highet), 353–56
summarizing, 565–66
  using your own words and word order when, 573–74
"Supersize Me: It's Time to Stop Blaming Fat People for Their Size" (Motluk), 520–23
supporting evidence, writing arguments and, 488
syllogism, 486
synonyms, 391–92

Tangney, June, "Condemn the Crime, Not the Person," 524–29
"Technology's Limits" (Komaroff), 98–102
thesis, 12–14, 71–89
  classroom activities using, 77–78, 84, 89
  definition of, 71
  readings
    "Anxiety: Challenge by Another Name" (Collier), 80–85
    "Most Important Day, The" (Keller), 74–79
    "No More Pep Rallies!" (Kralovec), 86–89
  suggested writing assignments, 78, 84–85, 89
  unified essays and, 91–93
  writing arguments and, 487
thesis statement, 12
  unified essays and, 91–93
"38 Who Saw Murder Didn't Call Police" (Gansberg), 230–35
time order (chronological order), 109–11
title, 19, 42
  references to, in beginnings, 137
tone, 242–44. *See also* diction and tone
topic(s)
  asking questions about your, 10–11
  focusing on a, 9–10
transitions, 188–209
  classroom activities using, 196–97, 203, 208–9
  readings
    "Becoming a Writer" (Baker), 199–204
    "On Being 17, Bright, and Unable to Read" (Raymond), 192–98
    "Why History?" (McCullough), 205–9
  suggested writing assignments, 197, 203–4, 209
Twain, Mark, "Two Ways of Seeing a River," 438–42
"Two Ways of Seeing a River" (Twain), 438–42

uncritical inference test, 469–70
understanding your assignment, 8–9
"Unforgettable Miss Bessie" (Rowan), 157–63
unity, 90–108
  classroom activities using, 96, 101, 107
  classroom activity using, 107–8
  readings
    "Meanings of a Word, The" (Naylor), 103–8
    "My Name" (Cisneros), 94
    "Technology's Limits" (Komaroff), 98–102
  suggested writing assignments, 96, 102, 108

verbs
  tense shifts, 25–26
  weak, 28
"View from the Bridge, A" (McDonald), 114–18
Viorst, Judith, "Friends, Good Friends—and Such Good Friends," 417–24
Vowell, Sarah, "Pop-A-Shot," 259–63

"Ways of Meeting Oppression, The" (King), 412–16
weak nouns and verbs, 28
Welty, Eudora, "The Corner Store," 121–25

"What Is Crime?" (Friedman), 394–97
"What's in a Name?" (Gates), 325–29
"Who Am I?" (Markoe), 264–69
"Why and When We Speak Spanish in Public" (Marquez), 472–75
"Why History?" (McCullough), 205–9
"Why We Crave Horror Movies" (King), 465–71
working bibliography, 556–57
"Wounds That Can't Be Stitched Up, The" (Russell), 151–56
writing process, 7–40
  editing, 21
  first draft, 18–20
  prewriting, 7–18
  revising, 20–21
"Wyoming Clouds" (Klinkenborg), 357–60

Zinsser, William, "Simplicity," 168–74

Student Essay Submission Form

We welcome students and instructors to submit essays for publication consideration that were written using *Models for Writers.* Send them with this Essay Submission Form and the Agreement Form on the back to: Models—Student Essays, Bedford/St. Martin's, 33 Irving Place, 10th Floor, New York, NY 10003.

Student's name ______________________________

Instructor's name ______________________________

School ______________________________

Department ______________________________

Address ______________________________

____

____

Course name and number ______________________________

Please indicate the chapter(s) in *Models for Writers* for which you would like us to consider this essay.

❑ Thesis	❑ Effective Sentences	❑ Process Analysis
❑ Unity	❑ Diction and Tone	❑ Definition
❑ Organization	❑ Figurative Language	❑ Division and Classification
❑ Beginnings and Endings	❑ Illustration	❑ Comparison and Contrast
❑ Paragraphs	❑ Narration	❑ Cause and Effect
❑ Transitions	❑ Description	❑ Argument

Agreement Form

I hereby assign to Bedford/St. Martin's ("Bedford") all of my right, title, and interest throughout the world, including without limitation, all copyrights, in and to my essay, ______________________________
______________________________ (tentative title), and any notes and drafts pertaining to it (the sample essay and such materials being referred to as the "Essay").

I understand that Bedford in its discretion has the right but not the obligation to publish the Essay in any form(s) or format(s) that it may desire; that Bedford may edit, revise, condense, or otherwise alter the Essay as it deems appropriate in order to prepare the same for publication; and that Bedford is under no obligation to publish the Essay. I understand that Bedford has the right, but not the obligation, to use and to authorize the use of my name as author of the Essay in connection with any work that contains the Essay (or a portion of it).

I represent that the Essay is wholly original and was completely written by me, that publication of it will not infringe upon the rights of any third party, and that I have not granted any rights in it to any third party.

In the event Bedford determines to include any part of the Essay in *Models for Writers,* I will receive one free copy of that work, if any, on publication.

This Agreement constitutes the entire agreement between us concerning its subject matter and shall inure to the benefit of the successors, assignees, and licensees of Bedford.

Student's signature ______________________________

Student's name ______________________________ Date ___ / ___ / ___

Be sure to provide us with time-stable information below. Please type or print clearly.

Address(es) ______________________________

____

____

Phone(s) ______________________________

E-mail(s) ______________________________

INSTRUCTOR'S MANUAL TO ACCOMPANY

PREPARED BY SARAH FEDERMAN

Instructor's Manual
to Accompany

Models for Writers

Short Essays for Composition

NINTH EDITION

Alfred Rosa
Paul Eschholz

Prepared by

Sarah Federman

BEDFORD / ST. MARTIN'S
Boston ◆ New York

Manufactured in the United States of America.

1 0 9 8 7
f e d c b a

For information, write: Bedford/St. Martin's, 75 Arlington Street, Boston, MA 02116 (617-399-4000)

ISBN-10: 0-312-44644-6
ISBN-13: 978-0-312-44644-4

Preface

The purpose of this *Instructor's Manual* is to help you use *Models for Writers* with the greatest effectiveness. We therefore provide for each selection in the book a fairly detailed analysis of the essay as a whole. In these sections of the manual, labeled *Essay Analysis and Discussion,* we try to share with you our experiences in teaching the essays—what to stress, what to explain, what to ask about, and what to expect generally from discussions. In addition, a typical analysis might do one or more of the following:

- explore one or more content issues
- point out stylistic features
- suggest classroom activities that reinforce rhetorical strategies
- suggest one or more other essays in the text that might be usefully taught in conjunction with the present one
- explain where students are likely to have difficulty understanding either content or rhetorical techniques

In addition, we provide in the section called *Questions for Study and Discussion* suggested responses to the questions following each selection. Our intent is to save you time, not to dictate answers. On occasion you may disagree with our interpretation or emphasis, but we trust that the suggested responses here will be useful at least as starting points. There are no substitutes for your own experience with each essay or for common sense about what will challenge and engage your students. Also included are suggested answers for the *Thinking Critically about This Reading* exercises and detailed discussions of what you might expect from each of the *Classroom Activities.*

The essays in *Models for Writers* are grouped into 18 chapters, each devoted to a separate rhetorical topic. Chapters 3 through 9 focus on specific elements of essays: thesis, unity, organization, beginnings and endings, paragraphs, transitions, and effective sentences. Chapters 10 and 11 concern some uses and effects of language: diction and tone, and figurative language. Finally, Chapters 12 through 20 explore types of essays: illustration, narration, description, process analysis, definition, division and classification, comparison and contrast, cause and effect, and argument.

The arrangement of the chapters suggests a logical teaching sequence, from the elements of an essay through the language of an essay to the types of essays. An alternative teaching strategy is to structure your course according to the types of essays, teaching other chapters as necessary or having students use them for reference. Finally, because each chapter is self-contained, you can design your own teaching sequence, omitting or emphasizing particular chapters according to the special needs of your class.

To help you use the book effectively, we would like to call your attention to the following special features:

Introductory Section on Reading and Writing Well. In Chapter 1, "The Writing Process," students learn useful questions that they can ask themselves as they undertake the writing process. By showing a student's essay in progress, beginning with developing an idea for an essay and ending in a final draft, the chapter allows students to see the writing process step-by-step. In Chapter 2, "From Reading to Writing," students learn how to become active readers. Annotated examples help students understand the best ways to prepare themselves to read a selection; read a selection for the first time; reread the selection; annotate the text with marginal notes; and analyze the text by asking questions. The chapter concludes with a discussion of using reading in the writing process. Here we include three annotated student essays that illustrate three types of essays—narrative, response, and analytical—that students typically write in college. In addition, the sample papers give students a good idea of the length and quality of writing they should be striving to produce. We suggest, therefore, that you assign the first two chapters early in the course and that you spend as much time as possible discussing the four student papers and their salient features.

Chapter Introductions. Before reading the essays in a particular chapter, students should read that chapter's introduction. There they will find an explanation of the rhetorical principle under consideration and a discussion of how it can be used. The information in the introductions will also help students to answer the questions and complete the writing assignments that accompany each selection.

Journal Activities. Preceding each reading are journal activities that prompt students to explore their own ideas and experiences regarding the issues presented in the reading.

Critical Thinking Questions. Each selection is followed by a prompt that encourages students to think critically about their reading by exploring—in discussion or in writing—the author's meaning and assumptions as well as the broader implications of the selection.

Visual Writing Prompts. Eighteen visual writing prompts are paired with professional essays, encouraging students to analyze connections between the print and visual texts.

Questions for Study and Discussion. The study questions for each selection focus on its content, its author's purpose, and the rhetorical principle used to achieve that purpose. Some of the questions require brief answers, and others are intended to stimulate class discussion. Because students' knowledge of rhetorical techniques and patterns will increase as the course proceeds, we have included for each essay one or more questions about rhetorical elements other than the one highlighted in the particular essay.

Classroom Activities. These brief exercises (requiring 15 to 20 minutes in most cases) enable students to work with each rhetorical element, technique, or pattern in the classroom, often in groups. The activities included here will help students develop thesis statements, organize sentences within paragraphs, use strong action verbs, work with connotation and denotation, use figurative language, use examples to document a generalization, use facts effectively, work with outlines for comparison and contrast, test cause-and-effect relationships, classify on the basis of distinctive characteristics, and build argumentative evidence. Frequently, these activities require students to engage in critical thinking and problem solving. We have used all of these activities in our own writing classes, and our students have found them helpful.

Suggested Writing Assignments. At least two writing assignments accompany each essay in the textbook. They offer students the opportunity to apply the rhetorical principle at hand. Often these assignments are related to the content of the essays as well; however, most can be assigned independently if you prefer not to assign all the readings.

Writing Documented Essays. An appendix on the documented research essay includes up-to-date instruction on using print sources and on using Internet sources, as well as guidelines for evaluating the authority and reliability of print and Internet sources. Instruction is provided on note taking—including summaries, paraphrases, and direct quotations—and on integrating borrowed material into papers. Also provided are models for using the most current Modern Language Association documentation style, including in-text citations and lists of works cited.

Glossary of Useful Terms. This glossary is located at the end of the book and provides students with concise definitions of terms useful for discussing the readings and their own writing. Wherever we have felt that information in the glossary might assist students in answering a study question, we have placed a cross-reference to the appropriate glossary entry next to the question.

Thematic Contents. If a particular essay evokes strong student response, this alternative table of contents makes it easier for you to choose thematically related pieces in other sections of *Models for Writers.* Nearly all the readings are entered under at least one subject heading, and many appear under two or three. Admittedly, some of these classifications may seem a bit arbitrary, but we believe that none are misfits. Beyond calling attention to the content of individual essays, this listing also allows you to point out different rhetorical approaches to common themes.

Online Reading Quizzes. The *Models* Web site—bedfordstmartins.com/models—features an online reading quiz for each selection.

Finally, we are very much interested in hearing from anyone who has constructive ideas about the content or use of either *Models for Writers* or this manual. We can be reached at the Department of English, 400 Old Mill, University of Vermont, Burlington, Vermont 05405.

Alfred Rosa
Paul Eschholz
Sarah Federman

Contents

part two **The Elements of the Essay**

CHAPTER 3 **Thesis 1**

Helen Keller, *The Most Important Day* 1
James Lincoln Collier, *Anxiety: Challenge by Another Name* 3
Etta Kralovec, *No More Pep Rallies!* 4

CHAPTER 4 **Unity 6**

Sandra Cisneros, *My Name* 6
Anthony Komaroff, *Technology's Limits* 7
Gloria Naylor, *The Meanings of a Word* 9

CHAPTER 5 **Organization 11**

Cherokee Paul McDonald, *A View from the Bridge* 11
Eudora Welty, *The Corner Store* 13
William Lutz, *Doubts about Doublespeak* 14

CHAPTER 6 **Beginnings and Endings 16**

Michael T. Kaufman, *Of My Friend Hector and My Achilles Heel* 16
Robin Marantz Henig, *Something's Off* 17
Ruth Russell, *The Wounds That Can't Be Stitched Up* 19
Carl T. Rowan, *Unforgettable Miss Bessie* 21

CHAPTER 7 **Paragraphs 23**

William Zinsser, *Simplicity* 23
Robyn Marks, *Raising a Son—With Men on the Fringes* 25
Mike Rose, *"I Just Wanna Be Average"* 27

CHAPTER 8 **Transitions 29**

David Raymond, *On Being 17, Bright, and Unable to Read* 29
Russell Baker, *Becoming a Writer* 30
David McCullough, *Why History?* 33

CHAPTER 9 **Effective Sentences 35**

Annie Dillard, from *An American Childhood* 35
Langston Hughes, *Salvation* 37
Caroline Hwang, *The Good Daughter* 39
Martin Gansberg, *38 Who Saw Murder Didn't Call Police* 41

part three **The Language of the Essay**

CHAPTER 10 **Diction and Tone 43**

Dick Gregory, *Shame* 43
David Sedaris, *Me Talk Pretty One Day* 45
Sarah Vowell, *Pop-A-Shot* 47
Merrill Markoe, *Who Am I?* 48

CHAPTER 11 **Figurative Language 50**

Robert Ramirez, *The Barrio* 50
Gary Soto, *The Jacket* 52
George Orwell, *A Hanging* 54

part four **Types of Essays**

CHAPTER 12 **Illustration 57**

Barbara Huttmann, *A Crime of Compassion* 57
Natalie Goldberg, *Be Specific* 59
Richard Lederer, *The Case for Short Words* 60
Christie Scotty, *Can I Get You Some Manners with That?* 62

CHAPTER 13 **Narration 64**

Henry Louis Gates Jr., *What's in a Name?* 64
Steve Brody, *How I Got Smart* 65
Maya Angelou, *Momma, the Dentist, and Me* 67
Kate Chopin, *The Story of an Hour* 69

CHAPTER 14 **Description 71**

Gilbert Highet, *Subway Station* 71
Verlyn Klinkenborg, *Wyoming Clouds* 72
Pete Hamill, *City of Islands* 74
Thomas L. Friedman, *My Favorite Teacher* 75

CHAPTER 15 **Process Analysis 77**

Garrison Keillor, *How to Write a Personal Letter* 77
Bill Husted, *Here's How to Revive a Computer Even after an Evil Wizard Kills the Beast* 78
Lars Eighner, *On Dumpster Diving* 80

CHAPTER 16 **Definition 82**

Lawrence M. Friedman, *What Is Crime?* 82
William Raspberry, *The Handicap of Definition* 83
Ellen Goodman, *The Company Man* 85

CHAPTER 17 **Division and Classification 86**

Martin Luther King Jr., *The Ways of Meeting Oppression* 86
Judith Viorst, *Friends, Good Friends—and Such Good Friends* 88
James David Barber, *Four Types of President* 90

CHAPTER 18 **Comparison and Contrast 91**

Mark Twain, *Two Ways of Seeing a River* 91
Del Miller, *Mac or PC: There Is Simply No Comparison* 93
K. Connie Kang, *A Battle of Cultures* 94
Bruce Catton, *Grant and Lee: A Study in Contrasts* 96

CHAPTER 19 **Cause and Effect 99**

Stephen King, *Why We Crave Horror Movies* 99
Myriam Marquez, *Why and When We Speak Spanish in Public* 100
Anna Quindlen, *Mom Quixote* 101
Norman Mailer, *One Idea* 103

CHAPTER 20 **Argument 105**

Thomas Jefferson, *The Declaration of Independence* 105
Martin Luther King Jr., *I Have a Dream* 106
Laura Rowley, *As They Say, Drugs Kill* 109
Mary Sherry, *In Praise of the F Word* 111

The Obesity Epidemic: Who's to Blame?

Greg Critser, *Don't Eat the Flan* 113
Alison Motluk, *Supersize Me: It's Time to Stop Blaming Fat People for Their Size* 114

Shame: Is It an Effective Punishment?

June Tangney, *Condemn the Crime, Not the Person* 116
Dan M. Kahan, *Shame Is Worth a Try* 117

Childhood Vaccinations: Should They Be Mandatory?

Barbara Loe Fisher, *Parents Should Be Allowed to Opt Out of Vaccinating Their Children* 119
Steven P. Shelov, *Parents Should Not Be Allowed to Opt Out of Vaccinating Their Children* 120

part two The Elements of the Essay

CHAPTER 3 Thesis

The Most Important Day (p. 74)

■ Helen Keller

Essay Analysis and Discussion

The first paragraph of this essay, although short, is vital to establishing focus and direction for the paragraphs that follow. The first sentence states the thesis, but without the two sentences following it, the essay would lose the unity Keller has achieved. To get students to see the connection between the thesis statement and the opening paragraph as a whole, and their relation to the rest of the essay, have them consider what each of the first three sentences accomplishes in regard to the other paragraphs. It may help to look at the stages of Keller's narration (as they are outlined in study question 6) to see if there is a correlation between those stages and the three sentences in the opening paragraph. The students' analysis should reveal that though the thesis statement focuses on a particular day, the essay can include discussion of other days and other events and remain unified because of the context established by the entire first paragraph.

Thinking Critically about This Reading

The light Keller refers to is the ability to communicate through language. Draw students' attention to Keller's metaphor at the beginning of paragraph 3 describing the ship lost at night in the fog, and to Keller's statement in paragraph 7 that "the living word awakened my soul, gave it light, hope, joy, set it free!"

Questions for Study and Discussion

1. Keller's thesis is the first sentence of the essay. Keller answers the question "What is the most important day in my life and why is that day important?" This question focuses Keller on a specific period in her life, that time when Anne Mansfield Sullivan opened up the world of words to her, which, in turn, let her think and communicate with others. Keller's thesis answers the first part of the question and her narrative explains the importance of that day.

2. Keller's purpose is to *tell* why the day that Anne Sullivan came to her was the most important day in her life.
3. For several weeks before Anne Sullivan arrived, Keller was angry and bitter. When that passed she fell into a "deep languor" (2). She compared the feeling to being a ship in a fog of darkness groping its way to shore.
4. Every new name gave birth to a new thought. Words would "make the world blossom for me" (9).
5. Keller understood the connection between words and the things they describe one day, after many such days, when her teacher placed one of Keller's hands under running water while she spelled the word *water* in the other. "Suddenly I felt a misty consciousness as of something forgotten—a thrill of returning thought; and somehow the mystery of language was revealed to me" (7).
6. On the first day, she meets Anne Sullivan and they embrace. On the next day, Anne Sullivan gives her a doll and spells the word *doll* on her hand until Keller is able to imitate the spelling. Several weeks later, Anne again tries to make the connection for Keller between objects and words (e.g., *mug* and *water* and *doll*) and is finally able to accomplish this at the well-house with the word *water* and the water itself.

Classroom Activity Using Thesis

Some questions that our students suggested include the following:

1. How serious is our campus wastepaper problem?
2. How much of our paper waste is currently being recycled?
3. How can our wastepaper be effectively used?
4. What is made from recycled paper?
5. What are the problems of collecting wastepaper on campus?
6. Is recycling paper waste an economic or an environmental issue, or both?
7. Does the campus newspaper use recycled newsprint?
8. What recycled paper products are currently being used on campus?
9. If we don't recycle wastepaper on campus, what will be the impact on our environment?
10. What other items, if any, are being recycled on campus?

Your students will come up with questions of their own, questions that perhaps focus on particular situations on your campus. Ask students to discuss what information is needed and where they would be likely to obtain that information to answer each of the questions here on recycling.

Anxiety: Challenge by Another Name (p. 80)

■ James Lincoln Collier

Essay Analysis and Discussion

Collier arranges his essay chronologically, from his youth to the present, to demonstrate his thesis that we can learn to overcome the stultifying effects of anxiety. At each major decision in his life, he uses examples from philosophy, psychology, and other peoples' lives to illustrate and strengthen his argument. The examples he chooses are common enough that the reader can sympathize with and relate to the author's point of view. At three different points, Collier also punctuates the essay with his rule and its corollaries, the conclusions he has drawn about anxiety and its relationship to learning. Ask students to think about some of the rules they have learned for themselves. Then ask them to describe, using examples, how these rules might have universal application. Remind them to use examples of situations that are easily identified by the other students in the class. They might try writing about lessons they learned over time, as well as those they learned quickly, after one hapless episode. How would the arrangement of material differ in that case?

Thinking Critically about This Reading

Collier's own experiences (see study question 3) echo his statement in paragraph 9 that "it seems to be a rule of life that you can't advance without getting that old, familiar, jittery feeling" and support the similar observation made by Kierkegaard. Ask students whether their experiences have led them to the same conclusions as Collier and Kierkegaard.

Questions for Study and Discussion

1. Collier states his thesis in paragraph 20: "The point is that the new, the different, is almost by definition scary. But each time you try something, you learn, and as the learning piles up, the world opens to you." Students will explain their own experience with Collier's thesis.
2. Collier explains extinction in paragraph 14.
3. Collier came up with his basic rule for himself after turning down an offer to work in Argentina one summer. He developed his first corollary as a result of reflecting on what he went through while interviewing famous people. He developed his second corollary as a result of his hesitating to accept a three-month assignment to work in Europe. By sharing the three experiences that led him to develop his basic rule and the two corollaries, Collier makes it easy for readers to accept his thesis. By the time readers reach paragraph 20, they are already familiar with the life situations that gave Collier his insight and understanding.

4. Collier means to demonstrate, based on his own experience, that we can overcome anxiety and in so doing can live a richer, fuller life.
5. Collier uses personification to depict anxiety as a traveling companion.
6. These paragraphs contrast with the first paragraph in Collier's essay to show that over time he has learned to overcome the kind of anxiety that kept him "safe" at home when he was a young adult.

Classroom Activity Using Thesis

Sentences 1, 2, 4, and 6 identify the topic and make an assertion about that topic that the writer must document in the body of the essay. Sentences 3 and 5, however, are weak as thesis statements; both sentences are too general and opinionated. By way of discussion, have students talk about what they would expect to read in an essay about each topic. Students' expectations for sentences 1, 2, 4, and 6 should be clearer than their expectations for sentences 3 and 5.

No More Pep Rallies! (p. 86)

■ **Etta Kralovec**

Essay Analysis and Discussion

Kralovec, an education expert, writes a passionate essay on how extracurricular activities in U.S. schools detract from students' learning, and she argues that such activities should not be funded by the schools themselves. You may want to ask students to consider Kralovec's thesis in the context of a school in which the vast majority of students pass standardized tests or go on to college. Do they think the argument against school-funded extracurricular activities is still as strong? Do they think her argument applies equally to all situations and schools? Why or why not?

Thinking Critically about This Reading

Kralovec cites instances of how time and money are taken away from classroom instruction. Ask your students to discuss their own thoughts and experiences and whether they think extracurricular activities added to or detracted from their education.

Questions for Study and Discussion

1. Kralovec's thesis is that schools spend too much money on extracurricular activities, often at the expense of educational basics: "Privatize school sports and other extracurricular activities, and remove all but basic academic studies from the classroom" (paragraph 2). Her solution

to the problem is to privatize extracurricular activities so that they don't bite into already cash-strapped schools' budgets.

2. Her purpose is to demonstrate the exorbitant costs of extracurricular activities and to encourage her readers to consider the merits of privatizing them.
3. Students will have different opinions about the feasibility of Kralovec's proposition. While she advocates for community groups and local businesses to sponsor school activities, students may doubt how and whether such a system would work. Students might ask: Who would organize the program? Would teachers who also work as coaches get paid? What if no community organizations or local businesses signed on? Would this cause schools to drop their extracurricular programs completely?
4. Kralovec discovered that the school's real expenses—insurance, transportation, salaries, equipment—for extracurricular activities was twice the initial estimate.
5. Students will disagree about how much money is too much. While $480,000 is a lot of money, it's important to note that the school's total budget was $4.8 million. The question of whether students are losing education at the cost of extracurricular activities is one you could have your students debate in class.
6. She cites a school in Searsport, Maine, where seven students were sent on an expensive golf trip in a school in which 70 percent of the students barely met basic academic standards. She suggests that students in schools in other industrialized nations score better than U.S. students on tests because foreign schools do not divert large chunks of their budget and class time to extracurricular activities.

Classroom Activity Using Thesis

Our students gave us these thesis statements as answers:

1. Extracurricular activities are important because they allow students to get to know each other better by forming communities around common interests.
2. Extracurricular activities enable students to expand their minds, work together, and be creative in a learning environment that isn't necessarily a classroom.
3. Extracurricular school activities are precisely that—extracurricular—and should not take up more than 10 percent of a public school's budget.
4. Private-sector funding of public school activities would lead to commercialization of the activities and the exploitation of students.

Your students, of course, will come up with other thesis statements or variations of the ones we have given. It's instructive to put all alternative theses on the board or overhead projector for analysis and discussion.

My Name (p. 94)

■ Sandra Cisneros

Essay Analysis and Discussion

Cisneros's essay is at once very simple and very challenging. Despite its brevity, it should yield several excellent discussion topics. First, its unity may not be apparent to many students, especially in paragraph 3. Cisneros's great-grandmother is vital to the discussion of her name, however, because of the obvious connection they have, not just in their given names but in their personalities as well. Students should understand the irony that two such strong-willed women should be named "hope." Also discuss why Cisneros presents her name so late in her essay. What does the reader think while reading the essay before she states her name? How does having to wait to consider why the name is like the number nine or a muddy color make the similes in the first paragraph more effective? Finally, students should enjoy the idea of choosing a new name. What does Zeze the X communicate to them about Cisneros?

Thinking Critically about This Reading

Cisneros states that Mexicans "don't like their women strong" (2). Before she married, Cisneros's great-grandmother was "a wild horse of a woman" (3); after she married, she became tame and docile and let the world pass her by. Cisneros does not want to lose herself the way her great-grandmother did after she married.

Questions for Study and Discussion

1. Cisneros's thesis is that she has inherited her grandmother's name, with all of its associations, but she does not want to be trapped by it. She states the thesis at the end of paragraph 4.
2. Cisneros's essay is unified in that each paragraph is logically related to her thesis. There are no digressions and there is no unrelated information. In the first paragraph, she presents the meaning and associations of her name. In the second, third, and fourth paragraphs she presents the family history of her name, and of her identification with the personality of her great-grandmother, if not with her ultimate situation. In the fifth, she establishes how she is unable to escape her name. In the sixth, she explains just how far she would go to escape it.
3. The name *Esperanza* is part of a culture that does not encourage strength in women. Using her name as the subject, Cisneros presents her heritage of cultural restrictions and her overwhelming desire to escape them.

4. The similes are open to interpretation, but students should demonstrate that some thought went into their answers. Most students, after having read the essay, will probably say that the similes give the impression that the narrator holds a negative opinion of the name, but other interpretations may be more complex.
5. Cisneros's tone is angry and defiant. She establishes it best in paragraph 2, where she attacks the Chinese for their view of women that parallels the Hispanic one. She also says bluntly that she will not be at all content with her great-grandmother's role in life. The tone helps her convey her desire to escape the associations that her name carries with it.
6. This is open to various interpretations, but Cisneros involves the reader by presenting intriguing similes and an intriguing personality associated with her name without revealing what the name is. The reader wonders what name is like a muddy color or the number nine, and by the time it is revealed, the reader is interested and aware of Cisneros's contempt for what her name implies.
7. Again, this is open to interpretation. Most students should pick up on the fact that it is unusual, dramatic, and hard-edged.

Classroom Activity Using Unity

Before starting this exercise, students should reread the introduction to Chapter 4, "Unity." Students can analyze their own paragraphs individually or they can exchange paragraphs with each other. In testing paragraphs for unity, students should look for sentences or portions of sentences that stray from the subject. Have students read their paragraphs aloud to the class and explain why their paragraphs are unified or how they need to be revised.

Technology's Limits (p. 98)

■ **Anthony Komaroff**

Essay Analysis and Discussion

Komaroff begins by describing Jessie, a longtime patient. He writes that on her first visit, he examined her thoroughly and prescribed medication for her high blood pressure. Paragraph 4 describes subsequent checkups while she was still in good health, during which they discussed personal matters. In paragraph 5, we learn that Jessie's health started to deteriorate after her daughter died. In paragraph 6, readers learn about Jessie's various medical conditions and the treatments used to help her. Paragraph 7 describes Jessie's final hospitalization and her death. Medical technology had done all it could for her. You may want to ask students whether they think the doctor could have done more at the beginning. Knowing that Jessie was far from home, might he have suspected that stress was partly to blame for her high blood pressure? Rather than simply medicating her, could he have suggested changes in diet and ways for her to acclimate herself to her new environment?

Thinking Critically about This Reading

Komaroff was able to better understand the needs of his patient—beyond what technology and medical devices could tell him empirically—because he got to know her on a personal level. He could give her better care because of their relationship.

Questions for Study and Discussion

1. Komaroff's thesis is stated in paragraph 3: "Technology had allowed me to make the diagnosis and prescribe effective treatment. But it was not only technology that earned her trust."
2. Komaroff's purpose is to show that the nuts-and-bolts of medical technology can serve the doctor-patient relationship only to a certain point. He wants to communicate the importance of the relationship a doctor has with his or her patients. The example of Jessie shows that by instilling trust and developing a relationship with patients, doctors can provide better care. Patients feel free to talk openly about their ailments, and doctors are able to tailor their treatments accordingly.
3. Had Komaroff used many examples, the power of the personal, one-on-one relationship between doctors and patients he advocates would have been downplayed.
4. Komaroff used a colonoscopy, MRI scans, and joint-replacement surgery. In December of 2000, Jessie had a heart attack that left her with fluid-filled lungs and failing kidneys. At this point Komaroff states, "We had run out of technologies" (7).
5. The details Komaroff includes about Jessie's life reflect his caring. He knew her family situation and remembers her daughter talking about her mother's fears. He also knew that after she lost her daughter Jessie looked to the church for support, and that her knee-replacement surgery enabled her to "walk down the aisle with other church elders" (5). He also uses the phrase "we had been lucky" (6) when referring to the number of medical options available to her. Using "we" rather than "she" demonstrates his feeling that they had gone through it together. Also, he was at Jessie's bedside when she died.

Classroom Activity Using Unity

This activity is meant to be somewhat amusing, but it should also be a good exercise for students who tend to get sidetracked in their writing. All of the extraneous sentences are closely related to the subject matter, but they add nothing to the essay's message, and most students will easily recognize the problem in someone else's writing, even if they have trouble identifying it in their own. The following sentences should be eliminated:

Paragraph 1	"Whether the walls . . ."
Paragraph 2	"Most of the students lived . . ."
	"Mr. Norant was known . . ."
Paragraph 3	"A cheerleader in college . . ."
	"Among those she fired . . ."

Discuss the reasons these sentences detract from the unity of the essay. Also, have students discuss what the other sentences contribute to the writer's argument.

The Meanings of a Word (p. 103)

■ Gloria Naylor

Essay Analysis and Discussion

In her essay, Naylor uses illustration to argue that there are two different definitions of the word *nigger*, depending on who is using it and to what purpose. In so doing, Naylor makes the larger point that all of language is similarly subject to interpretation and change depending on the context. Readers will notice that Naylor concentrates most of her essay on illustrating the lesser-known meaning of the word *nigger* as it is used in African American culture. This imbalance is based on Naylor's assumption that most of her readers will be familiar with the racist connotation of the word as it is used in the white culture. Students can choose another word that has both a familiar and a lesser-known meaning; then, using Naylor's essay as a guide, they can illustrate the ways in which the understanding of that word changes from culture to culture or from speaker to speaker.

Thinking Critically about This Reading

Naylor means that words in and of themselves are powerless. Not until a majority of people agree on the meaning of a word is it imbued with significance and power. In the larger white community, *nigger* has a very strong and specific racist meaning; in the smaller African American community, however, the word—when used by and among other African Americans—is a term of familiarity. The racist meaning of the word trumps its other meanings because more people recognize the power of its negative connotations.

Questions for Study and Discussion

1. The subject of Naylor's opening two paragraphs is language. While Naylor has the greatest respect for the written word, she considers the spoken word more powerful, coming at the instant of a thought and being expressed in the full dynamic interplay of all the senses. She points to the fact that words are simply arbitrary symbols that derive their meaning from the consensus of people who use them. She develops this thesis with a series of examples in the remainder of her essay.
2. Naylor best defines *nigger* in its role as a racial slur in paragraph 14: "a word that whites used to signify worthlessness or degradation." *Nigger* as used by African Americans is best expressed in the same paragraph: "Gathering there together, they transformed *nigger* to signify the varied and complex human beings they knew themselves to be."
3. Naylor means simply that the word *nigger* was used in her family in a context of love, admiration, and affection that allowed it to dwell there comfortably and unnoticed. In her third-grade class, she heard it expressed in a hostile context, for an altogether different purpose—as an insult. In other words, it was not the same word she had heard all her life and so she was hearing it for the first time.
4. Naylor includes details of her family's history, its structure, the neighborhood in which they all lived, the activities they enjoyed, the ways they earned their livings, and the substance of their conversations as a means of establishing the context in which their use of the word *nigger* arose. The little she offers in the way of a definition of the word *nigger* as used by the white community is disquieting to any reader who notices the omission and so is jolted to an awareness of not needing to be told what the word means.
5. Naylor could hardly have been faulted had she used an angry tone to describe the different meanings of the word *nigger*. However, she has chosen to use a level, objective tone—as if she were standing back casting a cool, refined glance at the phenomenon that has hurt so many of her people. In paragraph 3, when she recounts the moment she first heard the word *nigger* as a slur, Naylor describes the event rather matter-of-factly: "I remember the first time I heard the word *nigger*. . . . Had he called me a nymphomaniac or a necrophiliac, I couldn't have been more puzzled." Throughout her essay she analyzes the meaning of the word *nigger* as an anthropologist might, using the impartiality of the scientific method. It is

not until her final sentence that Naylor reveals the sadness and fatigue that we can assume came after who knows how long an effort to assimilate her initial feelings of confusion, shock, anger, and betrayal.

6. Naylor's final sentence is effective for reminding the reader once again that "in America" the primary use of the word *nigger* will be as a racial slur and is one that most readers do not have to sit on their mothers' laps to have explained.

Classroom Activity Using Unity

Paragraph 2 is the one that does not belong because it disrupts the unity of Gladstone's advice on building a fireplace fire. In paragraph 1 he gives the basic steps in building a fire. In paragraphs 3 through 5 he discusses three common mistakes that readers could make. Paragraph 2, which discusses the joys of a fireplace fire in winter and the need to properly maintain both the fireplace and the chimney, digresses from the writer's point. While the paragraph offers advice, the advice offered is not specifically about building a fire.

CHAPTER 5 **Organization**

A View from the Bridge (p. 114)

■ Cherokee Paul McDonald

Essay Analysis and Discussion

McDonald's essay is remarkable not only for the story he tells but also for the vivid description he uses. He organizes his narration chronologically and lets his story unfold through the use of dialogue between the narrator (presumably McDonald himself) and the young boy fishing. This dialogue enables McDonald to show us that the child is blind instead of telling us. Interestingly, the events that McDonald recounts occur within a half hour. Finally, take the opportunity that this essay offers to discuss with your students what it means to "see." How, for example, are the narrator and the boy using the word *see* in paragraphs 42 and 43?

Thinking Critically about This Reading

The narrator is both acknowledging the boy's thanks and reciprocating them. As he describes the tarpon carefully to please the boy, the narrator comes to his own renewed sense of wonder and appreciation for the beauty of the fish.

Questions for Study and Discussion

1. McDonald has organized his essay chronologically. The essay recounts an incident that took place in perhaps 30 minutes—certainly no more than an hour.
2. The kid wore wrap-around sunglasses (3). He was "fumbling" with his rod and reel (4); he could not see the shrimp by his foot (10); his fingers "felt" for the drag setting (16); he thought he had lost the fish when the line went slack (20); and he asked the narrator to tell him what the fish looked like (29). The narrator does not realize the kid is blind because he is preoccupied with his jogging and because the kid is a competent fisherman whose behavior does not arouse suspicion.
3. The narrator seeks to use words and phrases that are familiar to a child. He also looks for words that appeal to a sense other than sight. (For example, he starts to say that the fish is three feet long but then changes to the more concrete and sensory phrase, "as long as one of your arms" [33].) The effect is a description both accessible and vivid.
4. We learn that the kid is courteous; he says "please" (5 and 8) and "thanks" (12 and 42). He is, against all odds, a capable, determined fisherman (15, 24, and 47). Both the act of fishing and the fish itself give him tremendous delight. We see his joy in hooking and playing the fish (15 and 22), his pleasure in the narrator's description, and his desire to set the fish free (37).
5. The dialogue in this narrative plays up the shared interests between the narrator and the kid as well as their developing relationship. It gives the essay an informal tone. It brings the reader right into the scene, to see and overhear the event directly. Without the dialogue, the story would have lost its immediacy. The writer would have been reporting or telling us what happened instead of showing us.
6. A view is not just what is seen but a perspective, a way of understanding. The bridge spans the water, but it also represents the connection of respect and understanding that develops between the narrator and the kid.

Classroom Activity Using Organization

Ask students if they see any patterns in the information presented or if they drew any conclusions about these seven states. Depending on their answers (their purposes), students could organize a discussion of these seven states in several ways: (1) chronologically according to the date each state entered the union; (2) spatially from east to west, north to south, and so forth; (3) smallest to largest; (4) by population density; or (5) by impact on elections. This activity lets students discover that there are always several ways in which they can organize information, and that purpose is essential in making an appropriate choice.

The Corner Store (p. 121)

■ Eudora Welty

Essay Analysis and Discussion

Welty makes good use of detail and organization as she moves through the corner store of her childhood. In a few words, she manages to fill our minds as full as Mr. Sessions fills his shelves. Note how Welty uses sensory description to paint a picture that is real, without overusing detail. Also, students can analyze the way Welty acquaints us with Mr. Sessions without having him speak. Then students can discuss the author's use of hard detail as contrasted with her poetic impressions. The exercise will help them understand how difficult it is to say enough without saying too much.

Thinking Critically about This Reading

Mr. Sessions brings life and personality to the collection of things Welty sees and describes. He is the friendly man behind the counter who remembers his customers' weight and their favorite flavor of soda. The store gives the community a common gathering place and a point of common reference.

Questions for Study and Discussion

1. Students will find examples of chronological and spatial organization throughout the essay. Welty organizes the essay chronologically through the sequence of events from the time she enters the store until she leaves. Her body movement around the store and the movement of her eyes as she looks over the shelves and the counters are examples of spatial organization.
2. Welty realizes that a person who comes into a store out of the bright sunlight initially feels almost blind. Therefore, the first things that a person would be aware of are the odors—in this case, of licorice, dill pickle brine, ammonia, and untrapped mice.
3. Welty creates an impression of the old-fashioned plenty associated with a nineteenth-century country store by describing shelves, counters, and barrels stocked with the numberless goodies and smells available in such places.
4. Mr. Sessions is warm and friendly, a man who invites a child's hand to reach for a choice of penny candies, who knows what the child's favorite drink is, who weighs small children on his scale before they leave the store, and who will "remember what you weighed the last time."
5. Welty puts certain phrases in parentheses to set them apart. This information characterizes the era in even more detail than the rest of the essay.

A personal quality, which identifies the things that were especially dear to the writer, would be lost if these asides to the reader were left out.

6. Students should give reasons that demonstrate their understanding of endings.

Classroom Activity Using Organization

Using the principles of division and classification, students should establish general categories for the materials found in the desk and then distribute the specific items into the appropriate categories. The following is one possible arrangement:

writing/marking instruments: no. 2 pencils, ballpoint pens, mechanical pencil, highlighting marker, felt-tip pen
personal items: plastic comb, nail clippers, scissors, nail file, toothbrush
postage/mail supplies: book mailing bag, postcards, 8 × 10 manila envelopes, business envelopes, first-class stamps, postcard stamps, airmail stamps
items to hold things together: rubber bands, adhesive tape, paper clips, clasps, thumbtacks, bottle of glue
correction materials: eraser, bottle of correction fluid
miscellaneous supplies: 3 × 5 cards

Students will come up with categories of their own. For example, someone could argue that the scissors from the second category could be combined with the items in the fourth, fifth, and sixth categories to form the general category "desk supplies." There is no single correct answer; students should discuss the pros and cons of the various organizational plans put forth by the class.

Doubts about Doublespeak (p. 126)

■ **William Lutz**

Essay Analysis and Discussion

Lutz's piece provides an excellent opportunity for examining the importance of examples in a particular type of essay. In this case, it's hard to imagine Lutz being able to make his point without emphasizing the role of examples. To a certain extent, the examples *are* the point. You can follow your discussion of Lutz's essay with a class activity that identifies other topics that would require extensive use of examples. Then select one of those topics and have students, either as a class or in small groups, generate the specific examples that would support it. Finally, have students arrive at a tentative thesis that their list of examples suggests to them and sketch out an organizational pattern appropriate for such a purpose. They might begin with Lutz's organizational scheme and consider the degree to which it generally fits this kind of essay.

Thinking Critically about This Reading

Lutz doesn't provide a specific plan for combating doublespeak, but he suggests that familiarizing ourselves with its various forms will help us see through the misleading fog of language to the true meaning hidden beneath. You might consider asking students—individually or in groups—to develop plans of their own for combating doublespeak.

Questions for Study and Discussion

1. Lutz presents his thesis at the beginning of paragraph 2: "Doublespeak is language which pretends to communicate but doesn't." The rest of paragraph 2 expands on and clarifies this statement. Lutz reiterates his thesis about midway through the essay, in paragraph 9.
2. The four kinds of doublespeak are euphemism, jargon, gobbledygook or bureaucratese, and inflated language. Lutz's organizational pattern is to identify the type of doublespeak, define it, describe its function or its consequences, and then provide examples to illustrate. His approach seems well-suited to his subject matter because he acquaints readers with the information necessary to fully appreciate the significance of the examples.
3. Lutz suggests that jargon may be appropriate for people who work together in the same trade or profession, because it allows them to communicate more clearly, efficiently, and quickly.
4. Students' opinions about the effectiveness of Lutz's examples may vary, but chances are they will find his illustrations representative of the kinds of doublespeak that they have encountered in their own lives. Whether they feel that Lutz could have used more or fewer examples may depend on their own familiarity with the different kinds of doublespeak. In an organizational sense, Lutz appears to effectively balance his examples with discussion and analysis of their significance.
5. Changing the order of the first two paragraphs would diminish the effectiveness of Lutz's beginning. Without the context provided by the examples in paragraph 1, the discussion in paragraph 2 would seem abrupt and uninviting. The examples themselves offer an engaging introductory subject matter, but their presentation also establishes a slightly humorous and ingratiating tone.
6. Students may very well disagree on whether the serious claim at the end is justified by the body of Lutz's essay. On one hand, the sheer number of examples establishes the prominence of doublespeak as a phenomenon within our language. Lutz's discussion of what each kind of doublespeak intends to accomplish also supports his notion of how our perception of reality is altered. On the other hand, students may find some inconsistency between the humorous tone that underlies Lutz's discussion and the serious claim at the end.

Classroom Activity Using Organization

Least Heat Moon organizes his description spatially, moving from the middle of the rectangular room to the right and then to the shelves around the walls. That arrangement should make the students' sketches all roughly similar in terms of where the specific elements from Watts's store are located. But of course the real fun of the exercise is in seeing the differences that nonetheless emerge in the individual characterization of those elements, not to mention the students' varying degrees of artistic ability.

CHAPTER 6 **Beginnings and Endings**

Of My Friend Hector and My Achilles Heel (p. 140)

■ **Michael T. Kaufman**

Essay Analysis and Discussion

Kaufman's first paragraph is unusual and grabs the reader's attention. Two short sentences admitting prejudice contrast sharply with the finger pointing, subtle or not, that forms the backbone of most essays about prejudice. Kaufman's story is not dramatic or even noteworthy until the end, but he hooks the reader into bearing with him to find out the nature of his so-called "prejudice and stupidity." Have your students write a short personal essay that uses a concise, attention-grabbing first paragraph. Have them discuss the essays and identify the type of essay for which such a first paragraph might be most effective and tell why. Kaufman's ending stays with the reader for two reasons. First, it is a situation that everyone can empathize with because getting back in touch with an old, wrongfully neglected friend is something that most of us should do—but haven't. Second, it is an open-ended conclusion. The reader hopes that perhaps Kaufman will reunite with Hector somehow. Have your students discuss their reaction to the ending. How effective would the essay have been had there been a resolution at the end?

Thinking Critically about This Reading

Kaufman feels the need to apologize for the negative thoughts he had about Hector. Because of Hector's ethnic, financial, and educational background, Kaufman thought he might be a dock worker, for example—not a stage actor. As Kaufman himself states in paragraph 1, "This story is about prejudice and stupidity. My own."

Questions for Study and Discussion

1. Such an admission is unusual in a first-person essay, so it grabs the reader's attention and encourages the reader to finish the essay to find out what provoked such a statement. It also leads the reader to pay close attention to Kaufman's writing in hopes of discovering the roots of his stated stupidity. The second part of the question is personal experience.
2. Achilles was a Greek hero who had a weak spot on his heel, a fatal flaw that eventually killed him. Kaufman is referring to his own flaw, which is prejudice.
3. The essay is organized chronologically.
4. Kaufman's purpose is to demonstrate how easy it is to form prejudices and segregate oneself from other people based on assumptions. His organization helps him express his purpose by allowing him to trace when, why, and how his prejudice was formed.
5. Kaufman ignored Hector because he assumed him to be a physical laborer with whom he would have difficulty holding a conversation. It tells him that "tracking," as he calls it, may not be unusual, and it may be damaging to people from the entire range of socioeconomic "tracks."
6. Kaufman's ending is effective because it describes a painful situation that most people can identify with. By keeping the ending open-ended, he emphasizes the ongoing nature of his—and presumably many others'—problem.

Classroom Activity Using Beginnings and Endings

Students readily pick the second paragraph as the one they would use to start an essay. They like its opening sentence, which provokes their curiosity, and the anecdote used to introduce Hugh Troy. The first paragraph has the advantage of using one of Troy's stunts but suffers from an opening sentence that seems to come out of nowhere. The paragraph might make a good ending to an essay about Troy. The third paragraph is simply too dry, too matter-of-fact for a beginning. While a paragraph like this is sometimes necessary when writing a brief essay about a famous person, it should not come first.

Something's Off (p. 146)

■ **Robin Marantz Henig**

Essay Analysis and Discussion

Henig writes about losing her sense of smell and about her process of recovering it. She begins her essay with a startling claim—"A stinky old conch shell is what finally convinced me that I had lost my sense of smell"—grabbing her readers' attention by painting a clear and graphic image. Ask students to consider how Henig uses emotion to connect with her readers. For example, she writes, "I felt vulnerable" (paragraph 2), "so devastated by this particular loss" (4), "But I was heartbroken" (5). Ask students to comment on the role emotion plays in this essay. Do they think smell is an emotional sense? Why or why not?

Thinking Critically about This Reading

Henig means that most people—at one point, herself included—think they could probably live without their sense of smell. We don't often think of smell as being as important or pleasurable as the other senses: sight, touch, taste, and hearing. Ask students to rank the five senses in order of importance, and ask them to discuss their rankings. If they were forced to choose one sense to give up, which would it be and why?

Questions for Study and Discussion

1. Henig uses a startling claim to begin her essay. Students may also say she uses an anecdote. The essay begins with a bad smell and ends with a good smell.
2. Henig felt disconnected from the world around her. She could no longer tell her husband's mood from his smell or sense when food had gone bad. Ask students to consider other situations when the ability to smell is of vital importance—for example, burnt food, smoke, or leaking gas.
3. Henig missed the smell of her husband, of certain passing strangers, and of her daughters.
4. She had to assume that her "nerve endings had repaired themselves" (7). She exposed herself to strong fragrances and asked the person she was with what she was smelling. When alone she had to keep telling herself what smells surrounded her. She sniffed at spice containers in health food stores and at hot-dog carts on the street. At first she smelled only artificial fragrances like polish and shampoo. Then, certain smells did not register correctly. Detergent smelled sour and hot dogs smelled like soggy fur. With persistence, she eventually regained her sense of smell. She cried when first smelling, once again, freshly cut grass. She said she felt reunited with parts of herself.
5. The smell of fresh-cut grass reminded her of the "landscape of her childhood" (11). The smell of oil paints reminded her of her father; *L'Air du Temps* perfume of her mother. She cried because she reconnected to all the memories and associations she had with specific smells.

Classroom Activity Using Beginnings and Endings

Consider dividing students into groups of two or three, one for each of the types of beginnings outlined in the introduction to Chapter 6. Have students draft alternative beginnings to Henig's essay and comment on how that affects the rest of the essay. Ask how Henig's language, examples, and order would need to change to accommodate the new beginning. Also ask how the ending would need to change. Finally, have students revise Henig's essay and share their revisions with the class as a whole.

The Wounds That Can't Be Stitched Up (p. 151)

■ **Ruth Russell**

Essay Analysis and Discussion

Russell's essay offers the opportunity to discuss the issues of drinking and driving. Encourage students to share stories of how drunk driving has touched their lives or the lives of relatives or friends. These stories will help students empathize with the pain that Russell felt when a drunk driver almost killed members of her family more than two decades ago. Several years ago, when that same drunk driver became her neighbor, the old emotional wounds were reopened. Her outrage was rekindled when she witnessed him roar down the street into their parking lot, drunk again. Russell's outrage is not directed only at the drunk driver but also at a system that is lenient on DWI (driving while intoxicated) offenders and a society that jumps to their defense with lame excuses. Ask students to describe how they might feel if they were treated the way Russell was in paragraphs 11 and 12 after their family or friends were victims of a drunk driver.

Thinking Critically about This Reading

Russell relates these incidents to show that people are uncomfortable or unwilling to address the issue of drinking and driving in a responsible and meaningful way. Suggesting that the victims were injured because they were not wearing seat belts—and not because they were hit by a drunk driver—protects the drunk driver and, in a sense, condones his behavior.

Questions for Study and Discussion

1. The details of what the day was like are important to the writer because this was a day when her life and the lives of her family members changed dramatically. More important, by showing readers that nothing was unusual that December evening, she shows that there were no extenuating circumstances

to account for the accident. Quite simply, the other driver was drunk. The title captures readers' attention by getting them to think about the emotional and psychological wounds that remain unhealed as a result of something that happened on a seemingly ordinary December evening.

2. In paragraph 5 Russell describes her youngest brother as sitting "in the bed, a lonely little figure in a darkened hospital room." Although the black eye that the eight-year-old suffered in the accident will heal, the picture of him sitting alone in a hospital room lets the reader wonder how long the emotional scars will remain. The emotional impact of this image on readers prepares them for the description of the near-fatal injuries incurred by Russell's sister and mother.
3. Russell's tone is one of restrained outrage. Readers see her restraint and anger most strikingly in paragraphs 4, 8, 9, 10, 11, 12, and 14 as she articulates the deep wounds left from the accident and shows how townspeople questioned her and defended the drunk driver. Twenty-three years after the accident, Russell had believed that "the accident was ancient history"; she wasn't prepared for the way an encounter with the driver would reopen those old wounds. The irony of the driver's concluding remark ("Did I scare you?") does not escape readers.
4. Russell is making the point that "good guys" don't drink and drive. And, more important, good guys don't continue to drink and drive after a first offense. That excuse or defense is like saying that people are not responsible for their actions when they are drinking.
5. The encounter with the drunk driver recounted in the final paragraph happened on a December day much like the day of the accident. Implicit in Russell's telling of this bizarre incident is her outrage at society's treatment of repeat drunk drivers. The driver did not know when he made his offhand remark—"Did I scare you?"—that this question brought to the surface Russell's real pain over the accident 23 years earlier.

Classroom Activity Using Beginnings and Endings

Having students write alternative beginnings to an essay is a wonderful way to get them back inside their own writing. If students are having difficulty coming up with ideas for alternative beginnings, suggest that they read the opening paragraphs of six to ten essays in *Models for Writers.* You might want to start this activity by asking some students to read these paragraphs aloud to the class.

Students have told us that this exercise has given them new perspectives on their topics, ideas for ways in which they could revise their essays, and ideas for reorganizing their materials. By sharing the alternative beginnings with others in the class, students discover that a good opening paragraph really does make a difference for readers, especially when students are not required to read the essay.

Unforgettable Miss Bessie (p. 157)

■ **Carl T. Rowan**

Essay Analysis and Discussion

Rowan's essay offers students the opportunity to analyze the effective use of the dash. Many students have problems recognizing the proper place for this helpful form of punctuation and either use it too much or not at all. Rowan uses it in seven of his paragraphs, and for various purposes. Look over these instances with your students and have them identify which of the two most common reasons for using a dash each case falls under.

1. Use dashes to highlight parenthetical material, informal explanations, and afterthoughts that warrant emphasis.
2. Use dashes to signal a dramatic reversal of thought or tone.

When you've finished with Rowan's examples, have the students develop sentences of their own, using dashes in each of the ways described.

Thinking Critically about This Reading

Students will say that Miss Bessie taught Rowan about the importance of education, refusal to lower one's standards, and discipline. Miss Bessie provided Rowan with "the push and stimulation of a teacher who truly cared" (paragraph 16). She gave him inspiration and the belief that he could succeed.

Questions for Study and Discussion

1. Miss Bessie gave her students a sense of pride and self-worth by encouraging their talent and curiosity. In opening to them the worlds of literature, writing, self-expression, and a solid notion of this country's time in history, Miss Bessie taught young black children to stretch beyond the limits a segregated world had set for them. Rowan's opening paragraph is an effective beginning because it leads readers to ask, "What else did Miss Bessie teach him?" They need to read on to discover the powerful life lessons this petite dynamo of a teacher gave to Rowan and his peers.
2. The details of Miss Bessie's background appear in paragraphs 9 and 10. Rowan delays presenting this information so that he can first describe what Miss Bessie was like and why he is writing about her. This provides a stimulating opening and establishes a context for the biographical details because it is helpful to know what role Miss Bessie will play in the essay before being given information about her background.
3. In paragraph 1 Rowan describes Miss Bessie as about five feet tall and never more than 110 pounds. In paragraph 4 he notes that she had large brown eyes and in paragraph 12 that she was "frail-looking." Although

these characteristics do not seem to fit the image of the tough and towering figure from Rowan's school days, by the end of the essay they seem less inconsistent with the warm-hearted and compassionate teacher he looks back on as an adult.

4. Students' opinions may vary as to whether Miss Bessie's drinking influences their view of her. Rowan's feeling of a "new sense of equality" suggests that his discovery that she drank made Miss Bessie more lifelike, dispelling some of the larger-than-life images from his grade-school perception of her, while not diminishing her significance in his life.
5. Rowan's use of dialogue presents a more vivid picture of Miss Bessie's personality. Rather than relying on only a subjective, third-person description of her, Rowan allows the dialogue to provide a few more realistic glimpses into her character.
6. A firm, committed, wise, and caring individual emerges from Rowan's description of Miss Bessie. Some of the words used to convey this are *towering, tough* (1); *informed, dedicated, blessing, asset* (8); *essence of pride and privacy* (9); *bearing of dignity* (11); *softness and compassion* (22); *love and motivation, wisdom and influence* (25); and *wise, educated, warm-hearted* (28).

Classroom Activity Using Beginnings and Endings

When students are asked to write alternative beginnings themselves, they find that rhetorical questions, short generalizations, dialogue, and anecdotes seem to work best with Rowan's essay. For example, students offered these two beginnings:

> What for you makes a teacher memorable or remarkable?
> Miss Bessie was a giant among teachers.

Writing alternative beginnings for their own essays is an activity that frequently sparks significant revision. By looking at their writing from new perspectives, student writers discover for themselves the many possibilities inherent in their subject matter.

One effective way to use activity is to ask students to locate alternative beginnings within Rowan's essay before writing their own alternative beginnings. Our students nominated several alternatives:

1. dialogue—paragraphs 2 through 7
2. anecdote—paragraphs 17 through 19
3. humor—paragraphs 22 through 24
4. rhetorical question—paragraph 27
5. short generalization—paragraph 28

Discuss how each of these alternatives would work as a beginning in the context of Rowan's essay.

CHAPTER 7 **Paragraphs**

Simplicity (p. 168)

■ William Zinsser

Essay Analysis and Discussion

Freshmen are often surprised by Zinsser's suggestion to simplify, simplify. Many have come through high school writing courses believing that more is better and that the thesaurus is the basic tool for selecting vocabulary. To reinforce the notion of revising for simplicity's sake, have your students look over Zinsser's sample revision from manuscript on pages 172–74. Then, using examples from past student papers (or some other suitable source), present students with paragraphs needing simplifying. As students trim words or alter vocabulary or rearrange sentences, be sure they keep in mind the elements of an effective paragraph—controlling idea, unity, development, and coherence. When they've finished, analyze the deletions and changes and see whether they can identify common types of clutter.

Thinking Critically about This Reading

Zinsser points to "the clotted language of everyday American commerce: the memo, the corporation report, the business letter, the notice from the bank" (paragraph 2). He also gives the example of the airplane pilot, his college's president, and a 1942 blackout order and contrasts them with Thoreau's simplified prose. Zinsser suggests that writers need to think and write clearly, keeping in mind all the things that vie for their audience's short attention span.

Questions for Study and Discussion

1. As Zinsser states in paragraph 1, clutter is a writing disease, the symptoms of which include "unnecessary words, circular constructions, pompous frills, and meaningless jargon." In paragraph 3, Zinsser says that "the secret of good writing is to strip every sentence to its cleanest components." He then proceeds to give examples of "the thousand and one adulterants that weaken the strength of a sentence." Writers need to ask themselves: "What am I trying to say?" and then "Have I said it?" in order to eliminate clutter.
2. Each of Zinsser's paragraphs relates to his topic of clutter in writing and to his purpose of making readers more aware of clutter and its effect on writing. The main idea of each paragraph is as follows:

    1. "Clutter is the disease of American writing."

2. Most language of American commerce is unnecessarily complicated.
3. Words that serve no function need to be stripped from prose.
4. People need to express their thoughts in simple, straightforward language.
5. Roosevelt's example of clear English contrasts with the government memo.
6. Simplify as Thoreau does in his writing.
7. Clear thinking leads to clear writing and freedom from clutter.
8. Potential readers have a lot of competition.
9. When readers are lost, it's usually because the writer hasn't been careful enough.
10. Although readers might be forgiving at first, they usually don't stay with writers who make them work too hard.
11. Writers need to know what they are trying to say and cut everything that doesn't contribute to the intended meaning.
12. Thinking clearly is a conscious act that writers must force on themselves.
13. "Writing is hard work."

3. Paragraphs 4 through 6 illustrate the points Zinsser makes in paragraph 3 by providing examples of densely cluttered writing by highly educated people. He then presents simplified versions to underscore what he advocates.
4. Writers must ask themselves constantly: What am I trying to say? Have I said it? Is it clear to someone encountering the subject for the first time? These questions are important to Zinsser because good writing doesn't come naturally or easily. And the clear thinking that precedes it "is a conscious act that writers must force on themselves."
5. The first paragraph introduces the essay by defining *clutter* and establishing what Zinsser hopes to eliminate by writing his essay. It provides a necessary context for his thesis about simplicity. The final paragraph is a reminder that good writing does not come naturally but is the result of hard work. It is effective because it reemphasizes the importance of revision to successful writing.
6. "Clear thinking becomes clear writing; one can't exist without the other. It's impossible for a muddy thinker to write good English" (7).

Classroom Activity Using Paragraphs

Students should be immediately impressed by Zinsser's ability to ferret out and eliminate clutter in each of his paragraphs. This alone makes the paragraphs clearer and easier to follow because without the clutter Zinsser's craftsmanship shines through. At several points Zinsser edits out whole sentences—sentences that would have weakened the paragraph's unity. For example, in the first new paragraph he cuts the sentence "He *thinks* he knows what the writer is trying to say, but he's not sure," because it does not present an example of carelessness as each of the other sentences in the paragraph does. In that same paragraph, Zinsser uses the word *perhaps* to signal that he is presenting yet another example. Students should note how Zinsser uses the first sentence in each paragraph to refer back to a key idea in the last sentence of the previous paragraph.

One way to conduct this activity in class is to divide the class into groups of two or three and to have each group take responsibility for one of Zinsser's paragraphs. During class discussion, have the groups that worked on the same paragraphs present their findings and conclusions about Zinsser's editing changes.

Raising a Son—With Men on the Fringes (p. 175)

■ Robyn Marks

Essay Analysis and Discussion

Marks begins the essay faulting herself in paragraph 1: "Despite my best efforts, I am a single mother." She is raising her son in a single-parent home and is aware of the hurdles her son—and so many other young black men—have to overcome. Marks looks to many sources to figure out how to raise her son to become a "solid, productive adult" (2). For example, she cites academic studies in paragraph 3, her own work as a journalist in paragraph 4, the example of her brother in paragraphs 5 and 8, and all of the books written on the topic in paragraph 9. Marks talks about the men in her life who are providing her son with positive male role models, but she realizes that "everything Jason is, everything he trusts about who and what he can become, will come from me" (9). Consider asking students whether they think Marks, who is armed with firsthand personal and professional experience about the hurdles facing young black males, will provide him with what he needs. Do they think the direct involvement of a father is absolutely necessary if a child is surrounded with the love and support Marks is providing?

Thinking Critically about This Reading

Marks's firsthand experience as the sister of a young black man raised by a single mother and as a reporter who covers "crime and urban blight" (4) affords her a unique perspective on the hurdles young black males face. In paragraph 3 she cites demoralizing statistics on black men that solidify her worries for her own son.

Questions for Study and Discussion

1. Marks's purpose is to discuss the challenges black single mothers and their sons face, using her own experience as an example of a larger social issue: "[T]he majority of these boys and men were just like Jason, raised in a home by a single black mother" (3).
2. Student answers will vary. Ask your students to support their analysis by pointing to specific elements of the paragraphs they chose.
3. As a journalist "who has covered crime and urban blight" (4), Marks has firsthand knowledge of the problems facing young black men raised by single mothers. She has both personal and professional experience to support her concerns.
4. Marks feels responsible for continuing the cycle of fatherlessness in her family. "My grandmother eventually became a single mother, as did my mother and now me" (1). By beginning her essay this way, Marks gives readers insight into her anxiety and the lengths to which she'll go to help her son grow up to be a strong, respectable young man.
5. Marks puts the terms in quotation marks to indicate that society will not view her son as just another person or as an individual, but as a stereotype or a member of a group. Her concern that no matter what she does as a mother to instill values and respect in her son, his skin color will dictate—for many people—who he is.
6. This question should spark lively discussion. Some students will say that given the statistics and their own experiences, Marks's concern is justified. Others may say that Marks is overreacting and projecting too much into the future. Ask students to discuss what issues concern all parents—regardless of race or family makeup. What specific factors contribute to Marks's concern?

Classroom Activity Using Paragraphs

Here is one arrangement of the sentences:

> Athletes who overtrain find it very difficult to get in the flow. PGA golfer Fred Divot learned the hard way what overtraining could do. "I was playing well, so I thought with a bit more practice, I could start winning on the tour," Divot recalled. "Two weeks later, all I could think about was mechanics, and I couldn't hit a fairway to save my life!" Divot's case is typical, and most researchers believe that too much repetition makes it difficult for the athlete to reduce left-hemisphere brain activity. Athletes think about mechanics (left hemisphere) rather than feel (right hemisphere), and they lose the ability to achieve peak performance.

This ordering is based primarily on the transitional devices that link the sentences. Notice the repetition of words and ideas as the sentences progress. In the paragraph created, sentences 1 and 2 are linked by the word *overtrain*, whereas sentence 3 echoes the identification of golfer Fred Divot with a quote, followed by "Divot recalled." Sentence 4 continues the quotation. The beginning of sentence 5—"Divot's case"—refers to the issue addressed in the quoted material. Finally, sentence 6 repeats the words *mechanics* (sentence 4) and *left hemisphere* (sentence 5). The opening sentence gives the paragraph its main idea, and repetition in the sentences following gives it unity and coherence.

"I Just Wanna Be Average" (p. 182)

■ **Mike Rose**

Essay Analysis and Discussion

Students will likely find Rose's tribute to Jack MacFarland entertaining, but some may find it wordy or drawn out. Yet when they study the essay, they will find that each anecdote, each personal reference, and each seemingly casual statement directly relate to the topic Rose wants to present in a particular paragraph. Rose proves that you don't have to be overly concise or conservative in your writing to write an effective essay, but you do have to have a purpose and stick to it in each paragraph. Rose makes MacFarland and his own situation real to the reader while maintaining a flow in his essay that would be impossible to maintain with sloppy paragraphs. Have your students closely examine a paragraph of their choice and explain how each sentence relates to the paragraph's topic. If they write an essay about a teacher, emphasize the importance of using examples and anecdotes to liven up their essay—as long as those examples and anecdotes directly contribute to the paragraph containing them.

Thinking Critically about This Reading

Rose liked getting good grades from MacFarland because, he says, "I suppose I'd been mediocre for too long and enjoyed a public redefinition" (paragraph 5). MacFarland's grades meant more to him than other teachers' grades because he respected MacFarland. Unlike other teachers, MacFarland was hip and cool. Ask students to point to specific passages where Rose writes about MacFarland's cool style.

Questions for Study and Discussion

1. The title gives the reader a sense of just how much Rose's standards were raised by MacFarland. By the end of the essay Rose obviously rises well

above the average in a number of areas—he has exceeded his academic dreams.

2. MacFarland is a slob with wrinkled pants, a sorry tie, and stained teeth. Obviously, his abilities as a teacher have nothing to do with the way he looks.
3. (1) Jack MacFarland looked awful, but he was a very good teacher. (2) MacFarland's lectures were well crafted and intellectually stimulating, and his course covered a lot of ground. (3) He was able to handle the difficult students and earn everyone's respect. (4) MacFarland inspired Rose to work hard and do well. (5) Good grades from MacFarland were things of value. (6) MacFarland encouraged Rose to work to get into college. (7) MacFarland succeeded in helping Rose go to college.
4. Rose's second paragraph can be divided into two parts. In the first four sentences he discusses how MacFarland built up his students' knowledge of Western intellectual history. This background or overview material is necessary preparation for the analytical work that is discussed in the next four sentences of the paragraph. Rose's use of the pronouns "he" (MacFarland) and "we" (students) shows how the teacher led the way in the activities described in both parts of the paragraph. Rose's detailed accounting of authors, works, concepts, and activities prepares readers for the last sentence, "The man immersed us in language."
5. The transition between paragraphs 2 and 3 has to do with language—Rose's somewhat idyllic view in paragraph 2 and the real world of Mercy High in paragraph 3. The transition between paragraphs 3 and 4 brings the reader to what MacFarland did for Rose in particular. Rose shows what MacFarland did in class and how he interacted with others before he begins an in-depth account of his own relationship with MacFarland.
6. Rose introduces the reader to real people, kids like those everyone knows in high school. It makes the essay more entertaining, and it gives the reader a way to see what MacFarland had to contend with. By making them real to the reader, Rose shows the interaction MacFarland had with a variety of students, and the respect he earned from all.
7. Rose has difficulty getting into college because his grades are awful. He makes it by doing well in MacFarland's class and having him pull strings at his alma mater.

Classroom Activity Using Paragraphs

Once students select their topic sentences, have them make a list of all the details that come to mind that could be used in a paragraph. For example, for the topic sentence, "Signs of the sanitation strike were evident everywhere," a student's list might include "a discarded mattress, overflowing trash cans, littered streets, the smells of decaying garbage in dumpsters, piles of plastic trash bags curbside, rats venturing out in daylight, and flies everywhere." Next, have students write their paragraphs using only those details needed to show, demonstrate, or support the idea in the topic sentence. Finally, have several students read their paragraphs aloud—or better yet, put them on transparencies—for the class to discuss for unity, coherence, and development.

CHAPTER 8 **Transitions**

On Being 17, Bright, and Unable to Read (p. 192)

■ **David Raymond**

Essay Analysis and Discussion

Raymond writes openly and honestly about his experience growing up and struggling with dyslexia. While he was relieved to learn that he had a learning disability and was not "dumb," he feared that his classmates would ridicule him if they learned he was "going to a school for the retarded" (paragraph 10) to attend special education classes. Raymond's use of transitions is fairly sophisticated, so you might want to walk students through the essay once and, pointing out the transitions between paragraphs, answer Study and Discussion question 1 as a class. This exercise will help students understand that they may incorporate transitions in their own writing that are not dictated by a predetermined list of words and phrases.

Thinking Critically about This Reading

When asked, Raymond says he goes "to Mars" (12) when he leaves class to receive special instruction. He didn't want his classmates to know he was taking special education classes at another school. He states: "The bus also picked up emotionally disturbed kids and retarded kids. It was like going to a school for the retarded" (10). He was afraid that he would be considered retarded, a label he felt was worse than the label "dyslexic."

Questions for Study and Discussion

1. Transitional devices Raymond uses: Concession between paragraphs 1 and 2. Repeated key ideas between paragraphs 2 and 3. Concession between paragraphs 3 and 4. Reference to time between paragraphs 4 and 5. Repeated key ideas between paragraphs 5 and 6. Pronoun reference between paragraphs 6 and 7. Repeated key ideas between paragraphs 7 and 8. Reference to time between paragraphs 8 and 9. Repeated key ideas

between paragraphs 10 and 11, 11 and 12, 12 and 13, 13 and 14, 14 and 15, and 15 and 16.

2. Other examples include "but from where I sit," "unless you've been there," "I wish I were dead," "I guess I couldn't read," and "I didn't talk as good as other kids." These colloquialisms are the authentic expressions of a seventeen-year-old youth, and they add to the realism and credibility of the essay.
3. Raymond's tone is intimate and sincere and, although informal, serious enough to establish his central point. The colloquial expression suggests that his reflections are honest.
4. Dyslexia is a learning disorder in which the brain cannot interpret spatial relationships or has trouble distinguishing the difference between aural and visual information. The definition is not included because the essay is not about dyslexia. Raymond is writing about the effect on a child of being labeled as different or stupid.
5. Raymond's purpose for telling his story is to explain to teachers and parents what it is like to be dyslexic so that they will treat other children with this difficulty compassionately.
6. Raymond's story warns us that negative early-childhood experiences can have a devastating effect on a child's self-esteem, academic performance, and achievement, and that this effect can define us as adults.

Classroom Activity Using Transitions

The correct order for the sentences is 6, 4, 8, 3, 9, 2, 11, 1, 12, 5, 10, 7. Engage students in a discussion of the language cues that helped them arrange the sentences in a logical order. Students will readily point to transitions like *first* and *however*, the pronoun *this*, the repetition of key ideas such as "wetting down the surface" and "foreign material," and the organizational device "three steps."

Becoming a Writer (p. 199)

■ **Russell Baker**

Essay Analysis and Discussion

Few have gone through school without knowing a teacher like Baker's Mr. Fleagle—earnest, interested in his subject, eager to teach, but unable to communicate the joy of the subject to the class. The effectiveness of Baker's essay rests on his ability to describe Mr. Fleagle, and his description in paragraphs 2 and 3 is amusing, devastating, and full of imagery. Students should have a very clear notion of Mr. Fleagle's appearance, personality, and mannerisms from the description, and it should communicate to them the lesson Baker himself learns in the course of the essay—good writing can be funny and informal if it is clear and written with a purpose. It is through having so thoroughly established Mr. Fleagle as inept that Baker can make the ending surprising and effective, and it is easy for the reader to share Baker's joy and surprise. The paragraph transitions become particularly important in the telling of the development of the essay and its subsequent fate. Baker ushers the reader along in chronological order, but it is not a plodding account by any means. Baker bases his transitions on emotions and feelings, going from the joy of writing the essay to the anxiety of waiting for it to come back, to the joy of having it read. The reader can easily follow the progression, and the emotion-based transitions carry the reader on the same roller coaster Baker endured to the end.

Thinking Critically about This Reading

Seeing his classmates' reaction to his essay encouraged him: "I was feeling pure ecstasy at this startling demonstration that my words had the power to make people laugh" (12). He felt that he had "discovered a calling" (12). Baker thought so highly of Fleagle because he had "opened a door for me" (13).

Questions for Study and Discussion

1. Baker's transitional expressions, repeated key words and ideas, and pronoun references have been underlined in the following transcription of paragraphs 1 and 2.

    > The notion of becoming a writer had flickered off and on in my head . . . but it wasn't until my third year in high school that the possibility took hold. Until then I'd been bored by everything associated with English courses. I found English grammar dull and baffling. I hated the assignments to turn out "compositions," and went at them like heavy labor, turning out laden, lackluster paragraphs that were agonies for teachers to read and for me to write. The classics thrust on me to read seemed as deadening as chloroform.
    >
    > When our class was assigned to Mr. Fleagle for third-year English I anticipated another grim year in that dreariest of subjects. Mr. Fleagle was notorious among City students for dullness and inability to inspire. He was said to be stuffy, dull, and hopelessly out of date. To me he looked to be sixty or seventy and prim to a fault. He wore primly severe eyeglasses, his wavy hair was primly cut and primly combed. He wore prim vested suits with neckties blocked primly against the collar buttons of his primly starched white shirts. He had a primly pointed jaw, a primly straight nose, and a prim manner of speaking that was so correct, so gentlemanly, that he seemed a comic antique.

2. Make sure students note how Baker links the paragraphs to each other so that they flow chronologically without resorting to a plodding "Then I did this, then he did that" progression that many students fall into. Baker uses some very basic transitions—"This title," "When I finished it," "And he started to read," for example—but they are skillfully woven into the emotion of the story, so they lead the reader on without interfering with the flow of the narrative.
3. Baker's description of Mr. Fleagle paints an extremely clear picture of a teacher who will have trouble communicating with adolescents. Stuffy, prim, correct, antique—all are damning adjectives for teenagers. The repeated use of the word *prim* emphasizes the character of someone who appears out of touch with students—he sounds like the male equivalent of a stuffy old aunt whom children never want to visit because they must dress in uncomfortable clothes and sit up straight for what seems like hours on end. The description is important for the essay because it maximizes the impact of the later revelation Baker has in Fleagle's class. The man described in paragraph 2 seems incapable of inspiring anyone to do anything.
4. Mr. Fleagle's use of "don't you see" is ironic because the students obviously don't see the significance of what he's trying to say. In the end, however, Baker does see what Mr. Fleagle is trying to teach him, and it makes his epiphany that much more poignant.
5. Baker writes about the art of eating spaghetti, based on a happy memory of an evening spent eating spaghetti with relatives. He writes about it because he wants to and because it brings back good feelings for him. He doesn't want to turn his essay in because he thinks it violates all rules of formal composition—it is not respectable enough for Mr. Fleagle.
6. Baker repeats himself to communicate the sense of surprise and wonder he felt at the moment Mr. Fleagle read his essay. The reader understands the impact the event had on Baker much more clearly than if Baker had used a simple, emotionally neutral sentence.
7. Mr. Fleagle had demonstrated to Baker the power that his writing could have: It could make people laugh and enjoy the experience of reading or hearing it. Baker's prejudice that writing is not honest work made it difficult for him to think of writing as a career.

Classroom Activity Using Transitions

The lack of transitions between the three paragraphs in the exercise is painfully obvious, but writing them for text that is already there will teach students the kind of information and the techniques for linking paragraphs that are necessary for smooth transitions. There are no absolute right or wrong answers, but when a student reads the completed passage aloud, it should flow from paragraph to paragraph and be easy to follow. You might want to allow a little more time for this activity than usual, as it may take students a while to create effective transitions.

Why History? (p. 205)

■ David McCullough

Essay Analysis and Discussion

McCullough sees a problem with our understanding of American history and the lack of history instruction in our classrooms. He uses several examples from his firsthand dealings with college students as well as a study by the American Council of Trustees and Alumni to show that today's college students are woefully lacking in a basic understanding of American history. McCullough believes that history "shows us how to behave. History teaches and reinforces what we believe in, what we stand for, and what we ought to be willing to stand up for" (paragraph 7). Consider asking students the questions presented in the essay: Who was George Marshall? Where were the original thirteen colonies located? Who was the American general at Yorktown? Did their knowledge—or lack thereof—affect their reading of the essay? How did these examples serve to support his argument?

Thinking Critically about This Reading

McCullough feels that we can look to the past for examples of how to deal with current and future turmoil: "Think of what our predecessors endured and accomplished. Think of the dangerous times they knew!" (12). Periods of upheaval allow us to reflect on past events, learn from them, and chart a course for the future that is enriched with the knowledge of how we've gotten through difficult times in the past with a strengthened sense of who we are.

Questions for Study and Discussion

1. McCullough values American history and believes that not enough Americans know enough about it. He believes that knowing about our past will help us shape our future. McCullough says we now have a generation that is "to an alarming degree historically illiterate" (3). The use of the word *alarming* shows that McCullough values historical literacy and is concerned that students do not know enough about how we came to be. He goes on to remark that this ignorance is "like a disease, eating away at the national memory" (3). The word *disease* tells the reader that

McCullough believes that not knowing history can be dangerous. He talks about *warnings* (4) that have been sounded regarding this illiteracy. Ask students to comment on the connotations of the word *illiteracy.* What other word can they think of to describe our lack of historical knowledge? Is it as powerful as McCullough's word? Have them explain.

2. McCullough uses contrast between paragraphs 2 and 3: "Yet the truth is . . ." (3). Students may have different answers for the transition between paragraphs 3 and 4. They could argue that McCullough is using restatement when he talks about the warnings. Or they might say he is using example, citing the warnings as an example of how we have lost touch with the importance of history. McCullough uses time between paragraphs 4 and 5: "Two years ago. . ." (5). Between paragraphs 5 and 6, McCullough uses addition: "And there's been no improvement" (6).
3. The question in paragraph 2—"Who are we, we Americans?"—forces readers to think about how one could answer such a question *without* thinking about history. In order to answer the question, readers would probably have to discuss the past. McCullough uses the question to help readers see the valuable insights history can give into such powerful ideas. His question "But why bother about history anyway?" (7) enables him to put himself on the side of the majority, forcing the reader to think about and defend history. Some readers may find themselves answering the question. Others, however, may find themselves more drawn into the essay because they have asked themselves that question.
4. People need to acknowledge the events that have shaped the present. The study of history can inspire and motivate. Some students may say that lack of interest in or ignorance of history does not signify ingratitude. You may want to ask them whether there are other ways appreciation could be expressed. Does it go beyond reading about history? What about taking pictures of old buildings? Designing sets for plays set in historical times? How might learning about family history be a form of appreciation and gratitude?
5. McCullough says we must learn more about our history because it tells us who we are and how we got here, explores human nature and the human condition, and reveals our strengths and limitations. He also says that history teaches us about "cause and effect, about the simplest of everyday things—and the mysteries of chance and genius" (7). Some may add that history teaches us the possibilities for our individual lives, encourages social and political action, and inspires and touches our lives. Some may say that history can move us emotionally and make us more aware of our surroundings. Others may still not be moved by or interested in history. You may want to ask students how history influences our understanding of science, religion, art, dance, or literature.

Classroom Activity Using Transitions

The correct order for the sentences in E. B. White's paragraph is 4, 2, 5, 1, 3. The sentences in the paragraph follow in chronological order from that first summer in 1904 to the present. Students will point to the time markers "1904," "returned," "since," and "a few weeks ago." White uses pronouns skillfully as well; he moves from the family experience ("we" and "us") to the personal experience ("I"). Finally, White uses subtle references to previous ideas to link sentences together. For example, when he states "We returned there summer after summer," we know that the place he is referring to is "a lake in Maine." And that "this feeling" in sentence 3 relates back to his "wish for the placidity of a lake in the woods."

CHAPTER 9 **Effective Sentences**

from *An American Childhood* (p. 215)

■ **Annie Dillard**

Essay Analysis and Discussion

Dillard's essay charts two forms of childhood personal discovery. The more immediate is her discovery of the microscopic world, and the fascination that world holds for her. The more profound is her discovery of how she is to relate with her parents on matters of personal interest or passion. While Dillard's parents' reaction may strike some as aloof or uncaring—and probably would have been difficult for an extroverted child to handle—Dillard is careful to describe how it worked to open new avenues of exploration for her. With her curiosity and the right tools, "anything was possible" for Dillard. Note how she uses both complex and simple sentences to make the essay easy to understand, yet interesting to read. Students who believe that every sentence must be complex and dotted with commas, semicolons, and em dashes for an essay to be considered good writing will see ample evidence contrary to that notion. For example, the sentence "Mother regarded me warmly" is vital to understanding her parents' good will and willingness to respond positively to Dillard on a personal level. By limiting the sentence to those four words, Dillard makes it carry more weight. The reader knows that her mother's warmth is important enough to set apart from the rest of the text. Students can be encouraged to look at previous examples of their own writing—are there places where simple sentences would be more suitable than complex sentences? Or are there too many short, choppy sentences that detract from the flow of the essay?

Thinking Critically about This Reading

Dillard realized that she investigated things with her microscope because she liked to, not because she needed her parents' approval or praise. When her mother decided to stay at the table drinking her coffee instead of following Dillard down to her microscope, Dillard realized that she had her own life and interests, as did her parents.

Questions for Study and Discussion

1. Dillard writes with a child's voice to communicate her experience to the reader without adult cynicism or worldliness getting in the way of her sense of wonder and enthusiasm. It also sharpens the contrast between her reaction and her parents' reaction to her discovery of the amoeba. Dillard learns that she is not dependent upon her parents for a life; in paragraph 12, she says, "My days and nights were my own to plan and fill."
2. Dillard mixes complex and simple sentences in her first four paragraphs, interspersing her lists of materials and descriptions with short, pithy sentences that emphasize important points and make the paragraphs easier to read. The short sentences are the following:

   "Everybody needed a microscope." This communicates her childhood enthusiasm, as discussed in question 1.

   "One of the test tubes contained 'hay infusion'" and "This did not work for me." These sentences are used for variety. The first is a simple topic sentence, and the second emphasizes the problems Dillard began having with the material provided with the microscope.

   "Another test tube contained 'diatomaceous earth'" and "The kit's diatomaceous earth was a bust." These sentences perform the same functions as the preceding ones, with the use of the word *bust* emphasizing Dillard's disappointment.

3. It is not directly stated why the microscope appeals to Dillard, but it is obvious that she was a very curious child and wished to see for herself the things she read about. She perseveres through her early disappointments and is patient enough to wait until the weather is warm enough to pursue the field experiments that ultimately succeed for her.
4. Students should answer yes, in that Dillard uses a very simple vocabulary—aside from the necessary scientific terms—that is appropriate for a child's point of view. Words such as *bust*, *blobby*, *chance of a lifetime,* and *fuss over* maintain the informal tone.
5. Paragraph 12 is among the longest in Dillard's essay, yet surprisingly it consists of only three sentences. In sentence 1 she announces that she'd

"been handed my own life." In the second sentence she explains exactly what that meant. In the first half of the sentence she tells what her parents provided for her growing up, and in the second half she describes the freedom and independence that they gave her. The length of the second sentence reinforces the great value of the gift that Dillard's parents gave her. She concludes the paragraph with a short, punchy sentence stating that she was now free to plan and fill her own days.

6. The three short sentences in Dillard's final paragraph ("I had hit pay dirt." "Anything was possible." "The sky was the limit.") dramatically capture her excitement and delight. These short sentences surprise readers and focus their attention on the life lesson that Dillard learns.

Classroom Activity Using Effective Sentences

Although this paragraph describes a dramatic event, it is written in a way that makes it boring and difficult to read. The sentence structure is monotonously consistent, and, although all the necessary information is included, it is presented in such a way that the mundane has equal footing with the dramatic and unusual. You might wish to read the paragraph aloud to the class as it stands, then read the students' revised paragraphs aloud when they are done. Hearing the passage in both forms will give the students an auditory reference for what they need to do to create interesting and effective sentences.

Salvation (p. 220)

■ Langston Hughes

Essay Analysis and Discussion

In addition to Hughes's use of different sentence lengths and patterns in this essay, he varies the manner of his material, particularly for the scene at the church. To add a sense of the revival meeting's liveliness, he includes bits of conversation that enhance the essay's main idea. In paragraph 3 he presents the preacher's words; in paragraph 6, Westley's whispered mutterings; and in paragraphs 8 through 10, an exchange between the minister and Hughes's aunt. To illustrate the effects of these passages, read the essay aloud to your students and ask them to pay attention to what the dialogue contributes. Your discussion should focus, especially, on the dialogue's relation to the first and last paragraphs, and on how the inclusion of conversation helps convey Hughes's central idea. Students should also note that he includes only enough dialogue to serve his purpose.

Thinking Critically about This Reading

Hughes cries because he had lied to the congregation about seeing Jesus, because he regrets not seeing Jesus, and because he now doubts that Jesus exists at all. The irony is that Hughes's "salvation from sin" was based on a lie.

Questions for Study and Discussion

1. According to Hughes, salvation is being "saved from sin" when Jesus and the Holy Ghost come into your life. Young Langston "wanted to see Jesus." However, his salvation was more important to his aunt, who cared about his soul and didn't want to be embarrassed in front of the congregation by his being the only one left who had not been saved. Hughes expects to be saved because his aunt and the other townspeople had built up the expectation during the weeks of preparation for the revival meeting. In paragraph 3 we see the various appeals made by the preacher, and in paragraph 4 we see how the preacher's appeals are reinforced by the prayers and songs of the congregation.
2. Have students read portions of Hughes's essay aloud so that they can hear the rhythms that his sentences create. They'll see how the short, dramatic sentences punctuate the events of the evening, engaging readers in the emotions of the moment. Longer sentences, such as the one that begins paragraph 3, reinforce the ebb and flow of the preaching and singing at the revival meeting. Others, such as the third sentence in paragraph 11, reflect the unfolding of Hughes's thinking as he tries to decide whether to stand up at the revival meeting or what the whole experience means in the end.
3. If these two sentences had been combined, the dramatic effect of the reversal of thought and statement would have been lost.
4. The coordinating conjunctions in paragraph 3 are *and*, *and*, *and*, *and*, and *but*. Hughes uses coordinating conjunctions throughout his essay. When he wants to link closely related actions and not give any one of them emphasis, he does so in a long sentence. When he wants to link closely related ideas but give emphasis to each idea, he uses short sentences that begin with coordinating conjunctions.
5. The subordinating conjunctions in paragraph 15 are *for*, *for*, *because*, *because*, *because*, *that*, *that*, *that*, *that*, *since*. In this last paragraph Hughes reflects on the experience, and, therefore, makes explicit connections.
6. Some of the words Hughes uses to remind us that we are at a revival meeting are *sin*, *mourners' bench*, *preached*, *sermon*, *hell*, *prayed*, *Jesus*, *congregation*, and *wail*. In addition, Hughes uses traditional religious figures of speech such as "to bring the young lambs to the fold," "when you

were saved you saw a light," "lower lights are burning," and "all the new young lambs were blessed in the name of God."

Classroom Activity Using Effective Sentences

The six sets of short sentences can be rewritten as follows:

1. I can take the 6:30 express train or catch the 7:00 bus.
2. Miriam was tired after working all weekend on her research paper, for which she interviewed five people.
3. Juan did not have time to work out at the gym for over a month because his new job kept him busy every day.
4. Completely restored for the nation's 200th birthday, the Statue of Liberty, a gift of the French government over 120 years ago, welcomes newcomers to America.
5. The starting center on the basketball team, Carla is a tall, strong team player.
6. Betsy loves Bach's music, and she also likes Scott Joplin.

Have students put their rewrites on the board and discuss the ways in which each of the sets of sentences can be combined.

The Good Daughter (p. 225)

■ Caroline Hwang

Essay Analysis and Discussion

Caroline Hwang discusses a conflict many young adults can relate to, the conflict between their parents' hopes and dreams for them and their own aspirations and dreams. Her story has an added wrinkle, however—cultural differences that result from her being the child of immigrant parents. Caught between the Korean world of her parents and the American world in which she grew up, she sees her life as a series of compromises, a "life of halfwayness." Have students discuss their feelings about having "to choose between pleasing their parents and being true to themselves." Stylistically, Hwang's essay is interesting for its use of dialogue and for its sentence variety. For example, the dialogue in the opening seven paragraphs makes Hwang's dilemma real and gives voice to the Korean woman's cultural stance. Many of her sentences capture the hesitation or conflict in Hwang's own thinking about her situation. As a child of immigrants she is torn between her parents' dreams and her own.

Thinking Critically about This Reading

Hwang means that children of immigrants are caught between two cultures—in this case, Korean and American. She is suggesting that these children are the only generation to have a split identity. If Hwang herself has children in America, the children will be more culturally American and further removed from their Korean heritage than Hwang is.

Questions for Study and Discussion

1. Hwang most clearly and succinctly states her thesis in paragraph 18: "Children of immigrants are living paradoxes."
2. The incident in the dry-cleaning store pointedly shows Hwang's dilemma; she is caught between two cultures. The dialogue gives action and life to the incident. By having the store owner speak in her own words, pronouncing "Fxuang" as Koreans would, Hwang avoids the need to explain the incident herself. In paragraph 9, Hwang listens as her mother responds to the incident over the pronunciation of the family name. In both instances, dialogue allows Hwang to show, not tell the reader the attitude differences between her mother and the store owner.
3. Both short sentences capture Hwang's feelings, first in response to the storekeeper's unexpected question, and the second to the woman's cruel taunt. The two short sentences enhance the confrontational nature of this encounter.
4. Each of the sentences in paragraph 13 is structured to highlight the conflicts and contrasts that Hwang is experiencing in regard to her own identity. For example, in the first sentence "sacrifices" are contrasted with "opportunities," and in the second sentence her parents' thinking is contrasted with her own.

Classroom Activity Using Effective Sentences

This activity is an exercise in combining sentences. Encourage students to discuss the various ways in which each set of sentences can be combined—some ways are better than others—so that they can appreciate the flexibility of the English language.

1. Bonnie wore red shorts with pockets.
2. The deer hunter awoke at 5:00 A.M.; ate a quick breakfast of coffee, juice, and cereal; and was in the woods before sunrise.
3. After playing golf every weekend for years, my grandparents stopped playing last year, and now they miss the game.
4. If you fly over any major city, you will be appalled at the number of tall smokestacks you will see.

5. Most farmers were on the brink of declaring bankruptcy because most crops in the region failed during the three-month dry spell.
6. After work, I exercise, shower, and relax, and eat a light, low-fat dinner.

38 Who Saw Murder Didn't Call Police (p. 230)

■ Martin Gansberg

Essay Analysis and Discussion

Gansberg uses a third-person point of view in this essay because he was not involved in the events described. But third person is appropriate because it lets the facts speak for themselves. When you discuss this essay, mention that at no point does Gansberg editorialize about what happened to Kitty Genovese. Yet it is clear after reading the essay how he feels about the incident. Ask students how Gansberg manages to display his attitude about the lack of response to the attack, even though he uses the third person and interjects no opinions of his own. Have them look closely at his selection of details and ordering of events, and at his choices of diction. His use of dialogue is another important element in the narrative. After they've examined these aspects, students should see that although the facts seem to speak for themselves, deliberate choices about which facts to present help the essay achieve its purpose.

Thinking Critically about This Reading

Gansberg's title is very suggestive of his attitude toward the murder. Ask students to discuss how an alternative title, such as "Woman Murdered in Quiet Neighborhood," would have affected their reading. In paragraphs 24 through 31 Gansberg includes details of the attack, the police response, and the reluctant witnesses, which reveal that Gansberg is in disbelief that no one helped Kitty Genovese.

Questions for Study and Discussion

1. Gansberg's purpose is to show how apathy and fear have gripped the lives of New Yorkers, making them indifferent to the suffering of others. His use of narration has the advantage of illustrating the stark results of such apathy and fear, but the disadvantage of relying on readers to draw their own conclusions about the incident—conclusions that might not reflect what Gansberg hoped to achieve.
2. Gansberg's narrative of Kitty Genovese's murder begins with paragraph 7. As with Dick Gregory's essay "Shame," the introductory paragraphs establish

an appropriate context in which to consider the events of the narrated incident. Without that context, the neighbors' reactions to the attack on Genovese would not have as much emotional appeal.

3. The subordinate clauses that Gansberg uses include "who was called Kitty by almost everyone in the neighborhood," "although the railroad frowns on the practice," "which is in a Tudor building, with stores in the first floor and apartments on the second," "because the front is rented to retail stores," and "that marks most residential areas." The information that is essential to the story is contained in the main clause of each of the sentences in these three paragraphs.
4. Short sentences such as "She halted," "She screamed," "'Please help me!'" "Lights went out," "'I'm dying!'" "The assailant returned," and "It drove off" emphasize action and rivet the reader's attention to what's happening. Student responses about the impact of these sentences will vary. It is important, however, to have them explain why they selected the particular sentence that they did.
5. Quotes from eleven people in the essay lend authenticity to Gansberg's narrative and illustrate, through the words of those involved, exactly how appalling the situation is.
6. Gansberg uses a tone of controlled anger and subdued amazement. Although he describes events objectively in the third person, his arrangement of details and use of diction and dialogue hint at a more aggressive attitude toward his subject.
7. Gansberg might appear didactic if he were to analyze the meaning of his narrative at the end. Although he is forced to rely on readers to formulate an appropriate meaning for his essay, that is better than if he were to appear "preachy" and create hostility between himself and his audience. Students may or may not agree.

Classroom Activity Using Effective Sentences

One possible rewrite of the paragraph is as follows:

> Day care centers should be available to all women who work and have no one to care for their children, and not just to women who are raising their children alone or to families whose income is below the poverty level. This care should be reliable, responsible, convenient, and relatively inexpensive. Women who work must demand more day care centers. No woman should be prevented from working because child care facilities are unavailable.

You might want to put the activity paragraph on an overhead transparency so that you and your students can rework the paragraph together.

CHAPTER 10 **Diction and Tone**

Shame (p. 245)

■ Dick Gregory

Essay Analysis and Discussion

The heart of this essay is the incident Gregory relates about being shamed in front of Helene Tucker. Gregory chooses a chronological organization, but the chronology does not begin until the fourth paragraph because Gregory needs to establish a context for the incident in paragraphs 1 through 3. To give your students an indication of how vital such a context is to this essay, have them reexamine the first three paragraphs and consider what they contribute to Gregory's narration of the schoolroom incident in paragraphs 4 through 27, and what effect the removal of these three paragraphs would have on the essay. If you wish to narrow the focus of the discussion even further, ask them how the following sentences from those initial paragraphs interact with elements from Gregory's anecdote:

> "It was a lady's handkerchief, but I didn't want Helene to see me wipe my nose on my hand." (1)
>
> "Everybody's got a Helene Tucker, a symbol of everything you want." (2)
>
> "And she had a Daddy, and he had a good job." (2)
>
> "When I played the drums in high school it was for Helene and when I broke track records in college it was for Helene and when I started standing behind microphones and heard applause I wished Helene could hear it, too." (3)

After you've discussed the relationship between the opening paragraphs and the episode at school, have students analyze how those three paragraphs connect with Gregory's conclusion. The intent of your discussion should be to clarify what it means to establish a clear context for a narration.

Thinking Critically about This Reading

Gregory, when trying to impress Helene Tucker, told the class that his father would donate fifteen dollars to the community chest. His teacher humiliated Gregory by saying that if his father had that much money he didn't deserve relief, ultimately silencing Gregory by stating, "We know you don't have a daddy." This rebuke stung Gregory so greatly because he was revealed as a liar in front of the girl whose affection he so desperately wanted.

Questions for Study and Discussion

1. In the first three paragraphs of the essay, Gregory introduces Helene Tucker and tells of his infatuation with her. This information provides the motivation for his later behavior.
2. For Gregory, *shame* means "disgrace," in this case disgrace in an environment where he least expected to find it. Gregory was ashamed of his poverty and of not having a father; however, that day in school was the day "I learned to be ashamed of myself."
3. Students will likely say that Gregory's tone is angry or resigned. Ask students to discuss the meaning of the word *shame* and how Gregory's diction and tone relate that feeling to his audience. Ask students to find words and phrases that relate to cleanliness and dirtiness, or intelligence and stupidity, for example. What do these dualities convey? What do they reveal about Gregory?
4. The teacher thought Gregory was stupid, he said, but didn't stop to consider that he had trouble in school because he wasn't getting enough to eat at home. She also thought he was a troublemaker, again not taking time to consider that he was looking for attention he didn't get at home. Nevertheless, until the day of his shaming, he thought she liked him. "She always picked me to wash the blackboard on Friday, after school . . . it made me feel important." Ultimately she showed contempt for "you and your kind," and publicly humiliated him when she announced his secret to the class: "We know you don't have a daddy."
5. This is not a story about racism. In fact, there's nothing to indicate that his teacher wasn't black. The lack of money is the basis of Gregory's shame, just as it would be having money that erased it. Helene Tucker, the little girl who was light-complexioned, clean, and well-dressed, became the symbol of what he wasn't. "It wasn't until I was twenty-nine years old and married and making money that I finally got her out of my system."
6. Examples of Gregory's use of descriptive details abound in the essay. (By locating examples, students will become aware of how such details help to create vivid and interesting prose.)
7. Although Gregory introduces shame in the first sentence of his first paragraph, the focus of the paragraph is on the "love" (or crush) he has for Helene Tucker. He tells how this "light-complexioned little girl with pigtails and nice manners" made him feel good just being in her company. The final paragraph, in contrast, is dominated by shame. Gregory now felt as if "everyone had heard what the teacher had said, everyone had turned around and felt sorry for me." Gregory uses examples effectively to show how "there was shame everywhere." In a world filled with shame, there is no room for love. Gregory's final paragraph underscores the traumatic effect of the teacher's caustic words and therefore is an emotionally powerful ending.

Classroom Activity Using Diction and Tone

Synonyms for *eat, drink, sleep,* and *work* include the following:

eat: devour, nibble, feast, gorge, gobble, pick, dine, wolf, consume
drink: gulp, quaff, sip, chug, guzzle, imbibe, tipple
sleep: snooze, nap, slumber, doze, catch forty winks, turn in, hit the hay, crash
work: toil, labor, perform, serve, slave, sweat

Make four lists of verbs on the chalkboard. Classroom discussion should focus on the connotative differences between the verbs on each list. Students usually find it helpful to try using each verb in a sentence of their own. Also discuss how the verbs in each list convey more than the meaning contained in *eat, drink, sleep,* and *work*. For example, to *nibble* means to *eat delicately*. Have students translate the verbs on each list. The bottom line: Strong active verbs reduce the need to modify.

Me Talk Pretty One Day (p. 251)

■ **David Sedaris**

Essay Analysis and Discussion

Sedaris is known for his humorous and ironic essays. In "Me Talk Pretty One Day," Sedaris recounts his experience of taking French language lessons in Paris. His metaphors, similes, and anecdotes make this piece a funny essay, especially if it is read aloud during class. If students have trouble picking up on Sedaris's humorous tone, reading the piece aloud will help them hear the silliness that arises in his classroom. Consider asking students if they have ever been in a situation when they could not communicate effectively. How did they convey their thoughts? Did anything funny happen, such as a bawdy inversion of words?

Thinking Critically about This Reading

The fact that Sedaris can relate—in translation—his French teacher's insult is significant because it shows that he has learned enough of the language to be able to understand her rather obscure barbs. The teacher's cesarian section metaphor illustrates that she sees teaching as a painful process of trying to bring understanding to her students. It also shows that she is as pained by her students as they are by her.

Questions for Study and Discussion

1. Words and phrases that help Sedaris establish a humorous tone: "true debutant" (paragraph 1), "appears to be a ham sandwich" (1), "Pa Kettle

trapped backstage after a fashion show" (2), "weave a floor mat out of newspapers" (3), "a failed nursing student to inject me with horse tranquilizer" (3), "teeth the size of tombstones" (9), "Playmate of the Month data sheets" (12), "I love Tums" (15), "severe dermatological conditions" (15), "Lady Flesh Wound or Good Sir Dishrag" (18), "strap on my wooden leg" (23), "overheard in refugee camps" (25).

2. Student reactions will differ. Ask students whether they had trouble understanding Sedaris's humor. If they did, consider reading the essay aloud to the class. Ask them to discuss how hearing the broken French and English contributes to their appreciation of Sedaris's tone.
3. Students will have different impressions of Sedaris and his classmates. His most striking description of them is of refugees struggling to communicate. Point out to students that the class is filled with a very diverse group of people and that they have all come together for a common goal—to learn French.
4. Sedaris uses the jumbled words to illustrate his own inability to fully understand French. Had he included the "real" words instead, his sense of confusion and the drive he felt to learn the language would have been lost.
5. Sedaris's realization is that he can understand his teacher's words. He is able to understand several of her insults and states, "for the first time since arriving in France, I could understand every word that someone was saying."

Classroom Activity Using Diction and Tone

Our students have suggested the following menu descriptions:

tomato juice: spicy tomato juice; tomato juice with a wedge of lemon
onion soup: French onion soup; onion soup covered with cheese and slow-baked in a clay crock
ground beef: Salisbury steak; chopped sirloin smothered with onions and peppers
chicken: tender roasted chicken; lightly breaded, crispy chicken
peas: baby peas; petite farm-fresh peas
potatoes: tender, new potatoes; southern hash brown potatoes
salad: crisp salad greens; fresh garden greens lightly dressed with our house vinaigrette
bread and butter: fresh-baked, whole-grain breads and creamy butter
pasta: fresh, homemade pasta; pasta served al dente
ice cream: creamy gourmet ice cream; premium ice cream
tea: all-natural herb tea; selection of the finest teas from around the world
cake: sinfully delicious triple chocolate cake; delightfully light angel food cake with farm-fresh berries

Try to engage students in a discussion of what the various descriptions tell them about the foods as well as about the restaurants that have these descriptions on their menus. For example, which restaurants serve "hash browns" and which ones serve "tender new potatoes"?

Pop-A-Shot (p. 259)

■ Sarah Vowell

Essay Analysis and Discussion

This essay offers the opportunity for a short in-class writing exercise in which students describe one way they like to goof off or pursue what Vowell refers to as a "dumb-ass passion." Students should be instructed to write their descriptions in the language they would use if they were speaking with their friends, or perhaps with those who would share in the activity they describe. When they are finished writing, students can share their pieces, or at least parts of them that contain examples of the distinctive vocabulary they have chosen. The class can then consider how wide an audience the language of each piece might appeal to, and why.

Thinking Critically about This Reading

In Pop-A-Shot, players do not run, pass, or dribble; it's "basketball concentrate." In paragraph 8 Vowell states that Pop-A-Shot "is a baby game," "has no standard socially redeeming value," "is not about teamwork . . . or working together," "is not about getting exercise or fresh air," and "it costs money." In paragraph 9 Vowell states, "Pop-A-Shot has no point at all. And that, for me, is the point."

Questions for Study and Discussion

1. Although Vowell makes the statement with tongue in cheek, she does take seriously the need to goof off as one element in the pursuit of happiness.
2. Vowell believes there are two reasons she can shoot a basketball: black-eyed peas and Uncle Hoy. The backboard at her country home was nailed to a tree that grew on top of a hill, so if she missed a shot the ball would roll into a muddy drainage ditch for the kitchen sink containing, among other gross things, corn and black-eyed peas. Her Uncle Hoy was a girls' basketball coach and math teacher who made her practice free throws, only counting the ones that went through the basket with the geometrical precision of a swish.
3. Vowell's tone is informal and humorous. Words and phrases that contribute to the tone include *bogarts; stuck in an episode of* Friends; *bugs;*

topped; willy-nilly; trash-talking; moving-around-basketball; falling down on cameramen in between baskets; basketball concentrate; crack cocaine of basketball; the civic virtue of idiocy; Wa-wa-wa, little Pop-A-Shot baby; dumb-ass little passion; and *swish.*

4. Pop-A-Shot, according to Vowell, takes what she calls "moving-around-basketball" and condenses it into 40 seconds of its most fundamental element—shooting the ball into the hoop. In other words, it takes the essence of basketball—making baskets in a limited amount of time—and distills it into a denser, more compact form.
5. Most students will probably not see the paragraph about Joel's "real" basketball game as a digression, since it illustrates the difference between the pressurized situation of shooting free throws when the game is on the line in a "fairly serious adult basketball league" and the goofing-off quality of competition in the "dumb-ass passion" Vowell and her friends feel for Pop-A-Shot.
6. Vowell comes off as a person with a good sense of humor, a good relationship with her friends, and the ability to find fun in life despite obligations and responsibilities that can sometimes feel onerous. She is also capable of laughing at herself, as in her remark about being stuck in an episode of *Friends* or her celebration of the civic virtue of idiocy.
7. Vowell claims that the point of Pop-A-Shot is that it has no point at all, unlike such things as deadlines, bills, recycling, and phone calls. It offers the perfect opportunity to just goof off, thus freeing her from some of the stresses of daily life.

Classroom Activity Using Diction and Tone

This activity might take more time than usual, so be prepared to assign half of it as a homework assignment. When you introduce the activity, have the students think about how they speak to older and younger people, and, if possible, have them role-play the different ages and address each other in class, so that they can actually hear their tone. They will then have a good foundation from which to proceed with their paragraphs.

Who Am I? (p. 264)

■ Merrill Markoe

Essay Analysis and Discussion

Markoe writes a humorous essay about her experiences with Internet and magazine personality quizzes. The humor lies in her ability to connect to her audience on a very relatable subject. After all, most of us would like some insight into ourselves, either through horoscopes, fortune cookies, learning style inventories, or personality diagnostics such as the Myers-Briggs test. Ask students to consider how awareness of audience, as it relates to diction and tone, contributes to conveying humor. How might a humorous essay on "pop" personality quizzes for an audience of psychologists differ from an essay written for an audience of twenty-something magazine readers? For an interesting class discussion, try printing out a personality quiz from the Internet, or clip one out of a magazine. Ask students to take the quiz, score it, and then discuss their results. What purpose did each question serve in the analysis? How did the quiz attempt to understand the takers' personalities? Did they feel the results were accurate?

Thinking Critically about This Reading

Markoe means that the online quizzes provide the same type of diversion that horoscopes do: They provide a brief glimpse at insight and self-discovery. Additionally, we often turn to horoscopes out of habit, even though we know their messages will be cryptic at best. Horoscopes and quizzes provide us with a fleeting thrill—the chance to believe that something can tell us more about ourselves or our futures. "For about a minute and a half, the quiz glistens like a beacon of knowledge before you, offering answers to all the important questions in life" (paragraph 1).

Questions for Study and Discussion

1. Markoe feels that Internet and magazine personality quizzes are entertaining and harmlessly addictive but provide few meaningful insights and are often inconsistent. Her summary of all her results demonstrates this; "I am extroverted and reserved, passive and active, risk-taking and afraid of change" (16). The quizzes are "confusing" (13) and ask "seemingly irrelevant questions" (3).
2. Markoe's purpose is to poke fun at her own and others' use of these quizzes. Most students will say that Markoe does not see these online quizzes as a meaningful way to get in touch with oneself. The questions are often arbitrary and the results contradictory.
3. The idea that the computer quizzes could tell her things about herself that she did not know hooked her. But although these quizzes are meant to clarify, the more of them she took, the more contradictory her results became. She became as interested in the questions as in the results.
4. Most students will agree that her tone is humorous and sarcastic. Joking that at 1 P.M. she is still in her pajamas taking these quizzes, clearly not motivated to make positive changes in her life, she writes, "So there I was, alone in my house and suddenly a lot less attractive than I had been a few minutes earlier" (5). Clearly, since she had not left her computer, there was no way her attractiveness could really have changed. In

paragraph 10 she jokes, "I made the mistake of picking eggs and toast over cereal for breakfast."

5. The simile "as utterly seductive as the horoscope pages" (1) shows readers how addictive these quizzes can be. Even if they have never seen the quizzes, they can probably relate to the horoscope pages, which are often vague and contradictory. In another simile, Markoe shows the reader how tempting the tests look and how much hope they conjure up; "[T]he quiz glistens like a beacon of knowledge before you" (1). In the simile, "to recoup my losses, like a woman feverishly playing the slot machines" (5), Markoe shows the near-panic and compulsiveness with which one can continue to play.
6. Between paragraphs 4 and 5 she uses the transitional expression "So there I was" (5). Between 2 and 3 she uses a repeated idea, "I came to know of this one day" (3). She uses the transitional expression "Next" between paragraphs 8 and 9. These casual expressions and transitions keep readers feeling close to the author. Some students may like the repeated words or ideas because they keep them focused.

Classroom Activity Using Diction and Tone

Students' lists of words for each of the tones given will vary. Here are some of the words our students gave us:

humorous: laugh, joke, funny, surprise
angry: hate, sarcastic, fight, boil, humiliate
authoritative: dictate, judge, rule, control
triumphant: win, victor, celebrate, party, hard work
tentative: hesitate, unsure, undecided, reluctant

After having students compare their lists, engage them in a discussion of the connotative values associated with the words in each list. Have them focus on the verbs in their lists, and point out how well-chosen verbs influence the tone of a piece of writing.

CHAPTER 11 **Figurative Language**

The Barrio (p. 272)

■ **Robert Ramirez**

Essay Analysis and Discussion

Ramirez points out the sights of the barrio from a moving train that emerges in the "deep sleep" of night in the opening paragraph and reappears to the "yawns and restless stretchings" of a new dawn in the closing paragraph. Students can discuss this use of figurative language in asking four questions: Why does Ramirez use a train to establish a context for his description of the barrio? Why does he take us into the barrio only through the still hours of the night? What does he intend as the symbolism of the train and the street lamp? What do they add to his portrayal of the barrio?

Thinking Critically about This Reading

Ramirez goes on to say, "The barrio is a refuge from the harshness and the coldness of the Anglo world. It is a forced refuge" (paragraph 4). In paragraphs 5–10 he describes the institutions of the barrio and their importance in the community: the *tortillería, panadería,* corner grocery store, barbershop, pool hall, and *cantina.* These examples support his claim that the barrio is more than a home by illustrating that it is also a protected zone of culture, community, and family.

Questions for Study and Discussion

1. *Barrio* is a Spanish word that refers to a chiefly Spanish-speaking neighborhood (typically in a city) in the southwestern United States. Ramirez generally describes barrios as isolated communities "fenced off by railroads, canals, and expressways" (2). Because the barrio is a "refuge from the harshness and the coldness of the Anglo world" (4), members of the barrio have no desire to leave. All their needs are met within its confines.
2. The Spanish phrases, spoken as if the reader understands them, lend an aura of authenticity and color to Ramirez's essay. These words allow us to "hear" the people of the barrio. The other words connote warmth, community, intimacy, and friendliness. They are meant to emphasize the positive feelings of life in the barrio that are known only to its inhabitants.
3. "[T]his pulsing light . . . beats slower, like a weary heartbeat" (1). "[F]rom the angry seeds of rejection grow the flowers of closeness between outcasts, not the thorns of bitterness" (4). "[T]he warmth of the tortilla factory is a wool *sarape*" (5). "Their houses, aged and bent, oozing children, are fissures in the horn of plenty" (17). These metaphors are particularly apt because they compare things common to the barrio with other things that are relevant to it. The wool *sarape* is as common as the factory. The horn of plenty, broken and empty, is also a metaphor for the people of the barrio.
4. Ramirez uses a number of words and phrases that attribute human characteristics to the barrio and the daily train. These include "blinks" (1), "pulsing" (1), "weary heartbeat" (1), "grumble" (2), "arrest" (13), "ignore" (13), and "greets a new dawn with yawns and restless stretchings" (20).
5. Ramirez intends his comparison of the fences in the barrio with the walls of the Anglo community to symbolize the easy interaction among the

people of his culture as opposed to the isolation and separation of the Anglo world.

6. Had Ramirez begun his description of the barrio with the negative aspects of life there he would have risked having readers misunderstand the intent of his essay. Ramirez wants us to understand that life in the barrio is integral, satisfying, and necessary. He saves the sadder aspects of barrio life until the end, so that we do not confuse his desire for our understanding with a desire for pity.

Classroom Activity Using Figurative Language

Possible metaphors or similes for each of the items on the list include:

1. *a skyscraper:* huge glass needle
2. *the sound of an explosion:* rumble of distant thunder, cannon shot
3. *an intelligent student:* computer
4. *a crowded bus:* stuffed turkey, packed suitcase
5. *a slow-moving car:* snail, turtle, tank
6. *a pillow:* puffy cloud, flat pancake
7. *a narrow alley:* cave, tunnel
8. *greasy french fries:* slippery carrot sticks, glistening wet skin
9. *hot sun:* roasting oven, baking, sear like a flame
10. *a dull knife:* cutting with wooden utensil, frustrating as playing golf with the wrong club

Engage students in a discussion of the various figures of speech that they came up with for each item and have them decide which ones work best. They will see that good figures of speech are those that are fresh (not clichéd) and create a clear mental image.

The Jacket (p. 279)

■ Gary Soto

Essay Analysis and Discussion

Because this essay relies heavily on figurative language to help convey its point, you can use it as the basis for a classroom activity on figurative language that reflects the students' own experiences or points of view regarding adolescence. Working individually or in groups, students can create new examples of figurative language that serve the same purposes as those provided by Soto. For example, Soto begins his essay with the statement, "My clothes have failed me." Students should devise a statement that relies on personification and makes a similar point about the relationship between clothes and adolescence. In the same paragraph, Soto uses the simile "bitter as a penny" to describe feelings of envy for the happy couples at fifth- and sixth-grade dances. Students should come up with a different simile that conveys the same idea and is appropriate to the context Soto establishes in paragraph 1. They can then work through the essay, replacing each of Soto's examples of simile, metaphor, and personification.

Thinking Critically about This Reading

Soto's embarrassment comes from within himself. He feels the jacket is ugly and is so self-conscious about it that he attributes every negative—although common—childhood event to it. He feels he did poorly in school and was bullied and laughed at because he was wearing the jacket. Students may suggest that had Soto's mother given him the leather jacket he wanted, he would have felt secure and self-confident and wouldn't have let the "little things" get to him. Ask students to discuss a corollary situation: Imagine Soto really got the leather jacket. Do you think he would have ridiculed a classmate who had an ugly jacket the color of "day-old guacamole" (paragraph 2)?

Questions for Study and Discussion

1. Soto's jacket represents the insecurities he feels as an adolescent—insecurities concerning his appearance, his relationship with his peers, the way he is perceived by adults, his feelings about girls, and his overall need to fit in. By focusing his frustrations primarily on the jacket, Soto may avoid being overwhelmed by the emotional turbulence these insecurities can create.
2. The tree serves as a sanctuary for Soto, a place where he can temporarily escape the pressures of the adolescent world. In paragraph 10, he states that he would go to the tree and wait for something good to happen, or go there when he was upset "to think bad thoughts and watch my breath puff white and disappear." In other words, he was free there to act and think any way he wanted.
3. It is likely that Soto's mother bought him the jacket she did because that was all she could afford.
4. Soto's essay includes the following figures of speech:

   metaphor: *playground terrorist; propellers of grass*
   simile: *bitter as a penny; as if it were a stranger whose hand I had to shake; like an enemy; like braille; like a cup of crooked dice; like a scab*
   personification: *clothes have failed me; enough belts to hold down a small town; sleeve shriveled into a palsied arm; faces of clouds were piled up, hurting; my jacket, that green ugly brother who breathed over my shoulder*

Students' opinions about the purpose each figure of speech serves may vary, but they should recognize that, overall, Soto has selected elements within his examples that are appropriate for an adolescent's point of view. The figurative language helps to convey the emotional turmoil Soto experienced as a result of his jacket, so the essay would not be as effective without it.

5. In paragraph 3, Soto mentions his "mean brother." At the end of the essay, he refers to his jacket as "that green ugly brother who breathed over my shoulder." The connection between the two suggests that Soto's brother, like his jacket, was a source of adolescent discomfort in his life.
6. Students' opinions may vary widely on whether the jacket is the cause of Soto's grades falling or of his missing out on friendships with girls. This is a good question to explore as a class. The discussion should draw out contrasting views on whether clothes can, in fact, affect a person's self-esteem to the degree that they cause problems or whether they are only an outward manifestation of an underlying insecurity that was there to begin with and that is ultimately to blame for negative consequences.

Classroom Activity Using Figurative Language

Students might want to couple this activity with the prompt for journal writing that asks them to write about an article of clothing that had special significance for them growing up. Their attempt at personification can then convey the nature of that significance.

A Hanging (p. 285)

■ George Orwell

Essay Analysis and Discussion

Many students will find Orwell's essay very disturbing, but they should also find it relevant. It is interesting that, although "A Hanging" was written more than sixty years ago, it addresses some very modern issues, most notably that of capital punishment. It is a narrative, but it is also an extremely powerful and eloquent testimonial against the practice of putting a fellow human being to death. Notice how Orwell uses the two events that break the routine of the morning—the arrival of the dog and the prisoner's crying "Ram" on the gallows—to emphasize the awful nature of what is taking place. Yet, without those two events, the reader realizes, it would have been just another morning at the jail, an early morning routine that concludes with someone's death. Orwell's use of figurative language reinforces the bestial nature of the proceedings from the start—the condemned cells are "like small animal cages" (paragraph 1) and the guards handle the prisoner "like men handling a fish which is still alive and may jump back into the water" (2). Have your students look for other examples of figurative language. Also, discuss the ending with your students. Why do they think Orwell and the others felt so jovial and euphoric? What does the ending say about the jail workers and the jobs they must do?

Thinking Critically about This Reading

The variety of backgrounds underscores the universal approach to justice, and makes it apparent that no one culture is particularly cruel, bloodthirsty, or callous toward the kind of event that happened that day.

Questions for Study and Discussion

1. The appearance of the dog is dreadful to the executioners because it disrupts the routine. The dog disrupts the effort of the magistrates and other officials to carry out the execution in an orderly, reasonable fashion and to devalue and dehumanize the prisoner before he dies.
2. Neither the narrator's role nor the prisoner's transgression matters because Orwell is commenting on the practice in general, not on the legal aspects of this one case.
3. Orwell realizes that the prisoner is a human being, just like all the rest of them, and is experiencing life just as they are, even to the point of reasoning that puddles will make him wet, so they should be stepped around. The only difference is that his life is to be cut short. "One mind less, one world less" (10) means that for every human who is removed from the earth, there is one less unique perspective and understanding about the world.
4. Francis's story about the troublesome prisoner is ironic in that he was remonstrating the prisoner for inconveniencing those who were about to kill him!
5. "A sickly light, like yellow tinfoil" (1), "like the moustache of a comic man in the films" (2), "[the gallows] was a brick erection like three sides of a shed" (11), "almost like the tolling of a bell" (12), and so on.
6. The group is somber, almost automaton-like before the hanging (3 through 8) and ebullient, almost manic after the hanging (17 through 24). The superintendent was "moodily prodding the gravel with his stick" (3) and had a gruff voice; all are "aghast" at the glee of the dog. Afterward, it is a homely, jolly scene; the men are garrulous and laugh without knowing why. The shift in mood can be explained by the fact that they have gotten through this terrible event. Some students will notice that the police need a drink after the hanging.

Classroom Activity Using Figurative Language

This activity should not be terribly difficult for your students, but it will bring home how effective figurative language can be in communicating an image or atmosphere. Make sure they use familiar associations that communicate more to the reader than a simple description would. If you wish, have the students write a couple of similes or metaphors for the same actions on the part of those who are excited or pleased—how can they use figurative language to communicate a different mood from the same action?

CHAPTER 12 **Illustration**

A Crime of Compassion (p. 299)

■ **Barbara Huttmann**

Essay Analysis and Discussion

At the heart of Huttmann's dramatic and often shocking essay is the story of her young patient. In the beginning of her essay we meet him, a strong, confident, healthy young man. Then Huttmann proceeds in a chronological order to describe the rapid deterioration that ends in his death. Other things are happening as well: the collapse of his family and the nurse's own evolution from rule-abiding health worker to mercy "killer." Yet as dramatic as Huttmann's tale is, it remains a model of "show, don't tell." For Huttmann never asks us to weep—she moves us to tears with the details of the events she witnessed and the emotions she experienced. Even those who condemn her actions would be hard pressed to remain unmoved by the horrors that the young family experienced. Ask students to reread Huttmann's essay carefully to see how she sustains the dramatic atmosphere of her story. Which kinds of evidence were convincing and which were not? In the end, is she successful in convincing readers of the justness of her actions?

Thinking Critically about This Reading

Huttmann puts the word *life* in quotation marks to emphasize that the life her patient Mac was living was not one he wished to live. This emphasis also points to her argument that in situations like Mac's there really isn't a simple definition for life. Is it simply brain activity and respiration, or is there a question of quality and intent?

Questions for Study and Discussion

1. Huttmann did not have the legal right to end her patient's life. By that definition, she is a murderer. However, her defenders no doubt will point out that the definition of murder as the premeditated and malicious killing of a human being does not fit the circumstances of Huttmann's deed. She killed out of love, not hate, and the decision to do so was painful given her attitude that life is something that must be sustained and nurtured. As Huttmann wondered at the right of doctors to sustain life beyond reasonable

bounds, she no doubt questioned their right, and hers, to end it. That is why she argues so strenuously for a patient's right to make this terrible decision.

2. Huttmann's essay is as much a tale of her own struggle as it is the story of her patient's decline and death. She begins in paragraph 7 by telling us how often Mac had to be resuscitated and the terrible and grisly agony he went through. By paragraph 8, she is praying he will die but she has not yet thought of helping him to do it. In paragraph 9 she asks for a "no-code order," which only a doctor can issue. In other words, it is not illegal for doctors to allow a patient to die, only for a nurse to do so. When her request was refused, she contemplated the implications of failing to press the button. By paragraph 10, when Mac had undergone fifty-two codes, she began appealing to a higher court, a spiritual judge to question the necessity of her actions. She began to be haunted by the question that modern technology has made inevitable—Do we have the right to play God, not in taking life, but in sustaining it beyond all hope? Finally, she makes us witness her panic and fear as she makes the decision *not* to press the button. Her story is compelling and terrifying, and she spares us little of the terror she experienced in making her final decision.
3. As Huttmann explains in paragraph 18, a doctor may legally issue a no-code order. The hypocrisy for her is that the charge of murder is based not on intent but on which uniform a person wears.
4. In paragraph 7, Huttmann describes the work a team of nurses had to do over Mac's body: "The nurses stayed to wipe the saliva that drooled from his mouth, irrigate the big craters of bedsores that covered his hips, suction the lung fluids that threatened to drown him, clean the feces that burned his skin like lye, pour the liquid food down the tube attached to his stomach, put pillows between his knees to ease the bone-on-bone pain, turn him every hour to keep the bedsores from getting worse, and change his gown and linen every two hours to keep him from being soaked in perspiration." Such graphic descriptions are necessary to force the reader to see what Huttmann saw and, however feebly, to feel what Mac felt. She knows it is easy to make philosophical decisions about life and death from a distance. She wants to rub the readers' noses in the truth.
5. As her essay moves forward, Huttmann intensifies the story by going into lengthier detail about shorter periods of time. No doubt this is meant to parallel as much as possible the way in which Mac's pain escalated, not only in intensity but in the horror of its detail.
6. Quite simply, Huttmann means to say that as long as medical science and its practitioners have the means to keep patients alive and believe that they must do so, and as long as the decision not to resuscitate rests with the doctors, patients cannot legally choose to die.

Classroom Activity Using Illustration

This exercise has worked well in getting students to see the relationship between a thesis statement and what is necessary to make it credible and convincing. Of course, this exercise can also be used to have students generate a series of shorter examples, but here the focus is on the single example, which allows for some degree of depth and detail. You may want to have students think about possible examples and also compose one.

Be Specific (p. 306)

■ Natalie Goldberg

Essay Analysis and Discussion

Goldberg's message in this essay is simple and to the point—"Be specific." We all recognize when a writer is specific; the writing seems to come alive, to jump off the page. But beginning writers have difficulty being specific, using telling details. Goldberg offers some direct advice for students to start with: Give people and things names and provide a specific context (month, day, moment, etc.) for the situation about which you're writing. Not only does Goldberg give writers advice about being specific but she also demonstrates that advice in her own writing. In her final paragraph, Goldberg asks readers to "learn the names of everything: birds, cheese, tractors, cars, buildings." As a class exercise, generate lists of names for items in each of the categories she suggests.

Thinking Critically about This Reading

By being specific about what we call things, we can be sure to refer to those things correctly. Just as it is inaccurate to call Joe by the name of George, so it is with things. Goldberg says writers should refer to things by their specific names because "[w]hen we know the name of something . . . [i]t takes the blur out of our mind; it connects us to the earth" (paragraph 3).

Questions for Study and Discussion

1. Goldberg practices what she preaches in this essay. She's careful to "be specific." She "give[s] things the dignity of their names." And she set out to learn the names of everything, concentrating first on "the names of plants and flowers in my environment."
2. The lists help define the word *specific* because each list is made up of particular members of a general category. They forcefully show that names do, in fact, convey very precise images; each name on the list removes a

particular object from its category by bringing to mind a picture of that object in a setting furnished by the reader's imagination.

3. A writer needs to know not only the name of a particular thing, but the month, day, and moment of the context in which it is important (4). Precision in time is as important as precision in identity in making a subject real and immediate to the reader.
4. To know the name of something connects us to the earth—it makes us more awake and friendly toward the environment (3). It allows us to "penetrat[e] more deeply" into what is in front of us and to learn from it (5); it grounds us and makes us more attentive in a group (6).
5. According to Goldberg's example (addressing a person by her name rather than by "girl"), people—and by extension, things—are dignified when they are recognized by name as specific individuals instead of as members of a general class. "Integrity" implies uniqueness, wholeness, and self-worth.
6. Goldberg is addressing writers. In paragraph 4 she quotes William Carlos Williams: "Write what's in front of your nose." She mentions writing groups (6) and gives advice to "a writer" (7).

Classroom Activity Using Illustration

Possible answers for the blanks in each ladder of abstraction are pen, food, Native American, *The American Heritage Dictionary,* Essex Vocational/Technical High School, Tylenol Gel Caps.

For additional practice with being more specific, have students create their own ladders of abstraction (with one step on the ladder blank) and exchange them with classmates.

The Case for Short Words (p. 310)

■ Richard Lederer

Essay Analysis and Discussion

Many writers lose track of what writing is all about somewhere along the way. Instead of a medium of communication, it becomes a medium of vanity—the writer is out to impress readers with craft, not clarity. One of the easiest ways to spot this problem in a piece of writing is in its choice of vocabulary, as *use* becomes *utilize*, *try* becomes *endeavor*, and so on. Lederer's essay addresses this problem in two ways. He presents a standard, though eloquent, plea for the use of short words when long ones are not necessary. He supports his argument with evidence—academic studies that demonstrate that short words provide the foundation for the English language—and examples of great writing and speeches composed entirely of one-syllable words. Much of the impact of his essay, however, comes from how he illustrates his point in a more immediate manner. First, his four paragraphs of single-syllable words do a wonderful job of making his point that you can write well with only short words. Second, by presenting the student essays, he drives home the point that it does not take a great writer to make good use of short words—anyone's writing will benefit from using them where and when appropriate. Ask your students how many saw what Lederer was doing before he told them in the fifth paragraph of his essay. Have them reread the paragraphs. How does Lederer's use of all one-syllable words differ from his standard prose, as seen in the middle of the essay? Which is easier to read and understand?

Thinking Critically about This Reading

Such words can be called the "best" because everyone knows exactly what they are; if you use them, you do not have to worry about how advanced or specialized your audience is. The same advantage holds true for old versus new words.

Questions for Study and Discussion

1. Lederer says, "If a long word says just what you want to say, do not fear to use it" (paragraph 4). He is not trying to discourage the use of long words, but to encourage the use of more short ones where appropriate, as they can make essays easier to read and understand.
2. By having several quotes from those who are considered among the most effective writers and orators in history, Lederer proves that such great communicators do not seek to use long words just for the sake of showing off. Some of their best work is done with very simple tools. The inclusion of the ninth-grade essays demonstrates that it does not take the skill and polish of a great writer to use short words with great effectiveness.
3. Students have many choices—for example: "Big words can make the way dark for those who read what you write and hear what you say" (2). This metaphor communicates that the use of long words can obscure the meaning of what a writer wants to say, not make it easier to understand. "Short words are bright like sparks that glow in the night" (3) contrasts with the former piece of figurative language, communicating that short words are readily understood.
4. Students often feel pressure to come across as learned, formal, or smart in their writing, so they feel pressured to use fancy words. Lederer's point is that great writing often relies on short words, so the success the students have in completing the assignment supports his argument in favor of the use of short words.

5. Lederer's image of the sign will help readers retain the content of his essay. It is something that readers will remember even if they do not care to as they sit down to their next writing assignment.
6. Student responses will differ.

Classroom Activity Using Illustration

In a short piece of writing in which one is trying to explain or define a subjective or complex topic, an effective illustration is crucial to getting the point across. The ideal gift is a difficult thing to present to a reader, but the use of an example that captures the meaning of the ideal gift makes it concrete for the reader. You may wish to specify a particular situation—such as the birthday of a special friend, or a holiday with a relative—to help students narrow their choices.

Can I Get You Some Manners with That? (p. 316)

■ **Christie Scotty**

Essay Analysis and Discussion

Scotty asks readers to consider their own behavior with wait staff in restaurants. Using her personal experiences, she relates the different interactions she had in restaurants as compared with the professional world. Many students may have worked in the food service business themselves and may have firsthand knowledge. Ask students to look up the words *servant* and *server* in the dictionary. If possible, bring the *Oxford English Dictionary* definitions into the classroom. How did the meanings of these words evolve over time? Then ask students to brainstorm on each word for three minutes and jot down what comes to mind. You then may ask them this question: If someone is a "servant," is it ever okay to treat them as badly as Scotty felt some patrons treated her? While Scotty does not say so directly, what does she suggest is the best way to treat waiters and waitresses?

Thinking Critically about This Reading

Scotty wants to take potential business associates out to dinner so that she can see how they treat the wait staff. The dinner is a test: If her guests are rude, she will likely not want to continue doing business with them; if they are respectful, she will likely want to continue doing business with them.

Questions for Study and Discussion

1. Because they often find themselves answering such questions, students could have plenty to say about this. Some will say that people use the answers to evaluate the intelligence and potential of others. Some are bored

in their own jobs or even genuinely curious about what kinds of careers exist. While the question can be hard for the person answering, some people just use the question to start a conversation. You may also want to ask students why this question feels so hard to answer.

2. She says that some customers mumbled orders and did not look her in the eyes. Some interrupted her in midsentence to complain about the air conditioning being too cold or the sun being too bright. One man told her to go away because he was on the phone, then later asked what took her so long to get back to the table. The examples differ in that the first has to do with not acknowledging her, the second is about interrupting her and making demands in a rude way, and the third is about her being too attentive.
3. Because Scotty had had better experiences at the community newspaper, she knew she could be treated better. Also, she no longer felt that she did not deserve to be treated well. She says, "I came to expect friendliness from perfect strangers" (paragraph 11).
4. Scotty did find some rude treatment in the office setting. Her co-worker in advertising received calls in which people made direct and abrupt demands; "I called yesterday and you still haven't faxed—" (6) or "Hi, this is so-and-so over at the real-estate office. I need—" (7). Scotty hypothesizes that "[p]erhaps it was because their relationship centered on 'gimme,' perhaps it was because money was involved" (5). Students may agree, and you may want to have them cite examples from their own experiences. You may also want to ask whether her co-worker's personality may have been part of the problem. Students may say that when they did not enjoy a job they found themselves treated worse than when they loved it.
5. For Scotty, eye contact acknowledges the fact that she is a person as well as a food service provider. Students may say that being ignored is worse than being treated badly.

Classroom Activity Using Illustration

It's always a good idea to emphasize the five senses when having students describe or provide details. It is important to the success of this exercise that students be allowed to compare their lists of details for the object in question so that those having trouble generating details can see what others who find the exercise easier have done. As far as names for items are concerned, students should be made aware of the fact that having names for things has both positive and negative aspects. Certainly, common and proper names are a kind of experiential shorthand; when we have a name for something (e.g., Coke can) we don't have to spend a lot of time and effort signifying what we mean. However, the name of something can, for the writer, put the object at some distance from experience and lessen the importance and power of specific details.

What's in a Name? (p. 325)

■ Henry Louis Gates Jr.

Essay Analysis and Discussion

When examining this essay with students, have them note the vital role that dialogue plays in it once Gates arrives at the encounter between Mr. Wilson and Gates's father. Consider, in particular, the juxtaposition of the conversation Gates has with his father about why Mr. Wilson calls him "George" with the bit of dialogue that would spring up to break painful moments of silence when the adults in Gates's life were forced to acknowledge "one of those things." The first example of dialogue highlights the innocence with which Gates, the child, confronts a moment of racial awareness, while the second displays the more subtle, more sophisticated manner in which adults deal with similar moments.

Thinking Critically about This Reading

Gates's phrase "one of those things" refers to acts of prejudice and racism that African Americans face on a regular basis. It reflects Gates's purpose for his own story because such acts represent "a world that we could not affect but that affected us" (paragraph 12). He could not alter Mr. Wilson's attitude yet that attitude affected Gates significantly, as evidenced by his never again looking Mr. Wilson in the eye. Students' opinions on what the final statement means may vary, some believing it reflects Gates's resentment at Mr. Wilson's racist attitude, others seeing it as representative of Gates's diminished sense of self, knowing that Mr. Wilson views African Americans with contempt.

Questions for Study and Discussion

1. Students' views on the two opening quotations may vary considerably. Gates wishes to highlight how African Americans have been labeled, usually in a derogatory manner, while also recognizing the effect of such labels on self-identity among African Americans. Both quotations therefore connect with how Gates's experience hearing his father referred to as "George" affected his own sense of self.
2. Here, too, students may have differing views on Gates's reference to Trey Ellis's *Village Voice* essay. The key to their responses, however, may lie in how Gates frames the reference within the discovery that he had forgotten all about the incident when his father was called "George" until he read Ellis's essay. Chances are students will recognize the way in which

the things they read often trigger similar kinds of reminiscences. Whether they can envision themselves using such an opening approach in their own writing may depend, to some extent, on the amount and type of reading they do. One side benefit of Gates's allusion is that readers can refer to Ellis's essay in order to read another, perhaps more extensive, examination of the phenomenon of African American bynames.

3. Students' opinions about Gates's parents' own use of prejudicial words may vary. Before addressing this question, students may find it helpful to review Gloria Naylor's essay, "The Meanings of a Word," and in particular her discussion of words set within unique contexts and inflections, as well as her examination of her extended family's use of the term *nigger.*
4. The striking thing about the way Mr. Wilson is described in paragraph 4 is that despite Wilson's generally silent and unfriendly demeanor, Gates's father had managed to break through the brooding exterior to establish a kind of familiarity with him, enough so that they always spoke to one another. This makes Gates's discovery that Mr. Wilson calls his father "George" all the more confusing, and all the more painful.

Classroom Activity Using Narration

When discussing the results of this exercise, be sure that you examine the ways in which students deal with lapses in chronological order so that they avoid causing confusion for readers. Pay particular attention to the kinds of connections they make between paragraphs that show significant breaks in the chronological arrangement of events. After looking at students' strategies for narrating events out of sequence, discuss the variety of ways writers can achieve continuity and coherence when disrupting the chronology of their narration.

How I Got Smart (p. 330)

■ **Steve Brody**

Essay Analysis and Discussion

Brody uses the first three paragraphs of his essay to set up his point that sometimes a love of education is not born, it is made. The rest is a narrative presented chronologically to take us from his distaste for book learning to his "thirst" for it. This is a "one-joke" essay: The excerpts from the encyclopedia not only are used to support his thesis, but they also form the bulk of the dialogue with the girl Brody wants to impress. His lengthy discourses are punctuated with her short responses, which moves the narrative along smoothly. Brody makes good use of transitions to keep his story easy to read. However, just as frequently, he gets readers from paragraph to paragraph by moving them in time and space with transitions like "a few days later," "one day I was," and "and so it went." Students can study Brody's essay to observe his movement from one paragraph or one sentence to another with and without the use of transitional words.

Thinking Critically about This Reading

Brody's original incentive to read the encyclopedia was to impress his childhood crush Debbie. "I would henceforth become a seeker of facts. I would become chief egghead in English II and sweep the princess off her feet with a surge of erudition" (paragraph 9). After he failed to win Debbie's affections, Brody realized that he enjoyed reading the encyclopedia and had learned a lot. His second incentive was the quest for knowledge.

Questions for Study and Discussion

1. In each case, the following paragraph begins with a transitional term, such as *consequently, but, occasionally,* etc.
2. Dialogue always forces a writer to show and not tell. Brody's dialogue adds energy and life to his essay by letting the characters or players in this narrative speak for themselves. In witnessing the conversations between Debbie and the narrator and between Mrs. Larrivee and the narrator, we have a greater understanding of each person's personality and behavior and a greater appreciation of the humor in the situations than we would have had if Brody had simply reported what had happened. Notice that Brody is careful to start new paragraphs when speakers change and to use names or pronouns so that it's always clear who is speaking.
3. He had already "savored the heady wine of knowledge" and could not alter his course.
4. Brody's humor is affected by the stilted encyclopedia-style prose he tries to pass off as casual conversation.
5. Coleridge was an English poet (1772–1834). "The Rime of the Ancient Mariner" is probably his best-known work. It describes in "exotic and supernatural themes" the plight of a mariner, alone at sea with an albatross around his neck. Agamemnon, leader of the Greek forces in the Trojan War, was murdered by his wife Clytemnestra and her lover. Alexander Pope (1688–1744) was an English poet.
6. Brody's denial of any innate erudition at the beginning of his essay and his enthusiasm for learning at the end emphasize that the revelation of learning can happen to anyone and has little to do with higher intelligence. Also, by referring to Volume XIV, Brody reveals that he stuck to his resolve to read the encyclopedia.

Classroom Activity Using Narration

Students will point out that Brody devotes many paragraphs to his pursuit of Debbie and only two paragraphs to his realization that she already has a boyfriend. This activity provides an excellent opportunity to discuss emphasis and narrative time with your students. You might consider having students bring in sample narratives from their favorite books to show how different writers deal with these issues. Another idea would be to have students write about a shared experience, such as the first day in your class or a class field trip or presentation. Such an assignment would illustrate how each student emphasizes different pieces of the common experience.

Momma, the Dentist, and Me (p. 337)

■ **Maya Angelou**

Essay Analysis and Discussion

The editors of this text placed their own title on this selection from Angelou's *I Know Why the Caged Bird Sings*. Their title is appropriate for the content of the essay, but, given the complexity of Angelou's narration, other suitable options may also exist. This essay can, therefore, serve as a catalyst for discussion of how to choose an effective title. Ask your students to reread the essay with an eye toward providing it with a new title. Then, have them write suggested titles on slips of paper and turn them in so you can compile an anonymous listing on the board. Once you've completed the list, ask the students to vote on which title they like best, and when they've indicated their preferences, discuss why some titles were chosen over others. You will want to consider originality, ability to stimulate interest, and appropriateness to the content of the essay, as well as other factors the students may see as significant.

Thinking Critically about This Reading

Angelou goes on to say that on the white side of town, "[i]f the pain didn't di minish then, the familiar yet strange sights hypnotized me into believing that it had" (paragraph 6). Angelou's tooth began to hurt again when she passed the jail and encountered white children who taunted her. Angelou's pain relief is a metaphor for the contrasts between the black side of town (raw, painful) and the white side of town (protected, soothing).

Questions for Study and Discussion

1. Angelou's purpose is to show the kind of pain that bigotry and injustice inflict, and to show that such cruelty often fosters the desire for retribution in its victims.

2. The content of the two interchanges between Momma and the dentist is similar in that, in both cases, Momma exacts revenge on the dentist for his refusal to treat the young girl. But the way she achieves that revenge is different. In Maya's version, Momma "obliterates" the dentist with her angry words, rendering him weak and submissive under her power and authority. In Momma's version, although she speaks of the dentist and his nurse with contempt, the scene she describes is more subdued and less vengeful, but ultimately, more productive in getting Maya's toothache treated. The style of the two versions is very different. To use Angelou's words, the first displays an "eloquent command of English," both in the way Momma speaks and in Maya's description of events, while in the second, Momma uses her usual vernacular to recall the scene.
3. Angelou's chronological presentation helps her establish a clear and purposeful context for the scene at the dentist's office. In the narration leading up to the visit, she builds a sense of tension and frustration as she describes the pain of her toothache and her anxiety about approaching a white dentist. The chronological pattern also helps to juxtapose the two versions of what occurred between Momma and the dentist. The first-person point of view is crucial to the central idea of the essay because it shows Maya's desire for retribution firsthand, a desire that creates the fantasized version of the confrontation between Momma and the dentist. Her version becomes more poignant because readers come to feel what she is like and what motivates her, before they reach that scene. This makes the final statement more potent.
4. Angelou's essay contains the following similes: "as if a whitebreeze blew off the whitefolks and cushioned everything in their neighborhood" (6); "the way people hunt for shells" (18); "like little claps of thunder" (29); "like filling in a pie crust" (46); "like a piece of lint" (48); "thick as thieves" (48); and "like he was sitting on a pin" (48). Each simile works within its paragraph and all of the similes work together to provide a more vivid description of events.
5. Angelou's version of the episode describes what, for her, is a more just resolution of the situation: a Dodge City–style triumph over bigotry. The dentist is not only confronted, he is driven from town frightened and disgraced. To the child, it must have been a pale consolation that the dentist had to pay a few more dollars on his debt to the grandmother.
6. Angelou first uses exaggerated descriptions to indicate the magnitude of her pain: "I prayed earnestly that I'd be allowed to sit under the house and have the building collapse on my left jaw" (1); "seriously considering the idea of jumping in the well" (2); "I was certain that I'd be dead" (2); "the pain was more serious than that which anyone had ever suffered" (3). She then presents some startling metaphors to show her intimate connection to that pain: "I had frozen to the pain" (4); "the pain was my

world, an aura that haloed me for three feet around" (5). These references are important because they establish the extent to which she suffers physically; yet the physical pain subsides when Maya confronts the psychic pain of bigotry and injustice described in paragraphs 9 through 26, culminating in the dentist's refusal to treat her.

Classroom Activity Using Narration

Making a list rather than drafting is the important part of this activity. It's far easier for students to see a sequence of activities, and how it may be reordered, in list form than in a paragraph or essay. It is useful to discuss how drama is achieved through placement at the beginning or end of a sequence and what it takes to create a rising tension in a sequence of events.

The Story of an Hour (p. 346)

■ **Kate Chopin**

Essay Analysis and Discussion

Chopin lived in an era when women had few options. Those who did not marry and manage their family's household were referred to in pejorative terms such as "old maid" and "spinster" if they were known to be chaste, and as "eccentric" or worse if they had the hint of scandal about them. "The Story of an Hour" would not have much impact in these days of no-fault divorce and ever-increasing career opportunities for women, but, taken in the context of its time, it is a compelling story that raises many issues of the day. The journal prompt asks students to consider marriage on personal terms. Before students read the story, it may be a good idea to discuss what marriage meant for both men and women in the early 1900s. Some of them may know something about married life in that era, but they probably have not thought about it much as a reality. What is it like to be bound to someone with no hope of ever being released if the relationship sours? The swift progression of Mrs. Mallard's emotions—and she was married to a gentle man whom she was able to love at least some of the time—communicates how stifling the situation could be in Chopin's eyes.

Thinking Critically about This Reading

Her feeling of freedom is improper. One is not supposed to feel great joy so soon after the death of a spouse, so the natural reaction would be to fight it, at least initially.

Questions for Study and Discussion

1. Mrs. Mallard's friends and relatives see nothing other than pure grief at first, and they assume that she remains in that state. Her actual feelings are much more complicated. They include grief but are mixed with large portions of relief and joy.
2. Chopin is setting the scene in which Mrs. Mallard's epiphany is to occur. The descriptions distance the reader from the strong emotional nature of the situation. They establish that life is going on around her, even though she is in a state of suspended thought. The section effectively bridges the gap between the abrupt beginning of the story and the dominant reaction Mrs. Mallard has to her husband's supposed death, and it allows Chopin to acquaint the reader with Mrs. Mallard's physical setting.
3. The swift progression of Mrs. Mallard's emotions communicates the stifling effect marriage had on women. A more gradual, thought-out reaction would not have the same impact, because, once the grief has passed, the pleasure of regaining personal freedom is not a startling thing for the widow to feel. For her to feel it within an hour is startling, and by using the time element in her title, Chopin ensures that the reader does not miss the point.
4. The fictional narrative allows her to place thoughts in Mrs. Mallard's head, and it allows her to manipulate the events of the story to present her point. The psychology of marriage is something that would have been difficult for her to write about on a factual basis—especially in such a patriarchal society—but fiction is a medium in which she can present her point of view clearly and dramatically.
5. On an obvious level, Chopin couldn't have Mrs. Mallard narrate her own story because she is dead at the end. Chopin uses a third-person narrator so that we can observe Mrs. Mallard's reactions to the news of her husband's apparent death and her subsequent realization that she was now "free, free, free!" The third-person narrator's description of Louise Mallard as "a goddess of Victory" sets readers up for Brently Mallard's surprise appearance and for the final irony in Chopin's concluding sentence.

Classroom Activity Using Narration

The sentence progression is 3, 5, 2, 1, 4. Students may need to revise their first try at writing their own paragraph, because the exercise demands that the sentences be linked strongly to one another before they are scrambled. Writing about a progression of events without falling into a plodding, monotonous style of writing can be difficult, but students should try to make their paragraphs as interesting and smoothly linked as possible.

CHAPTER 14 **Description**

Subway Station (p. 353)

■ Gilbert Highet

Essay Analysis and Discussion

Highet's description of a subway station is an arresting piece to read because of the way he takes delight in the nauseating place. It is almost as though taking the time to examine it closely has imparted an interest value to the filth, the grime, and the murk. A good descriptive essay does the same thing for readers—no matter what it describes, it takes the time to examine something closely and carefully, and it communicates an impression that the reader may not have paused long enough to notice before. Highet's use of adjectives such as *leprous* and *abominable* gives the station an atmosphere that goes beyond dark and grimy—it makes it a place of interest because of its almost evil and unhealthy air. Students are asked to describe their classroom and other relatively familiar places in the exercises for this selection. Instruct them to take their time when they observe the places they choose to write about. After they make their lists of objects and adjectives, have them sit still for a while and just observe the details of their surroundings—they will probably notice more than they did in the process of writing things down.

Thinking Critically about This Reading

By *appreciate,* Highet means that he could take delight in a nauseating place. The sights pique his interest. He allows his eyes to linger, inspecting every aspect of the subway station.

Questions for Study and Discussion

1. The dominant impression that Highet creates is one of dirt, gloom, and neglect. The list of details will include lightbulbs "coated with filth," tiles coated with fifty years of soot, paint "peeling off like scabs from an old wound," and so on.
2. Students will give different responses to why Highet observes the subway station with zest and relish; he provides no explicit discussion of reasons in the essay itself. Perhaps he enjoys it because it yields such a rich tapestry of filth to observe—the closer one looks, the more dirt and neglect one can see.
3. The similes and metaphors are

   "as though it were a bolt hole in an abandoned coal mine"
   "paint was peeling off like scabs from an old wound"
   "looked like the hallway of a condemned slum building"

All of these descriptions convey powerful imagery and emphasize the disgusting nature of Highet's surroundings.

4. The advertisements include text from the Bible, a half-naked girl, a woman wearing a hat in the form of a hen sitting on a nest full of eggs, and a pair of girl's legs walking up the keys of a cash register. Allow students to have fun thinking of products that each of these might be advertising.
5. Highet is probably a regular rider of the subways. His eye for detail is acute, but his positive reaction to his surroundings indicates he is taking pleasure in observing familiar surroundings. If he were seeing it for the first time, he would likely recoil in horror and vow, when his train came, not to repeat the experience if at all possible. Instead, he says that the experience was over for the time, indicating he will soon be back to repeat it.

Classroom Activity Using Description

When you work on this activity with students, you may want to have them list the objects they see and connect them with adjectives that come to mind to describe them. When they decide what dominant impression they wish to communicate, they can use the objects that are related to the adjectives that best suit their purpose. Have the students compare their lists once they edit them down. It is likely that the students will be surprised that one room can yield such a large variety or range of dominant impressions.

Wyoming Clouds (p. 357)

■ **Verlyn Klinkenborg**

Essay Analysis and Discussion

Klinkenborg uses something as familiar as clouds and then adds levels of scientific background and poetic flourish to build a complex and powerful descriptive piece. Ask students to pick something to describe whether food (soup) or something in nature (trees) and try to mimic Klinkenborg's format. They can mix scientific information—soup cures for illnesses, for example—with vivid figures of speech to create a sense of drama. Klinkenborg uses clouds to give readers a sense of the Wyoming landscape; he makes clouds seem powerful when he writes of the "matron marching" (paragraph 5). How could this be done with trees, lakes, or other examples? How can something like rocks or snow seem powerful? Students could write about avalanches or flash floods.

Thinking Critically about This Reading

Klinkenborg means that the landscape of Wyoming allows the clouds to put on a spectacular show, which he goes on to describe in poetic detail.

Questions for Study and Discussion

1. Personification: "clouds have passed in migratory flight" (1), "the tight, blue-tinted hairdo of a matron marching westward in dudgeon across the sky" (5). Similes: "Mammatus clouds, as smoothly pebbled as a low-water beach" (4), "folded back upon themselves again and again like Damascus steel" (5). Metaphor: "metropolis of clouds" (1), "theater of wind" (1).
2. Students may say Klinkenborg uses logical and/or space order. He starts by discussing clouds and then moves in increasing intensity toward the buildup and release of a storm. He describes clouds generally in Wyoming, then the normal summer array, and then the storm process. What readers could find effective is how powerful and turbulent Klinkenborg makes clouds seem. He starts off softly and gently, and before readers realize it, they find themselves in the middle of a powerful storm with all sorts of unfamiliar shapes and forms.
3. Klinkenborg starts with a subjective and poetic description. By paragraph 3, however, readers realize that Klinkenborg has some knowledge of cloud types and storm terminology (*orographic, squall line, mammatus, pileus*). Klinkenborg, with the use of scientific tidbits, demonstrates that he and these clouds can be taken seriously. On the whole, students may see Klinkenborg as more poetic than scientific. He uses far more analogies and descriptive words than scientific terminology and references.
4. Students may enjoy and relate to the cloud analogies, saying that they too have found themselves pointing out clouds and assigning them shapes or names. Some are intense ("galactic gas jets") while others are humorous ("matron marching"). Students may find that the piece evoked various images and emotions.
5. Klinkenborg begins with an empty sky, moves through the theatrical play of the clouds, and ends as the clouds exit the stage. Students could say that the last image is a powerful one—how can something so large disappear? Students may or may not feel that this captures the essence of clouds for them. Some may consider the look of clouds from an airplane. They could describe this particular scene in a variety of ways—a war perhaps, or a herd of animals stampeding and then separating.

Classroom Activity Using Description

It's fun to see the variety of alternative terms the students are capable of producing, and it's helpful for some students to see that choosing the right word can make a very big difference in the effectiveness of their writing. Depending on the amount of time you have, this can also be a good time to teach students how to use a thesaurus, especially now that many students have this resource built into their word processing programs. Students should be made aware of both the pluses and minuses of using a thesaurus.

City of Islands (p. 361)

■ Pete Hamill

Essay Analysis and Discussion

Hamill gives readers a bird's-eye view of New York's five boroughs. In doing so, he asks us to look at and appreciate the area from this new perspective. Try reading the article aloud to students and ask them to close their eyes. How effective is the piece in evoking the images? Could they visualize it as well before hearing it read aloud? An interesting class discussion would come from demonstrating Google Earth (www.earth.google.com). If possible, go to a computer lab with a projector or use a classroom computer with Internet access and have students look up a familiar address—their home or workplace. The satellite photographs will provide an all-new view of this familiar place. Students can then write about how seeing from a new angle affects their perception of their surroundings.

Thinking Critically about This Reading

The simile provides readers with a sense of scale. Even if students have not seen the Statue of Liberty up close before, they are aware that it is large and can be seen from a distance on the ground.

Questions for Study and Discussion

1. A ground-based description would make it impossible for the reader to see the city in its entirety in one moment. Hamill's description would have to be a block-by-block, borough-by-borough analysis, creating a description much like a slide show.
2. Students will respond differently to this description. Hamill effectively gives readers a sense of spatial presentation.
3. These names serve as specific reference points for readers. For those who know the city, they evoke visual pictures as well as emotional responses. Hamill wants to evoke both and to keep his readers with him as he describes the city.
4. Hamill's diction is both general and specific. He refers to "Jamaica Bay" (paragraph 4) and "bright white beaches of Coney Island" (4). Other general and specific words include *Queens, Brooklyn, housing projects, Atlantic, subway track*, and *bridges*.
5. Hamill's description gives the reader the sense that New York is varied and large. With beaches, housing projects, harbors, rivers, and subway tracks, he paints a picture that combines the natural and the constructed landscape.
6. Hamill sees New York as an area filled with many well-known places, like Shea Stadium. He also has a great respect for the "geography and

history" (5) of the land—the history of "the harbor and the emerging port that drew the millions" (5). He also sees much contrast; Queens has "backyards and . . . the shimmer of tiny swimming pools" (4), while Brooklyn "is darker, older, a place of brownstone or brick, of aging tenements and ugly housing projects" (4). Some students may acknowledge that he seems to have more appreciation for the natural features, "the great harbor" (5), than for the architecture and infrastructure; "They lashed themselves together with bridges and miles of subway track" (5).

Classroom Activity Using Description

Different students will seek different pleasures from their favorite place. Communicate to them that while the appeal of the place may be obvious to them, it may not be obvious to other people, so they need to be careful in how they describe it. "Danger" may not be something that other people will understand as appealing, but the thrill and satisfaction of overcoming it is. "Serenity" is readily understandable, but what is it about the place that makes serenity possible there in a way that it is not possible elsewhere?

My Favorite Teacher (p. 365)

■ **Thomas L. Friedman**

Essay Analysis and Discussion

Friedman's description of Hattie Steinberg is built on examples that *show* the kind of influence she had on her students. As a class activity to demonstrate the role that examples can play in describing an individual, have students list important high school experiences involving teachers, good or bad. Once you have a sufficient number, discuss what each example reveals about the teacher-student dynamic, and have your students draw a descriptive conclusion about the teacher involved, based on the example. After completing this process for all the examples, you should have a list of experiences and conclusions that demonstrates the relationship between general observations and specific illustrations used to support those observations, or between *telling* and *showing*.

Thinking Critically about This Reading

Students may have varying interpretations of what Friedman means by this statement. Many of their responses will probably touch on the fact that the Internet provides information, but it doesn't help the user to develop character when it comes to applying that information.

Questions for Study and Discussion

1. Friedman's examples point out key aspects of his own career in journalism, thereby establishing the important role Hattie Steinberg has played in his life. His interview with an advertising executive for his high school paper, during which the advertising executive used a four-letter word that Friedman and Hattie decided to print, taught Friedman about the consequences of one's behavior. His description of his first published story for the school paper, for which he covered a lecture by and then interviewed Ariel Sharon, indicates the direction his career followed, focusing on issues in the Middle East. The *New York Times* was delivered every morning to Room 313. The paper exerted an enormous influence over his approach to journalism, beginning the professional path that led him from being Hattie's student to a successful columnist for the *Times*. Finally, Friedman's example about the "dot-com-Internet-globalization bubble" that burst impresses upon readers the real secret to success that Hattie passed on to him: fundamentals.
2. At the end of paragraph 10, Friedman presents characteristics that represent Hattie's understanding of fundamentals—reading; writing; arithmetic; church, synagogue, and mosque; the rule of law; and good governance. Friedman uses this series of items to illustrate how what Hattie taught about journalism applied to the larger concerns of life as well.
3. Examples of short sentences in Friedman's essay include

   "She wanted to teach us about consequences." (3)
   "Competition was fierce." (4)
   "His name was Ariel Sharon. First story I ever got published." (4)
   "She was a woman of clarity in an age of uncertainty." (5)
   "These fundamentals cannot be downloaded." (11)

   In each case, the short sentence emphasizes the key point developed in the paragraph in which it appears. Students' opinions about how the sentences affect them as readers may vary, but most will probably acknowledge the way the sentences contribute to the main ideas presented throughout the essay or the manner in which they create a sense of rhythm and fluency in the prose by varying sentence length and structure.
4. Friedman's repeated references to Room 313 reflect the deep impression the activities within that room made and the amount of time he spent there during high school. Now when he thinks of his experiences with Hattie Steinberg, he thinks of Room 313.
5. Students' opinions about which examples stand out for them and why Friedman chose those examples may vary. Whichever they select, however, the general idea conveyed should reflect Friedman's emphasis on Hattie's stern but principled and committed behavior toward her students.

6. Friedman believes that in the rush to make a lot of money quickly, the dot-coms "forgot the fundamentals of how you build a profitable company." Students may or may not agree with Friedman's assessment.

Classroom Activity Using Description

Here's an example of what students usually come up with for "a sports lover": never misses *Monday Night Football;* reads the sports page every day; uses dialogue with sports facts, comparisons, allusions; makes references to having played on teams in high school and college; gets *Sports Illustrated* or other sports magazines; has sports-related injuries; goes to sporting events; coaches Little League baseball.

CHAPTER 15 **Process Analysis**

How to Write a Personal Letter (p. 374)

■ **Garrison Keillor**

Essay Analysis and Discussion

Keillor has written the directional type of process analysis. He is instructing us in the art of letter writing. However, it suits the nature of the task that Keillor waits five paragraphs before he begins to list the actual steps in the process. First he wants to answer our silent questions: Why should I write? Who cares? What is a letter? Why is it important? Even as he takes us step-by-step from the first thoughts we give to our letter, to our signing it and stuffing it in an envelope, Keillor attends to the very personal, aesthetic nature of the task. Students can compare Keillor's thoughts about the writing process with Russell Baker's narrative about "Becoming a Writer" in Chapter 8. Ask students to underline key passages in both articles and map out the underlying approach each writer takes. Does one approach seem more effective than the other?

Thinking Critically about This Reading

Keillor is referring specifically to shy people who are unable to present themselves and their ideas in conversation.

Questions for Study and Discussion

1. Keillor thinks of a letter as a gift because it is given freely (or ought to be) and because it offers our friends a glimpse of the "real" us.
2. Keillor suggests that the first step in writing is to "get over the guilt of *not* writing. You don't 'owe' anybody a letter. Letters are a gift" (paragraph 6).

Large stationery is intimidating to the writer who thinks he or she has nothing to say, just as a plate filled with too much food is apt to take away a diner's appetite.

3. Keillor is writing a directional process analysis. He tells his readers that "We need to write" (3). Not only does he give us steps to follow when writing a letter, but also he anticipates problems that we might encounter and advises how to deal with them.
4. At the point that the writer's friend becomes real, he should write the salutation, take a deep breath, and plunge in.
5. Keillor addresses first the problem of not knowing where to begin. He suggests starting with the present. Next he says it isn't necessary to worry about form: "When you come to the end of one episode, just start a new paragraph" (12). Finally, Keillor advises the writer to ignore mistakes and keep going: "Let the letter cook along and let yourself be bold" (13). The three problems and their solutions are discussed in the order in which they would occur: the beginning, the middle, and the end of the letter.
6. By the end of the letter, the writer should know something he didn't know when he began, because "writing is a means of discovery, always" (13).
7. Students will be divided as to whether Keillor would consider an e-mail as much a "gift" as a traditional letter. Ask students to discuss which they would prefer to receive as a thank-you note or a party invitation, and have them explain why.

Classroom Activity Using Process Analysis

Preface this activity by telling your class that they need to avoid assuming knowledge on the part of the reader. Students are usually surprised at how difficult it is to write a process analysis so that a true novice can follow the steps. Even directing a simple task, like scrambling eggs, is a challenge when the directions are for someone who has never been in a kitchen. The student reviews should be stringent—"beat the eggs" could lead to disastrous results if not properly explained in the paper.

Here's How to Revive a Computer Even after an Evil Wizard Kills the Beast (p. 379)

■ **Bill Husted**

Essay Analysis and Discussion

Husted's article relies heavily on his ability to provide clear instructions. Ask students to identify three techniques he uses to simplify his writing. For example, would adding metaphors or using personification make the essay more complicated? Would using a more poetic style of writing as in "Wyoming

Clouds" by Verlyn Klinkenborg make it harder to stay focused on the details? For an interesting discussion, you might want to ask students whether they believe that computers will be easier or harder to fix in the future. Can Husted and people like him keep writing useful manuals, or are we doomed to rely on others to fix our machines? Car mechanics increasingly say that so much under the hood has become electronic, they cannot do as much to fix cars.

Thinking Critically about This Reading

Husted's statement serves as a warning to his audience. The statement calls upon those who have not had their computers crash to pay attention to his advice because they may need to use it one day. It also addresses those whose computers have crashed so that they will know how to fix the problem the next time it happens.

Questions For Study and Discussion

1. Husted uses a logical approach in organizing his essay, using checklist-like steps. This would also be a good approach for an essay about repairing cars or for one describing how to do a medical checkup.
2. Students may describe Husted's tone as friendly and cheerful, as when he uses the term "evil wizard" for his stepson. Phrases such as "a human hiccup" (paragraph 6) and statements such as "More machines get messed up from unneeded 'fixing' than by computer viruses or lightning" (6) keep the article light in tone.
3. Answers will vary. Some will say that mentioning the stepson is a lighthearted and playful way to begin. Others may defend it as a way of showing that these things can happen to anyone, even an expert. The stepson gives the essay context; otherwise it might read too much like an instruction manual.
4. Answers will vary. This could depend on a student's computer knowledge or interest in the essay. Husted uses few unnecessary terms; he does not fill the article with superfluous terminology. For new computer users, however, even this limited use of technical language could feel overwhelming.
5. Answers will vary. Even if his readers have not had their computer crash, he wants them to understand that it could. Equally important, he is writing to entertain his audience.

Students have fun with this activity. It's an exercise in following written directions. Even though each student is following the same set of directions, don't be surprised if their astro tubes don't look alike. Ask students whether any of the directions were difficult to follow, and, if so, how those directions might be improved. Ask students whether they relied primarily on the written or visual directions. Finally, recalling the specific directions in steps 6 and 9, have students fly their tubes.

On Dumpster Diving (p. 385)

■ Lars Eighner

Essay Analysis and Discussion

It is hard for anyone who has never faced homelessness to imagine life on the streets. Eighner, who became homeless after working and having a home for ten years, understands this. His essay about one aspect of homeless life, Dumpster diving—what he likes to call *scavenging*—incorporates concrete examples of the dangers and rewards of Dumpster diving. The image of pristine, still-frozen ice cream in a Dumpster is a powerful one, and one Eighner uses to explain the odd appeal of Dumpster diving. Discuss the final five paragraphs with your students, and how Eighner's essay may have changed the way they look at the material things that clutter everyone's life.

Thinking Critically about This Reading

Eighner means that those who Dumpster dive as a pastime to find free, interesting things have homes to return to and food to eat. They are the "dilettanti": dabblers only, not "the real deal." Those who Dumpster dive as a means of survival—the "professionals"—often don't have a choice but to eat others' discards.

Questions for Study and Discussion

1. Dumpster diving quite literally is jumping into large trash receptacles to find useful articles. Eighner says that he likes "the frankness of the word *scavenging*" (paragraph 3). It does not mislead in the way "foraging" does—it does not imply a gathering of natural goods; it implies living directly from refuse. He considers it a valid niche in society. A definition of scavenging is important enough for Eighner to include at the beginning because it establishes his view of this subject and because it establishes the frank tone maintained throughout the rest of the essay.
2. Eighner discusses the three main stages: the stage of shame and self-loathing; the stage of discovery, in which the scavenger discovers the wealth to be found in Dumpsters; and the stage of "professionalism," defined as being willing and able to eat from Dumpsters. Eighner provides vivid examples of the goods to be found in the Dumpsters that move scavengers through their period of shame. Such things as a working calculator and still-frozen ice cream indicate the thoughtlessness with which people throw things away (6). The discussion of food to be found and consumed in Dumpsters is more prosaic, but Eighner again provides specific examples.

Students will have different connotations for "dilettanti" and "professional," but they should indicate that there is a strong contrast between the two. Eighner establishes just how big a step it is to eat from Dumpsters by using these terms. Also, "professional" should imply that the person makes his or her living from it—that he or she is very good at it and that it is how he or she survives.

3. In paragraphs 4 through 12 Eighner describes the process of retrieving usable items from Dumpsters. New divers quickly discover that "people do throw away perfectly good stuff," and later they realize that "they must restrict themselves to items of relatively immediate utility." Eighner emphasizes the caution that is needed in evaluating edible items and confesses that even he makes an occasional mistake, resulting in dysentery. Eighner's title suggests a reflective, philosophical treatment of the subject. "How to Dumpster Dive," on the other hand, has the wrong feel; that title would suggest that Eighner is giving practical advice or directions, which he isn't.
4. Eighner has learned to take what he can use and let the rest go (13) and that material being is transient (14). He learned not to grab for objects just for the sake of having them, and he has found a peace that he believes eludes the "rat-race millions," confounded as they are by their consumer society (16). Eighner believes that Dumpster diving "has serious drawbacks as a way of life" (12). He suffers dysentery at least once a month.
5. Eighner discusses the concrete aspects of Dumpster diving to teach readers what it is like—what can be found in Dumpsters, how scavenging affects its practitioners, in what ways scavenging is a potential hazard, and so on. It is only from this base of knowledge that Eighner can then discuss the abstract, particularly the transience of material objects. For those who have never found such things as new running shoes or working calculators in Dumpsters, a discussion of transience may have little meaning. Eighner's concrete experiences give his abstract lessons credence.
6. Dumpster diving is a process. If the reader is able to understand how it is done, including its inherent challenges, problems, and rewards, it is then far easier to understand any lessons that may be learned from it. It is therefore a very effective strategy for Eighner to provide readers with a process analysis of Dumpster diving before presenting his conclusions or arguments regarding what he has learned from it. Students will give various answers to the question, but they should explain why it is important to present the process they choose before presenting a related conclusion or argument. Why is it important to present exactly what happens or how to do something before proposing an argument based on the process?

Classroom Activity Using Process Analysis

Recipes offer wonderful examples of directional process analysis, and Frances Mayes's recipe for lemon cake is no exception. Students will have various responses to reading this recipe depending on their interest or experience with cooking and food in general. Most will find it interesting to read because of its conversational tone and the writer's enthusiasm for the cake, but it's clear that the author assumes that the reader knows something about cooking. Although Mayes's recipe is interesting to read in paragraph form, it would be easier to follow if the ingredients were listed together followed by the individual steps for making the cake. Have students divide Mayes's paragraph into the individual steps they would follow if they were to make the cake. In the context of this analysis students might discover the need for directions such as preheating the oven or softening the butter and the need for an explanation on how the doneness test works, for example. Finally, this activity is sure to be a hit if you bring a lemon cake to class for a taste test.

CHAPTER 16 **Definition**

What Is Crime? (p. 394)

■ Lawrence M. Friedman

Essay Analysis and Discussion

Friedman offers readers a discussion of crime from a legal perspective. Many readers are surprised by what does not constitute a crime. On the other hand, Friedman points out that society decides what is a crime. This essay lends itself to some interesting writing activities. Have students pick two or three of Friedman's examples of non-crimes, such as breaking a contract, cheating on a spouse, poor driving, and overcharging at restaurants. Have them argue both for and against making these actual crimes, according to the legal definition. What would be gained or lost by doing this? Remind them of the different legal ramifications, according to the essay. You may also have them debate other issues, like the decriminalization of marijuana.

Thinking Critically about This Reading

Friedman states that society deems illegal that which upsets the stability of society. First comes the social judgment, then the legal judgment.

Questions for Study and Discussion

1. According to Friedman, crime "is a *legal* concept" (paragraph 3); what makes some conduct criminal and other conduct not is the fact that some acts, but not others, are "against the law."

2. In a criminal case, "society is the victim, along with the 'real' victim" (3). The crime can be punished without the victim's consent, and the state pays for the prosecution. In civil cases, the defendant cannot be incarcerated and does not receive a criminal record. The injured party manages and pays for the case, not the state. The case can be dropped.
3. Society is the victim because it has decided that the criminal act harms everyone, not just the individual. Student answers to the second part of the question will vary.
4. He cites lying, cheating on a spouse, overcharging on restaurant bills, and psychological abuse as examples of awful acts that are not considered crimes. He also cites breaking contracts, driving carelessly, slandering, and infringing copyrights as examples of acts that while detrimental to society are not considered crimes.
5. Friedman wants readers to remember that the legal status of a behavior does not necessarily determine the negative impact it has on the culture. Although breaking contracts or cheating on spouses can have a hugely detrimental effect on those involved, it is society that determines which acts are crimes. He wants readers to see the role they play in determining which acts are legally considered a crime rather than a civil offense.

Classroom Activity Using Definition

This is a simple exercise in critical thinking, requiring students to see a given item as being both a part of some larger class of items that share certain characteristics as well as differentiated from the other members of that class by certain distinguishing features. Not all students will be able to differentiate a tenor saxophone from other types of saxophones in the woodwind instrument class, so it may be necessary to have someone in the class who knows this narrower subject area offer assistance. (You may want to prepare yourself for the possibility that no one knows that the saxophone is a nineteenth-century invention of Adolphe Sax and that there are eight types of saxophone, each representing a different tonal range. Of these eight types, only four are widely used: the B-flat soprano, the E-flat alto, the B-flat tenor, and the E-flat baritone.)

The Handicap of Definition (p. 398)

■ **William Raspberry**

Essay Analysis and Discussion

Raspberry wants readers to consider how stereotypes can hold us back. In paragraph 2, he offers examples of how "black" is used as a compliment, and then in paragraph 3 shows how "black" could be used as an insult. This lends itself to an interesting discussion. Do positive and negative connotations apply to categories of identity other than race, such as gender, income, religion, political party affiliation, region, or sexuality, for example? Ask students to write about three categories they themselves fall into. What are the negative and positive connotations of those categories? Then, ask them to broaden those categories. How are they limiting? How could they be rethought and made more positive? How would students like to redefine them?

Thinking Critically about This Reading

According to Raspberry, because the definition of "black" is so narrow, black children feel that certain qualities are not theirs to have. Raspberry suggests that the definition of "black" causes African Americans to limit their aspirations to the areas of sports and entertainment.

Questions for Study and Discussion

1. Raspberry's purpose is to argue that the definition of what it means to be black is too narrow. He also argues that such a limited definition may encourage black people to feel that certain qualities are not theirs to have, such as being studious, judicious, educated, or well mannered, and that emulating and embodying these qualities can be seen as "selling out" or being other than black.
2. Some students will say his essay applies to everyone because he mentions Chinese people, blacks, and Jews. Because most of the article focuses on being black and challenging the assumptions about being black, readers could assume it is intended for a black audience; he clearly wants to improve black children's views of themselves. While writing to a white audience could prevent them from limiting black children, it is black children and their families who need to change the most. In paragraph 15 Raspberry writes, "Somehow, we have to make our children understand that they are intelligent. . . ." Here he tells us that his audience is other black parents. His good advice could be useful for all parents.
3. In paragraphs 1–4, Raspberry talks about both the positive and negative connotations of being considered "black." In paragraphs 5–7, he discusses the connotations of being considered "white" and how it can be used as a put-down among black people. In paragraphs 8–11, he asks readers to consider the possibilities if we could only free our children from the limitations of such narrow definitions of blackness and identity. In paragraphs 12–16 he talks again about some of the limiting assumptions black people make about themselves. He says that if they perpetuate these stereotypes, black children will surely fail.
4. Raspberry's point is that the negative and limited definition of what it means to be a black man has created a negative and, arguably, destructive model for young black men to emulate. He shows the effect of adhering to a limited idea of identity and self.

5. Raspberry wants people to rethink the stereotypes cultures have adopted and broaden the definition of being black. By challenging stereotypes, he challenges readers to stop limiting themselves. Just as whites cannot use their race as an excuse for poor math skills or lack of athletic ability, blacks can no longer blame their race for physical aggressiveness or poor academic performance. We need to broaden our definitions.

Classroom Activity Using Definition

Students' definitions of these terms will surely differ. Ask them to discuss how their definitions are similar and different. How do age, gender, ethnicity, religion, and socioeconomic status, for example, enter into our thinking when we think of definitions?

The Company Man (p. 403)

■ **Ellen Goodman**

Essay Analysis and Discussion

Ellen Goodman's essay, like W. H. Auden's poem "The Unknown Citizen," uses irony and sarcasm to expose Americans' penchant to become workaholics. She develops her definition of "company man" by carefully showing readers what Phil is as well as what he is not. Ask students if they make a distinction between a *company man* and a *workaholic*. Have them share their own experiences with a parent, relative, or friend who is a "company man" or workaholic and to describe the defining personality traits of that person. Explore the reasons why some people become overinvolved with their schooling or careers to the exclusion of other facets of their lives (for example, recreation, relationships, health, and so on). Finally, ask students what they think will be their own priorities after they graduate and take a job.

Thinking Critically about This Reading

This statement illustrates how small a presence Phil had in his own home and with his own family. Phil and his youngest son were, essentially, familiar strangers whose only commonality was that they shared a roof, much like neighbors in an apartment building who know each other by sight but speak no more than the occasional hello as they come and go.

Questions for Study and Discussion

1. Although some people look at a *company man* in a positive light—an employee who is reliable and shows extreme loyalty to his employer—Goodman does not. She calls Phil—the company man in this case—a "workaholic." For Goodman, the two terms are synonymous. A workaholic

is someone for whom work is a compulsion, one who takes the behavior of the workplace to an extreme, who never has a quitting time, and who sacrifices everything in life for the sake of a job. Ask students about the suffix *-aholic;* where else have they seen it used?

2. The phrase "Important People" ironically implies those who spend all their time on work and work-related events, trying to acquire money, position, and power.
3. Goodman uses this selection to issue a warning to those who are in danger of falling prey to the same circumstances that eventually killed Phil. The cold, detached tone of the essay matches the cold, detached attitude of Phil toward what really should have been the most important things in his life—his wife and children.
4. Goodman's unemotional tone enhances the irony and sarcasm of the essay. Her diction of irony and sarcasm is encapsulated in her descriptions of Phil. She writes about how Phil acknowledged weekends by wearing a sports jacket to the office instead of a suit. He is described matter-of-factly, being "of course, overweight by 20 or 25 pounds." He always ate lunch—egg salad sandwiches—at his desk. Have your students find other examples of Goodman's sarcastic and ironic diction.
5. The time of Phil's death is repeated to drive home the irony that he died at 3:00 A.M. on a Sunday, a time when hardly anyone is working at all.

Classroom Activity Using Definition

This activity encourages students to explore how connotations work, and how different people have different associations with some words. For example, some people think that a "go-getter" is a self-motivated, determined person, while others might see such a person as pushy, aggressive, or selfish. As writers, we all need to be aware of the connotations that our audience might bring to the words we use.

CHAPTER 17 **Division and Classification**

The Ways of Meeting Oppression (p. 412)

■ **Martin Luther King Jr.**

Essay Analysis and Discussion

In addition to being an excellent example of division and classification, King's essay is a model of how to achieve unity between paragraphs. To illustrate this, have students identify the topic sentence in each of King's paragraphs and make a list of those statements. They should come up with the following:

1. "One way is acquiescence: the oppressed resign themselves to their doom."
2. "There is such a thing as the freedom of exhaustion."
3. "So acquiescence—while often the easier way—is not the moral way."
4. "A second way that oppressed people sometimes deal with oppression is to resort to physical violence and corroding hatred."
5. "Violence as a way of achieving racial justice is both impractical and immoral."
6. "Violence is not the way."
7. "The third way open to oppressed people in their quest for freedom is the way of nonviolent resistance."
8. "It seems to me that this is the method that must guide the actions of the Negro in the present crisis in race relations."
9. "Nonviolent resistance makes it possible for the Negro to remain in the South and struggle for his rights."
10. "By nonviolent resistance, the Negro can also enlist all men of good will in his struggle for equality."

This list demonstrates how tightly King's ideas are connected as he moves from paragraph to paragraph. The supporting information that surrounds these topic sentences explains and strengthens the main idea of each paragraph, but it is the close connection between those main ideas that gives the essay its unity and makes King's logical argument, and the presentation of the ways to meet oppression, so easy to follow and understand.

Thinking Critically about This Reading

The "freedom of exhaustion" refers to a kind of giving up that engulfs the slave to the extent that he doesn't even "mind" his slavery any more, and if he doesn't mind, then he is "free" to do nothing about it.

Questions for Study and Discussion

1. King's purpose is to argue for nonviolent resistance. By classifying the types of resistance, King makes clear that there are essentially three ways to deal with oppression, and that for him only one of these options, nonviolent resistance, is viable.
2. The principle of division that King uses is the way oppressed people react to the oppression.
3. The order that King uses runs from the option that is easiest and least effective to the option that is most difficult and most effective.
4. Slaves become accustomed to being slaves. They will bear the ills slavery offers rather than risk other, unknown ills.

5. For King, one who acquiesces "increases the oppressors's arrogance and contempt" (paragraph 3). One who resorts to violence uses a means that "never brings permanent peace" (4). King shows that he does not favor acquiescence by using the following words and phrases: *resign* (1), *doom* (1), *prefer to remain oppressed* (1), *slaves* (1), *fleshpots of Egypt* (1), *worn down* (2), *give up* (2), *negative freedom* (2), *cooperate* (3), *evil* (3), *coward* (3), *inferiority* (3), *sell* (3). King shows that he does not favor violent resistance by using the following words and phrases: *resort* (4), *corroding hatred* (4), *momentary* (4), *temporary* (4), *impractical* (5), *immoral* (5), *humiliate* (5), *annihilate* (5), *thrives* (5), *bitterness* (5), *brutality* (5), *cluttered* (5), *wreckage* (5), *succumb* (6), *temptation* (6), *desolate night of bitterness* (6), *endless reign of meaningless chaos* (6). King shows that he favors nonviolent resistance by using the following words and phrases: *quest* (7), *truths* (7), *guide* (8), *rise to the noble height* (8), *loving* (8), *passionately* (8), *unrelentingly* (8), *full stature as a citizen* (8), *great opportunity* (9), *lasting contribution* (9), *sublime example of courage* (9).

Classroom Activity Using Division and Classification

Here are some possible classification criteria for the first group, Hobbies:

sports	sedentary activities
spectator sports	physical activities
participatory sports	

Friends, Good Friends—and Such Good Friends (p. 417)

■ Judith Viorst

Essay Analysis and Discussion

An analysis of the division-and-classification section of this essay will reveal two important features: its consistency in structure and its variety in development. For the most part, Viorst uses a three-step approach in her categories of friends: First, she defines the type of friend being discussed; second, she offers examples of the type; and third, she provides further clarification to reinforce her definition. The consistency of this pattern makes it easier to follow along as she goes down her list of numerous kinds of friends. She achieves variety in the ways she presents the further clarification in step three. She makes use of examples from women friends, dialogue from women friends, her own additional analysis, examples from her own experience, and various combinations of these to clarify the main points of her categories. Discuss this method of organization and development with your students and, when you've finished, see if they can offer additional supporting evidence for any of Viorst's categories, based on their own experiences. Then have them decide where that evidence would fit within the three-step structure of her essay.

Thinking Critically about This Reading

Students will likely realize that Viorst is saying that historical friends are important because, as she says, "we're still an intimate part of each other's past" (paragraph 15). Ask students to discuss the people they consider historical friends. How do they think their lives would be different if they didn't have these friends "who put us in touch with an earlier part of ourself"?

Questions for Study and Discussion

1. Viorst has come to see that friendships are "conducted at many levels of intensity, serve many different functions, meet different needs, and range from . . . soul sisters to . . . casual playmates" (3).
2. Viorst's purpose is to make her readers understand the many different kinds of relationships that fall into the general class of friendship. Classification is clearly an appropriate strategy because it helps to clarify the distinct types of friends.
3. Viorst's categories are convenience friends; special-interest friends; historical friends; crossroads friends; cross-generational friends; part-of-a-couple friends; men who are friends; and medium friends, pretty good friends, and very good friends.
4. Viorst states in paragraph 3 the principles of division that she uses in this essay.
5. Viorst numbers and labels each category and provides at least one memorable example of each type of friendship.
6. Viorst's tone is informal, almost conversational. It is certainly appropriate given her subject matter—friends—and her audience—*Redbook* readers, women 25 to 35 years old.

Classroom Activity Using Division and Classification

This exercise works wonderfully when students work in small groups to divide and classify the figures. Review the division-and-classification tree diagram on page 411 in the introduction to this chapter. Students can start by identifying all the variables—hair, eyebrows, position of mouth, necktie type, necktie shape, necktie design. Next, they need to decide which feature they want to use first as a basis for division. For example, one group might start by dividing the fifteen heads into two groups—one with hair, the other without. Then, they would divide these two groups, based on another category—say, necktie type. Students continue dividing and classifying until they exhaust the variables. Have students compare their division-and-classification tree diagrams. What conclusions, if any, can they draw from their diagrams?

Four Types of President (p. 426)

■ James David Barber

Essay Analysis and Discussion

This essay lends itself to an interesting comparison with Merrill Markoe's essay "Who Am I?" in Chapter 10. Ask students to read or reread Markoe's essay and consider whether Barber's personality evaluation seems to have more or less validity than what Markoe found on the Internet. Do Barber's groupings sound more valid, consistent, meaningful? If so, why? What makes his assessments more sound? Or, alternatively, are Barber's groupings just an interesting way to talk about past presidents?

Thinking Critically about This Reading

Barber means that presidents are individuals with their own senses of self, purpose, and legacy. Each person who becomes president makes a unique imprint on the office and hopes to shape it to his own personality. No president is a machine.

Questions for Study and Discussion

1. *Activity-passivity* relates to how much energy each man invested in his term. Was he up all hours of the night or did he go to bed early? *Positive-negative* refers to the attitude each held toward his work. Was he happy to be handling the issues and responsibilities of the presidency? Or, did leadership feel like a burden or a civic duty? The categories are like the x-axis and y-axis on a grid; leaders can fall into any one of the four quadrants. Because they are like quadrants, there is a great deal of flexibility within Barber's assessment.
2. *Active-positive:* These presidents enjoy activity. They tend to be productive and adaptive, with a positive vision of themselves. They want "rational mastery" (paragraph 7), moving toward "well defined personal goals" (7). *Active-negative:* "intense effort and relatively low emotional reward" (8). These men are "ambitious, striving upward, power-seeking. . . . Life is a hard struggle to achieve and hold power" (8). *Passive-positive:* "receptive, compliant, other-directed character" (9). These men want to be agreeable rather than assertive; they tend to have low self-esteem and superficial optimism. They want to be loved, appreciated, and to create good feelings. *Passive-negative:* These men are known for their "dutiful service" (10). They feel useless, have low self-esteem, and are in politics because they feel they are supposed to be. These men emphasize vague principles and want to stand above politics.
3. Barber starts with the most active presidents and moves down to those who are least interested in the office. In paragraphs 2 through 6, he sets

up the framework in which he will discuss the presidents and explains and justifies his outline. Paragraphs 12 through 15 give examples that correlate with the categories explained in paragraphs 7 through 10. Barber becomes more detailed as he continues.

4. He classifies George Washington as passive-negative because he sought stability rather than growth, was reserved, and wanted to leave office as quickly as he could. John Adams is categorized as active-negative because he took much action (he had the Alien and Sedition Acts passed and almost started a war with France) and was irascible, much given to work and worry. Jefferson is seen as active-positive: While he had problems, he "combined a clear and open vision of what the country could be with a profound political sense" (14). Barber calls James Madison passive-positive because of his compliance, his inability to stand strong against the warhawks, and allowing the nation to drift into war. He left the country close to bankruptcy.
5. Barber feels that a man's personal past is the strongest indicator for his "presidential future" (16).
6. Barber's categories provide a scheme by which to evaluate the effectiveness of presidents and the influence of their administrations on American history.

Classroom Activity Using Division and Classification

Barber uses words and phrases such as *aloof, withdrawing, stability, innovation, peaceful, worry, impatient, repression, tolerate, delightful humor, famous, compliant, urging combat, clear and open sense.* You may want to ask students how Barber's classification system could be applied to types of teachers, parents, or local government officials.

CHAPTER 18 **Comparison and Contrast**

Two Ways of Seeing a River (p. 438)

■ **Mark Twain**

Essay Analysis and Discussion

This selection from Twain's *Life on the Mississippi* is remarkable for the way that it shows how one's perception of something—in this case, Twain's perception of the river—can change with education. With Twain's knowledge of steamboat piloting comes the ability to differentiate between the "appearance" of the river and the "reality" of the river. What once appeared as "graceful circles and radiating lines" (paragraph 1) on the river's surface are now for Twain "a warning that that troublesome place is shoaling up dangerously" (2). Extend the discussion of Twain's experience to other arenas, and ask students to share times when knowledge has changed their views of something.

Thinking Critically about This Reading

The appearance of the river is one of beauty, poetry, and grace in the first paragraph, but in the second paragraph Twain describes the reality of the river. Now that he works on the river, Twain sees the river in a practical way, translating previously ethereal images into guidelines used by steamboaters.

Questions for Study and Discussion

1. Block organization is used in this essay. The only other option in a comparison and contrast selection would be a point-by-point organization, which would involve constantly going back and forth between the two views to show specific examples. This would ruin the narrative flow.
2. The analogy of a doctor being unable to appreciate human beauty because he or she has gained too much knowledge about the practicalities of human beings and their illnesses is effective and appropriate. In addition, by providing an example that is vastly different from his own experience—doctor and steamboater—Twain shows the reader a broad spectrum of examples. The reader realizes that, with almost everything, the acquisition of knowledge comes at the cost of losing an elemental—and innocent—response to beauty.
3. "Long, ruffled trail," "shone like silver," "boiling tumbling rings . . . as many-tinted as an opal," and "splendor that was flowing from the sun" are examples of simile and metaphor found in this essay. Have your students find others—all of paragraph 2 directly compares and contrasts with the views expressed in paragraph 1.
4. According to Twain, there are two ways to see the river, but one option is removed once the river becomes his place of "business." Becoming an adept steamboater was a triumph for Twain, but there was a trade-off. "I had made a valuable acquisition. But I had lost something, too . . . which could never be restored to me. . . . All the grace, the beauty, the poetry, had gone out of the majestic river!" (1).

Classroom Activity Using Comparison and Contrast

The key to this activity is to have students compile lengthy lists of descriptive details for each of the places they are comparing and contrasting. The more exhaustive their lists, the more they will see similarities and differences, and it is from the similarities and differences that they will draw conclusions. This exercise works well when students work in pairs. After fifteen to twenty minutes, have the students present their lists and preliminary conclusions to the class for discussion.

Mac or PC: There Is Simply No Comparison! (p. 443)

■ **Del Miller**

Essay Analysis and Discussion

Miller challenges a lot of the reasoning people offer for not buying a Mac. He focuses specifically on the Mac versus the PC. He also challenges readers to start thinking about why they choose what they choose and how many of these decisions are uninformed. Ask students if they could argue against the iPod in favor of other digital music players. What are the misconceptions about other players? Why do people head for the iPod?

Thinking Critically about This Reading

As Miller states in paragraph 4, "When I look around at what the bulk of the computing public actually uses their computer for, I see absolutely no reason why a significant portion of them couldn't switch to the Macintosh tomorrow and be perfectly pleased with the results." He cites file compatibility, games, and cost as reasons why Macs should be attractive to PC users.

Questions for Study and Discussion

1. Miller's purpose is to explain to a Mac-friendly audience why the general public tends to buy PCs instead of Macs and to answer key questions in the Mac versus PC debate. Some students will feel that Miller adequately addresses each of the concerns. He identifies the main objections and explains how Macs overcome each one. Some students will say that even though he does a good job of correcting misconceptions and arguing why a PC might be overkill for the average user, he does not make an overwhelming case for buying a Mac because he does not articulate how Macs are better or easier to use than PCs. While students may not be convinced to buy a Mac, they may be willing to consider one in the future.
2. Miller is writing for the Mac-friendly audience. His essay first appeared in MacOpinion.com, an online magazine for Mac owners, users, and enthusiasts, but students may say he is writing for the average computer user. Miller is passionate in his belief that Macs are a good choice for the average user, addressing and refuting each anti-Mac point in order to convince his audience.

3. Miller compares Macs and PCs on cost, program computing functions, game availability, and consumer perceptions. He organizes the article by first acknowledging the concerns that most people have about Macs, and then addressing each concern to demonstrate the Mac's ability to overcome it. He uses headings to help define his organization, opening the essay with the question "Why don't more people buy Macintosh?" This leads to the conclusion and final heading that there is "Simply No Comparison" when consumers consider computers.
4. Miller claims people do not buy Macs because "[p]eople don't even look at the Macintosh as an option" (21). People think they are too expensive, do not have enough software, and are not very compatible with other programs. People don't want the hassle of switching.
5. Miller provides information regarding cost, compatibility, and ease of converting. Because readers know he wants to convince them to try Macs, he chooses the types of differences that speak to their concerns. He could have spoken of the technical differences; this could have turned away the average computer user who cares more about cost and usability than technical details.
6. Most students probably expected Miller to make a case for one computer over another. However, it becomes clear that despite point-by-point comparisons in which the Mac prevails over the PC, Miller says that the reason PCs dominate the market is because the majority of consumers simply do not consider Macs and do not compare the systems. Miller argues that PC purchases are made by rote and that this would not be the case if consumers actually compared the two products.

Classroom Activity Using Comparison and Contrast

Students' opinions on the point of Britt's paragraph may vary. But one thing she no doubt hopes to accomplish is to undermine the sense of superiority that people often associate with being thin. She does this by contrasting the characteristics she has perceived in fat and thin people, organizing her paragraph by linking the physical characteristics of the two types with attitudes and behaviors. Ultimately, Britt shows that fat people are *not* "neurotic, sick, sad people."

A Battle of Cultures (p. 451)

■ **K. Connie Kang**

Essay Analysis and Discussion

Kang's comparison-and-contrast piece is based on conflict. The reference to the conflict in the first sentence indicates clearly that differences exist between African Americans and Korean Americans. Kang then contrasts the two cultures to explain the root causes of the conflict. Kang organizes her essay very effectively. Paragraphs 1 through 5 are used to establish the surface problems. Note how Kang makes paragraph 6 a very effective one-sentence transition into the cultural contrasts that underlie the problem. She can then explore what these differences are and how they contribute to the misunderstanding, such as the Korean cultural bias against smiling, in paragraphs 7 through 14. Paragraphs 15 through 20 suggest simple solutions to the problem and comment on the role of everyone in an ethnically diverse democracy. Have your students write a comparison-and-contrast essay based on conflict. Direct them to follow Kang's organization by beginning with the surface conflict, then making a transition to the contrasts that contribute to the conflict.

Thinking Critically about This Reading

Students will be divided on this question. Encourage class discussion by asking students to debate the issue. How many of the students think Kang is resorting to racial stereotypes, and how many think she is not? Ask students to cite examples from Kang's essay to support their position.

Questions for Study and Discussion

1. The "battle of cultures" referred to in the title is the clash between the Korean American and African American cultures in the Flatbush area of Brooklyn, New York, that "started with cultural misunderstanding and was compounded by a lack of bilingual and bicultural community leaders to intervene quickly" (3). Kang believes that "cultural insight" is missing in this drama. Three of the differences between Korean Americans and African Americans that Kang points to are (1) attitudes toward smiling, (2) attitudes toward money, and (3) the value of social conscience.
2. Kang states her thesis in paragraph 3. Her comparison and contrast of the Korean American and African American communities provides the "cultural insight" to understand this interethnic, inner-city drama. In her concluding paragraph, Kang reiterates the point of her essay: "[M]aking democracy work in a multicultural society is difficult but we have no choice but to strive for it."
3. After a long period of tension between the two groups, the African Americans are boycotting the Korean American grocers because a black customer said that she was attacked by a store employee.
4. Most Asian immigrants are ill-equipped to run businesses in the United States because they lack cultural and social knowledge of their new country. They are indebted to African Americans because of the civil rights work done by them, which means that Korean Americans face less discrimination today.

5. Kang is writing from the point of view of a Korean American, so she understands many of the elements of Korean culture that make it difficult to assimilate into American inner-city neighborhoods. She also understands the African-American point of view toward new Korean immigrants.
6. One element that makes it difficult for Koreans to adapt is that the "Confucian ethos lacks the value of social conscience" (16). Koreans tend to focus on themselves and their own success. They are not tolerant of other cultures and they don't reach out to people from other cultures, which has helped to exacerbate the situation in New York.

Classroom Activity Using Comparison and Contrast

Analogy can be a difficult strategy for students to understand and even more difficult for them to work with. It is good to stress, however, that a good analogy can be highly effective. Points to stress include the following:

1. The analogy normally relates a fairly abstract concept to a much more concrete and immediate subject.
2. An analogy is used to clarify, not to mystify.
3. The subjects of both sides of the analogy are not usually in the same class.
4. It is better not to create an analogy at all than to create one that is so bizarre or laughable that the reader is distracted by it.

Recently, one of our local television interviewers was heard attempting to clarify the difference between a proposal for a widespread tax increase and a proposal for a targeted increase as the difference between dust on everything and dirt in a flowerpot—a concrete analogy, all right, but hardly an effective one.

Grant and Lee: A Study in Contrasts (p. 456)

■ Bruce Catton

Essay Analysis and Discussion

Catton begins his essay describing Lee and Grant as two men with differences that not only encompass their own personalities, but embody the ideals that divided the North and the South during the Civil War. Beginning with paragraph 4, Catton uses a subject-by-subject organization of his material to elaborate on the personality of each man. Then, in paragraphs 10 through 12, he summarizes those differences using a point-by-point organization. Catton describes the similarities between the two men in the final four paragraphs, again in a point-by-point organization. By spending the better part of the essay describing the features that separated the two leaders, Catton heightens our expectations as to what the two men can possibly have in common. By using subject-by-subject to contrast them, he keeps them separate for twelve paragraphs. Then, using point-by-point to compare them, he draws them together within paragraphs and sentences as they were drawn together with the same purpose at the end of the war. Students can discuss to what extent the impact of the essay might have been lessened had Catton presented the generals' similarities first or if he had presented the entire essay in subject-by-subject or point-by-point contrast and comparison. Students can also plot the essay to see with what precision and equality Catton organizes his discussion of the two generals.

Thinking Critically about This Reading

Catton's identification of Grant as "the modern man emerging" is convincingly supported by his presentation of Grant as the mobile man, one of the adventurous entrepreneurial types whose wealth was due not to aristocratic, hereditary landownership, but to personal initiative and vigor.

Questions for Study and Discussion

1. As Catton sees it, the most striking difference between Grant and Lee was that Lee's first loyalty was to aristocratic society and the region in which it existed, whereas Grant would fight for society at large. Lee resisted change, while Grant defended national development.
2. The similarities that Catton sees between Grant and Lee are as follows:
    a. Both men were marvelous fighters.
    b. Both men possessed utter tenacity and fidelity.
    c. Both men possessed an indomitable quality.
    d. Both generals had daring and resourcefulness.

   Catton feels that their most important similarity was "the ability, at the end, to turn quickly from war to peace once the fighting was over" (16). Catton felt this similarity to be most important because it allowed the postwar unification of the country.
3. Catton first contrasts the diametrically opposed backgrounds of the two generals, demonstrating how social philosophy and regional mores determined the conflicting attitudes of the North and South. The later comparison, then, moves from conflict to union: We see that both men had "tenacity and fidelity," an indomitable fighting will, the ability to outthink the enemy, and the great soldier's ability to turn from war to peace. Because the similarity between these two men provides a natural conclusion to the essay, it is appropriate that similarities be discussed after differences. To end with contrast would leave the conflict unresolved.

4. The subjects of the paragraphs in the body of this essay are as follows:

    INTRODUCTION
        paragraph 3: Grant and Lee

    DIFFERENCES
        paragraph 4: Lee
        paragraph 5: Lee
        paragraph 6: Lee
        paragraph 7: Grant
        paragraph 8: Grant
        paragraph 9: Grant

    MOST STRIKING DIFFERENCE
        paragraph 10: Lee
        paragraph 11: Grant

    SIMILARITIES
        paragraph 12: Grant and Lee
        paragraph 13: Grant and Lee
        paragraph 14: Grant and Lee
        paragraph 15: Grant and Lee

    MOST STRIKING SIMILARITY
        paragraph 16: Grant and Lee

5. The profound "inequality in the social structure" (a landed leisure class supported by slaves) resembles the social structure of feudalism; also, a "class of men" with a "strong sense of obligation to the community" and its protection resembles the role of knights.
6. Paragraphs 2, 3, 8, 14, and 15: pronoun references; paragraphs 9, 10, and 13: conjunctions; paragraphs 4 and 11: transitional phrases; paragraphs 5, 6, 7, and 12: name repetition; paragraph 16: convention of order. These transitional devices make Catton's essay coherent and easy to read.

Classroom Activity Using Comparison and Contrast

This activity reinforces some of the fundamental tasks that need to be considered before continuing with the writing itself. It's good to stress yet again that time spent at this preliminary stage considering such important questions is not wasted but is an effort that will actually save time and ensure a better result in the long run. It is true for most of us that as we become more and more familiar with the writing process we think we can cut corners at the prewriting stage.

Why We Crave Horror Movies (p. 465)

■ Stephen King

Essay Analysis and Discussion

In his first sentence, King tells us we are all mentally ill; then he suggests that our love of horror movies helps us feel balanced because those movies provide a psychic release for our darker feelings. In paragraphs 8 through 10 King defines the nature of our insanity in more detail and explains how society forces us to deal with our darker emotions. Next, King suggests that because we cannot flaunt our meaner feelings, we need an outlet for them, through horror movies and the "sick" joke. He has gone through his argument twice, with more emphasis on explaining the nature of our illness the second time through. He presents a thesis—that we are all mentally ill—and then carefully uses our love of horror movies and the sick joke to prove it. The horror movie gives us permission to express our dark feelings; those dark feelings are forbidden; they are forbidden because they are (this is where he gets us) "crazy." Can students refute King's position using a cause-and-effect argument of their own? Or is he right?

Thinking Critically about This Reading

The horror movie maintains the status quo of the nature of good and evil and beauty and ugliness in our minds. It does not ask us to rework our values.

Questions for Study and Discussion

1. We crave horror movies to show that we are not afraid, to reestablish our feelings of being normal, and to have fun. Some people go to satisfy a morbid curiosity about how the horror will be effected or because they are aficionados of the macabre.
2. King compares the thrills and chills of the roller-coaster ride with the thrills and chills of the horror movie. Each propels you along, promising to reward your terror at the next turn; and each fulfills that promise, but when you least expect it.
3. Society applauds love, friendship, loyalty, and kindness because they "maintain the status quo of civilization itself" (9), King labels emotions that are mean and murderous as "anticivilization."
4. The sick joke and the horror movie both must appeal "to all that is worst in us."

5. King gives examples of strange behavior that occurs in all of us, moving from the innocence of people who talk to themselves to the potentially murderous lyncher. His last line suggests, as Freud did, that a darker, more menacing creature lies in wait beneath the civilized exterior we present to the world.
6. King's tone is humorously menacing. He, like the horror movie, likes to lead the viewer along, and then without warning spring at the viewer with a grisly thought or a shocking idea. His first and final sentences are meant to bring the reader up short. In between, students will find numerous examples: "If your insanity leads you to carve up women" (8), "The potential lyncher is in almost all of us" (9), "But if we deliberately slam the rotten little puke of a sister's fingers in the door, sanctions follow" (10). King goes so far as to repeat for us one of the more horrifying of the "sick" jokes.

Classroom Activity Using Cause and Effect

This activity, which our first-year students have found eye-opening, is useful in demonstrating for your students how easy it is while reading to make assumptions that are based on little or no evidence. The activity is also useful in alerting the writer to the care that must be taken not to imply more than he or she knows.

Answers:

1. T	4. T	7. ?
2. ?	5. ?	8. F
3. ?	6. ?	9. ?

Why and When We Speak Spanish in Public (p. 472)

■ **Myriam Marquez**

Essay Analysis and Discussion

Marquez explains why she and her family sometimes speak Spanish, arguing that they are just as much American as anyone else. You may want to ask students whether they agree with Marquez. Is speaking English an important aspect of being an American? What are the reasons for speaking English in America? For example, how does English enable people to both assimilate and contribute more productively to the American culture and economy? Is it hard to give back if you cannot participate?

Thinking Critically about This Reading

In paragraph 11 Marquez lists the contributions Latin American immigrants have made to the United States: fighting in U.S.-led wars, voting, holding political office, and paying taxes. She argues that participation, not necessarily assimilation, is what makes someone an American.

Questions for Study and Discussion

1. Marquez's thesis is that speaking Spanish, rather than English, with her family is a way of acknowledging her roots and respecting her elders and is not in any way meant to denigrate America. "Being an American has very little to do with the language we use during our free time in a free country" (7).
2. At several points, Marquez states the argument she will refute. For example, in paragraph 5 she writes that she does not mean to be rude; in paragraph 7, that being American does not require speaking English. She acknowledges that she understands the importance of English around the world and also the importance of immigrants. Each paragraph is a refutation of an argument she has heard against immigrants' not speaking English.
3. She uses *but* to stress the fact that she's challenging the point made in the preceding paragraph, in which she summarized an argument against speaking Spanish in an English-speaking country. Her use of *but* tempers the prior paragraph, while acknowledging the reality.
4. The essay is one of cause and effect. She begins by staying that she speaks Spanish with her family and then explains why she does so.
5. Student opinion will vary. Consider asking students to discuss why they think the founders did not make English the official language of the United States. Other countries have such laws, why not America?

Classroom Activity Using Cause and Effect

Causal chains can be confusing at first, and it is often difficult to distinguish between the ultimate cause, the immediate cause, and one or more of the effects when first developing the chain. It would probably help students to develop some chains as a class before they attempt to do so on their own. Take fifteen or twenty minutes and have the students work together to come up with causal chains that are relevant to their own lives, then have them take another ten minutes or so to develop one on their own.

Mom Quixote (p. 476)

■ Anna Quindlen

Essay Analysis and Discussion

Quindlen recounts her efforts to find the perfect Christmas gift for her son—a Mighty Morphin Power Rangers action figure. Part of what makes this essay effective is that Quindlen can show the insanity of hunting for toys at

Christmas, while herself being a part of the insanity. She comments on our culture without separating herself from it, which makes her a trustworthy and honest cultural commentator. Ask students whether they think she was silly to work so hard to find a toy for her son. Have they ever done something similar? Is her hunt part of the fun or is it just a waste of time?

Thinking Critically about This Reading

Quindlen is sad because she realizes that Christmas is a commercial and material enterprise. The anecdote of the woman at the cocktail party whose daughter stopped believing in Santa Claus illustrates what Quindlen hopes won't happen to her son. To perpetuate—and protect—her son's childish wonder about the Christmas season, she needs to buy him something. Her statement is ironic because people are supposed to be happy and full of joy around the holidays, not angry and pushed to violence.

Questions for Study and Discussion

1. She becomes tired, sad, stressed, and upset; "I grow weary" (paragraph 1), "I awaken in a cold sweat" (4), "I . . . return home, disconsolate" (5), "I am so sad" (6).
2. In paragraph 1, Quindlen tries to figure out why her son wants these toys so badly; "Driving home, I wonder whom to blame: retailers, manufacturers. . . . Every Christmas there is one plaything everyone desires and no one can get. Sort of like the Hope diamond." To her son, it is a desire greater than that for food or water, so she does not really care what caused it. She wants to fulfill his need.
3. By not reporting every day, she builds the intensity of the search. Some days other obligations probably kept her from looking for the toy, and leaving those "non-search days" out of her narrative elevates the sense of urgency. Time is passing, and with each day finding the toy gets less and less likely.
4. In paragraph 3, she quotes her son; "If I don't get Mighty Morphin Power Rangers, I'll know there's no Santa Claus." This conveys the son's desire as well as the reason for his mother's intense commitment to finding the toy. In paragraph 6, she quotes a woman whose daughter felt the same way as her son—she did not receive a Cabbage Patch doll, and "that's how she knew there was no Santa Claus." This intensifies Quindlen's need to fulfill her son's request. She also uses dialogue to recount her dream about the Princess of Wales. This helps the reader to feel the dream's intensity.
5. In the beginning she uses the phrase effectively to set up the organization of the essay. She shows all the actions she took to achieve her goal. At the

end, she repeats the phrase to show that the struggle is still not done. "I will persevere" is humorous in part because often people use this expression to mean they will achieve some monumentally important goal or feat of survival.

6. The title refers to Cervantes's *Don Quixote,* the classic novel of the "eternal optimist." Quindlen, through her title, relates her search for a Christmas toy to Don Quixote's "tilting at windmills"—an exercise in futility.

Classroom Activity Using Cause and Effect

The cause-and-effect pairs listed here are meant to provide students with familiar causal chains. All of them should be easy to develop along familiar pathways. The second part of the activity allows students to be a bit more creative. Have them develop as general a chain as possible for the mixed pair. An airplane having engine trouble on a specific vacation can definitely have the effect of making a vacationer nervous, but what elements of all vacations tend to make people nervous?

One Idea (p. 480)

■ Norman Mailer

Essay Analysis and Discussion

Mailer argues that TV advertising affects our attention spans and, therefore, the learning ability of adults and children. With less ability to concentrate, we are less able to acquire knowledge through reading. You might stimulate an interesting discussion by asking students whether Mailer would think that reading magazines or listening to the radio would also affect concentration. Magazines often include a number of articles on a variety of topics, and they include advertisements. The same can be said about radio. Do students think Mailer's criticism of television can apply to other media? Why or why not?

Thinking Critically about This Reading

In using the phrase "psychic strength," Mailer conveys his opinion that the mind, like the muscles of the body, "can be built up or allowed to go slack." Mailer believes that the ability to concentrate is the measure of a mind's strength.

Questions for Study and Discussion

1. Mailer states his thesis most clearly in paragraph 7: "I believe that television commercials have got to go."

2. According to Mailer, "If the desire to read diminishes, so does one's ability to read" (1). He means that if a person does not wish to read, that person will not read. As a result of not using the mental "muscle" that reading exercises, that person will become less and less able to focus and concentrate on what he or she does read. Mailer describes a cycle of mental atrophy.
3. Just as a muscle atrophies from lack of use, so does a mind. The less a person exercises his or her mind, the less that person wants to use his or her mind.
4. Mailer thinks that the disruptive nature of commercials cause "stagnation" and lethargy in children. Hours in front of the television mean hours spent eating, drinking, and watching ads.
5. In paragraph 6 Mailer states, "We have an economy that is stimulated by TV advertising. Yet the constant interruption of concentration it generates not only dominates much of our lives, but over the long run is also bound to bleed into our prosperity." Instead of training our children to be producers, the constant barrage of commercials is creating consumers with extremely short attention spans and lazy minds.
6. He thinks we should get rid of commercials, which finance free television, and that we should "pay directly for what we enjoy on television rather than pass the spiritual cost on to our children and their children" (7). You might find it interesting to discuss the television system in the United Kingdom, where people pay a license fee for each television set they own. The fees collected finance commercial-free network (BBC) programming. Do students think such a system would work in the United States? Why or why not?

Classroom Activity Using Cause and Effect

One of the difficult things about writing a cause-and-effect essay is that the effects are felt on many levels. The effect something has on you may not be at all the same as the effect it has on your neighbor, and it may affect society in ways that few people stop to think about in their daily lives. You can preface this activity with discussion with your students about the effects of another recent innovation that has swiftly become an important part of our society—cell phones. Have students identify the different effects cell phones have had on individuals, communities, and society as a whole.

The Declaration of Independence (p. 492)

■ Thomas Jefferson

Essay Analysis and Discussion

This essay can work well in conjunction with Abraham Lincoln's "Gettysburg Address" as an analysis of parallel sentence structure. The instances of parallelism in Lincoln's essay are accomplished either through repetition of word order within a single sentence or repetition of grammatical form in a series of sentences that make up one paragraph. Jefferson also relies on repetition of grammatical form, but develops the parallelism through a series of sentences, each of which serves as a paragraph in itself. This is partly because Jefferson covers more ground than Lincoln, but it may also reflect the difference in the essays' purposes. Have your students compare how the two types of parallelism are incorporated into these essays, and then discuss what effect the use of parallelism has on each. Lincoln's subtle and sonorous sentence structure, as opposed to Jefferson's more forceful and emphatic repetitions, may indicate the difference in tone between a dedication and a declaration.

Thinking Critically about This Reading

Government has power "to levy War, conclude Peace, contract Alliances, establish Commerce, and to do all other Acts and Things which Independent states may of right do (paragraph 32)." Students' responses as to what other purposes government may serve should show some understanding of the reasoning behind the Declaration. How do their recommendations differ from or agree with its basic concepts?

Questions for Study and Discussion

1. The self-evident truths that Jefferson puts forth in paragraph 2 are "all men are created equal," "they are endowed by their Creator with certain unalienable Rights," governments are instituted to secure these unalienable rights, and people have a right to throw off a despotic government. Once these truths are accepted, all the rest of Jefferson's argument follows logically.
2. Jefferson's argument can be stated in the following syllogism: *(major premise)* When a government is despotic it should be abolished and a new one established; *(minor premise)* the government of King George is despotic; *(conclusion)* the government of King George should be abolished and a new one established.

3. The major premise is presented as the consequence of self-evident truths and, as such, does not need to be supported.
4. In paragraph 31 Jefferson reviews the ways in which the colonies have attempted to make the British government aware of their problems.
5. The best examples of Jefferson's use of parallelism are found in paragraph 2, where he lists the unalienable rights, and in paragraphs 3 through 29, where he gives the charges against the king. Jefferson uses parallelism for emphasis; it establishes a rhythm that highlights each of the items in these lists, thus making the lists and the items memorable.
6. Examples of Jefferson's emotionally charged language include *wholesome* (3), *refused* (5), *inestimable* (5), *formidable* (5), *tyrants* (5), *manly* (7), *invasions* (7), *swarms* (12), and *harass* (12). Having established a sound logical argument, Jefferson uses emotionally charged language to call forth feelings of patriotism among the colonists.

Classroom Activity Using Argument

This exercise works well as a group activity. Before setting students free on one of the suggested topics or a topic of your own choosing, make sure they understand the dog leash law and waste pickup ordinance example provided in the text. This exercise gets students to focus on the essential pieces of an argument—in this case, three key points in favor of the writer's position (two logical and one emotional) and one point held by the opposition. After fifteen or twenty minutes, have several groups write their key points on the board or present their thoughts orally.

I Have a Dream (p. 498)

■ Martin Luther King Jr.

Essay Analysis and Discussion

The classroom activity for this essay refers to the variety of metaphors King uses in his speech. King's reliance on figurative language is pervasive, and his metaphors often appear in a parallel structure that contributes to the rhetorical flourish of the speech overall. Notice, for example, the final sentence in paragraph 1: "It came as a joyous daybreak to end the long night of captivity." Day and night are coupled in the metaphor to highlight contrasting circumstances. King follows this pattern in many of his metaphors. In paragraph 2, "a lonely island of poverty" exists within "a vast ocean of material prosperity." Following are more examples of King's technique:

"insufficient funds/great vaults of opportunity" (4)
"desolate valley of segregation/sunlit path of racial justice" (4)

"sweltering summer of the Negro's legitimate discontent/invigorating autumn of freedom and equality" (5)
"warm threshold/palace of justice" (6)
"desert state sweltering with the heat of injustice and oppression/oasis of freedom and justice" (13)
"mountain of despair/stone of hope" (19)
"jangling discords of our nation/beautiful symphony of brotherhood" (19)

Consider these examples as you examine King's more obvious parallel sentence structures (see question 4 below). Ask your students if they find the persistent metaphorical flourishes effective or if they believe such flourishes become overwhelming as the essay proceeds.

Thinking Critically about This Reading

By warning against "wrongful deeds," King is responding to a growing militancy within the civil rights movement. Groups such as the Nation of Islam and leaders such as Malcolm X advocated a more aggressive, confrontational approach to gaining equality, and did not rule out the use of violence if violence was directed at them. The more militant groups also felt that freedom and equality had to be fought for and won by African Americans themselves, without the aid of white sympathizers. King therefore wishes to emphasize his commitment to nonviolence and to integration in the battle for civil rights, fearing that any other approach could only be counterproductive in the long run.

Questions for Study and Discussion

1. King states his thesis at the beginning of paragraph 3: "In a sense we have come to our nation's Capitol to cash a check." He goes on to explain how the Constitution and Declaration of Independence promised freedom and equality for every American, yet America has defaulted on that promise, as evidenced by continuing racial injustice, by segregation, by the lack of opportunity for African Americans—in short, by the denial of freedom and equality.
2. The larger audience for King's speech is composed of everyone who listened to it on the radio or watched it on television, either at the time it was given or at any time over the years since he presented it in 1963. In many ways, King's speech also addresses posterity, signaling a period of momentous change in U.S. history and reminding those who come after him of the circumstances that created the need for such a pivotal event. The repetitions and parallel structures within King's speech catch the audience's attention and make clear his argument.

3. After King's opening, in which he refers to the promise of the Emancipation Proclamation, King highlights the degree to which that promise has remained unfulfilled. This sets up the context for identifying the purpose of the gathering he addresses and allows him to present his thesis in paragraph 3. The next stage in his argument emphasizes the need for demanding freedom and equality *now* and reminds the audience of African Americans' determination to secure citizenship rights. After cautioning against succumbing to bitterness and hatred, or "wrongful deeds," in the pursuit of equality, King then outlines some of the reasons why African Americans will not be satisfied until they are accorded their full rights as citizens. Next, King acknowledges the "trials and tribulations" that have brought people to Washington to protest, using that acknowledgment to set up his extended refrain of "I have a dream . . ." in paragraphs 10 through 18. He then finishes with a rhetorical hymn for freedom.

   King's organization suits his purpose overall, since the first part of his speech pays homage to the people who have gathered in Washington and acknowledges the conditions that have brought them there, while the second part finishes on a rhetorical high note full of hope and optimism, with the extended refrains of "I have a dream . . ." and "Let freedom ring. . . ."

4. The primary repetitions and parallel structures that appear in King's speech include:

   one hundred years later . . . (2)
   Now is the time . . . (4)
   We can never be satisfied as long as . . . (7)
   Some of you have come . . . (8)
   Go back to . . . (9)
   I have a dream . . . (11–18)
   Let freedom ring from . . . (21–26)

   These structures add to the persuasiveness of King's argument in two key ways. First, they make more memorable the ideas he presents, emphasizing through repetition the most important points of his argument. Second, each time King uses one of the phrases above, he connects it to something specific concerning the conditions of African Americans in the United States, or, in the case of "Let freedom ring," how pervasive such conditions remain. Thus, at the same time that he reinforces the main points of his argument he analyzes the nature of the problem he is addressing.

5. King's title emphasizes the spirit of hope and optimism that his speech engenders in the civil rights movement. It is particularly appropriate for the context in which the speech was given, since King verbalizes what is most likely the dream of all those present for the March on Washington in 1963. Students may have other opinions to offer on the suitability of King's title, as well as on possible alternatives.

Classroom Activity Using Argument

To choose the best quote for their paragraph, students will need to decide if they will use mostly persuasive arguments, logical arguments, or a mix of the two. The first quote will fit a mostly persuasive argument, the second a logical argument (let students know they can make up other statistics if they wish), and the third can be used for both. Make sure the students integrate the quote into the paragraph so that it directly supports the argument and suits the tone. Students may enjoy reading their finished paragraphs aloud—have them discuss which method of presenting the argument is the most effective for each subject.

As They Say, Drugs Kill (p. 505)

■ **Laura Rowley**

Essay Analysis and Discussion

Rowley arranges her argument into four sections: an opening statement, in which she presents the subject of her essay; the narrative, in which she gives an eyewitness account of the young man's death; her reaction to his death; and the conclusions she draws from the experience. The first three sections argue persuasively; by telling us her feelings and by forcing us to witness the man's agonizing and sudden death, Rowley makes an emotional case for not using drugs. In her conclusion, she is more logical, almost saying that it is unreasonable to witness or hear about an incident such as this and remain unconvinced. Students can go through the different sections to see what emotions Rowley inspires and what effect those feelings have on the reader. She says in her essay that friends remained unconvinced and thought it could not happen to them. What has Rowley done to ensure that her written narrative will be more convincing than her spoken one?

Thinking Critically about This Reading

Given the ironic tone of Rowley's introduction and the fact that her essay was first published in an issue of *Newsweek on Campus,* her audience is most likely college students. Ask students how engaged they would have been with Rowley's essay had she used a less ironic introduction.

Questions for Study and Discussion

1. Rowley uses very emotional, graphically disturbing language in her dialogue, her diction, and her choice of details. For example, "His face was grayish blue, his mouth hung open, rimmed with blood, and his eyes were rolled back with a yellowish color on the rims" (paragraph 22). The

dialogue adds drama, realism, and immediacy to her argument. The emotional, graphic language and the disturbing details are intended to shock readers into believing that drugs kill, that it can happen to anyone, and that they should change their behavior accordingly if they are using drugs.

2. Rowley wants us to consider that death by drugs can happen to anyone; she wants us to think about this fact and, if we are users, she wants us to stop.
3. Rowley is able to shock readers and force our attention to the issue with her eyewitness account of the death. Her friend seemed to agree with Rowley that witnessing such a death would be convincing enough to prevent anyone's using drugs again. Others saw no special meaning in the incident. They considered it a "freak accident" and learned little if anything from the young man's death.
4. Rowley may have chosen not to violate the man's privacy. However, his anonymity also gives an "everyman" quality to the story and underlines her proposition that what happened to him could happen to anyone. The young man's ordinariness distinguishes him from celebrity victims such as Len Bias.
5. Rowley shares openly her sense of helplessness and sorrow for the man who died and her concern for others who might die the same way. "It seemed irreverent to talk as the ambulance pulled away" (26). "My hands began to shake and my eyes filled with tears for someone I didn't know" (28). "If this death cannot make people think and change, that will be an even greater tragedy" (30).
6. Rowley's opening paragraph is apparently glib, which makes it shocking and grabs the reader's attention. The impact would have been diluted if the reader could have continued reading into the next sentence.

Classroom Activity Using Argument

Much of the success of any argument depends on the quantity and quality of the material brought to bear on it. Yet, even before going to the library or the Internet to search for information, students should be encouraged to engage in some essential critical thinking. While it is perfectly legitimate sometimes to cast a wide net in any search for information and issues, there are times when the search can be narrowed to save time and effort. Knowing how to ask questions related to the topic will get the search started more easily. In item 2, for example, the student might ask the following questions:

1. Isn't English the official language of the United States?
2. What is an official language anyhow?
3. What good is an official language?
4. Who wants an official language? For what reason?
5. Might it be the case that an official language is not desirable?
6. Do any states have state laws about an official language?
7. If so, which ones? What was the reasoning behind enacting such laws?

These same questions can be asked of just about any topic: Who? What? Why? Where? and When? So what? These are always excellent starting points.

As far as the question of where to obtain the desired information is concerned, it is good to remind students that it is sometimes helpful to use an encyclopedia as a way of gaining the most fundamental information in the quickest manner. Also, students should be cautioned to use only the most recently published information. An encyclopedia may be several years old and may not be accurate in stating how many states have passed English-Only laws. Newspaper indexes are a good way to get the most up-to-date statistics, but they should be checked for their accuracy. Finally, any information obtained from the Internet should be used cautiously, as the accuracy of such information is not always scrupulously checked. Using known authorities and disseminators, whether institutions or individuals, is always wise.

In Praise of the F Word (p. 510)

■ Mary Sherry

Essay Analysis and Discussion

Anything that involves short-term sacrifice to achieve long-term benefits is hard to sell in our society, and Mary Sherry knows it. But she also knows that her perspective as an adult literacy teacher carries weight when it comes to addressing those who would argue that failing is too traumatic for kids. In particular, note how she organizes paragraphs 2 through 4. She begins by saying what she does; she progresses to what she has learned about her school and what difficulties students and teachers there face; and only at the end of paragraph 4 does she bring up the word "failure." By the time she gets to that word, she has established her experience and credibility. She has also implied that the schools have, in some cases, failed their students by not being willing to fail them. Also note how paragraphs 10 through 12 comprise what is essentially a three-paragraph conclusion. Much of the text in the three paragraphs would be repetitive and unnecessary if Sherry felt she were addressing sympathetic readers, but it is clear that she feels that it is important to drive her point home. Discuss these and other techniques Sherry uses to persuade her presumably reluctant audience.

Thinking Critically about This Reading

By providing students with the opportunity to fail, teachers are enabling students to show that they can succeed. If students always pass, no matter how poor their work, the value of success is devalued. Students may disagree with Sherry's statement.

Questions for Study and Discussion

1. Sherry's thesis is that flunking kids—or even the possibility of flunking them—can motivate many of them in the short term and prevent many long-term problems. She uses her experience as both an adult literacy program teacher and a parent as evidence.
2. Sherry acknowledges the opposition to flunking in paragraphs 8 and 11, but her strong language—*cheats* and *excuses*—clearly shows how she thinks. She does not detail the reasons—mostly economic and social—for a policy of passing students, probably because she believes that such a discussion would get her argument off track by focusing on issues other than the students themselves. Sherry's experiences with students in her adult literacy program who have been "passed along" without mastering basic materials while in school argue strongly for a system that gets "tough" with students and encourages them with the threat of failure to make school a priority.
3. The "F word" can mean either failure or flunking. By calling it the "F word," Sherry implies that it has now become a taboo concept to flunk kids.
4. Sherry's audience is presumably educators and parents. It does not appear to be receptive to the "F word." Students should note the gradual introduction of the concept of failure, the long conclusion, and the personal examples.
5. Sherry has seen the results of passing marginally literate and illiterate students—severe problems after graduation and a need to go back to school. The second part is a matter of personal opinion.

Classroom Activity Using Argument

The reliability of evidence is, of course, what drives writers, scholars, doctors, lawyers, and researchers to do what they do. Finding more than one authority who agrees with the assumption of the reliability of a body of evidence sometimes can make a case for accuracy; sometimes such reliance only proves that scholars rely too heavily on the unexamined and untested work of their predecessors. A writer we know, for example, has been working on a book on the covered bridges of Vermont. Finding some discrepancies in the measurements of those bridges in source materials, he thought it necessary to take his own measurements. He found that not only were early published statistics inaccurate, but subsequent researchers and writers had relied on that information and republished it. The issue of reliability turns on the question, very often, of how much time a writer or other professional has to accomplish a given task. It should be made clear, however, that writing based on questionable information may so distort the conclusions that the whole endeavor becomes a waste of time.

Don't Eat the Flan (p. 515)

■ Greg Critser

Essay Analysis and Discussion

Critser argues against a public health policy that "therapizes" obesity and is afraid to tell overweight people to change their behavior. He suggests that the rate of obesity in the United States would be lower if public health officials addressed this problem the same way they do sexually transmitted diseases and smoking: using shame and stigmatization to encourage healthy choices and behaviors. If overeating—in essence, gluttony—were stigmatized, people would be less likely to overeat. Critser disagrees with the notion that "[t]elling people to not eat too much food is counterproductive. Worse, it leads to 'stigmatization,' which can lead to eating disorders, low self-esteem, and bad body image" (paragraph 9).

Thinking Critically about This Reading

Critser says that obesity can be blamed on gluttony, the unchecked "sinful" consumption of food. By calling consumers' attention to their unhealthy eating habits, food producers would be hurting their own business. The media rely on producers and advertisers for a large amount of their revenue, so it is against their best interests to encourage eating less.

Questions for Study and Discussion

1. Critser argues that overeating should be considered a moral issue, and that seeing it that way could work to alleviate the problem. Student reactions to this argument will vary.
2. Student reactions to such lawsuits will vary. Some students could argue that the lawsuit against McDonald's was justified because it resulted in the company's adding more healthy items to its menu. Consider discussing with the students how the threat of legal action can bring about positive social change, even if the case never makes it to court.
3. In the early twentieth century, the French encouraged education about food and published parenting manuals that addressed the issue of health and diet. This literature told parents they must "control the dinner table; all portions should be moderate; desserts were for holidays. Eating too much food was a bad thing" (12). Students might also suggest that the French are leaner because they eat less fast food, eat smaller portions in general, drink wine regularly, and eat a balance of carbohydrates and protein.

4. Critser means that the current attitude toward obesity is more concerned with the obese person's feelings than with his or her health. He says that telling an obese person to eat less is seen as an assault and not as sound advice. Critser puts "therapization" in quotation marks for emphasis.
5. The seven deadly sins are pride, lust, envy, anger, greed, gluttony, and sloth. Consider asking students to discuss how the sins are portrayed in the popular media.
6. *Flan* is the Spanish version of a rich French dessert called crème caramel. Critser is suggesting that Americans adopt the eating habits of the French, not just their decadent treats. While Americans love desserts, they should follow the French model and eat them in moderation only.

Classroom Activity Using Argument

1. either/or thinking
2. hasty generalization
3. post hoc ergo propter hoc
4. begging the question
5. false analogy
6. post hoc ergo propter hoc
7. oversimplification
8. oversimplification
9. begging the question
10. post hoc ergo propter hoc
11. either/or thinking
12. false analogy

Supersize Me: It's Time to Stop Blaming Fat People for Their Size (p. 520)

■ **Alison Motluk**

Essay Analysis and Discussion

Motluk argues that America's "obesogenic" environment is a major contributor to the rising number of the country's cases of obesity. According to Motluk, "the prevailing culture actually promotes obesity, making an unhealthy lifestyle the default option" (paragraph 3). A reliance on fast food, increasing portion sizes, and a de-emphasis on physical activity in schools, for example, have made healthy choices very difficult. For an interesting discussion, you could ask students to read Etta Kralovec's "No More Pep Rallies!" In her essay, Kralovec argues against school-sponsored sports at the expense of education. Students might be asked to consider how Motluk would respond to Kralovec's argument. Motluk says that physical activity, and therefore health, is sacrificed in order to achieve higher test scores.

Thinking Critically about This Reading

The irony is that the developed world is literally eating itself to death. Ask students to discuss the dichotomy between obesity in the developed world and famine in the underdeveloped world. What is their reaction to people eating themselves to death in one country and starving to death in another?

Questions for Study and Discussion

1. The "obesogenic" environment is one in which "the prevailing culture actually promotes obesity, making an unhealthy lifestyle the default option" (3). The components include diet, portion size, community design (no sidewalks), percentage of home-cooked meals, activity levels, and the social value placed on exercise.
2. Motluk feels strongly that obesity in the United States is a direct result of the environment. Because an unhealthy diet is the norm, making healthy choices becomes increasingly difficult. She cites increasing portion sizes, more meals eaten out of the home, communities that require citizens to drive rather than walk, and the decline in physical education in schools.
3. Motluk refers to differences in the portion sizes offered by McDonald's in the 1960s and today. In the1960s the average McDonald's meal was 590 calories; today, it is 1,550 calories. She also demonstrates how restaurants stand to profit by increasing portion sizes.
4. In this essay, Motluk addresses the rising rate of obesity in the United States, but she does mention in paragraph 2 that "the UK, Australia, and many other Western countries [are following] the U.S. lead." Obesity is a problem that many countries have to deal with.
5. Motluk implies that eating more home-cooked food and smaller portion sizes, as well as increasing exercise, particularly through physical activity in schools, would help alleviate the problem. Awareness of the obesogenic environment is the best way to avoid its pitfalls.

Classroom Activity Using Argument

Motluk considers the various factors leading to obesity in the United States. You may want to ask students to consider the question of why there are still many trim people. Why do many Americans, exposed to fast food options and stressed with packed schedules like everyone else, find time to eat right and exercise? What about all of the new diet foods? What accounts for the differences in behaviors?

Condemn the Crime, Not the Person (p. 524)

■ **June Tangney**

Essay Analysis and Discussion

One of the distinctions between Tangney and Kahan's essays is that Tangney distinguishes between shame and guilt. She claims that each has "very different implications for subsequent moral and interpersonal behavior" (paragraph 5). You may have an interesting discussion by asking students whether they agree with Tangney about the difference between guilt and shame. Is the difference more in the consequence than in the punishment?

Thinking Critically about This Reading

Tangney cites "recent scientific evidence" (4) that shows that those who receive shaming sentences have the same outcomes as those who receive standard prison sentences. Public shaming and stigmatization are counterproductive. While they may satisfy the public's thirst for brute and open punishments, they neither deter crimes nor prevent recidivism.

Questions for Study and Discussion

1. Shaming sentences are "sanctions explicitly designed to induce feelings of shame" (1) Judges choose these sentences over more traditional ones because the cost of incarceration remains high and the success rate extremely low. The judges feel they need alternatives.
2. Tangney believes that shame causes more harm than good. She believes there is a strong and important difference between shame and guilt, and that they lead to different behaviors and outcomes. Shame actually makes a bad situation worse by diminishing the person's sense of self and does not encourage better behavior. Guilt focuses on the bad behavior—not the bad person—and therefore encourages reparative action.
3. According to Tangney, "recent scientific evidence suggest that such attempts at social control are misguided. Rather than fostering constructive change, shame often makes a bad situation worse" (5).
4. Tangney answers the rhetorical question by stating, "Well, one way is to force offenders to focus on the negative consequences of their behavior, particularly on the painful negative consequences for others" (13). Students may also suggest asking offenders to think of a punishment themselves or asking the victims of the crime to suggest a punishment. Others may suggest educating the offenders on the effects of their actions.

5. Tangney says that other methods prove ineffective and perhaps destructive. "[T]houghtfully constructed guilt-oriented community service sentences are more likely to foster changes in offenders' future behaviors, while contributing to the larger societal good" (18). She thinks that any good community volunteer would welcome this positive outcome and not take it as an insult to his or her work.

Classroom Activity Using Argument

Audience is an abstraction for most writers. They have a vague sense of why it might be more helpful to say this or that, with such and such diction, but they don't really study the issue, the importance of not missing the target at every point in the writing. We find this exercise helpful in getting students to think more practically about the audience for their work. Types of evidence students should consider include the following:

1. A lot of basic information is conveyed if the audience is deemed by the writer to be uninformed on the subject.
2. Key terms and concepts are defined if the audience is uninformed.
3. Technical language is used if the audience is presumed to be familiar with the subject.
4. Unexamined assumptions that would not pass muster with less friendly readers would be offered if the audience is like-minded or sympathetic.

Shame Is Worth a Try (p. 530)

■ **Dan M. Kahan**

Essay Analysis and Discussion

Kahan makes an economic argument for the use of shaming punishments in place of imprisonment for minor crimes. Shame punishments are cheaper to carry out than incarceration, and they also allow convicts to contribute to the economy by making restitution to their victims or making child-support payments, for example. Ask students to read Greg Critser's essay "Don't Eat the Flan," which discusses how shaming people not to overeat could be an effective method for curbing obesity. Critser argues that using shame to combat gluttony is "a fundamental—and proven—public health tactic." Discuss with the class the differences and similarities involved in using shame in public health measures and in law enforcement.

Thinking Critically about This Reading

Kahan's argument is based on the economics of punishment for minor crimes—shaming punishments are as effective as prison sentences but vastly less expensive. Combining traditional sentences *and* shaming punishments, as in the case of sex offenders, negates the economic benefit of shaming sentences alone.

Questions for Study and Discussion

1. Kahan's thesis is stated in paragraph 3: "[W]hat the shame proponents seem to be getting, and the critics ignoring, is the potential of shame as an effective, cheap, and humane alternative to imprisonment."
2. "Steal from your employer in Wisconsin and you might be ordered to wear a sandwich board proclaiming your offense. Drive drunk in Florida or Texas and you might be required to place a conspicuous 'DUI' bumper sticker to your car. Refuse to make your child-support payments in Virginia and you will find that your vehicle has been immobilized with an appropriately colored boot (pink if the abandoned child is a girl, blue if it is a boy)" (1). Student opinions will differ regarding the question of the appropriateness of such punishments.
3. Kahan sees imprisonment as crueler than shame. In one sense, shame is less cruel for both the individual and society because it enables offenders to continue earning an income, compensating the victim, paying child support, and contributing to society. In paragraph 11, he states that "shame clearly doesn't hurt as much as imprisonment. Individuals who go to jail end up just as disgraced as those who are shamed."
4. Kahan cites a series of studies by Harold Grasmick suggesting that "the prospect of public disgrace exerts greater pressure to comply with the law than does the threat of imprisonment and other formal punishments" (9).
5. Students will have different reactions to Kahan's argument. Some might say they would like to hear about some experiences from the offenders themselves. Did shaming work in Wisconsin? Students may raise the question, not addressed by Kahan, "Will shame be more effective for some people than for others?" Others may agree with Kahan that shaming punishments are worth a try.

Classroom Activity Using Argument

A variation on this activity would be to focus specifically on the potential harm of violent content in entertainment. Assuming your classroom is technologically equipped for it, debaters can use examples from their own cultural milieu to illustrate their points.

Parents Should Be Allowed to Opt Out of Vaccinating Their Children (p. 535)

■ **Barbara Loe Fisher**

Essay Analysis and Discussion

Fisher is a parents' and patients' rights advocate who is arguing for parents to be given the ability to opt out of mandatory childhood vaccinations. One of her main concerns with the vaccinations is the possibility of harmful side effects. While Fisher and Shelov address the same topic, it might be interesting to explore with the class whether the audience seems the same for both essays. Fisher focuses on the parents' perspective while Shelov focuses on the public health perspective. Would either or both articles have been improved by either broadening or focusing their audiences?

Thinking Critically about This Reading

Her objection to vaccination is based on her assertion that some children could become sick or disabled—or could even die—as a result of the shots, and that very little is being done to ensure that these children are protected. She says that while infectious-disease rates have fallen, we now have an influx of neurological and autoimmune diseases that potentially could be connected to vaccinations.

Questions for Study and Discussion

1. Fisher's purpose is to argue against mass vaccination and to encourage more studies on the possible connection between vaccination and various ailments, such as autism.
2. She refers to the National Childhood Vaccine Injury Act of 1986, which acknowledged that vaccines could cause harm and shielded manufacturers against personal injury and wrongful death claims. Since 1990, Fisher states, twelve to fourteen thousand reports of vaccination-related injuries and hospitalizations were reported to the Vaccine Adverse Event Reporting System (VAERS). In the early 1990s the Institute of Medicine released a report confirming that vaccines can cause death.
3. Fisher claims that only "between 1 and 10 percent of all doctors make reports to VAERS" (paragraph 4), which suggests that far more cases exist than doctors actually report.
4. Her evidence for a connection between the increased rate of neurological and autoimmune diseases and vaccinations is that we administer vaccines when the brain and immune system are developing at the most rapid rate.

While she does not prove a connection, she says that it is dangerous to rule out the possibility.

5. Fisher claims that vaccination has been exempted from informed consent protections and vaccine makers' and doctors' liability because of "the notion that a minority of individuals are expendable in service to the majority" (13).
6. She wants to see resources dedicated to screening out children who could be hurt by vaccines. She also believes that parents, not governments, should make decisions about their children's health care.

Classroom Activity Using Argument

1. An effective syllogism establishes a connection between the major and minor premises. No such connection has been established in this attempt at a syllogism, therefore the conclusion may or may not be true.
2. This syllogism is valid and true.
3. This syllogism is valid and true.
4. The conclusion to this syllogism is not necessarily true because writers are not the only people who enjoy reading books.
5. The conclusion to this syllogism is not necessarily true because all incredibly sticky candy is not cotton candy.

When inexperienced writers become involved with presenting an argument, it is easy for them to lose track of logic as they write. The argument may seem to be clear in their heads, but it can become garbled on paper. When isolated and pointed out, the breakdowns in logic are easy to see, as this activity will demonstrate to students. They should have an easy time writing their own effective syllogisms, and the exercise will help them to think more about maintaining a logical presentation of their arguments as they write.

Parents Should Not Be Allowed to Opt Out of Vaccinating Their Children (p. 543)

■ **Steven P. Shelov**

Essay Analysis and Discussion

Shelov's essay addresses point for point almost every argument Fisher makes in her essay. Shelov couches the argument within the framework of public health. In order to protect all people, we must vaccinate. Fisher, however, focuses more on the individual: What happens to the child who actually does get hurt from the immunization? According to Shelov, incidents of vaccine side effects and death are wildly overreported and are unsubstantiated. According to Shelov, "It would be actual malpractice and poor public-health philosophy and practice to consider not immunizing our children against the potentially deadly infectious diseases" (paragraph 17). Which essay did students find more compelling? Why? Which position do they support, Fisher's or Shelov's? Why?

Thinking Critically about This Reading

According to Shelov, "Immunizations have a clear community benefit and, therefore, individual preferences should not be permitted to expose the public to the hazards of infectious disease" (15). Public schools are where members of the community—children—gather regularly in close quarters. A few children infected with a disease could quickly spread that disease among their classmates, their classmates' families, and then beyond to the wider community. In essence, the public school is ground zero for infectious disease, and mandatory vaccinations ensure that certain diseases, at least, will not spread.

Questions for Study and Discussion

1. Shelov states his thesis at the end of paragraph 1: "Allowing parents to opt out of vaccinating their children would endanger public health."
2. Some students might like the question-and-answer format, as it makes the essay easy to follow. Shelov answers many of the questions raised in Fisher's essay. Others may find that this format makes the essay too much like a Q&A session, rather than an essay. They might say it breaks the flow.
3. Shelov does acknowledge the media attention regarding adverse reactions to vaccinations. He then reiterates the point that no scientific studies link vaccinations to diseases such as autism. Moreover, he argues, the health of a few cannot be a justification for putting the health of thousands at risk.
4. Student opinion will vary. Consider asking students what method, other than comparison and contrast, they would have used to make Shelov's point. Why?
5. Shelov claims that no scientific evidence supports the claim that the hepatitis B vaccine can cause illness.
6. According to Shelov, "the major reason to prevent rubella in the community is to prevent exposure of pregnant women to children who have rubella. When contracted by a pregnant woman, rubella may infect her unborn baby, leading to a significant potential for mental retardation and a host of serious defects" (13).
7. People from countries where vaccinations are not mandatory or are not as rigid as in the United States could enter this country and spread disease. In 2000, children from the United Kingdom who were infected with measles entered the United States and put other children at risk of infection.

Classroom Activity Using Argument

Letters to the editor of a newspaper are usually very opinionated and do not rely on new information or the correction of erroneous evidence. Thoughtful, interesting letters, however, do present new information and new perspectives while recognizing other points of view. For this reason, students should be encouraged to go beyond their own opinions and bring new material or perspectives to light for the readers of the newspaper. Their letters will have a much better chance of being considered for publication when they send them to the newspaper.

Essay Submission Form

We welcome students and instructors to submit essays for publication consideration that were written using *Models for Writers*. Send them with this Essay Submission Form and the Agreement Form on the back to: Models—Student Essays, Bedford/St. Martin's, 33 Irving Place, 10th Floor, New York, NY 10003.

Student's name ______________________________

Instructor's name ______________________________

School ______________________________

Department ______________________________

Address ______________________________

____

____

Course name and number ______________________________

Below, please indicate the chapter in *Models for Writers* for which you would like us to consider this essay.

❑ Thesis	❑ Effective Sentences	❑ Process Analysis
❑ Unity	❑ Diction and Tone	❑ Definition
❑ Organization	❑ Figurative Language	❑ Division and Classification
❑ Beginnings and Endings	❑ Illustration	❑ Comparison and Contrast
❑ Paragraphs	❑ Narration	❑ Cause and Effect
❑ Transitions	❑ Description	❑ Argument

Agreement Form

I hereby assign to Bedford/St. Martin's ("Bedford") all of my right, title, and interest throughout the world, including without limitation, all copyrights, in and to my essay, ________________________ (tentative title), and any notes and drafts pertaining to it (the sample essay and such materials being referred to as the "Essay").

I understand that Bedford in its discretion has the right but not the obligation to publish the Essay in any form(s) or format(s) that it may desire; that Bedford may edit, revise, condense, or otherwise alter the Essay as it deems appropriate in order to prepare the same for publication; and that Bedford is under no obligation to publish the Essay. I understand that Bedford has the right, but not the obligation, to use and to authorize the use of my name as author of the Essay in connection with any work that contains the Essay (or a portion of it).

I represent that the Essay is wholly original and was completely written by me, that publication of it will not infringe upon the rights of any third party, and that I have not granted any rights in it to any third party.

In the event Bedford determines to include any part of the Essay in *Models for Writers,* I will receive one free copy of that work, if any, on publication.

This Agreement constitutes the entire agreement between us concerning its subject matter and shall inure to the benefit of the successors, assignees, and licensees of Bedford.

Student's signature ________________________

Student's name ________________________ Date ____/____/____

Be sure to provide us with time-stable information below. Please type or print clearly.

Address(es) ________________________

____

____

Phone(s) ________________________

E-mail(s) ________________________